At the Threshold

At the Threshold

THE DEVELOPING ADOLESCENT

EDITED BY S. SHIRLEY FELDMAN
AND GLEN R. ELLIOTT

HARVARD UNIVERSITY PRESS
Cambridge, Massachusetts, and London, England

First Harvard University Press paperback edition, 1993

Library of Congress Cataloging-in-Publication Data

At the threshold : the developing adolescent / edited by S. Shirley
  Feldman and Glen R. Elliott.
     p. cm.
   Includes bibliographical references (p.).
   ISBN 0-674-05035-5 (alk. paper) (cloth)
   ISBN 0-674-05036-3 (paper)
   1. Adolescence. 2. Puberty. 3. Adolescent psychology.
  I. Feldman, S. Shirley. II. Elliott, Glen R.
HQ796.A756 1990   90–33784
305.23′5—dc20   CIP

To our children, both adolescents
and adolescents-to-be
Andrew, Jeremy, and Michael Feldman
James and Mark Elliott
who confer on this project both
broader perspective and greater meaning

Acknowledgments

This volume is unusual in that it is the result of an intensive collaborative effort by the individual contributors that also reflects the comments of a number of other advisers and reviewers. As a result, we are deeply indebted to many people for its successful completion and wish to thank all those who helped with this endeavor.

The Carnegie Corporation of New York has generously underwritten the costs of preparing the manuscript. The idea for a work focusing on normal adolescent development arose out of the deliberations of the Carnegie Council on Adolescent Development. We are especially grateful for the continued encouragement and helpful suggestions of David Hamburg, President and Chairman of the Council; Elena Nightingale, Special Adviser to the President of the Corporation and our project director; Rubi Takanishi, Executive Director of the Council; and Vivien Stuart, Program Chair, Toward Healthy Child Development: the Prevention of Damage to Children. The Council regularly reviewed our progress, and their insightful comments were most stimulating.

We could not have completed our task without the ongoing counsel of our steering committee, who helped to guide the project from start to finish: Catherine Cooper, Sanford Dornbusch, Ellen Greenberger, the late John Hill, and Eleanor Maccoby. We greatly enjoyed the opportunities we had to work with them and know how much the book benefited from their thoughtful attention.

The Stanford Center for the Study of Families, Children, and Youth kindly offered to house the project, and we acknowledge the collegial working environment and thank the members of the Center for welcoming us.

Leslie Townsend, our administrative assistant, provided services too numerous to mention. Often she was the magnet that kept the myriad pieces of this project from flying apart, and she also made substantive contributions to the clarity and comprehensiveness of the work. In addition, Kristen Kerrigan helped with editing, and Betsy Scroggs and Janice Seagraves provided secretarial support.

We sought contributors who could write persuasively and well about their areas of expertise and then challenged them to do so in a few pages and for a broad audience. We were pleased that such uniformly talented and respected investigators agreed to participate. We thank them again for their patience with our repeated requests that they simplify and shorten their chapters, even as we asked them to include new topics.

Finally, we want to recognize the more than sixty professionals from diverse disciplines who anonymously reviewed drafts of one or more of the chapters. Their comments continued the challenge first issued by the Carnegie Corporation—that the volume describe research on adolescence in a way that transcended any single research specialty. We hope the result will serve as an invitation, and an enticement, for researchers from a wide array of disciplines to consider further the opportunities for studying this fascinating stage of life.

S.S.F.
G.R.E.

Contents

At the Threshold

1

CAPTURING THE ADOLESCENT EXPERIENCE

Glen R. Elliott and S. Shirley Feldman

The topic of adolescence is a confusing blend of the familiar and the unexplored. Each of us has experienced it personally; yet until relatively recently researchers paid it scant attention. Some of the most complex transitions of life occur during adolescence, as the body changes from a child's to an adult's, relationships with others take on new meanings and levels of intricacy, and individuals become increasingly independent. For most, adolescence is, or at least should be, a time of expanding horizons and self-discovery as skills are acquired for establishing adult roles.

Biological processes drive many aspects of adolescence. The bench mark of its onset—puberty—is common to all animal species, ushering in sexual receptivity and the capacity to reproduce. Interesting and potentially informative parallels exist between the maturational process in human beings and that in other animals, especially those having social structures. Studies of such commonalities underscore the critical importance of this part of the life course in establishing social skills, initially with members of the same sex and then with those of the opposite sex. For many social species such skills are honed in peer-oriented group interactions that are distinct from both earlier child-adult patterns and later adult pairings.

Likewise, social influences are pivotal in human adolescence because society shapes the expression of biological imperatives to a remarkable degree. For example, in the United States and most Western cultures adolescence is now viewed as extending roughly from age 10 or 11 through the late teens and even into the early 20s. At least for the past few decades it has also been characterized as a time of relative freedom, during which the principal social duty is acquiring an education. The perceived importance of formal education and the required duration of that process have lengthened the period of adolescence, and its cost has extended the time during which many adolescents remain financially dependent on their families. Even during the first part of the twentieth century adolescents were taking on adult roles and responsibilities at a much earlier age than most do now.

Adults' perceptions of adolescence often tend toward extremes. Many adults glorify it as a time of unparalleled potential, emphasizing the physical beauty, idealism, optimism, and enthusiasm of youth. Others typify the adolescent as a social rebel who is disrespectful, disorderly, hedonistic, and promiscuous—a view that coincides with Aristotle's lament about Athenian youth more than two thousand years ago. In part, such extreme views of adolescence flourish because this period of life has received little scientific scrutiny. As researchers have begun to explore the processes of growth and change, a more informed assessment is emerging of how biological drives and social prescriptions combine to define adolescence in the United States today.

As the succeeding chapters amply demonstrate, many disciplines are contributing valuable insights into normal adolescent development. Throughout this volume contributors have summarized the progress being made toward clarifying the underlying principles that shape the adolescent experience for most individuals. Beyond surveying what is known, the volume identifies major gaps in our knowledge and highlights some especially promising directions for research. The chapters were written for a multidisciplinary audience, so that people from a wide range of fields can learn about the ripe opportunities for investigation that normal adolescent development offers. The book is intended to provide an informative synopsis of research on normal adolescence not only for investigators but also for anyone else interested in this vital period of life.

Defining Adolescence

The period of adolescence now extends over so many years that it can be usefully subdivided into early, middle, and late substages. Early adolescence—ages 10 to 14—typically encompasses the profound physical and social changes that occur with puberty, as maturation begins and social interactions become increasingly centered on members of the opposite sex. Middle adolescence—ages 15 to 17—is a time of increasing independence; for a significant fraction of American youth it also marks the end of adolescence. Late adolescence—age 18 to the mid-20s—occurs for those individuals who, because of educational goals or other social factors, delay their entry into adult roles. In the United States and most other developed countries these subdivisions have been incorporated into the educational structure: junior high or middle school, high school, and college. Most of the chapters in this volume focus on the contexts and processes of early and, to a lesser extent, middle adolescence.

Not surprisingly, both biological and social factors help to define adolescence. For the individual, entry into puberty is the most widely accepted indicator of beginning adolescence. Most girls have a growth spurt signaling the start of puberty at about age 9-1/2; for boys the adolescent growth spurt begins, on average, two years later. Thus, as a group, girls mature sooner than their male peers. Still, within both groups some individuals mature much earlier and others much later than average. For the group, then, adolescent developmental processes may be occurring even though some individuals have yet to enter puberty. The psychological and social consequences of this readily observable and often emotionally laden variability in rates of pubertal development underscore the reality of adolescence as both a group and an individual phenomenon. With no meaningful biological markers to denote the end of adolescence, social factors define entry into adulthood; these typically include such events as marrying, joining the permanent work force, or becoming financially independent.

Adolescence is a stage of life distinct from either childhood or adulthood. This is true not just for human beings but for other species as well, especially primates. This observation strongly suggests that it is a time during which certain tasks need to be completed, among them becoming physically and sexually mature, acquiring skills needed to carry out adult roles, gaining increased autonomy from parents, and realigning social interconnections with members of both the same and the opposite sex. In addition, especially for human beings, society imposes specific expectations on the adolescent that shape some of these tasks—for example, by encouraging extended education in preference to early marriage and entry into the workplace.

In the United States today adolescence is characterized by marked age segregation and little regular interaction with adults. Peer interactions and peer pressures are particularly prominent. Compared with the situation of youths in other cultures and at other times, American adolescents now have an unequaled freedom of self-determination in many areas of their lives. For instance, they exert varying levels of control over how vigorously they apply themselves academically; the kind of friends of both sexes that they seek out; and the extent to which they adopt such risky behaviors as smoking, using alcohol or recreational drugs, and engaging in early or promiscuous sexual intercourse. Longer-range decisions that adolescents increasingly make for themselves include the length and type of formal education, career direction, and mate selection. What is of concern is that most early adolescents are making such choices while their thinking still tends to focus largely on the here and now rather than on longer-range eventualities. As a result, a better understanding of exactly how current attitudes toward adolescence affect immediate and long-term outcomes for individuals should be of considerable general interest.

The multitude of choices that young people face impels researchers to consider how adolescence prepares individuals for later adult roles as well as the ways in which the experience shapes and is shaped by the individual. Much more so than in earlier eras, youth seem to be instrumental in molding their own lives. The direct role of the family in moderating current activities and companions, let alone future careers and life-styles, has been greatly reduced. At the same time, the ability of relatives or other adults to offer advice about how to prepare for the future is vitiated by the rapid changes occurring in the work force and in family structures.

Social and cultural attitudes continue to influence many aspects of the adolescent experience. For some segments of society options are already fading as young people of 14 or 15 anticipate dropping out of school and looking for a job, or perhaps face the reality of an unplanned pregnancy. As a result, adolescent development needs to be examined not only at the level of fundamental processes but also in light of how those processes unfold in specific individuals and contexts.

Adolescence as a Pivotal Stage of Life

American society promotes adolescence as a distinct stage of life by means of a variety of mechanisms, among them compulsory schooling, child labor laws that prohibit early adolescents from entering the work force, and a separate juvenile justice system that metes out legal consequences of socially unacceptable acts partly on the basis of age. These and other social devices plainly define adolescents as "not adults"; and yet neither are they children. They are changing physically, maturing sexually, becoming increasingly able to engage in complex reasoning, and markedly expanding their knowledge of themselves and the world about them. These and many other factors foster an urge in them to gain more control over how and with whom they spend their time.

In recent years social conventions have granted adolescents greater self-determination at steadily younger ages, even as the diversity of socially acceptable life options has expanded. Current social expectations for youth are remarkably ambiguous. For example, adolescents typically pay adult fares by age 11 or 12 although they are restricted from seeing certain movies until after age 16. In most states one can get a driver's license and seek employment by age 16 and can marry, register to vote, and enlist in the armed forces at age 18, but one cannot legally purchase alcohol until age 21. Teenagers are deemed mature enough to decide whether or not to continue their education at age 16, but they receive markedly different treatment in the criminal justice system until they are 18 years old.

Neither the logic behind nor the appropriateness of each restriction is as relevant, perhaps, as is the sense that the total array conveys of societal uncertainty about adolescent capabilities. In the areas of work, sexuality, and political involvement—among many others—young people find themselves progressively more aware of and interested in their potential while receiving contradictory messages about their privileges and responsibilities. For example, when adolescents choose to work—and increasing numbers do so even while still attending school—they typically enter low-paying service jobs that provide little preparation for adult careers. Furthermore, few of them are expected to contribute to the family income; rather, their wages become discretionary funds for their own use. Similarly, dating is accepted and even encouraged among young adolescents, who have grown up on a heady diet of highly romanticized portrayals of sex in the mass media; yet at the same time, society's pervasive message is that successful adults postpone marriage and parenthood until at least their mid-20s. Similarly, the idealistic enthusiasm typical of the young can create tensions as they confront the pragmatics of the political process and the apathy or disdain many adults feel toward it. With few if any readily discernible guidelines, adolescents are left with the task of, but not necessarily the requisite intellectual and emotional tools for, reconciling immediate opportunities and desires with emerging long-range goals.

A central feature of the developing adolescent is the maturing capacity to modulate the surrounding environment and to select role models. The teenager's world widens markedly beyond that of the child. Schools typically become larger and more heterogeneous, especially with respect to ethnicity and socioeconomic status. Usually adolescents are also exposed to a larger number and variety of adult role models, both in school and elsewhere. With increasing access to cars and other forms of transportation, young people can travel much farther than before without routine adult supervision.

As this society has become more diverse, the number of roles and choices available to most teenagers has increased dramatically. Yet the criteria for selecting among them have become less obvious, as ideological or moral consensus has eroded in favor of pluralism. The tendency of the early adolescent to focus on the here and now further complicates the decision-making process. Sadly, the ever greater freedom of adolescence carries with it more risks and costs of errors in judgment. Dropping out of school, teenage pregnancy, sexually transmitted disease, drug addiction, homicide, and suicide are stark examples of the high social price that substantial numbers of youth pay for this freedom. Reasons for these demonstrably undesirable outcomes remain unclear, but their prevalence and adverse impact on individuals, families, and society strongly underscore the need for a better understanding of normal adolescent processes.

As influential as adolescent experiences are, they occur within the context of the overall life course. Children enter adolescence having been shaped by their biological and psychological predispositions and their experiences. Comparable events may have vastly different consequences, depending on those preexisting conditions. Taken together, the experiences of the child and of the adolescent are the mold from which the adult emerges. From a research perspective, then, adolescence needs to be considered as both a unique part of the life course and an integral element of it.

Part of the impetus for this volume comes from the widely held perception that adolescence today is a different, palpably more difficult process than it was only a few years ago. It is essential to establish what adolescence is like now and how the current situation differs from that of earlier times as well as to uncover the general principles that govern the process and help clarify why specific changes have had the observed effects. The successful elaboration of those interconnections should suggest points at which well-targeted interventions can promote more successful outcomes for young people who are having trouble traversing this stage of their development. Adolescence is the last stage of the life course during which society has reasonably ready access to the entire population, so such potential cannot be ignored.

Social Demographics

In the United States the adolescent population has fluctuated over the past several decades. During the 1980s the number of American youths between 10 and 19 years of age shrank overall, dropping from 35 million in 1985 to an estimated 33.8 million in 1990, with the number expected to rise again by the year 2000 to 38.5 million for an increase of 14% over the decade. Changes in the absolute number of adolescents have crucial implications for society in terms of the demands that will be placed on such disparate institutions as schools and colleges, the criminal justice system, consumer markets, and industry.

The United States is also undergoing striking changes in the ethnic and racial makeup of its adolescent population, in some instances much greater shifts than for older age groups. By the year 2000, 31% of adolescents will belong to a racial or ethnic minority: 12% Hispanic, 16% African-American, and 3% of Asian or Pacific Island descent. Distribution by ethnic group across the nation is far from uniform. For example, African-American youth are especially prevalent in the South, Asians and Pacific Islanders are concentrated in California and Hawaii, and native Americans and Hispanics are found predominantly in the West and Southwest. Changes in California are especially marked: minority youth increased from 27% of adolescents in 1970 to 43% in 1980, and by 1990 they constituted more than half the population in this age range.

The changing demographics are cause for some concern because of the status of minority ethnic groups in the United States. Disproportionate numbers of minority adolescents live in inner cities or in nonmetropolitan areas, where schools often are inferior, job opportunities are limited, and street crime is common. On average they come from families that experience relatively high unemployment and earn relatively low incomes; and they complete less formal education, experience earlier childbearing, and have higher birth rates than do nonminority adolescents. For example, in 1985, 43% of African-American children and youths lived below the poverty line, as did 40% of Hispanics. The number of minority youths living in poverty will probably continue to increase in the foreseeable future, owing to higher rates among minority families of conditions known to be associated with low economic status, including the prevalence of single-parent households and overall inadequate educational preparation.

The growing numbers of minority youth in this nation underscore the value of better understanding the effects of ethnicity on normal adolescent development. The contributors to this volume were charged to address such issues to the extent that available information permitted them to do so. Whereas much of the existing research on minority youth has focused on deviant behaviors, this volume assesses instead what is known about normal development for this population. As will become apparent, this topic has received far less attention to date.

Changing Contexts of Development

Most people would argue that being an adolescent today is a different experience than it was even a few decades ago. Both the perception of this change and the change itself attest to the powerful influence of social contexts on adolescent development. Where, with whom, and how adolescents spend their time and invest their energies affect who they are and what they will become. Thus the study of adolescence cannot be taken completely out of the societal setting in which it occurs, especially when that society is itself undergoing change.

Social change creates new experiences and opportunities for adolescents, and even well-established social institutions may be subject to marked changes over time. For example, during the 1950s the typical nuclear family consisted of a working father, a mother who was at home to care for the children and tend the household, and two or more children. That model is far from the reality of current family life for many adolescents. Reconstituted families, shared custody, single-parent homes, and never-married mothers are commonplace. Furthermore, such a simple recitation of different family structures fails to capture the instability that is inherent in many of them: a given adolescent may experience several of these family forms over only a few years. Such variations inevitably alter a young person's concept of family and therefore need to be recognized and researched, as does the more general impact of society's increasing acceptance of these alternative living arrangements.

Changes in social attitudes toward and expectations for adolescents have occurred in many spheres of adolescent life. A few examples readily serve to make the point:

• A high school education has become a minimal expectation, and schools have taken on a variety of social roles that go beyond education, among them health promotion, sponsorship of numerous peer activities, and even child care.

• The workplace, from which young people were removed a century ago, has once again become part of the lives of many adolescents. As we noted earlier, work for this age group is typically a part-time, low-paying, service-oriented activity that offers little meaningful contact with adults and is unrelated to long-term career aspirations.

• The proliferation of entertainment and leisure activities has also altered the adolescent experience: cable television, videocassette recorders, and markedly decreased social censorship have combined to expand dramatically the range of experiences to which the typical adolescent is exposed.

• Marked changes in women's roles mean that young people now see a much wider array of options for females. Many grow up in families in which both parents are employed.

• Access to illicit drugs has become a common feature of growing up, as has the danger of being physically victimized.

Growing up has always carried risks, but the nature of those risks is changing. Adolescents today are less likely than in the past to suffer debilitating or fatal childhood diseases. Increasingly the sources of immediate distress and long-term problems are becoming instead socially medi-ated conditions such as poverty and marital disruption. It is crucial to learn how changes like these affect ability of the young to navigate this crucial stage of development. Subsequent chapters address in more detail key aspects of social contexts in today's society and ways in which re-searchers incorporate consideration of such factors into their studies.

Methods of Study

The recent upsurge of exciting, informative research on adolescence is neither coincidental nor merely a result of new concerns about or awareness of teenagers. Adolescents present considerable challenges for researchers who wish to study them. For many phenomena of interest, obtaining reliable and meaningful information is difficult at best. Parents and teachers may be unaware of significant facts, and young people may be unwilling to participate in research or prohibited from doing so by concerned parents. Even those who agree to be involved in a study may be unable to provide precise and accurate observations of their own behavior and motivations. Still, innovative investigators have begun to establish the utility of some research techniques for gaining insights into adolescence.

One difficult but informative line of inquiry entails efforts to get adoles-cents to express their perceptions of and reactions to the world around them. Only they can talk about how they feel or identify concerns they may have about their immediate circumstances or describe their long-term plans and goals. Questionnaires remain the most common technique for much psychological and social research, but their usefulness depends on the creativity and perceptiveness of the person constructing the questions and on the willingness of subjects to answer them thoroughly and hon-estly. Interviews and daily diaries provide richer sources of information but are more labor intensive and can be more difficult to analyze. The range of data garnered by these techniques, in terms of both numbers of subjects and depth of assessment, is impressive. For example, national surveys of thousands of youths, especially if repeated over time, can help investigators capture general attitudes and spot temporal trends in a vari-ety of behaviors. Typically, such surveys provide factual data such as the extent to which adolescents are exposed to or engage in behaviors such as smoking marijuana, drinking beer, cutting classes at school, or dating.

Surveys can also help define how young people think. It is possible to explore explicitly how they go about solving problems, how they reason through moral dilemmas, and how much they know about social issues such as politics. Typically, questionnaires work well for eliciting responses about discrete events or for elucidating problem-solving styles. They are less helpful for obtaining accurate, detailed information about ongoing behaviors, for example, time spent on homework or watching television. The quality of the data hinges on whether the subjects respond honestly about thoughts or behavior that are more or less socially acceptable as well as whether they can accurately recall how much time they actually spent on a specific behavior.

At the other extreme, a few adolescents have allowed researchers to conduct an intimate assessment of their lives. For instance, in one such study volunteers recorded their activities and feelings repeatedly during the day for several weeks each time they were signaled to do so by a pager they carried with them. This labor-intensive, somewhat intrusive approach has been invaluable in helping to clarify the emotional intensity that can accompany seemingly trivial daily activities within families, such as carrying out chores or accommodating personal habits. Both types of research are needed to gain a full picture of adolescents individually and as a group.

Additional potential sources of information about young people are peers, teachers and other authority figures, and parents. They may be especially helpful in surveys of observable behaviors, such as how youths spend their time and with whom, as well as in studies of social interactions between adolescents and peers or adults. Investigators have demonstrated repeatedly, however, that different sources of information can yield quite disparate views of the same individual. For example, in a study of family cohesion and power relationships remarkably little agreement was found among the views of the adolescent, his mother, and his father. Although possibly confusing, such variegated perspectives may do much to reveal key processes, if they are analyzed properly.

Few studies have used research techniques that entail direct observation of adolescent behaviors. It is possible, however, to observe young people in their natural settings—for instance, at school, at football games, or at other places where they tend to congregate. Alternatively, they may be brought into a laboratory situation and observed alone, with peers, or with family members. Such observational studies, though expensive, have the significant advantage of enabling a trained investigator to verify objectively what happens in a given setting. Also needed is research that looks at the same individuals using different methodologies in order to establish the degree to which results from one type of study generalize to other situations.

Increasingly, biological measures are becoming available for studying adolescents. Investigators have long been able to measure such physical features as height, weight, strength, and stage of pubertal development. More recently, technological advances have enabled researchers to begin to measure biological substances from small samples of urine, saliva, or blood. Other techniques make it feasible to assess brain electrical activity and even brain structure safely and noninvasively. Incorporation of such methods into inquiries about adolescence has only just begun.

In addition to deciding what kind of information to obtain and how to acquire it, scientists must determine whom they should study and how often. The simplest—and by far the most common—approach involves gathering information from some readily available group in what is called a cross-sectional study. For instance, researchers might administer a questionnaire to a group of 11-year-old students in a nearby school. Cross-sectional research is common because it is informative, is less expensive than other types of studies, and can be completed fairly quickly. But it is limited in that results may apply only to the group studied. Suppose someone wanted to examine school attitudes and performance of early adolescents. The results of a study done in a school in which all of the students are white and live in intact middle-class families might reveal little about conditions in a racially mixed school or in an exclusive private school. By the same token, the results might vary depending on where the school is located or even on the ages of the students being studied. A number of these limitations can be overcome with the use of somewhat more elaborate cross-sectional studies, for example, by recruiting subjects across a wide range of ages from a number of different schools throughout the country.

Suppose this hypothetical study revealed that 11-year-olds had markedly different attitudes about suitable work roles for women than did 16-year-olds. It might be tempting to conclude that these observed differences reflect the effects of age and maturity. But other factors such as shifts in social assumptions about women also might cause the difference. Assessing developmental changes requires a research approach called the longitudinal study, in which the same group of subjects is observed repeatedly over time so that changes for each individual can be measured. Longitudinal studies are costly, requiring mechanisms for keeping track of subjects and for maintaining a research group long enough to complete the work. Still, they often are the only viable way to assess important issues about adolescence, because change is a central reality of that part of the life course.

Selecting the population for study can have both intended and unintended effects. For instance, the overwhelming bulk of research on normal youth has been conducted on middle-class white subjects, especially those living near universities. They were chosen, at least in part, because they were conveniently accessible and amenable to study. Minority youth are underrepresented in such research, although they are overrepresented in work that focuses on deviant behaviors such as delinquency, drug and alcohol use, teenage pregnancy, and dropping out of school. A crucial limitation that holds true throughout this volume is the extent to which researchers remain ignorant about normal developmental processes in diverse segments of society.

Focus on Early Adolescence

Rising interest among the general public and researchers alike makes this review of current knowledge about normal adolescent development timely. An explosion of activity in the field has led to new findings about its biological, psychological, and social aspects. The accumulating studies make possible a broad survey of what has been learned, the promising leads that are beckoning researchers, and the significant gaps that remain. Often new findings have built nicely on previous research; at other times the results have raised significant doubts about earlier beliefs. Furthermore, changes that have occurred in the United States over the past few decades pose new and challenging questions about the adolescent developmental process.

Key issues of adolescence, of course, are not new. The core developmental tasks remain: becoming emotionally and behaviorally autonomous, dealing with emerging sexuality, acquiring interpersonal skills for dealing with members of the opposite sex and preparing for mate selection, acquiring education and other experiences needed for adult work roles, and resolving issues of identity and values. Yet superimposed on these old issues are for many a set of new problems, some of which have already been mentioned. The complexities of the adolescent developmental process thus provide a challenging but compelling area for research.

This book draws mainly on research that strives to understand adolescents as a group, an approach that has the advantage of offering a reasonably coherent snapshot of adolescence yet tends to strip away the richness of individuality. The aggregate picture averages together active and passive youth, ebullient and depressed individuals, those living in supportive families and those mainly on their own from an early age. It also largely misses the adolescent voice that resonates with the joy and pain of growing up and articulates its confusions and moments of insights. Despite such limitations, this perspective was a pragmatic choice, accurately reflecting where the bulk of research lies. While practical and useful, this view is only one of many ways to consider this or any other part of the life course.

This volume undertakes a review of diverse research approaches, many of which are themselves the subject of numerous tomes. To simplify the task, we have limited consideration of pathological or deviant youth to a few instances that help illuminate aspects of normal development. In addition, we encouraged the authors to offer a broad overview and to rely on citations to steer interested readers to more detailed coverage of specific topics. Given the strict space limitations, they had to choose those examples of research that seemed to them most salient and most representative of key trends.

The authors were also charged to consider available research on all segments of the adolescent population, specifically including ethnic and racial minorities. One feature of research on these groups is that no consistent nomenclature yet exists for identifying discrete clusters of individuals with clear commonalities. For example, considering the Asian and Pacific Island populations as a unit ignores major differences among the various national backgrounds. In addition, terminologies change. Some researchers have begun to use the term *African-American* in preference to *black*. Because both are currently acceptable, we have elected to let each contributor decide which to use.

We begin with a look at basic processes of adolescent development, specifically biological and cognitive development. Part II focuses on some of the contexts, both general and specific, in which the changes of adolescence occur. These include the cultural and historical setting and ethnicity, as well as four specific areas that directly affect young people on a daily basis: the family, the peer group, the school, and work and leisure settings. Part III addresses processes and outcomes in adolescence and how these change during development. Many topics overlap; we have attempted to highlight those interactions while minimizing redundancy.

This work embodies a remarkable and heartening expansion of our understanding of normal adolescence. Much remains to be learned; yet it seems clear that adolescence is an appropriate and fruitful focus for scientific inquiry. The results of such studies are likely to inform society about the ways in which adolescence can be optimized both as an intrinsically rich experience and as the final training ground for adulthood.

PART ONE

Basic Foundations

Adolescence, especially early adolescence, is most easily characterized by the extraordinary physical and cognitive changes that occur as child turns into adult. They permeate every aspect of development during this stage, not only creating the impetus for myriad other changes in the young person's life but also influencing what resources he or she has to cope with those changes. Thus, it seems appropriate to include early in this volume two chapters that summarize recent progress in clarifying what happens to the adolescent body and brain—Chapter 2 on pubertal processes and Chapter 3 on adolescent thinking.

Clinical and basic scientists are making substantive gains in documenting the physical and cognitive processes that occur with the onset of adolescence. The work extends beyond mere recording of the typical sequence of events to increasingly more precise and detailed descriptions of the mechanisms that drive development. Such studies repeatedly bring home the important lesson that change seldom occurs along a single dimension. For example, although hormones are essential to stimulate physical maturation, their effects account for relatively few of the psychological and social features of adolescence. Similarly, progressive cognitive changes are well known; but they seem not to occur as sequentially or as independently of outside influences as was once believed.

The rapid progress being made in basic research on biological and cognitive processes is most heartening. Only as we both appreciate and are able to study the complex interactions between physical, psychological, and social processes can we expect to gain answers to the many pressing questions about normal adolescent development raised throughout this volume.

2

THE ROLE OF PUBERTAL PROCESSES

*Jeanne Brooks-Gunn and Edward O. Reiter**

In negotiating the phase of life between childhood and adulthood, adolescents face a number of developmental challenges, many of them involving reproductive events. As young people's bodies develop, they begin to incorporate such changes into their construction of self and must learn to cope with others' responses to their mature bodies. They also must learn how to respond to feelings of sexual arousal and, for many, questions about when and with whom to have sexual intercourse.[1]

Puberty itself is a key developmental challenge for adolescents. They must accommodate to the physical changes in a cultural milieu that, for girls, values the prepubertal over the mature female body. They must negotiate the loosening of childhood ties to parents and the move toward greater psychological and physical autonomy. As they do so, they must deal with sexual arousal and the beginning of relationships with members of the opposite sex, even as they are trying to develop a stable and cohesive personality structure for the regulation of mood, impulse, and self-esteem. How do boys and girls experience the social and biological changes that occur as they become reproductively mature? What does this experience mean to them and to others? How does it alter self-definitions and relationships? What are the effects on subsequent development in a variety of domains, including competence, psychopathology, and deviant behavior?

*We wish to thank the National Institutes of Health, the W. T. Grant Foundation, and the Russell Sage Foundation for their support. We are grateful for the comments of Michelle Warren and James Tanner. The help of Rosemary Deibler and Florence Kelly in manuscript preparation was appreciated.

1. According to a study of four groups of American teenagers, 60% had had intercourse by the following ages: white males, age 18; white females, age 19; black males, age 16; black females, age 18 (88).

Of particular interest is the vulnerable youth, for whom the onset of puberty may herald overwhelming challenges because of difficulties in coping with all the concurrent changes of early adolescence. To identify vulnerable youth, we look at predisposing factors such as culturally mediated beliefs about puberty, family circumstances, patterns of parental interaction, personality characteristics, and earlier preadolescent patterns of negotiating developmental challenges. Other contextually mediated factors include school transition, peer relations, and the "fit" between one's developing body and expectations about attractiveness or skill at sports.

Pubertal experiences, then, are part of the larger context of the life course. They occur most prominently in early adolescence (23), but pubertal growth often extends into middle adolescence as well (13). Behavioral changes may be influenced directly by physical processes, may be more generally related to the effects of age and grade in school, or may be linked to pubertal growth through social or contextual factors. Specific models have been developed to consider such possible interactions (23, 24, 76, 128).[2] Generally, more interactive models are replacing ones that were either mainly environmental or biological. Until fairly recently research focused on a limited set of biological and social changes as being age related and characteristic of all adolescents. That focus is changing. In addition to life events themselves, the timing and sequencing (tempo) of those events that mark the progression toward adulthood are now seen as critical in the definition of this particular phase of life and in our understanding of how the individual adapts to life changes.[3]

Finally, researchers in this area have been remiss in considering situational factors when comparing experiences and outcomes in different social classes and ethnic groups (and, in some cases, even boys and girls). In this sense pubertal research reflects the history of other rapidly evolving areas of human development (for example, early research on mother-infant interaction and peer relationships). White middle-class individuals are the first group to be studied, with more situationally based and culturally sensitive work following. We regret that we are able to say little about the pubertal experience of groups other than middle-class white youth,

2. The proclivity to make inferences about direct biological effects in the absence of appropriate designs is great, however, and some of the pubertal research fails to use sufficient caution. This is also true of the literature on menstruation (31, 124, 138). The specification of models testing direct and indirect biological effects of puberty would be extremely helpful.

3. Examining sequences of events, however, does not mean that their temporal ordering is invariable across individuals. The young adolescent may move into a middle school in sixth or seventh grade. She may begin to date as early as fifth grade, as late as twelfth grade, or not at all. Interindividual differences in the onset (and cessation) of pubertal processes are found, as is intraindividual variability in the timing and sequence of pubertal events.

but we are hopeful that, with the next generation of studies, more may be said in the near future. Also, this chapter, unlike the others in this volume, will provide more information about girls' than boys' experiences. Generally the only topics for which this occurs are those having to do with reproduction, including parenthood. This bias probably reflects societal beliefs that child-rearing and family roles are more important for females than males and, by inference, that pubertal change has more of an impact on girls than on boys (16). As Simone de Beauvoir so eloquently states:

> The young boy, be he ambitious, thoughtless, or timid, looks toward an open future; he will be a seaman or an engineer, he will stay on the farm or go away to the city, he will see the world, he will get rich; he feels free, confronting a future in which the unexpected awaits him. The young girl will be a wife, grandmother; she will keep house just as her mother did, she will give her children the same care she herself received when young—she is twelve years old and already her story is written in the heavens. She will discover it day after day without ever making it.   (44, p. 278)

History of Pubertal Research

Before turning to these topics, as well as describing the pubertal processes themselves, we must place pubertal research in a short-term historical context (15). Essentially until the 1980s almost no developmental work on the meaning or effects of puberty had been conducted (the notable exceptions are the California and the Fels Longitudinal Growth Studies). Two seminal works appearing in the 1970s highlighted both a lack of systematic study and the vital role of this life phase in healthy development (79, 104). At the same time, researchers examined whether "storm and stress" was an appropriate characterization of the experience and behavior of young adolescents, and whether changes in self-image during early adolescent transitions were best seen as continuous or discontinuous (117, 120). These studies seemed to assume that alterations in self-image and emotionality, if they occurred, would be due in part to pubertal changes as well as to the context in which these physical transformations occurred. Somewhat surprisingly, then, pubertal processes were not a subject of study in the 1970s. Then in the 1980s, starting with a 1981 conference on girls at puberty (23), this topic came into its own. During that decade at least six conferences were held on early adolescence, with the topic of puberty having a prominent place in each (24, 25, 76, 90, 101, 111).

Why did pubertal research languish? After all, the father of adolescent psychology, G. Stanley Hall, was writing on the subject in the early 1900s. Documenting pubertal rituals was a time-honored tradition in anthropology (113, 122). Physicians and physical anthropologists were busy cataloguing physical growth in a number of cultural settings, and endocrinologists were exploring the hormonal underpinnings of many of these changes (75, 153). While this is speculative, we believe that the lackluster response of behavioral scientists to the quite obvious manifestations of the transition from childhood to adulthood had to do with how pubertal changes are perceived and presented in our society.

First, many adults seem uncomfortable discussing puberty themselves and, by inference, believe that young people feel the same way. As Weideger recounts, many adult women report having been very upset about menarche ("I was afraid to tell my mother or friends; I was so ashamed," 166, p. 169). It is a short step from one's own discomfort to the belief that pubertal children do not talk about the changes and that puberty is a private, not a public (or at least highly salient), event. Many investigators have found it difficult, if not sometimes impossible, to work with or recruit potential subjects from schools for their research on puberty (17). In Brooks-Gunn's original early adolescent work, she had to contact the Central New Jersey Girl Scouts, since only a handful of public schools had granted permission to ask teenage girls about their menarcheal experiences and feelings (27). In her more recent studies concerning pubertal processes other than menarche (growth of breasts and pubic hair, weight spurts), she has collaborated with private schools because of the reluctance and discomfort of some public school administrators when faced by such topics (16).

Second, at a more individual level many parents, particularly fathers, report being uneasy about raising the subject of puberty with their offspring (the exception being mothers and daughters discussing menarche). Such feelings may be one reason why so many parents favor sex education in the schools (three-fourths to four-fifths, according to various national opinion surveys). In part, parents are prisoners of their own experiences. The number of women who report having been unprepared for menarche increases dramatically with age cohort (100): cultural beliefs handed down to immigrants from Europe often forbade such preparation (1); and sexual squeamishness may be as much or more a part of the American as the Western European experience, as demonstrated by differences in societal regulation of fertility (19, 92).

Third, even educational materials reflect society's ambivalence toward puberty. Much more explicit information is given to teenagers in many

Western European countries than in the United States (92). In West Germany, for example, the health-education pamphlet published by the Johnson & Johnson Company describes the pubertal process by showing photographs of girls in the five Tanner stages, just as medical texts do. In contrast, such graphic information is not included in any of the comparable health-education pamphlets published for American teenage girls; it is considered too controversial. In addition, pamphlets given to girls in the 1970s and earlier focus on concealment, reflecting societal beliefs (20). According to one booklet, menstruation is "a natural, normal part of life. Treat it naturally, normally, and you won't be embarrassed or upset each time it comes" (2). Another booklet states, "It's absolutely impossible for anyone to know you are menstruating unless of course you act stupid about the whole thing" (73). More recent materials are much less judgmental, perhaps reflecting changes in attitudes.

Such cultural messages are absorbed very quickly by our youth. Boys almost never talk about pubertal changes with their parents. One small study by Brooks-Gunn of pubertal boys found that only one had discussed first ejaculation with his father (62). None of the boys had told their friends that they had had an ejaculation (whether through nocturnal emission or masturbation). Indeed, for over four-fifths of the boys the study interview was the first time they had discussed this topic (information is typically transmitted via locker-room jokes and magazines). As one of the few scientists who have studied the topic explains: "Imagine an American boy coming to the breakfast table exclaiming, 'Mom, guess what? I had my first wet dream last night. Now I'm a man.' It is not without significance that such an imaginary episode is greeted in American culture with laughter" (141, pp. 333–334).

This cultural milieu has influenced the type of research that is conducted and perhaps the amount of useful work that is done (given the time and effort needed to obtain cooperation from the schools), as well as the responses of the pubertal child and significant others to physical change. (17) It also attests to the significance of these changes.

Physiological Changes of Puberty

Pubertal maturation is controlled by the reproductive endocrine system, which first operates in the fetal period. Events are controlled largely by complex interactions among the brain, the pituitary gland, and the gonads (ovaries in females and testes in males). The pituitary is a small organ at the base of the brain that receives signals from the brain and releases hormones into the bloodstream. These hormones, in turn, influence organs throughout the body, regulating growth and many other aspects of normal body function. Signals back to the brain, either through nerve pathways or by way of hormones in the blood, complete the circuit. Two systems of particular relevance to adolescent development are the hypothalamus-pituitary-gonadal axis, which regulates sexual maturation and reproduction, and the hypothalamus-pituitary-adrenal axis, which controls many aspects of the body's response to stress.

Before birth, gonads develop in males and begin to secrete hormones called androgens. Androgens set in motion a series of events that result in the development of male internal and external sex organs, and specifically in the formation of the hypothalamus-pituitary-gonadal axis. This process results in the birth of a boy; if it does not occur, the child is a girl (see Figure 2.1). After what appears to be a short burst of sex steroid activity in the first few months of life, this hormonal system then operates at a fairly low level until middle childhood (135, 136).

Two independent processes, controlled by different mechanisms but closely linked in time, are involved in the increase of sex steroid secretion in the prepubertal and pubertal periods. One process, adrenarche, involves production of androgens by the adrenal gland; this precedes by about two years the second event, gonadarche, which involves reactivation of the quiescent hypothalamic-pituitary-gonadotropin-gonadal system.

Physical Changes

Growth occurs during childhood and adolescence because of a complicated, harmonious interaction of multiple and diverse factors. Genetic influences, nutritional status, hormonal changes, and the presence or absence of diseases modulate the growth process both qualitatively and quantitatively during adolescence. The physical changes of puberty, extending from the preteenage years to the end of the second decade, have been carefully described (109, 110). Figures 2.2–2.5 illustrate the key changes, which occur in a continuous process. In girls, breast development is divided into five stages (see Figure 2.2). In boys, genital development is also divided into five stages (see Figure 2.3). Five stages of pubic hair growth have also been described for both girls and boys (see Figures 2.2 and 2.3).

Development of secondary sexual characteristics in girls. Breast budding, typically the first sexual characteristic to appear in girls, occurs at approximately 10.5 years. In one-fifth of girls, the appearance of pubic hair occurs prior to breast buds. The interval between breast budding and adult breast

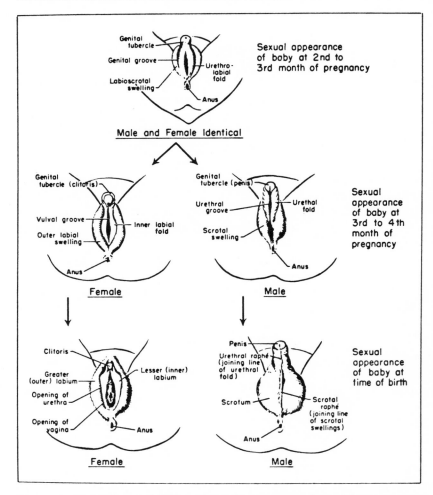

Figure 2.1. External genital differentiation in the human fetus. Three stages in the differentiation of the external genital organs. The male and the female organs have the same beginnings and are homologous with one another. (Reprinted from J. Money and A. A. Ehrhardt, *Man and Woman, Boy and Girl*, Baltimore: Johns Hopkins University Press [1972]. Copyright © 1972. Used by permission of The Johns Hopkins University Press.)

configuration is about 4.5 years and is similar whether girls mature at a younger or older age. Menarche (the first menses) occurs at approximately 12.5 years in the United States, about two years after breast buds appear. Menarche follows the peak height velocity, the age at which the most rapid growth occurs; in fact the time of maximum deceleration of growth

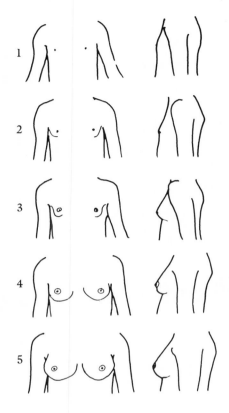

BREASTS

1. No breast development.
2. The first sign of breast development has appeared. This stage is sometimes referred to as the breast budding stage. Some palpable breast tissue under the nipple, the flat area of the nipple (areola) may be somewhat enlarged.
3. The breast is more distinct although there is no separation between contours of the two breasts.
4. The breast is further enlarged and there is greater contour distinction. The nipple including the areola forms a secondary mound on the breast.
5. Mature Stage Size may vary in the mature stage. The breast is fully developed. The contours are distinct and the areola has receded into the general contour of the breast.

PUBIC HAIR

1. No pubic hair.
2. There is a small amount of long pubic hair chiefly along vaginal lips.
3. Hair is darker, coarser, and curlier and spreads sparsely over skin around vaginal lips.
4. Hair is now adult in type, but area covered is smaller than in most adults. There is no pubic hair on the inside of the thighs.
5. Hair is adult in type, distributed as an inverse triangle. There may be hair on the inside of the thighs.

Figure 2.2. The five pubertal stages for breast and pubic hair growth. (From W. A. Marshall and J. M. Tanner, "Variations in the Pattern of Pubertal Changes in Girls," *Archives of Disease in Childhood,* 44 [1969], 291. Copyright © 1969 by British Medical Association. Reprinted by permission.)

PENIS AND SCROTUM

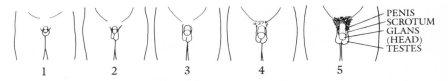

Stage 1: The infantile state that persists from birth until puberty begins. During this time the genitalia increase slightly in overall size but there is little change in general appearance.
Stage 2: The scrotum has begun to enlarge, and there is some reddening and change in texture of the scrotal skin.
Stage 3: The penis has increased in length and there is a smaller increase in breadth. There has been further growth of the scrotum.
Stage 4: The length and breadth of the penis have increased further and the glans has developed. The scrotum is further enlarged and the scrotal skin has become darker.
Stage 5: The genitalia are adult in size and shape. The appearance of the genitalia may satisfy the criteria for one of these stages for a considerable time before the penis and scrotum are sufficiently developed to be classified as belonging to the next stage.

PUBIC HAIR

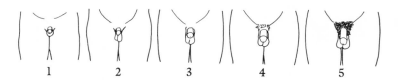

Stage 1: There is no true pubic hair, although there may be a fine velus over the pubes similar to that over other parts of the abdomen.
Stage 2: Sparse growth of lightly pigmented hair, which is usually straight or only slightly curled. This usually begins at either side of the base of the penis.
Stage 3: The hair spreads over the pubic symphysis and is considerably darker and coarser and usually more curled.
Stage 4: The hair is now adult in character but covers an area considerably smaller than in most adults. There is no spread to the medial surface of the thighs.
Stage 5: The hair is distributed in an inverse triangle as in the female. It has spread to the medial surface of the thighs but not up the linea alba or elsewhere above the base of the triangle.

Figure 2.3. The five pubertal states for penile and pubic hair growth. (From N. M. Morris and J. R. Udry, "Validation of a Self-Administered Instrument to Assess Stage of Adolescent Development," *Journal of Youth and Adolescence,* 9 [1980], 275–276. Copyright © 1980 by Plenum Press. Reprinted with permission.)

in height is most closely associated with menarche. The peak height velocity occurs before development of pubic hair in one-fourth of girls and in the initial stage of, or probably before, breast development in one-fourth of girls. The growth spurt begins approximately six to twelve months before breast budding, at a mean age of 9.6 years (see Figure 2.4). A wide variation exists in the sequence of events involving the growth of breasts and pubic hair and genital maturation, with a standard deviation of approximately one year for the onset of each given stage.

Development of secondary sexual characteristics in boys. The initial sign of sexual development is the onset of testicular growth, which occurs at about 11 to 11.5 years (Tanner stage 2). The bulk of testicular volume is attributable to the sperm-producing tubules, the mass of which is considerably greater than that of the sparse androgen-producing Leydig cells. In almost no cases does visible pubic hair develop during Tanner genital stage 2; 41% of boys are in Tanner genital stage 4 by the time pubic hair growth is first observed. Approximately three years pass between the first signs of

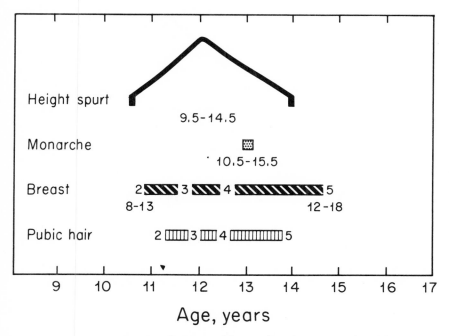

Figure 2.4. The developmental course of four pubertal processes for girls. (From J. M. Tanner, *Growth at Adolescence,* Oxford: Blackwell Scientific [1962], p. 36. Copyright © 1962 by Blackwell Scientific. Reprinted with permission.)

genital growth and the development of adult male genitalia, but a lapse of almost five years is still within the normal range. The peak height velocity is achieved by only a few boys by Tanner genital stage 3 but by 76% by genital stage 4. In boys the mean age at initiation of the adolescent height spurt is approximately 11.7 years—thus beginning shortly after the first evidence of gonadal maturation. The age of peak height velocity is between 13 and 14 years (see Figure 2.5).

Spermarche, which is the onset of the release of spermatozoa, has been estimated on the basis of age at finding spermaturia, determined by longitudinal assessment of urinary samples (99). Spermarche occurs between 12 and 14 years, at a rather early stage of pubic hair growth and within an extremely wide variation of testicular volume. Peak height velocity and maximum levels of testosterone production follow spermarche. Despite considerable variability of detectable spermaturia, this event does appear

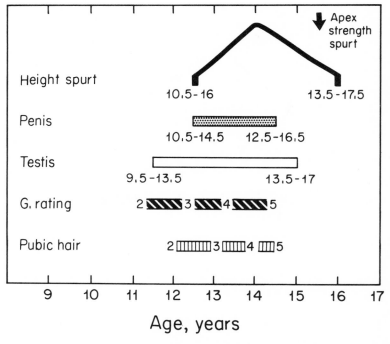

Figure 2.5. The developmental course of four pubertal processes for boys. (From J. M. Tanner, *Growth at Adolescence*, Oxford: Blackwell Scientific [1962]. Copyright © 1962 by Blackwell Scientific. Reprinted with permission.

to be relatively early. Most boys reach spermarche by age 14, despite the often sparse degree of systematic virilization.

Sex and ethnic differences in pubertal growth. The initiation of the pubertal growth spurt may be the earliest measurable physical feature in girls, occurring, as we have seen, about one year before breast budding. The growth spurt in boys does not begin until considerable gonadal development has occurred. This is why girls in the earlier stages of adolescence are taller than boys (see Figure 2.6). Boys are on the average about two years older than girls at the age of their maximum growth spurt, but the amount of height attained (10–14 inches, or 25–35 cm) and the velocity of

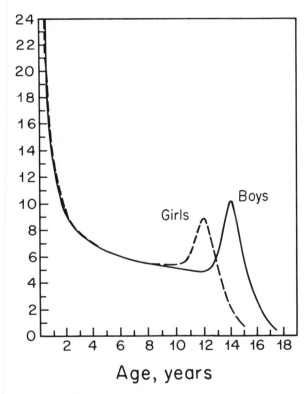

Age, years

Figure 2.6. Typical-individual velocity curves for supine length or height in boys and girls. These curves represent the velocity of growth of the typical boy and girl at any given moment. (From J. M. Tanner, R. H. Whitehouse, and M. Takaishi, "Standards from Birth to Maturity for Height, Weight, Height Velocity, and Weight Velocity: British Children, 1965," *Archives of Disease in Childhood,* 41 [1966].)

the spurt (2–3 inches per year, or 5–8 cm per year) does not differ substantially between boys and girls. The height growth spurt typically lasts about four years, with growth ceasing in girls at about 17 and in boys at about 20 years of age. The female growth spurt slows at menarche in midpuberty. In general, a girl can expect to grow 1 to 3 inches (3 to 7 cm) after menarche, and considerable pubertal sexual development may yet occur in almost fully grown girls. In contrast, a pubescent boy may not achieve his maximum growth until he has developed nearly adult genitalia. Pubic hair growth may also occur from midpuberty to late puberty in boys, while the process generally appears throughout the pubertal years in girls. The progression of pubertal growth is the same across ethnic groups.

Tempo or timing of pubertal change. Tanner has extensively described the substantial variations that occur in growth patterns—both the tempo of growth and the speed with which children carry out the entire growth process (155).[4]

Maturational timing seems to be the same across ethnic groups, provided nutrition is adequate. It is widely believed, however, that puberty occurs later among Asians than among whites. Brooks-Gunn completed a comparative study of dancers with national ballet companies in the United States, Western Europe, and the People's Republic of China, and found that the mean age of menarche was quite late for dancers, in comparison to population norms. The manuscript was criticized during the review process on the grounds that Asians have a later mean menarcheal age than whites. During a visit to China, however, she learned that the age reported in journals available to Western scientists was verified by several Chinese physicians and experts on sports medicine: menarche occurs at the same age in China for the population at large (at least in urban areas where nutrition is good and reporting of health statistics is extensive) as in the United States (81). The erroneous belief that it does not may be due in part to the fact that Asian females are generally lighter and smaller than their American counterparts;[5] therefore it is assumed that their physical

4. Tanner developed "tempo-conditional" standard growth curves in which individuals' growth curves may be expressed on a set of curves with varying rates, all derived from normal children. Despite being at the same height and weight at the initiation of puberty, and perhaps also at the conclusion of pubertal change, individuals experience the process at rates that vary dramatically.

5. Indeed, different weight norms (for height and age) have to be used to calculate weight percentiles for Chinese and American youth, given these differences. More generally, ethnic differences have been reported in weight, height, leg and arm length (proportional to overall length), skin-fold thickness, and possibly fat distribution. These differences have been reported in relatively well-nourished populations (57).

development is delayed. This is an example of ethnocentrism that one might expect to see applied to psychological events but not biological ones. Controversy also exists with respect to whether Africans and African-Americans develop earlier than other ethnic groups (57).

Brain Growth

Growth in brain weight proceeds through periods of varying velocity, with specific regions of the brain growing at different times in a pattern related in a complex way to the evolutionary age of the brain region (97). Early data suggested that brain cells increase in number from birth through age 2 or 3, after which little or no growth occurs. Later evidence suggests that brain growth extends well into adolescence and perhaps even further; questions as to amount, region, timing, and synchrony remain (46, 70). More recent qualitative studies demonstrate progressive differential maturation of nerve cells throughout childhood and adolescence (134). Sophisticated studies with magnetic resonance imaging confirm continuing changes in the structural functioning of the brain through midadolescence (89).

With respect to puberty and brain growth, Epstein (54, 55) has posited that while brain cell growth is essentially complete after the first two years of life, peaks and troughs in brain growth across regions occur throughout childhood and adolescence. Changes in head circumference over time are used as his proxy for brain weight and hence growth. He reports increases in head circumference around ages 10 to 12, after which a steep decline is seen for girls and a more gradual one for boys. These data have been criticized on several grounds, including analytic procedures (108), lack of replication (112), and lack of a sex difference, which would be expected if the changes had anything to do with puberty since boys develop later than girls (52, 126). It is more likely that "while discrete brain regions definitely progress through something like 'spurts,' in terms of such processes as the generation of nerve cells and of connections between them, different brain regions do so out of synchrony and in a reliable developmental sequence" (70, p. 552).[6]

6. Different developmental patterns for the two cerebral hemispheres are apparent. We wish to suggest that specific age-linked patterns parallel the cognitive developmental sequence described by Piaget (see Chapter 3 in this volume). Few data exist on how such changes might be associated with Piagetian stages in early adolescence (69). More generally, a great deal of research on hemispheric specialization and how it may be influenced by puberty has been conducted on spatial abilities. This work is attempting to explain the sex differences seen in spatial abilities by positing that boys, by virtue of experiencing a later

Studies of EEG activity from childhood to young adulthood have demonstrated a continuous process of growth, best described by an exponential growth function, along with discrete spurts in specific parts of the brain (157).[7] The sophisticated technological assessment of brain maturation is providing dramatic new descriptive data of brain growth and maturation; the relevance for hormonal, cognitive, and psychological changes still needs to be clarified, however.

The Endocrine System at Puberty

Hormonal control of pubertal growth. The endocrine system mediates interactions between nutrition and genetic makeup to influence growth and physical changes in puberty. Before secondary sex characteristics develop, concentrations of the pituitary hormones called gonadotropins—luteinizing hormone (LH) and follicle-stimulating hormone (FSH)—increase. Also noteworthy are the pulsating patterns in which the pituitary secretes these hormones over a twenty-four-hour period. Appropriate "bursts," or pulses, induce the ovaries and testes to produce increased levels of estrogens and androgens, which in turn stimulate physical growth. In addition, they stimulate the gonads to produce sperm in males and mature ova in females.

At about the same time, levels of growth hormones and a family of growth-hormone-dependent factors (the somatomedins) increase. Near the end of the pubertal process, perhaps in response to rising hormone levels, the production of these growth hormones seems to diminish. These growth factors are produced throughout the body by all dividing cells and act not only by classical endocrine hormonal means, having

---

puberty, have a longer period of functional lateralization (161, 162). Yet striking sex differences are found in only one aspect of spatial ability, that of mental rotations (103), and gender effects are seen prior to puberty (118). Many have tested the hypothesis that late-maturing girls have better spatial scores than their early-maturing peers, following Waber's premise and initial confirmatory findings. Effects, when found, tend to be small and are most likely to occur in studies using extreme samples (69, 118).

7. Of particular concern to students of puberty is Epstein's thesis (54) that acceleration of head circumference (and presumably brain growth) is associated with intelligence, which has not been found to be true (112). Epstein has gone on to suggest that learning is accelerated during periods of brain growth, and that middle school, a time when students are in a trough as to brain growth, may not be a particularly good time for learning new skills (56). Others have studied possible disruptions in cognition during early adolescence; while the ability to recognize unfamiliar faces may be lower in children aged 12 to 14 than in younger or older children (39), pubertal "dips" are not seen in any other of a number of cognitive abilities studied (see, for a review of this literature, 69; also 49).

circulated to the site, but also locally on neighboring cells or even on the cell that produces them.

It remains unclear how the hormonal, nutritional, and energy regulators of pubertal growth act together to initiate puberty. The associations between the sex hormones and the growth hormone–peptide growth factor system are being studied, especially connections between the growth factors and production of sperm or ova, and the role of local production and action of peptide growth factors in diverse tissues—skeletal and other— relative to material brought from distant sites.

Regulatory systems that control the reproductive endocrine system. Maturation of the reproductive endocrine system, which normally culminates in the production of sex steroids and sperm or ova by fertile adults, is regulated at multiple sites. Parts of the brain, including the cortex, limbic system, and complex neurotransmitter systems, modulate hypothalamic function. These influence the *hypothalamus,* which directly controls the pituitary by producing gonadotropin-releasing hormone (GnRH), which it secretes in rhythmic pulses. The *pituitary* synthesizes, stores, and secretes LH and FSH in response to continued stimulation by GnRH. And the *gonads* (ovaries or testes) respond by synthesizing and secreting sex steroid (androgens and estrogens) and producing sperm or ova. The hypothalamus also stimulates the pituitary to produce adrenocorticotropic hormone (ACTH), which causes the adrenal glands to increase androgen production (135, 136).

As we stated earlier, the hypothalamic-pituitary-gonadal system first functions during fetal life and early infancy (certainly in males and probably in females). It is then suppressed to a low level of activity for almost a decade and is reactivated during late childhood (94). Studies of newborn primates have suggested that this system may already be fully mature in males, but that its maturation in the female may extend into early childhood (130, 131). Such processes may operate in humans as well, although data are sparse. The role of the fetal gonads in producing androgens that alter maturity of the hypothalamus is currently under study.

Experimental and clinical studies support the hypothesis that the brain, not the pituitary gland or gonads, restrains the activity of the reproductive endocrine system in prepubertal children. This inhibition appears to be mediated through suppression of GnRH production and secretion (136). The number of hypothalamic GnRH cells and the production of GnRH do not differ in juvenile and adult monkeys, suggesting that the quiescent phase of reproductive function is mediated by some type of inhibitory mechanism (3). Intermittent, rather nonspecific excitation of hypothalamic GnRH-secreting neurons in prepubertal monkeys prematurely activates the pubertal process, providing strong evidence for regulation of the GnRH pulse generator and its secretory products by brain structures that regulate the hypothalamus (66).[8]

Neuroendocrine Control of the Onset of Puberty

Temporal definitions of pubertal events. As we have noted, the earliest manifestation of pubertal development in the male is enlargement of the testes, whereas in the female acceleration of height growth and breast budding are the first physical indications of puberty. In boys, increased evidence of testicular growth (or any other pubertal manifestation) prior to age 9 is viewed as being precocious and absence of any changes after age 14 as being delayed. In girls, onset of breast budding prior to age 8 or evidence of initiation of the pubertal growth spurt prior to age 7 is considered sexually precocious and the absence of these changes after age 13 to be delayed.

Extensive endocrinologic assessments of syndromes of sexual precocity and of delayed adolescent maturation have been undertaken. Of ongoing research interest are several relatively recent treatment approaches. The hypothalamic-pituitary-gonadal axis, prematurely reactivated in the syndrome of sexual precocity, is silenced by treatment with potent agonists of endogenous GnRH (74). These analogues of GnRH mimic the action of constant infusions of the native material on pituitary gonadotropin release; a process of "receptor down regulation" leads to an impairment of LH and FSH secretion (74). In the syndrome of delayed sexual maturation, therapy with replacement GnRH given in pulses has been effected (132). Accordingly, exploration of the regulation of hypothalamic, pituitary, and gonadal function is being undertaken in which administration of pulsatile GnRH has replaced the usual hypothalamic secretion profile. The recognition and study of such chemical manipulation of pituitary function has enabled investigators to inhibit selectively the reproductive endocrine axis in animals and assess varied growth and hormonal events at different stages of the pubertal process.

Timing of the onset of puberty. The average age at onset of puberty shows a secular trend over the past century toward earlier occurrence; the trend cuts across geographic and ethnic lines (154). This progressive decline in

8. The intimate ultrastructural and immuno-histochemical analysis of the arcuate nucleus and surrounding area of the hypothalamus remains to be carried out. The neuropharmacologic control of pulse generator function, whether by neural, neurohumoral, peripheral metabolic, or genome-determined circadian (or circhoral) periodicity is unresolved. Continuing assessment of this region of the brain with the application of DNA probes will lead to further definition of hypothalamic peptides involved with reproductive endocrine function.

the age of puberty is thought to be due to improvements in socioeconomic conditions; such a trend appears to have slowed or ceased over the last twenty years (154). Nutrition and weight early in life (the fetal and infancy periods) as well as nutrition and weight at the age of puberty may influence the onset of puberty (102). A critical amount of body weight or fat has been thought to trigger the onset (60), but much research does not support this hypothesis (43, 98, 146).

Although menarche is a relatively late pubertal event and is removed from those neural factors that influence both the production of gonadotropin-gonadal sex steroid and physical changes at the initiation of puberty, the possibility exists that some alteration of body metabolism, including the ratio of fat to lean body mass (somatometer), may affect central nervous system (CNS) restraints on the onset of puberty. Studies have characterized potential metabolic signals during maturation in monkeys (37, 150). Earlier use of alternative energy stores (amino acids and fatty acids) by the fasting juvenile primate, unlike the adult primate, perhaps related to increased rates of energy consumption or diminished availability of energy substrate, led Steiner and his co-workers to consider the linkage between metabolic alterations during maturation and the timing of the onset of puberty. Production of insulin, ketone bodies, and free fatty acids, along with alterations in the neural uptake of tryptophan and tyrosine, with consequent altered neurotransmitter synthesis, may be metabolic signals that affect the brain and, thus, temporally modify the onset of puberty.

Central nervous system control of the timing of puberty. Two mechanisms have been invoked to explain the prepubertal restraint by the central nervous system of gonadotropin secretion. One is a sex-steroid—dependent mechanism, a highly sensitive hypothalamic-pituitary-gonadal negative feedback system. The other is a sex-steroid—independent mechanism that can be ascribed to "intrinsic" CNS inhibitory influences (see Figure 2.7). In all likelihood both the inhibition of gonadotropin secretion in a highly sensitive manner by low levels of sex steroid throughout the prepubertal years and inhibitory action intrinsically mediated by the central nervous system, perhaps based on metabolic, body weight or composition, or other energy signals, interact to maintain the decadelong quiescence of the reproductive endocrine system.[9]

9. The physiological translation of the nutritional, sociological, and exertional influences on the reproductive endocrine system is obscure. Extensive studies of neuropharmacologic mediation of these modulators of pubertal onset, along with intrinsic (possibly genetic) CNS factors, remain to be carried out. Plant states that "the mechanisms that dictate the arrest and reawakening of the hypothalamic GnRH pulse generator remain a fundamental problem of developmental neurobiology" (131, p. 1782).

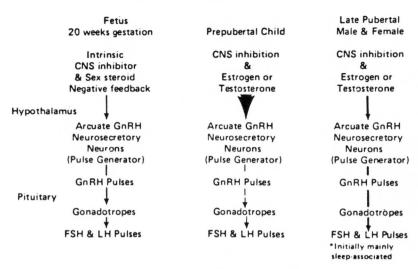

Figure 2.7. A schema demonstrating potential changes in the activity of the arcuate nucleus (medial basal hypothalamus) gonadotropin-releasing hormone (GnRH) pulse generator during development, the possible effects upon pituitary gonadotropes, and the hypothesis that the functional GnRH insufficiency of the prepubertal child is a consequence of central nervous system restraint by sex-steroid–dependent and sex-steroid–independent mechanisms. (From E. O. Reiter, "Neuroendocrine Control Processes," *Journal of Adolescent Health Care*, 8 [1987], 479–491. Copyright © 1987. Reprinted by permission.)

Current Issues

The central questions around which much of the current research revolves are relevant to matters of policy. These include: What is the pubertal experience like for teenagers today, and how does it differ from that in the past, both in the United States and in other cultures? How do pubertal experiences, in some circumstances and for some subgroups, trigger maladaptive responses? How may puberty, in conjunction with other events occurring during early adolescence, influence the emergence of developmental psychopathology? Can puberty (and in what circumstances and for what subgroups) rightfully be considered stormy and stressful, as it has been described since the dawn of adolescent psychology (77)? Does puberty herald an intensification of gender roles, and with it a truncation of role options and aspirations for girls, and is it thus more of a crisis for girls than for boys? And do changes in parental relationship with pubertal children have anything to do with subsequent differences in autonomy and achievement between male and female youth?

Meaning of Pubertal Change

Puberty may elicit a wide array of emotions. The child may feel alternately excited and frightened, pleased and dismayed, by the changes, and, given the rapidity with which they occur, bewildered as well. Physical change may be viewed as a cultural event that marks a transition. In nonindustralized societies, where educational demands do not postpone work and parenthood, the transition is made directly into adulthood. In developed countries, where educational trends delay entry into the work force, the transition is not to adulthood per se but to the intermediate phase that we call adolescence. Thus, the timing of taking on adult roles is associated with the way puberty is construed across cultures. When youth are expected immediately to become parents and working members of the community, puberty is often treated as a rite of passage, with various celebrations and ceremonies. Among the Arapesh of New Guinea,

a girl's first menstruation and the accompanying ceremonial take place in her husband's home. But her brothers must play a part in it and they are sent for; failing brothers, cousins will come. Her brothers build her a menstrual hut, which is stronger and better-constructed than are the menstrual huts of older women . . . The girl is cautioned to sit with her legs crossed. Her woven arm and leg bands, her earrings, her old lime gourd and lime spatula are taken from her. Her woven belt is taken off. If these are fairly new they are given away; if they are old they are cut off and destroyed. There is no feeling that they themselves are contaminated, but only the desire to cut the girl's connection with her past.

The girl is attended by older women who are her own relatives or relatives of her husband. They rub her all over with stinging nettles. They tell her to roll one of the large nettle-leaves into a tube and thrust it into her vulva: This will ensure her breasts growing large and strong. The girl eats no food, nor does she drink water. On the third day, she comes out of the hut and stands against a tree while her mother's brother makes the decorative cuts upon her shoulders and buttocks. This is done so gently, with neither earth nor lime rubbed in—the usual New Guinea method for making scarification marks permanent—that it is only possible to find the scars during the next three or four years. During that time, however, if strangers wish to know whether a girl is nubile, they look for the marks. Each day the women rub the girl with nettles. It is well if she fasts for five or six days, but the women watch her anxiously, and if she becomes too weak they put an end to it. Fasting will make her strong, but too much of it might make her die, and the emergence ceremony is hastened. (113, pp. 92–93)

The Mano of Liberia have a pubertal ceremony for boys:

The boys went through a ceremonial "death." In the old days they were apparently run through with a spear and tossed over the curtain. Onlookers heard a thud as he was supposed to hit the ground inside, dead. Actually, the boy was protected by a chunk of plantain stalk tied on under his clothes. Into this the spear was thrust. A bladder of chicken's blood at the right spot was punctured and spilled to make it all very realistic to other boys and women who could not resist the desire to see their sons, perhaps for the last time. Inside the fence *sa yi ge* (a ritual personage) and two assistants, all masked, caught the boys in mid-air, and dropped a heavy dummy to complete the delusion. The boys were actually unharmed and were quickly carried away into the deep forest which is the Poro grove. (83, pp. 13–14).

When puberty is not a rite of passage, the community typically does not acknowledge the event; instead, more private responses seem to be emphasized. In less industrial settings the advent of puberty may be seen as an economic and political event, in that marriage, which is expected to follow, may cement already existing interfamilial alliances or promote new ones. In addition, the girl's reproductive ability may be perceived as an asset by the father, who wishes to trade on her potential fertility. This fertility, which is inferred from the onset of menstruation, is important in societies where high birth rates are necessary, given labor-intensive agricultural methods and high rates of childhood mortality. It has been posited that chaperonage, bride-price, seclusion, and residence with the bridegroom's family before puberty are all means of regulating fertility prior to marriage and of realizing the economic value of the daughter to the family (122). Indeed, pubertal rituals are more likely to be celebrated in societies in which fraternal interest groups are absent and subsistence economic conditions prevail; in both instances alliances among kin are weak, increasing the value of using daughters as bargaining chips to strengthen them (122).[10]

10. Other, intrapsychic and status-role explanations have been offered for the frequency with which puberty is celebrated in many non-Western societies (35).

Regardless of the context and the form of the ceremony, puberty is celebrated in many world cultures. Somewhat surprisingly, then, either not much is said about puberty in developed societies, or else, at least until recently, it was cast in negative terms. As we have noted, the literature on menarche as recently as the early 1970s perceived the onset of menstruation as a crisis for the pubertal girl. This model was based on retrospective reports by adults of their pubertal experience rather than on prospective studies of girls themselves. Here is a typical adult report: "I had no information whatsoever, no hint that anything was going to happen to me . . . I thought I was on the point of death from internal hemorrhage . . . What did my highly educated mother do? She read me a furious lecture about what a bad, evil, immoral thing I was to start menstruating at the age of eleven! So young and so vile! Even after thirty years, I can feel the shock of hearing her condemn me for 'doing' something I had no idea occurred" (166, p. 169). In addition, the focus was on negative consequences, not on the fact that puberty is a part of growing up for all humans. Perhaps this reflected the psychodynamic and medical perspectives of most of the extant literature. Nonetheless, a reader might have found this view puzzling. After all, menarche was a mark of becoming an adult female. Was this necessarily negative? Did all girls resist growing up? Weren't there positive aspects to becoming mature? The crisis model was subsequently reframed as an examination of the *meaning* of menarche to girls as well as the transition from child to adult (27, 139).

A review of the early literature by Brooks-Gunn indicated that the adult psychoanalytic sources most often characterized menarche as anxiety producing and distressing (26, 45). Her subsequent research, along with that of others, aimed to determine how traumatic menarche actually was for girls, rather than relying on retrospective reports from clinical adult samples (see 11 and 71 for reviews of this literature of the 1970s and early 1980s). In general these studies suggested that girls experience an array of feelings—positive, negative, and ambivalent—as illustrated by a passage from Anne Frank's diary: "Each time I have a period . . . I have the feeling that in spite of all the pain, unpleasantness, nastiness, I have a sweet secret and that is why, although it is nothing but a nuisance to me in a way, I always long for the time that I shall feel that secret within me again" (59, p. 117). When we interviewed girls about how they felt right after menarche occurred (within two to three months), about a fifth reported only positive responses, about a fifth only negative ones, and about a fifth cited indefinite emotions such as "felt same" or "felt funny." The remainder experienced a combination of positive and negative feelings. About 60% were somewhat frightened or upset, although the intensity of these feelings was mild (139).

Given this research experience, Brooks-Gunn developed a less crisis-oriented framework for understanding the meaning of menarche (and, more generally, puberty), one that stresses the changes in self-definitions and relationships that occur as the child experiences puberty in a social setting. In one series of studies she and her colleagues found that girls construct a definition of the menstrual experience from various sources of information, of which direct knowledge of symptoms is only one. The fact that girls' reports of symptoms are correlated with their own premenarcheal expectations suggests that the direct experience of menstruation is interpreted in terms of previously formed assumptions. Moreover, individual differences in symptom reports can be predicted from the situation in which self-definitions are initially formed. Negative reports of symptoms in postmenarcheal girls in grades seven to twelve are associated with their being unprepared for menarche, being early to mature, and receiving information from sources perceived as negative. The definitions established during menarche may be difficult to change; subsequent menstrual experiences are perceived in terms of, and may be formed by, these definitions. Thus, perceptions of menstruation and information received during menarche and shortly thereafter may have long-lasting impact, as we saw with girls in eleventh and twelfth grade (12).

Meanings of Different Pubertal Events

Current research has expanded on these notions of the meaning of puberty to include events other than menarche and compare the meaning of different events.

Menarche. In general, menarche heralds gains in social maturity, peer prestige, and self-esteem, heightening awareness of one's body and increasing self-consciousness (65, 96, 144). As we have seen, girls report somewhat ambivalent but not very intense reactions to menarche. Those who menstruate early and those who are unprepared report more negative experiences at menarche than girls who begin at an average age and girls who are prepared (27, 71).

Girls almost never discuss menarche with boys or their fathers, but they do have extensive exchanges with girlfriends and with their mothers (27). Even among girlfriends, however, they remain reluctant to discuss menstruation immediately after menarche: premenarcheal girls expect to tell more girlfriends than they actually do tell, and one study found that only one-quarter tell anyone other than their mothers when they reach menarche. Little transmission of information seems to take place immediately following menarche, although later on friends share stories about symptoms and negative attitudes. Girls also may select friends based on perceived similarities with respect to menarche (28).

The usefulness of the research literature in helping us understand the significance of pubertal events to adolescents is limited by an emphasis on only one of the many physical changes that occur, on primarily middle school girls, and on an event occurring fairly late in the pubertal process. Research on links between behavior and puberty needs to focus as well on boys, on development of other secondary sexual characteristics, and on the onset of pubertal changes (but see, for exceptions, 31, 62).

Growth of breasts and pubic hair. The onset of breast growth is associated with positive peer relationships, greater salience of sex roles linked with reproduction, and a positive body image, while the onset of pubic hair growth is not (31). Possible explanations include the culturally mediated reproductive meaning attached to breast growth and its importance to others, given that breast development is easily observed while pubic hair growth is not. Our research gives credence to this view. When girls were asked about their reactions to pubertal change, almost all (82%) reported that breast growth was more important to them than pubic hair growth, primarily because "other people can tell" (21). In addition, more mothers talk to their daughters about breast than pubic hair development, and more girls are uncomfortable when discussions about the former are initiated.

Male pubertal events. Very little is known about the meaning of pubertal changes to boys. It is believed that the occurrence of ejaculation, or spermarche, is as significant for boys as menarche is for girls. In a small study midadolescent boys were interviewed with regard to their emotional reactions to the event, sources of information, and extent of peer discussion following the event (62). Emotional reactions to ejaculation were not very negative, although two-thirds of the sample did report being a little frightened, a response comparable to girls' reactions to menarche. Positive responses were stronger than negative ones. Although all boys were somewhat prepared, few sources were mentioned. Indeed, adolescent males may have more information about menarche than ejaculation, given the pervasiveness of health-education classes and their treatment of menarche. These boys, all of whom had had an ejaculation, were extremely reluctant to discuss the experience with parents or peers. None had told peers about their own experiences, although all joked about ejaculation generally. This secrecy may be due in part to spermarche's link to masturbation, a relation that does not exist for menarche.

Meaning of puberty to others. The meaning of puberty to others is typically measured indirectly, as in the study of parent-adolescent relationships as a function of pubertal status (85, 148, 149). Research asking parents about their reactions to pubertal change is sorely needed. Most young adolescents report that they are uncomfortable talking to their parents about pubertal processes (the exception being daughters discussing menarche with their mothers). In addition, girls are embarrassed or angered by their parents' discussing their breast development or their purchase of a bra (11, 34). This was illustrated in Brooks-Gunn's research by girls' interpretations of a picture showing a girl and an adult man watching as an adult woman takes a bra out of a shopping bag:

Story 1

The parents are probably saying that she needs a bra now, and she's probably embarrassed because of her father. And her mother went out and bought it for her.

Story 2

The mother's just went out and bought her daughter a new bra. And the daughter's probably feeling a little embarrassed that the father is probably standing right there, as well as maybe a little excited, I mean it's her first bra.

The father's probably feeling a little embarrassed, and maybe a little down that his daughter's growing up so fast.

And the story ends, the daughter gets the bra, and everybody lives happily ever after.

Story 3

She like went shopping with her mom or something, she got a bra.

Her dad is wondering what they got.

She doesn't want her dad to see.

Her mom took it out, and she was totally humiliated and embarrassed.

Her dad understood and stuff like that, but um, she thought it was really rude of her mother to do that, because, ya know, her mother was sort of teasing her and joking her and so was the dad.

And she was very embarrassed.

Finally, the fact that many adults were unprepared for puberty and did not discuss it with their parents may add to their discomfort, as we suggested earlier.

Timing of maturation. We know much more about the effects of maturational timing on the adolescent than we do about the meaning of pubertal changes. This is somewhat surprising since to understand the relative effect of puberty (that is, timing vis-à-vis one's peers), it would seem necessary to know how individuals generally incorporate societal and personal experiences of this universal set of events into their self-definitions. Again, we believe that ambivalence about puberty, in a society that attempts to ignore adolescent sexual arousal and has not come to grips with the short-term historical changes in sexual behavior, may in part determine the content of research. Hence, this ambivalence helps explain the focus on individual differences rather than the universal experience as well as determining what questions are more "acceptable" ("Are you early, on-time, or late with respect to your peers?" rather than "How physically developed are you, and how do you feel about breast growth, hair development, menarche, and so on?").

The question usually asked has to do with potential negative consequences of being "off-time" with respect to maturation, whether early or late. (This issue is investigated only for timing, although individual differences in duration or sequence may be significant as well.) Girls' and boys' progression through puberty is different, as we showed earlier in this chapter: girls typically have their growth spurt sooner and at different points in the process of developing secondary sexual characteristics than do boys (girls prior to menarche and breast stage 4 and boys after genital stage 4). Early-maturing girls and late-maturing boys are posited to be at greater risk for adjustment problems than other groups, given that they are the two most off-time groups, given relative gender differences in maturation (24).

Early-maturing boys seem to have an advantage relative to late maturers in many aspects of socioemotional and academic functioning, and some of these effects persist into adulthood (116, 125). Some seem to be more pronounced for boys of lower socioeconomic status (SES), for whom early maturation may confer greater prestige in athletics, but this focus may also have the effect of moving them away from academics (41). Thus, late-maturing low-SES boys are at a particular disadvantage with respect to self-esteem and popularity, given the value placed on physical strength, sports, and macho behavior. Interestingly, later in life the popular early-maturing boys may be at a disadvantage, given that the very attributes that increased their adolescent prestige also may tend to result in rigid, sex-stereotyped attributes in middle age rather than more flexible characteristics (125).

Early maturation does not seem to be an advantage for girls, even for a short time. The influence of maturational timing can be seen in physical development, preparation for and feelings about menarche, body image and self-image, and deviant behavior and relationships with parents and peers (girls have been studied more extensively in recent years, given conflicting results in the early longitudinal growth studies; see 24).[11]

Early maturers weigh more and are slightly shorter than are late maturers when pubertal growth is complete, and this difference persists throughout life. Early maturers may not be as well prepared for pubertal change as are late maturers. Early maturers are less likely to report that their father knew about their menarche and are less likely to tell their fathers about it directly (12). Since girls seem to choose girlfriends in part on the basis of physical status, early-maturing girls may have a smaller network of intimate friends (although we have little data directly addressing this theory). Early maturers seem to have a poorer body image than on-time or late maturers, at least when general measures of body image and weight-related indexes are used (9, 51). This is true of girls in elementary, junior, and senior high school. In addition, more eating problems, lasting throughout adolescence, are found among early-maturing girls compared to on-time and late maturers (29). In part, such differences may result because body build is associated with popularity; being thin is a desirable condition for almost all adolescent girls, and dieting is a common response to the current cultural demands for thinness. Early maturers, by virtue of being somewhat heavier than average, do not conform to the cultural values favoring thinness and the prepubertal figure. Thus it is not surprising that they may have a less positive body image (related to weight) and are more concerned about dieting than are later maturers, just as late-maturing boys are concerned about not having large enough muscles.

Early maturers, both boys and girls, may exhibit poorer emotional health than late maturers (14, 129). In addition, early-maturing girls who

11. While we know a great deal about the effects of being an early maturer (24), the literature suffers from various problems: different measures of pubertal status being used to classify individuals' timing (for example, bone age, menarcheal age, peak height velocity, secondary sexual characteristic development); the use of different percentile cutoffs to define early and late maturers (that is, across studies, between 15% and 30% of individuals may be defined as early or late); the use of normative or criterion-based classifications; and the use of age or grade distributions for pubertal events. In addition, comparisons between more deviant groups of off-time maturers (defined statistically, such as two standard deviations away from the norm, making up 1% to 2% of the population, or clinically, such as those children with precocious puberty), and less deviant groups (defined statistically, such as one standard deviation away from the norm, making up one-third of the population) are not made; almost all research focuses on the latter group, the more normative group of off-time maturers. Finally, with the exception of the California Longitudinal Growth Studies, little attention has been given to possible long-term effects of being an off-time maturer (see, for exceptions, 106).

experience negative events at home and in school are more likely to exhibit depressive affect than later-maturing girls who experience similar events (33). Girls also seem to be more negatively affected than boys by the confluence of events occurring during adolescence (128).

Early maturers, both boys and girls, may engage in adult behaviors (such as smoking, drinking, and sexual intercourse) at an earlier age than later maturers. They also seem to be somewhat more advanced with respect to dating than on-time or late maturers, at least in middle school. Actual pubertal status, however, does not seem to be associated with dating behavior (47, 63, 143); dating seems to be heavily age related and associated with peer behavior. By late adolescence differences between early and late maturers in dating and sexual behavior disappear for both boys and girls (91).

We know very little about the effects of maturational timing on parent-child relationships. Hill has reported stress in parent-child relationships for seventh-grade girls who had been menstruating for over a year (86), suggesting that some early-maturing girls may, at least in the short run, have difficulties with their parents (and vice versa). In addition, Steinberg and Hill report that boys at the apex of puberty experience more conflict with their parents than at other times during the pubertal sequence, although how timing enters the equation is not known (149).

Storm and Stress

Perhaps the most commonly held belief about puberty is that it heralds increased emotionality in the form of negative moods and swings in moods. While not as intense or extreme as popular accounts would have us believe, on average, increases in negative emotions do seem to occur between late childhood and late adolescence (whether mood swings increase as well is a fascinating but virtually unexplored issue).

Hormonal factors are postulated to account, in part, for the rise in negative emotions, probable through the activation effects of changes in hormone levels at puberty (8). Hormonal activation may influence excitability, arousal, or emotionality; these in turn may influence how individuals behave. Increased excitability and arousability may result in more rapid and/or intense mood fluctuations, or may render the adolescent more sensitive to environmental conditions. Accordingly, more negative emotions may be experienced following interchanges with peers or parents or other events that could be interpreted as disquieting. The sparse literature suggests that the production of hormones, but not the development of secondary sexual characteristics, is associated with emotionality, specifically aggressive affect in boys and both depressive and aggressive affect in girls (32, 121, 152; see also review, 123). These effects may be greatest when the endocrine system is being turned on. In a study of about one hundred early adolescent girls, negative affect was found to increase as the endocrine system was undergoing its initial large increments, leveling off or dropping after hormones had reached more adult levels. When interpreting such effects, one must take into account the actual magnitude of hormonal associations as well as their relation to social factors. For example, certain negative events may account for negative affect more than do hormonal factors (28).

Another caveat has to do with the possibility of bidirectional effects. We know that the hypothalamic-pituitary-gonadal axis is exquisitely sensitive to environmental conditions. For example, when women experience a considerable loss of weight (as in the case of anorexia nervosa), levels of hormonal secretions are suppressed, with the most obvious manifestation being amenorrhea and anovulatory cycles (that is, lack of menstrual cycles and cycles in which fertility is impaired) (164). In some adolescents experiencing anorexia nervosa or exercise-induced weight loss, a reversion to the prepubertal or early pubertal pattern of lowered-amplitude LH secretion with nocturnal LH spiking is seen. These changes are reversible with weight gain. Also, the genetic program for the timing of puberty may be partially overridden through environmental factors such as nutritional intake, weight gain or loss, and exercise (107).

Sexual Behavior

The other commonly held belief about puberty is that "raging hormones" increase sexual arousal and behavior. Sexual arousal is indeed associated with raised levels of testosterone in middle adolescence, for both boys and girls (159, 160). Sexual behavior, however, as well as sexual arousal, is socially mediated (19). For example, levels of testosterone are associated with sexual activity in boys, independent of secondary sexual development (160). But whether engagement in sexual intercourse increases androgen levels or androgen levels influence sexual behavior is not known. Also, situational effects, if added to the equation, may account for more of the variation in sexual behavior than hormonal levels. Initiation of sexual activity is closely associated with what is normative in one's peer group; so while very early sexual initiation may in part be hormonally influenced, by the time the behavior is normative, it is likely that social factors account for it (see 63 for a similar argument about dating behavior). Thus, even if hormonal effects are demonstrated, they must be evaluated in relation to situational effects before one can assume a direct relation between hormones and behavior. For a second example, prepubertal intercourse is becoming increasingly frequent among some groups of American boys (88), a fact that also illustrates the influence of peer norms. And for a final example, testosterone is *not* associated with some sexual behaviors in girls as it is with boys; perhaps social factors play an even greater role in how girls express sexual arousal (that is, in intercourse). More research on the roles of hormonal changes and social situations on sexual behavior is needed, especially given that the age of engaging in sexual intercourse is very early for some groups, contraception is used sporadically by the majority of youth, sexually transmitted diseases occur more frequently among teenagers than in any other age group, and the specter of AIDS increasingly haunts adolescents (see 18, and Chapters 13 and 17 in this volume).

Maladaptive Responses to Pubertal Growth

Thus far we have examined general behavioral responses to pubertal growth without considering the situational factors that may render a child vulnerable to negative effects of pubertal change. These factors are largely social, such as cultural preferences for thinness, societal pressures on girls to maintain a prepubertal figure in some professions and sports, and situational influences involving peers, school, and family.

Cultural preferences for thinness. Perhaps the most maladaptive response to pubertal growth involves the devaluation of the mature female body. The current extremely slender ideal for feminine beauty has so influenced women that many (from one-half to three-fourths) of adult females of normal weight believe themselves to be overweight (158, 167). Termed by some a "national obsession" (36), the pursuit of this ideal body affects eating behavior as well as self-perceptions. The 1985 Health Insurance Survey found that almost one-half of adult women across age and race were trying to lose weight (158).

Teenagers are affected by this societal preference, so much so that dieting and poor self-images increase as the body develops. Dieting is not the sole province of overweight girls and those for whom dieting is necessary for professional reasons (5, 6, 48). The ideal of thinness and the emphasis on the prepubertal look (58) are believed to contribute to the emergence of dieting at the time of puberty. Because of their desire to conform and their search for guidelines about how to behave, young adolescents may be particularly susceptible to popular mass media stereotypes, especially those values and images presented by the entertainment and fashion industries as vital elements of the "youth culture" (80). Confirmatory evidence found by research indicates that concerns about looks and body shape are paramount in early adolescence and that both boys and girls have these concerns. Numerous literary examples illustrate the depth of these feelings.

> The first imperfection of my skin—the first beginning of my slow, extended decline—had appeared the summer I turned sixteen on the night of a large family dinner party at our house. I admit I behaved badly.
>
> That night my father's newest employee, a clerk fresh out of Harvard Law whom I was very eager to meet, had been invited to dinner . . .
>
> [While carving the roast, my father] leaned over and dropped the first hacked slice of meat onto my plate. Then, on his way back up, he began to scrutinize my nearby face. With more disapproval than curiosity he suddenly said, "What's that?"
>
> "What's what?"
>
> "That on your cheek—there." He pointed at me with the carving knife.
>
> I winced away. I knew perfectly well what he was talking about. What he had picked out publicly to confront me with was something that, after causing me no end of anguish that afternoon I had decided was simply a pimple—a round, brown, ephemeral blemish which I had clumsily tried to cover up with dabs of my mother's make-up snitched from the jars lined up on her crowded dressing table. But, a novice in such methods, I had succeeded only in altering its color. It was no disguise for my father's eagle eye, though it might easily have hidden the imperfection from Alan Steiger, the young lawyer.   (142, pp. 84–86).

He wouldn't ask anyone else, he knew. It was too close to the prom. He put another piece of meat into his mouth. *Oh, God, what was wrong with him?* He thought everything had been going along fine. He would've asked her to go steady. Maybe that's why she broke the date, he thought. She knew they were getting to that point. Perhaps someone else had asked her. Perhaps she had just been using him all these months, just waiting for someone else to come along. Anybody. Anybody was better than Dennis Holowitz. *I'm so ugly, he thought, grinding the meat between his teeth. Ugly, I'm sick. I'm ashamed. My clothes are ugly. My face is ugly. My body is ugly. What am I doing alive? I always come back to this point. It's always there. This ugliness. I can't fight it. I'm running out of strength.* (168, pp. 82–83).

Brooks-Gunn and her colleagues asked adolescent girls to tell a story about a picture of a young girl standing in front of a mirror:

Story 1
She just took a shower and she wants to see if she is growing and all, and I guess she's just like seeing what she looks like. She's growing and she's just like looking at herself in the mirror.

Story 2
She probably thought, you know, she looked bad or something. So she looked in the mirror to see how she looked.

Story 3
She's wondering about what she should wear, and whether she should leave her hair like that, I mean it really looks like a really conservative type of cut.
She gets dressed, she goes to school, and after school she goes to a haircutter and gets her head shaved.

Story 4
She's looking at her face. And she's thinking, um, am I pretty. Um, and um, she's not really. She doesn't know really if she's pretty or not. She's kind of confused.

Professional and athletic demands. One of the possible negative outcomes of both physical development and its timing has to do with the expectations that adolescents have for their eventual appearance. The adolescent may perceive physical growth to be a sort of lottery, an outcome that cannot be known beforehand (80). That is, what will the ultimate shape and appearance of various body parts be? Looking at one's parents may give some hints but not the complete picture (correlations for heritability estimates for mother-daughter menarcheal age are in the 40s and 50s, for parent-offspring height in the 80s, and for parent-offspring weight in the 70s; see 64, 151). Expectations are not always fulfilled; such "mismatches" may set the stage for subsequent maladaptation. This is particularly true for those adolescents engaged in athletic or professional endeavors that require a particular body shape. Brooks-Gunn compared girls in dance company schools with girls in the general population in order to determine how the requirements of a particular social situation match up with individual physical and behavioral characteristics. With respect to dancers the demands are clear: they must maintain a low body weight in order to conform to professional standards and must devote a great deal of time to practice. Dancers are more likely to be late maturers than nondancers (61, 163). Being a late maturer may be particularly advantageous (as well as normative) for dancers, even though it has not been shown to be so for nondancers (30, 129, 143). In keeping with her premise, dancers who matured on time had poorer emotional health and body images and more eating problems than did the later-maturing dancers. Some sports also require (or prefer) particular body types, with similar results for athletes when the requirements call for thinness (18).

School and peer influences. Peer situations other than athletics, in conjunction with pubertal growth, may render an adolescent vulnerable to problem behavior. An example is the finding that, among sixth-grade girls, maturing early influences body image differently depending on whether they are in elementary or middle school (9, 144). A Swedish study found that, while early-maturing girls were more likely to drink and be sexually active than later maturers, the effect was related to having older friends, a phenomenon that was more prevalent among early than among late maturers (105). Presumably, early maturers actively sought or were sought by older adolescents as friends.

Parent-child relationships. Particular parent-child situations that may be sources of conflict are being studied; researchers want to know more about the intensity, meaning, and timing of conflict. Conflict and disagreement seem to be almost universal, though not intense (147). Such conflict is typically seen as temporary, as Hill's term "perturbation" implies (86). Parent-child relations are generally thought to be transformed as both parents and young adolescents renegotiate their relationship (72). While research has documented the nature of early adolescent relationships, discussion is sparse on actual developmental changes (from late childhood through late adolescence) and on the processes underlying them (14, 147).

Changes in parents' and children's expectations for one another may be as significant as changes in actual interaction patterns, although much less research has centered on the former. Children who are tall for their age group are expected by adults to perform more socially mature tasks (10). The fact that leadership and school achievement have been associated with children's and adolescents' height to a small degree (50) suggests the social stimulus value of physical characteristics (the role parents may play in the acquisition of such values has not been specified, however). As children enter puberty, parents may expect better-developed children to exhibit more socially adult behavior. For example, girls who are more physically mature than their peers may elicit more freedom from parents, thus making it likely that they will engage in dating earlier than other girls. These expectations may result in changes in interactions, although the process by which this may occur has not been studied.

Intensification of Gender Roles

Why is puberty seen as negative for girls while no mention of a similar crisis is found for boys? For boys, puberty is believed to expand role possibilities into the realm of work and achievement; for girls, roles are believed to be confined. In Chodorow's terms, boys are characterized as "doing" and girls as "being" (40). These distinctions, while believed to exist prior to puberty as a result of socialization, are thought to become pronounced at puberty, when gender-role divisions become apparent (possibly because of reproductive differences; see 87). Little research exists, however. Does gender-role intensification occur at puberty, and do girls really redefine themselves primarily in terms of reproductive roles while boys do not? If so, what are the processes underlying such self-definitional changes, and how do parents and peers contribute (16)?

Evidence that gender roles intensify at puberty is found in expectations for more "adult" behavior from pubertal children and increasing parental vigilance over girls after puberty. The author of *Kinflicks* gives us a vivid example of gender-role ideology for the pubertal female: "No more football? She might as well have told Arthur Murray never to dance again . . . I went upstairs, and as I exchanged my shoulder pad for a sanitary pad and elastic belt, I knew that menstruation might just as well have been a gastrointestinal hemorrhage in terms of its repercussions on my life" (4, p. 33).

Let us now consider how boys and girls also differ in terms of autonomy, intimacy, and emotional health.

Autonomy. As Erikson has suggested, girls may be more vulnerable to problems with autonomy than boys. Girls are believed to be more emotionally focused on and less individuated from their mothers than are boys (40, 93). Such differences may explain, in part, why girls are believed to speak "in a different voice"—more interpersonal, intimate, and relationally focused (67). Perhaps parent-child interactions occurring in early adolescence are different for boys than for girls. For example, observational studies suggest that girls are interrupted more and ignored more while boys assert themselves more as puberty progresses (86). That mothers seem to exert more power over their postmenarcheal than pre-menarcheal daughters, and that their use of power is associated with their daughters' compliance, suggests a partial explanation for the nonassertive behavior of girls in family interactions (34). More work on the process of autonomy for girls and boys, as well as on the antecedents for and consequences of parental behavior, is obviously called for.

Intimacy. At the same time, boys may be more vulnerable to lack of intimacy. Girls tend to have a smaller number of best friends, to whom they tell everything, while boys tend to have larger groups of friends with whom they engage in activities. While friendship patterns are being studied (see Chapter 11 in this volume), intimacy is not always the focus. Gilligan's work underscores the importance of intimacy to females (67); its lack in men is left to novelists and popular psychologists, who decry men's inability to form close relationships. Boys may be more vulnerable to intimacy problems that emerge, or become more salient, at the time of puberty. While this is speculative, the fact that it is culturally unacceptable to talk about male pubertal changes and the feelings they engender may be a pivotal issue in how males structure their friendships. In contrast, almost all girls today talk over pubertal changes with their mothers and their close girlfriends. Whether and how such differences influence disclosure and intimacy is not known, however.

Emotional health. Three of the best-studied and most prevalent psychiatric problems (and their less severe forms) are depression (depressive affect), conduct disorders (aggressive behavior and affect), and eating disorders (compulsive eating). All three are linked to gender, become more prevalent after puberty, and are associated with personality factors and situational events (see Chapters 16 and 17 in this volume).

Perhaps the most alarming outcome associated with the pursuit of thinness through dieting is the rising incidence of weight-related clinical syndromes among adolescent and young adult females (5, 6; see Chapter 17). Anorexia nervosa is an eating disorder characterized by behavior directed toward weight loss, by peculiar attitudes toward food, by distorted body image, and by an implacable refusal to maintain body weight. Occurring predominantly in females (90% to 95% of all cases), it is one of the few psychiatric disorders that can follow an unremitting course resulting in death. It is most likely to occur just after the pubertal weight spurt (78). Bulimia is an eating disturbance characterized by episodes of uncontrollable overeating, usually followed by vomiting, exercise, or laxative abuse to prevent food absorption. It occurs most frequently in late adolescence and early adulthood.

Severe depression is more likely to occur after puberty than before (38, 133). In addition, postpubertal girls are much more likely to be diagnosed as depressed than are boys, with these differences continuing into adulthood (140). Hormonal, sex role, and situational factors have been posited to account for these differences (25, 68, 119).

Conduct disorders and aggression are more prevalent among boys than girls from early childhood on, although they increase dramatically in early adolescence, suggesting that pubertal factors may exacerbate existing predispositions (which themselves are probably both biologically and socially mediated). In addition, younger boys with severe acting-out behavior problems are at much higher risk than girls for conduct disorders in adolescence and later in adulthood (see Chapter 16 in this volume; also 53, 137).[12]

Implications for Education and Future Directions

Studying the role of pubertal processes in the early adolescent transition has several implications for health and academic education. Pubertal children are not well educated about reproductive changes (19, 22, 84, 95). Courses in sex education and family life are not offered in all school districts, and in those that do offer them (about three-quarters nationally), education is not provided in fifth and sixth grade, the time when the majority of children are beginning to develop secondary sexual characteristics. Furthermore, existing programs are often brief and not particularly extensive. Programs have been shown to increase knowledge about reproduction without resulting in an earlier initiation of sexual intercourse (88). The specter of HIV infection may alter sex education in the schools. The fact that 94% of all parents want their schools to provide information to their children on the spread of HIV infection and AIDS (82) may offer an opportunity to expand the health-education curriculum more generally (18).

The off-time maturer, particularly the early-maturing girl, is currently provided little information about her maturational status. While children who mature extremely early or late are likely to come to the attention of a physician, early or late maturers within the normal range are not. These children may nonetheless have some concerns about being abnormal. A brief discussion outlining the sequence and timing of an event and the wide range of variations may be all that is needed to reassure many off-time maturers.

Parents, teachers, and school nurses could benefit from information about the potential pressures to date and to engage in adultlike behavior that pubertal children often face. Also, the knowledge that conflicts often

12. Prospective studies are necessary in order to understand the antecedents of these disorders, and, in a more normative sense, the less severe problems, as well as to see how the antecedents may differ for pubertal males and females. In addition, comparative studies of different sets of factors that may predispose a boy to be prone to aggression and a girl to depression, for example, are needed. Almost none exist.

surround the process of growing up may reassure parents and adolescents who find these altercations stressful. Finally, we need to let adults and teenagers know that some youths respond negatively to puberty and that certain factors and situations render them vulnerable to problems associated with pubertal change, such as the dieting and binging behavior seen in many segments of our society. Decreases in certain nutrients (for example, iron and calcium) at puberty may have long-term health implications, including bone weakness and hormonal problems (165).

With regard to academic achievement, we have said little about the role of puberty in cognitive development (see Chapter 3 in this volume). It is clear, however, that puberty may influence school achievement in a variety of indirect ways. Depressive affect and low self-esteem are generally associated with poor school performance; factors that increase the likelihood of poor emotional health may thus diminish academic achievement (128). Making the transition to middle school, a time at which academic demands increase, may be difficult for pubertal children, especially if the middle school begins in sixth grade (143). The confluence of multiple biological and social events seems to presage an increase in school problems and depressive affect (7, 145). Coping with family problems at the time of puberty may be especially difficult for girls, setting in motion a pattern of low self-esteem and school failure (127). Maturing early, for both girls and boys, may lead to a focus on dating and peer relationships, to the detriment of school achievement (106). While such factors have been shown to have short-term effects, little research addresses long-term school problems or factors that can either maintain a negative pattern or act as self-righting mechanisms.

While by no means exhaustive, this chapter sets out current approaches to the study of puberty as well as recommendations for future directions. In the biological realm we still do not understand fully the physiological mechanisms responsible for initiating and regulating neuroendocrine maturation and somatic growth, nor do we know how environmental factors may interact with biological ones to enhance or impede maturation. From a clinical perspective, the biological and social markers for severe problems such as depression, conduct disorders, and eating disorders are not well understood, nor are the reasons for their emergence or increase following the transition to adolescence. Few investigators have examined the role pubertal processes may play in cognitive change or the role of cognition in the emergence of negative emotions. Social-cognition perspectives are just beginning to be applied to the transition to adolescence, with this work being directed toward attributions and rule setting in the conventional, social, and moral realm. Other processes possibly associated with pubertal change (self-definition, social comparison, and so on) await investigation. Psychodynamic perspectives are regrettably rare in our research, even though clinical theorizing has been the basis for much of the current thinking on parent-child relationships, storm and stress, identity formation, and gender-role intensification, all topics of considerable interest. Not enough attention is being given to the progression from pubertal growth to sexuality. Across all topics too few cross-cultural and multiethnic studies have been conducted. Finally, the long-term implications of pubertal change and pubertal influences on behavior are just beginning to be studied.

3

ADOLESCENT THINKING

Daniel P. Keating

How does the thinking of adolescents differ from that of children or adults? Answers to this question are central to our understanding of adolescents and to guiding the policy decisions that affect them. The question is deceptively simple. It presumes agreement on what we mean by *thinking*. Scarcely a decade ago research on adolescent thinking could easily have been organized around a few central questions (56). Since then, accumulating evidence from a variety of perspectives has strikingly expanded the questions that must be considered and made consensus a more distant goal.

Loss of consensus is not unique to this field, nor should it be regarded as wholly problematic. In many areas that deal directly or indirectly with human cognitive activity, significant doubts have emerged about the nature and value of "certainty"—from philosophical inquiry into thinking (86), to mathematics, the "queen of sciences" (68), to the field of cognitive development (63). If in the past coherence was based on serious misapprehensions, then its loss is in reality a gain, for it invites us to ask important but previously ignored questions. Also, policy decisions based on misguided consensus can lead to unintended, and sometimes undesirable, consequences.

Resolving—or even confronting—fundamental theoretical questions about human cognition is beyond the scope of this chapter. Instead, my focus is more practical. Many cognitive researchers have shifted their attention away from purely theoretical questions, asked primarily in the laboratory, and toward more applied issues in which context and content play a central role (84). Much of the compelling new research arises from asking questions concerning matters such as the teaching of thinking and the chances of success for cognitively oriented intervention programs. And, in contrast to the decline of agreement regarding basic explanations, a reasonable consensus has begun to take shape about desirable goals in adolescents' cognitive performance in both academic and informal settings.

Finding a Framework

Two broad and complementary perspectives serve as a framework for this analysis: applied cognitive science and applied developmental psychology. The goal of the former is to turn the new and sophisticated methods of cognitive science to the analysis of real-world cognitive activity. The goal of the latter is related, in that it seeks to understand both the developmental sources of this activity and the relationship of cognitive development to other areas such as social and emotional development (84).

In addition, these applied perspectives focus on what we need to know in order to facilitate adolescent cognitive development. Through formal education, informal socializing agents (such as television), and broad social, cultural, and economic factors, society dramatically affects adolescent thinking. Designing policies that lead to desired outcomes requires critical examination of the nature of adolescent thinking and, at the same time, the social factors that shape it.

Many observers have bemoaned the low level of critical thinking among adolescents in a variety of academic fields, and have voiced concerns regarding the capacity of current educational practices to address the problem (30, 34, 57, 87, 88, 101). To the extent that such thinking is crucial for active participation in an increasingly information-based society—and there seems little reason to doubt that this is so—fundamental questions about the organization of formal schooling must be addressed. Insights derived from much of the current work in applied cognitive science, especially on the teaching of thinking, speak directly to this concern.

But the connection between formal schooling and adolescent thinking should not be overstated. There are many influences besides school. For example, the average adolescent in the United States watches over twenty thousand television advertisements annually, and advertisers, in an attempt to create goals or desires to be fulfilled by their products, often design ads intended to bypass or overcome adolescents' rational decision-making processes (78). We know far too little about the cognitive effects of mass media, whose technology continues to develop exponentially (cable television, MTV, VCRs, interactive video, and more). It is reasonable to assume, however, that the impact of these media will increase, and in ways that may be hard to predict. Olson (91), for example, has argued persuasively that literacy has had a major effect on human cognitive structures and processes. It seems safe to assume that the information technologies now coming into near-universal use will play a similar role.

Consider, too, the host of social policies that rely on a grasp of adolescent thinking characteristics. For many public health issues, for example, public education offers the major, and sometimes the only, effective means of intervention and prevention. To counter the health risks to adolescents posed by unprotected sexual activity or by drug use, to cite two prominent examples, we must rely to a significant extent on education. But we know relatively little about adolescents' decision-making competence in the real world (81). The available evidence suggests, however, that their potential for competent decision making is often greater than their performance in real situations, and that constraints on their performance derive from a range of social forces. Seen in this light, the problem of developing effective public health education requires that we understand as clearly as possible what types of messages adolescents can comprehend and use when needed.

One other key dimension of adolescent thinking deserves inclusion. As we consider issues affecting thinking, it is easy to assume that cognitive activity can be separated from other aspects of adolescent development. This would be a mistake. Cognitive changes are intimately linked to other developmental dynamics, and it is perilous to ignore them. These mutually influential links are perhaps impossible to unravel, but in concert they play a leading role in the effectiveness of interventions. As later chapters in this volume illustrate, changing perceptions—of the self, of the family, of peers, and of the broader society—influence and are influenced by the cognitive changes of adolescence.

Critical thinking, for example, may be as much a disposition as a skill (57, 88, 101, 106). It is thus likely to be influenced by the emerging sense of oneself as a consciously aware individual, by the value placed on such activity by significant others, and by the perceived opportunities to use it meaningfully in one's life (70). This interplay of cognitive growth with other areas of personal and social development has only recently emerged as a focus of research, but it highlights the necessity of integrating cognitive science and broader developmental perspectives.

Principal Questions and Methods

With this framework in mind, we can turn to the questions that organize the analysis of adolescent thinking. Note that this chapter has been broken down into sections for the purpose of explanation; this structure is not meant to suggest that the issues raised under different headings are independent of one another. On the contrary, one of the key themes in the review of current research is that these developments are fundamentally interdependent, especially when we concern ourselves with how adolescents function in real settings. The central questions are

- What develops, and how does it develop?
- What key factors affect adolescent cognitive development?
- How can we use this information to construct effective social and educational policies?

Before we turn directly to these questions, we should recognize that the answers are often closely related to the methods used to ask them. An extensive review of the implications of the differences in method for both theory and practice is beyond the scope of this chapter (34, 62, 63). A brief summary of some central issues, however, will place the research findings in perspective and will enable us to draw on the available literature in an integrative fashion, without concerning ourselves about its origins.

Individual Differences

Methods derived from *psychometric* or *differential* psychology were historically the earliest approaches to the study of adolescent cognition, and they remain the most influential in terms of practical impact on the lives of adolescents. Here the focus is on individual (and sometimes group) differences in the ability to perform well on cognitively complex tasks. The principal method is to administer standardized instruments, on which performance is analyzed in relation to broad population norms. Most of the available data on adolescent achievement are derived from these methods (100). Furthermore, the general public, including adolescents, understand that doing well on psychometric indicators such as the Scholastic Aptitude Tests is a major factor in educational and career success. These and similar instruments are used extensively for screening and selection.

Paradoxically, the practical influence of psychometric approaches has increased even as the theoretical underpinnings have come under ever sharper and less favorable scrutiny (39, 62, 113). One common theme is the difficulty of making inferences about cognitive competence based on the products of cognitive activity rather than on analyses of underlying processes and structures.

There is widespread concern regarding overreliance on such indicators of cognitive products in educational selection and advancement, and in curriculum development and teaching. Since such indicators often constitute the data for educational accountability, the types of cognitive skills that they emphasize—or ignore—can have dramatic effects on what and

how we teach adolescents. Frederiksen, for example, has argued that standardized tests contribute substantially to an educational bias in what is
taught and, hence, learned (38). Tests of critical skills and higher-order
thinking, for example, are difficult to create for mass administration. We
need to entertain the possibility that engaging in advanced thinking may
be more hindered than helped by current educational methods (57).

Because of their widespread use, however, psychometric test findings
do provide basic information on the cognitive achievements of large samples of the adolescent population, and they are often the criteria against
which other types of cognitive indicators are judged, whether implicitly
or explicitly. Little doubt exists about the reliability and replicability of
the performance patterns obtained with such methods; the major caution
is to avoid hasty inferences about what psychological constructs they
represent or explain.

Developmental Stages

In contrast to psychometric approaches, *Piagetian models* are based on a
different set of underlying explanations and have typically employed quite
different methods. The tenets of Piaget's theory are well described elsewhere (10, 14, 40, 51, 56, 58, 59, 97). Piaget focused on the development and
organization of logicomathematical operations through four major stages
or periods: the sensorimotor functioning of infancy; the preoperational,
largely egocentric thinking of early childhood; the concrete operational
logic of middle and later childhood; and the formal operational logic that
characterizes adolescence and adulthood. The cognitive operations within
any given stage are organized in a structure; thus, stage changes imply
shifts in underlying structure brought about through the constructive
interaction of the individual with the physical and social world. At the
stage of formal reasoning the structure is described as the coordinated
functioning of the sixteen binary operations of propositional logic (56).
This progression is presumed to be universal and invariable.

Inhelder and Piaget developed a number of tasks through which the
transition from the concrete operations of childhood to the formal operations of adolescence and adulthood can be indirectly observed (51). They
explored several major kinds of tasks drawn from the domains of mathematics and the physical sciences. Despite some initially supportive data,
most of the more recent evidence has tended primarily to raise doubts
about the validity of the original formal operations theory (17, 40, 56, 59,
77). Identifying underlying logic as the actual *source* of age-related changes
in performance has proved problematic. In particular, other potential

limitations on the cognitive abilities of preadolescents and early adolescents—such as memory capacity or efficiency, content knowledge differences, and task familiarity—are difficult to rule out.

A significant practical implication of this move away from stage models of formal reasoning and its development should be noted. A common use—or perhaps more accurately misuse (14, 58, 59)—of the Piagetian model within educational circles has been to view these developments as placing limits on the ability of adolescents to think logically or critically. Proposals to limit instruction until such forms of reasoning have the necessary maturational base (33; see also the section of this chapter on brain maturation) receive little support from the accumulating research literature (57). Indeed, the import of much of the research is that supportive contexts and early attention to the development of reasoning are precisely what is required to increase the likelihood of its emergence.

Much of the Piagetian legacy, however, benefits current work on adolescent cognition. The emphasis on adolescence as a transitional period in cognitive development remains justifiably influential. In addition, much of the systematic data on developmental differences in performance on a range of cognitive tasks derives from this approach.

Cognitive Processes

The *information processing* perspective has been both the source and the beneficiary of emerging critiques of psychometric and Piagetian approaches. In light of some of the difficulties encountered in both perspectives, many cognitive developmental researchers have moved toward some version of cognitive processing analysis (19, 36, 114). In general, the goal of an information-processing approach is to describe accurately the cognitive activities individuals engage in during the performance of various laboratory or real-world tasks.

There are many conceptions of human information processing. The majority of these have focused attention on a specific aspect of the processing system; attempts to describe the system as a whole are relatively rare. There are at least two reasons for breaking the information-processing system into a number of components. First, one might wish to validate in some way the reality of each of these hypothetical components. If so, it would be necessary to isolate the operation of one component while equating the functions of other components (experimentally or statistically). Second, one might wish to generate a plausible list of contributors to performance on some complex cognitive activity—higher-order thinking, for example. The former goal—validating the independent existence and contribution of various processing components—has been elusive (62, 114). But there is considerable value in the latter approach, which is primarily heuristic rather than theoretical. It affords systematic examination of relevant findings on adolescent thinking and is thus well suited to our purposes.

Cognitive Socialization

The three approaches just described concentrate on the internal structures of cognitive activity and changes in them. One other substantially different perspective is worth noting, even though its direct contribution to the research on adolescent cognition is minimal thus far: the *contextualist* or *cognitive socialization approach* described by Vygotsky (117). In this view social interaction, especially discourse, plays the key role in shaping basic cognitive structures and processes. An important theoretical distinction separates this approach from the other three (63): the major point here is that many differences in cognitive performance may be related to identifiable features of the cognitive environment.

To date this contextualist perspective has focused largely on broad environmental differences such as culture and social class (28), and has been criticized for exchanging psychological for sociological determinism (113). The most interesting questions have yet to be addressed, however; these focus not on broad demographic influences but instead on social interactions in which individuals engage—parent-child, teacher-student, and so on—and their effects on cognitive growth (12, 63). For example, a number of commentators have noted the role of small-group discourse in the formation of higher-order thinking in adolescence (87, 101). If it is true that the nature of social activities that adolescents experience plays a fundamental role in shaping thinking, then the educational and social practices that support or inhibit thinking are critical.

What Develops, and How Does It Develop?

Much of the research on adolescent thinking can be organized into broad categories. We can conveniently establish three distinct levels for describing the ways in which adolescents' thinking may differ from that of children or adults: basic processing capacity or efficiency; the knowledge base; and cognitive self-regulation. As we shall see, each of these has useful subdivisions.

As I noted previously, we also need to investigate the ways in which various features of the cognitive system interrelate. Such research may well provide the key to fruitful educational and social interventions in the future. Indeed, one common weakness of many interventions has been their focus on just one aspect of cognitive activity, on the assumption that changes could be generalized broadly. Failure to transfer, however, even to relatively closely related skills or tasks, has been the more usual finding (88, 89, 90, 101). Available evidence suggests quite strongly that shortcuts to significant cognitive growth turn out more often to be cul-de-sacs. On a more positive note, the evidence also suggests that cognitively richer and more integrated efforts offer substantial promise (49, 90, 101).

Basic Cognitive Processes

Changes with age in the speed, efficiency, or capacity of basic cognitive processing may contribute substantially to observed differences in much more complex performances (18, 60). To the extent that highly repetitive processes—such as those executed in working memory—are more efficient or have more capacity with which to operate, then more cognitive resources are available for other demands.

There are several kinds of evidence. A number of studies have examined developmental and individual differences in performance on experimental tasks designed to isolate features of cognitive processing (62). We might also expect such basic processing changes to be associated with features of brain maturation, and a number of researchers have explored this possibility (32, 115).

Cognitive bases. Findings are generally consistent in revealing age differences on a range of cognitive experimental tasks, with substantial changes occurring from late childhood to early adolescence and smaller differences thereafter (at least until late adulthood). It is less clear how to interpret these differences, for several related reasons. First, do such approaches succeed in isolating variations in fundamental processes and controlling for potential artifacts such as knowledge or strategies? Chi, for example, demonstrated that child chess experts showed better memory for chess locations than adult novices (25). Manis, Keating, and Morrison found that 12-year-olds were markedly better than 8-year-olds, and slightly worse than 20-year-olds, at allocating attention in a dual-task situation (80). This could be because the older subjects have more resources available (that is, through fundamental changes in efficiency or capacity), or because they are more skilled at directing available resources (indicating a change in strategy), or some combination of these factors.

A second concern is to determine the practical importance of such changes, assuming they can be clearly identified. Basic processing differences that explain few age or individual variations in more realistic, complex tasks are relatively less significant. There are some indications that as we develop "purer" measures of basic processing, they will explain fewer of the differences on more complex tasks (62).

Perhaps it is misguided to ask how basic cognitive processes change *independently* of changes in expertise. The evidence is overwhelming that growth in expertise is accompanied by, and to some extent dependent on, the automatization of basic processes in the relevant domain. It may be that adolescents do have more basic resources available, but it makes sense to ask how these compare to changes in automaticity resulting from concentrated efforts to acquire domain-specific expertise. In particular, it would be inappropriate to shape educational policies on the assumption that adolescents do not have adequate cognitive resources to acquire impressive levels of expertise (53).

Brain maturation. Several potential changes in brain development related to adolescent cognition have been proposed. The first of these focuses on possible brain growth spurts at about the time of puberty, and hypothesizes that certain cognitive functions are closely tied to such spurts (32). The second focuses on the relative development of the left and right cerebral hemispheres (115). A third proposal, less explicitly neurological in terms of proposed mechanisms, focuses instead on the timing of puberty as an enabling or inhibiting factor for developing advanced levels of certain kinds of abilities, especially spatial abilities (118, 119).

The most explicit argument for fundamental constraints on adolescent thinking is based on the neurophysiological work of Epstein (32). His argument, which linked changes in cognitive functioning indexed by Piagetian stage assessments to spurts in whole brain growth (phrenoblysis), has been examined by a number of investigators. It is crucial to examine this model because it has become widely influential in educational circles. The claim is that teaching cognitively demanding subject matter should be delayed until brain maturation is ensured (33).

Empirical and methodological critiques of phrenoblysis conclude that the claims of related periodicity in whole-brain growth and cognitive activity are not sustained by the original data, nor have other scientists been able to replicate many of the key findings (45, 83). Nor has the target of causal explanation—fundamental cognitive restructuring at the beginning of adolescence—been clearly isolated. Thus, even if a whole-brain growth spurt could be empirically established, it could not easily be linked to a specific type of cognitive restructuring.

Thatcher and his colleagues have examined the differential growth of the cerebral hemispheres (115), rather than focusing on whole-brain growth. On the basis of these findings they argue for five dominant growth periods from birth to adulthood in specific features of brain organization, and note that these overlap with broad Piagetian stages of cognitive development. The last two periods, from ages 11 to 14, and from age 15 to adulthood, primarily involve frontal lobe connections. Although they interpret their data as providing neurophysiological validation for cognitive stage theories, cautions similar to those mentioned earlier apply. Note too that many of the postchildhood transitions are not statistically significant (115, p. 1112).

A third hypothesis linking physiological changes to the development of adolescent cognitive activity states that differential maturation rates, specifically linked to brain lateralization, may be implicated in the different levels of spatial aptitude observed between boys and girls (118, 119). A meta-analysis of the numerous studies generated by this hypothesis reveals no convincing empirical support (79). Across a large number of studies, the differences in spatial ability between boys and girls did not change at adolescence. Major variations were observed primarily in mental rotation, and less so in spatial perception (79). Similarly, a review of numerous studies of verbal ability and brain lateralization found no gender differences at all (50). On the basis of these extensive reviews, a pubertal mechanism for explaining gender differences in abilities receives little support. Some slight overall maturation effects may yet be established, showing higher achievement among early maturers; but it is not yet clear whether these effects, if robust, should be explained in terms of cognitive factors, social factors, or some other influence (96).

The theoretical and practical implications of these findings differ somewhat. Theoretically, interesting suggestions about spurts in some facets of brain maturation associated with the adolescent transition continue to arise, although they have generally proved difficult to substantiate. Additional research to clarify these possibilities will be of interest. Serious methodological difficulties do, however, need to be recognized (47).

At a practical level, it is clear that using theories of brain maturation to guide educational or other interventions is, at best, premature. In particular, the practice of revising curriculum to lessen the cognitive challenges for preadolescents and early adolescents while educators await some specific physiological maturation is *not* supported by the best available data. Indeed, most evidence on the development of adolescent thinking suggests that such delays may actually be harmful.

Knowledge and Thinking

The most striking development in research on adolescent thinking in recent years has been a renewed interest in the role of knowledge and the relationship of knowledge to cognitive processes. Much of this has arisen in two contexts. First, an interest in the acquisition of expertise in specific domains has consistently revealed that the ability to reason effectively is crucially dependent on familiarity with the content about which one is reasoning (26, 42, 101). Second, attempts to find evidence of highly generalizable, content-independent formal logic among adolescents (and adults), through a variety of means including intervention studies, have been widely unsuccessful (56, 59, 77, 90).

Current research, however, does provide encouraging evidence that higher-order thinking among adolescents is attainable. The caution is that desirable cognitive outcomes are neither easily nor automatically attained.

Knowledge structures. It is useful to start with an overview of some of the major changes with age in adolescents' performance on a sequence of complex cognitive tasks. Reliable age differences can be observed in cognitive performance, and this evidence is of value in practical planning. In this discussion I shall consider several accounts of how best to understand these differences.

Across a wide range of content areas, from logical and mathematical topics (20), to moral reasoning (27, 102), to interpersonal understanding (61, 107, 109, 116), to social and political issues (see Chapter 18 of this volume), to the nature of knowledge itself (23, 66), there is substantial consistency in the ways in which adolescents, compared to children, respond to problems posed to them.

These broadly observed changes have been given a sometimes bewildering array of labels. One risk in choosing a label is that it is often interpreted (and intended) as an explanation for the shift. But in reality there are several plausible explanations for the same findings. Although the data are derived from grouped age differences, there is a further tendency to assume that such thinking is characteristic of most adolescents in most situations, an assumption that is not well supported by research (77).

With these caveats in mind, we can say that from early adolescence on, thinking tends to involve abstract rather than merely concrete representation; to become multidimensional rather than limited to a single issue; to become relative rather than absolute in the conception of knowledge; and to become self-reflective and self-aware. It should be emphasized that most of the evidence for such shifts comes from controlled situations in which complex problems are posed to participants and ample time for deliberation is afforded them. This probably tends to overestimate the sophistication of adolescents' thinking in everyday matters, which often tend to pose time-limited, dynamic, and personally stressful cognitive challenges (61).

This is a distinction of practical as well as theoretical and methodological significance. It is probably safest to assume that these shifts represent *potential* accomplishments for most adolescents rather than typical everyday thinking. Considerable research from the literature of applied cognitive science suggests that adolescents' (and adults') spontaneous thinking is rarely as systematic, reflective, or intentional as this characterization would imply (30, 34, 105). At a practical level, it would be foolhardy to assume that cognitive interventions for adolescents could rely on highly active and reflective engagement with demanding material. Yet attempts to encourage such higher-level engagement, if carried out systematically, do offer considerable promise.

One way to account for these broad changes in adolescent thinking is to maintain a central role for hypothesized structural shifts in logic—that is, a Piagetian change in core logical competence. To explain the findings that performance is dramatically affected by the content and context of the task, researchers have proposed a number of separate performance factors (14, 15, 92). For example, Moshman and Franks identify the ability to make valid inferences as the key logical shift; they focus on age 12 as a crucial turning point (85). But, as their data indicate, the age at which one ascribes this core competence to children's or adolescents' performance depends on the criterion used. Preadolescents (9 to 10 years old) do choose the correct conclusion from a set of premises when the conclusion does not conflict with empirical reality. But they perform poorly, and 12-year-olds somewhat better, when they must evaluate the validity of an argument whose conclusion is untrue in reality. Moshman and Franks use this latter criterion—the separation of a logically valid argument from empirical reality—as representing a "genuine grasp" of validity. But such a choice seems arbitrary; effective causal reasoning rarely uses this type of thinking.

Nor does this approach solve the conceptual problems involved in isolating fundamental shifts of logical competence. In particular, the claim that syllogistic reasoning tasks per se constitute a direct test of underlying logical competence cannot be validated (14, 58). It is interesting to note, however, that on such tasks it is typically between the ages of 11 and 14 that a majority of individuals first begin to meet some, though not all, criteria for achieving adequate formal logical solutions.

Two other interesting findings emerge from the continuing search for core formal logical competencies. First, it is evident that modest interventions have little impact; for formal logic even more sustained training may not have much of an effect (90). Second, the greatest difficulties arise when individuals are asked to reason in tasks for which there is no real content, and especially in which the logical solution to an argument conflicts with empirical reality.

This last point deserves further emphasis. Most real-world causal reasoning, including scientific reasoning, probably relies far less on abstract and formal logic than on pragmatic and informal thinking (71, 73, 90). For causal reasoning a sound grasp of empirical reality is as important as logic. In this view there is little point in trying to explain reasoning independent of a knowledge of content. It seems most likely that progress in logic among adolescents will occur when it is embedded in, rather than separated from, knowledge of content or subject matter (34). Future research should aim in this direction.

Beyond the search for fundamental shifts in logic, there are a number of other approaches for dealing with the broad transitions in adolescent thinking.

Case has described a model for joining neo-Piagetian or structural approaches with an information processing perspective (19). In this view teenagers do make substantial conceptual gains in a variety of content areas. Several related changes make these conceptual reorganizations possible. Adolescents have increasingly more cognitive resources available to them owing to the automatizing of basic processes, a greater familiarity with a range of content knowledge, an increased capacity of working memory, or some combination of these factors. Because of the reduced load on the cognitive system, adolescents become capable of holding in mind several different dimensions (or vectors) of a topic or problem, whereas previously they could focus on only one. This ability to generate and consider different representations of information creates an opportunity for broad conceptual reorganizations. From this perspective, shifts in the structure of knowledge are inevitably blended with changes in basic processing, content knowledge, and other developments. Whether it is possible, or useful, for research to try to separate these features remains an open question.

One reason for seeking to identify different cognitive features would be to learn more about the kinds of instruction that would assist in their development. Kuhn has explored the growth of scientific reasoning—that is, the ability of individuals to generate, test, and evaluate hypotheses about cause-and-effect relationships, and in particular to coordinate theory with evidence (73, 74).

Several significant findings have emerged from that series of studies. Overall, it seems that the ability to bracket one's own theory—that is, to hold different mental representations of "the theory" versus "the evidence"—emerges quite gradually, and is affected substantially by familiarity with content and the context of the task. In the basic paradigm individuals are asked to offer theories about what factors might cause certain effects. They are then presented with evidence bearing on the problem. By and large, children seem to be dominated by their naive theories. Evidence that goes against their belief is either ignored or transformed. Early adolescents seem to perceive some obligation to take evidence into account, but they still have difficulty maintaining separate representations of theory and evidence, and are likely to alter either or both in midstream. By late adolescence individuals have developed some skill at separating theory from evidence, but even then this process remains somewhat tenuous. In particular, the failure of evidence to conform to theory is apparently easy to ignore; the discovery of evidence that supports a rival theory usually leads to some alteration of one's theories (72).

Another key finding is that the similarities between adults and adolescents in drawing causal inferences are more striking than the differences, a point echoed by Koslowski and Okagaki (71). Even college students are far from perfect in evaluating evidence for theories. The powerful role that education plays in performance is also noteworthy. Non–college-educated adults, in fact, succeed at a level between that of sixth-graders and ninth-graders on several tasks in Kuhn's research (73). In general, though, the age differences I have noted are in line with much of the previous research on formal operations. The increases in performance are linear and gradual, with the 11-to-14 age range as the period during which a minority of generally successful reasoners becomes a majority.

These points should also be viewed in light of the work on children's intuitive theories about scientific knowledge (17). Although children often have limited or mistaken notions about a wide range of scientific or even everyday topics, it would be incorrect to assume that their theories are either wholly inconsistent or lightly held. The interaction between currently held theories and the ability to draw causal inferences may therefore be crucial. Poor performance by children and adolescents on many reasoning tasks may reflect relatively unsophisticated knowledge and an inability to suppress those habits of mind, as well as immature causal inference skills (73).

One other interesting finding is that during the transitional period early adolescents seem to reject the possibility that *any* reliable conclusions can be drawn. When early adolescents first begin correctly to give a "can't tell" response to logical syllogisms, they also give such an answer when, indeed, there *is* a valid conclusion—and one that younger children state quite readily (92). This sort of rampant relativism may be a necessary cost of becoming a critical reasoner, but it may have broader implications as well (23).

This pattern may be of considerable interest in future research. Baltes has described a life-span model of development that involves the dynamic interplay of gain and loss (4). This may aptly characterize important transitions in adolescent thinking, which we have usually looked at only in terms of gain. We have seen in several contexts—the "can't tell" response on syllogistic reasoning tasks, the difficulty encountered when valid arguments conflict with empirical reality, and the assertion that reliable conclusions based on reasonable evidence are not possible—that early adolescents react variably to the demands of critical thought. They tend to hold tightly to the idea that concrete reality is a guide to certainty. Later, as they accept the possibility of uncertainty and relativism, they may react by overgeneralizing this to a belief that *no* knowledge or reasoning is really reliable. At an extreme this may become a full-blown skeptical outlook (23) in which the value of knowledge itself falls into disrepute.

Two tentative connections for future investigation can be drawn. First, we can usefully categorize a number of these cognitive changes as reflecting a broad cognitive differentiation beginning in early adolescence. In general, differentiation in this sense means the increasing ability to hold several complex mental representations simultaneously. This cognitive differentiation may be closely related to other key psychological developments, particularly in the self-system (see Chapter 14 of this volume) and in relationships with significant others, both family and peers. That is, a broader process of psychological separation and individuation, which requires a relatively advanced level of objectifying the self in relation to others, may be intimately connected to the more traditional cognitive changes noted earlier. If so, this would imply close connections among cognitive, social, and emotional developments. Such mutual influences need to be explored further.

A second tentative conclusion is that the eventual resolution of this differentiation or objectification process may not always take the form of effective reintegration or coordination. In an interesting look at adolescents' and young adults' naive beliefs about physics, diSessa describes them as having "knowledge in pieces," even within specific domains (30). It is evident that the cognitive transitions of early adolescence effectively call into question many previously safe, "concrete reality" assumptions of childhood. But further developments are not *necessarily* in the direction of a more systematic and coherent understanding. In other words, knowledge may become more relative and abstract without becoming more systematic or principled. In challenging adolescents to forgo their obvious, intuitive understandings in favor of the depth of understanding that reasoning about causes can provide, there is an apparent loss but only a potential gain. We may need to approach the processes of integration more vigorously if this gain is actually to be achieved (30, 34, 121).

Another respect in which adolescent thinking becomes more differentiated is that specialized abilities and skills become prominent during early and middle adolescence. Evidence comes from research on the factor structures of psychometric abilities, and from studies of adolescents who are developmentally advanced in particular areas (8, 53, 55). Such domain specialization may be thought of as constituting distinct "intelligences" (39), or as resulting from differential patterns of cognitive socialization (63). The role of domain-specific content knowledge has recently emerged as a key to the growth of a wide range of thinking skills (42). The next section examines three related issues: adolescent misconceptions, adolescent thinking in social domains, and practical intelligence in adolescence.

Content knowledge. Substantial research indicates that adolescents often have strong misconceptions about the world. Some of the clearest evidence comes from science education (17, 30, 34). These misconceptions have been shown to exist in many topic areas, and they pose particular difficulties for education. Often the beliefs are deeply held, and the appearance of contrasting evidence or alternative views may have less impact than we might expect.

Linn refers to this as the resistance to changing one's "hard core" of ideas (77). She describes an adolescent who is asked to predict which of two blocks, which have the same volume but are of different weight, will raise the water level higher when placed in a container. The correct response is neither, since volume is the only relevant variable in this instance. After predicting that the heavier block would raise the water level higher, the adolescent was shown that, in fact, it raised the level to exactly the same point as the lighter block. The student's response: "Humm, the water went up the same in both the containers even though one of those cubes weighs more than the other. You must have *magic* water" (p. 79).

Understanding more about these misconceptions, especially for purposes of instruction, should be a significant focus of future research. It is not clear whether such misconceptions are well organized in coherent but misguided theories, or whether they tend to be local and unsystematic beliefs (30). In either case, if we are to help adolescents move toward more systematic and correct understandings, we must contend with their existing mental models. It should also be of interest to learn more about the presence of misconceptions in other content areas beyond mathematics and science. Teenagers' understanding (or misunderstanding) of their personal and social worlds is something we know less about, but it is of obvious practical significance.

There are a number of ways of understanding social and moral reasoning and its development (102, 109, 116). Three topics that have been of particular interest are perspective taking and its coordination (5, 107), moral judgment (27, 69), and adolescent egocentrism (31, 75).

Much of the growth in perspective-taking ability is typically and appropriately ascribed to early childhood (109). Selman, however, has proposed a model of perspective taking that continues to emerge in adolescence and adulthood (107). Drawing on the work of Kohlberg (69), Selman identifies four levels of perspective taking, beginning with simple egocentric judgments (the self's own viewpoint is the same as that of the other); moving to a self-reflective phase between the ages of 6 and 12, in which the individual recognizes the self as the possible target of others' perspectives; following this, there emerges sometime between 9 and 15 years a mutual or third-person perspective, characterized by the ability to engage in recursive perspective taking ("You know that I know that you know . . ."); and then on to a fourth level, which involves the understanding of a network of perspectives that binds individuals into a social system.

The principal data come from semistructured clinical interviews designed to draw out conflicts of perspective. The wide age ranges given for the characteristic emergence of the various levels may in part be due to the need for interpretive scoring. Some investigators have found relatively little systems-based reasoning, even by late adolescence. Mutual perspective taking may be the principal accomplishment for most adolescents and adults (61).

At a descriptive level this adolescent transition resembles similar transitions in the domains of person perception (5, 109) and in moral judgment (102). In describing other individuals, adolescents are more likely than children to suggest internal, psychological characteristics rather than external, physical features. And, when judging the motives of another's behavior, they are more likely to integrate both personal and situational factors. In the making of moral judgments, a transition to a conventional level involves the recognition of both individual and social factors in determining moral obligations. Postconventional levels involve deeper analysis of the respective rights and duties of individuals and societies in terms either of origins—the social contract—or of principles—universal ethics (69, 102). Like systems thinking in interpersonal relations, this last stage never becomes dominant even among adults, but by late adolescence a minority of individuals do show movement in this direction.

In all these areas a central theme emerges. In contrast with children, adolescents are more likely to consider both external and internal factors when attempting to understand or explain the behavior of the self or the other; and they are progressively more likely to integrate various features of the problem rather than merely summing or subtracting them. Yet their greatest difficulty occurs in the attempt to achieve an integrated understanding of their personal and social experiences (64, 65, 108). Indeed, such skills of coordination and integration seem to elude a substantial minority of individuals even into adulthood. This may be akin to the phenomenon of unsystematic or nonprincipled knowledge, or "knowledge in pieces," found in adolescents' conceptions of the physical world.

A recent challenge to the generalizability of these conclusions focuses on gender bias in the underlying conceptions of morality implicit in these systems. Gilligan has argued that concentration on an emerging moral logic of justice comes at the expense of understanding an emerging moral logic of care (41). At a more general level, researchers would profit from examining closely the socialization influences—both by group (gender, culture, social class) and by individual—on the styles and content of thinking (63). Especially in these content areas, attention to variations among individuals is likely to be at least as informative as a search for formal models of underlying structure.

Less thoroughly researched but of particular interest for adolescent cognition is Elkind's notion of adolescent egocentrism (31, 109). In this formulation the advancing cognitive capabilities of early adolescents, in particular their ability to take the other's perspective, leads to a specifically adolescent version of egocentrism. Teenagers may recognize that they are the potential focus of another's attention. Initially, however, they may overgeneralize this new understanding and assume themselves to be a focus of *most* other people's perspectives *much* of the time. Consequences of this overgeneralization are adolescent self-consciousness, or the assumption that one's everyday successes and failures are the focus of everyone else's thoughts: the "imaginary audience" and the "personal fable," in which adolescents construct elaborate fantasies that place them at the desired and dreaded center of attention. Although this model is intuitively appealing, there is as yet little substantive research to establish its validity (75, 109).

An issue that much of this research has failed to address is the connection between social or moral thinking and actual behavior. In the absence of such information, the practical and theoretical significance of age differences on cognitive tasks is unknown. One useful step is to seek connections between cognitive-level and real-world social competence. In Ford's study a significant correlation was found between adolescent social cognition and peer-rated social competence (37). The best predictors were self-rated interest in social goals and means-ends social problem solving. But most of the differences in social competence were not explained, raising the possibility that social cognitive expertise has yet to be tapped.

To the extent that research measurements fail to reflect the realistic contexts of social and moral thinking, we understand very little about cognitive activity. For instance, existing measurement approaches typically evoke reflective responses to static stimuli (for example, dilemmas), whereas most social interaction is dynamic and tightly time constrained (61). Methods that improve the contextual validity of social cognition research is a crucial next step.

Even less research attention has been given to practical intelligence—shifts in thinking about everyday matters—yet these issues may be of considerable immediate concern for the health and well-being of adolescents. Three representative topics are decision making, stress and coping, and career planning.

Are teenagers competent to make decisions that may affect them in critical ways? Given the organization of modern urban society, adolescents must make such decisions continually, regarding drug use, sexual activity, consumer purchases, and so on. Mann, Harmoni, and Power have summarized research on young people's decision making (81). Their conclusions coincide with the descriptions of adolescent thinking in a variety of areas already reviewed. Young and midadolescents are more likely than children to generate options, to look at a situation from a variety of perspectives, to anticipate the consequences of decisions, and to evaluate the credibility of sources. At each of these tasks, however, they are noticeably less skilled than late adolescents and adults; transitional periods tend to fall at about 11 to 12 years, and again at 15 to 16 years.

For example, Lewis presented students in grades eight, ten, and twelve with dilemmas regarding the choice of a medical procedure (76). The oldest group was most inclined to mention spontaneously a variety of risks (83%, 50%, and 40%, from oldest to youngest), to recommend consultation with an outside specialist with no vested interest in doing the procedure (62%, 46%, and 21%), and to anticipate future consequences (42%, 25%, and 11%). For instance, in response to a question about whether to have cosmetic surgery, a twelfth-grader noted: "Well, you have to look into the different things . . . that might be more important later in life. You should think about, will it have any effect on your future, and with, maybe, the people you meet." In contrast, the advice of an eighth-grader was more limited: "The different things I would think about in getting the operation is like if the girls turn you down on a date, or the money, or the kids teasing you at school" (pp. 541, 542). Both the gradual shift in perspective and the far-from-perfect performance of even the oldest group are similar to findings on other tasks. Weithorn and Campbell reported comparable findings: 9-year-olds, compared to 14-year-olds, give fewer reasons in response to dilemmas about pursuing various medical treatments, and show less understanding overall of the implications of differences among treatments (120). It should be emphasized, however, that the age variations must not be overstated: even children in the youngest group (age 9) were able to express a choice based on a reasonable understanding of outcomes.

The ability to generate and evaluate spontaneously a range of alternatives in making decisions shows a pattern of development similar to reasoning in formal and social domains. By early adolescence (11 to 12 years) a majority (or near majority) of individuals begin to show evidence of such abilities, although their capacity to integrate these various criteria is far from perfect, especially in situations presenting many attributes to be considered (67). By middle adolescence (14 to 15 years) most individuals make decisions in ways similar to adults—although it should be noted that adults' decision making also suffers from a host of well-studied biases and distortions (24, 73). Furthermore, the research has revealed age differences mainly in spontaneous generation and evaluation of evidence; there is no persuasive proof to date that even early adolescents are fundamentally incapable of carrying out the requisite procedures in adequately supportive environments.

Given the fact that protecting adolescents from having to make crucial decisions seems to be increasingly infeasible under our contemporary social arrangements, research that investigates the contexts in which sensible decision making skills can be acquired therefore seems warranted. It has been argued that our attachment to an imagined social order in which teenagers are immune from the necessity of making important decisions is itself a barrier to enhancing adolescents' decision-making abilities (81).

The ability to make decisions does not guarantee its use in practice, where breadth of experience comes into play. For example, there is ample evidence that driver training of various degrees of intensity is quite successful in raising the skills of 16-to-18-year-olds, both cognitive and psychomotor, to levels comparable to (and sometimes superior to) those of adults. But this training has been ineffective in reducing adolescents' markedly high rate of traffic accidents (99, 103). Where many public health and safety issues are involved, it is unwise to assume that the possession of skills ensures their appropriate use in real situations. Studies of the ways teenagers use skills in practical situations are sorely needed.

The ability to generate and evaluate a large number of choices is highlighted as well in another area of practical intelligence: coping with stress. Although there are a variety of ways of defining stress, stress reactivity, and coping, it is apparent that one major effective coping strategy is cognitive understanding and control (29). In his review of child and adolescent coping, Compas notes that both generating choices and means-ends thinking show important developmental trends and appear to be related to effective functioning in a variety of domains (29, 112). Similarly, Gouze, Strauss, and Keating reported the responses of young people aged 13, 16, and 21 to hypothetical requests for advice from acquaintances in ten different vignettes (for example, parents fighting with each other, a student who needs alcohol to get through the day) (44). The most notable age differences were seen in the number of solutions offered and in the cognitive sophistication of the advice on coping. This increased sophistication was most apparent in the ability to anticipate the consequences of various choices.

Understanding the sources of these observed age differences in the spontaneous consideration of options remains a major goal for researchers. One substantial program has investigated this topic in the domain of career exploration. Grotevant and Cooper have focused on the nature of family dynamics, particularly the process of adolescent individuation, as a key antecedent to effective functioning (46). They have tied this process to developments in the self-system (see also Chapter 14 in this volume). This research program highlights the role of factors that have not traditionally been deemed cognitive in our understanding of the activity of adolescents in the real world. In general, as cognitive developmentalists have cast their nets more broadly—into areas of informal reasoning, social and interpersonal reasoning, intrapersonal understanding, and so on—the evidence for pivotal effects that occur outside the narrowly cognitive system has accumulated.

In practical terms the information about the development of adolescent thinking in everyday life is modestly encouraging. There is evidence that early adolescents show reasonable thinking in appropriately supportive environments, and contributing factors are increasingly being identified. But it should be emphasized that realistic practice in using cognitive skills appears to be crucial.

Strategic knowledge. A number of the trends in adolescent thinking can also be understood as a result of the acquisition of specific strategic or procedural knowledge. In particular, the increased awareness of the consequences of one's decisions, the ability to carry out planning activities in problem solving, and the recognition of a variety of options when one is confronting complex issues have all figured prominently among the kinds of procedural knowledge more likely to be observed among adolescents than among children. Another broad change of special relevance here is the increase in self-awareness and reflectivity, which enhances the possibility of monitoring or regulating one's own thinking.

Again, however, the necessity of viewing these different sources of knowledge—strategies, content, and organization—as quite interdependent emerges clearly in the current research. Most programs of direct educational intervention designed to improve thinking skills are appropriately categorized as aiming at fostering procedural knowledge alone (11, 16, 22, 88, 89, 101). The hope is that through teaching problem-solving heuristics or habits of mind with a particular type of material—often not tied to any particular subject-matter content—students will also learn how to use these skills in a wide range of specific domains.

Convincing evidence has not been forthcoming, however. In many cases little formal evaluation has been made of programs designed to improve reasoning or critical thinking. Where careful evaluations have been done, the criteria are frequently the students' performance on materials exactly the same as, or very much like, the training materials. Although this may be a necessary first step in the evaluation process, it is weak evidence of a claim for the *general* advancement of thinking. The next and crucial step of transfer to quite different kinds of content has rarely been studied in any systematic way.

This is a significant educational concern, should the early research on expert knowledge systems be borne out. If content knowledge and procedural knowledge are inevitably intertwined, then programs of direct instruction in "general" thinking may be misguided at a basic level. For purposes of development, what we need instead is a better understanding of the acquisition of well-integrated strategic *and* content knowledge (34, 63).

Cognitive Self-Regulation

Two key features of cognitive activity are subsumed under this heading. The first is most broadly termed *metacognition*—the ability to monitor one's own cognitive activity for consistency, for gaps in information that need to be filled, for the accuracy of some procedural application, and so on. Attempts to teach metacognitive activity have encountered some of the same difficulties as (and sometimes overlap conceptually with) programs for direct instruction of thinking processes. Specifically, individuals often have difficulty transferring such skills to any content area outside that in which they were first learned (13, 21). Yet when such monitoring activities are developed in the context of particular skills such as reading, writing, or mathematics, some initial evidence suggests that instruction can be effective (93).

One might even suppose that an exclusive focus on metacognitive activities could be counterproductive early in the learning process in drawing conscious attention to activities that might better be allowed to proceed toward automaticity. In this sense metacognition may be a luxury of the expert. Once a difficult skill or domain has been mastered, attention can be given to whether or not the system is operating smoothly. The roles of generalized thinking skills and of cognitive self-monitoring in the development of adolescent reasoning thus require substantial additional investigation (114).

A second kind of self-monitoring is more problematic for cognitive development theories of any kind. If we conceive of thinking as purposeful and goal directed (117), then we must recognize that the goals of the test taker may not be those of the test giver, and the goals of the student may not be the same as those of the teacher. This intrusion of the individual's own goals, motivations, and commitments opens the gates of our typically closed-system models of thinking, learning, and teaching. Many constraints on reasoning and higher-order thinking may not be narrowly cognitive but may derive instead from motivations and dispositions (106; and Chapter 12 in this volume). If the habit of rational thinking is as much a disposition as a skill, then the circumstances that encourage adolescents to value it are as crucial as the instructional tactics for training it. Tracking the development of these motivational aspects that relate to cognitive performance remains a key topic for future research.

Factors Affecting Cognition

A number of factors that affect adolescent cognitive development have been noted. Here the goal is to compile those that are most significant for application to practice. Some factors are quite general in their influence on the majority of adolescents; others are more specific to particular groups; and still others operate at an individual level. As Bronfenbrenner and Crouter have argued, research has focused far more intently on developmental processes and structures than on the external constraints that impinge on and shape development (12). Future research on adolescent thinking will be enriched by greater attention to the study of cognitive activity when it is engaged with more meaningful content in more natural contexts.

Schooling

The most consciously organized social attempt to influence adolescent thinking is, of course, through formal schooling. Much of the research on the outcomes of schooling has focused quite naturally on standardized measures of achievement. Under such measures the incremental pace of achievement tends to slow at adolescence; annual increases hover around 0.15 standard deviation a year, as compared with increases at the beginning of formal schooling of about 2 standard deviations (1). This may be related to the nature of the skills being tested (38), in that children's rapid growth in basic skills is perhaps more readily quantified than higher-order thinking skills. Or we may be less successful at teaching higher-order thinking than basic skills.

A second concern for many North American commentators and national commissions is that the level of cognitive achievement is inadequate on several grounds: observed declines in performance over the last two decades; performance that is substantially inferior to that of students in other parts of the developed world; and performance that is in an absolute sense too low for the maintenance of a high-technology, information-based society. These concerns have given rise to many new initiatives on the teaching of thinking (88, 101).

But it is possible to identify some key elements that influence success (34, 87, 88, 101). Students need to be engaged with meaningful material; training of thinking skills must be embedded in a knowledge of subject matter, for acquisition of isolated content knowledge is likely to be unproductive; serious engagement with real problems has to occur in depth and over time; students need experiences that lead to placing a high value on critical thinking, to acquiring it as a disposition, not just as a skill; and many of these factors occur most readily, and perhaps exclusively, when students have the opportunity for real, ongoing discourse with teachers who have reasonably expert command of the material to be taught.

Detailed observations of adolescents' actual school activities (7, 43) reveal little in common with this list of effective cognitive factors. Some teachers in some schools on some occasions create these conditions, but in general there is a sharp discrepancy between what research shows to be useful and what the structures of schools permit in practice. Researchers must work on the problem from both ends: from the cognitive perspective, by developing better and more precise models of how cognitive processing, content knowledge, knowledge organization, and strategies combine to foster the acquisition of expertise in a variety of domains; and from the educational perspective, by discovering ways to increase opportunities for serious cognitive engagement by adolescents with teachers and with one another (87, 105). Reducing the complex array of institutional and other barriers is a major challenge.

Cultural Influences

The socialization of adolescent cognition does not occur exclusively in school. It may well be that a far greater influence comes from other cultural institutions and forces. Although this observation is so obvious as to sound trite, one would have difficulty finding recognition of it in the accumulated studies of adolescent thinking. We lack a research base on how thinking is affected by a wide range of powerful social forces, including the mass media, the organization of daily life (for example, the shopping mall culture), changes in family and community structures, and so on. Exploring such questions will require new methods of inquiry and analysis; but the importance of understanding how intentional and unintentional social policies shape the way adolescents come to think about their world warrants a significant investment.

Consider the pervasive example of television. As I noted earlier, the average adolescent watches some twenty thousand television advertisements each year (78). Both the content and the formal features of these messages encourage the processing of information in ways that are generally opposite to what we seek to develop through schooling (2, 78, 104, 110). The pace at which the information is offered is highly accelerated, so that rational or reflective thought cannot be employed. This is increasingly true of a range of visual media, although the most extreme expression is evident in television commercials. Irrelevant product information is introduced to suggest criteria for making decisions where no real differences exist. The need to sort through too much information is a significant hindrance for rational choice, and a common response is to avoid thinking at all. Indeed, that is often the advertisers' goal. Advertising is frequently designed to aim for the emotional level, with as little intervening cognitive processing as possible; an unanalyzed association between a product and a particular feeling is in fact the intent. Often, emotional states are rapidly invoked by images of social relationships—the happy teenage crowd at the fast-food outlet, the comfortable flirtatiousness of the crowd drinking their favorite beer—with the none-too-subtle message that the commodity can ensure attainment of this desirable state. These cognitive socialization factors—acceleration that undermines reflection, multiple irrelevant criteria that overwhelm thoughtful analysis, commodities that are portrayed as substitutes for human relationships—

are also features of much of contemporary culture beyond the mass media (III). If we wonder why adolescents have difficulty reaching the cognitive levels we deem important, we should consider what powerful social practices work against that attainment.

Some observers argue that the discrepancy between society's proclaimed goal of improved critical thinking among adolescents and the social and educational practices that seem more often to inhibit than to encourage it is an indication of which values are in fact operating (9). Research on adolescent thinking should seek to document more fully the effects of formal and informal socialization practices on the achievement of preferred cognitive outcomes. With solid evidence of this kind—some of which has already begun to emerge—there can be more informed public debate on the investments necessary to develop critical thinking.

We should also recognize that critical thinkers are likely to be, among other things, less impulsive as consumers, more demanding of meaningful work as employees, and more discriminating politically. It would be naive to believe that there is social unanimity on the desirability of these outcomes.

Cognitive Diversity

Because cognitive performance plays such a central role in our society's avowed meritocratic ideology, it is not surprising that controversies have arisen repeatedly with regard to comparisons between different groups. It is also not surprising that many of these empirical comparisons have focused on the allegedly deficient cognitive competence of our society's least powerful groups: women, racial and ethnic minorities, and working-class people. In any reading of this research, several caveats must be kept in mind. At the outset it should be noted that there exists no firm empirical basis from which to infer inherent differences between groups in terms of cognitive competence. Comparing of individuals from roughly similar backgrounds is fraught with interpretive difficulties; these problems multiply when group comparisons are made (28). It is not possible to attribute differences in performance between groups to basic cognitive deficiencies in the absence of a demonstrated model of how such basic processes can be assessed independent of knowledge and experience. Since we lack validated models of this type, speculation about fundamental cognitive differences is at best premature. The methodological obstacles to drawing such conclusions are extensive (28, 63).

Accordingly, this review is brief, selective, and largely descriptive. It focuses on those issues that may have some particular relevance to adolescent development and that suggest useful directions for future research.

Educational Achievement

Differences in educational attainment, whether indexed by years of school completed or by scores on aptitude or achievement tests, are clearly related to racial and ethnic group membership, and to the social class of the family in which the individual grows up. A nationally random sample of late adolescents and young adults in the United States was tested in 1980 for standardization of the Armed Forces Qualification Test (100). The test sampled content from academic and vocational areas. On the composite score whites performed significantly better than African-Americans and Hispanics. And within all groups the mother's educational level—used as one key index of social class—was a powerful predictor of achievement. When aggregated by social class, scores ranged among whites from the twenty-ninth percentile in the lowest group to the seventy-ninth percentile in the highest group. For African-Americans and Hispanics combined, the range was from the fourteenth percentile to the fifty-second percentile. These figures can be compared with geographic variation, which ranged from the sixtieth percentile in New England to the forty-second percentile in the East South Central states (Kentucky, Tennessee, Alabama, and Mississippi). As might be expected, the level of educational attainment was strongly related to test scores. In reading, for example, the grade-level estimate of tested achievement closely reflected actual educational attainment. For those with less than an eighth-grade education, the median reading level was a grade equivalent of 5.4; for high school graduates it was 9.2; and for college graduates it was 11.9.

What figures such as these indicate is straightforward: the highest levels of performance on standard educational achievement tests are obtained by adolescents and youth who come from the majority group in the society, who were raised in homes with the highest social-class status, and who themselves have stayed in school the longest.

Although some may find the figures themselves controversial, the more compelling need is to address the social problems they represent. Explanations of these and similar findings differ markedly according to theoretical perspective. At one extreme is the argument that such discrepancies, with their implicit marginalization of a substantial proportion of youth, are a predictable outcome of a profit-oriented economy and are necessary for its perpetuation (9). In stark contrast are those who view the pattern as the natural outcome of a meritocratic system that justly rewards cognitive competence—which, as it happens, is differentially distributed in nature (52). Although the weight of the evidence favors a socialization explanation of these group differences (63), any convincing account needs to be made specific and developmentally grounded.

There already exists substantial evidence that socialization differences have significant effects on cognitive activity. For example, Hakuta reported a longitudinal study of bilingual Puerto Rican children living in Connecticut (48). Equal facility in communication at home and in school, indexed by bilingual fluency, was important for a wide range of cognitive accomplishments into adolescence. Similarly, the socialization of cognitive styles and expectations for achievement has potent effects both in school and at work (1, 70).

Gender Differences

The value of exploring the role of socialization can be observed in the controversy regarding gender differences in mathematics achievement. Benbow and Stanley reported on a series of studies of mathematically precocious youth and noted robust differences among the proportions of boys with very high ability as compared to girls (ratios ranged from 5 : 1 to 10 : 1 in different samples) (6). They proceeded to consider several contemporaneous socialization explanations—for example, that girls take fewer math courses—and found them wanting. On this basis they concluded that the case for biological gender differences was strengthened.

Two arguments counsel against this conclusion and others like it. In logical terms, the finding that some socialization accounts fail to explain the results does not then increase the likelihood that a biological account is correct. And in empirical terms, there are a number of socialization accounts that are far more plausible than those considered by Benbow and Stanley. Baker and Entwisle, for example, report on a longitudinal data base examining parental expectations for academic achievement (3). In this study the role of parents in generating gender differences in expectations was apparent. These observations are supported by other research on parental and classroom socialization factors (94, 95). Although such research has not effectively accounted for all the observed gender differences in mathematical performance, claims that fail to take such influences into account are not tenable.

Overall, the direction of future research on questions about the sources of individual or group differences in cognitive attainment should become better defined as well-constructed longitudinal data bases are thoughtfully explored using causal structural models. Two prerequisites for such research apply. First, mechanisms are needed to support longitudinal and cross-sequential research, a procedure that is not generally feasible under current funding patterns. This is a commonplace observation among developmentalists, but for scientists specifically interested in cognitive socialization, the need is critical. Second, the cultivation of combined expertise in developmental science and in causal modeling, either through changes in doctoral training or through collaborative research, is essential.

Individual Differences

In any consideration of adolescent cognition it is vital to recognize the wide variability among individuals. For example, there is valid evidence that some adolescents (and preadolescents) are capable of remarkable levels of reasoning. Such precocity can be especially striking among mathematically talented youth, whether the assessment is of mathematical reasoning per se (53) or of performance on tasks of formal operational reasoning (54). Other evidence comes from the performance of preadolescents in domains that require quite advanced thinking and in which they have become expert (8, 35, 53).

Accounting for the sources of individual differences remains an elusive goal. Some current estimates of the heritability of indexes of general intelligence, though smaller than in previous work, are substantial—perhaps about 50% (98). Interestingly, to the extent that developmental estimates of heritability are available, they suggest that the combined adolescent and adult figures are generally higher than those for childhood or infancy (50%, 40%, and 20%, respectively). But it is important to bear in mind that heritability is a descriptive statistic that can change with alterations in the environmental context, and that speaks only to observable variations. It does not explain the cognitive or other processes leading to these outcomes.

In building models of the forces that shape cognitive activity, we must pay greater attention to specific social interactions in the home, at school, and in the culture at large. And we must remember that demographic factors are not developmental explanations. It is the nature of the interactions that counts, and this is imperfectly correlated with class, gender, and ethnicity.

Another set of factors involves the overall development of the individual. Adolescents differ in interests, motivations, and expectations. As they gain increasing independence, these aspects of the self tend more and more to determine how much effort and attention are devoted to various activities.

Directions for Research and Practice

Some of the most interesting research into adolescent thinking has addressed problems that arise in the real world, a focus that facilitates organizing this work to extract guidelines for practice and future research. For each of the themes discussed in this section I describe what we now know, how that knowledge can be used to give direction to social and educational policy making, and what major questions future research might address to shape this process more effectively.

Education for Critical Thinking

Ample evidence indicates that the adolescent transition is a crucial period in the development of critical thinking. Among the key cognitive achievements are

• Increased automaticity and capacity, which free cognitive resources for other purposes.

• Greater breadth of content knowledge in a variety of domains.

• Increased ability to maintain different representations of knowledge simultaneously, which permits new combinations of that knowledge.

• A broader range and more spontaneous use of strategies or procedures for applying or gaining knowledge, such as planning, considering alternatives, and monitoring one's own comprehension.

• An appreciation of the relativity and uncertainty of knowledge, which can support exploration and the seeking of knowledge.

Identifying adolescence as a crucial period for critical thinking may imply that such a development is isolated within adolescence and is automatic. On the contrary, the evidence is clear that neither inference is accurate. Unless there is laid down in childhood a solid basis of fundamental skills (such as literacy and numeracy) and reasonable levels of knowledge in core domains, the prospects for developing more advanced levels of reasoning seem remote. As we have seen, effective reasoning relies heavily on the availability of knowledge about which one is to reason, and on efficient access to that knowledge. For the subset of students who lack these fundamental skills and bases of information, potential gains in adolescent thinking are not likely to be realized. Similarly, the coordination and integration of these achievements is a major developmental task for all adolescents, and much of the research suggests that such systematization is often not achieved even in adulthood.

The transition to adolescence can be characterized as the opening up of possibilities for thinking about the world in a more fundamental way, which also involves yielding the certainty of childhood. This process of differentiation can be seen in many domains beyond the academic, including thinking about the self, relationships to others, and society. The transition during and beyond adolescence is more tenuous. It requires the systematic integration of knowledge and ways of knowing. In the absence of such integration, knowledge is often piecemeal and flawed with misconceptions; reasoning is often haphazard or absent; procedures are applied like algorithms, with no unifying understanding to act as a guide; and there is little motivation to seek explanations for one's experiences. Overcoming these cognitive obstacles in adulthood is possible, perhaps, but difficult. Education that fosters critical habits of mind in adolescence seems far more feasible developmentally.

In order to capitalize on adolescents' emerging cognitive competencies, however, education must include several key features. Acquisition of expertise in specific domains (content) and development of thinking skills (process) should be embedded within each other rather than competing for educational primacy, as is too often the case. Expertise can be defined as systematic and principled knowledge, in which an underlying explanatory structure organizes both content and procedures. In this sense a critical habit of mind is the most direct route to expertise because it seeks underlying explanations; and gains in expertise in turn render critical thinking possible by making relevant knowledge available in usable form. Developmental and educational research on how best to promote such integrated cognitive activity should be among our highest priorities.

Recall, too, that critical thinking is not just a technical skill but also a personal disposition. Communication of techniques and knowledge alone is not likely to be adequate unless there is a concurrent communication of their value. Teaching the value of thinking requires opportunities for substantive and meaningful discourse to convey the expert's or teacher's commitments, together with his or her knowledge and skills.

Contemporary practices for educating adolescents do not inspire confidence that these requirements are being met. Structural barriers such as class size, narrow test-based accountability, and complex scheduling dramatically reduce the opportunities for real discourse in schools to less than 10% of instructional time—and in some cases much less (43). In addition, the absence of discourse, combined with rigid accreditation procedures, means that there is often a poor match between the instructional level and the actual developmental level of the individual student.

Given these factors, how can we be surprised by low levels of adolescent cognitive achievement? Now that society has focused on the problem, two areas of applied research call for immediate attention. In the near term, we need to find effective adaptations within the existing educational structures that would allow for more discourse at or just above the student's developmental level (117), for the examination of meaningful material in greater depth over a lengthier period, and for the integration of content and process. In the long term, research on the social and political obstacles to a fundamental restructuring of education would be illuminating. Educational practices that operate in spite of rather than in synchrony with educational structures, even if they are effective, are likely to be short-lived.

Cognitive Socialization

Formal education is but one cultural agent that socializes adolescent thinking, and it may not be the most powerful. One of the largest gaps in research is in the sustained investigation of a host of factors that socialize young people's cognitive activity. Perhaps this gap reflects a psychological-determinist slant; whatever the reason, many questions of pressing practical importance have generated little research activity. It is helpful to consider broad socialization influences separately from those that are associated with differences between groups.

What lessons do adolescents learn from everyday social practices? It is sometimes easier to ask this question in areas where rapid historical change has taken place. Two prominent social forces, technology and community, illustrate the general point.

Earlier we considered the impact of one product of the information age: television. Certainly the advent of widespread personal computer use qualifies as similar in scope. It has become commonplace to note that such technologies have powerful effects on how we act and think. But these technologies are not static stimuli; the way in which they are used is the main determinant of how they affect cognitive (and other) development. Research on the cognitive effects of information technology must consider two broad questions: What is the effect of typical use patterns? And what use patterns are supportive of desirable cognitive outcomes? Passive consumption of commercial television may lead to attentional inertia, non-reflective thinking, irrational decision making, and confusion between human relationships and commodities. But how do adolescents actually use television? Are different patterns (channel flipping, VCR playback, MTV as background to conversation, family viewing with discussion) associated with different cognitive outcomes? Similarly, the installation of personal computers in classrooms or homes does not ensure any particular use of them. They can be aids to exploration or props for outworn educational routines (105).

With respect to changes in community life, the key questions center on how adolescents spend time with other people—principally their peers, their families, and other adults—and how those interactions shape their thinking. One common observation about modern society, particularly in the metropolises where an increasing percentage of adolescents live, is the decreasing coherence of the social fabric and the consequent "atomization" of individuals as separate from society. Symptoms include the geographic mobility of the middle and upper classes, especially the professional-managerial class, which can disrupt a sense of neighborhood or place; the stresses on family cohesiveness caused by poverty and economic marginalization; the lack of public gathering places, limited even in city centers to the commercial shopping mall as the sole option; and the prevalence of blended families, which tends simultaneously to increase complexity and decrease stability in the home. But again, facile connections between these social forces and cognitive outcomes should be avoided. What we need to know is what kinds of social interactions are actually encouraged or inhibited in these settings, how adolescents function in them, and how those interactions aid or deter cognitive growth and understanding.

Given the apparent popular consensus that thinking and knowledge are discouragingly underdeveloped among many adolescents, the temptation is to be pessimistic about the negative effects of societal influences, many of which are seemingly impervious to social or political controls. But seeking to understand in detail their impact on adolescent development offers more promising outcomes. Specifically, public education (in and out of school) can be designed more effectively to restore cognitive control to adolescents, both by inoculating them with critical habits of mind as a defense against social mindlessness, and by helping them to become effective users rather than passive consumers of technology. And if effective community structures are central to cognitive growth in nonacademic domains—and they probably are—an understanding of the crucial features can guide the creation of essential opportunities. In any case, a clearer grasp of precisely how our current social practices affect adolescents' thinking is a prerequisite to planning sensible policies.

Variations throughout history in the cognitive socialization of adolescents suggest certain practically and theoretically significant questions. Variations among individuals from different social groups are similarly relevant. To a considerable extent, successful cognitive achievement serves as a selection device for access to many of society's benefits, especially advanced education and desirable career paths. Working-class and certain ethnic minority adolescents, and, to a more limited extent, young women, perform relatively poorly on a variety of indicators used to assess such achievement. Although theories have proliferated to account for these results on the basis of biological differences, the reality is that, given our current state of knowledge, such claims remain entirely speculative. Direct evidence to support purely biological models has not been forthcoming.

But it is also true that many socialization arguments are equally speculative. What is missing from the discussion is hard evidence to link differences in socialization to different outcomes in a developmentally plausible way. Such evidence is more likely to be found at the level of specific social interactions, occurring repeatedly over time, rather than through more precise measurement of social indicators.

In seeking such evidence, researchers need to explore the features that define cognitively stimulating and well-structured environments. Again, not all features will be narrowly cognitive; social interactions that affect self-confidence, expectations for achievement, and a sense of purpose may be equally, or more, vital to cognitive growth. The systematic knowledge of, say, physics may be of limited value to an inner-city youth with severely limited prospects for employment. The evidence suggests that such factors are not trivial in explaining group differences in cognitive performance. But persuasive research into social influences is both labor intensive and time consuming, for it requires the study of complex events occurring over an extended period and demands sophisticated causal analyses of the resulting data.

Adolescent Thinking in Practice

In reviewing some of the descriptions I have cited of adolescent cognitive competence, one astute commentator noted that they did not sound much like any adolescents she knew! The discrepancy between the competence adolescents sometimes display and their actual performance in many everyday situations is of concern for both theory and practice. Models of cognitive activity built only on test or task performance in controlled situations may pertain only to those situations. Contextual validation of cognitive models is sought less often than it should be.

Available information suggests that most elements of competent decision making in many applied settings are achieved or achievable by early to middle adolescence. What factors assist or inhibit the transformation of this potential into actual performance? We need substantive additional research to answer with confidence, but some likely features can be identified. The opportunity to exercise realistic decision making seems fundamental. Since real-world decision making occurs under stressful circumstances (owing to time constraints, emotional involvement, and so on), and since stress in general may tend to reduce available cognitive resources, routinized skills are likely to be activated in these situations. Naturalistic studies of consumer decisions by veteran adolescent shoppers might be of considerable interest; on those occasions where impulse buying does not dominate, one may observe rather sophisticated cognitive activity. In contrast, many adolescents probably confront far-reaching decisions, such as those involving sex, drugs, or daredevil driving, with much less practiced consideration. The effectiveness of a variety of interventions to improve competent decision making, such as role playing and group social-problem solving, remains to be evaluated (82).

In a variety of academic domains the presence of naive theories incorporating substantial misconceptions has been well documented. Are there similar phenomena operating in other domains, such as social and practical intelligence? If so, what implications do they have for effective decision making? By analogy to the research on expertise, one possibility is that the mere presentation of "correct" information on serious public health issues, for example, may not suffice to alter beliefs. We stand to benefit substantially from research on adolescents' intuitive theories about many health-related choices and other significant behaviors.

Finally, we should be careful not to assume that teenagers' decisions that are objectionable to parents or to society at large are the result of incompetent decision-making skills. It may be that the decision making is quite effective; it is the purpose and intentions that differ. The decision of a mathematically talented ninth-grade girl to abandon mathematics may seem to reflect poor decision making. But it might indicate instead a stronger motivation to maintain peer relationships that would otherwise be threatened. The decision of an urban teenager to engage in drug trafficking, even at considerable personal risk, is not necessarily the result of failure to consider all the relevant information; it may be the outcome of quite sophisticated thinking about risk-benefit ratios in oppressive circumstances offering limited or nonexistent options. In these and many other examples we would surely wish that circumstances were otherwise. But ascribing objectively bad decisions to presumably deficient personal skills can be a subtle version of blaming the victim. In turn, this error can lead to social policies that are effective (and, not to be overlooked, expensive), such as public-education campaigns that are merely exhortatory, forestalling explorations of root causes and effective interventions. If we dislike the choices adolescents make, perhaps we need to give them better options from which to choose.

Cognition in Developmental Context

In focusing on changes in adolescent thinking we run the risk of viewing this activity in isolation from other developments. For every cognitive act there is a cognitive actor, and that person has many facets. Although much of the recent research on adolescent thinking has centered on domain-specific achievements, there has also been some welcome attention given to the way in which cognitive activity is interwoven with other psychological developments in a complex web. This is difficult but potentially rewarding research, and subsequent chapters will take up many of these themes.

Cognitive development is deeply embedded in the adolescent's view of the self, of relationships to others, and of the society and the world. Basic psychodynamic and family issues of separation and individuation are reflected as well as in the adolescent's increasing breadth of vision and decreasing sense of certainty. New and powerful emotions challenge the adolescent's emerging rationality and search for principles, but it is on those same developing cognitive skills that the adolescent must rely to make sense of unexpectedly complex feelings.

Constructing social and educational practices that support positive developmental outcomes in the face of this complexity is a daunting task. Two observations may help to make it seem only difficult rather than impossible. First, rigorous research that accepts the complexity of natural developmental phenomena seems more possible now than at any previous time. Advances in both research methods and mathematical analyses of complex data, and initial successes in applying them to real problems, are encouraging. The potential for obtaining solid scientific findings on crucial questions should provoke a flurry of research activity. Second, we need not envision a social structure that carries the adolescent all the way to critical thinking and consciously integrated self-awareness. There are good reasons to believe that if we provide the opportunities for progress toward these goals early in adolescence and remove unnecessary barriers to their later expression, they will become integrated in a self-sustaining cognitive system. Discovering and implementing policies that create opportunities and remove barriers can motivate researchers and policy makers alike.

PART TWO

Contexts

The inclusion in this volume of an entire section on the contexts of adolescence reflects the growing awareness within the field of the many ways in which outside factors can influence the course of development. In this regard, research into adolescence has been rediscovering a fact already well established with respect to the study of younger children. Seminal works by such investigators as Urie Bronfenbrenner, Glen Elder, Bill Wilson, Justin Wilson, and others not only point to the need to understand the role of contexts in molding child development but also demonstrate the feasibility of doing such research.

The chapters in this section illustrate the range of levels at which contexts can be studied. Chapters 4 and 5 address some of the broad social influences that help to shape the experience of youth within a particular society. The former offers an example of how a historical perspective can contribute to an understanding of adolescent processes; the latter addresses key issues of ethnicity and minority status and their possible impact on young people.

Chapters 6 through 9 consider some basic contexts in which all teenagers find themselves. Families, peer groups, and schools have been of considerable interest to researchers, and a picture of essential aspects of each of these contexts is beginning to emerge. Chapter 9 consists of three separate contributions that focus on other common influences—specifically those of work, leisure time, and the mass media. As this chapter documents, surprisingly little information is available on these topics, especially with respect to the young adolescent. In particular, the existing research literature fails to explore how teenagers spend their leisure time, whether with others or alone.

Absent from this section is any investigation of neighborhoods or communities. It is logical to assume that neighborhoods powerfully affect the ways in which adolescents fashion their lives. Factors of possible interest range from such pragmatic issues as available forms of transportation and perceived degrees of physical risk or safety to more abstract concepts of community spirit and support. Communities are also the source of churches and other organized social associations that often target teenagers and help to structure their activities outside school. Unfortunately, little research has been done into such issues as they relate to adolescent development, and we were unable to recruit someone to pull together the meager information that is available or to consider how work done on younger children might be extrapolated to youth. We hope that some future survey of normal adolescent development will find that the neighborhood has begun to receive the attention it richly deserves.

4

HISTORICAL PERSPECTIVES

John Modell and Madeline Goodman

Adolescence is, among other things, an organized set of expectations closely tied to the structure of adult society. It stands out from the other stages of human development as a period of preparation rather than fulfillment. Infancy is cherished in its own right; childhood and adulthood are seen as noble enterprises; and old age, we believe, is rightly brandy, not vinegar. But adolescence is a phase of imminence that is not quite imminent enough, of emergent adult biology that is not yet completely coordinated with adult roles, of hopes that are not yet seasoned by contact with adult reality, and of peer culture and society that mimic those of adults but are without adult ambitions or responsibilities. Adolescents are in a state of preparing themselves for adulthood by experimenting, studying, resisting, or playing.

Individual biological and psychological developments constrain the social construction of adolescence. The burden of this chapter is not to dispute the significance of adolescent development or the need to understand it in its own right. But historical evidence suggests that, over time, the organization of adolescence has changed far more profoundly than have the biological and psychological aspects of development (21, 25). This chapter offers evidence that changing social expectations for young people have been congruent with broad changes in the relationship of groups of people to one another, to production, and to the state. To understand adequately what adolescence *is,* we must also understand what adolescents are *supposed* to be and *why.* These questions can properly be answered only by placing them in a historical context. Our general argument is that the dominant political economy of an era helps define adolescence, both descriptively and prescriptively (10).

As we look at the emergence of adolescence as a social category in modern Europe and America, we shall survey two broad historical periods: the *early modern* period, approximately from the Renaissance to the end of the eighteenth century, a time when there was growth in both market-oriented agriculture and the nation-state; and *industrialization,* during the nineteenth century, when the rapid unleashing of new economic forms reorganized the relation of individuals to one another. These relations were subsequently modified by state, professional, and volunteer efforts to mitigate certain harsh consequences. After we give a brief account of the historically changing nature of adolescence, we shall look more closely at the twentieth century, a period of startlingly rapid change in economic, political, and social history, including the relations among age groups. We shall outline both the context and process by which adolescence has been socially defined and redefined.

This discussion emphasizes how the experience of adolescence is shaped by social class, in particular by educational institutions and labor-force conditions. It does not deal directly with the way in which gender influences adolescence, despite the fact that male and female youth often have been understood in distinct terms, and often behave differently. Nor does it examine how ethnicity affects the experience of adolescence. Other chapters will put more emphasis on these kinds of differences.

By understanding changes in the economic and social functions of the family in the last four hundred years of Western history, historians have tracked important alterations in the life stages of individuals. Initially, demographic data were used to construct life stages, for, even centuries ago, vital events were widely recorded. With care and skill these records have been aggregated to form collective accounts of life patterns. Subsequently, techniques were developed for interpreting aggregated census data and social bookkeeping records kept by the increasingly bureaucratized governments of the past two centuries. Over the last ten years or so a parallel sense of the ideological and cultural bases of the family and the life course has taken shape, together with a tentative reconstruction of the experience of adolescence itself.

Social-historical accounts are rarely definitive. Studies are inevitably local in time and place, and depend on the vagaries of making and keeping records. A rich account of context, rather than precise attention to theoretical specifications, characterizes historical work. Thus a chapter like this one, which depends on historical materials, must necessarily be interpretive; references are provided primarily to prod the reader's imagination.

Adolescence in Early Modern Europe

In the agrarian society and culture of early modern Europe and the American colonies, the family formed the main social and economic unit. For most people, personal life, community, and culture revolved around working on the land. Inheritance of property, for the peasantry, the gentry, and even the small but growing bourgeoisie, was the fundamental instrument of social placement. Concerns for lineage were emphasized in child rearing far more than they have been subsequently. Family was both the basic unit of economic production and the foremost instrument for social control and the maintenance of cultural stability. Although in most places the extended family did not predominate, families were often large, commonly augmented by servants and kin from beyond the nuclear unit. Infant mortality rates were high, and the emotional bonds associated with the modern nuclear family probably were muted (67, 83, 88).

Children had an important and highly visible economic role within the family, contributing to its economy, a generalization that holds across a wide range of economic levels and patterns. An economy of scarcity and a focus on lineage prompted the family to acknowledge the interrelatedness of their economic security and the current abilities of their able-bodied young children. Owing to a relatively undifferentiated economy, children were treated as miniature adults, distinguished from their elders more by their inability to command property than by any lack of adult capacities (20).

The agrarian world of the sixteenth and seventeenth centuries was one in which a child or youth learned early and fairly unambiguously, by example, the function he or she was expected to perform later in life. Concern with stages of life and precise age distinctions were not prevalent (34, 47, 50). Infancy, for example, referred to the period of material control over the child; infant schools of the early eighteenth century accepted children from the ages of 18 months to 6 years. The term *childhood* applied to anyone under 18, or perhaps 21. The term *youth* might refer to someone as young as 12 or as old as 24. The vagueness of the language speaks to the importance of actual tasks young people performed, underscoring the fact that what mattered in this society and culture was what one did and what one had rather than how old one was. It also reflects the general absence of institutions devoted to persons of any particular age. Although the word *adolescence* (or its equivalent) existed, it was not widely used before the nineteenth century. The word *youth* was preferred to describe what one historian terms the period of "semi-dependence," an extended stage defined by the economic status and role of the individual who was not fully dependent on his or her parents for economic support, who contributed to the financial stability of the family, but who was nonetheless not in a position to assume an independent adult role and set up his or her own household (34, 48).

This period between childhood and the attainment of adult status through marriage or inheritance was often long and drawn out, underscoring the strong connection between economic issues involving property and the control of fathers over the economic future of their children, especially their sons. Studies of inheritance practices in seventeenth-century New England indicate continuity with the premodern European pattern, where the father's life expectancy frequently determined when a young man could assume full adult status (34, 38). Legal and informal inheritance regulations, as well as the availability and relative attractiveness of alternative ways of attaining economic independence, modified this picture (7, 38, 77). On the whole, early modern transitions to adulthood were relatively unmarked by psychological traumas and personal crises. The outstanding exception—religious conversion—is a telling contrast to notions of modern adolescent crisis, in that religious conversion was understood to be not just an individual developmental stage but a public, communally sanctioned event.

The practice of "fostering out" youths—the removal of boys and girls, generally between 12 and 15 years of age, from the parents' home to live and work as employees in the home of another family in the community—promoted unconflicted passage through the teenage years. Even families who sent a member out to serve in another family might take in youthful employees themselves: the practice was considered not an economic expedient but a component in the upbringing of a youth. Service of this sort was common for the children of the landed, upper-bourgeois, and professional classes and even those lower on the social scale in England, in much of western Europe (but not in the Mediterranean world), and in parts of colonial America. The lower classes sent both girls and boys to live and work as domestics or apprentices in the home of their masters. In the landed and professional classes teenage children were often sent to boarding schools for analogous purposes (83). The practice was a widespread "tradition that reflected an older social order in which the boundaries between family and community were indistinct and in which households, places of both work and residence, were the basic units of social organization" (49, pp. 249–250). The practice served culturally, economically, and psychologically important functions. It trained individuals in specific economic roles while also removing the danger of potential intrafamilial conflicts (for example, of a sexual or generational nature). It denoted a period of dependence somewhat different from that associated with childhood; the apprenticed youth, though under the control of adults, was in a relationship of service, not filiality. On the symbolic level, the fostering out of youths served as a rite of passage, a ritual that introduced them into the adult world in a distinctly inferior status but at the same time with comforting constraints (79).

This picture of the early modern period was the ideal for stable times. In times of social change, phenomena emerged that bore some resemblance to what would later come to be identified as adolescence. To be sure, certain historians, while agreeing with this general outline, assert that young people in the past experienced many of the personal conflicts associated today with the onset of sexual maturity. They offer evidence to support the idea that adolescence was early recognized as a distinct period, and that something of a coherent youth culture occasionally existed. Davis, writing about sixteenth-century Lyons, argues that youth groups and youth rituals were prevalent and that medical literature, religious manuals, and popular printed material distinguished adolescence as a period of sexual maturation (19). Lyons' youth groups elected officials, organized carnivals and festivals, and performed demonstrations of public ridicule for cuckolds, scolds, and mismatched mates. These activities functioned both to control the conflicting sexual tensions of this stage of life and to socialize youth more fully into the "conscience of the community" (56, p. 21). Similarly, the seemingly spontaneous rise of male teenage confraternities in Renaissance Florence coincided with a demographic crisis and a perceived moral crisis in the family (19, 85).

Historians of England and America in the seventeenth and eighteenth centuries have recognized the existence of distinct youth cultures and periods in which young people were singled out as holding particular promise and hope for the society at large. A growing concern with youth sometimes served as a way for adults to respond to the pressures of cultural change. A great deal of evidence from New England confirms a general concern for over a century with the problems of youth, characteristically understood in a religious context. Sermons given by religious leaders reveal a view of young people as both a threat to the social order and a means of maintaining that order. One historian has commented that the shifting circumstances of life and the evolving character of the family prompted changes in religious experience, including a marked movement toward earlier and more emotionally profound religious conversion (38, 39; see also 17, 43). Religious preoccupation with the problems and promise of youth occurred in the context of a society that was becoming increasingly heterogeneous and secular, and in which there was not enough land to sustain the usual distribution of social roles within the community for a rapidly growing population. Authority in general, and parental authority in particular, was questioned as youths confronted new choices about what they ought to do in life. While the closing down of traditional opportunities placed a burden of choice on the shoulders of young people, its effect on adults was equally profound. Although youths now became responsible for making decisions about where they would live, what they would do, and whom they would marry, adults felt equally anxious and guilty over being incapable of leading their children securely into adulthood. Traditional roles no longer prevailed, and socialization by example became increasingly problematic.

Youth in the Age of Industrialization

By the early nineteenth century many young men in western Europe and America were confronting circumstances far different from those their fathers had known. The period of preparation for adulthood was much more difficult than it had been. What a young person had to do to become an adult was not necessarily harder than before, but it was far more uncertain and was frequently accomplished within institutional and other contexts in which youths were in close contact with one another rather than integrated with adults. Many farm families responded to shrinking economic opportunities by encouraging their sons to seek the formal education that might permit them to enter a profession or give them some advantage in business. Although student bodies were far less clearly defined by age than they would be in later educational institutions, the provincial academies and colleges provided a previously unknown context for the development of a youth culture. This withdrawal from social authority and control was often interpreted as turmoil and disorder by adults and frequently culminated in local, nonideological student rebellions (3, 34).

In a rapidly changing industrializing society the middle-class family became increasingly the "private" realm; it became the appropriate context for the expression of emotion and the cultivation of morality. Earlier in the century extrafamilial organizations and institutions tied lineage to community. The trend during industrialization was to focus attention on the isolated family, and mothers in particular, as having responsibility for the moral upbringing of their own children. As the economically productive outer sphere became the father's, the new family was identified as the mother's sphere (71, 81). Prolonged dependence of adolescents signified closer and more emotionally charged interaction between parents and children, which helped produce individuals who could perform successfully in society. Individual choice and initiative rather than inherited status and prescribed roles became characteristics of the nineteenth-century ideology of success. First and foremost among the attributes required was the internalization of self-government, self-restraint, and self-will. What one denied oneself as a youth would be repaid "with interest" in one's sound character as an adult. Contemporary adults believed that material rewards would be provided by an entrepreneurial society.

Within the intensely emotional, internal, and private world of the middle-class family, generational conflicts, particularly between father and child, were common. In one sense these intensely emotional struggles reinforced bonds between family members and underlined the socializing function of the family. The distinctive characteristics of the new middle-class household and its treatment of teenaged children formed part of a larger change in the view of children that developed throughout the century. Practices such as sacrificing for one's children and refusing to accept wages from them became one characteristic demarcating the middle from the lower classes in society. The period from 1870 to 1930 (later in European countries) marks the transformation in America from the nineteenth-century's "useful child" to the twentieth-century's sentimentalized "priceless child" (96). Only gradually did middle-class reformers succeed in making this conception the ideal of large segments of the working class as well (92).

The changes in the industrializing economic order and the expansion of choices open to youth came to be associated with the new environment of the city, to which young people of varied backgrounds had recourse. The city, growing at an ever-increasing rate, was considered by adults to symbolize the new economic relationships and morality of society and was thus perceived as a threat to order and tradition (20). Unlike the rural community, it was seen as a place for individuals—often youths—disconnected from the family unit, a place of and for strangers. And the public world it offered was increasingly viewed as threatening and dangerous, a place suited only for adults, from which children and young people ought to be protected (75, 78, 95). Working-class youth, especially when and where industrial employment did not command their attention, sought odd jobs and entertainment on the street, developing an age-based society that frequently aroused adults' anxieties (64, 66). In New York City colorful working-class youth types had emerged by midcentury—the Bowery B'hoy and G'hal—whose public displays of clothing, voice, and gesture reflected the simultaneous interpenetrating assertion of class, age, and gender distinctiveness: "A special mentality underlay these various expressions of youthful pleasure. It was this mentality—the way that the laboring people of the Bowery understood themselves in social and aesthetic terms—that made the avenue a coherent cultural milieu rather than just a place for good times . . . A unique blend of high-spiritedness and decorum, Boweriness was fundamentally mannered, enforcing its own standards of courtesy and polite conduct" (80, p. 94). If the predominant tone on the Bowery was truculent and masculinist, there nevertheless emerged from it small elements of a new path to adulthood for working-class women, one in which dependence, whether on family, social elites, or age-peer males, no longer went unquestioned.

In response to the threat of the city, a distinct family ethos emerged that was perhaps suitable to a mobile middle class but was increasingly proposed as normative for all urbanites. Within this new context youth moved from a semidependent to a fully dependent status. Industrial change led to a corollary decline in the practice of apprenticeship, a development that went especially far in America. Young people came increasingly to be seen as marginal. Their energy and vitality were often spoken of in sexual terms, and they were seen as threatening to the social order. Literature on the dangers of masturbation, for instance—aimed at the parents of adolescent males—abounded in America, beginning in the 1830s. As one contemporary wrote of this evil: "In the young . . . its influence is much more seriously felt . . .[They] cannot know how much their physical energy, mental vigor and moral sensibility have been affected by this indulgence" (78, p. 222). Sexual release was seen by many physicians and popular writers in the nineteenth century to be a drain on one's system, which "should be reserved to mature age . . . [and] even then . . . made but sparingly" (6, p. 179).

If middle-class adolescent boys characteristically struggled with their sexual appetites, their female counterparts struggled with their own equally disreputable appetitive urges. The dialectic of gender for the middle classes under industrial capitalism understood boys' adolescence as torn by the need to control their sexuality without weakening the aggressiveness that worldly success demanded. Girls' adolescence, by contrast, was stressful because the affectionate receptiveness girls were supposed to show toward their parents' loving provision (a portrayal in which food became increasingly central in bourgeois homes) was problematic. This was so because the expectation conflicted thematically with the development of personal purity that was so vital to the female adolescent project, a step anticipatory of the self-denial that middle-class women were supposed to offer as their particular contribution to the new economic order. Critical to girls' conflict was the contemporary cultural association of robust eating and urgent sexuality. A new disease, anorexia nervosa, emerged, a fitting emblem for an adolescence that was now seen as specific to class, age, and gender (9).

Extrafamilial institutions sprang up to help socialize individuals into the new corporate and bureaucratic world. These institutions—from the high school to the Boy Scouts to the sanatoriums for young neurasthenics to the settlement house—arose in the latter half of the nineteenth century to aid and encourage the family to fulfill the essentially middle-class child rearing deemed unattainable strictly within the family context. These institutions tended to create age-segregated peer groups. Within these adult-sanctioned groups adolescence could be recognized, named, analyzed, and perhaps channeled in desired directions.

Around the end of the nineteenth century the public high school was becoming an upward route into the American lower-middle class. By this date a sizable minority of urban, native-born whites attended high school at least for a while. In these relatively large, heterogeneous schools "the cultural system of the modern high school emerged in definite form . . . Sufficient numbers of students attended and graduated to support a complex matrix of peer-group societies for the first time . . . The total high school experience was romanticized as an episode of irreplaceable social and personal discovery. The high school popularized a new image of youth . . . as a creative and progressive life stage" (91, p. 150). Institutions like the Boy Scouts trained young men in behavior appropriate to ordered hierarchical organizations and aimed to instill "character" (57). The settlement house attempted to extend this notion of adolescence as emotional preparation for adulthood to young people whose period of preparation was seen as having been cut far too short by economic needs or by "the street" (1, 2).

Late-nineteenth-century character builders stressed the importance of developing strong will above all other components of masculine character, while simultaneously cultivating strength and self-control. "Boys were to be manly yet dependent, virtuous without femininity . . . to seek achievement but only as a form of preparation, for they must stay in school. They should know their place, and yet be bright and take initiative . . . With its goal of balanced growth, character building was an anxiety-driven struggle to have it both ways" (57, p. 32). Character builders formed a distinctive part of the new range of professionals who, while desiring to influence positively the socialization of boys and girls, also worked to secure a respected place for their expertise, their services, and themselves in the professional world.

No single individual did more to popularize and solidify adolescence as a critical developmental phase than G. Stanley Hall, whose enormous, didactic two-volume study *Adolescence: Its Psychology, and Its Relations to Anthropology, Sex, Crime, Religion, and Education* (40) was read widely in both the United States and Britain (20, 23, 50, 79). Hall's work on adolescence was strongly linked to the emergence of the academic discipline of psychology in the United States and formed part of his larger commitment to the field of child study. It contributed to the cooperation in America between academic psychology, the rapidly spreading public school bureaucracy, and the lesser groupings of professionals outside the schools committed to the task of aiding child development (65, 69).

Hall, along with the character builders and other professional organizations grounded in his theory, viewed adolescence as the period in which a person is most malleable. For Hall, the stage of adolescence represented a sort of rebirth of the individual, embodying both the possibilities and the uncertainties associated with radical change, and was thus congruent with an era of unprecedented social and economic change. Adolescence was a stage suited by its inherent developmental characteristics to the task of preparation for adulthood. In Hall's formulation the need was not simply to learn discrete adult skills but, virtually, to be reborn as an adult. To Hall and his followers each stage of life corresponded to the developmental process of the human race as a whole. Ideas of development and evolution more generally were central to the nineteenth century and reflected "a new experience of time as cumulative change," as opposed to an earlier understanding of time as cyclic; time came to be seen both as leading *somewhere* and as existing in some objectified space (56, p. TK). Adolescence was a phase of upheaval and trauma, storm and stress, corresponding to mankind's evolutionary progress from savagery to civilization.

These conceptions of adolescence conformed to a general shift during the nineteenth century from viewing the newly problematic youth as brash and troublesome to seeing them as vulnerable and in need of help. They also became a powerful justification for the institutional specialization and even segregation of youth, so they might more productively act out phase-specific turmoil understood as characteristic of their age. In this context precocity, once understood simply as an early blooming of adult capacities, came now to be viewed as a disease in need of curing (51). In turn, the view of precocity as a disease had profound effects on the development of another concept: juvenile delinquency. As a concept juvenile delinquency was dialectically related to adolescence: "The very traits that stigmatized certain youths as delinquent—namely precocity and independence of adult authority—were precisely the opposite of those embodied by the model adolescent" (34, p. 137).

Adolescence, as it developed conceptually in the late nineteenth and twentieth centuries, was first and foremost a middle-class creation. It was a notion that initially made sense in those institutional contexts for young people that promoted their socialization as adults able to hold their own in the competitive middle class. Initially, young people not of the middle class were often perceived as having no adolescence (34, 50, 57). The notion of juvenile delinquency, by contrast, pointed out the risks now seen as inhering in the adolescent period even for children not of the middle-class. Thus a need was seen for both conventional and remedial institutions to deal with adolescents and promote the general welfare. In the United States the degree to which these two kinds of institutions served young people of different classes tended to be obscured (73). Elsewhere the class distinction was explicit.

In early-nineteenth-century Britain young men had been among the most vigorous practitioners of "the instruments of misrule"—traditional charivari activities like noise making, mischief, and minor riot—organized to censure and limit truly deviant behavior but also dramatizing the tentativeness of the working-class' acceptance of the hegemony of the middle-class. After midcentury, however, urban police, ruling with the stick and usually a comfortable acquaintance with the ways of the working class from which they had themselves sprung, considerably restricted working-class youths' employment of the streets for such activities. As the century drew to a close, elites began pressing for benevolent institutions geared to the socialization—not merely the control—of these youths, toward the end of encouraging the children of the working class to develop into lawful adolescents, ready to accept and be influenced by formal education, in much the same way that middle-class youth were being socialized.

"This new generation of [middle-class] youth workers . . . felt themselves 'modern' in substituting for the schoolroom and chapel new extracurricular activities, but in the end they could not prevent conflicts between themselves and a sizeable part of the working youth," who proved reluctant to submit themselves without compulsion to the direction of their betters (35, p. 113). By the early years of the twentieth century (and considerably earlier in America), then, adolescence and adolescent problems were found to be typical not just of middle-class young people but of working-class youth as well. A classic study of working-class adolescents in Birmingham provides a case in point. Written at a time of increasing national insecurity over industrial and political competition with Germany, Freeman's 1914 study asserted that "adolescence is intended by Nature as the period during which the boy should learn to be a man"; thus, youth have needs not fulfilled by the "dead-end jobs" into which boys leaving school moved at 12 or 13 (31).

> We see [a] youth . . . in the years following school days as particularly susceptible to the influences of his environment. His awakened senses drink in impressions from everything with which he comes into contact, and these plough their furrow

deep in the texture of his consciousness. His knowledge is too
limited and his reason too undeveloped for him to grasp or
master his experiences . . . Meanwhile the various changes that
are going on in his body and soul force a thousand questions and
desires up into consciousness, and lead him to seek altogether
new relations with life. He is athirst for experience and knowledge. He will take whatever he can find. (31, p. 206)

To the ends of industrial, familial, and civic education, Freeman proposed
a new kind of part-day teaching institution, offering general education
that emphasized not abstract ideas but physical and moral education,
including sex education.

When their benevolence was rebuffed, as it commonly was, the social
workers who dealt with youth and those among the elites who supported
them condemned the adolescents as flawed or delinquent, and in so doing
promoted a delinquency scare that declined only as a modus vivendi was
gradually worked out between themselves and the working-class youth.
This arrangement divided working-class adolescents into two groups: on
the one hand, those who consciously aimed for "better things," voluntarily attended youth activities provided by the elites, and paid the proper
respect to their benefactors; and on the other, surly youths who preferred
the street, periodically judged by elites to be a threat to social stability (60,
79). As Humphries puts it, however:

Failure of working-class youth to respond to the education and
protective treatment thought appropriate for adolescents did
not lead to the abandonment of the theory of adolescence as a
crucial stage in character development. Instead, the concept of
adolescence was stretched to explain "precocious" and "antisocial" forms of behavior by reference to the incompetence of
working-class parents [although] . . . adolescent theories of personal crises . . . have little explanatory power when applied to a
working-class culture typified by group solidarity and a rapid
transition from childhood to adulthood. (46, pp. 17–18)

Transitions to Adulthood in Twentieth-Century Britain and America

At the turn of the twentieth century Great Britain was approaching the
brink of national decline, the United States the moment of steepest ascent.
In 1890, for example, when the British population was only six-tenths as
large as that of America, Britain produced approximately the same amount

of steel as did the United States. By 1900 Great Britain was producing only about half as much steel as the United States, having also been surpassed by Germany during the decade. By 1910 British steel production was only a quarter of America's. Britain now produced only half as much steel per capita as America, two-thirds again per capita less than a generation before. The United States achieved its remarkable gain in industrial productivity despite retaining almost one-third of its male labor force in agricultural occupations, a figure approximating that in England eighty years earlier.

British institutional structures tended to uphold existing privilege, whether deriving from family, from the empire and its bureaucracy, or from the industrial base that had initiated the industrial revolution a century before. British industry was far slower to adopt new production and marketing techniques than its American (and German) competitors. By contrast, American institutional structures, with less governmental and traditional authority to lean on, readily offered both prestige and material rewards to arrivistes using technological and economic innovation. The extreme stagnancy of the British industrial economy, accompanied between the two world wars by persistently high rates of unemployment, led to a strong trade union movement, with staunch intellectual and political allies from outside the working class. In addition, through much of the twentieth century the government made welfare provisions for those in temporary distress. The United States by contrast was slower than most of Western Europe to accept welfare capitalism. After the Second World War (and until recently) Britain opted strongly for state-generated full employment and generally more provision by government, while the United States at most times proved hesitant to create a completely elaborated welfare state, opting ideologically and politically for a more competitive capitalism. In America workers absorbed more of the costs, but mobility out of the working class was always assumed to be possible.

The evolution of modern capitalism and the modern welfare state in the twentieth century has extended adolescence and expanded its significance. We now turn our attention to three key transitions in the lives of British and American youth: leaving school, entering gainful employment, and marriage. The purpose of the comparison is straightforward: (1) to illustrate continued similarity over time (with variations on the theme) in the way the youthful life course has been organized in the two countries; (2) to suggest how behavioral differences in these transitions have influenced the meaning of adolescence in the two countries; and (3) to relate these national contrasts to the different ways in which the two societies have prepared, selected, and recruited young workers for the work force. The choice of the United States was an obvious one. The comparison with Britain was made partly for convenience, but partly because the contrast it offers is rather sharp. For instance, among some dozen Western nations surveyed for the 1960s and 1970s, the United States offered the most extensive education through late adolescence and Britain the briefest; Britain's rate of participation in the labor force for youths, initially almost the highest, shrank nearly the most rapidly, while that of the United States, initially rather low, grew more than any other (68).

Figure 4.1 presents an overview of age trends for the two nations. The average age of young men's transition out of school and into the labor force, and young women's transition into marriage are shown. Young men and women have tended to leave school at similar ages, but young women have often had a choice of paths thereafter—work or marriage—which complicate the analysis of their labor-force patterns. Women, however, marry at younger ages than do men. Consideration of age of marriage suggests the timing for both sexes of "getting serious" about moving toward family formation.

Two very broad patterns common to both nations dominate the graph: the upward movement in median age for leaving school and entering

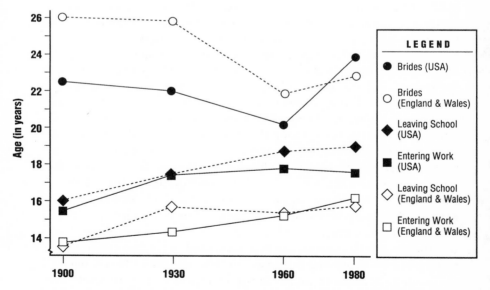

Figure 4.1. Trends in the median ages of transition, 1900–1980, England and Wales and the United States. (See Appendix for a summary of data sources.)

gainful employment and, until the 1960s, the decline in the median age at first marriage. In the past century the institutional structures that in some sense define the adolescent years have changed a great deal. At the beginning of the century most youth were in the work force, not at school. Good behavior was positively sanctioned not by promises of future utility and reward but by immediate payment and preferment. Bad behavior was sanctioned negatively not by physical or social humiliation but by the threat of dismissal. At the same time, marriage typically was far in the future, and a youth's commitment was solidly to the family of origin. Same-sex, like-age peer groups were based commonly on residential neighborhood and, as such, were typically socioeconomically homogeneous.

There were many points of tension in the turn-of-century transition pattern. For example, when youths glutted a slow labor market or a large cohort flooded a normal market, they found themselves both unsupervised and, at least for a while, unneeded. This situation periodically led to fears of a youth uprising (49). The modal adolescent increasingly found herself or himself at school, and his or her perceived needs and deficiencies changed accordingly. School, unlike the work force, is an age-segregated institution which, by its nature, focuses on socializing young people for adult roles. As a result, schools place a high premium on activity directed toward preparing for the future. Unlike the workplace, the prime axis of prestige in schools is age (teacher-student; higher grade–lower grade). In this setting adolescence has evolved as a transitional period of preparation for adulthood.

The marked decline in marriage age before 1960 was followed by an exceptionally sharp reversal after that date. Young people in Britain and the United States had, for a time, brought themselves closer to formalized claims of full adulthood and self-sufficiency by marrying at earlier ages. That early marriage has recently become relatively rare perhaps suggests a new, more comfortable institutionalization of late-adolescent patterns. Further evidence for this claim comes from the increasingly early age at which young people move into their own dwelling units, establishing an independence from parents that considerably precedes the setting up of new families. Relevant as well to the prolonging of adolescence are new mores incorporating an enlarged range of sexual and emotional intimacy outside of marriage.

Since the 1960s, youth have also been entering the work force before leaving school. The slowing or reversal of the trend toward delayed entry into gainful employment in the postwar years is an important development, initially interpreted as a response to the pressures on adolescents caused by extended schooling. More recently these trends have been seen as weakening the school's authority by placing more material resources in the hands of young people. It is considered especially alarming that wages have been used to purchase more youth-culture products and activities (37). In both countries the work force now challenges school as the main nonfamilial institutional context for adolescence. Whatever its limitations, the prevalence of adolescent work introduces a customer and market orientation into adolescents' day-to-day calculations.

The national contrasts that Figure 4.1 reveals are no less dramatic than the common trends. Throughout, the United States has demanded of young people more formal education and correspondingly later gainful employment. The differences in age at leaving school are significant: up to several years. This is not to imply, of course, that British children are accorded full adult status as soon as they leave school. But over the past century Americans have spent far more of their adolescence at school than have Britons. Correspondingly, Americans have worried far more about adolescents than have the British.

At the beginning of the twentieth century Americans married younger than did the British—about three years younger for women. As of the turn of the century in Britain marriages were taking place later in the life course, a trend that did not reverse direction for several decades. In contrast, even before 1900 more and more American marriages were taking place at early ages. Over much of the twentieth century most unmarried children in both Britain and the United States lived with their parents. If we can assume that courtship was a major activity for, perhaps, three years before first marriage, it is apparent that English parents early in the century experienced a considerable period of coresidence with adolescents. Although these youth were not yet engaged in courtship, they established other kinds of social ties outside the family. In contrast, even early in the century American parents had a far shorter experience of this phase of relationship with their children, seeing them pass more promptly from schoolchildren to young adults seeking a lasting intimate relationship with a member of the opposite sex. This pattern became more marked over time. (Eventually even the English began to approximate it.) Surely a longer period of residence with parents for young men and women with reasonably reliable, if modest, incomes provided more opportunity for the younger generation to observe and assimilate adult behavior, and for parents to recognize the process.

Most American readers will be familiar enough with the texture of the American dating system to recognize the ramifications of the national contrast. The American cultural practice of dating was, until the 1960s, an uncomfortable import in Britain. In the first three decades of the twentieth century American high schoolers evolved a clear set of prescriptions and proscriptions for selecting one another in heterosexual pairs, choosing shared activities (typically commercial entertainment), and engaging in intimacy in which controlled sexuality was a crucial feature. These components differentiated American dating from the parentally supervised courtship practices that it so rapidly replaced. By the 1930s this practice was shared in most, although not all, adolescent social settings in the United States, having initially been introduced by the middle classes in high schools and colleges (5, 8, 22, 26, 62, 93). Not until after the Second World War did most British adolescents adopt the American version of dating. Exactly comparable data are not available, but by the 1960s the typical ages for the onset of dating by adolescents was strikingly parallel in the two nations (72, 74).

One reason that prior to 1960 dating did not come to dominate in Britain as it did in the United States was that British boys were often without income while in school and had heavy material obligations to parents thereafter. "I've had two or three girl friends," reported a young school-leaver in the mid-1950s, "but they are too dear, especially if you are trying to save for a holiday" (11, p. 315). Holidays, characteristically, were to be spent with the boys, for the working-class male remained close to the neighborhood group that had sustained him through school well past the age at which his American counterpart was focusing eagerly on the dating scene. "Boys and girls often go out together in gangs, as much for display as for anything else"; this observation was still true when Leonard did her work in the late 1970s: "The earliest heterosexual interaction . . . occurred with transitory mergers of two single sex groups" (60; 55, p. 87). Leonard's fine study of young people in Swansea still retains a tone that contrasts with the situation in America, in fact noting explicitly that "my informants were always uncertain as to how to describe the less committed forms of interaction [with the opposite sex]: One could 'have a date,' or 'go out' with someone, but there is no norm corresponding to these phases. There is certainly no formalized, named, stage corresponding to American 'dating'" (55, p. 70).

In Britain, according to Leonard, working-class girls and boys lived in substantially different social and even cultural worlds, because girls were so positively oriented toward promoting marriage and boys so opposed (13, 32, 55). Adolescent females in Britain spent far more time in the parental home than did males, who were often on the street with the boys. Also, girls' school cliques were more school based than neighborhood based. They were, accordingly, far less durable, crumbling as soon as even one boy yielded to the charms of the most successful girl in the group. Boys' groups, by contrast, were so durable that they even survived their members' eventual marriages. The English male groups were far less oriented than their mixed-sex American counterparts to activities anticipatory of adulthood. Instead they engaged mostly in rowdy behavior.

Table 4.1 reemploys the transition data to examine another contrasting facet of the youthful life course in Britain and the United States in the twentieth century: the duration (for a cohort) of the period of transition, and the number of years elapsed between the (estimated) point at which one-quarter of a given cohort had achieved the given transition (left school, for instance) and that at which three-quarters had achieved it. The figures are, of course, arbitrary. The central 50% of a cohort are in no real sense "normal," nor are the outliers other than normal. Still, the number of years the central half of a cohort needed to pass through a given transition offers a simple and intuitive measure that permits national comparisons of trends over time. Obviously, some part of the difference (in leaving school, for instance) is the statistical product of variant regional, racial, and social class averages in timing. As a corollary, if these dif-

Table 4.1. Typical elapsed time (in years) between boys' school leaving and entry into employment, and young women's marriage, 1901–1981. (See Appendix for a summary of data sources.)

Year	Boys' school leaving	Boys' entry into work force	Women's age of marriage
England and Wales			
1901	1.1	2.1	10.8
1931	1.3	3.1	9.6
1961	1.5	?	4.6
1980	1.2	?	6.6
United States			
1900	4.5	3.7	8.8
1930	3.1	3.3	7.3
1960	3.3	3.6	4.1
1980	5.1	4.3	6.8

ferences were greater in one country than in the other, or if they displayed a strong trend, their sum would explain some of the patterns seen in Table 4.1. Nevertheless, the table crudely approximates the extent of the period of decision faced by young people.

In contrast to earlier observations about central tendencies, the length of decision periods in general has changed relatively little over time. The passage of a cohort out of schooling seems to have shifted its location within the adolescent years, but the transition itself takes about as long now as it did at the beginning of the century; the entry into work, too, has displayed no obvious trend. The passage into marriage, by contrast, has changed its pace in both countries. Initially quite a lengthy process—especially if men's marriage transitions rather than women's are being timed—the process tightened up quite dramatically over the first half of the century.

From the point of view of the experience of growing up, contrast in the pace of the transition from school to work suggests that the period we denote as adolescence may *feel* one way to most Americans and another to most Britons. British children leave school as though there were an appointed age; American children leave school as though they themselves were choosing when. Of course, there is an element of volition for many British children, and the American pattern is structured by larger factors. But the difference is a key to the structure of adolescence in the two countries. The pattern of entry into the work force stems largely from the school-departure pattern. Throughout most of the century British employers were, by American standards, remarkably well organized for accepting a large number of similarly qualified, like-age adolescent boys all at one time, and for incorporating them as a cohort into the world of work. The American work force, by contrast, receives a rather more differentiated group of youngsters in need of different kinds of training in how to be an employee.

Characteristically and enduringly too, cohorts of English boys have left school rather more abruptly than they have entered work, while cohorts of American boys have found jobs more promptly, whenever they have left school. The explanation seems to lie in the different ways that American and British employers have structured the work that they are willing to entrust to low-paid adolescent employees. British employers, with access to a pool of considerably younger children who have completed their education, have offered relatively few part-time and weekend jobs to youngsters still in school. British children have ended their schooling at a pace that is structured by the rules of the state educational system, and then have begun to search for a job. Typically, they have found this job relatively promptly; but some have not found it as quickly as others, and there has thus been the modestly greater age spread in job entrance in Britain than in the United States. As American adolescents have gradually turned their attention from school attainment to other forms of achievement, they have often taken jobs that supplement their school activities. American employers have long counted on a labor pool of this sort. As a result, entering the work force has taken place before leaving school.

Table 4.2 is also derived from the same estimates of transition ages. Here, what is compared across nations and over time is the degree to which major decision points have been compressed into a short period, as estimated by how many years elapse between the point at which three-quarters of boys have left school and that at which the first quartile of girls (whose activities are obviously relevant to what boys are feeling, and even what they are doing) have married. In the absence of longitudinal data, this is a useful way of indicating trends and differences in the youthful life course. Trends are straightforward and identical in the two countries: age at leaving school has crept up toward marriage age, and, in the United States, has passed it. Some of the agitation associated with adolescence is plausibly attributed to the many serious decisions young people must face. If so, the proximity of a series of such decisions must add to the burden of choice that throws young men and women anxiously on their own and their friends' psychological resources. Leaving school and marriage are highly consequential transitions (although both have become more easily reversible) (44, 63). The chain of decisions American young people must make suggests that the notion of a period of turmoil fits their situation but not the British. Only American youth, for instance, have had to decide whether to marry *or* to stay in school.

Table 4.2. Years elapsing between a relatively late age (third quartile) for a boy to leave school and a relatively early age (first quartile) for a girl to marry, England and Wales and the United States, 1900–1981. (See Appendix for a summary of data sources.)

| | Years Elapsed | |
Years	England and Wales	United States
1900–01	7.3	1.5
1930–31	7.2	0.0
1960–61	3.5	−1.3
1980–81	3.0	−0.6

Industrial development common to Britain and the United States, beginning around the turn of the century, explains much of the similarity in the evolution of adolescence in the two nations. Turn-of-the-century industry, at once more heavily capitalized than early industry and less dependent on skilled work, frequently required stronger backs than these youngsters had. Increases in the capitalization of industry rendered the labor of sometimes inattentive young workers risky and potentially costly. But new openings were created by the growth of retail and service businesses—jobs for messengers, for instance. Especially in such street trades as messenger-deliverer or newspaper hawker, these jobs were largely outside the supervision of adults, and often required literacy and numeracy. Thus the implied agenda for schools included instruction in conventional cognitive skills as well as the promotion of honesty and faithfulness to routine duty.

Industrial apprenticeship, which had once facilitated the transition from school to work in Britain, weakened in the face of industry's changing needs. By the 1930s the failure of apprenticeship in Britain was definitive, but memories of its value were sufficient that it was revived with considerable if imperfect success in the economic expansion that followed the Second World War. The creation of numerous dead-end jobs for young workers seemed to satisfy many of the needs of the working classes; but the jobs did not please reformers who were concerned with improving the nation's industrial skills and discipline (61, 79). A sense of an unstressful transition appears in postwar accounts: "I would have felt deprived if I had had to stay on [in school] . . . it is silly, terrible. A lad wants to start work when he is fifteen. He is grown-up, isn't he? He doesn't want to feel like a school lad all his life!" (11, pp. 80–81; see also 59, 94).

The more extended public schooling in the United States, and the upward trend in the age at leaving school even early in the century, made for a different child-labor problem. In Britain the need was to incorporate young people into work without destroying the scope of their capacities. In America the need was to keep youth altogether out of full-time work. Educators in the United States persistently pressed to be assigned the task of containing young people's energies. Curricular changes, including vocational education, were proposed so that schools might have something to teach that would hold the reluctant attention of its large numbers of students—old by British standards—who had already proven to their own and their teachers' satisfaction that they could not successfully tackle academic subjects. As the American high school had emerged in the mid-nineteenth century, it was designed to serve growing numbers of middle-class children of no longer secure property owners. By the turn of the century, industry, which had a large population of adult immigrants and native-born young men to draw on, had no use for the glut of working-class teenagers who annually left school. This led the high school to expand its clientele. Over two generations high school enrollment expanded, and eventually graduation from high school became nearly universal. The New York State Regents' Inquiry of 1938 concluded that "pupils who leave [high] school before graduation appear as handicapped from the standpoint of socially useful abilities as previous findings have indicated that they are from the standpoint of general aptitude and home background. Not only do they lack control of basic skills and of information needed for everyday living, but a great many of them are also judged incompetent to assume the duties of vocation or citizenship . . . And yet these boys and girls were free to leave the classroom as soon as they attained a specified chronological age" (24, p. 118). Dropping out was now a threat not simply to industrial efficiency but to citizenship as well.

When American school authorities urged children to stay in school, they reflected the ideological structures that held that extended schooling meant opportunity. The existence of widespread opportunities reconciled the national commitment to equality with the fact of equally widespread disparities in wealth and privilege. Merit, in the American system, would be recognized and rewarded; but it had to show itself in its own way, in its own time. It therefore was essential that since schools were the arena for adolescent achievement, as many children as possible should be encouraged to complete school. Over time, procedures were modified so that fewer children would be left back, and more remained with their supportive age peers. Academic curricula were supplemented by a variety of vocational courses, either as separate tracks or as optional pathways within variously comprehensive settings (54, 86, 87, 90). In America, in contrast to Britain, child labor was discouraged rather than aided by government officials concerned with the transition from school to work. Nor were industrial apprenticeship or industrial education ever serious alternatives to full-time formal education in this country.

The British concern for internalized codes of behavior appropriate to one's station in life contrasted sharply with America's interest in conveying to its citizens the sense of a capacity to master whatever situation might arise. At school, the British emphasis on right behavior found its most exacting expression in the character training that the particular rigors of hazing and field games inculcated in the famous public schools, which became so central to the British elite. When, in 1902, Britain first provided state-supported secondary schools, "the intention was to preserve as much as possible of the traditional grammar-and-public-school emphasis and spirit, and the assumption was that secondary education should be designed with university requirements in mind" (53, p. 372; 70). In the state-subsidized secondary schools, at least one-quarter of the places were to be reserved for high-achieving children whose parents could not afford the fee. Primary schools were to emphasize basic training in literacy, numeracy, and behavior suited to an industrial working class. As subsequent educational reforms prior to 1944 raised the minimum age for leaving school (to 14 in 1921, for instance, by abolishing the half-day provisions at ages 12 and 13), the primary schools contained but hardly educated the growing numbers of older students. These were young people not yet 14 years old, and therefore required to be at school, whose failure to gain entrance to a secondary school, or whose lack of interest in entering one, marked them as of no apparent academic promise. At the same time, compulsory education and the repression of child labor in America forced the abandonment of admission tests for all but a small minority of American high schools. As a result, the number of high schools and high school students grew rapidly, as did the heterogeneity of the high school student bodies.

Even when Labour party pressure in Britain led to the opening of state-subsidized secondary schooling for all takers in 1944, a new mechanism virtually guaranteed the sharp, class-based separation of students into an academically blessed minority and all others. This division in turn continued the prompt if voluntary exodus of most cohort members from school to work at what most Americans would consider a very early age. The mechanism was the famous eleven-plus exam, administered to all English schoolchildren during their eleventh year of age, designed to assess the student's quality of mind. A slightly older age was believed to be too late for most advantageous testing, because of the adolescent "tide which begins to rise in the veins of youth at the age of eleven or twelve" (53, p. 395). "Decisions which are critical for vocational choice are made at the age of 11 or 12, when they can reflect only the largely class-conditioned family environment of the child . . . Children are, in effect, graded 'superior,' 'mediocre,' or 'poor' in intelligence and attainments at the age of 11, educated accordingly for a few more years, and turned over for guidance into employment as manual or nonmanual workers as their schooling dictates" (29, pp. 85, 87). Since the recent abandonment of the eleven-plus, other mechanisms have channeled students into "appropriate" streams, where they, in turn, take up the more (but not overly) subtle cues that direct them out of school and into the work force. There is some evidence, however, that the comprehensive-school movement of the past two decades has finally begun to change this practice (30, chap. 11).

Turner's famous and fruitful contrast of the social-mobility logic under-lying the British and American class structures characterizes the English pattern as conforming to a logic of "sponsored" mobility, while the American system reflects a pattern of "contest" (89). The difference is apparent in the eleven-plus exam: the British selected a point at which natural abilities were thought sufficiently developed to differentiate among the nation's children. The largest part of what can be said to distinguish children has already been determined, in essence, before adolescence begins. The subsequent training each child receives is designed essentially to nurture and polish these already innate characteristics. In the United States there is (in theory) no such point: a young man or woman can always distinguish himself or herself by some achievement. Here the ideology and even much of the structure of secondary schooling has been designed to deny and modify the structure of inequality.

In America more than in Britain adolescence is understood (in Hall's sense, for instance) as a period of potentially great creativity. American children's adolescent years are marked by a number of highly consequential contests. Even the choice of which fields to contest in is itself significant and is seen as the young person's own decision. American adolescents, accordingly, matter much more to one another than do British children, both as competitors and as the allies they so badly need. The American extracurriculum, by design, teaches leadership and citizenship in the American sense: how to get along with a variety of people assumed to be coequals. Extracurricular events in America "are not the quiet activities of a small coterie of stamp-collectors or nature-lovers as in the British secondary school, but highly public activities which are felt to be very important by most of the pupils . . . Sports [to take a meritocratic realm in which the achievements of working-class youth gain universal recognition] are important in both Britain and the U.S. schools but, whereas in the U.S.A. games are watched by large crowds from the community . . . in Britain these games have no interest to the outside world and are not even watched by many of the pupils" (14, 36, 45, 84).

In both nations formal education serves in part to transmit parental status to young people as they grow up, equipping them by training and credentials for the occupational world. This transmission takes place at least in part through the universally observed greater "objective" success at school of children from higher-status families. But in neither country have all the best students been from the best families: school attainment has been partly a function of characteristics of the pupils themselves that cannot be explained by background. In the United States a study of graduating seniors in 1957 concluded that although socioeconomic background had a major impact on the extent of educational attainment, much the greater part of this was mediated by measured IQ, by the conduciveness of the home climate to study, and by internalized attitudinal factors, notably ambition. Of these, IQ was the most important. In England, by contrast, the characteristics of the school itself mattered a good deal, and mediated the impact of both socioeconomic background and measured IQ. The assignment of the student to one or another of the tripartite secondary school forms following the eleven-plus exam was highly consequential, while in the United States the impact of the school itself seems to have mattered relatively little. Here class background itself continued to operate rather significantly *within* the school, not because it differentiated students by academic achievement but because adolescents' membership in cliques was based on "personality," which often included class-based differences in style and outlook. In Britain school characteristics frequently outweighed family background, and choice of friends (within school) was hardly related to social-class background. Adolescence received its fullest expression within the American high school; British institutions gave adolescence no such scope, no such lasting significance (15; 16; 27, chap. 5; 28; 29; 41; 42; 52; 76, chap. 4).

The youth unemployment that has vexed Western economies since the early 1970s suggests that a new phase in the history of adolescence may be unfolding. Unemployment has impinged deeply on English working-class adolescence, transforming a "golden age of youth into a massive social problem" (12, p. 87). A 1986 study reports: "Leaving school and getting a job were mentioned by our sample as the first major steps in becoming adults. They had all left school, but those unable to find a job could not win from family, friends, and others adults the status and respect given automatically to a wage-earner, and so could not even start along the path to adulthood" (13, p. 191). A "deficiency model" of the British adolescent has come to replace one of sturdy acceptance, as scheme after scheme has failed to alleviate the growing problem. A recent youth placement program, for instance, aims to instill in the jobless school-leavers "all those abilities, bits of information, know how, and decision making which we need to get by in life" (4, p. 119; see also 18; 58). In the United States, by contrast, white adolescents, whether in school or graduates, have on the whole been increasingly welcome in the labor market, and find jobs early. The experience of black youth, however, resembles that of British youth, with employment even for high school graduates remaining elusive (see Chapter 8 in this volume).

Rates of unemployment are even worse for those who do not complete high school, especially minority youth from backgrounds of poverty.

Many Americans explain their problems as stemming from a deficiency model. Generally, though, Americans do not focus a great deal on lower-class adolescents as such. They worry rather more about the exceptional middle-class or near-middle-class adolescents for whom school itself may be a disorienting trial and who respond with "expressive alienation" from that institution (82, p. 2). A protracted adolescence, as we have seen, is understood in America to be a developmental period of considerable creative potential. But at the same time it is risky: in the 1950s, for instance, adolescent motivational failures lay near the core of the distinctively American imprecision about the class location of juvenile delinquency (33). Today's "cultural illiteracy" alarm, while nominally addressed to education institutions, indirectly indicts privileged adolescents who do not seem to care.

This chapter has sought to identify the relationships of young people to those strategically placed adults in society who largely define and redefine its social categories, including adolescence. Adolescence has implications for what ought to be as well what currently is. It carries implications about how young people should be treated in order to grow up to be the right kind of adults. Euro-American society in and after the Renaissance evolved a special status for young people that gave modest recognition to this period as one of preparation for adulthood. Youth roles were almost continuous with adult roles; ages of transition varied greatly from individual to individual, more according to circumstance than to prescription. With the industrialization and urbanization of the nineteenth century, the orderly progression of young people toward adulthood became so widely problematic that concerned middle-class adults elaborated a specialized vocabulary and set up special institutions for adolescents. The most critical component in this evolution was the spread of schooling necessitated by the new need for a literate urban work force. Schools amounted, among other things, to a template against which young people could be placed to judge the age appropriateness of their behavior.

At the turn of the twentieth century salient differences in these patterns had emerged in Britain and the United States. Major variants in the youthful life course and ideological differences in the two nations colored the way young people made the transition from adolescence to adulthood. These differences, like the class structures that underlie them, have proved remarkably persistent. Some twentieth-century patterns of adolescence have been strikingly similar in both nations. Stressful aspects of the transition to adulthood (leaving school, getting a job, marrying) tend to fall within a shorter period of time now, while the years of preparation for adulthood are fuller, tenser, and more overwhelming to the young people moving through them. Young people therefore need more guidance from caring and watchful adults.

These observations may be somewhat troubling to readers, for they argue that adolescence is a social construct, one that is changing even as we examine it. This notion should not deflect our attention. Rather, the malleability of adolescence points to the deep importance of understanding its attributes within a concrete context.

Appendix: Sources and Procedures for Transition Estimates

The broad comparisons and trends presented in Figure 4.1 and Tables 4.1 and 4.2 are based essentially on the adaptation of an approach used by demographers for estimating the time of vital events from cross-sectional data on current status by age. The underlying assumptions are that life-course transitions, such as marriage, are irreversible and affect more and more members of a given birth cohort year after year, until all who will ever make the transition have done so; and that during the period in which the transitions are taking place, there are no radical changes in age-specific transition rates. The first assumption allows one to infer median (and first-quartile or third-quartile) ages at transition; the second assumption allows one to treat single-moment, cross-sectional proportions in a given status as though they were the experience of a cohort undergoing the transition at that moment. Obviously, both assumptions—of irreversibility and of short-term stability of age-specific rates—are only relatively, not absolutely, true.

For these procedures to operate ideally, single-year-of-age data on each status in question would be called for. In fact, such data were available for only some of the transitions (least of all job entry) in some of the years studied (especially the more recent years), mainly for the United States. For some estimates only grouped age data were available, and linear interpolation was applied. In some cases where it seemed needed and appropriate, the age-specific experience of adjacent decades was used instead of the age-grouped parameters available for the year in question.

Education data for 1900–1 had to be based in part on retrospective accounts of educational attainment from the 1951 census of Great Britain and the 1940 census of the United States. These probably yield somewhat inflated claims for extensiveness of education, but they do by and large "fit" with the 1900–1 census data on labor-force participation. The most recent English marriage-age data are based on registration data, and are perhaps somewhat superior to, but not perfectly comparable with, those from earlier dates.

Relevant data were gathered from the following sources.

Schooling

Carr-Saunders, A. M., & Caradog Jones, D. (1937). *A survey of the social structure of England & Wales*. 2nd ed. Oxford: Clarendon Press, p. 114.

General Register Office (1925). *Census of England and Wales, 1921: General tables, comprising population, housing, . . . Welsh language*. London: His Majesty's Stationery Office, p. 174.

General Register Office (1952). *Census of Great Britain, 1951: One per cent sample tables*. Pt. 2. Table VIII.3. London: His Majesty's Stationery Office.

General Register Office (1964). *Department of Education and Science: Statistics of education, 1963*. Pt. 1. London: Her Majesty's Stationery Office, p. 10.

General Register Office (1966). *Census of England and Wales, 1961: Education tables*. Table 1. London: Her Majesty's Stationery Office.

General Register Office (1988). *Great Britain, Central Statistical Office: Annual abstract of statistics*. London: Her Majesty's Stationery Office, p. 78.

United States Bureau of the Census (1933). *Fifteenth census: 1930, population, general reports, statistics by subjects*. Washington, D.C.: U.S. Government Printing Office, p. 1098.

United States Bureau of the Census (1943). *Sixteenth census*. Vol. 4. *Population, characteristics by age*. Table 15. Washington, D.C.: U.S. Government Printing Office.

United States Bureau of the Census (1964). *Census of population, 1960*. Vol. 1. *Characteristics of the population, part 1, U.S. summary*. Washington, D.C.: U.S. Government Printing Office, p. 369.

United States Bureau of the Census (1975). *Historical statistics of the United States, bicentennial edition*. Vol. 1. Washington, D.C.: U.S. Government Printing Office, p. 370.

United States Bureau of the Census (1986). *Current population survey*, Ser. P-20, #408. Washington, D.C.: U.S. Government Printing Office.

Labor Force

General Register Office (1903). *Census of England and Wales, 1901: Summary tables*. Table 35. London: Her Majesty's Stationery Office.

General Register Office (1914). *Census of England and Wales, 1911*. Vol. 10. *Occupations and industries*. Pt. 1. Tables 3, 14a. London: His Majesty's Stationery Office.

General Register Office (1934). *Census of England and Wales, 1931: Occupation tables*. Table 2. London: His Majesty's Stationery Office.

General Register Office (1966). *Census, 1961, England and Wales: Occupation tables*. Table 2. London: Her Majesty's Stationery Office.

General Register Office (1973). Great Britain, Central Statistical Office, *Annual abstract of statistics*. London: Her Majesty's Stationery Office, p. 150.

General Register Office (1987). Great Britain, Central Statistical Office, *Annual abstract of statistics*. London: Her Majesty's Stationery Office, p. 120.

United States Bureau of the Census (1902). *Twelfth census . . . 1900, census reports, population*. Pt. 2. Washington, D.C.: Government Printing Office, p. 2.

United States Bureau of the Census (1904). *Special reports: Occupations at the twelfth census*. Washington, D.C.: Government Printing Office, pp. clxiv, cxli, 16.

United States Bureau of the Census (1933). *Fifteenth census: 1930, population*. Vol. 5. *General report on occupations*. Washington, D.C.: U.S. Government Printing Office, p. 115.

United States Bureau of the Census (1963). *Census of population, 1960: Subject reports PC(2)-6A: Employment and work experience*. Table 1. Washington, D.C.: U.S. Government Printing Office.

United States Bureau of the Census (1984). *Census of population, 1980: Detailed characteristics, United States summary*. Section A. Washington, D.C.: U.S. Government Printing Office, p. 118.

Marriage

General Register Office (1903). *Census of England and Wales, 1901: Summary tables*. Table 29. London: Her Majesty's Stationery Office.

General Register Office (1913). *Census of England and Wales, 1911*. Vol. 7. *Ages and condition as to marriage*. Table 1. London: His Majesty's Stationery Office.

General Register Office (1935). *Census of England and Wales, 1931: General tables*. London: His Majesty's Stationery Office, p. 141.

General Register Office (1961). *Census of England and Wales, 1961: Age, marital condition, and general tables*. Table 8. London: Her Majesty's Stationery Office.

General Register Office (1986). Great Britain, Central Statistical Office, *Annual abstract of statistics*. Table 2.5. London: Her Majesty's Stationery Office.

Kernan, K. M., & Eldridge, S. M. (1987). Age at marriage: Inter and intra cohort variation. *British Journal of Sociology, 38*, 45.

United States Bureau of the Census (1902). *Twelfth census . . . 1900: Population*. Pt. 2. Washington, D.C.: U.S. Government Printing Office, pp. 254–255.

United States Bureau of the Census (1920). *Fourteenth census of the United States, 1920: Population, general report*. Washington, D.C.: U.S. Government Printing Office, pp. 391–392.

United States Bureau of the Census (1933). *Fifteenth census, 1930: Abstract of the fifteenth census*. Table 15. Washington, D.C.: U.S. Government Printing Office.

United States Bureau of the Census (1961). *Census of population, 1960*. Vol. 1. *Characteristics of the population*. Table 176. Washington, D.C.: U.S. Government Printing Office.

United States Bureau of the Census (1984). *1980 census of population: Detailed population characteristics, United States summary*. Section A. Washington, D.C.: U.S. Government Printing Office, pp. 165–166.

5

CHALLENGES IN STUDYING MINORITY YOUTH

Margaret Beale Spencer and Sanford M. Dornbusch with the assistance of Randy Mont-Reynaud

The life experiences of minority adolescents in the United States are complicated by issues not faced by majority youth. Political, cultural, economic, and social forces interact in complex ways with such developmental concerns of adolescence as identity and self-image, increased autonomy, relations with peers, school achievement, and career goals. We shall consider these adolescent issues in relation to the historical, social, and cultural characteristics of specific American minority groups: African-Americans, Asian-Americans, Hispanics or Latinos, and Native Americans.

By adolescence, minority youth are well aware of the values of the majority culture and its standards of performance, achievement, and beauty. In contrast to younger children, adolescents evaluate their personal opportunities for attaining valued goals. For minority youth, adolescence is a particularly problematic juncture. This chapter surveys research that highlights the unique dilemmas of minority youth.

It is not surprising that, in contrast to the field of adolescent research generally, the study of minority adolescents necessarily involves far-reaching social issues such as racism, discrimination, inequality, and poverty. Social injustice (the denial of legal rights), social inconsistency (the institutionalized disparity between what is said and what is done), and impotence (the denial of efficacy) affect the aspirations, expectations, and achievement of minority youth (18, 98, 100, 101). Perceptions of prejudice, discrimination, and social inequity are significant aspects of the experience of minority adolescents.

While popular usage often equates the terms *minority* and *ethnic,* in this chapter they are not equivalent. Minority groups, like ethnic groups generally, share a sense of identity, a sense of belonging to a people with a common cultural tradition (29). In addition to this shared background, minority groups, in our usage, are targets of prejudice and discrimination. Racial and linguistic distinctions contribute to the high visibility of many minority adolescents, setting them apart from majority youth (48, 102). For example, those Hispanics who have darker skin or a more pronounced accent are more likely than other Hispanics to encounter prejudice and discrimination. Yet light-skinned Hispanics without accents are still members of a minority group. Race, color, and language do not define minority status, although they do contribute to it.

Current research on minority youth is diffuse, diverse, and frequently problem oriented, emphasizing such topics as teenage pregnancy, identity confusion, and academic underachievement. Much of this research focuses on a specific minority, or on comparisons between youth from one minority group and youth from the majority culture. Despite the abundance of such studies, there has been little integration of concepts and findings. We shall explore some of the factors contributing to this weakness.

The issues addressed here are general ones touching all minority youth, as well as some that are relevant for only certain minorities. Deciding which groups to study is a challenge faced by many researchers in this field. Rather than focusing on one or a few groups, we have chosen to present research on a broad spectrum of American minority youth.

Another challenge is that research on minority adolescence that takes into account the cultural context necessarily inherits the difficulties characteristic of cross-cultural work in general. For example, values and biases readily creep into studies of minority youth. In cross-cultural work more than in other research the values of researchers play a vital role in defining the issues, shaping the methodologies, and interpreting the results. Even scientists reflect the social milieu: notions of what is good or bad, important or unimportant, normative or deviant are culturally and perhaps politically motivated.

Biases operate at both the level of research and the level of minority youth experience. By adolescence, minority youth must confront the white culture and its values (91, 120). They are taught in public and private schools that have been characterized as supporting the cultural autocracy of the white middle class (14), in classroom contexts that are not adapted to minority learning styles (43, 60, 108), measured by tests that are sometimes culturally biased (114), and evaluated by teachers whose appreciation of their abilities may be hindered by stereotypes (23). Traditional research approaches fail to capture significant aspects of the environment in which minority youth grow to young adulthood. Perceiving bias among majority researchers, minority scholars often take a reactive stance (120). For example, Ogbu observed that "the research model of dominant group developmentalists is ethnocentric . . . It decontextualizes competencies from the realities of life" (97, p. 425). Value-free research may be impossible, but it is possible to acknowledge and reduce bias.

The confounding of minority status and social class poses an additional challenge to research on minority adolescence. In the 1960s a minority parent explained the distinction between race and class to her children. Her suggestion is instructive: "When they ask me why colored people aren't as good as whites, I tell them it's not that they're not as good; it's that they're not as rich. Then I tell them that they should separate being poor and being bad, and not get them mixed up" (20, p. 62).

Race and social class can interact in ways that exaggerate group differences, for minorities are overrepresented in the lower socioeconomic levels of American society. As a result, many researchers have given ethnic interpretations to phenomena that are largely the products of differences in social class. For example, decades of research on group differences in self-esteem often ignored the effects of socioeconomic background, thereby raising serious questions about interpretations of the results (51). When middle-income white children are compared with lower-income African-American children, the differences are striking but not informative because of this confounding (10, 120).

Although some minority youth are "middle class," economic advantage does not enable a youth to escape minority status. Middle-class minority adolescents still experience much of the prejudice and discrimination associated with minority-group membership (41, 92). Often characterized as a "model minority," Japanese-Americans may nonetheless experience stress associated with discrimination (92). Although middle-class minority adolescents have available more resources with which to counter the effects of prejudice and discrimination, they cannot avoid completely the impact of widespread stereotypes.

Although not all minority families are poor, poverty contributes heavily to adverse life experiences for many minority adolescents. A recent review has concluded that minority youth carry a disproportionate share of the stress of poverty and unemployment in America, and that these pressures may interfere with adults' effective parenting (83). Many of these adolescents are therefore doubly disadvantaged. Researchers on minority youth continually face the question of how to differentiate between the effects of social class and minority-group membership.

Social scientists studying minority youth inherit a traditional research base that is focused on negative outcomes rather than adaptive processes. Most research on African-Americans, for example, has been decried by Herbert Gutman as simply cataloguing "what was done to Blacks, what was done by Blacks and what was done for Blacks" (cited in 70, p. 168). A good deal of research on minorities has been conducted within the framework of a "deficit model." According to this model, minority youth perform poorly in school and later on the job because their family background is deprived, deficient, or deviant compared with white middle-class norms. Social scientists, for example, taking note of matriarchal households and absentee fathers, have tried to explain everything from truancy to teenage pregnancy as a product of "deficient" family structure. Too few studies have examined the triumphs of minorities in spite of poverty, social injustice, and inequities (81). A shift in focus may prove more productive for policy making than mere restatements of the sociocultural context of minority youth.

In the 1980s the social science research base on American minority adolescents was broadened to include suburban and rural African-American youth, supplementing our information about urban youth (6, 67). Research has expanded from an exclusive focus on low-income minority youth with many problems to include well-functioning adolescents from blue-collar families (69, 71). Studies of advantaged minority youth are emerging (13, 58, 108), and the growing African-American middle class has been receiving some attention (66, 118).

Although a more balanced research agenda is desirable, social scientists must not ignore the very real problems facing minorities today. Hispanics, for example, lag far behind most other ethnic groups in completing their education, with dropout rates nearly twice those for black and white youth (90). Adolescent Puerto Ricans and other Hispanics also have high unemployment rates (54, 133). The picture is similarly depressing for African-American youth (37). Compared with whites, African-American adolescents are more than twice as likely to be unemployed, are disproportionately likely to be arrested for delinquency, and are more than twice as likely to live below the poverty line (45). Of all minorities—including Asian-Americans, Pacific Islanders, Hispanics, and Native Americans—African-Americans have the poorest academic performance (109).

Research on minority adolescence demands interdisciplinary approaches, yet much of the available literature is one-sided, ignoring either cultural, environmental, or developmental variables. Furthermore, research emphases have varied with the political current of the times, resulting in a disjointed research perspective and little cumulative knowledge. The study of minority adolescent development must take into account psychological variables as well as the sociohistorical contexts of that development.

The life-span developmental approach, which combines biological, psychological, historical, and sociocultural perspectives, is thus particularly appropriate for the study of minority adolescents (4, 5). For minority youth, historical and sociocultural influences are especially relevant. Understanding minority adolescents requires further examination of the contexts of development, necessitating a broad ecological approach (15).

Sociocultural and Historical Influences

Minority groups are not homogeneous; they differ in their history and in their current sociocultural condition. For example, Cuban, Puerto Rican, and Mexican immigrants are all Hispanics, yet they had different reasons for migrating, came from divergent socioeconomic backgrounds in their native countries, and experience different rates and types of employment in the United States (90, 127). Native Americans are also heterogeneous and widely dispersed: more than two hundred tribal languages are still spoken, and approximately five hundred native entities are recognized by the federal government (65). There is also diversity among African-Americans. For example, adolescents of Jamaican background have had experiences quite unlike those of African-Americans from the rural South (81). Different groups face unique challenges and opportunities within the majority culture. They differ in their adaptive or maladaptive responses, with the effect of either buffering or increasing the impact of inequity. Thus, considerable variation within ethnic groups is the rule rather than the exception.

Demographic variables also influence minority adolescent development. Specifically, the size of the group, its relative distribution in the wider society, and its geographic location, whether urban or rural, are significant factors. Adolescents, for whom personal characteristics and acceptance by peers are central concerns, are particularly sensitive to the absence of fellow members of their minority in the community:

> "I'm the only Black in my Advanced Bio class. I'm the only Black on the soccer team. I'm the only Black in the band." (teenager in a suburban California high school, 88)

> "Sometimes you don't fit in. Like if you're a Puerto Rican on an Italian block." (129, p. 24)

The concentration of an immigrant group in an area increases its visibility and may increase the level of discrimination that it faces. Often a minority group is segregated within a geographic area, forming a cultural island within the larger social unit. This segregation may be involuntary, forced by discriminatory housing practices or by marked disparities in income; or it may be voluntary, arising out of the group's desire to maintain a supportive atmosphere in the midst of a society unaccepting of cultural differences.

The Chinese have long-established enclaves in New York, San Francisco, and other cities. Hispanics congregate primarily in three states: Puerto Ricans in New York and Mexican-Americans in Texas and California (46). Southeast Asian refugees, who initially were displaced widely throughout the United States in an effort to diffuse the burden of support, have mainly relocated to large urban centers such as San José and Los Angeles (17, 57). Immersion in ethnic neighborhoods often serves to buffer potential conflicts between the minority's traditional values and those of mainstream America.

One of the least-studied aspects of the minority experience among adolescents is the influence of community characteristics on personal and interpersonal processes. Ethnographic research has examined the interaction of community forces with such issues as school performance, career goals, identity, and conformity to dominant values. Examples include studies by Stack (123), Fordham and Ogbu (40), and MacLeod (72) among African-American youth and their families; research by Gibson (47) among Punjabi immigrant youth; and work by Matute-Bianchi (76) among Mexican-American and Japanese high school students. These studies of community values have provided insights into the mechanisms by which community forces affect adolescent development. Yet if we are to assess the relative influence of community pressures on adolescents, systematic studies comparing large samples are needed. Only such large quantitative studies can unravel the complex interaction of personal and familial factors with community characteristics and influences.

In one large-scale study Wilson points to a complex mixture of factors that produce an African-American underclass in inner-city communities (137). In particular, he found that the increased social isolation in concentrated areas of poverty and the lack of sustained interaction with individuals from mainstream society affect the perceptions of youth and the persistence of social problems. "The combination of unattractive jobs and lack of community norms to reinforce work increases the likelihood that individuals will turn to either underground illegal activity or idleness or both" (137, p. 60).

Within the inner city, young African-American males are increasingly unlikely to find legitimate employment, in part because of the lack of blue-collar jobs. Gibbs (45) notes that the community climate—the sense of kinship described by Stack (123)—is breaking down in the inner cities.

The combination of economic dislocation and discriminatory housing practices has deprived inner-city communities of necessary economic, social, and educational resources (10). The exodus of middle-income African-Americans from the cities to the suburbs has removed much of the leadership, leaving in its wake a shrinking tax base, a less educated political constituency, and a less extensive system of support from churches and other organizations (61, 137). The impact of these structural conditions on adolescent development needs further exploration.

In minority communities religious institutions are often influential (19, 49, 50). James Comer conveys the power and meaning of the African-American church through a boy's eyes: "The black church . . . was a place for participation and belonging. The deacons, trustees and ushers were ten feet tall on Sunday. This was not Inland Steel, Miss Ann's kitchen, nor the bank. This—the church—was theirs. In retrospect, the trustees were like the city board of finance and the deacons were like the city council" (22, p. 17).

African-Americans have indicated that their religious beliefs help them to get along with others and to accept the realities of the American occupational structure (115). Furthermore, African-American adolescents have reported that religion helps them in their family interactions. The church has been described as a structural bridge between the African-American family and entrance into the larger society (115). Lee's research documents the prevalence of strong religious faith within a sample of successful African-American students (67). Regular church attendance was a major factor in the lives of these youth, many of whom cited Jesus Christ, along with Dr. Martin Luther King, Jr., pastors, and deacons, as being important influences.

Studies in subgroups of other minorities have also found positive effects associated with religious participation. Moore and Pachon reported that Pentecostal churches among Puerto Ricans brought people together, promoted strong group identity, and improved coping mechanisms (90). Churches have been powerful sources of assistance to new Southeast Asian immigrants and their children; religious beliefs have been found to be associated with academic achievement within this group (17).

Although the view that religious institutions assist healthy adolescent development has intuitive appeal, solely positive effects of church membership cannot be taken for granted. Spencer reports that the church is no longer perceived as a major source of information about parenting strategies among lower-income families (121). In addition, a study of young African-American children indicated that belonging to certain denominations was associated with a decline in academic performance (12). These discrepant findings suggest the need for empirical studies of the role of religion in the lives of minority, particularly African-American, adolescents.

Another significant influence on the life experiences of minority adolescents is the political climate (17, 94). Political developments such as the expansion of school integration or the loss of industrial jobs frequently open or close windows of opportunity within the wider society. Sometimes instrumental changes manifest themselves as shifts in minority-group consciousness, such as the Black Power movement in the 1960s (106), the growing pressure by Hispanics for the election of more Hispanic officials, and the increasing unity among the diverse tribes of Native Americans. American society is changing rapidly, and the changes affect the ways in which minority adolescents perceive their personal situation, the position of their particular minority group, and both their short-term and long-term options.

Now that we have seen some of the demographic, historical, and sociocultural forces that are part of the background of minority adolescent development, let us turn to the subject of identity formation. We shall consider three major influences on adolescent development—family, peers, and schools—and end with a look at the types of future research that can improve our knowledge base and lead to the creation of informed social policy.

Issues of Identity

Adolescence is a crucial period for identity formation. "Identity, a conscious sense of individual uniqueness . . . and a solidarity with a group's ideals" (36, p. 208), is more problematic for minority adolescents, who often find themselves enveloped by the values and standards of the mainstream culture (91). In light of negative evaluations from the majority, the task of developing a positive identity as a member of a minority group may be difficult. When race is linked to membership in a minority group, the message from the wider culture may be, "If you're white you're all right; if you're brown, stick around; if you're black, stay back" (87, p. 98).

The adolescent's awareness of minority status is qualitatively different from that of the child (122). Very young children, for example, often think of their race and gender as mutable, something that may change as they grow (117, 122, 135). Many parents of minority children have confronted logic similar to that expressed by the adopted three-year-old African-American boy who held his white mother's hand, turned his palm over, studied it, and said, "When I'm big, I'm gonna be white all over, like you." Then he added, "And I'm gonna be a mommy when I get big!" (88)

In contrast to young children, adolescents have the ability to interpret cultural knowledge, to reflect on the past, and to speculate about the future (52, 53, 62). With cognitive maturity, minority adolescents are keenly aware of the evaluations of their group made by the majority culture (23, 40, 91). Thus the young African-American may learn as a child that black is beautiful but conclude as an adolescent that white is powerful (117).

The minority adolescent's awareness of such negative appraisals, of conflicting values, and of restricted occupational opportunities can affect life choices and the strategies selected for negotiating a life course. As one minority adolescent explained: "The future they see is shut off. It's closed. You're afraid to dream for fear of not reaching it, so you don't set up any goals, and that way you don't fail" (87, p. 91).

Minority youths' perceptions of themselves and their group are significant influences on socioemotional development. The "looking-glass self," in which one imagines the reactions of others to one's behavior and personality, affects the adolescent's identity development (25). For minority youth the stigmas of racial stereotypes, often reinforced by poverty, have the potential to distort the image in the mirror.

Yet negative evaluations of one's group need not portend a poor self-concept for minority youth, for minority status is only one of many potential influences on the adolescent's sense of self (26). In other do-mains—school, home, friends, sports—self-esteem may find positive ex-pression and encouragement (51). The impact of negative appraisals from the wider society may be countered by peers, parents, teachers, and other members of the youth's community (3, 7, 13, 26, 58, 117).

Still, many minority youth are faced with cultural devaluation of the symbols and heroes of their group. Chinese youth, for example, confront American role models who typically personify values antithetical to those of their immigrant parents (126). Adolescents, becoming sensitive to soci-etal inconsistency, are particularly affected by the conflict in values. A Chinese adolescent described her situation: "Chinese people had Chinese opinions. American people had American opinions. And in almost every case, the American version was much better . . . [but] there were too many choices and it was easy to get confused" (128, p. 191).

For other minority youth the problem is not conflicting role models but a lack of successful role models with whom to identify. This situation confronts many African-American youth in the inner cities. Sylvester Monroe, an African-American journalist, reflected on this issue, drawing on his own adolescent experience in an urban housing project: "If you were black, you didn't quite measure up . . . For a black kid there was a certain amount of self-doubt. It came at you indirectly. You didn't see any black people on television, you didn't see any black people doing certain things, and you couldn't rationalize it. I mean, you don't think it out but you say, 'Well, it must mean that white people are better than we are. Smarter, brighter—whatever'" (87, pp. 98–99). In response to such pressures, minority adolescents may strive to conform to white middle-class standards. Not all minority youth, however, have the option of fitting comfortably into the majority culture. For many, racial characteristics and skin color constrain their acceptance by white society, although for others the issue is not acceptance. As minority youth prepare for adult roles, their greatest desire is for just and equitable treatment (116, 120).

This issue of identity development for minority youth is further complicated by the value associated with a group's racial characteristics. Some youths find it easy—and desirable—to "pass" as whites; others cannot, or choose not to do so. For some minority females the white standard of beauty engenders self-denigration of their appearance (104). These are particularly significant concerns during adolescence, when physical characteristics are very much an object of concern. Adolescents in general are self-conscious and reluctant to stand out in a crowd. The visible minority youth has little choice.

Those minority teenagers who can interact easily or identify with the majority culture may find themselves rejected by their own group (3, 40, 47, 84, 85, 94). Overidentification with the white majority is commonly labeled pejoratively by minority groups. Native Americans who "act white" are "Apples"; Asians are "Bananas"; "Coconuts" describes that group of Hispanics; and African-Americans are "Oreos." The negative metaphors describe individuals who are racially "of color" but behaviorally "white" (84).

In terms of emotional development, adolescence is a time of constant, and often painful, comparison of oneself with others. Because the social network of the teenager is wider than the child's, adolescents are exposed more directly to the ideals and values of the majority culture. Compared to children, they are increasingly literate, have greater access to the media, and are more mobile, with greater physical freedom and financial resources to explore the environment beyond their immediate neighborhood. Even when they have a positive personal identity (51), minority adolescents may develop ambivalent or negative attitudes toward their own group. For example, African-American teenage girls who live in white suburbs are more negative toward their own culture than are younger African-American females (6). Other research suggests that Asian-American high school students are more negative toward their own group than are other minorities (103). Yet a 1985 study of African-American children through early adolescence noted a progressively more positive orientation toward their own group as the children grew older (122).

Minority adolescents clearly have a special task: to negotiate a balance between two value systems: that of their own group and that of the majority (14). Some youths reject the mainstream, forgoing the rewards that are controlled by the majority (40, 76); others denigrate their own culture and completely assimilate the values and behavior of the majority; and still others take the difficult path to biculturality.

Although young children are aware of some racial and cultural differences, minority individuals first consciously confront the issue of biculturality only at adolescence. This event traditionally has been described in terms of conflict, but social scientists now suggest that there is a double consciousness, an ability to perceive social interaction in terms of different standards and values (27).

W. E. B. Du Bois, writing at the beginning of this century, described the African-American of his day as "two warring idols in one dark body" (34). Internal conflict and tension were attributed to individuals who participated in two cultures simultaneously (124). This issue is raised by many individuals:

> "I wanted my children to have the best combination: American circumstances and Chinese character. How could I know these two things do not mix?" (128, p. 254)

> " 'Got one mind for white folk to see, 'nother for what I know is me." (Negro folk song, cited in 1, p. 194)

Stonequist's concept of the "marginal man" views him as "poised in psychological uncertainty between two (or more) social worlds" (124, p. 329). The marginal man was at home nowhere, belonging in neither group, yet wavering between both, uncertain how to act. A study of Mexican-Americans found that many members of this group were caught between two opposing cultures and often sought relief from their problems through alcohol (73).

In forging an identity, minority adolescents may choose among several strategies for dealing with their ethnicity: alienation, separation, assimilation, and biculturalism (104). Assimilation occurs when the belief systems and life-styles of a minority are replaced by those of the majority culture (107). In contrast, bicultural individuals shuttle successfully between their primary or familial culture and the dominant culture (107). Ramirez proposes a flexibility model, wherein the norms of both groups are available to minority youth and the standard used depends on the situation (107).

Bicultural competence may offer some advantages (113). For example, some bicultural Blackfeet Indians have been able to make situationally based choices of cultural orientations. With models from both their own ethnic group and the majority, individuals have had the advantage of a large repertory of skills and knowledge from which to draw (79).

Discussions of the experiences of Asian-American youth are cast largely in terms of conflict rather than biculturality (126). Work by Phinney indicates that Asian-American attitudes tend toward assimilation rather than ethnic pride (103). Conflict characterizes the feelings of Southeast Asian immigrant youth in particular (94). Adolescent Southeast Asians may not share the orientations of adult refugees, who still look back to their homeland and may feel exiled in America. Biculturality develops as a coping style, as a means of overcoming the feelings of helplessness that often overwhelm these youth. Nidorf characterizes this group as "struggling to select from both cultures those values and beliefs that will facilitate existence" (94, p. 421). There are frequently significant disparities between traditional values and American ideals of behavior. Nidorf notes:

> Effective coping often requires [youth] to embrace American values at the expense of values cherished by the parents. For example, in the United States we believe that the young person must develop autonomy from parents as a means toward achieving the strong sense of personal identity necessary for leading a productive life. However, the Southeast Asian youths are expected by their parents to remain indefinitely in a position of mutual interdependence with family members, their sense of self-worth and maturation established by subordinating their own needs and by assuming increasing responsibility for meeting the needs of family members . . . The confusing message received by refugee youths from their parents [is] "Become a success in the United States, but find a way to do it without becoming an American." (94, pp. 421–422)

Sung points out that many Chinese youth "perceive of their marginality as a dilemma. They are faced with a situation where courses of action are diametrically opposed or radically different . . . The choices are painful and more often than not immobilizing. Not having the maturity to evaluate or modify their courses of action or to adjust their values, they do nothing; the vacuousness of their . . . inability to decide is extremely uncomfortable" (94, p. 268).

Language is tied to issues of biculturality for many minority youth. Although a large number have made English their dominant language, their parents may still rely on the native tongue. Furthermore, these youths may be rejected by majority peers and teachers despite their efforts toward linguistic and cultural assimilation (48).

The adaptive consequences of biculturality vary from one social context to another and depend on many factors, such as majority attitudes, the strengths of the minority group, color and social visibility, the youth's own resilience or vulnerability, and factors within the family (112, 119, 121).

Family Composition and Processes

Minority-group families differ from majority families in their size, structure, and composition, their reliance on kinship networks, and their levels of income and parental education. These variables affect parenting behaviors (82, 105), family interaction processes (31, 33, 64, 74), and children's socioemotional functioning (83). Other research relates these family characteristics to adolescents' school performance (19, 32, 111). Thus, family environment is a mediating factor that strongly shapes the development of minority youth.

Large and extended families are more common among minorities than among non-Hispanic whites (138, 139). In 1980 families with five or more members accounted for 31% of Hispanic households but only 17% of the general population (63, 89). In addition, there are differences in the extent to which minority families interact with their extended-kin networks. African-Americans and Hispanics interact more with grandparents, aunts, uncles, cousins, and other more distant relatives than do non-Hispanic whites, and the support system among African-American extended kin is more active than that of other groups (56, 86, 123, 130).

Single teenage mothers particularly benefit from the availability of other adults to serve as surrogate parents. Research indicates that African-American adolescent mothers in extended families are more likely to remain in school than their peers who lack this support, and are less likely to rely on welfare. These young mothers also report more peer group support and more often say they feel in control of their lives than do African-American adolescent mothers living independently (21, 42). Advantages accruing to other minority adolescents from extended kinship networks have yet to be explored.

Single-parent families are much more common in the African-American and Hispanic groups than in the majority American population. In 1985 the proportion of children and youth living in single-parent households was 18% for non-Hispanic whites, 29% for Hispanics, and 54% for African-Americans (132). The proportion of children and youth who will live in a single-parent household before reaching age 18 is even greater;

these statistics merely suggest the magnitude of the population that will experience single parenting during at least part of their childhood.

The presence of a single parent is more likely to continue into adolescence for children of minority families than for those of non-Hispanic white families. Half of all African-American youth are likely to remain with a single parent for their entire childhood, in contrast to only 15% of whites (83). Single motherhood is clearly linked to poverty. Even among whites, about half the children living in single-parent households are below the poverty line. Among minorities, about 70% of African-American and Hispanic children being raised by single mothers are poor (39), and the number of these poor families has more than doubled since 1960 (134).

In comparison with the situation in two-parent households, single parents usually have more limited resources of time, money, and energy. We can speculate that this shortage of resources prompts them to encourage early autonomy among their adolescent children. For African-Americans, Asian-Americans, Hispanics, and non-Hispanics whites, granting adolescents more autonomy in decision making than is typical for their age is associated with negative outcomes such as high rates of deviance and poor grades in school (31). Thus, differences owing to family structure are partially explained by relating early autonomy in decision making to various outcomes. Poor school performance and a high incidence of deviance (truancy, running away from home, smoking, early dating, contacts with police, and arrests) among many minority youth can be explained in part by the association of single parenthood with this parenting practice (31, 32).

Similarly, within both minority and majority groups the extent of joint decision making between adolescents and parents helps explain the higher grades and lower rates of deviance of children whose parents are better educated. Those parents consult with their adolescents more often, and such a decision-making pattern is associated with positive outcomes across all ethnic and social-class groups. Minority parents, who are often less educated than majority whites, tend to employ joint decision making less often; this low frequency is associated, in turn, with lower grades for adolescents and greater deviance (31, 32).

Minority parents, like all parents, are responding to economic, social, and political conditions (7, 13, 19). Minority youth are more likely to come from disadvantaged and female-headed families (24). Although impoverished families often raise competent youth (55), poor parents risk having a diminished capacity for supportive and involved parenting, and thus tend to see an increased incidence of impaired socioemotional functioning among their youth (83). The absence of fathers can be explained in part by economic circumstances. Among African-Americans there has been a reduction since the 1960s in the male-female wage ratio (2, 136). Changes in industrial and occupational opportunities have reduced the capacity of minority men to support their families and, in turn, have affected their marriageability (45, 83, 137, 140).

A carefully documented review has examined how the psychological stress associated with poverty and unemployment adversely affects parenting behaviors. When parents are overburdened, they are less likely to display parenting behaviors that require patience (83). Parents who engage in practices that appear coercive may have valid motives for their behavior. Research is needed that goes beyond the study of behaviors to examine parental strategies and goals.

In spite of the difference in access to resources, there are striking similarities between competent adolescents from African-American blue-collar families and those from white middle-class families. Living in a competent, intact family facilitates highly adaptive levels of functioning among adolescents; family behaviors are more significant than the influences of class and minority status (71). It has been asserted that "middle-class Blacks are ardent defenders of the society's dominant values" (69, p. 131), but they typically do not have the same resources as whites to mobilize toward the shared goals.

Certain aspects of home life can serve to protect minority youth from social patterns of injustice (13, 58, 67). The community and family can filter out racist, destructive messages (7). Parents can provide alternate frames of reference to those presented by the majority (7, 117); they also can provide role models and encouragement.

Among some Asians subgroups parents are concerned that successful adaptation to mainstream society will undermine their cultural traditions and create problems in disciplining and controlling adolescents. A Southeast Asian refugee discussed his teenage daughter's behavior: "She complains about going to the Lao temple on the weekend and instead joined a youth group in a neighborhood Christian church. She refused to wear traditional dress on the Lao New Year. The girl is setting a very bad example for her younger sisters and brothers" (94, pp. 422–423).

Minority parents strive to protect their children from the world, since societal and peer influences often are perceived to be in conflict with the minority group's values. For example, Chinese parents are extremely conservative about dating, for both their daughters and their sons (126). Since the parents themselves have had no dating experience, parental control in this domain is seen as normative—at least by the parents.

> Good girls simply did not go out with boys alone, so the parents
> are very suspicious and apprehensive about their daughters dat-

ing, and watch them very carefully. For the daring girl who tries to go out against her parents wishes, there will be a price to pay . . . It is no easier for the Chinese boys. The pressure to succeed in school is even greater than for girls, and parental opposition to dating is even more intense . . . Naturally some children do not agree with their parents and have to carry on their high school romances on the sly. These children are bombarded by television, advertisements, stories, magazines and real-life examples of boy-girl attraction. The teenager is undergoing puberty and is experiencing the instinctive urges surging within him or her. In this society, teenagers are titillated, whereas in China they are kept under wraps until they are married. (126, p. 258)

The views and assumptions of minority parents reflect political and social currents. For example, there are different interpretations of the authoritarian parenting style that is frequently characteristic of African-American families (83). According to some, a socialization geared toward obedience and submission to authority was considered most adaptive for African-American children, given the roles they were expected to fulfill within the majority society (9, 11). McGoldrick pointed out that African-American parents who are strict in disciplining their children are preparing them for adulthood, for they believe that society imposes severe consequences on African-Americans who transgress (80).

Minority parenting is also affected by the activities and resources of adolescent peers. It is of great concern to minority parents that the peer group in inner cities can often offer tangible rewards for delinquent behavior to youths who feel alienated from society (45). Few legitimate routes to success are available for minority youth. Some who participate in the sale of drugs earn more money than their parents. Under such conditions, peer influences can easily outweigh parental control.

Peer Influences

During adolescence most youths turn increasingly to their peers. Minority teenagers, particularly immigrants, have additional motivation for doing so. Minority adolescents become aware of the differences between their own expectations, those of their parents, and those of the majority culture. And immigrant youth may begin to distrust their parents as they observe that their parents lack power and competence in the new society (94). The effect is compounded if the adolescent loses the ability to speak the minority group's language (38). These factors serve to strengthen the peer group, in place of the parents, as a source of emotional support and guidance. Peers may also play a role in furthering acculturation (28). The desire to be accepted, which is compelling among teenagers, is especially strong among refugee adolescents. For them the greatest threat is not the feeling of belonging to two cultures but the feeling of belonging to none (68, p. 173).

For many immigrant minority youth, peers from their own ethnic group provide a crucial sense of brotherhood or sisterhood within the new culture. Peer groups may form to oppose majority mores and to provide adaptive social supports that reduce feelings of isolation. Refugee youth, who may be living apart from some or all of their family, may form gangs as a substitute. The gangs permit the reenactment of traditional family roles such as protective older sister, older brother, and father (85, 94).

Young refugees, particularly those unaccompanied by family, often must rely on antisocial strategies to negotiate the departure from their homeland and to survive the wait in refugee camps. Gangs permit the continuation of previously adaptive behaviors such as fighting, stealing, and cheating, even though this may cause trouble for the adolescents in their new homeland (85).

For all adolescents, peer acceptance becomes an increasingly important goal. For minority groups, opposition has historically been a survival strategy. To be against anything white (that is, to be against the system at large) is one way for a minority group to define itself in the face of discrimination and racism (76). This can lead to a militant posture, which may be a form of coping (14). Peer dependence among Native Americans has also been described as a method of coping with feelings of isolation (30).

For some minority youth, acceptance by one's own peer group may hinge on rejecting the values and behaviors of the majority culture, particularly the culture of the school (40, 76). Some minority youth defy mainstream values, in particular positive school conduct, in an effort to maintain a separate and self-accepting ethnic identity. As Fordham and Ogbu note, however, placing African-American youths in a school with many high-achieving minority students relieves them of the psychological burden of "acting white" (40). In a context where academic achievement is normative for African-American youths, they can aim for success without being scorned by their peers.

The influence of peers often increases for adolescents who do poorly in school. When African-Americans, particularly males, fail in school, they try to appear successful to their peers in other domains. These youths may act "cool," adopting certain peer-oriented styles of walking, talking, and dressing. They may even identify with drug dealers and pimps as role models. By taking up "oppositional values," these youths define alternative standards of success and new paths for acceptance by their peers (51). Although sometimes adaptive in the short term, such behaviors usually lead to adverse long-term outcomes.

Minority Adolescents in Schools

Contrary to the popular stereotype, minority parents are interested in their youngsters' academic performance and strive to encourage them (70, 111). One ethnographic study, among academically successful rural African-American adolescents, reported strong parental support in the form of such comments as "Your education comes first," "I didn't get [an education], so I want you to," and "Go to school or find another house to stay at" (67, p. 133). Such sentiments are shared by other minority groups. A Mexican-American adolescent described her mother's efforts: "My mother keeps telling me: 'Ai, mi hija, tienes que sacar buenas calificaciones en la high school para que no te estes chingando igual que yo.' [Oh, my dear, you must get good grades in high school so you don't get screwed like me.] And you know she has a point. I don't want to be doing that. I've been in the cannery before. Just being there I can tell I wouldn't want to work there. I've got to do well in school so that I don't have to face this in my future" (76, p. 243).

Parenting practices may either support or detract from youths' performance in school. A recent comparative study of minority teenagers found that, after controlling for social class, punitive parenting and permissive parenting were both associated with poor grades. In contrast, authoritative parenting, which is characterized by setting limits in a context of warmth, was associated with better grades. Certain ethnic differences, however, were seen to affect the connection between parenting style and school performance, with the relation weakest among Asian-American adolescents (32).

Reports from Asian-American high school students of both sexes indicate that their families frequently practice authoritarian parenting. Such methods are significantly associated with low grades. Yet Asian-Americans as a whole receive high grades in school (32). The success of Asian youth in American public schools cannot satisfactorily be explained by a model of parenting style developed largely from white middle-class samples; a model that takes cultural contexts into account is needed.

In spite of parental encouragement, minority youth typically achieve lower levels of academic performance than do majority adolescents. Hispanics, for example, are nearly two years behind African-Americans in years of school completed. Their dropout rates are nearly twice those of African-American and non-Hispanic white youth. In addition, Hispanic students are frequently several years below grade level in American public schools (90, 109). In terms of grades and test scores, of all minority groups African-Americans average the fewest As and the most Ds and Fs in high school classes, and consistently have SAT scores that are lower than those of any other group (109). College enrollment rates held steady from 1976 to 1986 for African-American women but declined dramatically for men (45). This trend among African-American men is particularly disturbing since the proportion of African-Americans who finished high school during that same period increased from 68% to 76% (10). The perceptions of James Comer may be typical of the African-American's experience: "The school was, for many of my classmates, 'the white man's world.' I was aware of that very early. I can remember thinking that if Marshall Long can do so well in the Baptist Young People's Union Bible Drill, why could he not do the same in school? . . . I knew many other kids who could think fast, talk fast and act fast in the playground, in church and on the corner, who seemed to be immobilized in the classroom" (22, p. 20).

Ogbu (95, 96, 97, 100, 101) and Fordham (40) set forth a controversial set of ideas that relate the academic performance of minority youth to their perceptions of subordination and exploitation. The lack of equal educational opportunity within American society induces expectations of poor academic performance among African-Americans, according to Ogbu. Furthermore, teachers often underestimate and stereotype minority students, labeling them as educationally handicapped, and have generally low expectations for their academic performance (93). It has also been suggested that school culture and the culture of minority groups differ; school personnel and minority families and their children have difficulty bridging the gap (59, 60, 70).

The most distinctive aspect of Ogbu's thesis is his emphasis on the minority response to the perceived hegemony of white middle-class values in the educational system (14, 99). He portrays African-Americans and Mexican-Americans in the United States as far more likely to reject characteristic American attitudes and behaviors than recent immigrants who seek economic and political opportunities in the United States. Although many members of American minorities lead productive lives by both majority and minority standards, Ogbu has chosen to emphasize that some subgroups define appropriate behavior in opposition to white middle-class standards, particularly in the area of education.

According to Ogbu, minority opposition to the educational system stems from a lack of trust in the American social structure (100, 101). It makes little sense to strive to do well academically if one has no occupational opportunities. From the point of view of majority educators, dropping out does not make sense; education is supposed to be the road to upward mobility. Many researchers, however, believe that when minority youth give up in high school, this is a rational response to discrimination and perceived socioeconomic barriers (45, 95, 96, 97).

In fact, finishing high school—even completing some college—does not seem to bring the same job opportunities for minorities as for whites. For example, in terms of earnings and employment rates, African-American high school graduates do not do as well as white high school dropouts. In 1976 blacks aged 20–24 who had completed some college had higher unemployment rates than whites who never finished high school (45). Entwisle provides data showing that for youths without college degrees, racial differences in earnings increased between 1973 and 1986 (35). The number of job opportunities available to black and other minority adolescents in urban centers has sharply declined, owing to the shift from manufacturing to service industries, combined with the relocation of industries as well as middle-income residents to the suburbs (10).

Giving up in school because of a perceived lack of reward in terms of job opportunities is not only typical of African-Americans. There is evidence that some Hispanic high school students share a similar sense of futility. Matute-Bianchi's Mexican respondents expressed these views:

> "Mexicans don't have a chance to go on to college and make something of themselves"; "People like us face a lot of prejudice because there are a lot of people who don't like Mexicans"; "There aren't enough good jobs to go around"; "Some people, no matter how hard they try, just have bad luck" . . . to participate in class discussions, to carry books from class to class, to ask the teacher for help in front of others, to expend effort to do well in school—are efforts that are viewed derisively . . . by other Chicanos. Hence to adopt such features presents these students with a forced choice dilemma. They must choose between doing well in school or being a Chicano." (76, pp. 251, 255)

Many aspects of the American educational system have created difficulties for minority adolescents. A form of institutional racism prevails in many American schools, in that well-meaning teachers, acting out of a sense of misguided liberalism, often fail to challenge minority students. That is, knowing the handicaps that these adolescents face, some teachers accept a low level of performance from their minority pupils, substituting warmth and affability for academic challenge and high academic standards. Minority adolescents, like those in the majority, learn best when teachers combine warmth with challenging standards (8, 93). Teachers may expect minority students to fail and communicate these expectations to the students, who fulfill them (77, 78). The result is a form of racism without racists—teaching practices that result in poor minority performance (75, 77, 78, 93).

In contemporary American culture educators and parents tend to believe that innate ability, rather than diligent effort, is responsible for academic achievement. The emphasis on ability as the main predictor of differences in academic performance often traps minority youth in a vicious circle. Minority children who do not immediately perform well in the classroom are likely to be labeled low-ability or educationally handicapped students. Once they are placed in remedial classes, it is rare for them to be reassigned to higher levels later on (110). When minority youth are overrepresented in the lower tracks, the explanation given is their low level of ability and investment of effort; teachers' prejudices and practices are not considered (70).

In American high schools, African-Americans and Hispanics are overrepresented in the lower tracks and underrepresented at higher levels (109). The percentage of African-American students in the category of educable mentally retarded was double that of all other students in this category in 1980 (101, 109). Such labels become self-fulfilling prophecies, since when tracking errors are made—and there are many—only the parents of advantaged students are likely to protest. Minority parents and low-income parents are more likely to accept the track assignments endorsed by school personnel. Mislabeling and tracking serve to perpetuate social inequality.

Goals for Future Research

The projections that, by the year 2000, 31% of American youth will be members of minority groups (46, p. xi) demonstrate an immediate need for increased research on minority adolescents. The existing empirical literature is extremely variable; while a few topics have been extensively explored, others remain virtually untouched. Furthermore, the level of sophistication in theory and methodology is uneven. Changing political and social currents lead to abrupt increases or declines in research on "hot" topics. The fact that few studies rely on the measures and concepts developed by previous researchers in the field hampers the accumulation of knowledge. Much of the ethnographic literature provides useful insights, but it is limited in scope. Some adolescent minority groups, such as African-Americans and Hispanics, have received a good deal of attention, while other groups remain understudied.

A major deficiency of the research on adolescence has been its traditional focus on white middle-income youth. Since middle-class white families have supplied most of the data and shaped our general conclusions, it is not surprising that social scientists have tended to see mainstream white behaviors as the norm. Yet, if we are to develop sound theories of adolescent development with principles generalizable to diverse groups and situations, minority as well as majority youth must be studied.

The differences among minority groups provide a natural diversity of settings for comparative studies of adolescent development. Research among minorities can address three distinct types of questions: What differences exist among minority groups in the frequency of particular behaviors (such as authoritarian parenting)? Are there differences among minority groups in the relationship between certain behaviors and a particular outcome (such as the relation between parental involvement and academic performance)? And what are the most important minority-related factors (such as language use) contributing to differences in outcomes (such as social competence)? Minority groups differ in many respects; emphasizing just a few is mere social journalism. Only quantitative studies that use equivalent measures with samples from several groups can identify the relative contribution of particular behaviors and cultural contexts to group differences in outcome.

In spite of broad-based studies of community organization and its impact on minority adolescents (137), much remains unknown. First, most community studies are not comparative; few contrast youth from different minority communities. Second, community-level studies seldom include information on family, peer, and school interactions. It is difficult to assess the independent contribution of neighborhoods without a simultaneous examination of these other influences.

Traditional models of adolescent development fail to take this complexity of factors into account. The life-span developmental approach is uniquely suited to the study of processes and outcomes among minority adolescents. This perspective emphasizes the ecological context within which development takes place (15). The adolescent is seen as an active participant in a hierarchy of systems, from the microsystem of the family to the exosystem of government policy and the macrosystem of ideology (44). The life-span approach integrates biological and psychological factors with historical and sociocultural factors, seeking to understand the impact of changing contexts on individual development. For minority youth, whose development may be intertwined with issues of immigration, acculturation, poverty, and discrimination, this perspective is particularly appropriate. Such a systems approach to adolescent development can provide information for generating more comprehensive theories, reformulating developmental models of risk and coping, implementing intervention programs, and improving efforts to achieve educational and social equity.

We have reviewed some of the ways in which minority youth are different: in their historical and cultural backgrounds, in the visibility of racial characteristics, and in the demographics of their distribution within the larger society. One topic for future research is the way in which these elements interact with and contribute to the minority adolescent's socioemotional and cognitive development. For example, in regard to the key issue of identity, the normal adolescent process of self-scrutiny can be especially threatening for minority youth. Their growing awareness of the majority's evaluations of their group affects their sense of self. Commitment to a minority-group identity is an essential component of the self-concept that contributes to psychological adjustment. Accordingly, minority adolescents must explore the meanings of their ethnic identity or risk identity disorders (103).

Ogbu has suggested that the historical experiences of minority groups have a contemporary impact (100, 101). He has distinguished between immigrant minorities, who came voluntarily to America to improve their lot, and castelike minorities, who were involuntarily incorporated into American society by conquest or slavery. Ogbu attributes much of the poor academic performance of African-American youth to their historic distrust of the American system (40, 100, 101). Despite some criticism (16, 131), Ogbu's ideas have gained wide currency. There have been many careful ethnographic studies of relatively small samples of diverse minority youth (40, 47, 76, 125). These studies and their findings warrant large-scale testing, in which the values of African-American adolescents are compared with those of other minority youth.

One example of an undeveloped research topic is the effect of generational status on minority adolescents. There have been reports of high achievement among recent immigrant youth (17). Despite the language handicaps that plague new arrivals, many outperform earlier generations within their own ethnic group, as well as majority peers. Does acculturation render minority youth more susceptible to a relatively undemanding set of expectations for school performance? Or does the acculturated minority adolescent use different standards for assessing the future?

Current social organization and practices continue to present barriers for minority adolescents. In spite of progress in many areas, minority youth are still constrained in their opportunities and choices. Improving their circumstances requires a partnership between policy makers, service providers, and social science researchers. Research can help us understand the circumstances shaping the lives of minority adolescents. We cannot hope to make the necessary improvements in social conditions without better-informed social policies. Ideological statements are not enough. As Martin Luther King, Jr., put it, "What good is it to be allowed to eat in a restaurant if you can't afford a hamburger?"

6

COMING OF AGE IN A CHANGING FAMILY SYSTEM

Frank F. Furstenberg

The assumption that adolescent experience is shaped in important ways by family experience is widely embraced by developmentalists. While researchers appreciate the family's powerful impact on children's success in negotiating the period of adolescence, how that passage is linked to specific features of family structure and dynamics has not been adequately studied. Complicating the examination of this process are the profound changes that have been occurring in the family over the past several decades.

Most developmentalists are well aware of the findings of demographic and sociological researchers who have been charting the transformation of the American family. Still, the implications of these changes for adolescent development are just beginning to be recognized. In addition, the family is too often portrayed in broad brush strokes that miss the sharp variations across racial and social-class groupings (45). No children in the United States are untouched by the sweeping changes that have occurred in the family, but minorities and economically disadvantaged youth have been especially affected by certain features of the recent transformation (24, 78).

The aim of this chapter is to consider the implications of this transformation for adolescent development. What do the enormous changes in the timing of family events, the diverse organization of the family, and the emerging structure of kinship portend for the well-being of today's youth? This question is too broad for a single chapter. I intend to be selective, concentrating on topics that are relatively rich in empirical research, such as the timing of parenthood, and family disruption and reconstitution. In particular, the effects of these changes on disadvantaged and minority children will be highlighted. My disciplinary grounding will inevitably lead me to give more attention to the historical and sociological conditions that have altered the family form than the resulting internal dynamics within the family system. (Chapter 10 will deal with this latter theme more explicitly. Chapter 16 also pursues some related themes on youthful deviance.)

The first section of this chapter discusses some of the most conspicuous changes that have occurred in the American family over the past several decades. This serves as a prelude for considering how these changes have altered the typical experience of the later years of childhood and the early years of adolescence. I then assemble some of the evidence on whether and how these changes are affecting the subsequent adjustment of youths and young adults. This question has led troubled observers of the family to issue rather extravagant statements about the link between family change and adolescent well-being. The chapter concludes with an assessment of these claims as well as a discussion of some of the pressing policy questions raised by efforts to improve the circumstances of American families.

What Has Happened to the American Family?

Until the recent spate of historical research on the family, it was often assumed that family patterns in the United States and elsewhere were more or less stable until the industrial period. This notion has been thoroughly discredited by countless studies showing continuous changes in the family in earlier historical times (19, 20, 77). Also, it appears that there was no singular or common response to the onset of industrialization (42). Some patterns (romantic love, premarital sexual behavior, close affective bonds between parents and children, and the absence of multigeneration family units) that were once believed to be products of economic developments in the eighteenth and nineteenth centuries existed well before the industrial revolution (41).

Family historians have been unable to identify a period in America's past when family life was untroubled (20). Most are skeptical that the traditional family—what William Goode has labeled "the classical family of Western nostalgia" (40, p. 6)—ever existed in the form in which it is sometimes portrayed today: a stable, harmonious, well-functioning, supportive unit in which children were tenderly and skillfully guided into adulthood. Historical accounts provide abundant evidence that family life was often stressful, fractious, and repressive (73). Throughout the nineteenth century many children and youths were ill cared for and unsupervised. Mortality, morbidity, and extreme poverty often produced high rates of family instability. Uhlenberg estimates that survival rates of children to age 15 rose from .79 in 1900 to .98 in 1979 (81). The probability of a child's losing one or both parents has similarly declined from .24 to .05 during roughly the same period. In fact, conditions for children and families probably improved markedly and family life became *more* stable and *more* intimate in the twentieth century as mortality and morbidity declined and children became, in Viviana Zelizer's phrase, "emotionally priceless" (89).

We have much better empirical evidence to chart the course of family change during the twentieth century. Yet, as we shall see in the next section of this chapter, this change has not always occurred in a simple linear fashion, nor is it necessarily irreversible. Despite the need for interpreting even long-range trends with some degree of caution, I believe it is possible to reach some general conclusions about how transformations in our kinship system—marriage in particular—are reshaping the life course of children, thus altering our notions of adolescent development within the family.

Many observers contend that during the twentieth century the family—both the nuclear unit and the network of extended kin—has become an increasingly less prominent institution in the lives of children (18). Some would go further and contend that the influence of the family as a socializing agency for children has been seriously weakened. Such broad conclusions are usually rooted in a particular vision of "the good family" (80). Critics frequently respond that the family is a constellation of individuals who often have competing interests and conflicting agendas (74). From whose vantage point should we assess the changes that have taken place? Quite possibly the position of women in the family has improved while the position of men has not (40).

My concern in this chapter is to assess how family changes in the recent past have affected the situation of *children,* specifically those in the adolescent years. Is there reason to believe that family life has become more precarious for teenagers? Let us consider some of the trends in family life that may be altering the experience of growing up.

Recent Trends

It is possible to see quite different patterns of family change depending on the periods that are contrasted. Over the course of the twentieth century, however, certain major trends in family structure are apparent, especially if we bracket the anomalous period after the Second World War—the baby boom years—when the average marriage age suddenly dropped, fertility soared, and marital disruption slowed for a time. This era of domestic mass production was short-lived. The 1970s and 1980s saw a resumption of long-standing patterns (both in this country and in most Western European nations) in the way that families are formed, in the roles of men and women within families, and in the stability of family units (15, 51, 59). Let us consider each of these patterns in turn, and their relevance for the situation of adolescents.

Marriage Patterns and Family Formation

In previous centuries it was not uncommon for some women to marry quite young, especially in certain regions of the United States, but typically women married in their early 20s and men a few years later (9). Over time, the age variability in marriage patterns has diminished. During the twentieth century young people began to behave more like one another, perhaps because of the extension of education and the delayed entrance of youth into the labor market (62).

After the Second World War the marriage age dropped precipitously. In the 1950s well over two-fifths of all 19-year-olds were married, many after conceiving a child (67). Whether a rise in sexual activity drove down the age of marriage or whether the anticipation of abundant jobs and housing led young people to move more quickly into adulthood is a matter of some speculation (62). Whatever the causes of this "marriage rush," it lasted only briefly (12). The trend reversed by the 1960s; by the late 1970s the marriage age had returned to the level of a hundred years earlier; and by the late 1980s it stood at a twentieth-century high for women. In 1988 just 14% of all 19-year-olds had ever been married, compared to 40% in 1960 (84).

The postponement of marriage has contributed to the growing acceptability of premarital sexual activity during adolescence. No doubt the widespread availability of the contraceptive pill also affected attitudes and behavior toward premarital intercourse. By the late 1970s the once-strong link between sex and marriage had been severed, making the transition from virginity a central event for adolescents (43). Typically, the sexual debut now occurs many years before marriage; the gap between the two events has been steadily widening as the age at onset of sexual activity has dropped and age at marriage has risen. As a result, many more teenagers are exposed to the risk of pregnancy and childbearing outside of marriage (33, 90).

During the past several decades, while marital childbearing has decreased steadily and sharply, nonmarital childbearing has increased dramatically for adolescents. While teenage parenthood is not more common, *single* parenthood among teenagers is (50). In 1985, 13% of all babies were born to teenagers, of whom about three-fifths were unmarried (63). The birthrate among unmarried adult women has also increased rapidly as a growing number of baby boomers have reached their 20s and 30s. In 1986, 23% of all children were born out of wedlock, compared to just 5% in 1960 (64). This dramatic statistic is one reason why many demographers argue that the institution of marriage has weakened since the middle of the twentieth century (13, 18). Whether or not one accepts this characterization, the prevalence of early and nonmarital childbearing has had unmistakable consequences for the economic and social situation of children, a matter I shall discuss in detail in the next section.

The erosion of marriage is especially evident among African-Americans. Up until the 1950s blacks married as early as whites and were nearly as likely to wed overall. Blacks had higher rates of marital instability, but the racial disparity was not huge. Over the past several decades, however, black and white marriage patterns have diverged sharply (12, 24). Blacks are now much more likely than before to postpone marriage—increasingly, it seems, indefinitely. In 1987 only 12% of white women in their early 30s had never been married, in comparison to 34% of blacks (83). When marriage does occur, blacks experience much higher rates of disruption. Black women on the average spend only 22% of their lives in marriage, compared to 43% for whites (23). As we shall see, this disparity has profound effects on the family experiences of black adolescents.

Marriage statistics are not generally reported by socioeconomic status. Analysis of census data, however, reveals sharp differences in patterns of family formation among different social strata (78). The more education one has, the more one is likely to defer marriage, though not substantially less likely ever to marry. Despite the apprehensions of educated never-married women in their late 20s, most women (more than 85%) are likely to marry. But the postponement of marriage, often until careers are launched, means a growing proportion of college-educated women will not begin childbearing until their 30s. In 1985 women 30 and older accounted for a quarter of all births, the largest fraction since 1964. Some of this increase is simply due to the growing size of this baby boom cohort, but much of the increase is attributed to a rising proportion of first births to women in their 30s (63). The potential consequences for children of this emerging pattern of delayed childbearing are enormous, although the trend is sufficiently novel that not much is known as yet (3). Rossi has discussed some of the possible costs and benefits of delayed childbearing on the relationship of mothers to their adolescent children (72), and Parke has speculated similarly on the way that the timing of fatherhood might work to children's advantage (68).

Since later marriage and delayed childbearing reduce fertility, family size has become smaller, especially in contrast to the baby boom era. Fewer children are growing up in large families, and a growing number are only children. Among more recent childbearing cohorts the average number of siblings has dropped considerably (75). No agreement exists among researchers on the implications for adolescent development of growing up in small families, although most researchers would argue that having fewer children should permit parents to make a greater investment of both time and material resources in the children they do have (5).

The Reconfiguration of Marital Roles

Many family scholars believe that the driving force behind the dramatic shifts in the timing of marriage and fertility is the changing status of women outside the family. The entrance of women into the labor force, of course, began long before the 1960s, particularly for blacks (4). But the reconfiguration of work and family roles has been nothing short of spectacular in the last quarter of the twentieth century.

Between 1960 and 1987 the proportion of married women in their childbearing years who were in the labor market doubled. Those with children under 6 rose from 19% to 57% during the same period (83). In a short span of years it has become normal, if not normative, for women with children, even those with young children, to work. Many such women work only part-time, but large increases have occurred among full-time workers as well. Changes in working status among separated and divorced women with children have been more modest since the 1960s, in large part because these groups already had high levels of gainful employment. Female heads of household are now only slightly less likely to be in the labor force than male household heads.

While women have greatly increased their participation in the labor force, it is not so apparent that men have assumed a greater share of domestic chores. Cross-sectional studies of time use among family members indicate that husbands have been reluctant to take on household responsibilities, including child care. For all the talk about the greater involvement of fathers in child rearing, it is difficult to produce much hard evidence that parental responsibilities have become more widely shared (57). Perhaps it is too soon to detect a trend toward more symmetrical parenting, but most comparisons over time show that fathers still play a minor role in day-to-day family responsibilities. Unfortunately, most of the available data from household time budgets and surveys is not detailed enough to show whether fathers increase their commitments to child rearing as children enter adolescence. Elsewhere I have argued that a bifurcation is occurring in the involvement of fathers in the family, with some becoming more involved while others are retreating from any paternal involvement by avoiding marriage altogether (34).

There is a dearth of information on how the new division of labor within the family is affecting the exercise of parental responsibilities. One area that has been examined is the sexual socialization of children—what children learn about sex and birth control from their parents (26, 61). If this area is at all typical of the division of labor between mothers and fathers, we are forced to conclude that the socializing role of fathers is small compared to that of mothers. Even for boys, fathers are much less active in communicating sexual information than mothers, although they may have a considerable indirect influence on their sons' attitudes and values (50). Later in this chapter I return to the question of how family processes have been affected by the reorganization of family roles.

Marital Disruption and Conjugal Succession

Historians looking back on the twentieth-century family will undoubtedly debate how the rising incidence of marital disruption contributed to shifts in the timing of marriage, rates of fertility, and the breakdown of a gender-based division of labor. Elsewhere I have argued that the institutionalization of divorce and remarriage—the pattern of conjugal succession—is an intrinsic part of a broad configuration of changes in the kinship system that are rooted in cultural movements and economic conditions that began long before the twentieth century (29). Throughout Western Europe and North America family relations have become more discretionary; a greater premium is placed on emotional gratification and a lower value on obligation and authority. When it comes to forming and dissolving families, individuals have been granted more power to make personal choices (59).

Voluntary marital dissolution was still a rare event at the start of the twentieth century; by midcentury it was more common though still widely censured; today it is regarded as an unfortunate but inescapable risk of matrimony. It is well known that at least half of all marriages will end in divorce. Few couples entering marriage today are committed to remaining in an unhappy relationship, even for the sake of the children (79). The great majority of adults disagree with the view that couples should stay married because their children might be harmed by divorce.

Many children now spend at least part of their childhood in a single-parent family (8, 35, 48). As I noted earlier, more than a fifth (14% of whites and 60% of blacks) are now being born to unmarried parents. By age 16 close to half of those whose parents are married will see the dissolution of that marriage—a little less than two-fifths of the whites and three-quarters of the blacks (10). Rates of both nonmarital childbearing and marital disruption increase as education decreases (66, 78). More than two-thirds of the children of mothers who do not complete high school will spend time in a single-parent family, as compared to slightly more than a third of those whose mothers are college graduates (10).

The duration of single parenthood is a substantial fraction of most children's lives. Five years will elapse for nearly half before their mothers remarry. Since the interval between first and second marriage has been growing and the period of single parenthood is thus lengthening, many children are unlikely to see their mothers remarry before they reach adolescence (7). Thus it is safe to conclude that increasing numbers of teenagers are facing the complex task of negotiating stepfamily life.

Black children are more likely than whites to be raised by a single parent. Their parents are more inclined than whites not to marry at all and, when they do wed, to experience more marital disruption and to have a lower incidence of remarriage. Not only are black women less likely to remarry than white women, but those who do remarry are slower to do so than whites (66). Thus, in 1986 only two-fifths (39%) of black children under 18 were living with two parents, in comparison to two-thirds (66%) of Hispanic and more than three-quarters (79%) of non-Hispanic white children (84).

Even though white children are less likely than nonwhites to live with a single parent, those who do often encounter complex family situations. Since their parents are more likely than blacks to remarry quickly, many risk living through the dissolution of a second marriage. Close to half of all white children whose parents remarry will see the breakup of their stepfamily before they are out of their teens. The children of less-educated parents experience somewhat higher rates of stepfamily dissolution. Overall, at least one child in ten growing up today will undergo this sequence of events; and this does not include the growing number of children living in even more temporary arrangements resulting from informal unions (28).

When stepfamilies are formed, children acquire a complex set of relations. Somewhere between two-fifths and half of these children will have a stepsibling, although most will not typically live with him or her. And for more than a quarter, a half-sibling will be born within four years (7). Thus, about two-thirds of children living in stepfamilies will have either half-siblings or stepsiblings. Little is known about the impact of these relations on the functioning of the family, but studies are currently under way to probe the significance of stepfamily life on the development of children (47). Certainly the difficulties of managing rivalries, establishing trusting and supportive relationships, and restraining sexual attraction all become heightened issues in complex family systems (69).

Another consequence of the growing pattern of conjugal succession is the wider network of kin created by divorce and remarriage (36, 52). A large number of children growing up today will have more than two sets of grandparents and accordingly be connected to more than two extended families. The few studies on the importance of steprelations as emotional supports or sponsors are not terribly informative. It remains to be discovered how often these potential kinship ties become influential in children's lives. One study indicates that young children are often quickly assimilated into the wider kinship network of their stepfamilies, while adolescents are only occasionally integrated into their stepparents' families (35). No study has yet examined the meaning of these stepfamily ties throughout the course of childhood, adolescence, and later adulthood.

A growing number of children whose parents never marry or marry only briefly may, by contrast, be experiencing a shrinking family world. Typically, children raised by a single parent have limited contact with the extended kin of their noncustodial parent (usually their father's family). Divorce has the effect of strengthening the maternal line at the expense of the paternal line, unless the noncustodial father maintains an active presence in the child's life. In a study of grandparenthood, Cherlin and I discovered that relations between children and their maternal grandparents intensified following divorce (assuming maternal custody), while paternal grandparents maintained only ritual relations with their grandchildren (14). For adolescents, who often see less of their grandparents than younger children, marital disruption had the effect of severely curtailing intergenerational ties.

This matrilineal tilt evident in the society at large is especially marked among black children, whose contact with biological fathers is frequently episodic or nonexistent. Persistently high rates of nonmarital childbearing and marital disruption, combined with a low incidence of remarriage, produce an imbalance in the kinship network, limiting the flow of resources to black children from their father's family (76). Whether this factor adds to the disadvantages of black youth in attaining higher education or entering the labor market has not been adequately examined. Several studies of the long-term consequences of disruption on the educational attainment of young people suggest that the contribution of resources, both economic and psychological, from fathers may be a key contributing factor in the educational achievement of young adults (37,

46, 60). High rates of disruption among less-well-educated whites and Hispanics may restrict the flow of kinship resources through the paternal line, thus reducing social mobility. But limited contributions of middle-class fathers to their children's support may also heighten the risk of downward social mobility (1, 87).

Family Change and Adolescent Well-Being: Macro-Level Studies

We have seen evidence of a transformation in the family which suggests that the changes that have occurred are part of a new kinship complex, sometimes referred to as the postmodern family. Higher rates of employment among women have encouraged the postponement of marriage, driven down fertility, forced some realignment of marital roles, and permitted divorce. These changes have in turn promoted increased participation by females in the labor force. A common thread linking all these changes is reinforcement of personal choice and gratification as a primary principle governing family relations.

I have only hinted at what these changes might imply for the well-being of children and youth, if indeed well-being is linked to the stability of the family. This is a matter of some dispute. There are those who believe that a direct link exists between family change and the incidence of adolescent problem behavior. The assertion that family disintegration is the principal cause of rising rates of academic failure, delinquency, suicide, substance abuse, and sexual license strikes a familiar note. Throughout American history observers have perceived the declining strength of family ties as a source of youthful misbehavior. Even during the 1950s, in the heyday of domestic tranquillity, this theme was popular. In the 1960s family breakdown was widely blamed for the rise of youthful protest and deviance (25, 55). More recently some demographers and sociologists, citing macro-level trends in family stability, have asserted that the restructuring of the American family may be jeopardizing the welfare of teenagers.

This argument is forcefully advanced by Uhlenberg and Eggebeen, who contend that family changes, most notably marital disruption and the entrance of mothers into the labor force, may explain the decline of adolescent well-being as measured by a wide array of problem behaviors during the period from 1960 to 1980 (82). Uhlenberg and Eggebeen cite familiar statistics to show that school dropout rates, a decline in SAT scores, and a rise in substance abuse, delinquency, homicide, suicide, motor vehicle accidents, abortion, and nonmarital childbearing among teenagers all occurred over the same twenty-year period when parental involvement in child rearing was waning. They suggest that the loosening of parental control and commitment has resulted in the rise of adolescent problem behavior.

At first glance the coincidence of these trends in family change and the welfare of youth seems striking. A closer look at the data, however, undermines much of the Uhlenberg-Eggebeen thesis (32). First of all, most of the indicators of problem behavior began to improve in the late 1970s, yet more children than ever before were exposed to marital instability and maternal employment in the 1980s. Second, black youths experience different trends from whites, confounding the simple link between problem behavior and the strength of family ties. Despite the proliferation of single-parent families among blacks, black adolescents have been showing improvement on many of the indicators (academic performance and delinquency rates, among others) for more than a decade. Finally, problem behavior among adults under 40 closely parallels the adolescent trends. Strong historical effects were operating during the 1960s and 1970s that were felt by both teenagers and young adults. It is implausible to trace the sources of fluctuating rates of problem behaviors directly to changes in family structure that were taking place at the same time. An adequate explanation must account for period effects that seem to have shaped the behavior of a broad spectrum of age groups.

Historians may argue that some of these changes can be explained by the political and cultural shock of the Vietnam War and the Watergate era. The questioning of authority, the loosening of social controls, and the support for experimentation and innovation were part of the zeitgeist of this era, which may have stimulated both changes in the family and risk-taking behavior. In short, the weakening of cultural and social constraints created an environment that tolerated both institutional innovation and personal exploration.

Demographers add another dimension to this historical and cultural account. The rapid increase in the size of the youthful population strained the resources of institutions organized to regulate and serve the population of teenagers and young adults. The inability of schools and the labor market to incorporate what Norman Ryder called "the barbarian horde of youth" created discontent and alienation (16, p. 45). Preston has shown that economic resources shifted from children and youth to the elderly during this same period (71). He argues that the decline in welfare of the young over the past several decades has been matched by an improvement in health and social advantages among the elderly. He contends that lower fertility rates ultimately weakened the political position of families with children, while the growing electoral power of the elderly has resulted in their receiving a larger piece of the public pie, thus diminishing the share available to children and adolescents.

There are those, however, who believe that family trends may not have uniformly worked to the disadvantage of children. Zill and Rogers report that many trends for adolescents, especially in health and education, have shown steady improvement. And the most marked changes for the better have occurred among minorities. They point out that increased parental education, smaller family size, and the improved economic status of women may produce benefits for children that offset some of the negative effects of family instability. As they conclude in a paper describing the changing well-being of children: "Many people in the United States believe that: the institution of the family is falling apart; the condition of children is deteriorating; and, changes in the family, especially increases in divorce, single parenthood, and maternal employment, are the principal causes of the ills of children. But all three of these assumptions are challenged by the trend data reviewed [here]" (91, p. 95).

Family Change and Adolescent Well-Being: Micro-Level Studies

The broad correlation between family trends and adolescent well-being provides at best mixed support for the view that adolescent behavior is being adversely affected by changes within the family. This macro-level analysis, however, does not directly address the question of whether changes in the form and function of the family are affecting the socialization process and the welfare of children. A more searching test of this proposition requires a micro-level inspection.

On some topics, notably teenage childbearing and marital disruption, quite a bit of research has been carried out. The consequences for children's well-being of maternal employment and shifting gender roles within the family has been less extensively studied, but a body of research does exist on these topics (44, 56, 72). Far less is known about the implications of delayed childbearing, although a little has been written on the effect of maternal age on child-rearing patterns (3, 17).

It is not my intention to review in detail the substantive findings from any of these bodies of research (see Chapter 10 in this volume). Instead, I want to comment on the problem of drawing general conclusions from available studies about the effects of family changes on adolescent development. Very few studies actually establish a convincing link between family environment and the socialization of children. Finally, I also want to provide some impressions of the contribution of family changes to the socialization process of young people today.

The Impact on Children of Early Childbearing

The vast literature on teenage childbearing focuses for the most part on the effects of premature parenthood on the mother and, to a lesser extent, on the adolescent father. Not until the last decade or so has equal attention been given to the children of young parents (2, 30, 50), and just a handful of studies actually examine the special problems the offspring of teenage parents have in negotiating their own adolescence. Nonetheless, there seems to be good reason to suspect that these children tend to have more problems in academic achievement and general behavior, and may themselves be more prone to early parenthood, than the offspring of more mature parents. (It is not so clear that postponing parenthood beyond the 20s confers any advantages for children.)

The Baltimore study of children of teenage parents, with which I have been associated, shows, for example, a high incidence of problem behaviors ranging from school failure, substance abuse, running away, delinquency, anxiety and depression, and early parenthood among the offspring of teenage mothers (31). Comparisons with national data confirm the impression that children born to adolescent parents are at high risk for these problems (31, 49). Many investigators have concluded accordingly that early childbearing may pose special risks for children because teenage parents are less competent care givers, possess fewer material resources, offer a less stable family environment, are less desirable role models, or experience more competing demands on their time. Yet the evidence demonstrating any of these specific links is tentative at best.

Researchers have shown that children of early childbearers differ on a variety of outcome measures from children of later childbearers. A "state" (early childbearing) is associated with a difference in "rate" of behavior (for example, infrequent vocalization among infants, a high incidence of temper tantrums among toddlers, or the early initiation of sexual activity among young adolescents). This states-and-rates approach provides little insight into the mechanisms that might account for the differences it reports. Moreover, it tends to exaggerate the differences between the two populations by ignoring the overlap across groups or the variation within groups. While the risk of school failure or delinquency is two to three times higher among the children of teenage mothers, the majority of these youngsters do complete high school and manage to avoid serious problems with the law (31).

In tracing the links from family structure to family process to outcomes, we encounter another problem familiar to some developmentalists: teenagers who become mothers are different in a variety of ways from those who delay parenthood. To the extent that they antedate the child's birth, these preexisting differences (selective recruitment) may account to some extent for the outcomes. Let me illustrate. We know that teenage mothers are often less academically able and motivated than their peers who are not parents. To what extent would these differences in academic competence and commitment affect children born to these mothers regardless of the timing of the birth? Since we cannot randomly assign some mothers to begin childbearing early or late, we are compelled to use indirect statistical techniques to sort out the *selection bias* from the special environmental effects directly linked to the experience of being a premature parent.

Even if selection bias can be estimated, we still need to identify the particular mechanisms that explain why certain children are disadvantaged by having a teenage mother and others are not. Studies of children at risk who succeed offer a promising strategy for isolating the conditions in children and families that amplify or mitigate the impact of early childbearing. In the longitudinal study of adolescent mothers and their offspring in Baltimore, it was possible to identify the presence or absence of specific resources that influenced the impact of premature parenthood on children's success in adolescence (31). The offspring of teenage mothers fared better in their own teenage years if their mothers had received family support during the early stages of parenthood; if educational and family planning services were provided; and if their mothers had managed to return to school, enter stable marriages, and restrict further childbearing. In short, the mothers' access to resources and their ability to manage the transition to parenthood mediated the conditions under which their offspring flourished or floundered.

Tracing the processes by which events in the parents' lives improved or undermined their child-rearing skills identifies only some of the reasons why certain children fare better than others. Differences among the children themselves obviously account for a good part of the variation as well. The Baltimore study found, for example, that vocabulary test scores and data on behavior problems collected in the preschool years were strongly related to school performance and risk-taking behavior in adolescence. It seems likely that differences in temperament and cognitive skills condition the effect of early childbearing, although little data has been collected on the types of children who are prone to experiencing problems in later life.

In all likelihood a certain amount of turnover occurs among the children with problems linked to early childbearing. That is, some children start out exhibiting difficulties that subsequently subside over time as their mothers' lives improve or their family circumstances change. For instance, although close to half of the teenagers studied had failed a grade by high school, by the time they were between the ages of 19 and 21, two-thirds had graduated and another sixth were close to completing high school. Almost all the youngsters in the study were sexually active by middle adolescence, but only a third became parents as teenagers. Many children seem to alter the trajectory of their lives from their early to their later teens, but we know relatively little about how this shift in the life course is negotiated. Examining these discontinuities provides one way of exploring the socialization processes linking family events and outcomes for children.

Delayed Childbearing and Its Effects on Children

As I reported earlier, a growing number of parents, men and women alike, are postponing childbearing until their 30s or even later. For the same reason that teenage parenthood is thought to be a disadvantage, delayed childbearing may benefit children if it means that parents possess greater resources when they launch a family (68). The available evidence is insufficient to draw any lessons about how socialization is affected when parenthood is delayed, although some tantalizing findings appear in Rossi's comparative study of the management of adolescent children by older and younger parents, which found that the two groups of parents may have different perspectives on problem behavior (72). Yet an unpublished thesis by Nord reviewing the literature on the effects of parental age at birth indicates no strong evidence favoring the children of older parents (65). Her analysis of the National Survey of Children also failed to produce results showing that the children of delayed childbearers experience fewer problems as adolescents. The skimpy literature on this topic will, no doubt, be augmented in the future as the growing number of later childbearers stimulates interest in this topic.

The Impact of Marital Disruption on Children

There is no lack of literature on the consequences of marital disruption. Over the past decade or so hundreds of studies have been carried out to determine the effects on children of divorce, as well as other forms of marital disruption such as separation, death of a parent, and single parenthood. Several excellent summary reviews have tried to extract some general conclusions. These reviews suggest that children of divorce are at higher risk for experiencing a variety of developmental problems during late childhood and early adolescence, including school failure, delinquency, precocious sexual behavior, and substance abuse (11, 22).

Both clinical and short-term longitudinal studies provide substantial evidence that almost all children experience some degree of trauma when their parents separate (86). For some the difficulty continues or even grows over time (85). Most children seem to recover from the initial distress in a period of several years, although there is some evidence that the delayed effects of divorce appear in late adolescence or early adulthood as young people begin to establish permanent relationships and form families of their own (11, 38). The most striking question for developmental researchers is how to explain these divergent patterns by identifying processes that can be traced to differences among individual children, their immediate family environments, their peer relations, or the larger social world of school and neighborhood.

The most sustained research on this topic has looked at gender and age effects that may mediate the impact of divorce. A number of investigators, following the early leads of Hetherington and her colleagues (11) and the clinical team of Wallerstein and Kelly (86), have compared the responses of boys and girls to family disruption. Boys are presumed to be at greater risk when contact with the father is curtailed. A 1987 review of this body of studies suggests, however, that the early results of clear-cut gender differences in response to divorce may not hold up in the findings of large-scale studies that have looked at a wide range of outcomes (88). Divorce may well produce negative effects for boys that are later offset when their mothers remarry. There is some evidence that girls may find their mother's remarriage more stressful than boys. The differential response of boys and girls to the disappearance of fathers and the appearance of stepfathers is a promising hypothesis, but it may still be too crude to distinguish when outcomes will be favorable or unfavorable for children. To tease out gender differences in response to divorce, it may, for example, be necessary to examine in finer detail the circumstances surrounding the loss of a father or the acquisition of a stepfather, such as how parents prepare children for family change, how former spouses handle their relations and their respective child-rearing responsibilities, and so on. I suspect this same lesson applies to the search for age effects. A number of researchers have tried to establish differences in response to divorce depending on the child's age at the time of disruption. A number of investigations have, in fact, shown that preschool children do experience more intense and more lasting effects from a parental separation than children in later childhood or early adolescence (22, 86), although Wallerstein and Blakeslee report a reversal of these earlier findings (85). Several competing hypotheses may explain these outcomes. Younger children may simply be more vulnerable to the effects of divorce; they may be exposed to less competent caretaking after a divorce; or couples who divorce early might themselves be different. Until the various theoretical implications of age have been examined directly, it will not be possible to say just how much age matters or why it may matter for some children and not others.

In addition to examining gender and age, researchers have pointed to a wide range of other possible mediating factors that may explain why some children seem to recover from the initial trauma of divorce while the condition of others worsens over time. Without summarizing in great detail the results of the studies, I have listed some of the circumstances that may alter the outcome of divorce for children.

Personal characteristics of the child. There is good reason to suspect that preexisting differences among children may explain some of the apparent effects of divorce. The interaction of temperament and stressful family conditions surrounding the marital breakup could account for divergent patterns of adjustment. Exploring this hypothesis requires longitudinal study. One of the few that have examined children's characteristics prior to divorce reveals that the children most affected by a divorce were already troubled prior to the dissolution (6). This finding raises the possibility that problem children may intensify family conflict, increasing the risk of divorce. Thus, some of the effects of divorce on children may result from selective processes that put troubled children at greater risk of experiencing their parents' divorce in the first place. It would be especially promising to examine this hypothesis during adolescence, a period when many families undergo elevated levels of stress.

Characteristics of parents who divorce. Parents differ in their ability to manage a divorce successfully. Most go through a period of depression, grief, and anger following a divorce. How quickly they recover and how much these feelings interfere with their child-rearing patterns is an open question. A number of studies have shown that parental skill in protecting children following a divorce may be a vital asset to the children (86).

The varying capacities of parents to cope with marital disruption again points to the need to distinguish the influence of preexisting patterns from influences that result directly from marital disruption. If parents who divorce are different to begin with from those who stay married—and we know that they are—then we must be aware that different outcomes for children that seem to be related to divorce could be the result of what I referred to earlier as selective recruitment. Again, longitudinal studies will help us sort out the effects of prior differences in parents, child-rearing patterns, and other family processes that may be associated with divorce.

The process of divorce. Many investigators have speculated that family conflict produces more adverse effects on children than divorce itself (70). A number of studies comparing children exposed to chronic conflict in intact families with the children of divorce reveal similar levels of problem behavior. These results suggest that conflict leading up to divorce may be one of the most potent factors in children's subsequent well-being. Conflict generally subsides following divorce, which may account for why children's adjustment improves over time. But what about children exposed to continuous conflict owing to litigation or lack of cooperation between their parents in the aftermath of the divorce? More research is needed on the long-term consequences of the way that parents continue to collaborate after they are no longer married. Some manage to share parental responsibility successfully, but most do not. The prevailing pattern is that fathers decrease their involvement in child rearing over time. A large proportion have little or no contact with their adolescent children, and those who do rarely take an active role in supervising them. This relatively low level of involvement may explain why researchers have had difficulty establishing a strong link between paternal contact and behavior during late childhood and early adolescence (34).

The economic effects of divorce. One of the major results of divorce is that it impoverishes children, at least for a time. Close to nine out of ten children reside with their mothers following a divorce. Most women do not earn enough to support a family, and the contributions of fathers living apart from their children are generally meager. As a result, many children experience a drastic decline in their living standard.

Many investigators have attempted to study the economic effects of divorce by treating income as an exogenous factor; that is, they often control for the effects of economic status while examining social and psychological processes. But the impact of reduced living standards on children in single-parent families deserves further examination. Loss of income often results in residential moves, school changes, shifts in child-care arrangements, curtailed recreational opportunities, and a variety of other changes in life-style for both mother and child. We have yet to learn how these changes are perceived and responded to by children. The low level of child support may help explain differences in educational attainment between children from disrupted families and those from stable marriages. Most states do not even require child support for children over the age of 18, and fathers are often unwilling to provide economic assistance to college-age adolescents.

Remarriage and stepfamily life. Many children whose parents divorce will acquire a stepparent before they reach adulthood, most often during adolescence. As I mentioned earlier, researchers often confound the experience of divorce with the subsequent involvement in stepfamilies. In fact, children may adjust well to divorce and poorly to their parents' remarriage or vice versa. Few generalizations can be made about how stepfamily experience affects development, although some girls may experience greater difficulties around the time of their mother's remarriage than boys (88). Stepfamilies pose special problems for adolescents who are in the process of sexual decision making. Some research suggests that parents' dating and cohabitation practices may influence the initiation of sexual behavior in their adolescent children, especially girls (11). But evidence is not yet sufficient to conclude whether it is remarriage or divorce that most affects adolescent sexual experience.

Long-Term Consequences of Marital Disruption

Much of the research on marital disruption examines the short-term effects of divorce and remarriage on children. A growing number of investigators, however, have begun to look at the impact on the transition to adulthood and adjustment in later life. Mounting evidence reveals that marital disruption seems to affect later patterns of family formation and attitudes about marriage and childbearing. Even though they report fairly conservative attitudes toward divorce, children who have grown up in single-parent families are more likely than those from intact marriages to have children early in life, to marry while they are young, and to divorce (38, 60).

As I have indicated, serious methodological problems plague many of the studies that have been done to date on the effects of divorce and remarriage on children. It remains to be seen how much the process of disruption or its aftermath affects children directly and how much of the presumed effects of divorce are really the result of preexisting differences that would lead to the same outcomes whether or not divorce occurred. With careful longitudinal investigations we are likely to make some headway on determining the effects of divorce as well as on the more important issue of how, why, and when divorce or remarriage is harmful to children's development.

At present we may be overestimating to some extent the impact of divorce on children by not taking selection bias into account. But it is equally plausible that our studies underreport the effects of divorce by measuring only visible and easily detectable outcomes or by failing to trace long-term consequences that show up only in adulthood. While almost all studies suggest that divorce is a critical event for children, it still remains unclear how much it shapes their subsequent life course. I suspect that we are likely to conclude that the lifelong significance of divorce is likely to change depending on subsequent events and their interpretation. Marital disruption sets off a chain of experiences, but these are sufficiently variable that, by itself, the impact of disruption may be only a modest predictor of later outcomes.

Work Roles and the Well-Being of Children

Suffice it to say that the various conceptual and methodological problems plaguing the literature on early childbearing and marital disruption apply just as well to other areas of family change. The voluminous research seeking to measure the impact of maternal employment on child development has suffered from the same sorts of limitations. Efforts to identify the consequences initially treated maternal employment as a discrete event rather than a transition that initiated a complex chain of events in family organization. By now many researchers have concluded that mothers' employment per se does not have any powerful or uniform direct effects on children (44, 56).

This does not mean that the breakdown of the gender-based division of labor in the family and the reorganization of family roles has had no consequences for the course of children's development. But assessing these consequences requires a careful consideration of such mediating conditions as the mother's (and father's) response to work, the demands of the job, the father's willingness to participate in child care, the availability of high-quality care outside the home, and a myriad of other factors that determine the meaning of maternal employment for different family members (58). Of course, many of these conditions are not specific to particular families but are defined by cultural and social conditions outside the family. These are subject to continual change and redefinition as public attitudes about women's work evolve and as institutional support for working women grows.

How can we generalize about the current effects of women's work on children using data from the 1960s or early 1970s, a time when relatively few women with young children were employed full-time? The answer is that we cannot. Our research must be more historically and culturally specific, taking into full account the changing external and internal conditions that specify the meaning of family change for all family members (80).

One final caveat should be mentioned for researchers trying to trace the effects of changing family circumstances on the socialization process or for policy makers trying to interpret the impact of these changes on the well-being of children. Often we look for a single "bottom line": Is a working mother good or bad for children? What are the negative effects of marital disruption for adolescents? Will late childbearing improve or worsen the life chances of children? The search for a summary answer is understandable, but it may not be completely informative. Family changes may not only have dissimilar effects on different children but may also produce mixed outcomes for the same child. Maternal employment can produce children who are independent and resourceful but others who are deprived and neglected. Characteristics of the child, the parents' responses, and the options available to children produce varying results that overwhelm any general effect of maternal employment. Moreover, even if a general response were to be identified, it would be subject to change as cultural and political conditions adapt to a new division of labor within the family.

Family Change and Public Policy

The evidence that changes in the family have generally compromised the health and welfare of youth is mixed at best. Certain family changes have probably produced net benefits: later age at marriage and delayed childbearing have promoted higher educational attainment and lower fertility among parents. It is difficult to show any general effect of women's participation in the labor force on the well-being of children and adolescents, which is not to deny that particular types of children in certain circumstances may either profit or suffer from having mothers who work. It is more certain that early, nonmarital childbearing and marital disruption affect some children adversely, if only because single-parent families are often economically insecure and live in a disadvantaged social environment.

I have discussed a number of problems in establishing causal pathways between events such as early childbearing or marital dissolution and specific behavioral outcomes for children. It seems likely, however, that investigators will continue to find that single parents, especially teenagers, have greater difficulties managing the responsibilities of child rearing, particularly if they reside in disadvantaged neighborhoods with inadequate child care, poor schools, limited recreational opportunities, and an active street culture that offers young people opportunities for illegal activity.

Should we and could we deter nonmarital childbearing and discourage marital dissolution? Disagreement exists over the advisability of using public policies as a tool to favor certain forms of family structure. At the margins there is probably general agreement that it is appropriate to discourage early childbearing. While delaying childbearing would not eliminate most nonmarital parenthood, it probably would reduce the amount of public funds required to support children born to single mothers by guaranteeing that more single parents would be educated and employed by the time their children were born.

Thus far, programs to prevent premature parenthood have not been notably successful. As we have seen, rates for teenage parenthood outside of marriage have risen for whites and remained at a high level for African-Americans in the past decade. In part this trend has been caused by a sharp increase in early sexual intercourse and a sluggish and ambivalent response to pregnancy prevention through public education and contraceptive services (43). As is well known by now, the United States has a much higher rate of teenage parenthood than other Western nations, at least in part because educational and family-planning services are less readily available here (53). It is probably not too optimistic to believe that a more realistic approach to managing youthful sexual behavior might ultimately reduce the number of early, unplanned births, substantially benefiting minority children, especially African-Americans.

But teenage parenthood is only one aspect of single parenthood. Even if early childbearing were eliminated altogether, it would decrease the proportion of children who spend part of their childhood in single-parent families by only 10% to 20%. The problem is created predominantly by marital dissolution, a condition that may be less easily prevented. Most Western nations have seen a tremendous increase in divorce over the past two decades, although by international standards the U.S. divorce rate remains exceptionally high (13).

While we are able to identify some of the sources of the rising rates of divorce, it is far more difficult to imagine policy solutions for reversing the trend. Divorce, as I have argued elsewhere, appears to have become an intrinsic feature of the American kinship system (29). While we may not be able to reduce substantially the incidence of divorce by public policy measures, we might devise means of mitigating some of the obvious economic disadvantages created by marital disruption (and, incidentally, nonmarital childbearing as well).

The amount of child support paid by noncustodial fathers is abysmally small. Compared to fathers in other Western nations, American males contribute little income to their children, and far fewer men pay anything at all. The legal and cultural sanctions for coaxing fathers to furnish support are apparently much more effective in Europe (54). Our more privatized family system permits fathers to abrogate their parental obligations. The idea of garnishing fathers' wages, long practiced in some

European countries, has only recently been tried in this country. A highly discretionary system that requires single mothers to establish and enforce support agreements is gradually being replaced with a more standardized system of enforcement. If fathers knew that they would have to pay to raise their offspring, both nonmarital childbearing and marital disruption might be deterred to some extent. At the very least, a more effective system of child support would reduce (though certainly not eliminate) the degree of disadvantage for children in single-parent families (37).

Should we do more to offset the disadvantages of growing up in a single-parent family? In his book on reducing the rate of poverty in families with children, Ellwood argues that a multipronged strategy will be necessary (21). Assurance of child support through federal and state programs that replace Aid for Dependent Children by guaranteeing a minimum payment regardless of the amount provided by the nonresidential father is an attractive proposal that is under experimentation in several states. If child support were supplemented by an increased minimum wage and guaranteed employment for single mothers, most families might be pushed above the poverty level.

Ellwood's strategy for assisting single parents is to upgrade the economic programs that reach the broadest strata of impoverished families. He advocates general, noncategorical programs, an idea that might have broad political appeal. This plan might be extended to social services as well. General programs—child care, preschool education, and medical insurance—that are partially or fully subsidized for single-parent families have the best chance of reaching the greatest number of children in need. While single-parent households do have special problems, these problems may be addressed by providing services to both one-parent and two-parent families. Noncategorical assistance for all low-income households avoids the pitfall, perceived by many conservatives, of creating incentives for nonmarital childbearing and divorce.

Raising the economic level of single-parent families will help mitigate some of the disadvantages associated with marital disruption and nonmarital childbearing. But even if economic parity existed between two-parent and one-parent families, children living with a single biological parent are not likely to fare as well as those who are raised by both parents (37). If, as some researchers suspect, the ability of single parents to supervise their children is diminished, a parent's capacity to manage may be augmented by training, by assistance from other adults, and by strong support from child-care programs, schools, and youth services. To date we know relatively little about the extent to which effective supports reduce the incidence of problem behavior among children from single-parent families. Studies evaluating such programs could have policy import and contribute to our knowledge about social conditions that mediate the impact of family change on children.

The Future of the American Family

Social scientists have never had great success in projecting family trends. In the 1940s no one foresaw the emerging marriage rush and baby boom. Then in the early 1960s few if any demographers anticipated the incredibly rapid reversal of these trends, the accelerated entrance of mothers into the labor force, the rise of nonmarital childbearing, and the spectacular increases in the divorce rate. This failure should give pause to those who read the demographic tea leaves looking for signs of family change. Almost anything is possible, if recent history serves as a guide.

Some experts are predicting a swing back to the traditional family—a lowering of the marriage age, a reduction in the number of working mothers, a decrease in divorce, and so on. My own best guess is that we could, and perhaps already do, see minor fluctuations that might oppose some of the most dramatic trends, but I suspect it is equally likely that we are in store for more cohabitation, higher rates of nonmarital childbearing, later marriage, and further postponement of parenthood. I believe that family diversity is here to stay. This means that many, if not most, children will have to cope with unpredictable family experiences. If we are going to provide some measure of certainty and security, we must be prepared to lend greater social and economic support to families in transition. If we are creative in rendering this assistance, it will strengthen rather than undermine the role of the family in the child's life.

7

PEER GROUPS AND PEER CULTURES

B. Bradford Brown

In the eyes of many adults, adolescents seem to have a passionate herding instinct. They shuffle in packs from home to school to shopping centers to street-corner hangouts. In rare moments of physical isolation from peers, they maintain connection with friends through use of their favorite technological invention (well, perhaps second favorite, right behind the Walkman or boom box), the telephone. They insist that dressing, talking, even walking like everyone else their age is a profound statement of their individuality.

Although certainly an exaggeration of the realities of teenage life (46), such an image underscores the salience of peer groups as a major context of teenage behavior and development. Peer groups are not unique to adolescence, nor do they first appear at this stage of life (77). Yet there is something special about their role in adolescent development, or at least the attention they command from adults, that invests peer group relations with a prominent place in studies of adolescence.

For some time, however, adolescent peer groups have suffered an image problem. The profound impact of Coleman's treatise on the adolescent society (40), intermittently reinforced with mass media portrayals of the disturbing uniformity of youth, have lulled researchers and policy makers into a false assurance that the character of teenage peer groups and peer culture is well charted. Many feel comfortable regarding the peer group as a social-structural proponent of the conformity and single-mindedness of young people. There is persistent, contrary evidence, however, that there are *multiple* peer cultures, which encompass and encourage the diversity that truly characterizes young people's value systems and behavior patterns. Although such evidence is compelling, many researchers remain blithely wedded to the task of describing a uniform, homogeneous, singular adolescent peer culture.

In other facets of adolescent peer relations, such as friendship, we have witnessed a dynamic growth in insight since the early 1970s. Research on peer groups, however, has remained remarkably stagnant (118), largely, I think, because of the unsettled debate over the basic nature (uniformity or diversity) of youth culture. Before the study of adolescent peer groups can move forward, researchers must discard their false images of teenage peer culture and strive for a more sophisticated conceptualization of peer groups. This shift will direct attention to a new set of questions: What accounts for the emergence of peer groups and peer cultures in adolescence? How do teenagers come to understand and find their place in this peer system? How stable is the system? Does the structure of peer groups or the pattern of interrelationships among peer cultures remain consistent throughout adolescence? Do young people commonly shift their allegiances among peer crowds? How do peer groups affect individual behavior and psychological well-being? Finally, can or should adults attempt to structure adolescent peer cultures or manipulate a teenager's place within the peer system? These questions form the agenda for this chapter.

Roads Too Well Traveled: Laying the Youth Culture Theme to Rest

" 'Teen-agers' are not adolescents in a total society of all ages; they are a race with a distinct plumage and music . . . Such a subculture . . . is a language and mores *against* the adults, or at best excluding them, as if they were a foreign tribe, probably hostile. In principle, every teen-ager is a delinquent" (71, pp. 18–19). With these words Paul Goodman captured a perspective on adolescence that has flourished for decades (59, 106), fueled primarily by Coleman's landmark study of teenage values and lifestyles in ten Chicago-area high schools in the late 1950s (40). This study seemed to provide evidence supporting Parsons' (106) characterization of youth as irresponsible, hedonistic, and recalcitrant in the face of adult expectations—forming a unified, monolithic culture opposed to adult society. In Coleman's data and conclusions three factors sharply differentiated the adolescent peer culture from adult society. First, adolescents' career aspirations reflected youthful hedonism rather than a concern with making substantive contributions to society. More boys, for example, desired to become famous athletes or jet pilots than missionaries or atomic physicists, and more girls aspired to be famous actresses than schoolteachers. Second, criteria for popularity with peers devalued academic achievement in favor of characteristics less valuable in the eyes of adults, such as athletic prowess or membership in the "leading crowd." Third, parents and children seemed to espouse opposing views on such issues as the most desirable characteristics of a friend or dating partner. Coleman concluded that adolescent peer culture drew teenagers into a preoccupation with the present and, therefore, alienated them from adult society. Despite sizable community (and, of course, individual) differences in his findings, Coleman chose to emphasize the predominance of a monolithic adolescent peer culture that was oppositional to that of adults.

Debunking the Myth of the Youth Culture

Later studies picked up on each of the three major factors apparent in Coleman's results. Adolescents' rejection of responsible adult careers became, in the later work of Keniston, an alienation from adult institutions and value systems. After observing successive cohorts of youth remain uncommitted to an adult society whose values they could not accept (87) or work diligently to transform adult institutions into something more compatible with their own aspirations (88), Keniston attempted to institutionalize the monolithic youth culture as a normative phase of adolescent development. He proposed "youth" as a stage of life to be negotiated between adolescence and young adulthood. Keniston acknowledged "youth" as a provisional life stage, not necessarily experienced by all adolescents (88). Nevertheless, his argument lost its appeal when succeeding cohorts of teenagers in the late 1970s and early 1980s eagerly embraced conventional adult norms and career patterns (83) with a zest reminiscent of Friedenberg's (67) portrayal of youngsters in the 1950s. This left observers pondering whether the monolithic, oppositional nature of the youth culture of the 1960s was a historical aberration rather than an enduring characteristic of the adolescent peer culture.

Meanwhile, other researchers were attempting to replicate Coleman's findings on adolescents' criteria for popularity among peers. In some cases results were consistent with Coleman's (60, 63, 130). Other studies, however, produced curious anomalies. Although a study of Canadian youth reported criteria for being popular much like Coleman's, the overwhelming majority of students said they would prefer to be remembered as an outstanding student rather than as a great athlete or a popular person (68). In other words, students knew the norms of the popular crowd but failed to endorse them. Other researchers found differences by gender, grade level, and/or extracurricular participation in the importance of high grades, good looks, athletic ability, and personal qualities for popularity among peers (12, 28, 123). Equally problematic were Cohen's reanalyses of Coleman's own data, which found evidence for not one but three different value orientations among students in Coleman's sample (38). Such differences called into question the pervasiveness and consistency of youth-culture norms among adolescents.

Coleman's third factor—the opposing value system of parents and peers—laid the groundwork for studies that addressed three common presumptions about the impact of a monolithic youth culture on parent-child relationships. First, in the seemingly inevitable situations in which parents and peers give conflicting advice, peer pressure would consistently overpower parental influence and thus drive adolescents away from adult values. Second, rapid social change would so transform the future that teenagers would become unified in a set of values and aspirations alien to the parent generation (33). Third, the ability of peers to wrest adolescents' allegiance away from parents would vault teenagers into deviant activities.

In fact, however, little support was found for any of these expectations. Studies of real or hypothetical situations in which parents and peers offered conflicting advice indicated that teenagers do not routinely acquiesce to peer pressure. In fact they are more likely to follow adults' than peers' advice in matters affecting their long-term future (for example, college choices or career planning), and they actually rely on their *own* judgment more often than that of either peers or parents (13, 85, 93, 116). Furthermore, Dornbusch found that adolescents faced with conflicting parental and peer advice often choose to follow the group that they believe is most likely to learn of their choice (52). Thus, whatever evidence we find of adolescents' inclination toward peer conformity may simply be a sign that peer groups are better detectives than parents.

As for the hypothesized "generation gap," studies across several decades show consistent evidence of a strong *congruence* between parents and teenagers in political, religious, and moral values (6, 53, 61, 86, 103, 127, 132, 134). Thus, even if the peer culture does attempt to wean adolescents away from their parents' value systems, the evidence is that its efforts are unsuccessful. Other studies have reported that peers usually *reinforce* rather than contradict parental values (3, 86, 129). Indeed, Cooper et al. found that adolescents tend to replicate in their friendships the pattern of relationships they have with family (42).

Finally, there is the question of whether peer groups draw teenagers away from the influence of parents and into deviant activities. In cases where peer group norms are in obvious opposition to prevailing adult norms, such as in delinquent gangs, researchers have found that adolescents are not so much being pulled away from adults by the deviant crowd as driven to this crowd by parents' ineffective child-rearing practices (36, 50). Dishion and Patterson provided longitudinal evidence of how parents' inability to imbue youngsters with effective social skills contributed significantly to their involvement in delinquent adolescent peer groups (51, 107).

Redirecting Research to the Multiplicity of Peer Cultures

In the face of all this evidence, why does the notion persist that there is a monolithic, hedonistic youth culture that pulls students away from adult values and norms? For their tendency to focus on small but vocal, controversial, and oppositional segments of the adolescent population, the mass media must shoulder some of the blame. So too must social scientists who, for unknown reasons, have ignored the tremendous diversity of values and interests that exists among adolescent peer groups (85). It seems easy to forget that there is as much variation in values and aspirations within the youthful generation as between young people and adults (132).

Perhaps, however, the greatest obstacle to letting go of the notion of a monolithic youth culture is the lack of a good model with which to replace it. How can one characterize and explain the diversity among adolescent peer groups? Some have argued that teenage peer cultures, like those of adults, are organized along socioeconomic lines. In Britain, for example, social class has been the major dimension delineating peer groups, including deviant subcultures (2, 33, 76, 90, 131). Adolescent peer groups seem to be made up of neighborhood rather than school associates; the socioeconomic homogeneity of neighborhoods and the British sensitivity to social position encourage youths living near one another to coalesce into crowds. Such crowds appear to incite young people to act out tensions among the social strata that adults have learned to sublimate (72).

Some have proposed a similar conceptual scheme for American peer groups. Hollingshead (80) and, more recently, Polk (108) have suggested that American youth culture can be divided into at least two segments: one located at the high school and composed mainly of middle-class, college-bound youth; the other consisting of working-class and lower-class youth who are no longer in school. There are two weaknesses to this scheme, however. One is that most American high schools boast not one but a diverse array of peer groups with quite distinctive values and interests (26, 47, 85, 92, 109). The other is that social strata are not so neatly separated by school walls, or even by peer group boundaries (38). Whereas some crowds are dominated by one social class (preppies, greasers), other are quite heterogeneous (jocks, nerds) (47, 92, 119).

There also have been efforts to characterize adolescent peer groups along two or more dimensions. Loeb proposed that adolescent peer groups—cliques and crowds, as well as peer culture in general—could be rated according to their degree of informality and their degree of member participation in decision making (94). As it turned out, one dimension predicted the other in this scheme because both dimensions were determined by how adults socialized adolescents. Although this scheme might account for different interaction styles in various adolescent peer groups, it does not explain why certain crowds—the populars, the brains, the partyers, the nerds—keep cropping up in various ethnographic descriptions of adolescent peer culture. In this regard, Rigsby and McDill's scheme is more appealing (110). They proposed two orthogonal dimensions on which teenagers could be rated: commitment to the formal (adult-controlled) reward system of the school, and commitment to the school's informal (peer-controlled) status system. From this the authors identified four generic peer cultures: well rounded, studious, fun culture, and uninvolved.

Rigsby and McDill's conceptual scheme strikes me as particularly promising because it recognizes that orientations toward peer and parental or adult values are best conceived not as endpoints of a single dimension but as separate orthogonal dimensions. Groups of adolescents who coalesce at various points in this two-dimensional space begin to define different peer groups or youth cultures (15). The *expression* of such a culture, however, is probably mediated by other factors, including gender, socioeconomic status, ethnicity, and community and nation of residence—not to mention historical events. Thus, peer groups are characterized not as monolithic and static but as divergent and dynamic. The relation of peer culture to other contexts of adolescents' lives is not fixed and invariant. A peer group's values may be quite compatible with, contrary to, or even independent of a young person's school and family.

In short, as we abandon the notion that youth are united in a generational culture that stands in opposition to adult society, we must seek to understand the multiplicity of adolescent peer groups and peer cultures that are constantly adjusting to historical and sociocultural circumstances. Thus, researchers must question anew how peer groups and peer cultures come into being and are transformed across adolescence; how individuals find, maintain, or adjust their place within this peer system; and how experiences in the peer group affect adolescents' attitudes and behaviors.

Setting the Stage: Conceptual Labels for the Adolescent Peer System

Before we explore what researchers have learned and identify facets of adolescent peer groups and peer cultures that need closer examination, some clarification of my conceptual scheme is in order. One problem with previous research is that the term *peer group* has been used rather loosely. It has been applied to everything from patterns of interaction with one friend to an individual's tie with her or his entire age cohort or generation. Because of the confusion engendered by such broad use of the term, some restrictions and distinctions must be imposed. First, my discussion of peer groups will *not* include two-person relationships (for example, dating partners or a pair of friends). These interactions are better understood in the context of research on friendship and dating or romantic involvements (see Chapter 11 in this volume). Second, one can distinguish between institutionalized and informal peer groups, that is, between groups for teenagers that are set up and controlled by adults (such as formal youth clubs or sports teams) and those initiated and controlled by teenagers themselves. This chapter deals only with the latter type of peer group.

Third, small, relatively intimate groups of peers are identified and defined on a different basis from the larger clusters of adolescents to which researchers often refer. Typically the small groups are *interaction-based* entities, comprising a limited number of adolescents identified as a group because they "hang around" together and develop close relationships. This sort of group shall be referred to as a *clique*. Cliques can vary in size, intimacy, and openness to outsiders (56, 73). Generally, however, they remain small enough to allow for regular interaction of all members, to ensure that all members understand and appreciate one another better than do people outside the clique, and to permit members to regard the clique as their primary base of interaction with groups of age mates (55, 100).

In contrast to cliques are *crowds,* which are larger, *reputation-based* collectives of similarly stereotyped individuals who may or may not spend much time together. By reputation-based I mean that an adolescent's crowd affiliation denotes the primary attitudes or activities with which one is associated by peers. It can also be a commentary on one's status among peers or level of social skills. Crowd labels common among secondary school students reflect these characteristics: jocks, brains, loners, Asians, rogues, druggies, populars, nerds, Mexicans, and so on. Whereas clique norms develop from within the group (98), crowd norms are imposed from outside the group and reflect the stereotypic image that peers have of crowd members (24). Because crowd labels theoretically group together individuals with similar characteristics, clique members often may share the same crowd affiliation. Yet the distinction drawn here between a clique and a crowd is quite different from Dunphy's, in which crowds are simply an amalgam of several cliques (55).

To appreciate the nature and dynamics of cliques it is helpful to differentiate between two types of such groups. *Activity cliques* are peer groups that adolescents are thrust into by circumstance: study groups at school, cabins at camp, and so on. A *friendship clique* is a group of associates the adolescent chooses for himself or herself. Because group functions and compatibility of members differ dramatically in these two types of cliques, differences in group dynamics can be expected as well.

A final distinction is between a *membership group*, the clique or crowd to which an adolescent belongs (or is considered part of by peers), and a *reference group*, the crowd that serves as a guidepost for determining one's values and actions or measuring one's abilities. For many adolescents the membership group is also the reference group, but it is dangerous to assume that this is always the case. A nerd who hopes to become a popular may be more heavily influenced by the popular peer culture than by the norms of the nerd culture.

Distinguishing between institutionalized and informal peer collectives, dyad and group relations, cliques and crowds, activity and friendship cliques, and membership and reference groups gives researchers a more powerful framework within which to explore the dynamics of adolescent peer groups and peer cultures. The distinctions help us, for example, to sort out the various theoretical perspectives from which researchers have addressed the question of how and why the peer group system emerges and begins to capture adults' attention in early adolescence. It is to this issue that I now turn.

The Emerging Character of Adolescent Peer Groups

It is no startling discovery that peer groups begin to appear as a key dimension of social relationships well before adolescence (105). Yet changes in the character of peer group relations that somehow occur between childhood and adolescence transform peer groups into a more prominent and, for many adults, foreboding context of adolescent development. Information on the nature, timing, and precipitating conditions of peer group transformations is remarkably limited (121), but four major changes stand out.

Changes from Childhood to Adolescent Peer Groups

First, peer interactions consume a larger amount of an individual's time, and peer associates account for a larger proportion of one's central social network in adolescence than in childhood. In a typical week, even discounting time spent in classroom instruction (23% of an average student's waking hours), high school students spend twice as much of their time with peers (29%) as with parents or other adults (15%) (46). Same-sex peers make up the largest single category of significant others for adolescents; peers, including opposite-sex friends, account for 40% of the significant-other network (11). The corresponding withdrawal from adults occurs early in adolescence: Garbarino et al. reported that by sixth grade, adults (excluding parents) accounted for only 25% of early adolescents' primary social network—and only 10% among early maturers.

A second change is that adolescent peer groups function more autonomously—that is, with less adult guidance or control. (Remember that we are talking about informal peer groups, not youth organizations controlled by adults.) Childhood peer groups are anchored in the neighborhood, where they can remain under the close supervision of parents (105). Adolescent peer groups are more likely to be anchored at the school, under the less watchful supervision of teachers. Membership cuts across neighborhoods, and teenagers make a more conscious effort to escape the presence of adults when interacting with peers. Even at home, parents watch with amusement as their adolescent children transform closets and bathrooms into makeshift phone booths to ensure that conversations with peers remain private.

Third, as adolescents distance themselves from adults, they draw closer to peers of the opposite sex. The proportion included among significant others grows steadily throughout adolescence (11). Strict gender segregation, a hallmark of childhood peer groups (77), stands in sharp contrast to the mixing of sexes that appears to be a major rationale for the restructuring of peer groups in adolescence (55).

Finally, peer interactions expand beyond dyadic and clique relationships to acknowledge the presence of the larger peer collectives that I label crowds. Adolescents seem to agree more on the norms or stereotypic traits and behavior patterns of crowds than on precisely who belongs to each one. Nevertheless, the emergence of crowds marks the appearance of peer *cultures,* which are often the focus of adult concern about peers as a context of adolescent development.

Sources of Change

Collectively these four changes transform peer groups in adolescence into an increasingly complex heterosexual social system that is a central component of teenage social relations and increasingly autonomous from the adolescent's other social spheres. What precipitates these changes?

Quest for identity. One factor is teenagers' need to crystallize a sense of identity. As adolescents strive to relinquish psychological dependence on parents, peer groups become a temporary replacement until fully autonomous (psychological) functioning is possible (27, 62). Some regard the central psychological task of early adolescence to be locating a peer group that is not only accepting and supportive but also compatible with one's dispositions and interests (100). It is sensible, then, to expect cliques to become more salient and also distant from parents in adolescence, as they take on the role of substitute source of psychological dependence. It is equally sensible for crowds to emerge as identity prototypes with different life-styles and value systems for teenagers to explore.

Some research evidence supports this psychological agenda: clique membership is a significant predictor of adolescents' psychological well-being and ability to cope with stress (75). But tight-knit cliques are more characteristic of girls at moderate levels of ego development who are still struggling to achieve an autonomous sense of identity (74). In addition, the importance attached to belonging to a crowd peaks in early adolescence, then drifts downward with age as dissatisfaction with the demands for conformity associated with crowds intensifies (21).

Puberty. In addition to this psychological agenda, biological factors contribute to the transformation of peer groups. Certainly puberty prompts a heightened interest in the opposite sex and a need to adjust peer relations to allow for more heterosexual interactions; thus, the opposite sex is incorporated into one's cliques and crowds. But pubertal development also seems to prompt teenagers' withdrawal from adults and their increasing focus on peer relationships (70, 114). In fact, females who mature early may be drawn into heterosexual peer relations before they are psychologically ready for them; they often associate with cliques of older peers, who encourage their participation in sexual and delinquent activities (95).

Social-cognitive development. Erikson (62) and Newman and Newman (100) argue that adolescents seek out the peer group best suited to meeting their needs for emotional support and exploration or reaffirmation of their values and aspirations. This presumes that adolescents can evaluate crowds on the basis of not only their behavior but also their normative values and styles of interaction. Crowds are essentially categories of individuals based on intentions and personality dispositions as well as on typical activity patterns. It is doubtful that these social-cognitive characteristics emerge much before adolescence (4, 104, 117), and their appearance may contribute substantially to transformations in the peer group system.

Of course, not all adolescents develop these social-cognitive skills at the same time or to an equal degree (79), which may account for differences in teenagers' ability to fit into a crowd or draw on its resources to promote adaptive behavior (75, 95, 100). Furthermore, because the character of crowds involves subjective evaluations, individuals with equivalent person-perception or group-perception skills may perceive the peer group system in quite different terms. Brown and Mounts reported significant ethnic differences in which groups students named as the major crowds in their high school and how they distributed classmates among these crowds (25). For example, whites were more likely than blacks to mention a black crowd and to assign a large proportion of students to this crowd.

Social-structural perspective. Major changes in the structuring of peer groups may result not only from these facets of *individual* development but also from adolescents' attempts to adapt to the new *social* world to which adults subject teenagers. With the transition into middle school or junior high school, students generally move from a structure based on self-contained classrooms (in which most of their time is spent with the same small number of age mates) to one in which they confront a much larger, constantly shifting array of peers, many of whom are strangers. It becomes hard to know all one's classmates personally, and it is difficult for old friendships to survive if conflicting class or activity schedules prevent associates from seeing one another often (9). Bonds with adults at school also begin to dissipate. Students typically spend just one hour a day with each teacher, and adult supervision is looser than in grade school as teachers and administrators move to encourage some sense of autonomy and personal responsibility among students (58, 81, 112).

Moving into this environment, early adolescents seek strategies for negotiating the rush of new peer relationships. Securing one's place in a clique prevents a student from having to confront this sea of unfamiliar faces alone. Including members of the opposite sex in one's circle of friends ensures participation in the heterosexually oriented series of school-sponsored social activities (mixers, proms). And developing a categorization scheme for peer crowds or peer cultures helps one to negotiate relationships with peers who remain acquaintances or strangers. In other words, most major changes in peer groups can be seen as efforts to cope with the new school structure thrust on youngsters at adolescence. The depersonalized and complex routine of secondary school increases the young teenager's need for sources of social support and informal exchanges.

Of course, the notion that schools form the locus of peer group interaction, and therefore the major social-structural influence on the adolescent peer system, is both culture bound and class bound. In other nations in which secondary schooling is highly selective or segmented by ability or social status, as well as in portions of the American population in which dropout rates are high, the influence of school structure may be sharply reduced. The point here is that changes that endow the peer system with a distinctive character in adolescence probably happen more because of than in spite of the nature of other major contexts in adolescents' lives. So, in studying adolescent peer groups researchers need to remain mindful of how they affect and are affected by teenagers' participation in school, family, work, and other large social situations.

Thus, the unique character of adolescent peer groups and peer cultures seems to be a response to forces of change within the individual as well as changes in the social environment. Teenagers construct a peer system that reflects their growing psychological, biological, and social-cognitive maturity and helps them adapt to the social ecology of adolescence. Of course, not all cliques and crowds are healthy environments for adolescent development. Let us now turn to the question of what determines the type of peer group and peer culture in which a teenager will become involved.

Finding One's Peer Group Niche

In a fashion similar to Erikson's depiction of late adolescents seeking an "occupational niche" to help consummate identity development (62), one can speak of a teenager's need to locate her or his "peer group niche"—a position among peers that is uniquely one's own but that fits into the larger fabric of peer social life. To date, however, there has been little research to guide our understanding of this process. The extensive literature tracking childhood cliques and exploring the consequences of children's sociometric status on peer relations (see, for example, 1, 64, 111) stops short at adolescence. A major reason is that the observational and sociometric methods employed to assess children's social skills, peer acceptance, and cliquing patterns were developed for small, circumscribed populations of peers (such as elementary school classrooms) and are unsuitable for the larger network of peer relations that adolescents confront in comprehensive secondary schools. Deriving new methods applicable to larger peer collectives is a hurdle that researchers still must surmount.

Factors governing adolescents' selection of friends (proximity, similarity, and so on) will probably figure heavily in their integration into a clique (see Chapter 11). It is also probable that an adolescent's level of social skills will influence the ease with which he or she locates a circle of friends and comes to occupy a central position within the clique. Thus, there should be considerable congruence between what is to be learned about adolescents' entry into cliques and what has been learned from work on adolescent friendship patterns and studies of childhood clique relations.

Another issue seems to be how adolescents fit into a crowd. Erikson's suggestion that the identity crisis be negotiated by "trying on" various identities (62) implies that adolescents should shift their affiliation from crowd to crowd, sampling the prototypical identity each crowd offers. In reality, adolescents' ability to choose and change crowds may be too constricted to accommodate Erikson's ideal process. This is because, in a sense, adolescents do not select a crowd to join so much as they are thrust into one by virtue of their personality, background, interests, and reputation among peers. The preadolescent whose life is dominated by sports seems destined for membership in the jock crowd. The Mexican-American who typifies to peers the characteristics of Hispanic culture can hardly escape being labeled as part of the Mexican crowd.

How well can one predict adolescent crowd affiliation from preadolescent characteristics is a fascinating but virtually untouched area of research. Investigators have discovered significant associations between crowd affiliation and a set of personality traits (82) as well as patterns of family interaction (57), but longitudinal studies are needed to establish the causal direction of such associations. Recent sociometric studies of children (see, for example, 66) have found it useful to differentiate between aggressive and nonaggressive rejected boys. The distinctions drawn between the two groups are remarkably similar to adolescents' discriminations between druggies (or toughs) and nerds (24), but determining how well childhood sociometric status predicts adolescent crowd membership also requires longitudinal studies that simply have not been conducted. The need for such research is unquestionably high: if researchers can determine childhood precursors of entry into dysfunctional peer groups, interventions can be designed to help redirect children into healthier peer environments in adolescence.

Constraints on adolescents' choice of crowd affiliation include other less malleable personal and environmental factors. Adolescent peer cultures may not simply mimic the adult socioeconomic system, as Hollingshead claimed (80), but social class does seem to figure heavily in membership in certain crowds—especially higher-status groups among girls (40, 56). In schools with a diverse ethnic composition or a visible ethnic minority group, ethnicity can become a major dimension along which crowds are defined (25, 92). In Brown and Mounts's study of multiethnic high schools, between one-third and one-half of minority students were associated by peers with ethnically defined crowds—rappers (blacks), Asians, Hispanics, and so on—but the rest were classified into reputation-based groups such as populars and nerds (25). It remains to be seen why ethnicity is the major defining characteristic in the eyes of peers for some minority students, whereas activities, interests, or social standing among peers stands out for others. Also, although the mixing of genders that characterizes adolescent peer relations in general is apparent in most peer crowds or cultures, there are still some crowds (including high-status groups) in which the membership is predominantly male (for example, jocks, farmers) or female (for example, populars). More broadly, adolescents are restricted to crowd categories recognized by peers. In one rural school, students had no difficulty assigning their classmates to crowds until they came to one boy. "He's sort of in a crowd by himself," they mused. "At other schools you'd call him a punker, but we really don't have any punkers here—except for him" (18).

Some might suppose that because crowd labels are little more than vague, stereotypical categories, and because the constraints on selecting a crowd for oneself are substantial, the crowd niche would matter less to adolescents than their clique niche. Remember, however, that clique affiliation indicates merely who an adolescent's close friends are; crowd affiliation indicates who an *adolescent* is—at least in the eyes of peers. It is a very personal evaluation of the adolescent by those whose opinions matter. Thus, it is not surprising that adolescents resist being labeled or pigeonholed as part of one crowd (128).

Teenagers must struggle with the tension between having no crowd affiliation—no clear image or identity among peers—and suffering with an image they dislike. Ianni discovered this tension in his observations of jocks and freaks in one upper-middle-class suburban high school (81). Freaks appeared to resent being labeled freaks by the jocks because of the implicit hostility inherent in the label as the jocks used it. Nevertheless, they seemed to appreciate being called a freak by fellow freaks. As Ianni noted, "If a freak did not want to be recognized as a freak, he would not adopt the dress, manners, and loose lifestyles of the freaks" (81, p. 20).

One finds, however, that a teenager's crowd affiliation is not always obvious or clear-cut (128). For some teenagers there is widespread consensus among peers about their membership in a particular crowd, and they seem happily ensconced in the group. Others understand that peers associate them with one peer culture (their membership group) but seek desperately to be accepted by another culture (their reference group). Still others defy labeling, by either peers or themselves, as they float among crowds with opposing interests and images (20). Rather than struggling to pin down each teenager in one or another group, researchers might choose to regard these cases as alternative responses to the task of finding a peer group niche.

For teenagers who successfully locate an acceptable niche, who form a supportive network of clique mates and settle into a crowd whose image is compatible with their activities and aspirations, peer groups promise to be a highly adaptive context in which to negotiate adolescence. For those who either falter in these tasks or choose a dysfunctional crowd, peer groups c n have maladaptive consequences. The processes are not simple and are certainly not well understood by researchers. To make matters more complicated, they do not appear to be stable, in view of the dynamic features of adolescent peer groups to which I now turn.

Transformations in Peer Groups and Peer Group Relations

Those who have described the adolescent peer group system often have regarded it more as a painting than as a moving picture—a stable, enduring social system through which each generation of teenagers dutifully passes. The actors change, but the play remains the same. At a broad level of abstraction this is quite true. But individuals change during adolescence, and this change may precipitate transformations in the structural or interpersonal aspects of their environment. There is growing evidence of transformations in family relations during adolescence (78, 97, 124). Researchers need to explore whether or not a similar process takes place in the peer context. Do patterns of interaction within and between cliques or perceptions of crowds remain stable during adolescence, or are there systematic transformations throughout the teenage years?

Transformations within Cliques

Although, theoretically at least, cliques are founded on principles of reciprocity and equality, members' positions and interrelationships are not all alike. Dunphy pointed out that cliques often have multiple leaders, each serving different functions (55). Others have differentiated between levels of centrality in clique membership, such that some members occupy core (leadership) positions, others are at the periphery of the clique, and the rest occupy a middle ground (73, 75, 119). Differential positions within cliques and the existence of peripheral members ("hangers-on" or "wanna-be's") mean that clique membership is always in a state of flux. In this respect, adolescent cliques are inherently unstable entities.

In research on adolescent cliques, concern with stability and change has focused on the microanalytic level, charting the degree of stability in relationships among members over a short period of time (several weeks or a few months). Two classic observational studies of early adolescent boys in summer camps examined the formative stages of cliques (114, 120). Both studies found that much of the group's earliest interaction was oriented toward establishing a dominance hierarchy. Within the first few days of camp, occupants of the highest and lowest rungs of the hierarchy became apparent; the positions of all other group members were settled soon after. Past this formative stage, relations within the clique (both dominance and friendship patterns) remained quite stable.

Curiously, however, observations of *girls* in summer camp revealed no evidence of a stable dominance hierarchy, but instead showed a pattern of shifting coalitions across the clique's natural history (113). There are three reasons why studies of boys in summer camps may overstate the stability of cliques. First, they deal only with activity cliques, which are undoubtedly more stable in membership and probably more susceptible to dominance hierarchies than friendship cliques, where voluntary, mutual selection breeds more of a norm of equality and reciprocity.

Second, the summer-camp setting contrasts sharply with the more typical social ecology of adolescence, in which teenagers encounter constantly shifting clusters of peers throughout the day—from class to class in school, between different school settings (classroom to lunchroom to extracurricular contexts), and between school and family or other community settings. In each case somewhat different social skills predominate (academic abilities, finesse in social interchange, athletic prowess), and the authority structure within the group may shift as the talents necessary to succeed in the setting change. Sherif and Sherif, for example, observed one clique in which the leader temporarily relinquished his position when the group played basketball (119). Consciously or unconsciously, the leader recognized the superior talents of another member in this activity. By contrast, a dominant member who tries to push authority beyond the limits of his or her abilities risks censure or ostracism from the clique. Cusick recounted a case in which the leader encouraged off-task, frivolous behavior from his clique mates during class time that they were supposed to be spending on a group project (47). Everyone in the group received a poor grade on the assignment; when the teacher's comments seemed to confirm the group members' sense that the leader had acted irresponsibly, they effectively ousted him from the clique.

The leader's fate points up a third shortcoming of the activity cliques that are the focus of summer-camp studies: they do not allow individuals to shift membership between cliques, or to belong to none at all. Developmental patterns of clique membership are becoming a hotly debated issue. On the one hand, an investigation found that the proportion of adolescents claiming membership in a clique increased between sixth and eighth grade (45). On the other hand, sociometric analyses of clique structure in one school revealed a sharp decline from sixth to twelfth grade in the proportion of students who were definitely clique members and a corresponding increase with age in the percentage labeled "liaisons" (121). These were students whose primary social ties were to peers in a variety of cliques, or for whom most close associates also existed at the margin of one or more cliques. Similarly, unpublished Scottish data indicated an increase with age in the proportion of girls preferring to organize their social life around one close friend rather than a clique (see 122). As researchers pursue this debate, they may encounter a set of mediating factors. For example, Eder's data imply that membership may be more firm and loyal among adolescents in certain crowds (such as populars) than others (for example, the average crowd) (56).

Transformations between Cliques

Dunphy's study of Australian adolescents remains the classic work on structural changes in relationships between adolescent cliques (55). In a five-stage model Dunphy described how isolated, single-sex cliques characteristic of early adolescence build closer relationships with opposite-sex cliques. Then they tie into a loose association of several cliques to allow for larger social activities, only to dissipate again at the end of adolescence into isolated but now fully heterosexual cliques. The validity of Dunphy's stage model is rarely questioned, even though his work has never been formally replicated. Understandably, the environment that Dunphy studied differs from the social ecology of today's American peer cultures, which leaves several important issues in need of further research. For example, are the sequence and timing of structural changes in clique interrelationships consistent across peer crowds or cultures? Do brains and nerds traverse the sequence in the same way as blacks and populars? Are cliques constrained from combining with groups in other crowds, as playwrights would have us believe (in, for example, *Grease* and *West Side Story*), or are such integrations possible provided the "social distance" (difference in perceived norms and actual activities) between crowds is not too great? Is the integration of opposite-sex cliques determined strictly by the heterosexual attraction between certain members, as Dunphy implied? When someone from the popular crowd starts dating someone from the average crowd, do both entire cliques begin to merge, or does one partner have to abandon his or her clique mates to legitimize his or her image as a new member of the other one's crowd? What determines who makes the move: the status of the crowd? the gender of the individual? Elaboration of Dunphy's basic developmental scheme is sorely needed.

Transformations in Crowds or Peer Cultures

I have argued that whereas cliques are behavioral phenomena, defined by observable interaction patterns, crowds are more cognitive phenomena, in which assignments are determined by judgments about someone's personal characteristics. It is not surprising, then, that transformations in teenagers' conceptions of crowds are reminiscent of the sequence of developmental changes in social-cognitive skills. Early adolescents seem to focus on concrete behavioral components of the peer group system. They can readily identify the membership of major cliques among classmates (32), but they have a more primitive understanding of crowds. In one study, sixth-graders who were asked to name and describe the major crowds in their school gave labels that focused on group leaders or recess activities (Aimee's group, "jump rope" crowd, "play kill" crowd); by contrast, most students in eighth and ninth grade labeled crowds by their general dispositions or interests (jocks, nerds, and so on) (18).

More careful and comprehensive interviews also showed that, from preadolescence to middle adolescence, the focus of teenagers' open-ended descriptions of crowds in their school shifted from behavioral patterns to dispositional characteristics (101, 117). In O'Brien and Bierman's sample, making abstract and relative comparisons among crowds (such as arranging crowds into a status hierarchy) was quite common among eleventh-graders but rare among fifth-graders (101). Students' sensitivity to their place in the crowd system—that is, their ability to predict accurately which crowds peers would place them in—also seems to increase with age, although this is more true of members of certain crowds (such as jocks and druggies) than others (such as unpopulars) (20). It remains to be seen in future studies whether groups such as unpopulars lack the social-cognitive sophistication of other groups or simply prefer to ignore the undesirable label placed on them by peers.

Not all changes in the conceptualization of crowds are linear. Brown and Clasen found that, when students were asked to name the major crowds in their school, the proportion of responses that fell into typical crowd categories (that is, those excluding hybrids and uncodable crowd names) climbed from 80% in sixth grade to 95% in ninth grade, then fell steadily through twelfth grade (18). Interestingly, this pattern parallels age differences in susceptibility to peer pressure (7, 19).

Along with the changing conceptualization of crowds, there are shifts in students' assessments of the salience of crowd membership. Both J. C. Coleman (39) and, more recently, Brown, Eicher, and Petrie (21) found a steady decline in adolescents' ratings of the importance of belonging to a crowd and a mounting concern with age about the ways in which remaining close to a crowd stifles self-expression and identity development. In addition, many ethnographers have commented on the tendency of high school seniors to develop a sense of unity that dissipates or transcends crowd boundaries (92, 128). It is therefore unfortunate that most ethnographies have focused on samples of seniors, who may underestimate the degree to which crowd affiliation separates students.

Information on transformations across adolescence in individuals' crowd affiliation is more limited, but it seems doubtful that Erikson's notion of "trying on" various identities through shifting crowd affiliation is a common practice. First, there are constraints on movement among crowds (17): not all crowds are equally receptive to new members (56, 92), and peers may resist a student's efforts to change his or her image radically. For example, druggies who have gone through a rehabilitation program may not win acceptance by other crowds despite apparent changes in attitudes and behavior. They must live down their reputation and suffer the skepticism of peers in other groups, as well as their own crowd, that their conversion is only temporary. Second, there is considerable individual variability in how closely a teenager is associated by peers with just one crowd. True consensus on someone's crowd affiliation is rare (18); more often, students are located by peers in two or three crowds, although one crowd may be mentioned more frequently than others. Because crowd affiliation is so subjective, charting changes in crowd affiliation is a difficult and inherently imprecise task.

It is also worth noting that the range of crowds available to adolescents also may shift across time. Historical events may give birth to novel crowd types (the beats of the 1950s or hippies of the 1960s) or cause the reputation of certain crowds to undergo a metamorphosis, such as the transformation of the "politicos" in one high school from an antiestablishment, radical group in the late 1960s to one remarkably supportive of the school administration several years later (92). Curiously, however, a standard set of crowds seems to flourish in all historical eras, including, as I have already mentioned, jocks, populars, brains, delinquents or alienated youth, and nerds. Their constant presence in listings of peer cultures is an issue that warrants investigation.

Consequences of Peer Group Affiliation

Of course, for many adults the primary concerns about peer groups are the ways in which, and the degree to which, they influence the behavior and well-being of adolescents. A common image seems to be that of adolescents enduring a constant and rather overwhelming barrage of peer pressure to conform to group norms, with this pressure serving to impede rather than assist personal growth. Yet, given the diverse and dynamic nature of peer groups and peer cultures, this image of steady and uniformly negative pressure does not seem valid. There is no denying that peer pressure figures heavily in the lives of American adolescents, but questions abound about the details of peer pressure and other types of peer group influence, including their source, magnitude, direction, mode of expression, and impact on teenagers.

Conceptualizing and Measuring Peer Influence

A vigorous advertising campaign to combat teenage drug use has been waged by encouraging adolescents to "just say no" to drug use, or profess, "Drugs are not my style." Implicit in this campaign is the misguided notion that peer pressure to use drugs is direct and overt. Empirical evidence suggests, however, that peer influence usually operates in a much subtler fashion (119). When asked to describe pressures to use drugs (especially alcohol) at parties, teenagers' responses are very consistent: "It's there if you want it, but nobody gives you a hard time if you don't. Like, no one comes up and shoves a beer in your hand and says, 'Here, drink it!' Of course, if everybody else is drinking you may feel a little weird just sipping a soda."

In struggling with the task of conceptualizing peer influence on adolescents, a number of researchers have concluded that there are two influence processes, although the two they articulate are not always the same. Deutsch and Gerard distinguished between *normative* influence, or pressure to conform to the positive expectations of another, and *information* influence, or pressure to accept information from another as evidence of reality (49). It appears that, in peer groups, normative influence is stronger, but only among those who are motivated to be part of the group. Kandel differentiated *modeling,* in which adolescents imitate peer behavior, from *reinforcement,* in which adolescents adopt the values of peers, which then affect choices of behavior (85). In examining influence patterns in friendship dyads, Kandel found that modeling was a stronger influence with reference to drug use. Berndt argued that whereas past research has focused on *normative* influence (a teenager encouraging a friend to adopt her or his values and attitudes), the stronger source of influence (especially toward positive behaviors) is *interactional;* that is, we are influenced most by friends who provide support and avoid conflicts (8).

Beyond recognizing that we have yet to settle how peer influences work, the lesson to be learned here is that peer influences are multidimensional, more often subtle (through modeling behaviors and being supportive or establishing group norms) than direct, and contingent in their impact on the adolescents' willingness to be influenced. Finally, it appears that peer influence takes different forms in each major arena of peer interaction (54, 73): close friendships, cliques, membership groups, and reference groups.

Regrettably, most investigators have ignored the challenge of properly conceptualizing peer influence and have adopted instead a wholly un-acceptable measurement strategy, namely equating degree of similarity between friends with peer influence. The assumption is that the more similar teenagers are to their friends, the more they have been pressured to adopt the friends' attitudes or behaviors. But researchers have consistently shown that similarity stems primarily *not* from processes of peer influence but from adolescents' inclination to choose like-minded peers as friends and the tendency of peer groups to recruit as new members individuals who already share the group's normative attitudes and behaviors (37, 54, 84, 85, 96, 99).

Key Findings from Past Studies

A few efforts have been made to measure peer group influences in a more sophisticated fashion. In these, four basic findings stand out. First, teen-agers are not uniform in their susceptibility to peer influence. In submit-ting subjects to contrived or hypothetical situations of peer pressure, investigators have found rather consistently that susceptibility is higher among early adolescents than younger or older age groups (7, 10, 41, 44). Gender also has been a factor, but not with a definitive pattern: studies using contrived situations to examine implicit pressure from a general set of peers suggest that girls are slightly more susceptible to peer pressure than boys (44, 91), whereas those using hypothetical situations to gauge explicit pressure from friends report higher susceptibility among boys, especially in antisocial situations (7, 19). Also, Costanzo found susceptibil-ity to peer influence to be negatively correlated with adolescents' confi-dence in their social skills (43). Even at the height of susceptibility (that is, in early adolescence), the inclination to follow friends is much weaker in antisocial than neutral activities (7). Yet to be examined are many crucial factors, such as how susceptibility relates to dominance or leadership status, social-cognitive abilities, and crowd affiliation. But the clear implication of work to date is that the inclination to conform to one's peers is subject to significant individual, developmental, and situational variability.

Second, adolescents' perceptions of the peer pressures they encounter are also quite variable. In asking teenagers to describe the degree and direction of (rather explicit) pressures from friends, Brown and his colleagues found that, whereas reports of pressure toward peer involvement and conformity to group norms were quite consistent, pressures in other areas (misconduct, involvement with school and family) varied substantially by age, peer group affiliation, and even community of residence (14, 23, 34). Although pressure toward misconduct (drug use, sexual activity, minor delinquency) increased throughout adolescence, it remained substantially lower than pressures in all other areas. In fact, pressure to finish high school was the single strongest influence from friends that respondents reported. In the most general terms, however, perceived pressures seemed to reflect the diversity of norms inherent in the adolescent peer group system, and they followed a developmental trajectory different from that observed in studies of susceptibility to peer influence.

A third finding is that even among adolescents inclined to accede to peer influence, peer pressure does not seem to *dictate* adolescents' behavior. One study indicated that susceptibility to peer pressure and the degree of pressure adolescents actually perceived from friends accounted for less than half of the variance in self-reported peer involvement (7%) and misconduct (43%) (19). The authors conceded that their means of measuring peer pressure may have underestimated its impact on respondents' behavior. Yet, even with measurement strategies that overstate peer influence, correlations with individual behavior are not overwhelming. For example, studies of tobacco and alcohol use routinely present the smoking and drinking habits of close friends as a valid measure of peer pressure, even though similarities in patterns of drug use probably result from selection of friends as well as pressure from friends. Measured this way, peer pressure accounts for between 10% and 40% of the variations in teenagers' smoking and drinking behavior (5, 89).

Finally, we have learned that peer influence does not operate independently of experiences in other contexts. Susceptibility to peer pressure varies among adolescents exposed to different family structures and parenting styles (125). There are also significant differences across communities in levels of perceived pressures, even among adolescents in similar types of crowds (34).

Debating the Direction of Peer Group Influence

All four findings suggest that peer group influences are neither uniform nor overwhelming, but the question remains whether peer pressure and peer group affiliations are primarily limiting or liberating forces in teenagers' lives. The tendency has been to view them as dysfunctional or as sources of constraint. A controversial ethnographic work on black teenagers' efforts to avoid the crowd label "brainiac" illustrates this stance. Fordham and Ogbu argued that among lower-class blacks, high academic achievement was equated with "selling out" one's ethnic identity (65). In response to intense pressure from peers not to "act white," bright students in the all-black school they observed either became underachievers or hid their achievements from peers by becoming a comic or cutup in class in front of peers. Fuller reported a similar phenomenon among black girls in a British school (69). Of course, "brain" is a label avoided by most white students as well because of its association with "nerdish" characteristics (16), but the larger issue here is how peer groups serve to enhance the opportunities and self-concept of certain adolescents at the expense of others. In addition to the dominance hierarchy within cliques (114), there is a status hierarchy among crowds that helps account for the uneven distribution of privileges and resources among students in high schools (15). Larkin, for example, recounts how a popular crowd running a school's talent show rejected acts from lower-status crowds in favor of crowd mates whose auditions exhibited clearly inferior talent (92). In the face of such uneven access to social recognition, it is not surprising that self-esteem varies directly with the position of an adolescent's crowd in the status hierarchy (22).

Of course, such an example pales by comparison to the images most adults have of antisocial peer groups—images, of course, that are emphasized by news media: rival inner-city gangs maiming one another to protect their turf, "skinheads" attacking members of minority groups, boys on a rampage of assault through city neighborhoods. We realize now that serious delinquency, along with heavy drug use, is concentrated in a small number of adolescent cliques and crowds (31, 109, 119, 126). Yet, although they make up a small proportion of the teenage population, such antisocial peer groups are a matter of grave concern. In most cases, however, it does not appear that they are composed of "all-American kids" turned bad by peer influence. Instead, aggressive children, who are readily labeled as such and rejected by most of their peers, gravitate toward one another and coalesce into cliques well before adolescence (29, 30). Group norms reinforce members' antisocial behavior patterns (102), but the group also provides emotional and instrumental support so that members do not necessarily suffer from low self-esteem (99). In other words, antisocial peer groups do not redirect members' behavior patterns but reinforce predispositions that predated group membership. Peer influences contribute to the antisocial behavior of these adolescents, but they do not cause it. Of course, the same can be said of peer influences in more positively oriented groups.

There are those who maintain an optimistic perspective on peer influence. Newman and Newman contend that peer group expectations "may be perceived by the adolescent as a force drawing him to be more than he thinks he is, to be braver, more confident, more outgoing, etc." (100, p. 269). Clasen and Brown emphasize that adolescents perceive more pressure toward self-enhancing activities (school achievement, peer socializing) than antisocial or self-destructive behavior (35). Johnson found that crowd affiliation in junior high school predicted students' subsequent vocational identity in college, a fact that suggests that peer group membership or pressures may nurture adolescents' future occupational inclinations (82).

Directions for Future Studies

The question, then, is not whether peer pressure and peer group affiliations are basically positive or negative forces in teenagers' lives, because they are obviously a mixed blessing. The challenge for researchers is to clarify how and in what circumstances peer groups aid in or detract from healthy development. In pursuing this challenge, investigators should be mindful of three insights gleaned from previous studies. First, in charting the nature and extent of peer group influence, it is unwise to rely heavily on either adolescents' assertions or adults' impressions. The American emphasis on individualism and developmental press toward autonomy may encourage teenagers to underrate peer pressure, and parents' preoccupation with deviant activities may cause them to overlook more positive aspects of peer group affiliations. It is imperative to develop more sophisticated and sensitive measures of peer influence, perhaps through greater reliance on ethnographic or observational methods.

Second, conceptual and measurement schemes must allow for multiple forms of peer influence. The same form may not predominate at all levels of peer group interaction.

Finally, concern over the impact of clique or crowd affiliation must be tempered by the recognition that peer groups sort adolescents according to personality dispositions and behavior patterns. In other words, peer group differences are not wholly a function of peer influence but are partially a reflection of preexisting individual differences. The question of interest, then, is how peer influence reinforces or redirects adolescents' behavior, and how it fosters continued growth or impedes development.

The Place of Adults in Adolescent Peer Groups

From time to time researchers and policy makers have debated whether or not adults should intervene and attempt to exercise some control over adolescent peer groups (40, 47). Once the myth of the monolithic youth culture is debunked, this debate becomes moot. For better or worse, adults and adult institutions *do* intervene in teenage peer cultures. Evidence showing that child-rearing practices can predispose children to choose certain peer groups has already been presented (51). Adults have a vested interest in perpetuating peer groups that fulfill particular functions at school (100). Larkin observed the collusion between one crowd and the school administration that helped maintain the crowd's power base in the peer system (92). Ethnographers have recorded parents' complaints that certain crowds get preferential treatment or a disproportionate share of resources from the school or adults in the community (48).

We are beginning to understand how the organization of schools affects preadolescent peer group relations. Hallinan found that the size of cliques varies as a function of the size of elementary and middle school classrooms (73). Schwartz observed differences in peer-interaction patterns between students in high-ability versus low-ability classes—differences that were consistent across schools that varied in socioeconomic and ethnic composition (115). High-track students emphasized their shared group status and collective identity, whereas the lower-track children engaged in competitive, derogatory interactions. Cliques emerged within rather than across tracks, so that students of low ability were effectively cut off from the healthier peer-interaction patterns of high-ability students. Because these were the formative stages of adolescent peer group formation, it is likely that these differences were carried forward to secondary school; but just how secondary school structure affects teenage peer groups remains to be seen. For example, the relative emphasis that teachers and administrators give to sports, academics, or particular extracurricular activities may help define the types of crowds that emerge in the school, or at least their relative status. Adults' efforts to break down or maintain racial barriers may also influence the degree to which ethnicity becomes a major defining characteristic of crowds (for example, whether or not blacks, Hispanics, Asians, and so on form readily identifiable peer cultures).

Strong parental investment in activity-based crowds—booster clubs for sports teams that help define the jock crowd or for performing groups that define the "band fags"—should alter these peer groups' behavioral norms and orientation toward adults.

Yet, adolescents' quest for autonomy and their need to construct a peer environment that is somewhat distinct from the adult world (62, 133) limit the degree of adult intervention that is acceptable. By examining how adults attempt and manage to influence crowds from a distance, researchers can increase our sense of how peer groups and peer cultures fit into the more adult-oriented contexts of teenagers' lives.

For some time, the tendency among researchers, educators, and policy makers has been to regard peer group relations as a disparate dimension of the adolescent experience—the locus of deviance and daring amidst other contexts that emphasize stability and conventional wisdom. But as information on peer groups accumulates, the similarities between this and other contexts of teenagers' lives become more striking than the differences. Like families, peer groups are best conceptualized not as a unitary entity but as a complex network of relationships. Cognitive and pubertal changes that transform family relations in adolescence also seem to have a major impact on the structuring of peer groups and the emergence of peer cultures. Social class and ethnic background not only influence students' academic orientations and opportunities in high school, but also shape the peer group system and delimit an individual's potential clique and crowd affiliations.

Beyond these superficial similarities there is evidence that other contexts have a more direct impact on peer groups. Parenting practices affect adolescents' orientations to peer cultures (51, 125), and the school environment helps define the array of peer groups that emerges in a community (34).

In other words, the false image of a universal, monolithic youth culture is giving way to a picture that is far more exciting: peer groups and peer cultures form a complex and dynamic context for adolescent development, one that is responsive to developmental changes characteristic of adolescence, and one whose structure and influence on adolescents is mediated by their gender and ethnic background, by their experiences in school and family, and by historical forces that shape their environment. By abandoning simplistic notions of peer groups, researchers and policy makers are in a much better position to discover the reality of teenage peer relations and recognize the potential for peer groups to serve as a crucial context for personal growth during adolescence.

8

SCHOOLS AND THE ADOLESCENT

Doris R. Entwisle

For adolescents a clear distinction separates "learning" from "schooling." Secondary schools certainly prompt some cognitive development and learning, but by adolescence the pace of cognitive development is slow—probably one-tenth as rapid as in elementary school (53). The major effect of secondary school is to create an environment that brings economic, political, and social forces to bear on *all* phases of development: the physical, by way of athletic and other programs; the social, by way of peer groups and organized activities; and the personal, emotional, moral, pre-vocational, and political, by a variety of means. Although enormous strides have been made in understanding cognitive processes over the past few decades (see Chapter 3 of this volume), little of the existing research pertains directly to secondary schooling.

The means by which schools shape the various strands of adolescent development are often unclear or controversial, in part because these strands are closely interwoven. For example, the transition from elementary to junior high school comes at about the same time as the onset of puberty. A major task for the future, then, is to improve our understanding of the reciprocal influences among these developmental strands. How does the pace of socioemotional development affect cognitive development, for example; or how does the political environment affect vocational aspirations? Furthermore, adolescents' personal and school histories extend backward in time, so paper personae in the form of school records shadow adolescents into secondary school. A key issue is the extent to which youngsters' growth is constrained, if at all, by the developmental trajectories into which they were launched *before* secondary school. Research "snapshots" of secondary school students are simply not sufficient for understanding adolescents and their schooling in any comprehensive fashion, because students' prior life experiences and the futures they have in mind for themselves matter too. Students who intend to go to college will function better because of that intention, while students who see only a bleak job market ahead may be tempted to drop out.

While this chapter will attempt to clarify how schools affect the process of adolescent development, its scope is necessarily limited. It does not deal with those pressing social issues that adolescents often bring with them into the school setting, such as drug and alcohol use; sexual behavior, including teenage pregnancy and AIDS; and delinquency and violence.

The chapter is organized around three major themes which are derived more from current knowledge of adolescents and their schools than from a set of logical principles. First, what effect does the schooling *process* have on development? By what means and to what extent do schools prompt adolescents' cognitive growth and other development? Second, what role is played by the *ecology* of the schools? How does the physical and social climate of a school intersect with adolescent development? Third, how does adolescents' schooling fit into a *life-course perspective?* How is the schooling of adolescents affected by earlier schooling, and how does the secondary school experience set the stage for development to follow?

Because researchers in each of these genres are concerned with different outcomes, the focus of their studies varies considerably. Research on school processes consists mainly of large-scale quantitative studies originally undertaken in response to interest in how schooling may both affect youngsters' life chances and promote social equity. Research on the ecology of schools, by contrast, focuses mainly on aspects of the organization of schools as institutions (for example, age grading, tracking) and on the social organization of student bodies (for example, minority enrollment). Finally, the more recent life-course research integrates aspects of the process and ecology themes but retains its own distinctive flavor. This perspective considers the school in relation to other social institutions such as the family and the workplace. It is particularly concerned with *change:* how, for example, do the physical and emotional life transitions that adolescents experience affect their schooling, and how does change in schools affect personal development?

Using these three themes as a backdrop, this chapter will highlight both current knowledge and topics that deserve further inquiry in order to frame a research agenda. Among the variables that have received inadequate attention are minority versus majority status and gender. Both are major determinants of school continuation.

The Schooling Process

Educational Attainment

Many large-scale studies of secondary schooling have focused on educational attainment (14, 52, 102, 103, 104). These studies are remarkable for their consensus that first, the effect of school quality (for example, library size) on differences in students' achievement is small; and second, achievement-test gains, on average, are small in high school (about 0.12 to 0.15 standard deviations per year) (53).

Ability and social class. The process approach to studying schools focuses on how adolescents fare as they are "processed" through them, and how their material and personal resources are converted into the credentials that govern their future life chances. Process research focuses on the number of years of schooling completed because it is the single best predictor of later occupational attainment. Individual attributes (for example, academic ability) and the family's socioeconomic status are the major constructs used to account for individual differences in achievement. A typical study of this genre (see 2 for a readable summary) assessed a national sample of forty thousand youths in 1955 and again in 1970, evaluating the effects of background variables such as sex, academic ability, and socioeconomic status. This study and others like it have found that ability and social class both contribute to school outcomes, although they tend to influence different kinds of outcomes. Ability is the dominant influence on class standing and self-concept; ability and social class contribute equally to the number of years of schooling completed; and class is the primary determinant of how parents, teachers, and peers influence students. For example, curriculum tracking is influenced more by social class than by a student's ability.

Both the school process genre and other styles of research come to the same conclusions about educational attainment. In a composite ten-year overview of the economic status of five thousand families making up a nationally representative sample, Duncan found that parental status affects children's subsequent socioeconomic standing primarily through its influence on the level of children's education (20).

Explaining background effects such as social status is problematic because the mechanisms of transmitting status through high school experiences are complicated. Perhaps these effects result from the efforts of high-status parents; or perhaps school counselors act as gatekeepers. "School quality" or "teacher quality," as measured by library size, the number of teachers with advanced degrees, and the like, has very little effect when the intake variables, or the students' own characteristics, are adequately controlled.

Noncognitive traits. Noncognitive traits are not included in most school process studies. In general, when factors such as anxiety, occupational aspirations, and outside interests are added to process models, they seem to make little difference (41, 84). While all have small effects, no particular factor seems more crucial than the others in its impact on school attainment. Effects of temperament and similar characteristics on educational performance during adolescence may be small because the major results of such variables are felt early in the schooling process, are factored into early achievement in primary school, and then affect later performance indirectly (27). While the impact of temperament, sociability, and similar factors on outcomes such as grade-point average and gains on test scores have been investigated, outcomes such as academic self-image have been neglected.

Extracurricular activities and sports. Extracurricular activities have also been studied as "add-ons" to the basic school process models. Using Equality of Educational Opportunity (EEO) data, Hanks and Eckland found that participation in athletics neither depresses nor particularly improves academic performance (44). For the majority of students, sports have little relevance, although this finding may not hold for blacks. Participation in other extracurricular activities, however, has relatively strong and favorable effects on academic performance and achievement, perhaps because such activities link students to the larger society of the school, especially to teachers.

Ethnic and gender differences in attainment. Minority students have native languages, dialects, and values that differ from those of the majority population, and they frequently experience either institutional or more individual discrimination. It is nonetheless essential to recognize diversity in the educational experience of various groups. Some, such as Asian Indians, Chinese, and Japanese, on average do better in school and attain higher levels of formal education than whites, while others (especially Puerto Ricans and Mexicans) compare less favorably (72). Parents' level of education and father's occupation also appear to be significant factors in minority group differences in educational attainment. Furthermore, intercohort comparisons show that the attainment of recent foreign-born cohorts is not much different from that of older foreign-born cohorts (72).

While some individuals in the less educationally advantaged minority groups do achieve academic success, researchers know very little about how and why this occurs. Information on the nature of the schooling process for minorities is derived mainly from comparisons between blacks and whites (19, 59, 90). In those comparisons, socioeconomic background seems less a factor for blacks than for whites, but particular racial differences in the schooling process are hard to pin down (40). Research on the ways in which families and schools interrelate and on the dynamics of student-teacher interaction in mixed-race classrooms offers several clues. It may turn out that ethnicity primarily affects school performance early, and then that effect is carried along. The impact of integration, for instance, appears to be felt most in the early years (70).

Both ability and socioeconomic status have been examined with respect to gender. Ability is more important than socioeconomic status for determining males' educational attainment (2), but the reverse is true for females. Even more discouraging, though, is the fact that women do not receive as much schooling as men even when ability and background are controlled. Although females have higher grade-point averages in high school, they do not complete as many years of schooling as males by age 30 (51). No doubt pressures to marry or have children, as well as sex-role stereotypes discouraging women from intellectual or scholarly pursuits, contribute to women's lower levels of education.

Dropouts

Preventing students from dropping out of school is a topic of considerable policy interest. It has, however, received less scientific study than other aspects of secondary schooling because most of the large-scale school process studies were based on students who remained in school. Analyses of more recent data (such as *High School and Beyond,* a national sample of high school sophomores followed for several years), indicate that the same factors that predict dropping out predict college attendance (87). Able students and those from advantaged backgrounds are more likely to stay in school than are their less advantaged counterparts; when these factors are controlled, however, blacks and Hispanics are *less* likely to drop out than non-Hispanic whites. In fact, when blacks and whites with similar test scores and high school grades are compared, blacks are actually somewhat *more* likely than whites to finish high school, to go to college, and to complete a college degree (1). Similar comparisons can be drawn with Hispanics. Despite even larger initial disparities in grades between whites and Hispanics, a small difference in college attendance favors Hispanics, even when statistical adjustments have been made. Put another way, the poor academic preparation and disadvantaged economic background of minority youngsters may account for their high dropout rate rather than factors such as greater family disruption or dialect differences. This is important news for educators and counselors of adolescents. Part of the handicap for minority students who experience family problems (including teenage pregnancy) is the widespread perception that school failure inevitably follows. A black woman who became pregnant as a teenager resists this stereotype: "I have beat the odds . . . I no longer wish to participate in this study of Blacks who are supposed to end up on welfare" (37, p. 146). Nevertheless, among minority students, competing needs such as for early work experience, and other factors such as heavy dating, increase the likelihood of dropping out (87). Early identification of potential dropouts is of utmost urgency. There is as yet, however, no solid prospective study of a "typical population," beginning in grade one and following students into high school. Nonetheless, the available evidence indicates that students with poor grades in elementary school, and those exhibiting in-school delinquency and truancy in the early grades, are likely to drop out of high school (69, 110, 115).

The Relationship between Education and Earnings for Minorities

Although more minority youth are staying in high school, the earnings of those who have only a high school education have decreased sharply over the past two decades (65). In fact, for males with less than a college degree, the earnings differential between whites and minorities has significantly increased (see Table 8.1). Students sense these trends. The realization that a high school diploma does not provide much currency in the mar-

Table 8.1. Racial breakdown of percent change in real mean annual earnings of civilian males 20 to 24 years old, 1973–1986 (1985 dollars).

Educational level	Race		
	Non-Hispanic White	Black	Hispanic
Dropouts	−42.4	−60.6	−27.3
High school graduates	−24.4	−43.8	−34.5
Some college	−11.4	−42.7	−21.2
College graduates	−5.6	+6.5	N.A.

Source: 120, p. 21.

ketplace, that the job market is bleak, or that it places little value on their current schooling lowers students' morale and makes them highly skeptical about the usefulness of schooling (114). In fact, for youth who do not go to college full time, high school grades and test scores have little effect on wages, even though employers benefit from the greater productivity of higher-achieving students. A major reason for this, Bishop states, is that employers rarely use school records when they make hiring decisions, either because they do not request the information or because schools are slow to respond (7).

Schools alone cannot make up for the pathologies of the larger society; it is an almost impossible task for some high schools to help students maintain a sense of self-worth and identity securely rooted in their prospects for the future. The emergence in many communities of partnerships between schools and businesses does seem to offer hope, however.

Implications for Future Research

The existence of particularly effective schools (those that produce the greatest gains on standardized tests), is sometimes seen as evidence that differences among schools *do* affect the achievement of poor and minority children. So far, however, research on effective schools has been plagued by conceptual and methodological shortcomings that call into question both the findings of the research and its utility as a model for future studies (92, 95). To begin with, the research does not invoke a conceptual model; even more problematic, though, are the difficulties with assessments of educational outcomes, the major criteria used so far. Using this research to draw conclusions about differences among schools is premature, although such studies may serve as sources of hypotheses for future testing.

More research on large aggregates of secondary students is probably not going to be productive. If we are to obtain a better understanding of educational issues related to gender and minority status, more work is needed on the specifics of classroom climate and school procedures (subjects I take up in the next section). There are provocative hints in the literature about factors that may play a role in students' achievement. Both the ethnic composition of the school and teachers' expectations appear to affect the performance of minority students. While teachers of low-achieving minority students have been found to be insufficiently challenging (85), desegregated settings apparently help blacks develop ambitions and aspirations for the future (50). In short, the features of schools that have to date been neglected in school process models may be critical.

Among the areas that urgently need further study are the impact of parental efforts, the social structure of desegregated schools, and the determinants of academic achievement in females. While researchers know that parents play a role in promoting the high achievement of some minority groups, the data are not yet conclusive. Parents' interest in and knowledgeability about the school appear to help (99), as do parental efforts to instill an awareness of racial barriers in black youth (8). In a similar vein, more studies are needed to understand school social structure in desegregated settings (42). We need to know more about how school climate, peer norms, situational opportunities, and costs to students of ethnic mixing shape social relations among adolescents in mixed settings. Similarly, we need to know more about how females interact with peers, teachers, and parents inside classrooms and elsewhere. Despite decreasing sex-related differences, there is still a well-documented performance gap in mathematics (33), the subject most relevant to high-level technical jobs. Subtle influences by parents, teachers, guidance counselors, and peers seem to explain the task values, performance levels, and curricular choices of girls, especially with regard to mathematics (22, 89).

Teachers can be a significant source of motivation for all students. Teachers' attitudes and support can make a difference. Brad, an 18-year-old just graduating from high school, puts it well: "My English teacher my junior year was one of the best teachers . . . She was tough; oh, wasn't she tough . . . So I respected her; almost feared her, but not quite—there's a fine line there. She liked me; I liked her. And she was tough and I knew it, so I worked up to her standards" (60, p. 462).

Social Ecology

While the process approach focuses mainly on the ways in which adolescents' backgrounds and personal characteristics help or hinder them as they are processed through schools, the social ecology approach emphasizes how social and organizational characteristics of the school impinge on adolescent development. What characteristics of schools seem to foster students' growth? This question has prompted considerable ethnographic and case-study research on secondary schools (66, 68). Such data is a valuable source of hypotheses because it provides the "thick description" that other styles of research cannot. This question has also prompted comparative studies of schools and classrooms on both a large and a small scale. For analytic convenience let us distinguish factors of *school organization* (for example, age grading and tracking) from those of *social demography* (for example, single-sex schools and minority enrollment).

One landmark study by Rutter and his colleagues combined the school process and school ecology approaches (97). It examined twelve London inner-city secondary schools, and by means of interviews and direct observation assessed a broad spectrum of outcomes, including academic achievement, school attendance, and delinquency. Although other research generally shows that the more able students are not held back academically by being placed with less able students, and the less able profit from learning with the more able, the Rutter study indicates that the social mix of students brought into a school, in particular the proportion of "problem" and less able students, seems to have a tipping point. As long as the proportion of such students is relatively low, they profit from associating with those who are more able or better off than themselves. Too high a proportion of problem students, however, leads to increased delinquency rates and poorer performance. This study also highlights factors such as good school standards, well-conducted lessons, and the existence of positive adult role models that improve students' performances.

Social Climate

In some ways a school populated by adolescents resembles a miniature society. Students have specialized roles assigned by gender and by "generation" (school class); in addition, the school is socially stratified according to how the individuals within it are valued, and symbolic rewards accrue to students in relation to this social stratification. The formal organizational structure of the school, supposedly in parallel with its pedagogic functions, may or may not conform with its social organization, however. For example, leaders among the student body in some schools have little concern for academic goals.

The consensus now is that adolescent subcultures are rather diverse and loosely structured (74). This view differs from Coleman's findings based on his pioneering study of the social ecology of high schools. He described an "adolescent society" in which students turned to peers rather than to parents for support, and in which students' values in some schools were diametrically opposed to those of the staff (13). More recent studies suggest that adolescents are profoundly influenced by parents, often more so than they are by peers (45, and Chapter 7 of this volume), and that social organization within schools is not as monolithic as Coleman's work suggested. Since adolescents are exquisitely sensitive to peers and peer group sentiments, effects of the informal social organization of the school on youngsters' socioemotional and academic development could equal or surpass effects of the school's formal organization (tracking, curriculum structure, and the like).

Teacher and Classroom Characteristics

There is little indication that traditional measures of teacher quality such as years of experience, advanced degrees, and various kinds of certification matter much; this is probably because the way those resources are deployed is a function of the bureaucratic environment (64). A multitude of studies in recent years suggest that a more important influence on achievement is the actions and attitudes teachers display in the classroom; the emphasis on academics, time spent on task, teachers' expectations, and classroom structure have all been related to differences in academic achievement (see 96 for a review). Regular homework assignments and evaluation of homework and class work are important, and such matters as covering material mandated by the curriculum may be critical. For example, in a recent nationwide study, low achievement in mathematics was explained to a large extent by the fact that students had not been taught the material covered in their texts (117). Very large variations between classes were noted in the extent to which core topics in the eighth-grade curriculum were taught. At the same time, a rigid concentration on curriculum may be counterproductive; flexibility on the part of the teacher and involvement of the students in activities probably are essential for fostering those aspects of cognitive development that are the hardest to measure, such as creativity, self-direction, and the ability to weigh and use evidence. Teachers must strike a balance between sticking to the lesson and allowing students to explore and be creative. Although much of the research on teacher and classroom characteristics has focused on the later years of elementary school (11, 12), it generalizes readily to secondary schooling and is a major focus of current research with adolescents.

Ability grouping in junior and senior high school is common. Yet findings on ability grouping (or tracking) are mixed (38). It is likely, but not certain, that tracking affects achievement, probably by creating variations in students' academic experiences. For example, the most successful and most skilled teachers are more often assigned to teach high-track classes. High-track students attain more advanced schooling, perhaps because they are exposed to more of the information needed for succeeding on college entrance exams. In addition, some evidence indicates that tracking counteracts racial and sexual inequalities because the assignment process favors blacks and females (39).

But tracking almost surely has costs that are hard to measure. One is that low-track students attempt to differentiate themselves from peers by distinguishing themselves as "smarter" than others. A dialogue between students in a low track during informal class time went as follows:

Kelvin: What page are you on?
Sandra: 47.
Kelvin: I'm way ahead of you. I'm smarter than all of them.
Sandra: No, I'm smarter than you.
Kelvin: No you ain't.
Sandra: You didn't even pass your test.
Kelvin: So, you can't catch up to me.
Sandra: Yes I could little boy.   (100, pp. 107–108)

Subtle effects of the classroom context contribute to sex-related differences in achievement, although research at the secondary level is sparse. Much of the gender gap in mathematics that emerges in the secondary years may have its origins in family and classroom experiences several years earlier, although the specific linkages have yet to be spelled out. In elementary school, for example, boys' grades and test scores are the same as girls', but teachers make more academic contact with boys and spend more time with them in math (63). Teachers' and parents' attitudes favoring boys in math in the early school years (28) may account for boys' advantage in the secondary years (22).

Differences in teachers' interactions with male and female students in mathematics classes are not universal at the secondary level (12), but where they do exist, they follow an increasingly distinct pattern with age. At the upper high school level, boys are the object of more disciplinary remarks but also of more jokes, personal statements, encouragement, and praise than girls. In lower-level high school classes the same patterns appear, although to a lesser degree, while in junior high few sex differences of this sort have been reported. Brophy believes that no conclusion can yet be drawn concerning the quality and quantity of differences by sex in science and mathematics instruction at the secondary level (12). They may be most pronounced for high-ability students (21), the more so because males are more likely than females to be assigned to high-ability groups in math (43).

Recent research indicates that the family plays an important role in the development of children's attitudes toward math, a significant determinant of the motivation to continue studying the subject. In particular, mothers (not teachers or fathers) are the critical socializers of sex differences in students' math attitudes and achievement. Mothers believe that math is harder for their daughters than for their sons and communicate this belief to their children. This expectation then affects the students' likelihood of persevering in math. Eccles (Parsons) found that students' motivation to continue studying math is predicted most directly by the value they place on mathematics courses and by their anxiety about math (21). The fact that adolescent girls place a lower value on math courses and therefore take fewer and lower-level math courses than boys is of wide concern because it precludes them from entering many careers later on.

School Organization

Age grading. Age, a major determinant of social organization in all segments of society, has particular prominence in schools. In the past few decades the decline in the age at which youngsters reach puberty has coincided with the emergence of the middle school. This new kind of school organization (grades six, seven, and eight or, less often, grades five, six, and seven under one roof) is designed to offer an environment that accommodates the special characteristics and needs of early adolescents. Research that justifies the middle school organization is hard to find, however.

Like most other major changes in the organization of schools, the shift to middle schools has been prompted more by intuition and political pressures than by scientific evidence. In theory, middle schools can adjust to the wide diversity among students at these ages. Becker found, for example, that grouping classes by ability and exposing students to multiple teachers benefit the more socioeconomically advantaged students in middle school, while their counterparts from less advantaged backgrounds do better when they are instructed by a limited number of teachers (6). But at present, middle schools generally do not combine these patterns. Instead they are split about equally between the elementary school pattern of self-contained classrooms and heterogeneous ability grouping and the high school pattern of separate ability tracks and multiple teachers (79). While one might not wish to use socioeconomic status as the sole determinant of middle school organizational patterns, they nevertheless could be tailored more than they are now to the learning needs of students of different backgrounds and abilities.

One particularly pressing need is for middle school learning environments to be matched to the developmental needs of students. Are current middle schools succeeding in this endeavor? When the school structures for seventh-graders in 6–8, 7–9, K–8, and 7–12 schools are compared, organizational structures of the 6–8 schools are found to differ substantially from those of the 7–9 schools (10). In terms of size, for example, the typical seventh-grader in the 6–8 school is one of 611 students, while the typical seventh-grader in the 7–9 school is one of 905 students. Smaller size sets the stage for a variety of adaptations in staffing, scheduling, and grouping, so the seventh-grader does not become "lost" in the school and is provided with strong, close adult support. Also, 6–8 schools are less departmentalized than 7–9 schools, although departmentalization is still the dominant pattern (in 79% of the 6–8 schools, compared to 96% of the 7–9 schools). Teachers of seventh-graders in 6–8 schools are more likely to engage in team teaching, to be subject-matter specialists (except in math), and to teach only one grade than are teachers in 7–9 schools. Thus, organizational factors in the 6–8 schools are more likely to promote academic and social development. But tracking—a potentially negative influence on the development of adolescent self-esteem and social relationships—is actually more prevalent for the typical seventh-grader in the 6–8 schools than in the 7–9 schools (10).

Relatively little research has compared the transition from elementary school to junior high with the transition from elementary to middle school. If the middle school transition were to precede the onset of puberty by a sufficient time, the piling up of multiple stresses (school change coupled with the rapid physical changes of puberty) might be avoided. We do not know this for certain, however. The question is further complicated because the shock of transition seems to affect girls more than boys (105, and Chapter 2 in this volume).

It is also worth noting that the appeal of the middle school structure may have little to do with the needs of the students themselves. Educators sometimes promote changes in schools to divert public attention from troublesome issues (such as the drop in SAT scores over the past few decades). The rise of the middle school also stems in part from an understandable desire to keep elementary schools devoted to prepubertal students. Many girls in grades five and six are pubertal and even postpubertal. While keeping them in K–6 elementary schools may not cause problems for the mature students themselves, it may create difficulties for the younger children.

Another latent but strong incentive pushing large urban school systems toward middle school reorganization is concern about dropouts. An earlier transition to middle school leads to an earlier transition to high school. When students move on to high school from middle school (at age 14), they are still far enough below the legal leaving age of 16 to effectively defuse the option to discontinue school. But when they make the transition after junior high (at age 15), they are less than a year away from the leaving age, and many find it easy to be come truants—de facto dropouts.

Public versus private. Lively debates have lately centered on the relative advantages of public as compared to private schools. The controversy began when Coleman, Hoffer, and Kilgore concluded that private schools are better than public schools at fostering achievement and at providing equal opportunity across ethnic and minority lines (15, 16). The conclusion that differences between the two types of schools are large has been challenged (56). In reanalyses of the data reported by Coleman and the others, Jencks (53) and Willms (121) concluded that juniors and seniors learn slightly more in private schools but that the evidence on equalization of opportunity for ethnic groups is only suggestive. Critics concede the need to examine other outcomes, however, such as differences between public and private schools in fostering religiosity, character building, and so forth.

Studies contrasting public and private schools also shed new light on how schools work. For example, it has been reported that Catholic schools, by restricting students' track choices, tend to counteract social differences among students (62). If schools offer many choices among courses, social differences are accentuated because information about the consequences of those choices is not equally available to all students.

A related issue—single-sex versus coeducational schools—has received much less research attention, in part because the number of single-sex schools in the United States has decreased in recent decades. In Britain, where the state educational system includes both kinds of schools, neither seems to have any marked advantage in terms of scholastic achievement (96). Previously optimistic findings showing that females and minorities learn more in reading and science in single-sex schools are questionable because of the selective intake of the schools (62, 93). That is, students in single-sex schools often have parents who have gone out of their way to provide an alternative kind of schooling for their youngsters; these parents may also do other things to help their children achieve. Thus, some of the presumptive effectiveness of such schools may be attributed to the special characteristics of their student bodies.

School size. No evidence that educators' intuition can be dead wrong is more compelling than that on the popular recommendation to expand the size of high schools (17). Subsequent research has unequivocally shown that relatively small secondary schools enhance personal development and prosocial behavior among adolescents (4), although school size makes no difference in achievement on standardized tests (14, 97). A student body between 500 and 1,000 students is now seen as optimal. Although the average size of high schools was estimated to be 787 in 1980–81, a size that is seen as optimal, the statistical "facts" are misleading. Relatively few high schools are actually this size; many are small (below 500), especially in rural areas, and many in urban areas have thousands of students. Averaged together, the data on high school size produce a falsely optimal picture.

Smaller schools have the advantage of offering more chances for each student to be featured in a key role. Because small schools have a limited pool of students available for activities, even marginal students are integrated into the social structure. Almost all schools have a newspaper, a student government, a band or orchestra, and so on, and the number of influential positions may not be much larger in a huge school than in a small one. It also appears that a small school is more responsive to its students: it is more flexible in both rewarding and punishing them, and it encourages more student participation in governance. Several studies have also found less negative behavior in small schools (80, 81). Finally, the effect of this socialization seems to persist. Students who have attended relatively small high schools go on to participate more actively in political, religious, community, sports, service, and other social activities (67).

Social Demography

More than 14 million students were enrolled in high schools (grades nine through twelve) in 1985 (118), with about 27% enrolled in schools with fewer than 300 students. Actually, over half of U.S. high schools and a little under a third of high school students are found in rural areas (9), a demographic pattern that has received remarkably little attention. Furthermore, severe poverty among youth is concentrated primarily in rural areas, not in the inner cities (20), and is especially severe in the South.

Ethnic and cultural diversity. Secondary school is the stage of schooling at which a particularly glaring gap appears between America's ideals of social equity and its disturbing failure to live up to those ideals. Before students reach the age of puberty, their schools tend to be rather homogeneous in terms of socioeconomic status, and both parents and students seem relatively open to ethnic pluralism. These circumstances may explain why attempts at desegregation have so far been most successful at the elementary level. In contrast, secondary schools span the time in life when many students are beginning to take a serious interest in members of the opposite sex. At this stage parents and students alike feel threatened by ethnic and cultural diversity in schools. These threats are usually perceived along ethnic or religious boundaries—black/white, Jew/non-Jew, and so on—but an even more powerful dividing line, and one not so explicitly recognized, is socioeconomic status. Middle-class parents often try to provide their children with relatively affluent peers by taking up residence in school districts where the level of family income is high or by placing their youngsters in "exclusive" (private) schools, either parochial or independent. Although the quality of instruction may be nominally at issue in these decisions, the basic force motivating parents is to provide their children with a competitive edge later in life in both the labor market and marriage. Parents often withdraw youngsters from integrated urban schools and place them in mixed-race private schools or in private schools where the level of religious diversity actually exceeds that in public schools; the difference is that average economic status is higher in these private schools.

Minority representation. Two causes can be identified for increases in minority enrollment in high school: a proportionately greater increase in numbers of black and Hispanic young people in the population compared to other groups; and a decrease in minority dropout rates, partly as a consequence of improving performance of minority groups relative to whites (55). The gap separating national test scores of blacks and whites, for example, has steadily diminished over the past two decades, and school attainment of most minority groups has improved relative to whites (72).

Reviews of desegregation research consistently report weak effects and find the benefits of desegregation to be less in secondary school than at earlier levels (30, 46, 91, 98, 111). Nevertheless, Jencks and Mayer conclude that the effects of a school's racial composition on its students' educational attainment are uncertain (54). From data collected in 1965 and 1972, the most recent available, they determined that northern blacks learned more in predominantly white than in predominantly black schools, but southern blacks did not. And despite agreement by most experts that a school's racial mix does not affect white students' achievement, they saw the evidence on this topic as equivocal. They did note, however, that whites who graduated from racially mixed high schools in 1972 were as likely to attend college as those who graduated from all-white high schools.

Desegregation plans with a metropolitan scope show greater gains in achievement for blacks, perhaps because such plans foster socioeconomic as well as racial integration. Generally, blacks' achievement is increased in schools that are mostly white (70), perhaps because teachers in predominantly middle-class desegregated schools pace their teaching to what they see as the average level of the class—which is higher than the level they would expect in a segregated black school (18). Minority students who have experienced desegregation seem to move more often and more successfully in desegregated settings as adults (78), and are more likely to work at white-collar occupations than are blacks who attended all-black schools (54). It is hard to tell whether this is a consequence of school experience per se, of parental motivation, or of socioeconomic status.

Large-scale studies of the effects of desegregation and race are seldom linked to internal classroom dynamics. Integration at the classroom level is more critical than integration at the school level, but classroom segregation often occurs owing to tracking by ability groups. Although teachers report that their behavior is the same toward black and white pupils, observations show that whites receive more praise and have more opportunities for sustained interaction than do blacks (70). Perhaps teachers have a socioeconomic bias independent of ethnicity; this would also be more disadvantageous for blacks than whites because blacks are generally not as well off as whites. Furthermore, a high school's average socioeconomic level may have a substantial effect on how much black (but not white) students learn (54).

A promising finding for minority groups is the consistently favorable impact of cooperative learning (109). When students work together in mixed-race groups, *all* students show improved problem-solving skills, perhaps because such groups promote equal-status contact, favorable norms, and other conditions that are otherwise difficult to achieve. Cooperative learning improves achievement, self-esteem, and intergroup relations for both white and minority children, probably because it fosters positive peer interaction. Although this kind of research was carried out with younger students, it has promising implications for secondary school students as well.

Implications for Future Research

More research is needed on the ways in which teachers interact with their classes. Detailed cross-national comparisons of secondary schooling practices are proving fruitful (116). Such research has highlighted the importance of the actual amount of instruction students receive, particularly in mathematics, a subject to which many American teachers give short shrift (117). More work is also needed on how well-known principles of human learning (intention to learn, distribution of practice, overlearning, and the like) can be used to improve classroom instruction.

More rigorous comparisons of transition effects for middle schools as compared to junior high schools are long overdue, and much more research is needed on how to tailor the organization of middle schools to the needs of early adolescents. We also need to know more about how characteristics of the student body such as level of ability or preparedness influence schooling (5). For example, schools and school districts that enroll less able students may adopt easier texts and set lower goals, even for those students who are exceptionally able.

School size is a particularly promising field for more research because it is directly controlled by school systems, and because the structure within a school can mitigate the effects of size. In many middle schools, for example, a separate administrative structure (vice principal, counselor, secretaries) and a distinct portion of the building are provided for each grade so as to personalize the treatment of students. A large, impersonal school may have a negative impact on teachers as well as students, with more teacher disaffection leading to more time lost from work, more requests for transfer, and less adequate instruction, although there is no research directly addressing this question. The effects of large schools on parental involvement also need investigation.

In relation to desegregation, future research should focus on the classroom level. Also, we know very little about how socioeconomic status interacts with ethnicity and race to affect schooling: little attention has been given to integration across socioeconomic boundaries except in terms of tracking studies. We do not know, for example, *why* blacks do better in schools that are mostly white or of a high average socioeconomic level (70).

Research is needed on "stopper" variables—rewards that change parents' and students' priorities (122). Besides superior curricula, these could include payments for students to stay in school or credits toward college expenses, as in the Lange-supported program in New York, which offers a free college education to elementary school students provided they do well and stay in school.

Life-Course Approach

The life-course approach offers a perspective that is enormously useful in understanding adolescents and their schooling because it emphasizes the way in which development is embedded in a social and temporal context. With respect to education, the life-course approach emphasizes the interaction between individuals and their school environments. It can thus embrace topics that fall into the area where family and school overlap, such as the consequences for adolescents' schooling of parents' marital disruption or of household moves. It also embraces the overlap between maturational processes and schooling, so that the timing of puberty is studied in relation to school change. Researchers have been particularly interested in the impact on a child of moving from a comfortable elementary school environment to a new, larger, more impersonal social milieu at a time when many students are struggling to deal with the physical and psychological changes of puberty. In addition, although most research asks how schools affect adolescents, the life-course perspective forces us to turn the question around and ask how adolescents affect their schools. This approach gets at the heart of the schooling process because it emphasizes the reciprocal and ongoing interactions between students and their schools.

This perspective expands and enriches the discussion of many of the topics covered earlier in this chapter. It calls attention to the effect of age-grading on students; and it emphasizes that life transitions, including those from one school to another, are times that students may find particularly difficult because a developmental mismatch can occur. For example, junior high school teachers often become more controlling at the very time when children are seeking increased autonomy; and the large, impersonal junior high school is not compatible with the needs of young adolescents for social recognition. The life-course perspective also directs attention to the longer-term consequences of schooling.

Early adolescence is associated with the change from elementary to middle or junior high school, middle adolescence with the transition into high school. The end of high school (through graduation or dropping out) is often taken as the first of a series of life events marking the transition into adulthood. The parallel between segments of the life course and the organizational structure of schools is no accident; schools are graded strictly by age, and students are "off-time" if they have been retained at any point along the line. At present it seems better not to hold students back, for then they have fewer friends and perhaps a lower opinion of themselves. Being off-time in school also leads to greater absenteeism (119) and is a direct predictor of dropping out (87). The impact of retention is a topic that cries out for more research.

Changing students' performance trajectories at the high school level is difficult. Despite the many uncertainties of the 1966 Coleman report, it convincingly established that, whatever the factors that hamper the schooling of minority and disadvantaged students, they take effect early (14). Bringing about significant improvement in adolescent achievement will probably require improving earlier school performance (3, 27). There is strong persistence in achievement trajectories, and the effects of social background are greatest at the earliest levels (71). And the social ecology of early schooling affects students later on as well (29, 47, 61, 113). More and more evidence indicates that the preschool years and the earliest grades are the most cost effective times for intervention.

School Transitions

Transitions are critical periods for students because they are points of maximum discontinuity and change. The transition into junior high often requires a shift from the intimate neighborhood elementary school with self-contained and personalized classrooms to the bureaucratized junior high with many teachers and hundreds of classmates. Transitions may also involve redefinition of social roles (26). Moving from elementary to junior high school increases stress for adolescents in part because students move from being "top dog" to "bottom dog" in the school social system (94, 105). But transitions are also strategic periods for study because variability among individuals tends to increase during such periods. Just as in a bicycle race a hill spreads cyclists out so it becomes easy to see who is leading and who is falling behind, so life transitions such as changing schools similarly challenge students, and differences among them tend to widen.

Early longitudinal studies of the transition from elementary school to junior high found that self-esteem of white females decreased with the change from sixth to seventh grade, but that of white males did not; black youngsters of both sexes seemed to negotiate the transition well in that their self-esteem increased (106, 107). These early studies did not find a decrease in self-esteem for white females moving to seventh grade in K–8 schools. In more recent work, when seventh-graders who had switched to junior high were compared with others still in a K–8 school, it was the junior high students who showed certain adverse effects such as negative attitudes toward school, lower self-esteem and fewer leadership roles for girls, and more victimization of boys (105). Furthermore, unfavorable outcomes for both sexes were noted in terms of participation in extracurricular activities, grade-point averages, and math achievement scores. In addition, many youngsters in junior high schools, especially girls, did not recover in middle adolescence from these earlier declines. Early-developing girls in grades six and seven performed less well academically and manifested more problem behavior in school than did late-developing girls.

Multiple changes such as divorce, a household move, and a switch from one school to another seem to put a considerable burden on an adolescent going through puberty and a school transition simultaneously. With regard to schools, developmental readiness must also be considered; children can be thrust too early out of childhood and into adolescence. The move to a large, impersonal junior high school at age 12 or 13 may just be too soon for some youngsters. The proximal social climate (teachers' attitudes, peer group status) is probably most significant for predicting how school change will affect students (83). Literature on classroom environments suggests that important grade-related changes in the school social environment accompany a general pattern of decline in schoolwork. After the move to junior high, students perceive critical differences: they report that teachers care less about them, are less friendly, and grade less fairly than elementary teachers (23, 24). Furthermore, when students move into junior high, the size of the student body increases; students are given fewer opportunities for interaction with the teacher; and student-teacher relations deteriorate. Grouping by ability becomes more rigid, grading becomes more rigorous, teachers exercise more control, and so on. All of these factors illustrate a lack of fit between the developmental needs of the adolescent and the educational environment (25); in other words, the social structure of the typical junior high greatly increases the psychological burdens on students at a time in life when their self-image is fragile.

Despite the increasing prevalence and popularity of middle schools, no scientific evidence validates the sweeping switch from junior high schools to middle schools. Simmons and Blyth's findings indicate that the better choice would be to return to the earlier K–8 and 9–12 pattern of school organization (105). To the extent that pubertal stress is a factor, then delaying the school transition until later in puberty would help the students adjust. More research is needed on social-structural factors that increase or reduce the stress of the transition out of elementary school, as well as on school size. For less able students, a less complex and more intimate organization seems preferable because it permits peer networks from elementary school to be maintained (see my discussion in the next section). The issue of school size for middle school students is probably even more critical than it is for high school students, but no studies have addressed this issue. In fact, relatively small school size, more than the range of ages or the need for fewer transitions in K–8 organization, could account for the relative advantages over other arrangements. Being in a secure, predictable, and responsive environment over the vulnerable years may be the best aid for young adolescents' affective and socioemotional development.

Peers and School

Peers are widely recognized as influencing adolescents' schooling. The school process models conceptualize peers as involving mainly a single best friend or at most a highly select few, whereas the school ecology approach conceptualizes peer effects in terms of popularity (weak ties). School process models estimate relatively weak effects of friends on a student's plans to go to college, perhaps because support from good friends is unconditional. In contrast, school ecology studies find that being in the "leading crowd" affects school performance strikingly: it enhances academic performance in schools where academic success is valued but weakens performance in schools where good grades are a social liability (13).

Peer climate is very much implicated in escalating stress during the transition to junior high: changing schools is painful because it disrupts peer networks and challenges peer group standing. Peer group issues need to be taken seriously because they significantly affect achievement and behavior. Youngsters who are rejected by school peers are at higher risk for dropping out later (88); there is also more delinquency among those who do not remain with the same peers (97). In one study, for example, students whose peer networks were preserved over the transition to high school exhibited greater academic success, better adjustment, and fewer psychological problems in comparison to a control group that experienced the "usual procedures" that disrupt peer networks (35). Furthermore, a four-year follow-up revealed that twice as many control-group students as experimental-group students later dropped out (34).

School Discontinuation

A youngster's decision not to stay in school is a turning point that determines life chances for years to come. Numerous studies have identified the characteristics of students at risk of dropping out. Less able students, older students, and disadvantaged youth are all more likely to drop out, as are youth from the South and West (87). Not surprisingly, those with less investment in school, as indicated by early work experience (for males) and many absences, are also more likely to drop out. In addition, tenth-graders are more likely to drop out of predominantly black than predominantly white schools, even with socioeconomic background controlled (54); perhaps this results from the prevalence of different norms in these schools. Finally, accelerated role transitions such as teenage parenthood generally have negative effects on school continuation (37) for both blacks and whites alike (87), especially for females. Another cost of adolescent parenthood may be the disruption of peer networks, which could also have a negative impact on the decision to stay in high school.

Many other factors associated with dropping out of school have been identified. What is lacking, however, is an understanding of the process or causal sequence that explains how these factors operate. For example, does being off-time lead to students' being labeled "slow," which then leads teachers and parents to expect less of individuals who have been retained? Does the retained student suffer from lowered self-esteem, which then interferes with subsequent efforts to learn? Equally important, however, is the need to identify those factors that guard against dropping out of school. The research to date has hinted at several such factors and has indicated that parental encouragement most strongly affects continuation decisions at the end of high school (71). More research is urgently needed to confirm and expand these results.

Family and School

Focusing on the life course reveals our lack of knowledge about the overlapping roles of family and school (see Chapter 6 of this volume). Families provide models for students, intentional or unintentional instruction, home environments that can favor or deter academic pursuits, and financial resources that can encourage or discourage staying in school. The emotional tone of the family setting may also help or hinder students. For example, stress and disorganization at home increase susceptibility to infections (82) and thus to greater absentee rates. In addition, the transition into junior high may coincide with the time of peak conflict between parents and adolescents and thereby accentuate the stress of the transition.

Events within the family such as marital disruption or household moves are known to increase the difficulty of the switch to junior high (108). Early research on family disruption and general school performance suggested that the effects of disruption are short-lived and most severely affect younger children, but more recent findings are less optimistic. In a national sample of white respondents, divorce was associated with relatively low educational attainment for children of both sexes (57). Children living with remarried mothers and stepfathers have more discipline problems at school than children living with both natural parents, with the effects of remarriage particularly negative for girls (58, 73, 101). The mechanisms by which divorce affects achievement in school are not fully understood, but there are several potential routes. Children in stepfamilies are less likely to receive help with homework (36), and children of single parents may have to spend a lot of time helping with younger children and performing household tasks. In addition, families often move soon after marital disruption and continue to experience more moves than do two-parent families (75). If normative transitions from one school to another are challenging, unexpected moves from school to school may be even more so, because they do not necessarily occur at a grade-change point and probably involve breaks with friends and peers.

Living in a mother-only family decreases the likelihood that youngsters will complete high school, and the longer this living arrangement continues, the greater the risk (76). Data from the 1980 census indicate that living with a single parent substantially diminishes the likelihood of a student's being enrolled in high school, even with current family income and mother's education controlled (77). For children of both sexes, living in a mother-only family increases the odds of dropping out of school by 122% among whites and by about 30% to 55% among other groups (blacks, several Hispanic groups, Native Americans). Living in a father-only family is not associated with dropping out of school among blacks, but it does increase the odds of dropping out by about 75% among Cubans and Asians and by about 50% among Mexicans and Puerto Ricans.

Compared to children in two-parent families, those in one-parent families have lower grade-point averages and more behavioral difficulties, but only minimally lower IQ (48). Single parents as a group tend to have lower income and less education than other parents, but factors besides these may affect school attainment. These include students' psychological difficulties after the separation of their parents (76), and the more negative perceptions that teachers have of children from single-parent homes (31). Although single mothers are more likely than married women to be employed outside the home, this in itself does not seem to have deleterious effects on youngsters' school achievement, except possibly for middle-class boys (123); in general, maternal employment is associated with better performance by children (49).

There is a tendency for parents to withdraw from school affairs after their children have left elementary school (112), but parent involvement affects school performance in a positive fashion regardless of age. Considerable research shows that parents' participation increases the effectiveness of schools at all levels (32), and middle school principals often try to maintain the involvement of parents who have been active in elementary school affairs. Although we know of no direct evidence, parental involvement may account for some of the advantages of relatively small school size. Parents as well as students are probably more active in smaller schools because of undermanning; they must pitch in and make costumes for school plays, help raise funds for school trips, drive students to athletic events at other schools, and the like.

Implications of the Life-Course Perspective for Future Research

There is a need to study individual students' life trajectories over the adolescent years, when students experience various kinds of changes at school and other stressful events. How is it that some children not only cope well over the adolescent years but appear to be strengthened by life events that are defeating to others? We need to know more about family influences on adolescents to understand their vulnerabilities and resilience in the face of stress and their ability to cope at school and elsewhere.

More research investigating peer group support and its relationship to school transitions would also be fruitful. It seems likely, for example, that peer support and gender and ethnicity interact; that is, students whose status is traditionally low (females, blacks) may be more adversely influenced by transitions (51), in part because they are more "affiliative" but also because their social status is lower and more problematic than that of white males.

We need more research investigating specific aspects of the classroom environment related to student "fit" and to teachers' actions. For example, it has been found that even when children themselves had weathered the transition from elementary to secondary school, secondary teachers rated their competence lower than elementary teachers rated a comparable group who had not made the transition (86).

More study of the early predictors or precursors of dropping out of school is essential. Although there are some studies predicting dropout from elementary school (69, 115), there is no broad-based prospective study of dropouts with data back to grade one or earlier. We need to understand the long-term effects of factors such as repeating a grade and excessive absenteeism. Right now there is strong political pressure to hold youngsters back (a policy that makes a school system's average test scores look better), although research findings on this issue are equivocal.

Future Directions

Knowledge about adolescents and their schools is fragmented, in many cases weak, and generally without much theoretical foundation. Some gaps are particularly notable. One is the lack of attention to issues such as the effect adolescents have on their schools. Most of what we know pertains to how schools affect adolescents—the old "socialization" approach. Life-course ideas, which strongly emphasize the role of individuals in shaping their own development, should create a better balance. We need more studies on the dialectic of development, in which notice is taken of how students and schools reciprocally influence each other.

Another major gap is the lack of theory. Schools as they are organized at present are not in accord either with theories of pedagogy or theories of control. Researchers are even at odds about the major typologies to apply to schooling. For example, there is disagreement as to whether an "adolescent society" actually exists, and if so, how critical it is for understanding schooling (see Chapter 7 of this volume). Our knowledge of adolescents' schooling is rarely linked to the psychology of learning or to cognitive research more generally (see Chapter 3 of this volume), although there are some promising leads along this line. The dearth of theory contributes to problems at every level; in the absence of theory it is difficult to integrate findings from different studies, to reconcile those that disagree, or to set research priorities. The life-course approach, although not a theory itself, has appeal precisely because it at least offers a set of concepts and a unifying perspective, thus opening up promising new lines of investigation in schooling research.

The large-scale quantitative studies of secondary school achievement have left a rich legacy, especially in telling us what is *not* important about schools. Differential contributions by schools to cognitive growth are extremely small at the secondary level, and recent controversies over private versus public schooling only reinforce this conclusion. The process of school achievement from this perspective is mainly driven by students' background and personal characteristics, especially their ability and socioeconomic status.

One likely reason for this is that students bring lengthy personal histories with them into secondary schools. By then their achievement trajectories, attitudes toward school, and outlook on life are fairly well set. Another reason is that cognitive growth at this stage in life is relatively slow (although this fact has perhaps not received the emphasis it deserves). Staying in school, however, is important for later success; additional years of education are still a ticket to many of life's advantages.

The value of a college education now seems on a par with what a high school diploma was worth a couple of generations ago, although not having a college education now seems to carry a heavier penalty in terms of expected earnings, particularly for minorities, than not having a high school education did previously. For reasons that have little to do with secondary schools themselves, a high school diploma cannot ensure young people even an entry-level job. Students and their teachers sense this truth but are powerless to deal with it. So as more and more education is required, secondary schooling becomes mainly a path toward opportunities for further education.

Recognizing the secondary school's limitations, we can at the same time list some of the qualities or circumstances that increase the ability of the secondary school to do its job well. One is size, with smaller and more intimate schools recommended on several counts. Another clear recommendation is to establish organizational patterns that overcome or diminish barriers to high performance by female students and minorities. Fracturing peer groups or coupling a school transition with pubertal change seems undesirable in general but is particularly harmful to girls. Careful attention to the student's individual schooling history, including peer group affiliations, is one effective route for improving students' school experience. Another route is to examine the specific nature of the classroom environment. How are teachers actually covering the curriculum, setting standards, and the like? As one would expect, youngsters in classrooms where teachers cover more of the curriculum learn more.

The social ecology of classrooms (or other units smaller than schools) is a particularly fertile area for more research. The use of peer tutoring, cooperative mixed-race learning groups, and other approaches that break down socioeconomic and racial boundaries within schools seem promising. Coaching students about how "the system" works is an additional way to help minority groups. Ethnographic or middle-range studies like that of Natriello and Dornbusch (85) reveal the discrepancies between parents' and students' perceptions of classroom behavior. It is important for teachers and others to realize that stressful life events such as divorce are probably no more disadvantageous, and may be even less disadvantageous, for minority than majority students, when level of economic disadvantage and other factors are taken into account.

The life-course perspective emphasizes the overlap between families, schools, and work. Family events such as marital disruption and household moves have negative consequences for school performance, as do dependence on welfare and teenage pregnancy (37). Yet individual success stories do occur despite what seem overwhelming odds. To understand why this occurs, we need to know more about how social change in the larger society affects adolescents and their schools (see Chapter 4 in this volume).

Valuable insights from the life-course approach include the importance of maintaining peer group structure across transitions and changing those aspects of classroom practices (such as more stringent grading) that intensify the difficulty of school transitions. The timing of transitions is much better understood than current school policy would indicate. There is serious question, for example, whether transitions to middle school are easier than transitions to junior high. So far a K–8 and 9–12 pattern of school organization seems optimal.

The life-course approach points out the interdependencies among various strands of development. School process models and research on school ecology have, with few exceptions, laid principal emphasis on achievement; they have generally ignored the biological and psychological aspects of human development, although obviously these interact with schooling. Achievement in math seems more negatively affected by the stress of transition than does verbal achievement, perhaps because the former is more closely tied to instruction in school. Additional research is obviously necessary on these factors, and particularly on the impact of school structure on females and minorities. Psychological and physical well-being and self-image are particularly vulnerable at transition points, and these are closely linked to the timing of puberty. At a more micro-level, we need to know more about the particulars of the interaction between psychological well-being and cognitive development.

School process research generally suggests that variables of personality type affect school outcomes very little, but this may not be true for particular phases of development or remain true when causal sequences over the life course are more carefully specified. Students will not always be happy, nor should they necessarily be, in the sense that challenge, if it is genuine, involves some degree of discomfort. At the same time, adolescents need schools where they can achieve a sense of satisfaction and where their growth can proceed in meaningful ways.

9

LEISURE, WORK, AND THE MASS MEDIA

Gary Alan Fine, Jeylan T. Mortimer, and Donald F. Roberts

In most research on adolescence, the family, school, and peer group are considered the major settings in which the socialization and development of young people occur. The structure and interpersonal dynamics of families, the factors that affect academic achievement, and the values and social influences of the peer group have received most of the attention. Yet this vision of adolescence fails to capture certain vital aspects of young peoples' lives. Adolescents spend a significant portion of their time engaged in leisure activities, including those that involve the mass media, as well as a substantial amount of time in the part-time labor force. This chapter draws attention to the nature and consequences of these activities.

Leisure activities occur in many settings and interpersonal contexts. For example, in one study of middle-class high school students it was found that leisure pursuits, such as socializing with others, engaging in hobbies and sports, and listening to music and watching television, accounted for 15% of youths' time at school, 47% of their time at home, and 58% of their time with peers (40). Leisure and media-related activities also take place in such informal settings as street corners, shopping malls, and neighborhood playing fields, and occur not only when adolescents are in the company of friends and family members but also when they are by themselves.

Informal paid work often begins prior to adolescence, and takes place in either the home or the neighborhood. During adolescence, however, young people move into the formal work place. With this change of venue comes a concomitant change in the interpersonal context of work. The work of children is often conducted in the presence of, or supervised by, adults; for girls it often involves the care of younger children. Adolescent work, in contrast, is highly segregated by age, and indeed has been described as "a bastion for the adolescent peer group" (81, p. 79). While many youngsters do work mainly in the company of their peers, a substantial number carry out their work activities alone.

Research on leisure, mass media, and work tends to be framed within a functionalist perspective which emphasizes that human activities serve purposes and have consequences. Work and leisure activities are believed to reflect current cultural values and to influence future tastes, attitudes, and behaviors. Research within the functionalist tradition considers both immediate and long-term consequences of the way in which adolescents play and work.

Studies that focus on short-range or adolescent outcomes address such issues as the influence of sexually explicit lyrics in popular music on adolescent sexual conduct, the effect of teenagers' participation in team sports on cooperation and competition in other contexts, and the effect of part-time paid employment on students' performance in school. As the last example implies, researchers sometimes turn their attention to the nature of the activities that work and leisure pursuits may displace. For instance, does part-time work take time and energy away from studies? Does television viewing supplant reading? Implicit in these questions is the notion that certain activities are more valuable, or have more important consequences, than others. Studies that focus on long-range adult outcomes or the socialization of future behavior consider issues such as the effect of adolescents' participation in sports and hobbies on adult leisure activities, or the impact of early job experience on the earning power of young adults.

Teenagers, however, are rarely concerned about the socialization function of their leisure and work activities. They engage in leisure pursuits because they are fun or they fill time. Not surprisingly, adolescents' moods are most positive and their activity level highest when they are participating in leisure activities rather than attending class or working at a part-time job (40). Nonetheless, many teenagers derive some enjoyment from their jobs, and are prepared to work long hours in order to earn the money that enables them to have fun in nonwork settings.

It is difficult to provide an integrated review of knowledge about leisure, mass media, and work during the adolescent years. Researchers in these fields come from different disciplines—sociology, communications, psychology—and these various disciplines have fostered somewhat different questions and methods of inquiry. Fruitful cross-disciplinary work has been carried out in many areas of adolescent development (for example, in this volume see Chapters 2, 5, and 17), but interdisciplinary research has not yet occurred in the area of work and leisure. Consequently, this chapter consists of three independent sections, each written by a different author.

Adolescence and Leisure

Youth is usually associated with a lightness of being, unbearable or not. Particularly in contemporary Western cultures (69, 102), adolescence is a "protected" status. High school and college seem the country clubs of the young; leisure serves as the emblem of their existence. Yet, in giving our children freedom, we expect them to take it seriously. When they do not, we find ourselves with a "youth problem." When generations do not mimic those that have come before or adapt themselves to the cadences of the adult community, elders intervene. Eventually the reality of work may be the most effective socializer of all; much "leisure deviance" is transitional (67, 164).

If adolescence is defined as a distinct time of life, the relevance of leisure becomes clear. Aside from schools, leisure is the social institution most closely associated with the world of adolescence. Although leisure can be understood as the sum of behaviors beyond social constraint or biological demand (*free* time), leisure can also be thought of as a "thing in itself"— not an absence but a presence.

Through the lens of leisure, adolescence can be conceptualized by several metaphors: adolescence as activity, adolescence as experience, adolescence as community, adolescence as culture, and adolescence as market. These images permit us to explore the dimensions of what leisure means to the adolescent and how it is used. Particular forms of leisure that characterize the period of time we call adolescence are highly culturally determined. Until two centuries ago the concept of adolescence was unknown in many societies, including western Europe and North America (see Chapter 4 in this volume). The expansion of schooling and the delay of participation in labor markets provided the structural and economic conditions that permitted this period of leisure. The leisure-time behavior of adolescents derives from reflections, translations, and inversions of adult and childhood activities.

Sex roles define leisure behaviors: teenage boys and girls have different leisure preferences (40). While one must be careful not to make claims that gender differences are universal, such differences in adolescent leisure are evident in the United States (35, 64), Nigeria (3), Sweden (51), Australia (68), Great Britain (24), and among Israeli Jews and Arabs (63). While differences between the sexes are not always consistent, there is a strong tendency for boys to prefer sports and vigorous activities. Preferences are primarily cultural. While there may be some physiological differences that affect interest in certain sports and physical activities, even here the primary feature that differentiates boys from girls is the relatively greater social support boys receive for participating in sports (103, 186).

Social class (and sometimes race and ethnicity) also seems to influence the kinds of leisure activity in which adolescents engage (51, 62, 71), although the evidence here is mixed (74, 149). While there has been little research on racial factors in leisure behavior, Stoll and Inbar's study of southern black and white adolescents suggests that sports and games are a particularly significant form of socialization for blacks, primarily because they can inculcate achievement values (177).

Adolescence as Activity

Because they enjoy relatively more free time and fewer responsibilities than adults, adolescents have large blocks of time to fill. Csikszentmihalyi and Larson found that, with the exclusion of sleeping, 40% of the time of their sample of American adolescents was spent on leisure (including socializing, sports and games, watching television, and so on); in contrast, 29% of their time was "productive" (spent, for example, working, studying, in class), and 31% of their time was spent on maintenance activities (errands, eating, and the like) (40). Adolescents choose leisure activities that they enjoy, given the cultural milieu in which they are embedded, and given the possibilities that their resources allow.

Some social worlds are set aside (by tradition at least) as domains where adolescents dominate. The boundaries are admittedly somewhat porous, so preadolescents and young adults may be included as well, but the major players are adolescents. Sports, games, and activities involving music are among the primary leisure arenas in which adolescents (typically males) participate. The sphere in which the adolescent presence is perhaps most notable is that of sports (34, 47, 98, 160), especially team sports. A series of ethnographic descriptions of adolescent sports underline their power to focus adolescent interest (97, 187). The sports world is still in practice a predominantly male world from which females may be excluded (21, 85), despite growth in the proportion of female participants since the enactment of Title IX.

Adolescents are the main participants in games and hobbies, particularly those that require considerable free time. In an ethnography of fantasy-role games, most players were high school students who left that intensive social scene behind only when they got a full-time job, became engaged, or began college or even graduate school (59). Video game parlors and pinball arcades are also populated by adolescents (101, 113, 136). As with sports, adolescent boys control these public leisure scenes. Girls' leisure activities have been less well studied, perhaps because they frequently occur in private settings rather than in public (119). Obtaining descriptions of the leisure patterns of girls requires further research (46, 95, 195).

Adolescence as Experience

Recognizing that adolescents engage in certain sets of behaviors more than other people do still does not explain why *these* activities? How are leisure activities experienced, and what values do they reinforce? Obviously those activities in which adolescents engage are those that they find enjoyable, or those that address their perceived needs and values (135, 138, 189). While space does not permit a detailed treatment of these needs, we should note that leisure activities allow adolescents to deal with the challenges of aggression and sexuality or to come to terms with both the desire for group membership and the need for solitude (40, 59, 145, 150).

Many motivational studies ask adolescents to complete a leisure preference survey from which various factors are extracted; these factors are then labeled by the researcher. Such an analysis generally does not provide access to the *lived experience* of adolescents, but the themes uncovered appear to have some validity, even when researchers disagree as to the number of relevant factors and how they should be named. Kleiber, Larson, and Csikszentmihalyi distinguish between "relaxed leisure" and "transitional activities" (104). The latter are those activities (sports, arts, hobbies) that prepare one for the serious aspects of adult roles and involve concentration and challenge. Ellis and Rademacher, analyzing the same data, find that a five-factor solution is also valid (50). Their five factors are learning activities, fantasy and imagery, transitional or expressive activities, resting, and socializing. This solution implies that analyses utilizing only two categories group together too many dissimilar activities, leading to an undifferentiated vision of adolescent experience.

These analyses of self-report questionnaire data should be supplemented with in-depth interviews, personal accounts, and texts from realistic novels (38, 152, 190), in which the immediate, locally situated experience of leisure can be understood. These detailed accounts, while posing problems of generalizability, add depth to the breadth of survey material. Since many adolescents are self-conscious about the "meaning" of their experiences, these data may reveal unexplored dimensions of adolescent self-image.

Adolescence as Community

In Chapter 7 of this volume B. Bradford Brown describes the relationship of adolescents to their peers (see also 17). Here we emphasize that much adolescent leisure takes place in the company of peers. We recognize the adolescent pastime of "hanging out." Adolescents value their peers; their peer network provides a community in which the dangers of performance failure are considerably reduced (105), notably in the challenging transition between childhood and adulthood. These peers represent a supportive audience for leisure; adolescence represents in this sense a "staging area" (58) in which crucial themes of age and gender are acted out.

The idea of community can be stretched beyond interpersonal relations to incorporate spatial implications. Ethnographies of adolescent gangs and informal groups reveal that adolescents do not just hang out, but they hang out in carefully defined and limited locations; many adolescent groups have a "territory." This is particularly noticeable in the case of youth gangs (4, 90, 95, 182), but it applies to nondelinquent adolescents as well (168). The sense of place may be as significant as the activity itself. The existence of a place of one's own, carved out of public territory, tells adolescents that they are a meaningful community. This is their location for leisure.

At one time (and still in some communities) the street corner was the preferred location for meeting and greeting. For many middle-class suburban adolescents the mall has replaced the corner (6, 99). While it was considered somewhat dangerous and unseemly for teenage girls to congregate in public places, a well-lighted, enclosed location such as a mall is now deemed more suitable. This change in environmental structure, along with changes in values, may make groups of adolescent girls more visible.

Teenage parties represent small-scale scenes in which the community can define itself and, through the actions of the participants, create a status structure. While little work has been conducted on parties (117, 167, 169), Clark argues that dance parties are significant in socializing black adolescents in cross-gender relations (30). The presence of peers in a semipublic situation puts a brake on excess intimacy and provides a moderately painless way for individuals to become sensitive to one another's feelings. Games such as spin the bottle provide a structure in which sexuality and interest in the opposite sex can be explored (179). By the end of adolescence, sexuality becomes hidden and drug and alcohol use becomes more public. In addition to teaching interpersonal skills with members of the opposite sex, parties provide an opportunity for "recreational deviance" (5, 105). Generally both sex and drugs are first provided in peer communities.

Adolescence as Culture

In any consideration of "youth," the term *culture* often comes to mind. Beyond activity, experience, and community, adolescents share meanings.

The idea of youth constituting a special, distinctive cultural category seems to be a product of the period of the Second World War. Talcott Parsons contended that youth constitutes a distinct social category with its own values—hedonism and irresponsibility (146). He traced these values to societal affluence and to the development of a set of information channels that link adolescents.

Scholars debate the extent to which there exists a single, unified youth culture based on the age of a population cohort (34, 116, 172), as opposed to a set of youth cultures that are grounded as much in class, gender, and ethnicity as in age. Those theorists who speak of a unified youth culture claim that the social conditions of youth (for example, years of schooling, degree of parental control) lead to a distinctive set of attitudes and cultural symbols (53, 131). Yet Brown argues that it makes little sense to speak of a monolithic youth culture—especially within a heterogeneous Western society (17). Just as adults have subgroups with their own cultural symbols, so do adolescents.

Through their identification with these group members, teenagers develop a shared sense of what constitutes proper *style* (91). This collective knowledge is most evident not in political formulations or in delinquent behavior but in identity claims (44, 181). While American researchers have tended to focus on the psychological conditions of adolescent leisure, their British colleagues have explored the cultural components of adolescence—the display of age categories. In particular they have chosen *not* to focus on middle-class teenagers; instead these researchers conduct ethnographic research with working-class youth.

Public symbols, such as hairstyle, clothes, and other identity claims (60) and badges of membership, in conjunction with leisure pursuits, have the effect of making youth categories more evident, both to members and to adults (61, 171). Those who argue for a class-based youth culture situate the development of culture in the political economy of society—the economic structure that channels youths into different forms of work and leisure as a function of production needs (15, 31, 130, 192). Youth culture cannot be separated from class culture (or the culture of gender). Tanner, in analyzing the proliferation of the British mods and skinheads of the 1960s, argues compellingly that both groups were ostensibly "working-class youth cultures," but actually represented different class factions with different needs in a rapidly changing British society (180). The mods, typically engaged in semiskilled manual occupations or low-status white-collar jobs, emphasized that middle-class cultural style to which they had a peripheral relation. The essence of their style was a "parody" of consumer society (91). The skinheads, more closely tied to working-class communities, celebrated and exaggerated working-class culture through their cultural styles, reflecting a collective sense that they were particularly threatened by the impact of social change and denying, rather than coming to terms with, bourgeois life-styles. A quick glance at tastes in music, clothing styles, and sports suggests that the less class-conscious American scene also has had distinct youth subcultures, such as punk, New Wave, yuppie, Ivy, and hippie styles. Racially based youth cultures may be the most dramatic example of these distinct traditions. The cultural symbols they adopt serve as markers that indicate who are members and who are outsiders.

Adolescence as Market

Once postwar baby boomers reached adolescence, it became clear that they represented a large market. This demographic bulge, coupled with Western affluence and the availability of considerable leisure time, made this group an inviting target for a variety of entrepreneurs (157). Given that adolescents save less than other age groups (100), their purchasing power is magnified. Virtually all of their money is spent on discretionary luxuries much connected to leisure (81).

Entrepreneurs, seeing this, appropriate the indigenous symbols of youth leisure, rebellion, and revolt, and translate them into consumer goods. The incorporation of black leather jackets or blue jeans into mainstream fashion is an indication of the change in cultural meaning of the identity symbols of an outsider group. The youth-oriented black markets of Eastern Europe indicate how powerful this urge to profit from culture can be (12). In addition to marketing symbols of youth subcultures, they provide a range of external cultural goods that can be used by style-conscious adolescents.

Perhaps the area in which a leisure-based adolescent market is most apparent is music. Since the 1950s the music industry has been largely underwritten by teenagers' cash (42). It is an industry to which numerous young people aspire and for which many train (13). With the possible exception of the other leisure industries of sports, movies, and television, there is probably no legal occupation in which a youth can earn so much and gain such public fame.

The industry requires a continuous stream of new products, music that, if it is to succeed, must be defined as innovative. Music preferences are fluid—one might say mercurial—but they are always central to identity for adolescents (30, 86, 105, 148). The disco craze of the late 1970s, the fashion for crossover country music, the popularity of Michael Jackson, the Beatles, or Elvis indicate the role that commercial music can play in defining youth. Recording companies must be sensitive to shifting tastes, even if their judgment is largely guesswork. These cultural texts (even if they are understood only as slogans) provide content for youth cultures. Again, one should emphasize that few musicians appeal to all adolescent groups; like adolescent cultural taste, taste in music is often segmented by class, gender, race, or region. In addition, musical entrepreneurs create spaces in which adolescents can gather (107, 163) and in which community can be enacted.

We cannot separate adolescent leisure from the economic structure in which such leisure is embedded. Economic realities affect activities, experience, community, and culture, just as components of adolescent leisure influence the market structure.

Leisure Socialization

Leisure, like all life experiences, socializes participants. But to what end? With respect to adolescent leisure, one can claim that leisure may have, under certain circumstances, three distinct effects: (1) Adolescents may be socialized to the adult world (that is, to the normative structures of society); (2) adolescents may be socialized to an oppositional youth culture; or (3) adolescents may be socialized to an oppositional adult world.

The prevailing view among American students of adolescent leisure is that leisure provides an arena in which young people are socialized to those challenges that will face them as adults. Leisure, despite all of its expressive, hedonistic functions, is fundamentally instrumental (138, 139). Organized as it often is outside the control of adult-dominated institutions (family, church, school, workplace), leisure provides opportunities for adolescents to structure their own lives. It brings the youth to an accommodation with a world outside home (105).

Some researchers extend this argument by suggesting that youthful leisure is a means of anticipatory socialization to future status (150, 156). Researchers have amassed considerable evidence that involvement in extracurricular activities affects later educational and occupational achievement and social integration (89, 142, 143, 174), although these studies typically examine boys' participation in extracurricular activities at school. Involvement in adolescent leisure may even have continuing effects twenty-four years later (70). Researchers found, for instance, that for the male subsample, both high school extracurricular activity and socializing were positively correlated with adult occupational prestige. No leisure factors were significantly associated with the occupational prestige of employed females, although for the whole female subsample socializing was negatively correlated with level of education. The greater involvement of women in the labor market and in a wider variety of occupational roles, however, may change this finding.

Others argue that although adolescent leisure can socialize participants, those effects are not to society as a whole but to particular class and gender positions within that society. The critical (Birmingham) school of British ethnographers sees an intimate connection between the leisure of the "lads" they study and their economic prospects. The leisure activities that youths have access to and are led to choose fit them into adult positions at work (95, 116, 180). If leisure is not necessarily causal, it is a facilitating variable.

Several researchers, discussing the socializing components of adolescent leisure, see this socialization as primarily internal. Early adolescents are socialized into their own youth cultures, and these have distinctively different values from the adult world. Roberts, Noble, and Duggan suggest that for adolescents, unemployment is not debilitating or stigmatizing, given the norms of their (working-class British) community (158; see also 92). Young people demand flexibility and leisure opportunities built into their work. Their allegedly poor work habits are, in effect, a different model of what the relationship between work and leisure should be. These values require a reconceptualization of unemployment. The worrisome hooliganism of British soccer fans has been seen as a particular response to adolescent needs—an attempt to develop an age-based status and sense of control in the face of adult pressures (115). The value structure of a particular cohort can be distinctively different than that found among other age groups.

Policy Issues

As must be evident, the discussion of adolescent leisure depends on the presuppositions of the researchers as well as on the particular social position of those being studied. During the past few decades there has been a call, particularly by American researchers, for more "leisure counseling" (66, 170). Others demand a greater involvement of social institutions such as schools in developing leisure programs (62). These researchers believe, despite somewhat uncertain support from the data, that leisure contributes to successful adolescent development and adult adjustment. This belief is particularly likely to be emphasized when leisure is seen as a bridge to the adult world (105). The response from this perspective is to involve experts in the leisure of teenagers, not to dismiss the subject as a matter of secondary importance (93, 116). In some instances this involvement may promote government control or direction in the leisure worlds of adolescents.

Doubters, however, noting the past failures of government attempts to control adolescent leisure (33, 131, 134), suggest that a laissez-faire attitude is preferable. Some domains of adolescent life should indeed be controlled by teenagers themselves—an approach that avoids increasing government bureaucracy and services for the sake of uncertain outcomes.

Adolescent leisure has been a source of concern for adults dating back to ancient Greece. The concern with pool halls mirrored in *The Music Man* later attached itself to pinball palaces, bowling alleys, rock concerts, head shops, video game parlors, and other locations in which adolescents gather. We worry about fantasy role-playing games, comic books, competitive sports, pornography, drinking, punk rock, unisex clothing, and, always, sex; adolescents are prone to "controversial leisure" (140). At times (during the 1930s) we have worried that there was a "poverty of leisure"; at other times (during the 1960s) we worried about too much leisure (138). Adults, because of their power over adolescents, have opportunities to turn the image of adolescent leisure into a folk devil, which must be eliminated or tamed in the name of societal stability and moral propriety.

In developing policies about adolescent leisure, we must stress caution and restraint. It is easy to react with anxiety or outrage at the doings of adolescents—sometimes to the satisfaction of adolescents themselves. Researchers should continue to describe patterns of adolescent leisure and analyze the connections to the other social spheres in which young people and adults function, recognizing that most, though not all, leisure styles are both transient and relatively innocuous. We owe it to our children to know them, to understand them, and to appreciate their cultural differences. We also owe them the presumption of trust. Leisure is rarely a social problem, though it is frequently seen as such. Careful research can dissipate the fog of misunderstanding, leading to a sympathetic resolution of the economic, medical, physical, and social problems that do weaken the fabric of adolescence.

Adolescence and Work

In studying adolescence, social scientists have given primary attention to the family, school, and peer group as central contexts for development. These emphases are very much in accord with a traditional view of the life course in which work follows the completion of secondary schooling. Yet secondary education and employment are increasingly becoming simultaneous activities. In the United States from 1953 to 1983 the percentage of boys aged 16 and 17 who were in the labor force while attending school increased from 29% to 36%; among girls, the corresponding figures actually doubled—from 18% to 36% (183). By 1987, 41% of high school students were in the labor force (184). But these official reports may be quite conservative estimates of the number of adolescents who work. When gauged by self-report, about 60% of high school sophomores and 75% of seniors indicate current or very recent employment (7, 8). In addition, in 1987 only 7% of a national sample of seniors reported that they had never worked for pay (8, 41, 114).

In the depression era young boys entered the labor market to help their families cope with the economic crisis brought on by unemployment of the main breadwinner (48). Girls, however, traditionally had lower rates of participation in the work force. The most recent statistics, as well as data obtained from student surveys, indicate that gender differences may have disappeared (8, 184), although Cherlin and Furstenberg's National Survey of Children (aged 11 to 16) indicates that girls are less likely to report employment than boys (196).

White students' employment rates are higher than those of minority groups (183). Among young people aged 16 and 17, the rate of employment for blacks is a little more than half that of whites (for boys, 23% as opposed to 42%; for girls, 24% compared to 42%). We know very little about other differences between ethnic groups in teenage employment. One study of ninth-graders found that the proportion of Hmong students from Laos who reported holding a steady job for pay (12%) was considerably smaller than the corresponding figure for the non-Hmong (52%) (122).

Adolescent employment is now frequently characterized as a middle-class phenomenon (81, 197), and there is some evidence that children of higher socioeconomic status begin to work outside their own homes at younger ages than their counterparts from more disadvantaged backgrounds (127). Not only are middle-class students more likely than lower-class teenagers to live near suburban shopping malls and other locations where "youth jobs" can be found, but they are also more likely to be successful in competing for jobs wherever they are found.

The intensity of employment, as measured by hours per week, also varies by social class and by gender. There is evidence that youths from lower socioeconomic strata, when they do find jobs, work longer hours than middle-class youths (165), and that boys work longer hours than girls. For example, among boys the typical employed sophomore spends fifteen hours working each week, while seniors work twenty-one hours; typical girls of the same ages work eleven and eighteen hours respectively (110). Given the amount of time committed to work, Greenberger and Steinberg (81) argue that for many students, adolescence can no longer be considered a "moratorium," a time for experimenting with different identities and exploring new interests.

The Meaning of Adolescent Work

The influx of students into the labor force has generally been viewed as a good thing. Seeing youth work as a means of counteracting the isolation of young people in the rather artificial environment of the school, which provides little contact with real-world problems and mature working adults (other than teachers), several national task forces have called for even more participation of young people in the labor force (23, 133, 144, 194). Adult commentators often stress the positive outcomes of youth employment. The potential benefits are legion: enhancing self-confidence and developing responsibility; making adolescents feel useful; adding to knowledge of the working world and the use of money; creating high occupational aspirations; and engendering positive work values and an appreciation of the value of education. Even the most simple tasks require some mobilization of effort and self-discipline (173). Through employment students learn the importance of coming to work and completing tasks on time, following directions, and being dependable. They learn to operate equipment and develop skills that may prove useful in later employment (27).

This sanguine view is supported by Elder's study, *Children of the Great Depression* (48). Boys whose parents had suffered economic losses were drawn into the labor force to help support their families; girls in similar circumstances benefited the family economy through labor-intensive housework and child care. These children, when compared to those who were not economically deprived, manifested a range of positive outcomes in adulthood, including (for boys) strong crystallization of occupational goals and career commitment. Elder and Rockwell attribute these benefits to the self-confidence gained from helping the family during its time of crisis (49). It is clear, however, that the historical context of employment for teenagers has changed.

Young people themselves, when asked about their motivations for employment, emphasize the monetary rewards, which tend to be used for immediate personal consumption or savings. Greenberger and Steinberg, in fact, argue that because most adolescents do not have to assume basic living expenses, working for the minimum wage generates a large disposable income that supports a high level of self-indulgent consumption (81). When asked how they spend their money from their jobs, employed ninth-graders most often said to buy clothing (70%); the next most frequently mentioned purpose was "to buy other things—like records, tapes, sports equipment, stereos, TVs, bikes, etc." (65%). This was followed by entertainment (62%); only 22% were saving for their future education, and only 7% admitted to giving money to their families (125). Adolescent contributions to the family coffer are generally quite rare (8), but more frequent among blacks than whites.

The Nature of Youth Work

The positive rhetoric surrounding the employment of young people appears to be predicated on the image of the apprentice actively learning a craft or skill under the guidance of a more experienced master. In previous eras young people worked on the farm, in factories, and in the crafts in positions that led to adult careers (81), but today teenagers work primarily in the retail and service sectors in positions earmarked for youth or for other transient workers. These positions provide little opportunity for advancement or for exercising authority, and the pay is low (79). Girls typically receive lower wages than boys (80). Tasks are often simple and repetitive (stocking shelves, cleaning, carrying), and therefore require little training, special skill, or knowledge acquired in school (82, 141). While the rhetoric of youth employment stresses the benefits of working cooperatively with others, Greenberger and Steinberg's research indicates that many youth jobs involve little interdependence with other workers, that, in fact, much time is spent working alone (79). The youth workplace, furthermore, is highly age segregated, offering little opportunity to emulate, or even have contact with, responsible adults.

Despite this general picture, it does not appear that adolescent workers uniformly view their jobs negatively. Some claim substantial autonomy at work: nearly half of Greenberger and Steinberg's sample of students in grades ten and eleven "felt they had some say in deciding what they themselves did at work" (81, p. 94). When Mortimer and Finch asked ninth-graders, "How much control do you have over the way you spend your time at work (over the order and the amount of time you work on the various part of your job)?" 56% answered "complete control" or "a great deal of control." Close to half described their jobs as "very" or "somewhat" challenging, and found them to be meaningful and important "almost always" or "often" (125).

Indirect Effects of Work Experience

Because of the central importance of the family, the peer group, and the school in adolescent development, it is likely that the impact of work experience will be largely mediated by these contexts. That is, the effects of adolescent employment will depend on how employment affects experiences and relationships in these sectors. If adolescent work limits the time spent with, and diminishes attachment to, parents, or interferes with developmentally valuable activities—whether academic or extracurricular—at school, the effects of work might then be considered indirect, operating through these experiences. Before considering the effects of employment on individual outcomes, we should first turn to the ways employment impinges on other adolescent relationships and activities.

Employed adolescents have been found to spend less time with their families than do nonworking teenagers (84), and boys who are working tend to have less close relationships with their family members (176). It has also been reported that working adolescents have less close relationships with peers (176). It seems that work likewise draws students away from school: employed students have been found to spend less time on homework, to be absent from school or tardy more frequently, to cut class more, and to be less involved in extracurricular activities (81). Further research should attend to the causal chains—both direct and indirect—through which adolescent work experiences affect key developmental outcomes.

Direct Effects of Employment

The formation of work-related orientations and identity are critical developmental tasks of adolescence (39, 52). In adolescence, awareness of one's distinctive abilities relative to peers emerges; a cognitive map of the occupational world is formed (73); and educational and occupational aspirations are developed. At this time critical decisions are made regarding courses to take in school (choices about math, science, and foreign languages may foreclose or facilitate later educational and career options) and track placement. Since orientations and accomplishments in adolescence set the stage for a lifelong process of socioeconomic achievement (55), social scientists have given primary attention to the effects of employment on achievement-related factors: to grades obtained in school, to the academic self-concept, to educational and occupational aspirations, and to early socioeconomic outcomes.

Greenberger and Steinberg's survey of workers in four California high schools is the most extensive study of youth work to date (81). In their sample, employment was associated with punctuality, dependability, and personal responsibility (77, 176). Consistent with these findings are those of D'Amico, who has reported evidence from the National Longitudinal Survey of the Labor Market Experience of Youth that employment at low intensity (less than twenty hours per week) lessens the likelihood that a student will drop out of school (41). Economists who have investigated attainments in the years immediately following high school have also noted that teenagers who were employed while in school have more stable employment histories and higher incomes than previously nonemployed youth (65, 121, 124).

Others, however, have pointed to achievement-related disadvantages of early employment, arguing that taking on adultlike responsibilities in the work setting interferes with making more beneficial educational investments. Analyses of data from the Youth in Transition Study, a national longitudinal study of adolescent boys followed from the tenth grade to five years beyond high school, found that those who had worked during high school had lower grade-point averages, less positive academic self-concepts, lower educational and occupational aspirations, and lower educational attainments five years after high school than those who had not worked (124). Those who were employed longer while in high school were more disadvantaged. Prior variables (socioeconomic background, ability, earlier academic self-concepts and achievement levels) could not explain these differences.

Since employed adolescents may work for few or many hours, it is important to examine the effects of the degree of investment in work for both contemporaneous and subsequent achievement outcomes. The Youth in Transition data indicate that adolescent educational and occupational aspirations diminish as hours spent working in high school increase (56). Time spent on homework, reported enjoyment of school (176), engagement in extracurricular activities, and grade-point average likewise appear to suffer with overinvestment in paid work (41, 110). Greenberger and Steinberg found that students who put in long hours at work (more than fifteen hours per week in the tenth grade and twenty per week in the eleventh) had lower grade-point averages (81). But other evidence with respect to grades is mixed (41, 96, 110, 165, 175, 176). Greenberger and Steinberg have argued that the absolute decline in grade point attributable to teenage employment is rather small. They further suggest that employed students maintain their grades, even while working long hours, by manipulating their schedules to avoid courses (for example, math, science, and foreign languages) that require a heavy investment of time. It could be that older students (seniors as opposed to juniors and sophomores) are more adept at selecting courses or that they have more opportunity to do so. Data from the Youth in Transition study indicate that long work hours depress grades for sophomores and juniors but not seniors (56).

Marsh reported that the average number of hours worked during the sophomore, junior, and senior years of high school had a negative effect on sixteen of twenty-two outcomes, including high school attendance, scores on standardized achievement tests, staying out of trouble, the number of academic credits obtained, academic self-concept, completion of homework, educational aspirations, and the likelihood of going to college (114). In his analyses, which used data from High School and Beyond's large representative sample of American youth, relevant background variables and the lagged dependent variables were controlled.

Finally, given the kinds of jobs most readily available to the young, working at this age can foster orientations that are precisely the opposite of those anticipated by the proponents of youth work. Greenberger and Steinberg found employment to be related to cynical attitudes toward work—for example, the notion that a person is "crazy" to do more work than he has to (81).

Relatively little attention has been given to developmental outcomes not directly related to career planning and achievement: for example, more general dimensions of the self-concept (self-esteem, personal efficacy), happiness, depression, and stress. Employment may create stresses and overloads for many young people at a stage of life when they have not yet developed adequate coping mechanisms. Greenberger and Steinberg present some evidence that working promotes escapist habits and means of coping with stress, mechanisms that may be counterproductive in the long run and detrimental to health as well (81). Employment was found to be associated with the use of cigarettes and marijuana (81, 175). Stressful work was related to alcohol and marijuana use for both sexes, and to school absences among girls (83). The National Survey of Children found that employed girls of 15 and 16 who worked long hours expressed less satisfaction with their lives than their nonemployed counterparts (196).

There is also evidence that adolescent workers, and especially those whose hours are long, engage in more school-related misbehavior (cheating, class disruption) and other forms of deviance (drug trafficking) (78, 161). In fact, the employed adolescent has opportunities for deviance not available to nonworking peers, such as providing goods and services to friends without pay, stealing money or goods, and misreporting on one's time card (161, 162).

Areas for Further Work

Although considerable research has examined the topic of youth employment, there are major deficiencies in the design of several prior studies. First, many of the findings thus far described are based on cross-sectional comparisons of workers and nonworkers; longitudinal research is sorely needed to separate selection effects from the consequences of working. That is, while the evidence clearly points to hours of work as a factor in reducing student achievement, those who are less academically able or interested in school may choose to work longer hours. Second, some research is based on nonrepresentative samples (for example, restricted to a particular social class); and many studies do not contain enough cases to compare racial and ethnic groups meaningfully. Third, investigators have sometimes preselected the cases to be studied, thereby introducing unknown biases. For example, in the most influential study to date, Greenberger and Steinberg examined mainly middle-class white youth, and compared middle-class students who had worked for the first time in grades ten and eleven with students who had never worked (81). Left out of the picture were all the students working at the time of the survey who had worked before the tenth grade, as well as those who were not working at the time but had held jobs earlier. Some of their findings emphasizing the detrimental consequences of working may be specific to those who begin to work relatively late in adolescence and may be less relevant to those with longer work histories.

Aside from these methodological problems, there are serious substantive gaps in the literature. A large body of research on adults has demonstrated that highly autonomous and substantively complex work has positive psychological outcomes, including those directly related to work (such as job satisfaction, degree of involvement, and intrinsic occupational values), as well as more general personal traits (for example, intellectual flexibility, self-esteem, self-confidence, self-directed orientations, trust in others, and less anxiety) (57, 106, 126, 128). Although many young people work alone, free of close supervision, their tasks are generally quite simple and repetitive. If adolescents respond to work similarly to adults, we would not expect these kinds of jobs to be developmentally beneficial.

In addressing this question, we must take into account the way young people themselves view their work. What may seem simplistic and repetitive from the standpoint of an objective observer may have a phenomenologically different meaning. We noted earlier that many youths describe their jobs quite positively. Work of any kind may be seen as a means of demonstrating responsibility and adultlike status, a way of preparing for subsequent careers, and a source of prestige among peers. Alternatively, it may have little salience but be viewed as just a way of earning some spending money, with few lasting consequences. These orientations could become self-fulfilling prophecies.

While Steinberg and his associates found few significant relationships between the objective characteristics of adolescent jobs and personal outcomes (175, 176) it is premature to conclude that what happens in the workplace makes no difference to adolescent development. Adolescents who take on jobs in formal employment settings are entering a new social role that is directly relevant to a central set of psychosocial tasks confronting them at this time of life. In some ways the new role of worker is similar to that of student (45, 129). But it involves quite different social definitions, rewards, and responsibilities. There is evidence that people are most vulnerable to change immediately after entering new social roles (87, 137, 185), and that young adult workers (ages 16 to 29) are more responsive in both positive and negative ways to the impacts of autonomy at work than older employees (111, 126).

We must pay much closer attention to the features of youth employment to understand fully the consequences of working. If adolescents' jobs are substantively complex, autonomous, and interesting, one might expect more positive outcomes; but if they involve little challenge or independence, negative results may follow. Mortimer and Finch found that autonomy and an intrinsic motivation toward work both have positive consequences for adolescent self-esteem (123). The amount and quality of contact with adults and peers on the job must also be considered, along with the novelty of these contacts. As Greenberger and Steinberg suggest, we must ask whether relationships at work—with co-workers, customers, or clients—expand the young person's social horizons, allowing contact with categories of persons who would otherwise not be encountered (81). Do these persons stimulate new perspectives? Do they channel youth in the direction of positive, prosocial behaviors, or do they stimulate deviant or harmful actions?

Researchers have given little attention to variations in the outcomes of working that may be conditional on gender, minority status, and socioeconomic background. In thinking about their future, girls tend to make vocational plans that are closely tied to their conception of themselves in future family roles. Decisions regarding marriage, the number and spacing of children, and the division of labor between the spouses become foremost considerations. It is unclear what effect employment among adolescent girls may have in the development of sex-role orientations and plans. Employment has been found to increase girls' (but not boys') self-reliance (77, 78) and intrinsic occupational values. It may have gender-specific implications for occupational aspirations as well.

While minority students are less likely to be employed than whites, the possibility of finding different consequences contingent on race or ethnicity remains to be explored. Because members of minority groups have greater difficulty in making a successful transition from school to permanent work, the meaning of early jobs may be quite different for them. For the minority student, or the student from a socioeconomically disadvantaged background, adolescent work experience may be a way of gaining skills and contacts that promote future occupational prospects. Williams and Kornblum, in their ethnographic study *Growing Up Poor*, note that "the most sought-after jobs are those that will 'look good when you apply for another job'" (191, p. 35). White, college-bound students may have quite different attitudes toward their part-time jobs.

The situation is further complicated by the adolescent's age. Most research has been restricted to adolescents in grades ten through twelve. Although most students now start working for pay outside their own homes by the age of 12 (127), we know little about the consequences of employment earlier in adolescence or about the nature of the adolescent "work career." Are there differences between those who make the transition from informal neighborhood-based work (babysitting, yard work), generally the first introduction to paid employment outside the home, to employment in formal employment settings (businesses and other organizations) earlier rather than later in their careers? Does the timing of this transition make any difference for subsequent outcomes?

Some preliminary evidence from a longitudinal study of one thousand ninth-graders in a midwestern city, mostly aged 14 and 15, indicates that the duration of the adolescent work history has some positive outcomes, especially for boys (127). Among boys, starting work early was found to have significant positive effects on grade-point average and educational plans (when the intensity of the work, or average number of hours worked per month, socioeconomic background, race, and mother's marital status and nationality are controlled). The National Survey of Children data show that employed boys aged 11 to 14 were happier than their nonworking counterparts. Teachers were also less likely to view boys of this age as behavior problems if the boys were employed six or more hours per week (196). These findings about young adolescents are definitely unexpected, given the predominant pattern of prior research findings based on older cohorts of youth.

Bronfenbrenner, in *The Ecology of Human Development,* contends that the effects of a given context on a person depend on more than what occurs in that context (16). They are also contingent on experiences and events in other settings (88, 198). We know very little about the ways in which policy-related interventions could alter the negative impacts of youth employment and promote more beneficial consequences. Whereas policies aimed at reducing the number of hours students are advised, or permitted, to work may seem to be reasonable, many adolescents are able to work long hours without suffering a decline in academic achievement. We need to know more about the reason for this variation. Is it located in the types of work experiences encountered; in stable ability-related, motivational, or other personality traits; or in the behaviors of work supervisors, teachers, parents, or other adults? Bronfenbrenner has argued that activities will have more beneficial personal consequences if they are understood and supported across developmental settings. Does it make a difference, as Greenberger and Steinberg suggest it does (81), if students are able to discuss their work experiences in their classes with teachers and peers; if teenagers can share their work experiences with their parents; or if parents approve or disapprove of their children's jobs? The answers to questions such as these must inform the development of social policy affecting the work experience of youth.

Adolescence and the Mass Media

A large empirical literature indicates that the mass media—television, radio, newspapers and magazines, records, video, and films—play formative roles in American teenagers' lives. Surveys demonstrate consistently high levels of media use. Experiments and field studies confirm that young people aged 12 to 18 learn from the media, that they voice concerns and attitudes that echo themes common in media messages, and that they behave in ways that reflect media content. Nevertheless, models of adolescent development have not guided research into the use and effects of the mass media, and the existing research tells us remarkably little about the role of the mass media in adolescence. Empirical work uses teenagers to examine media effects but seldom employs the media to investigate youth. It examines how teenagers respond to portrayals of violence, to political campaigns, or to sex-role stereotypes but seldom operates from the premise that adolescence locates abilities, interests, needs, and tasks that are uniquely relevant to how teenagers use and respond to media and messages.

Recent constructivist conceptualizations in media research, however, argue that the psychological and social baggage that audience members bring to the media plays an influential role in their use and interpretation of, and responses to, media and messages. To the extent that adolescence is conceived of as a special developmental period with unique needs, events, and demands, it is reasonable to assume that perspectives and tasks associated with the fundamental concerns of adolescence will influence how teenagers respond to media content (54).

Types of Outcomes

Research on adolescents and mass media can be organized in terms of time-related and content-related studies. The former are largely descriptive characterizations of kinds and amounts of media use. A few studies of this type address displacement issues, exploring whether the mass media take time from other activities. Fewer still view media use as a legitimate dependent variable (for example, as an important element in understanding how adolescents spend their time, or as an indicator of family and peer relations).

By far the most common type of research addresses whether and how exposure to different kinds of media content influences audience beliefs, attitudes, and behavior. Such research typically has an administrative or policy-oriented bent; it tends to respond to perceived or anticipated "social problems" (such as congressional calls for investigations of the impact of television violence). Often effects research is critical of media content, looks for presumed negative effects, and assumes a moralistic tone. Insofar as effects research has been conducted with adolescents, it is usually because the special status accorded minors in our society makes them a focus of policy-oriented research, or because they represent semicaptive samples of convenience, or both. Studies typically concern such issues as whether individual and social well-being are threatened by frequent or explicit portrayals of violent or sexist or racist behavior, or of sexual innuendo, or of consumerist values. Let us consider each of the two types of outcome in turn.

Time-related outcomes. If the amount of time devoted to an activity indicates its importance, then there is little question that the mass media play a significant role in adolescents' lives. Unfortunately, only one national sample survey has been conducted in the last decade (14), a period during which technological advances have changed the media environment dramatically. Nevertheless, numerous small-scale investigations, reviewed by Comstock and associates (36), Greenberg (76), and Roberts and Maccoby (155), reveal that teenagers typically spend a third or more of their waking hours with one or another of the mass media, either as a primary focus or as background for other activities.

Estimates of adolescent television viewing range from two to four hours per day, with a great deal of variation around the averages. Some watch little or no television, while others view as much as eight hours daily. Viewing peaks in early adolescence, then gradually declines in response to increasing interest in competing media and the demands of school and adolescent social life (36, 112, 120).

As television viewing declines, the use of music media—radio, records and tapes, music video—increases to four to six hours per day by middle adolescence. Again, the amount of listening varies greatly depending on such factors as age, peer group and family relations, and other time demands, but the stereotype of the "wired teenager" contains more truth than fiction (18, 20, 28, 178). As teenagers get older, movie attendance increases (over 50% of young people aged 12 through 17 report at least monthly attendance), and in recent years viewing of videocassettes has emerged as a common adolescent activity, with various studies reporting from five to ten hours per week (75, 188).

The use of print media also grows throughout the teenage years. Newspaper reading begins at around age 11 or 12 and gradually increases until 60% to 80% of late adolescents report at least some daily newspaper reading. Similarly, magazine and book reading slowly climbs until over a third of high school juniors and seniors claim daily magazine reading and over 20% daily reading of nonschool books, reports substantiated by sales figures for teen-oriented books and magazines (14, 32). Comic book reading, however, declines steadily from ages 10 to 18.

When time devoted to all of these media is combined, even allowing for instances when reading and listening, or even reading and television viewing occur simultaneously, the average adolescent spends roughly eight hours daily with some form of mass media.

Of course, one is hard-pressed to find an "average" adolescent. Large individual differences characterize all forms of teenage media use. In addition to the age differences just noted, such factors as gender, race and ethnicity, family socioeconomic status, and intelligence all locate differences in which media are used, to what extent, and for what purposes. For example, females tend to watch more television and listen to more music than do males; blacks view and listen more than whites, with black females forming the most avid audience (19, 20, 76, 178). Brighter teenagers are more likely to read the newspaper and news magazines and to watch television news (26, 166); print use is positively related and television viewing negatively related to family socioeconomic status, but listening to music manifests no relationship. The family communication environment—the degree to which a family makes an effort to maintain harmonious social relations and the degree to which it stresses examination and testing of new ideas—predicts both the kinds of media and the content that adolescents select (25).

Different mass media serve different social and psychological functions at different stages of adolescence. Television is a family medium, frequently viewed with parents and siblings. This may explain why adolescents who report difficulties with peers and with social relationships tend to be heavy television viewers, as well as why older teenagers engaged in establishing independence from the family watch less (109). Listening to music is largely an individual activity, occasionally engaged in with friends but seldom with the family (108), although peer groups exert a strong influence on musical preferences (159). There has been almost no research on the topic, but movies and video cassettes appear to be peer group media. Schramm, Lyle, and Parker long ago described adolescent moviegoing as a social activity (166), and video cassettes seem to serve the same function. Adolescents commonly rent and watch videos in groups, and one suspects that the combination of pressure and bravado inherent in the adolescent peer group context helps to explain why much adolescent video viewing involves R-rated and even X-rated films.

Concern is often voiced that time spent with the mass media, especially television, adversely affects other activities, particularly schoolwork. This *displacement hypothesis* posits that television viewing replaces more "valuable" activities such as reading or homework, thus harming academic performance. Reports of negative relationships between amount of viewing and various measures of adolescent academic performance, however, seldom withstand controls for third variables such as socioeconomic status and IQ. Moreover, the few studies that examine the relationship between television viewing and academic performance over time generally fail to find evidence supporting causal interpretations of the correlations. It appears that poor academic performance is at least as likely to engender viewing as the reverse (94, 132, 153). Although watching television takes time from the use of similar media such as radio and the movies (just as video cassette viewing may diminish time spent watching broadcast television), the bulk of time devoted to the medium comes from unmeasured activities, those marginal or "unimportant" pastimes that seldom receive attention when social scientists measure time budgets. It remains to be examined whether such marginal activities are really unimportant, or whether the kinds of "down time" they represent play a significant role in adolescent development (132).

Content-related outcomes. Many discussions of mass media presume large and direct effects of content. They commonly assume that viewing x hours of television violence (or commercial appeals or sex-role stereotypes) or hearing y hours of "pro-drug" (or pro-sex, or pro-rebellion) music will almost automatically lead viewers or listeners to accept and adopt the attitudes and behaviors manifested in what they see and hear. All that exposure, it is argued, must engender massive effects, especially among youngsters, who are particularly vulnerable (9, 72, 151, 193).

Empirical research, however, paints a somewhat different picture (118, 155). People can and do learn from media messages. Children, adolescents, and adults have all been shown to acquire a wide variety of information, ideas, attitudes, and behaviors from the mass media, particularly from television. Moreover, a growing literature details how various content characteristics (portrayal of consequences, model attributes, salience and complexity of information, and so on) and context characteristics (presence of a co-viewer, opportunity to practice, cues in the performance setting) influence the probability of both learning and acting on media messages (11, 36, 147, 155). But even experimental studies, which ensure high levels of audience exposure and attention, and measurement situations engineered to elicit enactment of what has been learned generally produce relatively small effects (18).

One reason for the absence of large effects is that most studies leave the definition of what constitutes a relevant or meaningful outcome to whoever conducts (or funds) the study. Thus, a teenager who learns fear from a television portrayal of violence will be counted as "unaffected" by a researcher interested in television's influence on aggressive behavior. And whether aggression or fear (or some other "lesson") is learned, or even perceived, depends as much on the viewer as it does on the manifest message.

The mass media are no different from other information sources in that there are tremendous variations in what people attend to, in what sense they make of it, and in the conditions that mediate subsequent action based on what has been absorbed (10). Just as parental advice may engender dramatically different responses from a first and a fourth child, so too a television situation comedy may affect the beliefs and behaviors of a child in seventh or twelfth grade, a boy or a girl, a black or a Hispanic teenager in quite different ways. Differences in perspective, need, abilities, and interests all exert strong influences on how information is processed. The question, then, is not whether adolescents learn from the mass media, but which adolescents learn what, under which conditions, and, most important, to what end.

Adolescent Development and Media Effects

Models of adolescent development sometimes differ in the number or nature of fundamental tasks they posit, or in the labels attached to those tasks. Most concur, however, that the central work of adolescence includes developing a positive body image, beginning to achieve economic and emotional independence and freedom from authority, more completely defining sex roles and learning about relationships with the opposite sex, preparing for future occupational and family roles, and developing civic competence (1, 37, 54).

An individual-differences approach guided by models of adolescent development seems particularly appropriate. Since adolescents generally are at least entering the latter stages of cognitive development, their seeking and processing of information is more a function of what they are motivated to do than of what they can do. Moreover, the teenage years are a period of intense information-gathering activity about the future, characterized by increasing control over ways to satisfy information needs. Finally, and perhaps most important, adolescence is a time when one or another of these developmental issues is likely to consume much of a given teenager's social, psychological, and cognitive energy (54). It follows that the mass media serve as increasingly useful sources of information for teenagers, and that the particular developmental issue an adolescent is confronting significantly influences which aspect of a media message he or she attends to and how it is processed.

Information relevant to various adolescent developmental tasks is readily available in the mass media, indeed often within the same message. For example, a single episode of a situation comedy portraying a family crisis over one child's threat to drop out of college and another's dilemma about whether or not to kiss on a first date may present quite different messages to adolescent viewers confronting different problems. One viewer may attend to the nature of the parent-child interaction, seeking new ways to assert independence; another may focus on the arguments for and against completing (or even beginning) college; a third may view the show solely in terms of behavior with the opposite sex in anticipation of the coming weekend's possibilities. What each one takes *from* the program will be affected by the individual perspectives, needs, and concerns that each brings *to* the program—all at least partly mediated by the particular developmental task (or tasks) being dealt with at any given time. Obviously various other content-related, contextual, and individual factors such as peer and family relations, personal experiences, and intellectual abilities will also intervene in the learning process. Nevertheless, models of adolescent development will help to guide and sharpen questions about the effects of the mass media on teenagers.

Many studies have used teenagers to examine the effects of media content, and some of those studies are relevant to the developmental tasks listed earlier. For example, experiments demonstrate that adolescents exposed to televised portrayals of sex-role and ethnic stereotypes or unusual occupations or the Bill of Rights are more likely than unexposed counterparts to learn about, and sometimes behave on the basis of, the information (29, 75). Similarly, correlational studies show that teenagers who attend more to news and public affairs media are more politically knowledgeable and active (26), that girls who watch a lot of television espouse more traditional sex-role beliefs, that frequent soap opera viewers give higher estimates of actual rates of divorce and illegitimacy, that viewing crime-action shows correlates positively with knowledge of arrest rights but negatively with attitudes favoring civil liberties (22, 43).

We also know that different teenagers respond differently to the same media messages. Television violence, for example, has more of an impact on white than on black teenage boys, possibly because so many action-adventure protagonists are single white males. Similarly, girls are more accepting than boys of nonsexist portrayals of female behavior, while boys (but not girls) who view a great many soap operas tend to express concern about the fragility of relationships (2). Several reviews summarize this literature (29, 36, 76, 147, 154, 155).

Missing, however, is any extensive consideration of how adolescent development influences teenagers' selection and interpretation of media messages, and any empirical research that proceeds from the recognition that adolescence locates interests, needs, perspectives, and tasks that are uniquely relevant to how teenagers use and respond to media. Until work proceeds from this perspective, our understanding of the role of the mass media in adolescent development will remain sketchy at best.

In the same vein, we need to recognize that the term *media research* is a misnomer. With the exception of work on types of media use and on adolescent political socialization, most research focuses on television; the other media are largely ignored. This is no trivial oversight considering that adolescents spend more time with radio than with television, that much of radio and many films, videos, and print materials are produced primarily for adolescents, and that those media aimed specifically at teenagers tend to be used either in isolation or within the peer group, places where parental or other adult mediation is least likely.

Finally, it is time to conceive of media use as a dependent as well as an independent variable. Between the two questions "What is rock music doing to our children?" and "Why are our children devoting so much attention to rock music?" the answer to the latter may be the more informative. It is necessary to ask whether and how various mass media messages influence adolescents' beliefs, values, and behavior. But it also seems wise to ask what their behavior with regard to the media tells us about their knowledge, beliefs, and values.

The three disparate areas of research reviewed in this chapter draw attention to the importance of leisure, mass media, and work in the lives of today's adolescents. Young people clearly value these activities, at least as can be judged by the amount of time teenagers voluntarily choose to devote to them. To date, however, research findings on these topics have been limited in that they are derived from studies that are atheoretical, and based on cross-sectional and correlational data. As a result, the findings lack the impetus and direction that can come from theories that seek to identify and systematize the key broad questions. Furthermore, cause and effect remain intertwined, so that it is virtually impossible to disentangle, for example, whether devoting many hours to violent fantasy games causes typical teenagers to become more violent, appeals to adolescents already fascinated with violence, or has minimal effect on actual behavior.

This brief review underscores the need for attention to what adolescents do when they are not in formal educational or family settings. Leisure and work settings offer potentially exciting new dimensions to many of the central questions about development that are addressed throughout this volume. Effective utilization of such opportunities will require innovative methodologies and research designs. One key point, however, is clear: the time is ripe for researchers to broaden their focus to include a wider range of activities and sites in which adolescent development occurs.

PART THREE

Psychosocial Issues

The bulk of research on normal adolescent development has sought to identify and elucidate key processes that characterize this phase of life. Among these are physical and sexual maturation, major changes in relationships with family members and with peers, and a growing awareness of and interest in both oneself and the wider world. The chapters in this section examine what investigators have learned about such vital issues, discuss gaps in the existing literature, and point to some especially promising leads for future research.

The first several chapters parallel earlier ones on context. For example, Chapter 10 discusses the role of the family in helping adolescents achieve autonomy and connectedness. Chapter 11 describes the diverse processes of peer relations that occur within the context of peer groups. And Chapter 12 focuses on issues of achievement and performance, many of which are played out most powerfully in the school. The possible effects of ethnicity and minority status are so important and pervasive that available information is reviewed in each of the chapters.

Chapters 13 to 15 highlight processes that largely serve to define the individual. These include burgeoning sexual awareness and interest, an emerging sense of self, and maturing coping styles. Chapter 16 considers how a better understanding of teenagers who engage in behaviors that may be problematic for themselves or society can illuminate fundamental aspects of normal development. Chapter 17 surveys the topic of health, indicating what is known about how adolescents deal with matters that may affect physical well-being, both immediately and over the long term. Finally, Chapter 18 considers the impact of young people's heightened attention to societal processes. As these chapters amply document, researchers are making exciting progress toward elucidating the central tasks of adolescence, even though much remains to be done.

Despite the impressive array of topics included in this section, some crucial aspects of adolescence are conspicuously missing from both the existing literature and this volume. Most notably absent is the adolescent voice. Too little, still, is known about the internal life of the individual teenager. The picture presented often implies a sense of rationality and purpose that seems more likely to have been imposed by the adult viewer than by adolescents themselves. Interestingly, little is known yet about how young people become aware of and begin to try to deal with emotions, despite the obvious importance of affect in all aspects of life. Also needed is more research on how they acquire a defined set of personal values and a sense of morality. In short, the field has done much to define and study the key components of adolescence, but it has been much less successful in considering those aspects that help to make this period of development such an intensely personal and powerful experience for each of us.

10

AUTONOMY, CONFLICT, AND HARMONY IN THE FAMILY RELATIONSHIP

Laurence Steinberg

Although the popular and clinically influenced stereotype of the adolescent's family as a crucible of intrafamilial tension and hostility has not been confirmed in empirical studies of teenagers and their parents, research has shown that the second decade of a child's life—and, in particular, the first few years of this decade—is a critical time for the realignment and redefinition of family ties. Parent-child relations do not seem to be reconstituted in any dramatic way during the transition from childhood into adolescence, but they nevertheless are transformed in subtle yet significant respects (11). The purpose of this chapter is to examine the nature of and influences on this set of relational transformations.

It is important to note at the outset what this chapter will *not* cover. Although I will consider the ways in which various demographic factors—especially household composition—may moderate patterns of relational change during adolescence, studies of the impact of these demographic factors in their own right are reviewed by Furstenberg (see Chapter 6 in this volume). Similarly, while the implications of changing family dynamics for adolescent development will be noted from time to time, more thorough discussions of the family's role in adolescent development are to be found in Chapters 12 through 16. Finally, because this chapter, like the volume it is a part of, emphasizes research and theory about the developing youth as an individual, I do not focus on the family as a system, nor do I examine marital or sibling relationships in families with adolescent children. Although crucial transformations in these relationships may occur during the teenage years, space considerations preclude coverage of these topics.

Theoretical Considerations

The Psychoanalytic Legacy

I want to note at the outset the profound influence that psychoanalytic models have had in shaping and defining the empirical agenda in this area. The work of A. Freud (23), in particular, has directed the attention of students of adolescent family relations to describing and understanding the process through which adolescents detach themselves from their parents. According to this view, the process of detachment, triggered by the biological changes of puberty and their sexual sequelae, is characterized by intrafamilial storm and stress, and adolescent rebellion is viewed as both an inevitable and normative response to this "second oedipal" event (1). From the analytic vantage point, the development of autonomy during adolescence is conceptualized as autonomy *from* parents; parent-adolescent conflict is seen as both a normative manifestation of the detachment process and as a necessary stimulus to the process; and parent-adolescent harmony, at least in the extreme, is viewed as developmentally stunting and symptomatic of intrapsychic immaturity. Indeed, as Freud wrote:

> We all know individual children who as late as the ages of fourteen, fifteen, or sixteen show no . . . outer evidence of inner unrest. They remain, as they have been during the latency period, "good" children, wrapped up in their family relationships, considerate sons of their mothers, submissive to their fathers, in accord with the atmosphere, ideas, and ideals of their childhood background. Convenient as this may be, it signifies a delay of normal development and is, as such, a sign to be taken seriously. (23, 264–265)

The implications of the psychoanalytic view of adolescence for the study of family relationships have been many. The chief legacy is the notion that conflict and detachment, rather than harmony and attachment, characterize normal family life during this period of development. As a result, most research has been biased toward the study of the extent to which, the ways in which, and the reasons why adolescents and their parents grow apart, to the exclusion of research on the ways in which close family ties are maintained (or perhaps become even closer). Far more is known about the nature of parent-adolescent conflict and ideological differences between the generations than about the nature of parent-adolescent closeness or intergenerational similarity. As will be evident, this imbalance is especially ironic in light of research on representative populations of young people and parents which indicates that harmony is a far more pervasive feature of family life during this period than is contentiousness (18, 40, 49), and that the values and attitudes of adults and youth are more alike than different (13).

A second influence of the psychoanalytic view concerns the issue of discontinuity (12). The theory holds that detachment abruptly terminates the latency, or preadolescent, period. In response to the resurgence of latent drives—mainly, but not exclusively, sexual drives—the formerly obedient and respectful young adolescent "regresses" to a more psychologically primitive state and turns spiteful, vengeful, oppositional, and unpredictable (23). As Adelson and Doehrman note: "The boy may suddenly turn surly or sullen or cocky or competitive or scornful vis-a-vis his father; the girl may treat her mother with withering scorn or her most patronizing, brittle 'friendliness,' or may be overcome with dark, inexplicable rages" (1, p. 101). An important implication of this disjunctive view of adolescence is the belief that a prior history of parent-child harmony is more or less irrelevant to the development of parent-child relations in adolescence; the overpowering libidinal forces of puberty are believed to imperil even the most sturdy of relational foundations. This emphasis on adolescent upheaval and its unpredictability has steered researchers away from studying the continuities between family relations in childhood and those in adolescence. Perhaps as a consequence of this view, no studies exist of the ways in which earlier family characteristics (for example, levels of harmony or conflict) moderate the nature of the family's transition into adolescence.

Neoanalytic Revisions and Extensions

Orthodox analytic views of the detachment process have given way to more tempered neoanalytic theories that emphasize the process of adolescent individuation rather than detachment. The primary proponent of this theoretical orientation is Blos, who has written extensively about the "second individuation process"[1] of adolescence (7; see also 39). Individuation occurs as the young person develops a clearer sense of self as psychologically separate from his or her parents. Neoanalytic perspectives generally minimize the behavioral storminess of the adolescent's movement toward emotional and behavioral emancipation and emphasize instead the somewhat more pacific process through which the adolescent develops a new view of himself or herself and parental figures (1). In Blos's view, the individuation process is marked by the repudiation of parents; but much

1. The first individuation process is held to occur during infancy.

of the process is cognitive, not behavioral, and successful individuation is not necessarily accompanied by overt rebellion or oppositionalism (38).

Recent Theoretical Developments

Since the middle 1970s a new look has appeared in the literature on family relations during adolescence, one that for the most part disavows the orthodox analytic view and further transforms the neoanalytic perspective espoused by Blos and others. This new look, which is mainly empirical and somewhat less theoretical (or at least less grandly theoretical), begins with the premise that major realignments in family relations occur during the adolescent years, but it challenges the view that these realignments necessarily occur against a backdrop of distantiation or emotional detachment. Rather, the thrust of these more recent writings has been to emphasize, first, that most adolescents develop responsible autonomy without severing their emotional bond to their parents (27, 34); second, that differences between families resulting from demographic and individual factors influence the way in which family relations are transformed (47); third, that changes in family relations must be understood in light of the psychological development of the parents as well as the adolescent (58); and fourth, that the family must be viewed as a system of intertwining relationships rather than a collection of independent dyads (26).

Much of the recent empirical work on transformations in family relations at adolescence has examined parents' and adolescents' behavior toward one another either through studies of interaction patterns (15, 29) or through self-reports (62, 72). The neoanalytic perspective on family relations, however, draws attention to the fact that much of the readjustment in family relations at adolescence is intrapsychic, not only interpersonal (34). Changes in the teenager's and parent's conscious and unconscious *images* of each other, therefore, may be just as significant as changes in their behavior toward each other. Accordingly, students of family relations during adolescence must attend to subjective and subtle, as well as objective and overt, indications of changes in parent-adolescent conflict, harmony, and autonomy. Unfortunately, empirical research has rarely addressed this issue systematically, and researchers have seldom examined the relation between subjective and objective indexes of transformations in family relations.[2]

2. Some of the more insightful treatments of the issue of cognitive realignment may be found in Collins (11), Youniss and Smollar (72), and Hill and Holmbeck (34). Also, Smetana (60), whose work is discussed later in this chapter, has provided a cognitive-developmental perspective on transformations in family relations that may serve as a basis for rapprochement between the cognitive and analytic viewpoints.

Central Issues

Consider the following excerpt of an interview with a 12-year-old girl, conducted as part of my own program of research:

I WAS WONDERING ABOUT THE WAY THAT YOU AND YOUR MOM TREAT EACH OTHER NOW. IS IT THE SAME AS IT WAS A FEW YEARS AGO, OR DO YOU NOTICE ANY DIFFERENCE IN THE WAY SHE TREATS YOU?

>Yeah, she treats me—she seems to trust me more with things. Like leaving me alone with my sister at night when they're away.

WHAT ABOUT THE ARGUMENTS OR FIGHTS THAT YOU HAVE? HAVE THOSE CHANGED AT ALL?

>I guess I argue more with her.

WHY DO YOU THINK THAT IS?

>I'm not sure.

WHAT KINDS OF THINGS DO YOU ARGUE ABOUT?

>When I'm supposed to go to bed. She tells me to clean up my room and I don't want to. I want to read a book or play with my friends.

DO YOU TREAT YOUR MOM DIFFERENTLY?

>Yeah, I guess so. I guess I used to not yell at her back. But now I do.

SO WHEN SHE YELLS AT YOU, YOU YELL BACK. DOES SHE YELL AT YOU MORE THAN SHE USED TO?

>I don't think so . . . We don't really have more arguments; it's just that I yell back at her when we do have arguments.

HAVE YOU NOTICED ANY CHANGES IN YOUR OPINION OF HER, WHAT YOU THINK OF HER? HAS THAT CHANGED SINCE YOU WERE LITTLE?

>Maybe. When I was little, she was just my mother. Now she's more of a real person. I don't know. She still seems like she did when I was little, but now besides being the one who takes care of me and stuff like that, she's like everybody else. She has a career and all that kind of stuff too.

Is this passage best understood in terms of the development of autonomy, changes in the nature of parent-child conflict, or in the manifestation of parent-adolescent harmony? In my view the interchange has implications for understanding all three. Accordingly, the review that follows is organized not around the separate topics of autonomy, conflict, and harmony but rather around several fundamental issues that cut across all three domains. I begin with an examination of the view that storm and stress is normative.

Storm and Stress

I noted earlier that a key legacy of the psychoanalytic view of adolescent development is the belief that family relationships deteriorate during this period and that adolescent rebellion, conflict with parents, and detachment are all normative. A careful examination of the evidence on this issue is critical, because policy makers, practitioners, and parents need to know whether and to what extent familial stress is predictable and normal. Insofar as the public believes that adolescence is a time of normative disturbance in the family, families in distress will be less likely to seek professional help. And insofar as policy makers and personnel in funding agencies subscribe to this view, organizations will be less inclined to support programs and research aimed at preventing difficulties that are erroneously believed to be inevitable or at ameliorating problems that are mistakenly thought to remit spontaneously after adolescence.

The weight of the evidence to date indicates that the portrait of family storm and stress painted by early analytic writers is unduly pessimistic. Several large-scale surveys of adolescents and parents indicate that approximately three-fourths of families enjoy warm and pleasant relations during these adolescent years (49). The vast majority of teenagers are likely to report admiring their parents, turning to them for advice and counsel, and feeling loved and appreciated by them (50). Of the one-fourth of families who report less-than-happy relations, a large majority have experienced prior family problems (54).

It appears, therefore, that only a very small proportion of families—somewhere between 5% and 10%—experience a dramatic deterioration in the quality of the parent-child relationship during adolescence. Not surprisingly, family relations are more likely to be strained (both prior to and during adolescence) in households of delinquent or psychologically disturbed youth. The view that adolescent detachment and family stress are inherent features of domestic life may thus accurately describe families of teenagers with problems but may not apply to the normal population of young people and their parents. There is reason to believe, therefore, that families who experience a marked worsening in the quality of their relationships are likely to be in need of professional attention.

It is not known whether these estimates of the prevalence of family problems, derived almost exclusively from studies of firstborn adolescents from white, middle-class families, can be generalized to other populations, but there is little reason to assume a priori that family relations are inherently more strained in nonwhite, non–middle-class households. Although research on these populations is needed, it would be prudent to begin from the premise that neither storm nor stress is normative for them either.

While we can confidently say that conflict is not the norm in white, middle-class, intact households, it does appear that strained or distant parent-adolescent relationships may be more prevalent among single-parent households and stepfamilies than in biologically intact households (47; see also Chapter 6 in this volume). Even in these populations, however, parent-adolescent discord is not the norm; it is more accurate to say that the proportion of families who report difficulties at adolescence is simply smaller in biologically intact two-parent homes than in others. More to the point, variations within family-structure groups are likely to be more substantial than are differences between groups (71).

Current information on how parent-adolescent relations may vary as a function of household composition is limited in several respects, in part as a consequence of the excessive use of the "social address" research design, which merely contrasts adolescents raised in different family structures without examining intrafamilial processes (9). First, although the popular press often makes sweeping comparisons between two-parent, intact households and all other groups combined, there is considerable diversity within the population of nonintact families that is all too often overlooked. For example, the category of adolescents in single-mother households includes some living with a divorced or separated single mother; some living with a widowed mother; some living with a mother who has never married; some living with a mother and an unrelated adult male; and some living with a mother and a member of the extended family. These variations in household composition are likely to affect the nature of parent-adolescent relations, but they seldom are examined systematically (but see 16 for an exception).

Second, cross-sectional comparisons of families that differ in household composition do not tell us whether the nature of the relational transformations that occur at adolescence differs as a function of family structure. For example, studies indicate that familial discord (47) and adolescent detachment (55) are greater in single-parent homes and stepfamilies than in biologically intact two-parent homes; and that parental permissiveness is greater in single-parent than two-parent homes (16, 21). But these studies do not tell us whether these differences arise from, or are related in any systematic way to, features of the adolescent transition. Parent-child discord and distance and parental permissiveness may be greater at all points in the family life cycle in nonintact households.

Several researchers have followed families with adolescents through the process of divorce or remarriage, a more difficult, but likely more fruitful, approach (31; see also Chapter 6 in this volume). Generally these studies suggest that teenagers have less difficulty coping with parental divorce than do younger children but more difficulty coping with parental remarriage. Remarriage appears to be especially hard on adolescent girls; several studies suggest that adolescent-stepfather relations are more strained among daughters than sons (24, 56). Even these studies, however, do not examine how divorced or reconstituted families negotiate the transition into adolescence, or whether the pattern of relational transformation experienced in these households at adolescence differs from that observed among biologically intact two-parent families. Given the continued high rate of divorce and remarriage among parents of school-aged children, it is imperative that social scientists interested in transformations in family relations at adolescence initiate longitudinal research that begins prior to the teenage years and follows families of different structures through the transition. They must ask whether detachment is more likely to occur in these households at adolescence, or, alternatively, whether youngsters growing up in nonintact homes enter their teens with more distant relationships with parents.

There is some suggestion in the literature that familial strain may be more characteristic of relations between firstborn children and their parents (33). The reasons remain unclear, although studies of parental images of adolescence suggest that parents may have different expectations before their firstborn reaches adolescence than they do as their subsequent children become teenagers (10). One hypothesis worthy of investigation is that a self-fulfilling prophecy may operate whereby novice parents of teenagers expect, provoke, and find more oppositional behavior in their youngsters than do parents who have already experienced an older child's adolescence. Whether a similar process helps account for the family-structure differences discussed earlier (that is, whether single parents or stepparents may have different expectations for adolescence) is another interesting but unresearched question.

Far less is known about whether family relations in adolescence vary systematically across ethnic groups. The little research that exists, mainly on African-American teenagers, suggests that researchers must attend to the ways in which the prevalence of households headed by the mother, the relatively more matrifocal orientation in general, and the widespread use of extended family networks among African-American families may moderate patterns of relational change in adolescence (6). Because most studies of African-American adolescents have not systematically separated the effects of ethnicity and socioeconomic status, however, we must be cautious about generalizing findings derived from studies of low-income minority youth to more affluent minority populations. This caveat notwithstanding, it is important to note that theories about "normal" interpersonal development based on an image of the relatively isolated two-parent nuclear household may not apply to young people growing up under other circumstances.

Is Detachment Desirable?

There is strong evidence against the view that detachment from family ties during adolescence is desirable. The prediction derived from analytic models, of course, is that adolescents with close relations to parents should show stunted psychological development. Yet the empirical evidence is directly antithetical to this prediction: Teenagers who report feeling relatively close to their parents score higher than their peers on measures of psychosocial development, including self-reliance and other indicators of responsible independence (65); behavioral competence, including school performance (32, 43; see also Chapter 12 in this volume); and psychological well-being, including self-esteem (28, 43; see also Chapter 14 in this volume). Not surprisingly, they score lower on measures of psychological and social problems, including drug use, depression, and deviant behavior (4, 22, 37; see also Chapter 16 in this volume). This finding is robust across socioeconomic and ethnic groups. Although the argument has been made in clinical circles that a moderate degree of closeness is preferable to too much or too little, studies of nonclinical populations do not support the hypothesis that the parent-adolescent relationship can be so cohesive as to be enmeshing (cf. 44). There is some evidence, however, that teenagers whose parents are excessive in their use of guilt-inducing and other psychologically controlling techniques may suffer developmentally as a result (43).

In view of the clear and consistent evidence that detachment from family ties during adolescence is neither normative nor desirable, we must ask why this notion persists. A quick pass through the child-development section of most bookstores indicates that this viewpoint is indeed alive and well; most of the titles of books aimed at parents of teenagers suggest that adolescence is something for parents to survive rather than enjoy.[3] In view of the very reasonable hypothesis suggesting that parental expecta-

3. For example, an examination of titles turned up the following: S. Hayman, *Adolescence: A survival guide to the teenage years* (New York: Gower, 1986); R. Kolodny et al., *How to survive your adolescent's adolescence* (Boston: Little, Brown, 1984); P. Buntman & E. Saris, *How to live with your teenager: A survivor's handbook for parents* (New York: Ballantine, 1982); and D. Powell, *Teenagers: When to worry, what to do* (New York: Doubleday, 1986).

tions may influence the quality and nature of parent-adolescent relations (12), more research on the sources of information sought and used by parents, as well as the impact of this information on parenting practices, is needed. It would also be fruitful to examine whether and in what ways the mass media continue to promote the view that adolescence is an inherently difficult time during which detachment from parental ties is the norm.

It is impossible to discuss expectations about adolescence (whether held by parents, practitioners, scientists, or adolescents themselves) without acknowledging the role of the broader social context in shaping these beliefs. We know from the work of the many cultural anthropologists who have studied adolescence that expectations and beliefs about "normal" adolescence, and about "normal" parent-child relations in particular, are highly variable across cultures. We know less about variations among ethnic groups within contemporary American society, but we do know, for instance, that expectations concerning the appropriate ages at which various "autonomies" should be granted vary considerably across ethnic groups (21). It is likely that expectations concerning the expression of harmony and conflict vary as well.

Historical forces also shape attitudes and beliefs about adolescence (19; see also Chapter 4 in this volume). During the late 1960s, for example, it is likely that the attention given by the mass media to the "generation gap" contributed to parents' anxieties about their ability to influence their children's values; stereotypes of adolescents as rebellious and oppositional were probably strengthened during this era. Today, concerns over crack, AIDS, and school crime create different anxieties, with their own implications for understanding the genesis of parental belief systems. My intent in challenging the storm-and-stress model of adolescence is not to imply that contemporary parents' worries about their youngsters' exposure to drugs, sexually transmitted diseases, and violence are unwarranted or unjustified. There is a crucial difference, however, between portraying the world in which adolescents currently live as a potentially dangerous place (which is accurate) and portraying adolescence as an inherently stressful time for the individual or the family (which is not). It is essential that we understand how best to keep these two messages distinct.

Alternatives to the Detachment Model

Part of the difficulty we encounter in debunking the myth of storm and stress is that a suitable substitute has yet to be completely articulated. Virtually all scholars writing about family relations in adolescence agree that transformations in the parent-child relationship do occur during this period, that families vary in the ways in which their relationships are transformed, and that these variations are likely to influence the young person's mental health and behavior. Several writers have attempted to describe these transformations in terms other than of storm and stress or detachment, and their work offers promising leads for a new theory of normative transformations in the parent-child relationship.

Moving toward an interdependent relationship. Youniss and his colleagues have argued that transformations in family relations at adolescence reflect the adolescent's growing understanding of his or her *interdependence* within the family and the parents' willingness to engage in a process through which close ties are maintained but the young person's individuality is not threatened (72). Both parent and adolescent actively participate in the mutual and reciprocal process of redefining the relationship. Transformation of the relationship from one of unilateral authority to one of cooperative negotiation is necessary for the adolescent's social and psychological development to proceed on course; a severing of the parent-child bond jeopardizes this process. In healthy families adolescents remain responsive to parental authority and continue to seek parents' advice, but they do so in a context of greater freedom. The parents, at the same time, retain their authority through "giving more freedom to adolescents by recognizing their personal needs and capabilities . . . It is clear that parental relationships have not been discarded nor have they lost their binding power. In fact, the adolescents said that the transformation helped to bring them and their parents closer" (72, pp. 162–163).

This suggests that, if emancipation does occur at adolescence, it is more likely to be manifested in subtle changes in parents' and adolescents' conscious and unconscious images of one another than in dramatic changes in behavior. According to several studies (61, 65, 70) adolescence is a time for the shedding of childhood (and childish) conceptions of parental omniscience and omnipotence, a finding consistent with the work of Blos and other neoanalytic theorists. As children get older, for instance, the gap between their description of an "ideal" parent and their characterization of their own parents widens (12, 20). But as Smollar and Youniss (61) point out—and in contrast to neoanalytic theory—the realization that one's parents are far from ideal does not necessarily lead to a rejection of their authority or a repudiation of their wisdom (72). Instead, once the relationship has been transformed, parental authority and wisdom are seen in more balanced, and probably more accurate, terms.

A handful of studies point to the very different roles played by mothers and fathers in their relations with adolescent sons and daughters. The overall picture suggests that the four parent-adolescent dyads may be characterized by quite different types of relations and may undergo quite different sorts of transformations in adolescence (25, 29, 33, 62, 71, 72). Mother-daughter relations are the most affectively charged, characterized by high levels of both closeness and discord, and by a high level of shared activities. Mothers' relations with sons are also high in conflict and harmony but are not characterized by the same level of joint activities. Fathers appear to have emotionally "flat" relations with their teenagers in comparison to mothers, and share few activities with daughters. In general, the father-daughter relationship appears to be the outlier, distinguished by its affective blandness and relatively low level of interaction (62). An investigation by Gjerde reminds us, however, that assessments of maternal and paternal behavior must take into account the context of the interaction (25). In families with adolescent boys, for example, the adolescent's interaction with his mother is more positive when the father is present, while his interaction with his father is more positive when the two are alone. We do not yet understand the reason for this difference.

Temporary "perturbations" in the family system. Youniss and Smollar's work on mutuality in the parent-adolescent relationship does not fully address the emotional and behavioral aspects of the process of relational transformation. Although the end result of the transformation may be a happier and more mature parent-child relationship in which cooperative negotiation and mutual respect is the norm, the road traveled toward this destination may have its share of bumps and potholes. A different group of writers, including Collins (12), Hill (33), and Steinberg (63), have focused on the emotional and behavioral manifestations of the process through which family relationships are transformed, especially during the critical early adolescent years. According to these writers, early adolescence in particular is a period of temporary perturbation in the family, characterized by heightened bickering and squabbling (especially between mothers and teenagers) and diminished levels of positive interaction (between teenagers and both parents). The nattering is generally over mundane issues of daily life; the lessening of positive interaction typically takes the form of fewer shared activities and less frequently expressed affection (33, 36, 46, 62).

Several researchers have shown that temporary periods of perturbation in the family system occur at around the onset of puberty (33, 51, 62, 63, 67). These researchers interpret transformations in family relations in terms of the family's adaptation to the adolescent's physical development (33, 62). Generally speaking, pubertal maturation leads to a modest increase in distance in the parent-adolescent relationship, a finding that supports the psychoanalytic proposition that the somatic and hormonal changes of puberty set in motion a series of intrapsychic and interpersonal processes that culminate in the adolescent's successful individuation from parental objects and engagement in intimate relationships with age-mates.[4] Although the distancing effect of puberty on parent-adolescent relations is observed in several studies, the magnitude of the effect is modest, and the studies in no way suggest that puberty provokes familial storm and stress (63).

Collins has written about the perturbations that occur in the family system in early adolescence as well, but from a cognitive-mediational perspective (12). Here the focus is on understanding the expectations that parents and children have for one another's behavior, the ways in which these expectations may (or may not) change during adolescence, and the impact of violations of expectations on parent-adolescent interactions. Violations of expectations take two forms. First, patterns of behavior established prior to adolescence engender expectations (typically on the part of the parent) that may be violated as the child becomes older. Second, new expectations may be formed by both parent and child, but they may be discordant. Perturbations in the family system result, he argues, when expectations are violated, and violations are more likely to occur during periods of rapid development. As I noted earlier, more research on the nature of, and bases for, parents' expectations of adolescence is needed.

Because perturbations in family relations typically do not threaten the emotional cohesion of the parent-child bond, the fact that families pass through such periods should not be taken as evidence of adolescent detachment. Indeed, we must ask whether and how periods of realignment—even when accompanied by conflict—may contribute in *positive* ways to the psychosocial development of the adolescent. As Cooper correctly points out: "Although conflict is often considered an indicator of incompatibility, current research provides evidence that conflict can function constructively when it co-occurs with the subjective conditions of trust and closeness and their behavioral expressions" (14, p. 183).

It is all well and good to discuss the positive function of conflict in the parent-adolescent relationship, but we must not lose sight of the fact that the important question is not whether conflict is functional or dysfunctional but under what circumstances conflict is likely to be one or the

---

4. Interestingly, at least one study has shown that distance in the parent-adolescent relationship may itself accelerate pubertal maturation in girls (63). Social influences on the rate and timing of puberty are discussed in Chapter 2.

other. There undoubtedly are families in which conflict is unhealthy, either because it is pervasive, because it does not occur against a backdrop of emotional closeness, or because it escalates regularly into angry fighting or physical violence. But research suggests that these families are in the minority. Most parents and children who enter adolescence with a sturdy foundation of trust and a strong bond in all likelihood negotiate the transition with relatively little cost (albeit with some increase in daily hassling), and youngsters may actually benefit from the interchange and dialogue that accompany disagreement. This process may facilitate movement toward the more mutual, reciprocal relations described by Youniss and Smollar (72). Families whose emotional foundation is shaky to begin with, however, may find the period of perturbation too much to bear and may fall into deeper levels of disengagement and detachment. Future research on perturbations in the family system and their consequences for adolescent development should examine preadolescent variations in parent-child closeness as a factor that may moderate the impact of conflict on individuals and the family system.

The enduring attachment bond. A third set of writers has attempted to cast the parent-adolescent relationship in terms derived from attachment theorists such as Bowlby (8). These writers, including Greenberg, and Kobak and Sceery, have suggested that early attachment relationships help foster working models of interpersonal relations that are carried, albeit in modified form, over the life span (26, 41). If this view is correct, variations in the security of youngsters' attachment to their parents prior to adolescence should influence the way in which family relations are transformed during the adolescent passage. Thus far, with one exception (2), attempts to extend the attachment paradigm to adolescence have focused on assessing individual differences in attachment security and examining the implications of these differences for mental health and psychological functioning, rather than on developmental changes in the meaning or manifestations of the attachment bond (26, 41). It remains to be seen whether the working model of relationships that the young person brings to adolescence influences the pattern of relational transformation experienced by the family. A reasonable (but untested) hypothesis is that the successful movement toward healthy interdependence and the negotiation of temporary periods of perturbation are more likely to occur in families in which teenager and parents are securely attached.

Positive Functions of Parent-Adolescent Conflict

I noted earlier that disagreements over family rules and other mundane features of everyday life may become more frequent during early adolescence than before or after, but that in most families this discord does not diminish the emotional attachment between adolescents and their parents. The frequency of disagreements increases between childhood and early adolescence, remains stable through middle adolescence, and declines somewhat thereafter (45). Although studies employing different methodologies yield different estimates, it appears that the typical teenager and parent quarrel about two times weekly, or about twice as often as the typical husband and wife (45).

An examination of the sources of disagreement between parents and adolescents casts doubt on many widely held notions about the nature of intergenerational conflict. It is widely believed that adolescents and parents hold conflicting views about political and social matters, and that this divergence in values and attitudes is a primary source of intergenerational tension. This is not the case today, nor was it the case during the height of the political and social turbulence of the 1960s and 1970s (13). The clarity of hindsight indicates that the nature and existence of a generation gap was grossly overstated by the popular media, and that calls of alarm from blue-ribbon commissions writing in the 1970s (53) about the pervasiveness of a counterculture and the widespread rejection of adult values by American youth were exaggerated. Indeed, as Montemayor points out, the topics that adolescents and parents argue about have changed little since researchers began examining this issue over sixty years ago (45). Squabbles about curfew, household chores, and school responsibilities are the most commonly mentioned sources of argument, even in studies conducted during historical periods in which adolescents and adults were alleged to argue frequently over more lofty concerns than dirty laundry.

Despite the banality of most family disagreements, several writers have suggested that this sort of low-level quarreling serves an important purpose in the adolescent's development. Steinberg, arguing from a sociobiological perspective, has suggested that this bickering and squabbling at puberty is an atavism that ensures that adolescents will spend time away from the family of origin and mate outside the natal group (64). Parent-offspring conflict intensifies at puberty in most other species of primates, and it is possible that the tension experienced by humans has an evolved basis. Because the squabbling occurs within the context of a close emotional relationship, it may force the adolescent to look outside the family for intimate companionship without breaking ties to parents.

Holmbeck and Hill have offered a complementary perspective on the adaptive significance of parent-adolescent conflict that draws on both psychoanalytic and social learning theory (36). They argue that conflict promotes adjustment to developmental change through intrapsychic as well as interpersonal processes. At an intrapsychic level, the conflict may facilitate individuation. Recalling the work of Youniss and Smollar (72), one might argue that the intrapsychic emancipation that permits the adolescent to develop a more mature and more realistic appraisal of his or her parents—and ultimately a more mature and more mutual relationship with them—is helped along by a temporary period of heightened squabbling. These frequent disagreements, in the context of a strong attachment, force the adolescent to come to terms with parental fallibility and, consequently, relinquish childish dependence on mother and father. At an interpersonal level, the conflict arising between adolescents and parents at puberty may serve an informational function (36). Disagreement may be a mechanism through which the adolescent informs his or her parents about changing self-conceptions and expectations.

Smetana has offered a cognitive-developmental perspective that is also instructive (60). She contends that parent-adolescent conflict is best understood in terms of the different ways in which parents and their children understand and define family rules, events, and regulations. Using the results of an extensive series of interviews, Smetana demonstrates that the growing frequency of conflict in early and middle adolescence is related to the development of advanced levels of social reasoning. She cites two reasons. First, as young people develop, they are increasingly likely to view issues that they and their parents had once defined as matters of social convention (for example, "In this family we all make our beds every morning") as matters of personal choice ("Since it's my bed, I'll decide how often to make it"). Because parents are likely to maintain a conventional stance toward these issues, conflict ensues. The conflict is not so much over the issue as it is over the *definition* of the issue (that is, a matter of personal taste versus one of social convention).

Second, during early and middle adolescence young people pass through a period of cognitive development in which they cast social conventions as arbitrary—including social conventions that regulate the sundry matters that parents and teenagers squabble about (see Chapter 3 in this volume). Thus, even when both the adolescent and the parent define an issue of contention in conventional terms (that is, there are "rules" that govern one's behavior), the adolescent may be unlikely to adopt the parent's convention (for example, "Your friends may dress that way, but mine don't"). The following excerpt of one of Smetana's interviews, with a tenth-grader, will sound annoyingly familiar to most parents of teenagers:

WHEN CLEANING YOUR ROOM COMES UP, IS IT THAT YOU DON'T WANT TO CLEAN YOUR ROOM?

> I don't care whether I clean it up or not, it's just that, it's a big issue with my mother, she gets really upset about it.

WHY?

It's just that way, because I'll go, "I don't care," and she says, "Well I do," and then it keeps going.

WHY DO YOU THINK SHE MAKES YOU CLEAN IT THEN?

I don't know . . . I don't know, she keeps saying, "All little kids have to clean their room."

WHAT DO YOU THINK ABOUT THAT?

She's probably right, but I don't think I should have to, I don't think I should have to like make sure there's nothing gross in there . . . and have to clean up an entire room. (60, p. 105)

Frequent disagreements, however minor, are understandably sources of tension and stress to many parents of teenagers (57, 59). Studies have found that parents of adolescents are likely to feel less adequate and more anxious about parenting than parents of younger children (3, 35, 68). Reports of parental stress are highest in early adolescence and are related to youngsters' demands for more independence and, presumably, to conflicts that arise over issues of autonomy (59). In addition, distance between parents and adolescents may diminish marital satisfaction (66) and provoke midlife reappraisal and self-evaluation, especially among parents with a teenager of the same sex (57), and especially among parents without a strong orientation toward work outside the home (58).

As Cooper points out, however, the process of disagreeing—so long as it takes place in the context of a close parent-child relationship—may contribute in important ways to the adolescent's psychosocial development (14), despite its impact on parents' peace of mind (see Chapter 15 in this volume). For example, adolescents' identity development and interpersonal skills are more advanced in families in which members are willing to express their own points of view and tolerate disagreements with one another (15). Similarly, adolescent ego development is greater in families in which discussions are characterized by relatively frequent discourse that reflects problem solving, empathy, and acceptance, and relatively little interchange that is devaluing, judgmental, or constraining (30). These studies recall the finding, noted earlier, that adolescents whose parents use excessive amounts of psychological control may suffer somewhat in the development of competence.

Tolerance of disagreement and the discord that may ensue is apparently a key feature of parent-child interaction in families with psychosocially healthy adolescents. The combination of conflict and cohesion is critical, however: "When family conflict is hostile, impulsive, and inconsistent, and prone to escalation to high intensity, children feel neglect and lack of love, and avoid interaction with their parents. Thus, contentiousness alone may not be the distinctive feature of dysfunctional conflict, but whether or not conflict occurs within a context of relational cohesion" (14, pp. 183–184). This notion is consistent with available data on the disproportionate prevalence of abusive relations between adolescents and stepparents (24). Although the level of squabbling in these dyads may be no greater than that between adolescents and biological parents, stepparents and adolescents may lack the affective cohesiveness that prevents low-level bickering from escalating into dysfunctional discord and abuse. More research is needed on identifying families predisposed toward dysfunctional conflict, and on the processes through which functional disagreement escalates into dysfunctional discord. Patterson's work on the escalation of family conflict from simple problems of noncompliance to serious problems of physical violence (52) serves as a useful starting point for the study of adolescent-parent conflict and its vicissitudes.

Cooper's contention that it is not the presence of conflict per se that is the issue but the context in which conflict occurs (14) suggests that researchers should focus more on the study of conflict resolution than on conflict genesis. Unfortunately, researchers have spent far more time and energy on the latter than on the former. The limited available data on conflict resolution suggest that if negotiation and discussion are essential components of functional conflict, most parents and teenagers are missing opportunities to facilitate the adolescent's development. According to a telephone survey by Montemayor and Hanson, nearly half of all adolescent-parent conflicts are "resolved" by one or both parties withdrawing from the incident, nearly 40% by one person simply telling the other what to do, and only 15% through negotiation (48).

Studies of conflict resolution would appear to be indicated, but it is not clear how to overcome some inherent methodological difficulties. Laboratory studies of family interaction processes in which family members are asked to discuss an issue or plan an event yield rich information on the processes of discourse, but they typically force artificial conflict resolution and do not permit withdrawal (33). These tasks probably tell us very little, therefore, about the extent and nature of conflict resolution in everyday situations. Researchers may want to consider alternatives to laboratory studies of interaction processes, as well as ways of revising interaction task instructions to permit irreconcilability and allow for parties to withdraw without reaching agreement.

The Power of Authoritative Parenting

Thus far I have suggested that adolescents thrive developmentally when the family environment is characterized by warm relationships in which individuals are permitted to express their opinions and assert their individuality. (One might label these characteristics *warmth* and *psychological autonomy*). A third component of functional parenting, *demandingness,* has also been identified (43). Demanding parents expect mature behavior from their adolescent, set and consistently enforce reasonable rules and standards for behavior, and when necessary discipline their youngster firmly yet fairly. The constellation of warmth, psychological autonomy, and demandingness, first identified and described by Baumrind (5), has been labeled *authoritative.* Adolescents who grow up in authoritative homes score higher on indexes of psychological development and mental health, however they are defined (32, 43). Although most studies of parenting practices and their outcomes do not disentangle the effects of warmth, psychological autonomy, and demandingness from one another, it appears that the absence of parental warmth is associated mainly with deficits in the domains of social skills and self-conceptions; the absence of psychological autonomy with deficits in the domains of self-reliance and competence; and the absence of demandingness with deficits in the domains of impulse control and social responsibility (43).

The authoritative pattern may be contrasted with three other prototypes: the *autocratic* or *authoritarian* pattern, characterized by high levels of demandingness but low levels of warmth and psychological autonomy; the *indulgent* pattern, characterized by low levels of demandingness, high levels of warmth, and a laissez-faire attitude toward decision making; and the *indifferent* or *uninvolved* pattern, characterized by laissez-faire decision making and low levels of demandingness, but low levels of warmth as well (43).[5] Research on developmental differences among adolescents growing up in these four types of family environments is summarized in Maccoby and Martin (43) and will not be reviewed here. Suffice it to say that youngsters raised in indifferent households are at greatest risk for psychological dysfunction and involvement in various problem behaviors (drug and alcohol use, delinquency, sexual precocity), and that youngsters raised in either autocratic or indulgent households are likely to score somewhere between those raised in authoritative and those raised in indifferent households on measures of social competence, self-reliance, self-esteem, and other indicators of psychosocial development.[6]

5. In many discussions of Baumrind's perspective, the "indulgent" and "neglectful" groups are combined and discussed under the label "permissive." But because the effects of permissiveness vary as a function of the level of parental warmth, grouping these two together leads to confusing and inconsistent findings. It is recommended that "permissive" be used only as the antithesis of "demanding" and not as a label for a constellation of parenting practices.

6. A word or two is in order on the difference between psychological and behavioral

Much of the work on the benefits of authoritative parenting has been conducted on samples of white, middle-class youngsters growing up in two-parent households. Given the consistency, over time and across studies, with which youngsters from this population who are raised in warm, democratic, and demanding environments outscore their peers on measures of psychosocial development and prosocial behavior, it does not appear that further research on the consequences of authoritative parenting *in this population* is necessary or warranted. It would seem timely to initiate research on the *determinants*, rather than the *consequences*, of authoritative parenting practices.

Whether these same principles apply to other populations of adolescents and parents is an exceedingly important question, and one that must be answered before large-scale attempts are made to alter parenting practices in an authoritative direction. The recent work of Dornbusch and his colleagues demonstrates that the deleterious consequences of autocratic parenting for adolescent school performance appear to cut across ethnic boundaries (17). The positive consequences of authoritative parenting and the negative consequences of indifferent parenting hold up across socioeconomic groups and family structures as well. More research in this vein, with different outcome variables, is certainly needed. Such research should adopt a longitudinal design, beginning prior to the child's entry into adolescence and following the family through the critical early adolescent transition. There is ample reason to hypothesize that many of the benefits of growing up in an authoritative family environment—at least in contemporary America—transcend the boundaries of socioeconomic status, ethnicity, and family structure, but we must keep in mind that this remains a hypothesis.

In view of the apparent power of authoritative parenting, several researchers have asked whether the parenting practices that make up this style can be taught. The most critical work in this area comes from Patter-

---

control and their respective effects on the developing adolescent. Some readers may find it inconsistent, or perhaps confusing, that the two forms of control appear to have opposite effects on the adolescent. (Many researchers do not distinguish between these different forms of control, which is clearly a mistake.) Adolescents appear to be adversely affected by psychological control—the absence of "psychological autonomy"—but positively influenced by behavioral control—the presence of "demandingness." Too little behavioral control may leave the youngster without adequate guidance and supervision and may, as a consequence, expose him or her, especially in contemporary society, to an array of developmentally risky temptations and dangers. Too much psychological control, in contrast, may facilitate dependency and impede the development of psychological competence and self-direction. The challenge for parents—and it may be a difficult one—is to grant sufficient psychological autonomy to their child without being behaviorally permissive.

son and his associates (52), who have developed an effective treatment program for distressed families with an aggressive, delinquent, or noncompliant child. The program focuses on the training of demandingness—supervision, monitoring, limit setting, and the like. Patterson's program is unlike conventional family therapy, because it emphasizes the tuition of constructive child-management practices rather than the analysis of underlying interpersonal dynamics. Specifically, the program is designed to teach parents how to convey to their children clear expectations for acceptable and unacceptable behavior, how to monitor their children's behavior, how to respond consistently and swiftly to noncompliance, and how to reward prosocial behavior. One of the most encouraging findings reported by Patterson's team is that participation in this training program leads not only to a decrease in problem behavior among the target children but to significant improvements in the behavior of their siblings as well (42). To date the long-term effectiveness of this program is unknown, as is its effectiveness in inner-city communities. Research on the efficacy of this and related approaches is urgently needed.

Future Directions

Conventional models of familial storm and stress and adolescent detachment are being replaced, however slowly, by a number of promising perspectives that are more tempered and optimistic. As research from these new perspectives continues to develop, researchers should explore ways of disseminating findings of these studies to parents and practitioners, whose views of adolescence are likely to be somewhat anachronistic and unduly pessimistic.

Although empirical research has not supported the view that adolescence is an inherently contentious period for the family, recent studies of young people and their parents indicate that major transformations in the parent-child relationship occur during the second decade of life. While these transformations do not threaten the integrity of the emotional bond between young people and their parents, they may be associated with a temporary period of perturbation or realignment in the parent-adolescent relationship, especially during the early adolescent years.

The period of disequilibrium, likely triggered by the biological and cognitive changes of adolescence, is characterized by a somewhat diminished level of positive interaction between teenagers and their parents and a concomitant increase in bickering and squabbling. Although this period of perturbation may take a temporary toll on the psychological well-being of parents, for most families it leads within a few years to a redefinition of the parent-child relationship from one of unilateral parental authority to one that is more cooperative and reciprocal. Among the factors most likely to moderate the pattern of this relational transformation are the affective quality of the parent-child relationship prior to adolescence, the structure of the family (whether intact, divorced, or remarried), and the expectations about adolescence held by parents, teenagers, and the society in which they live. Unfortunately we know very little about the ways in which childhood attachments, family structure, and individual expectations affect the family's transition into adolescence, nor has research examined the nature and sources of these expectations. Research on these issues is much needed.

In general, healthy adolescent development is facilitated by a parent-child relationship that maintains a strong affective bond while tolerating disagreement and the expression of the young person's growing sense of individuality. A style of parenting that has been labeled authoritative, characterized by parental warmth, democratic parent-child interaction, and parental demandingness, is consistently associated with positive developmental outcomes in young people. Conclusions about transformations in the parent-adolescent relationship and the implications of variations in this process for adolescent development, however, are limited by the restricted range of populations included in most research. Although there is good reason to suspect that authoritative parenting has positive consequences for most adolescents, research on nonwhite and nonintact families is urgently needed.

As we look to the future and to the changing demography of the United States (69), it becomes essential to study the new models of the parent-adolescent relationship in more heterogeneous samples of families. The next generation of research must examine whether and how variations in socioeconomic status, family structure, and ethnicity influence the ways in which families adapt to adolescence, and it must explore the ways in which these demographic factors moderate the developmental outcomes of familial adaptation. This is not to say that the current literature, with its foundation in studies of white, middle-class families, is too compromised to be of value; nor is it to suggest that studies of group differences in family processes should replace studies of family process and its developmental outcomes. As research on families with adolescent children proceeds, however, we must not lose sight of the changing social context in which families live and the implications of this change for the study of family relations.

11

FRIENDSHIP AND PEER RELATIONS

Ritch C. Savin-Williams and Thomas J. Berndt

Countless writers from Aristotle's day to the present have extolled close friendships as the most rewarding and satisfying of all human relationships. For many adolescents relations with friends are critical interpersonal bridges that move them toward psychological growth and social maturity. Chapter 7 of this volume reviewed literature pertaining to the nature and effect of peer groups as a context for development. The focus in this chapter shifts to a consideration of the peer relationship itself. Our primary intent is to examine the close, intimate friendships with peers that have special significance because of the support they provide to adolescents and the influence they have on their behavior and attitudes.

Youniss and Smollar characterize friendships as important, enduring, relatively problem-free peer relationships in which the participants understand one another and learn new things (121). Although young children do not draw a sharp distinction between friendships and other peer relationships, differentiation grows more acute during adolescence as various qualitative aspects of friendship increase in importance (105). Peer friendships may cross barriers of race, sex, social class, and age; in addition they may be relatively plentiful or sparse, intense or superficial, stable or unstable. Despite these variations, friendships are usually perceived by both adults and youths to be crucial for a full and rich adolescence.

Friendship and Adolescent Development

Forming relationships with parents and other adults is a central element of the unique developmental tasks of childhood; but by adolescence the role of peer friendships as a source of activities, influence, and support increases rather dramatically. Although adults often want to monitor adolescent peer interactions, most parents encourage these relationships because they recognize how enjoyable friendships are to young people and how essential, in Western societies, success in forming and maintaining peer relations is to social and psychological adjustment (cf. 96).

Parents and friends contribute significantly but in different ways to an adolescent's development (121). Youth seek the approval and guidance of parents in forming standards, values, and educational or occupational goals (74). With friends, they learn of an extrafamilial reality and experience a life that is uniquely their own. With parents, adolescents are likely to talk about progress in school and career goals; with friends, they talk about problems in dating, views on sexuality, personal experiences, common perspectives, interests, and doubts. Because teenagers seek approval from their parents, they do not want to appear childish, foolish, or inferior to adults. Thus they are far more likely to be self-disclosing and open, to "tell everything" about the self, to friends than to parents (121).

In part, this increased importance of peer friendships is reflected in the amount of time adolescents spend with friends. In the United States teenagers average twenty hours per week of nonclassroom time with peers, compared to the two to three hours reported in Japan and the Soviet Union. Interactions with peers during adolescence occupy more time for many youths than interactions with family or solitude. Moreover, the frequency of interactions with friends continues to increase throughout adolescence as time spent with parents decreases (40).

In describing the nature of friendship, adolescents typically mention two features not commonly found in children's descriptions. First, friends must be *loyal* to one another; they should not "talk about you behind your back." Commitment and genuineness in attitudes, values, and interests are demanded. Second, much importance is attached to the *intimacy* of friendships—that is, to the ability to share one's thoughts and feelings with a friend (3, 17, 42). Indeed, intimacy is often treated as the prototypical feature of adolescent friendships, especially among girls. With increasing age there is also an increase in the number, complexity, flexibility, and precision of constructs used to describe friends, a development that reflects advances in cognitive, linguistic, and role-taking skills (104).

These developmental features of peer friendships begin, according to Sullivan, with the evolution of "chum" friendships during early adolescence (114). He proposed that such friends increase one another's self-esteem; provide information, emotional support, and advice; and help and support one another. Friends also contribute to an evolving sense of identity, of having a place in the world (120). Through self-disclosure, and by allowing oneself to become vulnerable before a coequal, adolescent friends share with one another their most personal thoughts and feelings, become sensitive to the needs and desires of others, and, in the process, acquire a deep understanding of the other and the self. This intimacy, according to Sullivan, has critical significance for future interpersonal relationships (including romances), and is crucial both to developing a sense of connectedness with others and individuating the self.

Various studies (see, for example, 61, 94, 108, 120) have reported that this intimacy or emotional closeness and trust are more characteristic of girls' than boys' relationships at all ages. Buhrmester and Furman have suggested, however, that the sex difference may be more one of style than substance; boys form friendships "in which sensitivity to needs and validation of worth are achieved through actions and deeds, rather than through interpersonal disclosure of personal thoughts and feelings" (22, pp. 111–12). Even though the sexes do not differ in the number of friends individuals have, males seem more willing than females to make new friends in new environments. Girls often appear to have more exclusive friendships and to be less likely to make new friends when they already have reciprocated friendships with other girls (49).

Adolescents typically report that they enjoy their activities with friends more than any other (40, 118). With friends, they feel that they are understood and can fully be themselves (121). Friends spend much time together simply talking about themselves, other adolescents, or events in the wider world. They relax, joke, watch television or videos, and participate in sports. These moments of enjoyment and companionship contribute to a generational sense of belonging with others who are respected and liked. Through interactions with friends, social skills such as the ability to empathize with and understand the point of view of others are learned and practiced (95). Knowledge concerning various aspects of the self can also be increased through comparisons with friends. Early adolescents engaged in friendships are more likely than those who are not to be altruistic, to display affective perspective-taking skills, to score high on tests of intelligence, and to maintain positive peer status (31, 80).

Several theorists and researchers, however, have expressed doubt concerning the basic premise that close friendships of the type described by Sullivan (114) are beneficial for adolescents' development. Mechanic has argued that intimate relationships that involve extensive sharing of personal feelings or worries may be harmful for psychological adjustment (81). He proposes that frequent conversations with friends concerning personal problems leads to a heightened introspection about feelings that is rarely healthy and may contribute to an increase in physical or psychological illness. Adolescents' friendships are valuable precisely because they are *not* like the intimate relationships praised by Sullivan. In Mechanic's view, adolescent friendships are beneficial when they involve young people in exciting activities, distracting them from a preoccupation with themselves.

Rubin focuses on the friendships of children rather than adolescents, but he too feels that friendships have potentially desirable as well as problematic features: "Through their relationships with one another, children are likely to learn not only how to get along with others but also how to reject others ('You can't play with us'), to stereotype them ('There's dummy Dwayne'), and to engage in regressive or antisocial behavior" (95, p. 11). Rubin suggests that intimate friendships "give rise not only to self-acceptance, trust, and rapport, but also to insecurity, jealousy, and resentment. The fact of the matter is that children's closest friendships manifest all of the prominent features of close relationships among adults, including their destructive as well as their constructive elements" (95, p. 11). Friendships may not necessarily be bad in themselves, but close relationships with some friends may have negative effects on children. For example, adolescents who develop close friendships with classmates who have negative attitudes toward school are likely to display negative attitudes and undesirable behavior at school themselves (1).

Although empirical support for these features of friendship is scarce and occasionally equivocal, we shall examine them in some detail because of their potential significance in promoting the kinds of behaviors, attitudes, and values that evolve during adolescence. It is not our goal to review everything that is currently known concerning the features of adolescent friendships; several comprehensive reviews are already available (for example, 4, 6, 68). Rather, our focus is on questions that we believe are of significance to those concerned with policy issues for adolescents.

Characteristics of Supportive Adolescent Friendships

Number of Friends

Experts in adolescent development disagree as to the number of friends that is optimal for promoting healthy development. Is one close friend ideal, or do adolescents benefit from having several or many close friends? It is generally known that the number of best friends usually peaks in early adolescence at about four to six and declines thereafter (55, 93) until adulthood, when typically there is one best friend, a few close friends, some good friends, and a much larger number of colleagues or acquaintances.

Having more than one close friend is obviously an advantage if one quarrels with a best friend or if the best friend is unavailable when companionship, advice, support, or information is needed (41). Yet having many friends is not necessarily better than having a few close friends, or even no friends; having multitudes of friends may indicate a fear of being alone or an inability to establish close, intimate relationships. Children with many friends tend to be popular and have positive reputations with their classmates; but by early adolescence many of these friendships will have ended, and the quality rather than the quantity of friendships will be most significant (8, 57). Moreover, friendships can be impediments to growth if they are established with those who fail to show desirable attitudes such as self-reliance and plans for future education (51).

Perhaps more important than number of friends per se is their perceived availability in times of need and the characteristics of those friends (for example, whether or not they are supportive). Among adults, a single intimate relationship with a confidant with whom one can share thoughts and feelings is just as effective as multiple relationships in helping one cope with stressful events (36). It is not possible to judge whether the same conclusions hold for adolescents, because researchers have seldom distinguished between the number and the quality of friendships, frequently ignoring the distinction between the terms *best friend, close friend,* and *friend.* Nor have researchers often considered the possibility that characteristics of individuals other than sex and age influence the quality of friendships.

Stability and Reciprocity

Two opposing assumptions can be made concerning the stability of adolescent friendships. The first is that adolescents form and end friendships frequently, often for the slightest of reasons. The second is that in adolescence one forms lifelong friendships. The relative stability of adolescent friendships is a significant issue for two reasons: first, the developmental outcomes of having stable relationships are generally perceived to be positive, and second, the ability of a friend to influence an adolescent's behavior and values is likely to be greater when the friendship is stable. The first point is our concern here; the second will be discussed in the section on friends' influence.

Epstein found that two-thirds of the youths in her study did not have a stable, reciprocated friendship during a one-year period (52, 53; see similar findings in 34, 67, 95, 97). The stability and reciprocity of short-term friendships did, however, increase from early to late adolescence, more so for female than for male adolescents. Reciprocated friendships were more stable than unreciprocated ones, and the category of friends was more stable than the category of best friends. Epstein concluded, "Stability is neither typical nor required for best friendships across the life span" (55, p. 151). Contrary findings, however, have been reported by Berndt and associates, who found most friendships to be stable over a school year (9, 10).

The failure to maintain the same friends over time has been attributed to both environmental and personal factors. Environmental factors include the transition from middle school to high school (8, 55) as well as school structure or composition. These transitions affect friendship patterns because they expose the adolescent to a larger array of social networks, academic work groups, curricula, and reward structures. Changes in friendships after a school transition appear to be fortuitous: adolescents are more likely to maintain past friendships if they are assigned to the same school or the same classes in the new school (8). Among African-American adolescents in a predominantly white junior high school, whose reciprocated friendships were based on neighborhood rather than school, school was not found to be a place conducive to forming or maintaining contact with friends (31).

Other studies have noted the role played by personal characteristics in determining the stability of adolescent friendships. During childhood, shared activities are critical in forming and maintaining friendships. By early adolescence, however, stability of relationships is best predicted by the willingness of friends to help and support one another, perhaps because new social demands are placed on adolescents (and thus more peer help is needed), and because advanced cognitive factors are being developed (for example, an increased capacity for abstract reasoning and for recognizing the needs of others) (25). Friends in a stable relationship tend to have similar attitudes and behavior such as political orientation, educational aspirations, marijuana use, and participation in delinquency (72). Friends who share positive attitudes toward their relationship and have frequent contact prior to school transition are more likely to remain close afterward (8).

Another major determinant of stability is the relative quality of the relationship. In a longitudinal study of youths making the transition from high school to college, both the number of and the degree of satisfaction with high school friendships were found to decrease dramatically (109). These failures were attributed to poor communication patterns and low self-disclosure among friends. Maintaining friendships requires social skills such as the ability to initiate interactions, reveal personal information, display affection and support, and avoid major negative assertions (although modest conflict may enhance friendships). Males are far more likely than females to report feeling lonely and dissatisfied with both old and new friends because of deficits in these skills.

Stable friendships have several *short-term* benefits. On most school-related (achievement and behavior) measures, those who had stable friendships with similarly high-scoring peers out-performed all others (51). Adolescents with stable friendships tend to have positive reputations with peers, enjoy popularity, and be judged as well behaved by teachers, both before and after a school transition (8, 24). Conversely, adolescents who make new friends immediately after the transition are judged by teachers to be disruptive and by peers to be aggressive. These findings suggest that the rapid formation of new friendships in a new setting may not always be a sign of healthy adaptation but may instead reflect past failures in other relationships.

The *long-term* consequences of having stable or unstable, reciprocated or unreciprocated friendships during adolescence have not been investigated. We believe this omission needs to be corrected if the significance of friendships for adolescent development is to be better understood. One point of view is that changing friendships during adolescence is desirable because development proceeds at different rates for different individuals, and therefore adolescents who were similar when they became friends may not have much in common later. Rather than maintaining this established friendship and not growing, or even regressing, adolescents may be better served by making new friends (17).

Similarity of Friends

The benefits of friendship may depend not only on the stability of the relationship but also on similarities or dissimilarities among friends. Because of natural changes in the environment that occur during the course of adolescence, the possibility of encountering diversity increases dramatically: youth move from small, neighborhood elementary schools to large middle schools or junior high schools and high schools; physical mobility (for example, driving) becomes more possible; and growing freedom from parental restraints may open new options for contact with peers unlike oneself. Yet Epstein notes that during adolescence friends become *more similar* on a growing number of traits, especially if the friendship is reciprocated and long-lasting (55, 56).

This similarity may be due to the ways in which the social world of adolescents is organized. Settings such as neighborhoods are frequently segregated by social class, race, attitudes, and values; schools are similarly segregated by tracking, extracurricular activities, reward structures, and methods of instruction. Thus, youth are generally exposed by chance to a homogeneous pool from which to select their friends (35). The preponderance of same-age friendships may be due to the large number of opportunities for interactions with other adolescents of a similar age, for age grouping is the norm in most schools, team sports, and youth programs. In other less age-based cultures, and among nonhuman primates, mixed-age groupings among youth are more common (97, 119).

Similarity among friends may also be explained by personal preference. For example, participating in athletics increases exposure to peers who possess similar athletic abilities and particular types of values (for example, physical fitness), attitudes (competitiveness), and status (usually high). Adolescents may also seek friends like themselves in order to increase the supportiveness of their friendships. Similarities in age, social class, and race among friends reflect this consideration. Teenagers may prefer same-age friendships because they want equality with their friends in respects such as status and maturity (120). Beyond noting the obvious fact that friends' similarities in race and social class reflect racial and class segregation in classrooms and schools as well as larger segments of society, Schofield also suggests that interracial friendships are uncommon because racial differences are confounded with differences in achievement and interpersonal behavior (100). Such differences increase the likelihood of conflict within any friendship involving individuals of different races (see also 50). For example, middle-class white females appear particularly intimidated by the ritual insults of working-class African-American females (101). Thus, the critical element in forming friendships may not be race, social class, age, or sex per se but the need of adolescents for friendships that are relatively safe, familiar, and trouble free.

Friends are also similar in respects other than sociodemographic characteristics, which may serve as initial guides before a more fine-tuned process of discovery takes place (56). With increasing age, adolescents show greater concern with the deeper qualities of a person, such as character, attitudes, beliefs, and values (103, 121). For example, high school friends tend to have similar attitudes and behaviors involving drinking, smoking, church attendance, number of evenings spent at home, and dating (34). Friends also tend to be alike in their orientation toward educational aspirations, academic achievement, and preferences for music, entertainment, and other common activities (38, 40, 53, 72, 75, 84). Equality (115) and similarity (4, 120) in friendship are instrumental in giving adolescents a sense of competence and self-validation.

It is also true that adolescents sometimes prefer friends who are different from themselves. Kandel found that adolescent friends were more similar in their behavior, such as illegal drug use, than in their attitudes, for example, favoring the use of marijuana (73). But divergence was greatest on psychological characteristics such as closeness to parents, self-esteem, and social isolation. If one is unpopular or of low status, then befriending a dissimilar peer may be advantageous (70). Adolescents, especially males, from low-income families occasionally choose friends higher in socioeconomic status to improve their own social status; the latter may "select down" to obtain recognition of superiority (52). Dissimilarity among friends may also result from qualities considered relatively unimportant by the individuals themselves. For example, a student athlete may primarily value athletic ability in a friend and not care whether that friend has high or low grades.

But are friendships based on dissimilarity healthy for development? Are mixed-age friendships, in particular, beneficial or detrimental to an adolescent's development? An adolescent with friends of various ages could, perhaps, avoid becoming immersed in the conformity of the youth subculture and instead develop the various interpersonal skills and social perspectives of those older or younger. Yet a common fear, especially among parents and school officials, is that such learning will be negative, that older youths may encourage younger adolescents to engage in delinquent behavior or early sexual activity. In fact, early sexual and delinquent activities are more frequent among young teenagers who interact with older youths (18). It is not known, however, whether such associations guide the youngsters to delinquency or whether they are already delinquency-prone.

Magnusson's longitudinal study of eighth-grade girls lends support to those who fear the influence of older peers (78). Early-maturing girls developed friendships with those chronologically older but biologically similar to them. Because of these associations the girls were more likely than their peers to engage in a number of norm-breaking behaviors, such as playing truant, getting drunk, ignoring parents' prohibitions, and pilfering from stores. These results emphasize the role of older friends as transmitters of norms. The long-range consequences of these patterns were also evident: as adults (age 26 years) the earliest developers were most likely to have borne a child and were less likely to be vocationally and educationally oriented than peers who developed later. Also of some concern is the psychosocial maturity of youths who select predominantly younger adolescents as friends (114). A common but untested assumption is that adolescents are best able to develop age-appropriate behaviors and social skills in the context of same-age groupings.

Friends are usually of the same gender. Indeed the label "best friend" is generally reserved for same-sex friends. Sex segregation in free play and peer groupings is the norm from preschool through the pubescent years (77). Both biological and socialization processes play a role in this development through differential play styles of the sexes and their unique modes of exerting peer influence. One outcome of these same-sex interactions is a strong sense of gender identity based on same-sex group membership. By adolescence other-sex relationships are frequently perceived as qualitatively different, or as dating opportunities (113). Other-sex friendships, especially during early adolescence, may be viewed as impediments to evolving gender-appropriate behaviors, characteristics, and interests. These relationships are frequently characterized as infrequent interactions with low levels of intimacy (22, 55, 65, 100).

Yet for some adolescents these dissimilar relationships may be neither romantic nor insignificant. For example, gay and lesbian youth may seek out friends of the other sex not for romantic potential but because of similarity of interests. Although the vast majority of both white and African-American gay and lesbian adults reported that they had a close same-sex friend during their childhood and adolescence, the percentage was still somewhat lower than for matched heterosexual men and women (2). The former were less likely than the latter to "pal around" with children of the same sex and were more likely to have a close friend of the other sex from grades one through eight. Recent research with gay and lesbian youths aged 14 to 23 documents the prevalence and the importance of other-sex friendships for "coming out" and the enhancement of self-esteem (98).

Similarities among friends may merely indicate that the social world of adolescents is structured in ways that typically provide opportunities for interactions with others who are alike in significant respects. But adolescents also prefer friends who are similar to themselves because they expect a friendship to be a relationship among equals. The relative developmental benefits of having similar and dissimilar friends are as yet little understood or documented.

Personal and Environmental Determinants of Friendship

Other than the variables previously discussed—number of friends, stability of friendships, and similarity of friends—researchers have addressed few of the determinants of close and supportive friendships during adolescence. It is nonetheless apparent that variations among adolescents in eliciting supportive friendships are not purely random, nor are they derived entirely from environmental causes. Adolescents' own characteristics determine in part how supportive their peer relations are. For example, youths who rated highest in popularity, sociability, and positive attitudes about their relationships with peers were found to be best able to maintain their friendships despite a school transition (8). Indeed, stable friendships may not be an independent contributor to so much as a symptom of adjustment, itself a stable characteristic, after the junior high transition. These findings, however, do not alter the fact that loss of supportive friendship is often precipitated by environmental factors beyond an adolescent's control. When friends attend another school, any interaction during the school day is virtually precluded.

Personal characteristics may themselves be influenced by experiences in previous social relationships or by genetic factors. In regard to the latter, adolescents who are genetically predisposed to express sociability and extroversion may be more likely to maintain harmonious interactions with friends than those inclined toward shyness or poor impulse control (99). In regard to the former, Gold and Yanof noted, "Friendships are significantly influenced by the values concerning and capacities for intimacy nurtured in the parent-adolescent relationship. Though not necessarily replicating parental relationships, peer relationships bear some resemblance to them" (63, p. 654). In their research they found that adolescent girls who viewed their mothers as an appropriate model reported intimate, affectionate, and mutual relationships with their closest girlfriends.

Additional evidence that links the kind of relationships one has with one's parents with how one conducts friendships is provided by Sroufe's longitudinal study of attachment (reported in a personal communication, May 1989). Preadolescents and early adolescents were classified as secure or anxious on the basis of histories of parental attachment during their first year. As assessed by observational measures and counselor ratings, the youths securely attached to their parents were likely to have healthy peer relationships. For example, they were rated higher in peer social competence, had more friends, participated more in peer group activities, and were less likely to be socially isolated than the anxious youths.

Thus, one's ability to establish active and healthy peer friendships is based on personal characteristics as well as on one's history of positive interpersonal relationships. Researchers do not yet know the degree to which establishing positive friendships and peer relations is based on genetic or traitlike characteristics as opposed to learned behaviors that may be easily altered through intervention or conscious effort.

Potential Benefits of Close Friendships

Sullivan was the first major theorist to emphasize the contributions of close friendships to adolescent development (114). He proposed that intimate conversations with close friends increase adolescents' sense of self-worth and the accuracy of their understanding of other people. More recently, Rubin has suggested that interactions with close friends facilitate the learning of social skills, lead to more accurate self-evaluations through comparison with other people, and foster a sense of group belonging (95). Because there is little empirical evidence that directly establishes the effects of friendship on adolescents' behavior and development, many of the conclusions drawn in this section must be considered tentative.

Not all writers have wholeheartedly adopted the general hypothesis that close friendships have positive effects on adolescent development. Because most researchers have examined only the correlations between friendship and various aspects of behavior or adjustment, they have been unable to demonstrate a causal link. Significant positive correlations do not unequivocally demonstrate that friendships influence adolescents' adjustment; these correlations could instead indicate that better-adjusted adolescents are successful in forming and maintaining friendships. As McGuire and Weisz have stated, "It may be reasonable to contend, in contrast to Sullivan's hypothesis, that a child's greater initial sensitivity to others' feelings and his helpful behavior cause and sustain friendships" (80, p. 1483). Data from longitudinal studies could clarify this issue, but such data are rare (7). In general, however, close and supportive friendships appear to have beneficial effects on several aspects of adolescents' psychological, social, and academic adjustment.

Supportive Friendships and Psychological Adjustment

Adolescents who have satisfying and harmonious friendships typically report positive self-esteem, a good understanding of other people's feelings, and relatively little loneliness (79, 80, 91). Similar results are found for white and African-American youth, both middle class and lower class (27, 32). These findings imply that the relations between the qualities of adolescents' friendships and psychological adjustment do not differ markedly across racial and social-class groups.

Nevertheless, the qualities of adolescents' friendships may not be linked to their psychological adjustment to the same degree or in the same direction for all groups of adolescents. Hirsch and Reischl have suggested that adolescents in some types of families may find support from friends to be harmful or at best ineffective (69). As might be expected, they found that perceptions of friends' support in coping with problems at school were positively related to self-esteem when the adolescents were from normal families. But this relationship was slightly reversed when the adolescents came from families with one clinically depressed parent. Hirsch and

Reischl speculated that the latter adolescents felt anxious about their friends' views of their parent and about the future of their friendship. These speculations are valuable because they attempt to define the processes that account for positive or negative relations between measures of friends' support and psychological adjustment.

Exploration of possible sex differences in the relationship between friends' support and adjustment would also be valuable. As we noted earlier, researchers have consistently found that adolescent girls perceive their friendships as more intimate and emotionally supportive than do adolescent boys (6, 121). Knowing whether this difference has any impact on the relation of individual differences in friendship to individual differences in adjustment would be both theoretically and practically significant (43).

Supportive Friendships and Social Adjustment

Adolescents who have satisfying and harmonious friendships tend to be popular with their classmates, have positive views of them, and behave in ways that reflect advanced levels of social skills. In a study of lower-class African-American seventh-graders, those who perceived their friends as supportive had more reciprocated friendships, were more popular with their classmates, and were more often nominated by their peers as individuals who could successfully manage such social situations as arranging a double date or representing classmates in a meeting with teachers (27; see also 28). Two other studies found that adolescents with an especially close and satisfying friendship behaved more generously toward a classmate when playing a game or completing a task than did adolescents without such a friendship (79, 80).

Berndt and Hawkins assessed the friendships and social adjustment of one group of junior high school students on three occasions (8). Adolescents who described their friendships as most supportive also viewed their relationships with the rest of their classmates positively, although these correlations were stronger at the end of seventh grade than at earlier times. Moreover, students' perceptions of their friendships were positively related to changes over time in attitudes toward classmates as a whole. This finding can be interpreted as evidence that friendships have a causal influence on attitudes toward classmates. Apparently adolescents who began with a positive view of their close friendship group developed an increasingly positive view of their entire set of classmates.

Adolescents who viewed their classmates positively also assumed that their classmates viewed them positively, a finding that is consistent with another longitudinal study of adolescents making the transition to junior high school (111). Sixth-grade girls who believed that their classmates valued them highly had high self-esteem in seventh grade. This result illustrates the links between social acceptance and aspects of psychological adjustment such as self-esteem.

Longitudinal data on the relationship of friendship to social adjustment are limited. Although there is little doubt that friendships are associated with certain aspects of social skill and adjustment, the evidence for positive relations between friendship and indicators of social adjustment (for example, popularity) is not clear-cut (80). More research is needed to clarify the inconsistencies in available data. We especially need research in which both adolescents' friendships and multiple facets of their social adjustment are assessed on repeated occasions.

Supportive Friendships and Academic Adjustment

Adolescents with satisfying and harmonious friendships tend to behave appropriately in school, are motivated to do well, and often receive high grades. Teenagers who perceive their friendships as supportive have higher achievement-test scores, report-card grades, and behavior ratings from teachers, are more involved in school, and place more value on what they learn there (8, 82). Although early studies included mostly samples of white, middle-class adolescents, the relationships hold more generally as well. For example, lower-class African-American teenagers who perceived their friends as supportive were shown to have high grades and achievement-test scores as well (27).

By contrast, one study found that a measure of perceived support from friends and other peers was unrelated to a composite measure of school adjustment based on students' grades, conduct, absences, and other indexes (43). Furthermore, among lower-class African-American adolescents in a senior high school, perceptions of support from peers (not just friends) were negatively related to grades (29), perhaps because the peers themselves devalued school achievement (27). This suggestion is analogous to Ball's hypothesis that close friendships may reinforce negative attitudes toward school in low-achieving adolescents (1). Although plausible, current data are too incomplete to justify either accepting or rejecting this view. One problem with both studies is that neither Ball (1) nor Cauce and associates (29) used specific measures of the closeness or quality of the friendships.

On balance, the available data suggest that young people with positive and supportive friendships usually show positive attitudes and behavior in school as well. One plausible explanation is that teenagers enjoy opportunities for interactions with their friends at school. Consequently, when they have especially close and satisfying friendships, they are likely to have a favorable impression of their entire school experience. Another possible explanation, one that reverses the presumed causal direction, is that adolescents who have adjusted well to school also have advanced social and social-cognitive skills and are therefore better able to form and maintain close friendships than students who are less well adjusted. Again, longitudinal studies designed to examine these hypotheses could clarify the degree to which each one captures the truth.

When viewed as a whole, research findings are most consistent with the view that friendships are positively associated with the psychological, social, and academic adjustment of both male and female adolescents from a variety of racial and social-class groups. Yet because relevant data are derived from correlational studies, the findings do not demonstrate that close friendships have a causal impact on adjustment. Tests of that hypothesis with longitudinal designs, experimental designs, or short-term interventions are needed.

Peer Relationships and Status in the Peer Group

In addition to their close friendships, most adolescents have relationships of some kind with larger peer groups, such as school classmates, cabinmates at summer camp, and athletic teammates. Since the 1930s researchers have attempted to summarize these relationships with indexes of adolescents' social status in a particular peer group. Investigators typically ask adolescents to name those whom they especially like and especially dislike. While indicators of social status can be derived in many ways, two major approaches are most often used (23, 37).

The first and simplest approach is to total both the number of positive and negative nominations that an individual receives. The negative nominations are then subtracted from the positive nominations. The resulting score can be treated as an index of the adolescent's popularity, social acceptance, or social preference. Until the 1980s most researchers used a variant of this procedure to assess the relation of adolescents' social status to other variables ranging from aggressive behavior to unusual first names (cf. 68).

In the second approach to the measurement of social status, each adolescent's totals for positive and negative nominations are used in combination to assign the adolescent to a specific social-status group. Most attention in recent years has focused on three groups: popular, rejected, and neglected. Popular adolescents receive many positive nominations and few negative nominations relative to their peer group as a whole. Rejected adolescents receive many negative nominations and few positive nominations. Neglected or isolated adolescents receive few positive or negative nominations. The primary advantage of this classification procedure is that it allows researchers to distinguish unpopular adolescents who are truly disliked (rejected) from those who are neither especially liked nor disliked (neglected).

Several studies have shown that unpopular and rejected children and adolescents are the groups most likely to be aggressive, to drop out of school, to engage in criminal behavior during adolescence or adulthood, and to show mental illness in adulthood (88). At the other extreme, popular children tend to be more intelligent, more socially skilled, less involved in conflicts with peers, and more sociable (68). In adolescence they tend to be leaders in activities, have more athletic ability, and are likely to experience puberty before the majority of their peers (97). The behavioral profile and long-term prognosis for the neglected adolescent is less clear. Although several studies suggest no long-term negative consequences, the failure to separate the neglected from the rejected status groups in many studies reduces the adequacy of the data base (88).

The relationship of social status to concurrent behavior (for example, aggression) and adult outcomes (for example, mental illness) could be explained in two ways (88). On the one hand, low status in the peer group may reduce adolescents' opportunities for learning social skills that contribute to the socialization of desirable behaviors and mental health in adulthood. For instance, adolescents who are rejected by peers may have neither the opportunity nor the incentive to learn techniques for influencing others that are more diplomatic than a kick or a punch. On the other hand, low status in the peer group may not have any direct effect. Some adolescents may have low status because their preexisting psychological or social handicaps cause others to reject them. These handicaps then manifest themselves in poor adult outcomes. Stated more succinctly, the alternative positions differ as to whether they view low status as causal or merely symptomatic. Parker and Asher have argued, however, that the alternatives should not be treated as a strict either-or choice (88). To some extent low status may be a symptom of preexisting difficulties, and to some extent it may be a cause of future difficulties.

The two perspectives on social status are especially crucial for this chapter because they raise questions concerning the kinds of relationships that low-status adolescents have with their peers. In particular, is low social status related to features of adolescents' friendships?

On theoretical grounds a relation between the two might be expected because often the same behaviors are associated with high social status and good friendships. For example, popular teenagers are typically less aggressive than rejected ones (26) and adolescents prefer to make friends with peers who are relatively nonaggressive (3, 85). Moreover, intervention programs designed to teach children and youth how to make friends can also have positive effects on their social status (14, 83). In general, adolescents who have the social skills necessary for achieving high social status can be expected to have considerable abilities to form and maintain close, harmonious, and supportive friendships.

Other theorists, however, emphasize the distinction between friendships and social status (23). They suggest that there is no compelling reason why popular children, who have many friends, will also have supportive or harmonious friendships. Basing her study on participant observation in one junior high school, Eder concluded that the rivalry induced in adolescent girls by the desire for high social status frequently created conflicts and tensions in the friendships of very popular girls (46).

Evidence that popular adolescents have more supportive friendships than less popular peers was noted in a previous section of this chapter (and see 27, 28). In addition, rejected children perceive their peers as less supportive than do popular children (45), whereas perceptions of support do not differ significantly between popular and neglected children. One difficulty in drawing conclusions from this study is that the measures of support referred both to friends and to other classmates. Adolescents who are rejected by their classmates are likely to be aware of their classmates' negative attitudes toward them and thus tend not to view their classmates as supportive. Their perceptions of their own friendships may be rather different.

Some studies, however, have found either a weak relation or no relation at all between measures of social status in the larger peer group and measures of the quality of close friendships (8, 80). Other researchers have shown that adolescents' popularity is not related to the number of reciprocated friendships that they have or their identification as members of friendship groups (26, 57). These studies, however, assessed only the quantity and not the quality of friendships.

Because the findings of recent research are mixed, theorists of both persuasions can find evidence consistent with their views. It remains unclear how the two theoretical positions might be reconciled or integrated. Research illuminating this conceptual and empirical puzzle would be highly valuable. In addition to settling the theoretical questions concerning the skills and attributes that are instrumental for friendships and social status, this research would clarify the links among different facets of adolescents' peer relationships.

Research on the connections between friendship and social status would also be of practical significance. Low social status has repeatedly been diagnostic of psychological, interpersonal, and academic difficulties in childhood and adolescence (88). If the features of young people's friendships are largely independent of their social status but are related to measures of adjustment and development, then identifying adolescents at risk would be more accurate if both friendships and social status were assessed. Alternatively, if the features of friendships are related to social status, then researchers can potentially determine whether friendship or social status is more strongly or more directly linked to developmental outcomes. The answers to these questions would, in turn, guide the formulation of strategies for preventive interventions or treatments for adolescents experiencing problems with peer relationships.

Romantic Relationships

Another variety of peer relations is the peer romance. Apart from their sexual aspects, however, the nature of romantic relationships has been generally ignored by researchers. By junior high school, interest in friendships with the other sex increases, especially among girls, although members of the other sex never constitute the majority of best-friend nominations (55, 65, 100). For girls, these relationships are usually with older boys and boys from other schools. There is, however, a qualitative difference between these romantic relationships and friendships (113). It is exactly this qualitative difference that is overlooked in the research literature.

What is known is of a more quantitative nature. Romantic relationships begin to emerge during early and middle adolescence, and most, although certainly not all, adolescents experience dating prior to graduating from high school. While numerous statistics indicate how many adolescents date, what activities they engage in, the prevalence of sex in romance, and racial and social-class differences (see Chapter 13 in this volume) little is known about the interpersonal aspects of romantic relationships.

Sullivan believed that early adolescent "chumships" offered an opportunity to practice interpersonal qualities that would carry over into romantic relationships (114). Within these same-sex friendships one could learn self-disclosure and experience the benefits of intimacy. Dunphy viewed the friendship clique and crowd in a similar light; indeed, Dunphy believed these same-sex friendships begin to disintegrate as members become involved in heterosexual dating (44). Those who do not make this move are likely to be labeled as odd or developmentally delayed and are rejected by peers.

Thus it is generally believed that skills learned in developing and maintaining friendships, such as showing intimacy, are further developed and expressed in romantic involvements. Dating has been viewed as serving a number of other developmental functions, some of which overlap with the benefits of friendship. An early review lists the four major functions of dating as entertainment, socialization, prestige enhancement, and courtship (112). Additional functions served by these relationships include identity and prosocial development (107) in that relating to someone else enhances sensitivity to and empathy with needs that are different from one's own. Several investigators have demonstrated that, with age, all dimensions of intimacy increase for other-sex relationships (22, 108). In the latter study female-male couples moved from the least intimate relationships in fifth grade to most intimate in eleventh grade. Thus altruism, intimacy, and identity receive critical attention and support during adolescence in relationships with members of both the same and the other sex.

The onset of relationships with the other sex may, however, have negative ramifications for same-sex friendships. The temporary decline between fifth and seventh grade in intimacy scores for same-sex friendships may be due to interference from other-sex relationships (42, 108).

There is some indication that, regardless of the intimacy scores of these new relationships, they are not able to withstand much disruption. A longitudinal study of youth during the summer before college and continuing for the first three semesters of college found that nearly one-half of all high school romantic relationships ended, and the remaining ones became less satisfying, when one partner entered college. Because deficits in interpersonal and communication skills are more common for males, four times as many men as women reported feeling lonely and dissatisfied with both old and new friends and romantic partners. Successful new relationships were initiated because of the need for companionship and were found to increase in affection, support, and modest amounts of conflict (109).

Beyond such factual aspects as age at onset and frequency of dating, romantic relationships between adolescents remain an open field for researchers. Issues that need to be addressed include the similarities as well as differences among adolescent same-sex and other-sex friendships and romances (both prior to, during, and after the romance); how such relationships are experienced by lesbian and gay youth, adolescents of color, and youth of various social classes; an empirical demonstration of the proposed developmental functions of romantic encounters, especially as they affect mental and social well-being; and a study of the phenomenology of dating.

Friends' Influence on Adolescents

Extent and Direction of Influence

The influence of friends extends beyond concerns of immediate relevance such as clothes, entertainment, and companionship to include behaviors, attitudes, and beliefs that have important consequences for an adolescent and his or her society (4, 22). For example, best friends influence adolescents' educational aspirations and their use of alcohol, marijuana, and other illicit drugs (73). In terms of drug use, a review of the literature found that the relative influence of friends and parents varied depending on the drug (62). Friends were critical influences in decisions to use marijuana, parents for use of other illicit drugs, and both for alcohol. For those who had never smoked cigarettes, initiation was best predicted when both friends and parents smoked, when levels of parental support were low, or when friends had low expectations for success, both general and academic (30). The ability of friends to influence the behaviors and attitudes of adolescents is magnified when adolescents perceive that their parental relationship is negative (parents do not like them) or deficient in support and guidance.

When relations with parents are positive, Hartup's "synergistic" model (68) best explains the relative influence of friends and parents. Hartup argues that there is little disagreement between parents and adolescents as to basic moral principles, future educational and career aspirations and goals, and self-control; the discord usually emerges over relatively trivial matters and over fundamental developmental issues that are related to status within the family and identity outside the family network. In these latter situations the influence of friends may become quite important. Kandel's early research illustrates the synergistic model (71, 74). In situations in which the mother wanted her child to attend college but the child's best friend had no such plans, half the adolescents in her study reported no college plans; in the reverse situation (mother opposed to college, best friend in favor), only 21% of the adolescents planned to attend college. Thus, the influence of the parent appears to be greater than that of the best friend on educational plans. When both the mother and the best friend were in agreement, then there was nearly complete concordance: 83% had college plans when both influences were in favor, while only 8% had college plans when both were opposed.

A central question concerning the influence of adolescents on one another is whether nonselected peers are as influential as friends (35). Relatively few researchers or policy makers have drawn this distinction between peers in general and friends, yet the difference can be critical. For example, lower-class girls attending a health clinic reported that their knowledge of and beliefs concerning contraception and pregnancy were similar to their parents' and not their peers'. But when a distinction was made between friends and peers, girls who perceived that they were at odds with their friends but not necessarily with peers in their beliefs and myths about sexuality tended to be those least likely to use contraceptives (87).

Reports from the mass media and from parents suggest that peer norms contribute primarily to delinquency, drug use, and other undesirable behaviors. Many intervention programs are predicated on the premise that peer influence propels the adolescent toward rather than away from undesirable behaviors. Yet when peer influence is assessed in terms of similarity between friends or increases over time in friends' similarity, the nature of their influence is as likely to be positive as negative (see also Chapter 7 in this volume). Adolescents who did not smoke cigarettes believed that their friends would disapprove if they started smoking; if they already smoked, then their friends tolerated their behavior but did not approve of it (Urberg, personal communication). Adolescents rarely expected their friends to favor, much less pressure them to begin, cigarette smoking. Several other investigators have reported that friends may also pressure adolescents to study hard, achieve good grades, and attend college (20, 52). Researchers have also demonstrated the influence of friends on social understanding and a sense of identity (120), on the capacity to form and maintain egalitarian relationships (6), on positive mental health (92), and on prosocial behavior (68).

We should also remember that the influence of friends is reciprocal: adolescents are influenced by their friends, and they in turn influence their friends. The final outcome of this mutual process is often a compromise in which friends become more similar to one another. Often this compromise does not change the average position of the group members (52, 72). At other times one outcome—through discussion or argument—may ultimately come to seem more attractive or persuasive and be endorsed more strongly than another (11). In such cases evidence suggests that the compromise position is more likely to be prosocial than antisocial.

Conditions that Increase Friends' Influence

Friends are most likely to be influential if the friendship is stable, reciprocated, and exclusive. Epstein emphasized that long-standing friendships, especially for males, are likely to influence a number of school-related measures such as achievement and satisfaction with school (51). Even after the friendship wanes, the influence remains, although to a lesser degree than that of current friends. Reciprocated friendships are also more influential than nonreciprocated friendships on some measures of school attitudes and performance (for example, low achievement and lack of self-reliance). That is, adolescents are likely to be influenced in their behavior and attitudes by peers whom they would like to have as friends.

If an individual has many friends, the power of any one friend is less than if he or she were the sole confidant (35). The influence may also be domain specific. For example, a friend who is well known as a fashion trendsetter may be most influential in how an adolescent dresses, while another friend who is a teammate on an athletic team may influence diet. Teenagers are affected not only by a best friend but also by the small group of friends with whom they spend much of their time (35, 48, 55). Many youths have several friends who may all differ in their attitudes and behaviors. Although the closest of these friends may have the most influence, other friends are also likely to share some influence.

It should also be noted that adolescents sometimes act out of their own inclinations, independently of friends, family, or peers (68). In research on family and peer influence, a significant number of adolescents "abandoned the provided response categories and spontaneously added 'myself,' 'personal opinion,' . . . to emphasize independent choice" (102, p. 11). Thus, independent judgment is also found in adolescence.

Processes of Influence

Longitudinal studies have shown that the similarity between friends at any one time is due partly to the selection of friends who are already similar and partly to the influence of initially dissimilar friends on one another (35, 51, 72). Epstein demonstrated the power of peer influence over a one-year period by showing that initially low-scoring students improved in their academic adjustment when they had high-scoring friends (51). There was little change among those who initially had friends with scores similar to their own (either low/low or high/high). The fourth case—high-scoring youths with low-scoring friends—demonstrated the potential negative influence of peers: the grades and self-reliance of these high scorers fell over the course of the school year. Other research has shown that friends within a clique were more similar to one another than to other peers on a number of attitudinal and personality characteristics (for example, desire to be remembered as a brilliant student), and new clique members became more similar over time to the original group members (34). Finally, a longitudinal study of stable friends, former friends, and friends-to-be regarding marijuana use, political orientation, delinquency, and educational aspirations indicated that assortative pairing (similarity in selection) and socialization (peer influence) were essentially equally responsible for similarity between friends after time (72). Thus, friends both reinforce the status quo and provide a vehicle for change.

On the whole, writers who lament or praise the effects of friends on adolescents' behavior say almost nothing about how this influence or power is applied or why it is effective. It is assumed, although not well documented, that the practice of spending an enormous amount of time together and exchanging many ideas through conversation induces friends to imitate or model one another's behaviors, attitudes, and values. These attributes in turn are socially reinforced through praise, recognition, and increased status (72, 73). The difficulty of assessing these social conditioning processes is so formidable that they are frequently assumed rather than tested.

One exception is the research of the social anthropologist Eder, an innovative and provocative investigation of how power and influence are conveyed among adolescents (48, 50). Because friends share a wide range of experiences, information is learned primarily through observation and disseminated through interactions. Among working-class and middle-class adolescents aged 10 to 14 observed in a middle school lunch room, Eder found teasing among friends: "Its ambiguous nature allows adolescents to express liking, communicate social norms and release embarrassment in an indirect manner" (48, p. 27). Through openly teasing one another about sensitive issues such as weight, appearance, homosexuality, and romantic relationships, the youths were able to express an opinion without being held directly accountable for hurting a friend (50). Another study found that by means of indirect gossip about nongroup members and humorous teasing of friends, African-American adolescent females conveyed information about "norm violators" (64). Teasing increases feelings of closeness and solidarity among friends, allows creative processes to be expressed, maintains gender boundaries, and teaches adolescents how to initiate romantic interactions (58, 97, 101).

French and Raven have proposed other mechanisms that may give one person influence over another (59). Friends have *coercive power* when they have the ability to punish others for noncompliance with a suggestion or command. This power seems to be assumed, explicitly or implicitly, in most research. Observations in natural settings indicate that *overt* coercion is rarely used among adolescents as a technique for changing one another's behavior. Conformity to peer group norms (110) or to the desires of a dominant peer (97) occur with relatively little external pressure in the form of physical threats or sanctions, except under unusual circumstances, for example, when all members of the group join together in a fight or when the dominant adolescent displays bullying or antagonistic personality characteristics. Through ridicule and other means of expressing disapproval peers can, however, exert *subtle* coercive power to lower or raise an adolescent's self-esteem or group status (48, 60).

Second, friends have *reward power* when they control outcomes that others desire, such as the opportunity to share problems with friends, to call on friends for help, to receive compliments or other responses that boost self-esteem, and to have fun in activities with their friends. The influence that friends have rests in large measure on their ability both to confer these rewards and to withdraw them.

Individuals possess *referent power* when others admire them and want to be like them. Adolescents become friends in part with those they want to be associated with and whom they perceive as popular, good at athletics, skilled at fighting, or outstanding in some other way (97, 110). Referent power contrasts sharply with the notion of peer pressure. Friends may have referent power even when they do not exert pressure. No threats, bribes, or other forms of punishment or reward are necessary for effective referent power. Even interacting with one another may be unnecessary.

The last two types of social power described by French and Raven, *legitimate* and *expert power* (59), might appear to be of little significance in terms of the influence of adolescent friends. Legitimate power depends on the existence of formally established, hierarchically organized social institutions. Friendships, however, are not formal social institutions and do not have an explicit hierarchical organization. Indeed, adolescents emphasize the equality among themselves and their friends, which is inconsistent with accepting some individuals as experts, unless the interpretation of expert power is broadened. For example, teenagers (especially females) may maintain a belief in overall equality among friends but behave in a contrary, power-oriented fashion (97) or acknowledge that certain individuals have areas of special expertise (116). Those who know more about playing basketball, arranging a party, or stealing a car would naturally have additional power and influence when youths are engaged in these activities. In addition, adolescents may change their views after discussions with friends, not because they feel pressured to do so but because friends gave them information or advice that was convincing.

No single construct can encompass the multiple forms of peer influence on adolescent behavior. Occasionally single friends or groups of friends control an individual's behavior by means of punishment or threats. More often friends reward those whose behavior is consistent with their norms and withdraw rewards from those whose behavior violates the norms. Even when friends do not exert pressure, young people are likely to conform because they want to be accepted by their friends and because they admire individuals who live up to the group's norms. In still other cases individuals follow suggestions made by others because they believe the suggestions are reasonable. Few of these forms of influence, however, have been explored in theories or research focusing on the positive and negative effects of friends' influence. In addition, the potency of these influence processes may vary according to the age, sex, social class, race, and personality attributes of the youths; by the various phases in the course of the friendship; and by the particular effect being investigated. Few of these issues have been addressed.

Implications for Research

For the most part adolescents thoroughly enjoy the time they spend with friends. Such times are sources of fun, activity, and support. We now take for granted that peers are significant in the lives of adolescents, but little is really known about the development of enduring, meaningful peer relations or of the continuities, rather than the discontinuities, of peer relations among youth (108). In some areas researchers are now ready to embark on fine-tuned analyses (for example, on the meaning of intimacy for boys), while in others (such as the existence, nature, and meaning of other-sex friendships) the ground for investigation is still quite fertile. Several of the major research needs in and policy implications of peer relations during adolescence are reviewed below.

Research Needs

The preponderance of evidence suggests that close and supportive friendships have beneficial effects on psychological, social, and academic adjustment in adolescence. Nevertheless, more research is needed before this conclusion is taken as an established principle and used as a basis for practice in educational or clinical settings. In the planning of future research on the contributions of friendships to adolescents' behavior and development, six issues merit special attention.

First, the features of adolescents' friendships must be assessed directly rather than simply assumed. In several studies in which friendships seemed to have negative effects on adolescents' adjustment (see, for example, 1), the features of these relationships were not measured systematically. A careful assessment might have revealed that these friendships were not perceived by the adolescents themselves as especially close, harmonious, or supportive. In other words, less well adjusted youths may appear to be negatively affected by their friendships because they actually lack the kinds of friendships assumed to be most effective in promoting a good adjustment to life.

Second, the most important dimension of friendships, in theory, is closeness or support (7, 114). Researchers, however, have occasionally assessed the number of friends that adolescents have (57) or the frequency of their interactions rather than the degree of support (40). Yet teenagers with many friends do not necessarily enjoy the kinds of intimate relationships that are usually assumed to be most beneficial for development. Similarly, a youth who has frequent interactions with friends is not necessarily receiving support from those friends. Scattered research findings suggest that, during adolescence, spending a lot of time with friends is associated with poor adjustment to school and antisocial behavior (8, 39, 40). To paraphrase a well-worn (and sometimes misleading) adage, it may be the quality rather than the quantity of the time spent with friends that is most important.

Third, additional data are needed on the relationship between the features of adolescents' friendships and specific aspects of their adjustment. These data could be valuable for clarifying the inconsistencies in the findings of previous research. For example, additional studies could determine whether there are particular conditions in which the relation between friendship and psychological adjustment differs for the two sexes. This information would, in turn, be useful in judging whether the problems a specific adolescent has with his or her friends are likely to be symptomatic of fundamental problems in psychological adjustment. In other words, the information would help to define the predictive validity of friendship measures for adolescents with specific characteristics or adolescents in specific groups.

New data could also suggest when friends' support is most effective and when it is ineffective or even harmful. For example, we need to identify family circumstances in which the support of friends is negatively related to an adolescent's self-esteem (cf. 69) or inadvertently increases psychological stress. If there are replicable conditions in which friends' support is negatively related to academic achievement (cf. 29), more focused investigations could clarify the kinds of interactions with friends that decrease achievement motivation or increase alienation from school.

Fourth, cross-sectional data must be supplemented with longitudinal data or data from experimental interventions in order to offer a firmer foundation for conclusions about cause and effect. Longitudinal designs are particularly valuable because they can show not only how friendships affect adolescents' adjustment but also how adolescents' adjustment affects their friendships. For example, entering seventh-grade students who were perceived by their classmates as especially sociable had formed more supportive friendships by the end of the year than other students (8). Conversely, students who were viewed by their classmates as particularly aggressive and disruptive at the beginning of the year had increasing conflicts with their close friends during the course of the year. These findings provide a corrective to theories (see, for example, 114) that refer only to the effects of friendship on adjustment by demonstrating that friendship and adjustment have reciprocal influences on each other.

Fifth, the processes assumed to account for positive (or negative) effects of friendship on adjustment must be clearly defined in theory and directly measured in research. Several theorists have claimed that friends rarely give support intentionally to one another; rather, support is obtained as a by-product of participating in close relationships (89, 117). In this view merely having friends and interacting with them give adolescents a sense of belonging and security that increases their well-being. Thus, identifying how friends support one another is equivalent to specifying how close friends behave with one another.

An alternative view is that specific types of interactions can be classified as "supportive transactions" (76). Adolescents who participate in these interactions with friends by definition receive support. From this perspective understanding the processes by which friendships contribute to development is equivalent to investigating what occurs during supportive transactions, and with what consequences.

Most probably the truth lies somewhere in the middle. Intimate conversations among friends, for example, may cover a variety of topics and serve primarily to bolster adolescents' sense of being respected or valued by another person. In other cases these conversations may be focused on a single problem. An adolescent may, for example, want advice on how to tell his parents that he is flunking three classes, or that she is worried that she might be pregnant. In terms of research planning, recognizing the difficulty means presenting a priori hypotheses concerning the processes that link features of friendship to some aspect of adjustment and then measuring those processes directly.

Finally, more attention must be given to the characteristics of adolescents who are friends. Some evidence is available on friendship among white adolescents, African-American adolescents, and youths whose families differ in social class. The existing data suggest that there are more similarities than differences across these variations, but this conclusion depends on only a handful of studies. In addition, virtually no attention has been given to friendships among adolescents below the poverty line or from very wealthy families, or among youth of color other than African-Americans. An essentially unaddressed question emerges when we consider issues of romance. Should relationships with members of the other sex be interpreted as "dating opportunities" or as legitimate friendships? In most cases the former perspective has been taken. Not only does this view negate the experiences and feelings of most lesbian and gay male adolescents (98), but it also gives credence to the stereotype that adolescents cannot establish friendly relations with members of the other sex that are not tainted by sexual desire. These friendships may play a special role in the development of identity, empathy, and altruism during adolescence, but these hypotheses have not been investigated systematically (107).

When examining the characteristics of adolescents, researchers must move beyond merely citing categorical variables such as age, sex, and race. Although these variables are relatively easy to assess, little is known concerning their effects or their importance. In short, the literature on peer relations during adolescence is based primarily on a *social address model,* in which characteristics of persons and their relationships are viewed as a product of environmental factors with little attention given to the processes whereby this occurs (19). The observational research of Eder has begun to document the processes by which race and social class operate in peer relations among adolescent girls (48). She found that through exchanges of "ritual insults," African-American working-class girls convey to one another what is valued and normative while displaying their own wit, intelligence, and self-defense skills. More research of this type is needed.

Differences that exist within person or class categories are frequently masked by comparisons of group means. One excellent example is the research of Youniss and Smollar (121). Like others, they found that female adolescents self-disclosed more than males and were more oriented toward meeting the emotional needs of friends. On careful examination of the data, however, they found that this sex difference was directly applicable to only one-third of the males, who seemed devoid of intimate, trusting peer relationships. These males made friends for pleasurable association and shared activities; they kept relationships "light" by withholding whatever self-doubts or personal concerns they may have had. The other two-thirds of the males were nearly identical to the females in patterns of relating to peers. Thus, one could conclude from a comparison of means that female adolescents are more socioemotionally peer oriented, but such a conclusion simplifies and distorts the reality of adolescent peer relations because it misconstrues the nature of the vast majority of male-male peer interactions.

We believe a perspective that focuses not on preconceived class variables but on patterns that emerge from the data that cut across our usual notions of categories will open the floodgates to a creative and increasingly sophisticated examination of the nature and function of peer relations during adolescence. If we must compare the sexes, social classes, and races, then an emphasis on processes—for example, what it is about one's social class that accounts for variations—is highly desirable. Such a focus will increase our understanding and our ability to predict developmentally significant outcomes.

Implications for Intervention

Issues raised in this chapter in regard to the positive and negative influence of peers have particular implications for interventions designed to increase the beneficial effects of peer relations. First, in regard to peer influence, relations with peers can be a source of stress and disruption in the life of an adolescent (21). Peers may encourage behavior or attitudes that are uncomfortable or that can cause her or him to make decisions such as to defy parental wishes or to try something novel or frightening. An adolescent may also strive so hard for peer approval that conformity overshadows individuality. Little is known about the strain of peer relations, even for those who are neglected or rejected. Studies seldom provide useful answers to crucial but controversial questions such as how the degree of friends' influence changes with age, the processes by which friends influence one another, and the variations owing to personal and environmental factors.

Little is also known concerning the therapeutic benefits of friendships. Many positive attributes have been correlated with good peer relations, but few studies have evaluated causal hypotheses. Friendships may foster intimacy; but it may also be true that youths who have the skills to be intimate are most likely to seek out friends. Peer relations may enhance the individuation process; or individuated adolescents may simply be more likely than alienated or enmeshed individuals to establish friendships. In relatively few studies of peer influence can the causes be sufficiently separated from, or even be assumed to be prior to, the effects.

Interventions that reduce or minimize the disruption of adolescents' friendships would appear to be desirable. Also, because variations in peer support depend partly on personal characteristics, interventions that focus solely on changes in the social environment may be only moderately effective. Some teenagers who do not have supportive friendships may need only to interact with peers and adults who encourage them to form friendships, but others may need training in the skills that contribute to forming and maintaining friendships. Although current theories do not clearly identify the skills needed for obtaining support from friends, both the basic and specialized skills required for participating in social relationships and for seeking particular types of support from friends may play a role. Attention to both the personal and the environmental influences on the ability to obtain support from friends may be the touchstone for an optimal intervention program.

Forming successful peer relations is a critical aspect of healthy development (54), but researchers are just beginning to explore populations of youth who are without supportive peer relationships. Neglected and rejected youths are in special need of attention in terms of basic research and intervention programs. In his research Hansell noted that isolated youths were dissatisfied with school life, had high rates of tardiness and absenteeism from school, and were rated by principals as coping poorly with the stress of student life (66). The research of Olweus with thousands of Norwegian and Swedish youths 8 to 16 years of age demonstrated that bullies tend to be anxious, passive, and insecure (85, 86). They feel ashamed, unattractive, and abandoned, without friendships.

Social scientists need to provide the impetus, if not the programmatic skills, to develop friendship-enhancing programs for rejected and neglected adolescents (13, 14, 16). Through training, practicing, and evaluating social skills (conversational, prosocial, and self-disclosure skills, recognition of others' needs), the interpersonal competencies necessary for successful peer relations might be enhanced (21). It may be that rejected youths are deprived of the opportunity to learn social skills through positive peer contact (15). In several innovative studies of social-skill training Bierman and her associates have improved the peer acceptance of children and early adolescents who had previously been rejected by their peers. Examining whether this improved status extends beyond the six-week follow-up period, and in settings other than the school, is an urgent research need.

Issues of the relative positive and negative merits of peer influence and the nature of supportive peer relations remain to be resolved. Conforming to peers may restrict individuality, freedom of expression, personal development, and future aspirations (54). Having no friends may be preferable to having "bad" friends. An adolescent may learn negative behaviors to keep friends, or be so concerned with initiating or maintaining friendships that she or he feels rejected, jealous, or isolated. We believe, however, that the evidence supports the notion that the ideal is a few close, intimate friendships that are secure, stable, and reciprocated.

Close peer relations are essential during adolescence. Friends seek a shared understanding, openness, trust, and acceptance (121). In addition, emotional and social needs are met, and problems are worked out. This "consensual validation" is a "reciprocal process whereby two persons seek to understand their world through a mutual exchange of ideas, feelings, and thoughts that are offered to each other for comment, discussion, or evaluation" (121, p. 129). Because the process requires equality in give-and-take, friends are the key to consensual validation. The ultimate developmental outcome should be individuation, a feeling of being separate from and yet connected to others. One should discover in friendships one's uniqueness.

12

MOTIVATION AND ACHIEVEMENT

Valanne L. Henderson and Carol S. Dweck

One of the most fundamental issues in adolescence is that of achievement. Why do some students blossom while others, equally talented, seem unable to handle challenges? This chapter focuses on the psychological factors (apart from ability) related to achievement—factors that foster either adaptive achievement behavior that allows students to reach their fullest potential or maladaptive achievement behavior that may result in a failure to fulfill that potential.

Adolescence is a critical time for achievement. It spans the kinds of changes and challenges that research has shown bring out students' adaptive or maladaptive achievement tendencies. These changes and challenges occur at precisely the time when students need to lay the groundwork for future achievement. Change is perhaps the defining characteristic of adolescence, since it is occurring in nearly all the fundamental areas of life. From within, important biological and cognitive changes are taking place (see Chapters 2 and 3 in this volume). From without, there are different types of social relationships (see Chapters 7 and 11) and new sorts of academic work to pursue (see Chapter 8). These new social and academic pressures force adolescents toward different roles, often involving increased personal responsibility (see Chapter 14).

As adolescents move into these new, more adultlike roles, their perceptions of their lives may change (see Chapter 14 for a fuller discussion). The game of life is being played for real now. Adolescents may begin to view current successes and failures as predictors of future outcomes in the adult world. Moreover, as demands intensify, the different areas of the adolescent's life may come into conflict. Social pursuits may cut into the time needed for academic endeavors, or ambitions in one domain may undermine the attainment of goals in another, as, for example, when academic achievement leads to social disapproval (52, 77).

Whether or not the individual adolescent is able to adapt effectively to these new academic and social pressures is determined, in part, by psychological-motivational factors. The role these factors play in achievement is now known to be more central than was once believed. People have commonly thought that academic achievement was largely the result of intellectual ability. Whether individuals meet, fall short of, or exceed their intellectual potential, however, is often mediated by other psychological factors that influence academic performance (25, 28, 38; see also Chapters 3 and 8 in this volume). These factors collectively constitute achievement motivation.

Motivation is more than simply the desire to do well, although in common parlance this is usually what is meant by the term. Instead, motivation consists of a variety of psychological processes that determine whether a student will pursue achievement goals, which achievement goals will be pursued, and how effectively they will be pursued. This chapter will attempt to capture and identify these motivational factors and to explore how they interact to foster adaptive achievement behavior. The discussion will focus on academic achievement, documenting that these motivational factors play an important role in predicting academic achievement over and above actual intellectual ability, and, indeed, that motivational factors are not necessarily related to ability (18, 19, 25). In fact, a student who is less bright than others but who has an adaptive motivational pattern—that is, one who is persistent, is able to maintain effective learning strategies and a positive attitude toward academic tasks—may turn out to be a high achiever. In contrast, some of the brightest students who have maladaptive motivational patterns—the ones who give up easily, do not use good learning strategies, and do not enjoy academics—may fall considerably behind and fail to fulfill their potential. For example, many bright girls who excel throughout elementary school begin to lose their edge in adolescence; this decline is accompanied by (and perhaps caused by) debilitating motivational patterns. A maladaptive motivational pattern may lead to the failure to invest effort in studies, avoidance of difficult classes, preferences for nonacademic activities, and negative emotional responses to learning situations.

Toward a Unifying Model of Achievement Motivation

Excellent reviews of research on achievement motivation already exist (3, 4, 6, 25) and are beyond the scope of this chapter. Rather, we present one current motivational framework whereby we attempt to integrate many of the central ideas from other theoretical positions and then discuss how this framework is useful in understanding some of the changes and problems that emerge in adolescence.

In the past, the motive to achieve was considered a personality trait (45, 73). This trait was believed to be activated by environmental or situational cues when valued outcomes were at issue (9). Early conceptualizations focused on the single-factor trait of achievement motivation. A hypothesized need to succeed was thought to be engaged for highly valued outcomes. Individuals who had higher motivations—that is, those who actively pursued success—were more often successful than those who had lower levels of achievement motivation. Such conceptualizations, although extremely useful, failed to describe the precise motivational processes that account for adaptive or maladaptive achievement behavior, to explain what thoughts, feelings, and goal-directed behaviors people experience in the process of achievement. The challenge, then, has been to discover what particular psychological factors or processes predict adaptive responses in achievement situations and who, despite a desire to do well, may be more vulnerable to debilitation, alienation, and anxiety.

The motivational process model depicted in Table 12.1 emphasizes the relationship between the beliefs that individuals hold and the adaptive and maladaptive coping patterns they display (see 26). It is based on research

Table 12.1. The motivational process model: specific components and their relationship to behavior.

THEORY OF INTELLIGENCE	GOAL ORIENTATION	CONFIDENCE IN INTELLIGENCE	BEHAVIOR PATTERN
ENTITY THEORY (intelligence is fixed)	PERFORMANCE GOAL (to gain positive judgments of competence)	IF HIGH --------------→ BUT	MASTERY ORIENTED Seek challenge High persistence
		IF LOW----------------→	HELPLESS Avoid challenge Low persistence
INCREMENTAL THEORY (intelligence is malleable)	LEARNING GOAL (to increase competence)	IF HIGH OR LOW --------------------------→	MASTERY ORIENTED Seek challenge (fosters learning High persistence

in academic achievement that shows how the beliefs people hold about their intelligence orient them toward pursuing certain goals, and how these goals shape their thoughts, feelings, and behavior in achievement settings that pose challenges or obstacles. To summarize briefly, this research has demonstrated that children who believe that their intelligence is a fixed trait (entity theory) tend to pursue the goal of documenting that trait (seeking positive evaluations of their abilities and avoiding negative ones, or performance goals) and tend to be more vulnerable to discouragement and debilitation in the face of failure because they see failure as an indictment of their intelligence. In contrast, children who believe that their intelligence is a malleable quality—one that can be developed through learning (incremental theory)—tend to pursue the goal of increasing their abilities (learning goal) and remain vigorous and effective in the face of obstacles because they see obstacles as a natural part of the learning process. In fact, the maladaptive and adaptive behavior patterns can be distinguished from one another through three types of characteristic responses: emotional responses, cognitive responses (thought patterns), and behavioral responses (achievement-related actions).

Achievement Behavior Patterns

This model grew out of research on achievement behavior in middle childhood (18, 19, 22, 27). In this research, children manifested two different responses to difficulty or challenge: an adaptive mastery-oriented pattern and a more maladaptive "helpless" pattern. Children displaying the two different responses showed equal ability and interest in a task prior to encountering difficulty. Only when the experimental task posed obstacles, and the children were facing failure, did the two patterns clearly emerge (18, 19, 27).

In the helpless pattern, children seem trapped by the experience of difficulty. They conclude that their difficulty is a failure and that this failure is indicative of low ability. That is, these children attribute their difficulty to a lack of ability. They often say things like, "I'm not very smart at this," even though they have recently demonstrated their ability through multiple successes. Moreover, once the difficulty is viewed as a failure indicating low ability, the children feel anxious or upset about the situation, and their performance falls apart. They may lapse into less sophisticated problem-solving strategies, slackening their effort as well as losing sight of the task objectives. While it is possible that withdrawing effort from difficult tasks may sometimes be adaptive in the short term, in that it allows the individual to maintain self-esteem, such coping strategies seem maladaptive in the long run. The habit of routinely withdrawing effort when challenged may hinder individuals' attempts to realize their personal or academic aspirations, given that virtually all valuable pursuits require people to overcome obstacles en route to success.

The mastery-oriented pattern provides a dramatic contrast to the helpless pattern. In the mastery-oriented pattern, the children, far from losing sight of the task objectives, remain extremely task oriented. Instead of becoming concerned about their ability, they become concerned with their learning strategies. Mastery-oriented children often instruct themselves to think carefully, to pay attention, and to remember past feedback (3, 18, 19). These children report feeling challenged and excited by difficulty rather than threatened and anxious, and they are able to maintain their positive outlook. They continue to use effective problem-solving strategies and may even teach themselves more sophisticated strategies, so that performance is maintained or improved.

Thus, research indicates that the helpless pattern is characterized by failure-oriented cognitions, negative affect, and deterioration in performance, whereas the mastery-oriented pattern is characterized by task-oriented cognitions, positive affect, and stable or improved performance. Although these patterns were first documented in a laboratory setting, they have been found to have a significant impact in natural settings, such as the classroom, when challenging or confusing new material is presented (64; see also 15).

These patterns may well describe adolescents' reactions to the challenges, obstacles, and setbacks they encounter as they negotiate the transition from childhood to adulthood. If so, some bright students who manifest the helpless pattern may fall short of their potential, lower their aspirations, or lose their zest for academic pursuits. Indeed, the more challenges, confusion, or obstacles the transition poses, the more marked should be the divergence between helpless-pattern and mastery-oriented students.

Before we turn to a discussion of the psychological factors that may underlie these patterns, we should highlight some aspects of the behavior patterns just presented. The helpless pattern is characterized by viewing difficulty and errors as failures and attributing one's failure to a lack of ability. Attribution theory suggests that one's explanation for success and failure is influential in determining whether or not one continues to invest energy and effort in pursuing valued outcomes (101). Indeed, many studies have found that low achievers blame their failures on a lack of ability but do not credit their successes to high ability, while high achievers do credit their successes to high ability (37, 69; see also 19). Although the attribution of failure to a lack of effort is not as clearly related to high academic achievement (37, 69), training low-achieving students to attribute failure to a lack of effort can help to boost persistence, self-efficacy, and other aspects of motivated behavior (7, 14, 22, 83). In large part these individual differences in attributions and their emotional and behavioral concomitants can lead to more intensive research into the psychological factors that predispose children to react in these different ways.

Implicit Theories and Achievement Goals

What psychological factors have been found to underlie these patterns of behavior? As we have noted, recent research has demonstrated that the conceptions of intelligence children hold and the goals they pursue may "set them up" for the helpless and mastery-oriented behavior patterns (1, 10, 26, 30, 60, 61; see also 23). If a child believes that intelligence is a fixed thing (an entity theory), he or she tends to be concerned with showing that entity to good advantage in order to receive positive judgments by performing well (performance goals). As Figure 12.1 indicates, holding an entity theory and performance goals increases children's vulnerability to the helpless pattern, especially when they have low confidence in their abilities. Performance-oriented children seem to be attempting to validate their intelligence and often display an attitude that questions, "Am I smart enough to do this?" That is, they appear to be trying to find out how much of the entity (intelligence) they have. To the extent that they focus on assessing their abilities, difficulties or failures become functional indicators of low competence and may trap the child into the negative evaluations and expectations characteristic of the helpless pattern. That is, when the child is concerned with obtaining positive judgments of his or her abilities but increasingly believes a negative judgment is forthcoming, the helpless behavior pattern may emerge (2, 10, 30, 61). In addition to creating this general vulnerability to the helpless behavior pattern, the combination of an entity theory and performance goals may also create vulnerability in another way. When children are overconcerned with documenting their ability, they are often willing to sacrifice opportunities to learn, especially if the process of learning involves making mistakes or becoming confused (10, 30). Not only do these students give up in the face of difficulty, but they may avoid challenge altogether.

In contrast, having an incremental theory and learning goals seems to foster the mastery-oriented pattern (5, 30). Children who believe that intelligence is a malleable quality that can be developed through effort (incremental theory) tend to be more concerned with developing that quality through learning new skills (learning goals). Children who hold incremental theories and learning goals seem to focus on the questions "How do you do this?" and "What can I learn from this?" Difficulties are not perceived as failures or indications of low ability; rather, errors may be seen as providing feedback about their effort and their strategies for mastering the task. Thus, the incremental theory and learning goals seem to foster the mastery-oriented pattern. What is most striking is that students who lack confidence in their abilities but hold an incremental theory and learning goals are also mastery oriented; in fact, they are sometimes found to be most invigorated by challenges in spite of their lack of confidence (10). Finally, with an incremental theory and a learning goal, the child may be willing to appear incompetent in order to learn and actually may believe that appearing to be incompetent by making errors is part of the learning process (10, 30, 61).

Although there is a clear relationship between theories of intelligence and the goals children tend to favor (6, 10, 26, 60, 75), goal selection is also strongly influenced by situational factors. Obviously, some situations favor pursuit of performance goals, others are more suited for learning goals, and still others permit simultaneous pursuit of both. Both goals are important and seem to exist in everyone's repertoire. The evidence indicates that when the situational demands are high, individuals can be induced to adopt either goal (1, 30). But when the situation does not provide cues favoring either goal, an entity theory of intelligence biases the individual toward performance goals, while an incremental theory biases the individual toward learning goals.

The motivational-process model thus utilizes three major variables— theory, goals, and confidence—to predict, and perhaps explain, behavior in achievement settings. In summary, the implicit theory of intelligence orients individuals toward particular goals that, in combination with confidence, foster adaptive or maladaptive behavior.

Although only two theory-goal-behavior patterns have been described, others may exist. These two patterns clearly do not characterize all of the people all of the time. In fact, several researchers have identified a variety of attributional styles that seem to be related to particular sorts of goals and self-perceptions (32, 82). In addition, work currently under way seeks to identify other implicit theories of intelligence (46) that, together with these attributional styles, achievement goals, and self-perceptions, form clear theory-goal-behavior pattern relationships. Even so, the model we have described provides a framework for understanding and integrating past research and theories of motivation. For example, a study conducted by Wolf and Savickas indicated that students who had an integrated time perspective (that is, who were oriented toward long-term goals and outcomes, who carefully planned and structured their time to facilitate attainment of goals, and who were optimistic about the future) were more likely to manifest a behavior pattern similar to the mastery-oriented pattern, whereas students who had a less integrated time perspective were more likely to manifest learned-helpless types of behaviors (104). This result is interesting because the incremental theory, which orients individuals toward learning goals, should also orient the student toward more long-term objectives, and in particular to looking for mastery and improvement over time. In contrast, the entity theory, which orients individuals toward performance goals, should keep the student very much rooted in immediate outcomes.

Other areas of research that may be illuminated by this framework include those of intrinsic motivation and locus of control (17, 59). Incremental theorists should be more intrinsically motivated because they value learning per se. They should also have a greater sense of control because they believe that ability can be acquired through their actions. Viewed in this way, the research in these areas is consonant with the motivational-process model in a number of ways. Several studies have indicated that adolescents who pursue knowledge for its own sake (who are intrinsically motivated) have higher academic achievement scores, whereas "need-for-achievement" measures show no unique relationship to achievement apart from intrinsic motivation (65, 103; see also 36, 43). Other research shows that feelings of a lack of control over the environment are associated with anxiety, while a feeling of being in control is related to positive attitudes toward school and greater enjoyment of novel and creative tasks (5, 74, 85, 96; see also 78, 79, 100). Of course, more research must be done in order to establish a link between theory, intrinsic motivation, and a sense of control over outcomes (see 26 for a discussion of these issues).

Like other models of motivation, the motivational process model presupposes that the student values achievement. If students do not believe that achievement is important, they will not actively pursue achievement outcomes. On a general level, a low evaluation of achievement may underlie the decision not to continue one's education beyond high school or to drop out of school altogether. At a more specific level, a sense that particular tasks are not important may underlie those expressions of boredom and demands for explanations of utility so common in adolescence. Whether or not the individual values achievement in the same way that society values it, and why an individual might devalue achievement, are questions a theory of motivation must be able to address. Such issues are especially important in the area of adolescent achievement motivation. Why do some students quit school even though they clearly have the ability to succeed academically? Why do some elect to escape reality through the abuse of drugs and alcohol? The partial answer this theory offers is that low confidence and the belief that intelligence is fixed may predispose individuals to devalue achievement and to avoid achievement situations in defense of their self-esteem. That is, if students believe that they lack the ability to be academically successful and cannot do anything to acquire that ability, they may decide that academic success is not important to them rather than accept the belief that they are inadequate in a crucial area. Such a hypothesis remains to be tested empirically.

Basing one's conclusions on the findings reported thus far, one might expect that the theory of intelligence adolescents hold as they make the transition to adulthood is particularly critical. First, they may believe that their successes and failures are predictive of their future performance as adults, and that it has become increasingly necessary for them to do well. For example, a student may come to believe that an index of academic performance such as high grades is a good predictor of occupational success or income as an adult. Second, the situations students face are likely to be confusing and are always changing. It may seem as though the rules of the game have altered—that life is guided by a different set of principles from those that were familiar when they were children. As the question "Are my abilities adequate?" is repeatedly addressed in this context, adolescents may have difficulty generating and maintaining confidence in their abilities. For those who hold incremental theories, the increased importance of success and the uncertainty of achieving it may spur a heightened orientation toward learning and mastery, heralding a time of growth. For those given to entity theories, such a time of uncertainty may be more difficult. The increased importance and unpredictability of success heighten the salience of performance goals, pose a threat to their confidence, and thus may be distressing rather than invigorating. A combination of entity theory, performance goals, and low confidence may well prime these students for the helpless behavior pattern. In adolescence the helpless pattern may involve performance debilitation in the form of declining grades, expressions of anxiety, avoidance of courses that are difficult or potentially confusing, and devaluation of academic pursuits. Hence, these motivational factors may predict whether high achievers will remain high achievers and whether previously low achievers will blossom in the new school environment.

A Study of Motivation and Achievement

One study examined the applicability of the model depicted in Table 12.1 to the early adolescent transition (47). Its findings support the notion that, as adolescents move into a more demanding environment, the implicit theory of intelligence they hold is a powerful predictor of their academic adjustment and achievement. Students were followed over the first few months of the seventh grade, their first year of junior high school. Their implicit theories and their confidence were measured, as were their grades and their level of anxiety. The results showed that, predictably, entity theorists earned significantly lower grades than incremental theorists, regardless of prior achievement. Also as predicted, entity theorists reported significantly higher levels of anxiety.

Predicting Academic Achievement

The model we presented earlier suggests some very specific predictions about achievement. Past research has shown that theory and goals are not consistent predictors of actual achievement in elementary school. Yet, in the face of confusing change and heightened importance of outcomes during adolescence, the student's implicit theory of intelligence should begin to predict academic performance. For example, as entity theorists face key outcomes and find their confidence shaken by confusion or changes in academic structure, they are apt to succumb more often to the helpless behavior pattern. Over time these entity theorists should become less able to master academic tasks, and should thus show declining grades. Therefore, entity theorists in general, and those with low confidence in particular, should have lower grades in junior high school in comparison to their incrementally oriented classmates.

Henderson and Dweck report the grades of four groups of students, divided according to assessments of their theories of intelligence (incremental or entity) and their confidence in their intelligence (high or low) (47). The students' sixth-grade achievement scores were measured in order to determine how much the motivational factors contributed to seventh-grade grades over and above what was accounted for by the students' past achievements. (Even though past achievement scores might already have reflected motivational variables, the challenges of the new school setting could be expected to push the groups even farther apart.)

The average grades for each of the four groups are presented in Figure 12.1, along with the grades the students "should" have received according to projections based on their sixth-grade achievement scores.[1] The incre-

---

1. These groups did, in fact, differ in their prior achievement. Whether this difference was due to the theories the students endorsed or resulted from prior achievement the design of the study cannot determine. Nonetheless, the seventh-grade achievement analysis indicated that the groups were driven apart, with group differences increasing in the predicted direction.

Predicted Grade Point and Actual Grade Point

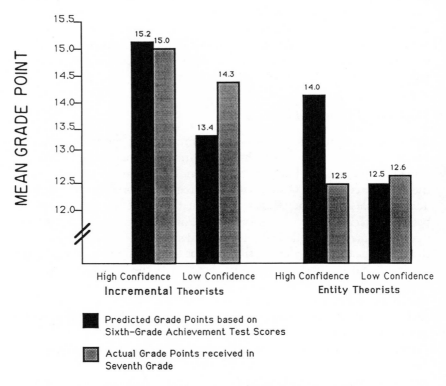

Figure 12.1. Mean Grade Point by theory of intelligence and confidence in intelligence.

mental high-confidence group, who were expected to do well because of past achievement scores, did indeed do quite well in school, earning the highest grades of any group. Similarly, the entity low-confidence group, who were not expected to do well, did not do well at all. The most interesting groups, however, were the incremental low-confidence group and the entity high-confidence group. Although the former group were not expected to do particularly well, their seventh-grade grades were quite good relative to those of other groups, and in fact were not much lower than those of the incremental high-confidence group. In contrast, the entity high-confidence group, who were expected to do rather well, ended up receiving quite low grades, about the same as those of the entity low-confidence students.

The surge in achievement for the low-confidence incremental theorists is consistent with past research that suggests this group is the most invigorated by challenge (10). Although early studies also had shown that high-confidence entity theorists tend to avoid or be defensive in the face of a challenge that may undermine their sense of ability (10, 30), actual performance debilitation was not predicted.

Apparently, then, the way students think about their intelligence may affect their ability and desire to master academic material. Although current evidence is only correlational, it does suggest that a belief in a fixed intelligence may inhibit the desire or disrupt the ability of a student to master academic material, whereas a belief that learning new material increases one's intelligence may actually promote academic mastery. Even more encouraging is that the student's belief is a significant predictor of adolescent achievement over and above the effect of prior performance, a factor that may already reflect motivational effects.

Predicting School Anxiety

Another important area of prediction arising from this model of motivational processes concerns anxiety related to school. Although it is now clear that adolescence is not necessarily a time of storm and stress (see Chapter 15 in this volume), some students are indeed more anxious than others. Some of this anxiety may be owing to a more vulnerable, more easily threatened sense of self-esteem. It seems likely that those students who hold an entity theory feel threatened when they fear that they may not be winning positive judgments of their intellectual capacity. The more threatened students feel by confusion, error, or difficulty, the more likely they are to experience anxiety in the general situation that evokes the feeling of threat. Again, this should be especially true if the student already doubts his or her intellectual ability, as do the low-confidence entity theorists. In accord with this logic, Henderson and Dweck found that the combination of an entity theory and low confidence predicted the highest levels of anxiety in a group of seventh-graders (47). That is, as the model predicted, these students were most vulnerable to the emotional concomitants of the helpless pattern, expressing more feelings of anxiety than any other group. Was this result due to the lower achievement of these low-confidence entity theorists? That is, did lower grades contribute to higher anxiety? Surprisingly, actual achievement, as measured by grades, did *not* have a significant effect on subsequent anxiety over and above the effects of theory and confidence.

These data, like the data for seventh-grade achievement, are potentially important results. First, they provide evidence that the motivational-process model is able to predict real-world (as opposed to laboratory-evoked) emotional responses in adolescence. These data indicate that in their everyday lives low-confidence entity theorists report a high degree of anxiety. Although causal links still must be established, it seems that students' theories about intelligence and their confidence may truly have an impact on their coping resources. If so, it may be possible to improve the academic performance and allay the anxiety of underachieving students by directly addressing the issues of implicit theories and related goals (cf. 22, 84).

Further research is needed in order to explore and integrate aspects of this and other models of achievement motivation. In particular, research is needed that examines the causal relationships among theory, confidence, academic performance, and anxiety. If it is shown that adolescents' theories do indeed play a causal role in achievement, then there is a clear need for research that examines the ways in which the potential effects of an implicit theory of intelligence can be modified.

Beyond Academics

Thus far we have focused exclusively on the motivation for academic achievement; indeed, when people talk about achievement motivation they are generally referring to academic achievement. As Maehr has suggested, however, achievement motivation can be involved in any activity where, first, there is a standard of excellence (meaning the activity can be evaluated in terms of success and failure); second, the individual is in some sense responsible for the outcome; and, third, there is some level of challenge and, therefore, a sense of uncertainty (68). Thus, one can aspire to an athletic standard of excellence (athletic achievement motivation), or to an artistic standard of excellence (artistic achievement motivation), or even to a social standard of excellence (social achievement motivation). Perhaps motivation needs to be considered relative to the area of endeavor. Research in the academic domain suggests that specific academic motivation measures (self-concept of academic ability) are better predictors of actual academic achievement than are global measures (general self-concept) (12, 55, 72, 88, 89; see also 42, 70, 86). Is it the case, then, that each domain operates under a specific motivational system and that individuals may show widely discrepant motivational patterns in different areas? For example, do individuals have different implicit theories in the different domains, or do they tend to hold similar theories across domains? The evidence seems to suggest that an approach that allows for domain specificity may be more fruitful in understanding human behavior. Even when individuals do hold similar theories across domains, they may have different confidence levels and, therefore, may display different behavior patterns. Further research is needed to address these questions fully.

Whether individuals have domain-specific or domain-general motivational tendencies, it is important to ask whether or not the concepts useful for the academic domain can be adapted to understanding and predicting behavior in other domains.

In the social domain, Goetz and Dweck looked at social behavior in the face of challenges and setbacks and found quite similar behavior patterns—a mastery-oriented pattern and a helpless behavior pattern (35). This was the first evidence that a model developed for the academic domain might be extended into the social domain. Later studies documented the relationship between students' implicit theory of personality (whether personality is a fixed thing or a malleable quality) and behavior and between social goals (learning/development[2] or performance goals) and behavior in situations involving mild social rejection. In these situations, just as with academics, students with an incremental theory of personality and learning/development goals were more likely to manifest mastery-oriented behavior than were students who believed that personality was something that could not be changed (66, 76). An analogous model of motivation may indeed explain some aspects of social behavior. In fact, in the study of adolescent achievement motivation discussed earlier (47), an entity theory of personality and low confidence were associated with anxiety in the same way that an entity theory of intelligence was associated with anxiety. Most notable were the results indicating that students who held entity-type theories in both domains and had low confidence were especially anxious in school, providing further evidence that the social domain may be understood within this sort of framework.

Although no one has yet examined the athletic domain using a similar model, it seems plausible that students who view athletic ability as something that can be developed are more likely to pursue athletics—even in the face of difficulty—than are students who hold that athletic ability is unchangeable. Some support for this version of the model can be found in

---

2. In the social domain one can have a goal not only to learn social skills but also to develop social relationships. Therefore, we feel that *development* better describes the social goals that are equivalent to learning goals in the academic domain.

a study by Rotella, who reported that the young athletes who came closest to maximizing their potential were those who behaved much like the mastery-oriented students we described earlier (81). These athletes dedicated off-season practice time to overcoming their weaknesses. Rather than viewing these weaknesses negatively and being anxious about them, they saw them as offering opportunities for growth and instituted systematic training programs to overcome their deficits (see also 34).

In the arts, performers are constantly in situations that strongly favor performance goals—a perpetual "now or never" life-style. If performers view their artistry as a fixed, unchangeable entity, performance situations may cause extreme anxiety and even debilitation in the face of difficulties. Yet many truly great artists refer not to their talent but to their "craft" (39, 90), and focus on ways to fine-tune their performing skills, to develop their techniques so as to capture more fully the essence of their art in their performances. Such observations illustrate the need for more research in a variety of domains in order to clarify the role that motivational variables play in achieving standards of excellence.

Another question that arises from the examination of different achievement domains is whether or not these domains interact with one another. The discussion presented here centers on the interaction between the social domain and the academic domain in adolescence. More precisely, it concentrates on the question of whether or not social goals interfere with the attainment of excellence in the academic domain.

One way to research this question is to examine the academic performance of adolescents in schools with different social contexts—for example, single-sex schools and coeducational schools. Evidence from studies in this country and others indicates that there may indeed be some interference between social and academic goals. Generally these studies have shown that students in single-sex schools have a higher level of academic achievement than do their counterparts in coeducational schools—sometimes as much as a year's difference in achievement (41, 58; see also Chapter 8 in this volume, but see 71 for an opposing view). This seems to be true even when the single-sex schools are state schools and have equivalent demographic characteristics to those of the coeducational schools, as in Jamaica and New Zealand (41, 54). Perhaps even more relevant to the issue of cross-domain interference are data showing that students in the single-sex schools generally have more positive attitudes toward academics, are less likely to pursue or express sexually stereotyped academic preferences, and are less preoccupied with "rating and dating" during school time (41, 54, 58).

These effects of social context indicate that social concerns can interfere to some extent with academic achievement, especially when those concerns involve members of the opposite sex. Further support for the interaction idea comes from Henderson and Dweck (47). When social-motivational variables were included in the analysis (theory of personality and confidence of personality, or how likable students believe they are) in addition to the academic-motivational variables, the predictive power of the motivational process model improved by 40% in the prediction of seventh-grade grades. Without a reciprocal influence between the two domains, no such improvement in prediction of grades should have been observed.

It is essential to pursue these interference effects in research. If a student shows debilitation in a nonacademic domain or is feeling defensive or anxious about that domain, it may affect his or her ability to maintain mastery-oriented behavior in academics. It is possible that by determining which other domains most strongly affect the achievement of academic standards, researchers and educators might be better able to identify and aid students who are experiencing difficulty.

Motivational Factors and Gender Differences in Achievement

A number of differences exist between the academic achievement of boys and girls. Generally, girls get better grades than boys throughout the elementary years, especially in the verbal subject areas; they also show an ability in math at least equal to that of boys. As girls move into the adolescent years, however, they begin to slip in math and science and earn fewer top marks than boys (20, 29, 31, 49, 67). This is especially true near the peak of the ability distribution (8; see also Chapter 3 in this volume). It is as if the brightest girls lose their edge and stop earning the high grades they used to receive. Why is this? Research has indicated that it is here, at the height of the ability distribution, that the motivational differences between boys and girls are greatest (62, 91, 95). Of course, a number of other factors may contribute to this gender difference (see Chapter 8 in this volume), but we will focus our attention on the motivational factors and how they may play a role in creating gender differences in achievement.

What variations exist in the motivational pattern of bright girls as compared to bright boys? In a study of eighth-graders, Leggett found that bright girls were twice as likely as bright boys to endorse an entity theory of intelligence (60). Furthermore, of those girls endorsing the entity theory, three-fourths preferred academic tasks that were easy enough to ensure success (thus demonstrating a performance goal with low confidence). In contrast, none of the boys endorsing an entity theory desired such easy tasks, preferring difficult ones that would show how intelligent they were (performance goal with high confidence). If these girls are more likely to hold an entity theory and performance goals with low confidence, they become more vulnerable to the helpless behavior pattern. Indeed, Licht and Shapiro showed that bright girls (compared to other girls and bright boys) were more likely to attribute failures to lack of ability and to show performance debilitation (64).

Can this finding provide insight into the long-standing gender difference in math and science achievement? Indeed it may. Students who tend to show the helpless behavior pattern find especially difficult subject matter that involves confronting and conquering potentially confusing new material. Math, over the years, repeatedly requires the student to master new skills and new conceptual frameworks, and thus may often engender the kind of confusion that could trigger the helpless pattern. In contrast, verbal subjects (after the basic skills are mastered) do not tend to introduce wholly new skills or new conceptual frameworks but rather require students to apply skills they have already mastered to increasingly difficult material. In a study designed to mimic mathematics learning using a nonmath subject, Licht and Dweck found that students displaying the helpless pattern did well if there was no initial confusion (as might be the case in verbal subjects) but were severely debilitated by initial confusion (as might be the case in mathematical ones), and the brightest girls were most debilitated by this confusion (62). Thus, bright girls showed a striking difference in the mastery of the *same* material depending on whether they had experienced a period of confusion.

In summary, bright girls may view ordinary difficulties in math and related subjects as indicating that they lack ability and may come to doubt that they can do well in these subject areas. Instead they may focus their energies on subjects that allow them to apply skills they have already mastered—that is, subjects that make it easier for them to maintain confidence in their abilities. In this way an increasing differential may emerge between girls' achievement in mathematical and in verbal areas—*not* because their actual mathematical abilities are wanting but because their belief in these abilities has waned. Such a conclusion illustrates that certain motivational patterns render some children well suited to the novelty and challenge of math and similar subjects and render others averse to these experiences.

Gender differences in motivational patterns may also be linked to particular feedback practices that are typical of the elementary classroom (24, 62). These practices may inadvertently lead girls to believe that difficulty, confusion, or setbacks indicate lack of ability, a point of view typical of the helpless pattern. In contrast, boys may be oriented toward nonability attributions when they encounter difficulty (see 62 for a full discussion). Yet in spite of the evidence that these attributions of low ability may be fostered by classroom feedback, there is also evidence that students can be trained to overcome the helpless behavior pattern. Dweck found that the learned-helpless behavior pattern could be broken by training individuals to attribute their failures to lack of effort rather than of ability (22; see also 7, 14, 83). Surprisingly, she also found that giving helpless-pattern students extensive experience of success (in order to raise their confidence) did not alleviate the pattern, and in some cases actually exacerbated the problem. Thus it is not that these students need to receive lots of positive feedback but that they must learn to accept negative feedback as a source of information for future efforts rather than a judgment about their ability. Indeed, it may be the lavish success that bright girls experience in grade school that leaves them unprepared for and shaken by the challenges they must confront in adolescence. These girls may need to become oriented toward a new motivational framework in which challenge indicates an exciting learning opportunity rather than a threatening and potent indictment of their ability.

Ethnicity and Motivation

Although much research has documented differences in achievement among ethnic minority groups—with some groups showing disappointing achievement in many areas (for instance, African-Americans and Hispanics) and others showing impressive achievement (for example, Asians)—few studies have been able to pinpoint the precise motivational factors contributing to these differences. Several questions can be addressed with existing findings, however. Are the variables in the motivational process model sufficient to explain an ethnic group's achievement pattern (that is, do theory of intelligence, goals, and confidence lead to adaptive or maladaptive achievement behavior)? If not, what other factors may affect motivation: Do some factors work against valuing academic goals, or is achievement embedded in another cultural framework that modifies its character? For example, does the culture favor group goals over individual goals and so apply pressure incompatible with individual achievement? And finally, might factors other than motivational ones be contributing to ethnic group differences? For example, are the skills needed for achievement available to members of the ethnic group? Are the members of the ethnic group socialized and educated to allow them to pursue their goals effectively?

Stevenson, Lee, and Stigler have conducted cross-cultural research examining the differences in achievement among American, Chinese, and Japanese children (93). In general, Asian children performed much better than did American children. In addition, the parents of the Asian children strongly believed that success was due to effort, whereas American parents believed success was due to ability. The Asian parents' greater emphasis on effort as a means to success may promote an incremental theory of intelligence that enables their children to become more mastery oriented (see also 48, 50). This same cultural bias may hold as well in Asian-American communities and families (99).

Despite the impressive achievement of Japanese students, some aspects of their achievement-related behavior are inconsistent with the incremental theory as we have described it. For instance, many Japanese students are driven to work hard at their studies so that they may perform well on exams, but they may be less able to think originally or analytically in nontest situations (99). Those students who fail to gain entrance to the best universities may become extremely depressed or even suicidal (98). Once they do gain entrance to a university, students no longer apply themselves to their studies; they do not seem to be driven to master knowledge any longer (51, 99). This may be because Japanese students are assured of graduating once they gain admittance, regardless of their performance (51). These observations seem more consistent with an entity-theory orientation. Closer examination of Japanese culture suggests to us, however, that the high achievement motivation may be embedded in a moral framework. In the Japanese culture it is important to honor one's family. For the child this means being a good student and gaining acceptance to the best schools. If one is a good student, then one brings honor to the family and is therefore a good person. If one does not succeed academically, one brings shame on the family and is not a good person (102). Therefore, the mastery-oriented academic behavior may be driven by an entity theory and performance goals in the moral domain, with all the vulnerabilities and liabilities that the entity theory entails.[3] Hence, the model of academic achievement presented in Table 12.1 would need to be expanded to take account of the fact that, for Asian-Americans, academic achievement may be embedded in other social-cultural issues.

3. We must note here that we are not suggesting that the Japanese students are not achieving. Obviously they are (see 93). Nor are we suggesting that Japanese schools are less effective than American schools; the reverse is more probably true. What we are highlighting is that academic motivation is valued and evaluated within a cultural system, which is not the same across all cultures. Americans tend to value individual achievement and success, whereas the Japanese tend to value the smooth functioning of the social unit and personal modesty.

It is not clear whether the disappointing achievement of many African-Americans is due mainly to motivational patterns or to a lack of skills necessary to fulfill achievement goals. Certainly in the athletic domain African-Americans have shown outstanding achievement. What might be hindering success in the academic domain? Is the poorer performance of African-Americans due to a bias toward adopting the more maladaptive components of a motivational system (such as an entity theory with low confidence) or to a failure of the educational and socialization agents to provide the skills that will enable the students to attain academic goals? It is unclear whether ethnic or cultural factors favor the adoption of one or the other theories of intelligence, since research on black cultural values seems to suggest the availability of both theories of intelligence (13, 40, 56, 57, 87). In line with the motivational process model, however, Bowman and Howard suggest that black parents who, like the Chinese and Japanese parents, stress the importance of effort in surmounting obstacles (that is, who teach their children that there are fewer opportunities available to blacks and that blacks must therefore work harder than whites to do as well) have children who do better academically than the children of black parents who do not present this mastery-oriented stance toward difficulties (11).

In addition to specific motivational factors, the requisite skills and knowledge may not be as widely available to African-American youth. Jencks and Mayer suggest that although many black youths have high aspirations, those most fully embedded in black culture (for example, those who attend all-black schools) may lack the skills they need to realize those high aspirations (53; see also 16). It has been suggested that training low-achieving black students in metacognitive types of learning strategies (such as concentrating, getting main ideas, using self-tests and other study aids to monitor and modify one's learning behavior) may improve achievement and increase academic motivation (44). We have stressed the adaptive nature of pursuing certain achievement goals, but adopting these goals without possessing the means for achieving them is not sufficient for academic achievement. It would appear, then, that a research approach that systematically examines motivation and skills may be called for (see 44).

Finally, there is some question regarding whether the lower achievement of Hispanic adolescents might be due to a clash in cultural values. Although more work is needed on motivational processes among Hispanic youth, it is widely known that the Hispanic community tends to value the group over the individual (21, 80, 97; see also 33). Perhaps the individualistic achievement goals of our society, which are the focus of the model presented in Table 12.1, are antagonistic to more group-oriented goals. How such values affect the structure of the motivational system is an empirical question that still needs to be addressed. Nevertheless, if group goals are favored in the Hispanic community, then it may be important to advance group goals that also promote individual achievement. Perhaps utilizing some of the educational strategies from Japan and China may have a beneficial effect on Hispanic children's achievement, since many of these strategies emphasize the individual's role in promoting the achievement of the group, both in the classroom (by having the students help one another) and in the society (by emphasizing the value of learning to the economic well-being of the nation).

The issue of ethnicity is vitally important. Ethnic (and socioeconomic) factors have an impact on academic performance, but whether and how these factors affect the structure of the child's motivational system is a question that must be addressed in future research.

Future Directions

Throughout this chapter areas calling for future research have been noted. A number of issues are in serious need of analysis with a motivational process framework, among them the origins of the motivational patterns, their stability, and their long-term consequences.

First, more research is needed if we are to understand what sorts of factors in a child's life are most important for determining which motivational patterns the child displays—most particularly, what experiences with parents and teachers foster particular theories and goals. Experimental work by Ames (1) and by Elliott and Dweck (30) shows that highlighting normative evaluation (for example, how one child's performance compares to another's) rather than individual learning and mastery fosters the adoption of performance goals and increases the child's vulnerability to the helpless behavior pattern. Further studies of real-world practices and their effects would be informative for a full understanding of the issue of origins.

Another set of research questions involves the matter of consequences: Where will a particular theory lead the individual? Some possible consequences were identified in the study by Henderson and Dweck (47), but much more work needs to be done. For example, how does the relationship between motivational variables and grades vary over time? In the short term, one can ask whether the high-confidence entity theorists will recover from the slump in their grades. In the long term, one can ask where theory, goals, and confidence lead. One can hypothesize that the incremental theorists are more likely than others to go on to college, to attend more challenging colleges, to pursue more sophisticated courses of study, and to graduate. If so, then it becomes even more important to understand how to help students cope adaptively in the long term.

Our society places a high value on academic achievement. Traditionally America has been a nation of "the best and the brightest," a nation "in search of excellence." These values remain strong today, especially as we are challenged from without by other nations for scientific and technological leadership and from within by the academic underachievement of many of our youth. As a society we are seeking to understand how best to foster academic excellence in our children and at the same time promote a zest for learning and emotional well-being. It is to be hoped that a greater understanding of motivational processes will enable us to help individuals in our society fulfill their intellectual and human potential.

13

SEXUALITY

Herant Katchadourian

Reproductive maturation is the most distinctive feature of the transition from childhood to adulthood. It is also potentially the most problematic. As children negotiate the decade between the attainment of reproductive maturity in the early teens and the taking on of mature roles in the early 20s, adults do not seem to know how to deal with adolescent sexuality any better than adolescents know how to deal with it themselves.

This gap between the biological maturation of sexuality and the social acceptance of its behavioral expression (or its social maturation) is a source of many of the problems associated with adolescent sexuality. This discrepancy between biological and social maturation is an issue that must be understood in its evolutionary, historical, biological, and social contexts (50).

Although the problem is not new, the second half of the twentieth century has seen the widest separation in human history between the timetables of biological maturation and the socially acceptable expression of sexual behavior. Since adolescents control neither their biological nor their social schedule of development, the "problem" of adolescent sexuality is hardly one of their own making.

Most discussions of adolescent sexuality focus nonetheless on its problematic aspects, particularly with respect to teenage pregnancy, (25, 52, 53, 59) and sexually transmitted diseases, most recently AIDS (9). These are serious health problems (see Chapter 17 in this volume), but we cannot deal with them effectively without an adequate understanding of the normative aspects of sexual development in adolescence.

Our understanding of early adolescent sexuality is currently quite inadequate since most studies deal with older teenagers (10, 55). The few that do include early adolescents in their samples do not look at them separately. Most research is based on limited samples and suffers from the bias of time as well. The sexual experiences of today's young people may be radically different from those of previous generations. The parents of tomorrow's adolescents—who came of age themselves during the sexual revolution—may deal differently with the sexuality of their adolescent children than did parents of previous generations. Nonetheless, much of what we have to say about early adolescent sexual behavior is extrapolated from the study of older teenagers carried out in the past.

Adults traditionally harbor the wistful wish that the inevitable awakening of sexuality in youth should occur as late, and cause as few ripples, as possible. This leads to a let-sleeping-dogs-lie mentality, or an ambivalent acceptance of the realities of adolescent sexuality geared to containing and controlling it. There is an underlying fear that adolescents are sexually crazed, promiscuous, and irresponsible. Problems associated with their sexual activities are thus often blown out of proportion. Such views do not allow a clear understanding of the natural developmental process or a compassionate and effective way of coming to terms with its negative consequences.

Other problems have to do with obstacles to the study of childhood and adolescent sexuality. Standard investigative methods, such as direct observation, verbal inquiry, and experimental manipulation, are themselves perceived as socially unacceptable forms of sexual interaction with youngsters. Adolescents cannot be studied without parental consent and their own cooperation. This double hurdle seriously skews samples that do get studied. Retrospective analyses of past adolescent behavior of adults have their own drawbacks (18).

Like the rest of this volume, this chapter attempts to combine social science expertise with policy concerns regarding youth. This essentially behavioristic approach slights the intrapsychic processes that underlie adolescent development. It neglects the subjective dimension, the thoughts and feelings of adolescents themselves. There is little in these pages that delves beneath the behavioral surface or conveys the bittersweet emotions of adolescent love; the urgency and intensity of its sexual passion, the frustrations and anxieties of its fulfillment.

Patterns of Sexual Behavior

The transition from childhood to adult sexuality through adolescence entails a great many changes. Early adolescents are barely out of childhood; late adolescents are almost adults. Thus, while a youth of 13 and one of 19 are both nominally teenagers, their sexual behaviors cannot be lumped together. Furthermore, individual differences set adolescents apart by levels of biological maturity as well as by their social, economic, and ethnic backgrounds. When we compare adolescent sexual behavior in different cultures and different historical periods, we encounter even greater diversity (21).

In the light of all this we find that very little can be said about adolescent sexuality that would apply to most individuals, let alone everyone, in this age group. Moreover, the lives of teenagers are in flux, as if they were marching across a bridge from the shore of childhood to the shore of adulthood. This sense of being in transit, suspended in midair, imparts to adolescent sexuality its fluidity and unpredictability, and its exhilarating as well as its exasperating character.

The physiological capacity for sexual arousal and orgasm is already present in children of both sexes (14, 51). It is not clear when and how such reflexive responses become eroticized. Typically, the linkage between physiological changes, such as erection or vaginal lubrication, and subjective feelings of sexual arousal is well established by the time of puberty. Activities that elicit these physiological and psychological responses are considered to be sexual behaviors. (For a general introduction to sexual functions and behavior, see 43). The antecedents of adolescent sexual behaviors are discernible, or are assumed to be present, in childhood. But what appears to be the same behavior, such as masturbation, may have different motivations and fulfill different functions in childhood, adolescence, and adulthood.

Sexual activity in preadolescence (up to age 10) takes the form of play consisting usually of self-exploration, genital manipulation, and comparable activities with opposite-sex or same-sex partners. Although it is convenient to describe such behaviors as heterosexual or homosexual play, they do not as yet reflect definitive sexual orientations. In the Kinsey studies (carried out over four decades ago), sex play among white boys was found to reach its peak at 39% by the age of 12; among white girls the peak came earlier, at age 9, involving 14% (47, 48).

A study of African-American preadolescents describes this period as a time of ongoing sexual activity (83). The sexual interactions of this sample of boys and girls (mean age 10 years), however, were largely restricted to holding hands, hugging, and playing games with sexual overtones. Sexual behavior becomes more explicit as a child crosses into puberty. Sex ceases to be a form of play and has serious social and reproductive consequences. Against this background we can now take a closer look at what early adolescents do sexually, when, and with whom.

Autoerotic Behavior

Autoerotic behaviors consist of sexual fantasy, nocturnal orgasm, and masturbation. These behaviors are quintessentially adolescent. Yet they both antedate adolescence and persist beyond it into adulthood.

Erotic fantasy. Erotic fantasy is by far the most common sexual activity indulged in as such or as part of other sexual behaviors such as masturbation and coitus. In the Coles and Stokes sample (ages 13 to 18), 72% of teenagers admitted to having erotic fantasies: 94% of these involved television figures or movie stars, 28% rock stars, 17% imaginary people, and 57% boyfriends and girlfriends (13).

The prevalence, explicitness, and intense erotic charge of fantasies are part of the upsurge of sexuality in adolescence and presumably are related to the hormonal changes of puberty (3). Cognitive and other psychological changes are also assumed to play a significant role.

Sexual fantasies fulfill a number of important functions in adolescence (and continue to do so in adult life). First and foremost they are a source of sexual arousal. Pleasurable in and of themselves, they enhance the enjoyment of other sexual activities as well. Second, fantasies act as substitutes for the satisfaction of sexual needs and goals that are either unattainable or best avoided. Given the limited opportunities most teenagers have for sexual experience, this compensatory wish-fulfillment function of fantasies is especially crucial for them. Third, fantasies provide an opportunity for teenagers to confront their sexuality, allowing them to recognize the nature and strength of their impulses, their sexual preferences, and their commonality with others, as well as their personal idiosyncrasies. Finally, sexual fantasies perform a rehearsal function and act as a form of anticipatory coping.

Romantic and erotic fantasies are sustained by the prevalent themes and images available in the popular culture. The shallow romances of soap operas on television and in movies, the suggestive and explicit lyrics of rock music, the nudity of soft-core pornographic magazines, and the vulgarity and violence of hard-core pornography are often the raw materials from which adolescent fantasies are currently fashioned. The influence of the mass media in the sexual socialization of teenagers is of singular importance.

The very assets of erotic fantasies may turn to liabilities. If fantasies consistently act as substitutes for real-life interactions, they may deter the person from establishing age-appropriate social ties. The monologue of autoerotism may compete with the dialogue of sociosexual discourse.

Sexual fantasies can be quite troublesome for some adolescents. Their intensity may be frightening, their forbidden aspects guilt provoking. Since teenagers are not likely to share such thoughts with others, those with even innocuous fantasies may think they are "queer," "weird," "perverted," or somehow different. Although young people may make determined efforts to curb their fantasies, they may not be able to push out of their mind their more disturbing erotic thoughts. But even these experiences may prove useful for learning how to manage sexual desire and the anxieties it can engender.

Nocturnal orgasm. Erections in sleep (usually during REM periods) can be observed in prepubescent boys (16). A similar vasocongestive response occurs in women during REM periods (22), but the precursors of this process in puberty have not been studied in girls.

Nocturnal orgasms with ejaculation (wet dreams) appear following puberty. Because of their involuntary nature, they have been thought of as a safety valve to release pent-up sexual tension. But nocturnal orgasms are too infrequent to serve such a purpose. In the Kinsey sample they accounted for 2% to 3% of the total sexual outlet for females and 2% to 8% for males (47, 48), although most people experienced them at one time or another. When orgasms through other means become less frequent, nocturnal orgasms do not become significantly more frequent by way of compensation. Therefore, the conventional advice that teenagers should let nocturnal emissions "naturally" relieve them of pent-up sexual tensions is not realistic. Like menarche for girls who are unprepared, nocturnal emissions can be disconcerting for boys, and the telltale evidence of the ejaculate a source of embarrassment.

Masturbation. Erotic fantasies are closely linked to masturbation; fantasies may lead to masturbation and the wish to masturbate in turn conjures up erotic fantasies (33). Fantasies are used regularly by at least half of adolescents during masturbation. But 11% of boys and 7% of girls say they never fantasize when stimulating themselves to orgasm (77). The lack of elaborate fantasies does not mean lack of all erotic imagery, however. Like fantasy, masturbation provides a readily available, safe, and secure sexual outlet. It allows for the release of sexual tension and is a means of exploring one's own sexuality. It is useful in itself as well as a form of rehearsal for sociosexual interactions with others.

Masturbation is the most common source of orgasm in adolescents of both sexes, serving as the source for their first ejaculation among boys in two out of three instances. In the Sorensen sample (aged 13–19), most girls who masturbated had started at about age 12; most boys dated their first experience before age 14 (77). In the Coles and Stokes sample the proportion who said they had masturbated was 46% for boys and 24% for girls (13). The consistently higher percentage figures among boys probably reflect a true gender difference, although they may also be due in part to a greater willingness on the part of boys to report the behavior. It may also be that some girls do not have the knowledge or the language to describe the self-stimulation they engage in as masturbation. The severe social condemnation of masturbation and the presumption of negative health consequences that characterized attitudes in the past have been largely abandoned. Yet a certain amount of guilt and shame continues to be attached to the practice, even by adolescents themselves (77).

Sociosexual Behavior

Petting. By the time they get to high school, most adolescents have crossed the line from autoerotic to sociosexual behaviors. Petting represents a significant advance in the interpersonal aspects of sexual behavior because it requires the ability to negotiate and share sexual experiences. The component activities of petting follow a fairly predictable progression from the less to the more intimate interactions. Hence at successive ages the percentage of boys and girls who have engaged in a particular sexual activity (such as kissing) gets progressively larger.

Oral sex. The practice of oral sex is now fairly common in adolescence. Among students in grades ten to twelve, 50% of males and 41% of females engage in cunnilingus, and 44% of males and 32% of females engage in fellatio (64). Boys reportedly enjoy both experiences more than girls (13). Some adolescents refuse to engage in oral sex even if they have had sexual intercourse because they see it as a more intimate activity, or because of other concerns. Some use oral sex as a substitute for coitus to avoid pregnancy, while others use it for its own sake.

Sexual intercourse. The most important sexual milestone that heterosexual adolescents achieve is the initiation of sexual intercourse. Not only is coitus generally considered by heterosexuals to be the most satisfying of all sexual relations, but it also has the most significant personal and social consequences (38). Couples who engage in coitus cross a line that irreversibly alters the character of their relationship. Pregnancy and sexually transmitted diseases make coitus a high-risk activity if the proper precautions are not taken. For these and similar reasons the prospect of coitus among adolescents, especially at the younger ages, raises serious social concerns.

There are very few studies that provide data on coital behavior in early adolescence. Those that exist show coitus to be a sporadic and relatively rare experience. Two studies report that fewer than one in ten teenagers of both sexes had engaged in coitus before age 15 (40, 54). A more recent study reports 12% of boys and 6% of girls aged 13 having had coital experience (13). Studies of older adolescents indicate first intercourse to have occurred on the average at about 16, usually within the context of a steady relationship (84).

Since the late 1960s adolescents have become sexually active in greater numbers and at younger ages (42, 85, 86). Nonetheless, age continues to be a good predictor of when teenagers will initiate sexual activity. Results from a national longitudinal survey show that by age 15, about 17% of boys and 6% of girls are no longer virgins; at age 18, 67% of boys and 44% of girls are sexually experienced; by age 20, the figures go up to 80% for males and 70% for females (60).

In the Coles and Stokes sample, the reactions of boys and girls to first intercourse varied considerably (13). Girls generally had more negative reactions than boys: 1% of boys and 11% of girls said they "felt sorry" afterwards; 60% of boys and 23% of girls said they were "glad." Nonetheless, subsequent coital experience was reported to be generally quite positive: about 80% of boys and 70% of girls said they enjoyed sexual intercourse a great deal.

These and similar data show coital experience to be tinged with some negative reactions, particularly for girls, but on the whole to represent a positive experience for sexually active teenagers. Ethical, medical, and social concerns notwithstanding, sexual intercourse appears to be in the process of becoming part of the normative experience of adolescent development in the United States.

Homosexual relations. Just as some children engage in sex play with members of their own sex, it is not unusual for adolescents to have homosexual contacts with peers, and sometimes with adults or children. Typically such encounters are of an exploratory and transient nature; they do not, as such, lead to a homosexual orientation in adulthood, although most adult homosexuals usually trace their sexual orientation back to adolescence (5).

Despite the recent liberalization of social attitudes, many adolescents (boys more so than girls) continue to disapprove of homosexuals, and some are quite hostile to them. Lesbians are viewed with more tolerance. In view of these attitudes, self-reports of homosexual behavior tend to be particularly unreliable (13). In the Sorensen sample, about 5% of boys and girls aged 13 to 15 reported having had one or more homosexual experiences (77). For 56% of boys and 32% of girls who had had such an experience, it occurred at ages 11 to 12. For girls the partner was most likely to be about the same age (63%); for boys the partner was just as likely to be younger or the same age, and in 12% of cases it was an adult.

Many, but by no means all, adolescents who are openly gay face special problems. The revelation or discovery of their homosexuality resulted for one group of gay teenagers in strongly negative reactions from parents (43%) and friends (41%). They were discriminated against by peers (37%), verbally abused (55%), and physically assaulted (30%) (70). Many of them had problems in school, engaged in substance abuse, ran away from home, or got into trouble with the law. Nearly half had contracted a sexually transmitted disease (70). Despite increasingly tolerant social attitudes toward homosexuality, there are currently few resources to help gay teenagers cope with the special stresses of their lives.

Determinants of Sexual Behavior

What a teenager does sexually, with whom, and when is a function of biological and social factors. Most studies have focused on when teenagers engage in first coitus (59). Yet, teenagers do not typically "go all the way" without prior experience of other sexual behaviors at increasing levels of intimacy. Although primarily related to first coitus, the determinants of adolescent decision making pertain to the broader range of adolescent sexual behaviors as well.

Effects of Puberty

It has long been assumed that the sexual awakening of adolescence is related to the biological changes of puberty. There is in fact a clear association between the signs of pubertal development and the initiation of adolescent sexual activity (80, 83, 87).

The influence of pubertal development on sexual behavior may be both direct and indirect, and somewhat different for boys and girls. The direct influence of puberty is ascribed to the activational effects of hormones on the nervous system. For instance, levels of testosterone are correlated with sexual behavior in boys, regardless of the level of development of secondary sexual characteristics (81). In girls a similar association links testosterone levels and sexual interest but not sexual behavior (82). This suggests that social influences tend to inhibit the behavioral expression of the enhanced sexual interest of girls at puberty.

The indirect effects of puberty depend on the stimulus value of secondary sexual characteristics. For instance, the development of breasts in girls and signs of physical maturation in boys make them more sexually attractive and more likely to be drawn into sexual interactions (75). In this respect, female hormones (in particular estrogens) are critical in bringing about bodily changes in girls. But their potential effects on the brain, and hence their direct impact on sexual behavior, is unclear.

Biological factors are essential for the development of adolescent sexual behavior, but their effects are dependent on social influences. Biology defines the limits within which sexual interactions take place. Their social context shapes the particular behavioral patterns and imparts meaning to them. Thus, the initiation of a given sexual behavior, such as coitus, is highly dependent on what is normative in the adolescent's peer group (26). At low levels of sexual development and motivation, a teenage girl is less likely to be influenced by the sexual behavior of her friends; but at higher levels of hormonal readiness, peer behavior becomes more influential.

Similar correlations apply to dating behavior. The age at which teenagers generally begin to date is determined by the biological schedule of pubertal development, which establishes the baseline. But for a given boy or girl, level of pubertal development is not necessarily the determining factor. Individuals will begin to date when their friends do, or in response to social expectations with respect to their age, regardless of their level of biological maturity (20, 29). With boys, the level of pubertal development and the sexual behavior of friends are also influential. But unlike with girls, the influence of friends is not contingent on boys' level of maturity. In other words, with higher levels of development, the sexual behavior of friends does not increase in importance for boys (75).

Effects of Ethnicity and Socioeconomic Status

Sexual intercourse is more prevalent among black than white adolescents at all ages; blacks become sexually active earlier than whites (4, 63, 87). In a sample of young people aged 11 to 17 (mean age 13.6), 77.3% of black males, 39.1% of black females, 24.9% of white males, and 10.3% of white females reported that they had had engaged in sexual intercourse (6, 8).

Why these differences exist is not entirely certain. There is evidence that black girls mature somewhat earlier than whites, but the difference is too small to provide a biological explanation (57). Social explanations include economic factors, differences in the acceptability of early sexual behavior, the effects of family and neighborhood environments, and the ethnic composition of schools attended by teenagers (1, 36, 57, 78).

Black teenagers who become pregnant can expect a more favorable reaction from the baby's father than whites (65% against 43%) as well as from their peers (70% against 40%) (57). The more accepting attitudes may be due to the prevalence of the practice and may act in turn as an inducement for it. Since sexual attitudes and values are usually assessed among teenagers who are already sexually active, however, their views are likely to be influenced by their experience (59).

Effects of Religious Affiliation

Sexual values are closely tied to religious affiliation: religious observance is linked with sexual conservatism or restraint (17, 37). What is significant here is not the particular religion or sectarian association but the extent to which an individual is committed to its teachings.

Personal and Interpersonal Factors

Early sexual experience is more likely among teenagers of lower intellectual ability and academic achievement, who lack educational goals; conversely, higher academic performance and motivation are connected with postponement of sexual activity (17, 36, 57, 58). Again, antecedent and effect may be difficult to separate. Sexual activity may be a distraction from academic work, just as lack of academic ability and interest may incline teenagers to seek satisfaction from sexual activity.

Not much is known about the personality factors that may have a bearing on when a teenager first engages in sex. In one of the few prospective studies available, it was possible to isolate a number of factors that were associated with early sexual activity. Characterized as "transition prone," adolescents in this group placed a comparatively higher value at an earlier age on becoming independent and a lower value on academic achievement and religious beliefs. They were less disapproving of problem behavior in others and themselves, and therefore more tolerant of deviance (38, 40).

Teenagers typically claim that their sexual experiences are not the result of premeditated, conscious decisions but that they just "happen" (12). The degree of impulsivity and the ability to delay gratification are hence key factors in determining if and when an adolescent will become sexually active.

The interpersonal context of sexual activities has not received sufficient attention. The experience of falling in love may or may not be associated with sexual contact. The loved one may be a distant and unattainable figure (a movie star or rock musician) or a known person. Even when peers are involved, adolescent love often entails distant adulation rather than actual personal intimacy. But many teenage couples who are in love may become sexually intimate. Being in love typically acts as a precondition and justification for engaging in sex in the contemporary peer culture.

Adolescents also engage in casual sex. Boys are more likely to do so than girls, who place a higher premium on intimate relationships. In the Coles and Stokes sample, close to a third of nonvirgin boys claimed to have slept with someone they "didn't really know," as against a fifth of the girls (13). Boys were also more likely than girls to have had their first coital experience with a casual acquaintance (37% against 17%).

Although most sexual interactions between teenagers involve mutual consent, various forms of coercion may also occur, ranging from psychological pressure to rape. In the Coles and Stokes sample, 14% of the sexually active girls reported having been raped—a quarter of them before 10 years of age. In 16% of cases the rapist was a boyfriend, in 30% a more casual friend. The use of coercion and various self-justifications for it appear already established among boys by the time of adolescence.

Sexual Socialization

In the more traditional perspective, the biologically based sexual drive erupts at puberty and is channeled into socially constructed patterns. An alternative model, which more behavioral scientists adhere to, gives greater primacy to social processes in the shaping of sexual behavior. In this view biology provides the physical "machinery" and hormonal factors prime the predisposition to act sexually. But when, why, and how a person engages in sex is learned within a particular sociocultural setting (see Chapter 2 in this volume). As a result, there is a wide diversity in sexual behavior across cultures (23, 32) as well as within the various socioeconomic, ethnic, religious, and other subcultural segments of a given society.

Gagnon and Simon exemplify the social processes approach by considering sex to be a socially "scripted" activity (27). In this view sexual expression is governed not by biological impulses as such but by the complex interweaving of "cultural scenarios," "interpersonal scripts," and "intrapsychic scripts." The sexual script acts as a record of past sexual activities, a standard for present behavior, and a plan for the future regarding when and with whom one has sex, and what one does sexually, in a given set of circumstances (74).

Sexual Identity

A key outcome of sexual socialization is the formation of a person's sexual identity, which becomes an integral part of the sense of self (see Chapter

14 in this volume). First, there is a basic perception of oneself as a sexual being. Linked to it is the idea of one's sexual attractiveness (sexiness) to others as well as what one finds sexually attractive in others (44).

In addition, sexual identity encompasses sexual orientation and gender identity. Sexual orientation, which may be heterosexual, homosexual, or bisexual, becomes consolidated in adolescence. Gender identity pertains to masculinity and femininity. Its roots are laid in childhood, but its definitive manifestations take shape in adolescence (45, 56).

Adolescence is a crucial time for the consolidation of gender identity and sexual orientation, but much remains to be learned about the developmental processes that shape these aspects of the personality. Uncertainty about the relative significance of biological and psychosocial formative factors prevails with respect to both (5, 69).

Parental Influences

The role of parents in the sexual socialization of children is taken for granted. But since there is usually little direct communication between parents and children on sexual topics, it is unclear how such socialization takes place. It may be that parents convey their sexual attitudes indirectly, through the example of their own behavior, or in the context of broader issues. For instance, a middle-class family may foster principles of self-restraint and postponement of gratification in general. The youngster is then expected to apply these precepts to sexual behavior. The attitudes and expectation of teenagers with regard to academic achievement tend to mirror their parents' level of education and aspirations for their children. The higher academic goal orientation of youngsters from better-educated, more affluent families in turn makes it less likely that they will engage in coitus at an early age. Girls who emphasize academic achievement and strive to please parents and teachers may be less interested in boys and in turn less interesting to them (12).

A strong relationship exists between a mother's own sexual experience as a teenager and that of her teenage daughter (63). Family composition and intactness have a further bearing. Girls from single-parent families are more likely to become sexually active at an earlier age than those who grow up in two-parent families (37, 63, 87). Does the sexual behavior of a single mother act as a model? Is it the lack of parental supervision that is at issue? Or is it more specifically the absence of the father (as a controlling figure or in some other role) that engenders the propensity for early sexual activity in the children? Insufficient research has been done on these issues for us to judge (66).

The way parents relate to teenagers provides further clues to sexual behavior. The daughters of mothers who fail to show affection while setting firm limits are more likely than others to engage in early sex. Also, daughters grow more distant from their mothers after they have engaged in sex. Both the decline in closeness and the initiation of sex may result from increased independence (59). Sexual acting out may be used by rebellious adolescents as a way to express defiance and autonomy (30). Sex may become a weapon with which to provoke or humiliate parents.

Some studies have correlated the initiation of early sexual activity by teenagers with poor communication with parents and lack of parental support (39). Teenagers who have close relationships with their parents delay sexual activity (37). Consistency of values between children and parents, a sense of family connectedness and support, and close ties at home are all linked to a lesser likelihood of adolescents' becoming sexually active (40).

Nonetheless, the causal role that communication plays is far from certain. Parental discussion of sexual matters may occur after the teenager has initiated sexual activity (63). One study of the level of communication about sexual topics before the initiation of sexual activity found no relationship with the behavior of daughters. For sons, discussions with the mother were associated with lower levels, but with the father with higher levels, of subsequent sexual activity (41). This may be because fathers implicitly encourage sexual activity among their sons, while mothers may discourage it.

Communication about sexual matters between parents and children is part of the larger issue of sex education in the home. Sexual conservatives maintain that whatever instruction children receive in such matters should be imparted by their parents. This would ensure that the information is conveyed within the context of a family's moral values. Yet it is doubtful how often or how effectively such instruction is given in the home.

A study conducted in the late 1970s in the Cleveland area showed very little meaningful and positive sex education taking place at home. Fathers were particularly uninvolved in the sexual education of their children. Both boys and girls directed their questions (usually related to pregnancy and childbirth) to their mothers. When parents responded to these questions, they usually dealt with them on a one-time basis rather than as part of an ongoing dialogue (71, 72).

Parents often do not know what to tell their children about sex because they lack accurate information themselves or are uncertain of their own sexual values. Other parents have very clear convictions about sexual morality but have difficulty persuading their children to adhere to them. Confronting the emerging sexuality of teenage children makes some parents particularly uneasy (73). Others fear that broaching the subject may stimulate, encourage, or frighten their children, or somehow lead to a loss of innocence.

It has become standard practice to berate American parents for their failure to educate their children about sexuality. But there is no evidence that parents in other comparable cultures do a significantly better job. Perhaps there are deeper reasons why it is hard to talk to one's own children about sex no matter how well informed or enlightened a parent may be. Talking about sex is a form of sexual interaction, and its avoidance may be part of the incest taboo. The adolescence of children often coincides with the middle age of parents. Both are periods of transition, with their particular anxieties, including sexual concerns. To expect parents to tend personally to the sexual instruction of their teenage children while they themselves are in search of answers in their own lives may be unrealistic. Nonetheless, the liberalization of attitudes brought on by the sexual revolution of the 1960s may be reflected in the greater willingness of new generations of parents to deal with their children in this area (31).

Peer Influences

The effect of peer relationships in sexual development, like the influence of the family, is taken for granted, although it may not be fully backed by research evidence (34). The influence of the peer culture complements the influence of the family in socializing the teenager (see Chapter 11 in this volume). But the two may also conflict. This is particularly true during periods of rapid social change when generational values diverge, as was the case during the 1960s (54). The peer group gradually supplants the family in the sexual socialization of the adolescent. Even if teenagers do not engage in sexual relations, their sexual attitudes are likely to be influenced by the peer culture through the information (and misinformation) it provides and the values it transmits.

What are these values? The adult perceptions of adolescent sexuality tend to stereotype it as hedonistic, impulsive, and irresponsible. Teenage love is seen as impetuous, turbulent, shallow, a transient infatuation ("puppy love"). Adolescents have a more positive and idealized view of themselves. They see their sexual and romantic interactions as spontaneous, honest, and idealistic, in contrast to the seemingly more calculating, manipulative, hypocritical, "uptight" sexual associations of adults.

Major gender differences are already discernible in adolescents with regard to attitudes toward sex and love. Even in elementary school, girls begin to learn about commitment and emotional intimacy through same-sex friendships, whereas boys learn about sex first and about its relational components later (79). In adolescence this difference is seen in the greater willingness of boys to engage in casual sex, while girls are more concerned with relationships. While both sexes value intimacy and love, males in general tend to be more sexually permissive than females. A negative feature of gender differences can be seen when the double standard is applied to teenagers. Boys who are sexually active tend to be characterized as "studs" while their female counterparts are seen as "sluts."

Peer influence is often claimed to be a potent factor in determining when an individual initiates sexual intercourse. For instance, in a 1986 poll conducted by Louis Harris, one thousand teenagers were asked why they had not waited to have sexual intercourse until they were older. The top four reasons given by adolescent girls were peer pressure (34%), pressure from boys (17%), curiosity (14%), and "everyone does it" (14%). Boys cited peer pressure (26%), curiosity (16%), "everyone does it" (10%), and sexual gratification (10%). The countervailing considerations for not engaging in sex were the danger of sexually transmitted diseases (65%), danger of pregnancy (62%), fear of discovery by parents (50%), and fear of having their reputations ruined with friends (29%) (68). Research in this area, as in this case, usually relies on the reports of individuals with respect to their own behavior and attitudes as well as those of their friends, without independent validation (34).

Friends are less often relied on as a source of information on reproduction than parents (15% against 23%). The percentage figures for peers and parents are the same (17%) as a source for contraceptive information. But for other sexual behaviors, peers (particularly same-sex peers) constitute the primary source more often than parents: 32% against 12% with regard to questions about masturbation, and 26% against 14% on homosexuality (13).

Generalizations about adolescent sexual values are difficult to make since adolescents differ from one another as much as adults do. The sexual behavior of teenagers is also difficult to predict from their attitudes and normative beliefs. Young people are grappling with inconsistencies and conflicts between their parents' beliefs, their own beliefs, and their behavior. Being in a state of flux, they have uncertain guidelines and a need to explore and experiment, and they are increasingly subject to peer pressure, all of which makes their behavior unpredictable and seemingly erratic.

The perception of teenagers of how sexually liberal and active their same-sex peers are is an important predictor of their own sexual involvement (15). This perception need not necessarily coincide with the actual behavior of peers; it is sufficient for a teenager to believe that his or her friends are engaging in sex for this perception to act as an incentive.

There may be a more direct relationship to the actual sexual behavior of a best friend through a "homogeneity bias" that marks such relationships. For example, in acquiring or developing a close friend, a girl will be influenced by shared sexual values and behaviors. Virgins are more likely to become best friends with other virgins. If the friend becomes sexually active, the girl may be faced with two choices: to terminate the friendship or to follow her friend's example and lose her own virginity (6, 8).

Boys and girls who are popular with opposite-sex peers are often those with the highest levels of sexual involvement. This pattern holds true for whites but not for blacks, for reasons that are unclear (63). White boys seem more likely than blacks to be influenced by the sexual behavior of peers and to choose their friends on that basis (7). Girls are generally more likely than boys to be swayed by the actual or presumed sexual behavior of their peers, especially their best friends and their boyfriends (7, 15). Here again peer influence is less compelling among blacks; it is white girls who are generally most susceptible to peer influence.

The influence of undesirable friends has been a common fear of parents and teachers. Sometimes it provides a comforting explanation as to why one's son or daughter has "gone wrong." Yet it is often difficult to separate the influence of friends from the choice of particular friends in the first place (see Chapter 11). The relationship is often reciprocal: the sexual behavior of the adolescent helps determine the crowd he or she runs with (62); conversely, the sexual behavior patterns of the crowd influence the behavior of the individual associated with it.

Adolescent Sexuality and Society

Social institutions such as schools and churches, the mass media (especially television), advertising, and the cultural environment as a whole all contribute to the sexual socialization of the teenager.

Sex Education in Schools

Until fairly recently sex education was practically absent from the school curriculum. Only since the early 1970s have a large number of programs been developed to impart information about sexual functions (particularly reproduction and contraception) and sexual relationships. Their aim is to inform, as well as influence, teenagers' attitudes and behaviors (46).

While these attempts at sex education may have proved highly controversial at the local level, national public opinion polls show that the majority of adults favor sex education in schools (28, 61). Adolescents themselves express strong support for it (31, 65). A sample of 179 school districts in large cities found that three-quarters provided some sex education in their high schools and junior high schools (76).

There are considerable similarities in these programs: 94% promote rational and informed decision making, and 77% provide information about reproduction (34). In junior high school the topics typically covered are sexual anatomy, the physical and psychological changes in puberty, reproduction, dating, and sexually transmitted diseases (67). Teaching about contraception is more likely to start at the high school level.

Most programs are short (ten hours or less) and are usually integrated into courses in biology, health science, or physical education. Consequently, fewer than 10% of students are exposed to comprehensive sex education programs in school (49). A number of community organizations such as Planned Parenthood, churches, and youth groups (YMCA, Boys Scouts and Girl Scouts) also offer sex education programs.

Given these efforts to educate and the quantity of sexually related materials to which youngsters are exposed, one would expect American teenagers to be quite knowledgeable about sex. Generally, though, they are not, even about elementary facts. It is this ignorance combined with widespread sexual activity that is alarming (13).

Sex education programs that go beyond the perfunctory level do increase students' knowledge. They may also influence their attitudes, making them more tolerant of the sexual values and behavior of others. But they usually have no demonstrable effect on timing of first sexual intercourse and frequency of subsequent sexual activities (49). But among teenage females who are sexually active, sex education is correlated with lowered pregnancy rates. One study estimates that about 60% more white females and 70% more black females would have become pregnant had they not received sex education (24, 88).

Serious efforts at sex education are so new and so difficult to evaluate that we need more time to assess their effectiveness. We must recognize that influencing teenage sexual behavior calls for more than education about reproduction. There is more to sex than the "plumbing" of the reproductive system. The interpersonal aspects of sex—its pleasures, anxieties, and satisfactions—are what give meaning to sexuality.

Recent attempts at more comprehensive sex education include programs in family life education (where sexuality is but one of the issues addressed), family communication programs, decision-making training, peer-related programs, and other approaches that aim to impart knowledge and influence attitudes. More specifically preventive interventions provide access to contraception (such as in school clinics) and, even more generally, involve programs that enhance individuals' options with respect to broader issues (59).

Sexual Themes in Popular Culture

Following the liberalization of laws on pornography and the shifts in public attitudes during the 1960s, a wave of sexually explicit materials flooded the marketplace (2). Such themes and images in advertising, on television, in films, videos, song lyrics, magazines, newspapers, and myriad other forms make it inevitable that teenagers are exposed daily to sexual materials and messages. The separation of the artistic from the pornographic, the innocuous from the harmful in all this material is a source of ongoing controversy (19).

Sexuality and Social Deviance

In American society the lingering traditional ideal is one of premarital sexual abstinence, followed by a lifelong commitment to a monogamous heterosexual partnership in marriage. Romantic attachment, mutual sexual satisfaction, and parenthood are the basic components of this idealized model.

This ideal makes little allowance for sexual experience in adolescence. Although public attitudes toward teenage sexuality have become considerably liberalized, sexual activity is still associated by many with social deviance, and the loss of virginity in adolescence is perceived as socially problematic. On the one hand, socially deviant youth tend to be sexually more active than others. Early sexual experience is linked to other forms of deviance, such as delinquency and alcohol and drug use (see Chapter 16 in this volume). But, on the other hand, a substantial proportion of the adolescent population that would not otherwise be considered deviant is now sexually active. This represents a schism between the current realities of adolescent life and traditional societal expectations.

Teenagers who are victimized by adults also suffer the consequences of deviant status. Those who are sexually abused are keenly aware of their aberrant experience. Those who are trapped into the pornography industry or prostitution are seriously alienated from the social mainstream and relegated to a life of degradation and deviance. All of these considerations add up to an urgent need for society to confront the realities of adolescent sexuality in all its ramifications and to try to come to terms with them.

Future Directions

American society dealt with adolescent sexuality in the recent past mainly by trying to suppress it or ignore it. Adults now seem to have lost control over the sexual behavior of adolescents. For better or worse, sex in adolescence is here to stay. So the task has shifted to containing the damage. Adults, however, are not of one mind about this. In some quarters there is a positive acceptance, if not a celebration, of adolescent sexuality, in others a determined attempt to reinstate traditional expectations ("Say no"). But among the majority of people concerned with adolescents, there is an uneasy uncertainty about what sexual values to espouse, what limits to impose, and what behaviors to welcome.

In a pluralistic and individualistic society like that of the United States, we are unlikely to reach consensus on how to deal with adolescent sexual behavior. If we are going to face up to it and its problematic consequences, there has to be at least some common understanding of the nature of adolescent sexuality, the best ways of approaching its study, and the public policies required for its social management.

A Balanced View

To begin with, the emergence of sexual behavior in adolescence may have to be accepted now as part of the normal process of becoming an adult physically and psychosocially. Therefore, adolescent sexuality as such cannot reasonably be seen anymore as a "problem." It becomes a problem only when sexual behaviors lead to undesirable consequences. So the question is no longer whether or not adolescents may engage in sexual experiences but what sorts of sexual behaviors are healthy, moral, and socially desirable, and which are not.

Concerns with the problematic aspects of adolescent sexual activity are well taken. Adolescent pregnancy and sexually transmitted diseases can have serious and long-term consequences. Urgent and sincere efforts must be made to deal with these issues. Nothing less than the future of the nation's youth is at risk. But these concerns should not overwhelm the equally pressing need to understand, nurture, and regulate the flowering of sexuality during adolescence in ways that are consistent with current realities, social values, and individual freedoms. We are a society that places considerable value on sexual gratification. It is essential that we understand the role that adolescent sexuality plays in the creation of sexually healthy and competent adults. To this end many questions remain to be answered: To what extent does adolescent sexual experience help develop more rational and reasonable approaches to selecting a mate? How can it reduce sexual incompatibility and conflict, thereby strengthening marital and other committed relationships in the future? How can the tendency toward sexist, exploitative, or violent sexual behaviors be discouraged during this crucial formative stage? What are the costs and potential risks entailed in permitting, encouraging, and guiding adolescent sexual behavior? What are the gains and the costs of suppressing it?

Long-standing social attitudes have relegated sexuality to a special category of human experience. It is time to end this quarantine. Sex must take its rightful place among other bodily functions and human experiences. Sexual attractions and interactions make sense only within the broader context of interpersonal relationships with peers, parents, and other significant adults. Likewise, sexual values and moral principles must be an integral part of the individual's broader ethical orientation.

Problems for Research

We must recognize at the outset that research into early adolescent sexuality will continue to present formidable obstacles. In addition to traditional sources of resistance on the part of parents, increasingly stringent standards for conducting research with human subjects are likely to put severe limits on what can be done in this area. Biomedical and behavioral scientists in partnership with parents and others concerned with the welfare of youth will have to devise methods of inquiry that permit meaningful investigation.

At the biological level, we need to know more about the maturational patterns of the sexual response cycle and the effects of hormones and neurotransmitters in stimulating and sustaining sexual behavior. At the behavioral level, we need to know a great deal more about the onset and patterns of sexual activity and about the demographic, socioeconomic, and interpersonal aspects of these sexual behaviors, especially sexual intercourse. Studies will have to be carried out in ways that can separate antecedents of sexual activity from consequences. Much more needs to be learned about the processes underlying these associations.

At the psychological level, the role of sexuality needs to be further elucidated with respect to basic issues such as ego identity, self-esteem, competence, and other key aspects of adolescent development. Cognitive factors are equally critical in determining the capacity of teenagers for decision making, moral reasoning, anticipating the consequences of one's actions, and determining risks. These and other related issues require much more study.

Education

It is likely that the threat of AIDS will make sex education virtually mandatory, especially if the epidemic begins to make substantial inroads into the adolescent population. On the positive side, this should generate funds and may help overcome any residual resistance to sex education programs. On the negative side, it will further reinforce the feeling that society takes an interest in sex education only because sex is seen as a problem.

Sex education must become better integrated into the school curriculum. It cannot be very effective if it is tucked away wherever it will cause the fewest ripples. At whatever level it is started, and however many hours are allotted to it, the teaching of sexuality must be approached no differently from other subjects. Children learn in progressive installments; there is no reason why they should not do likewise in learning about sex.

If the overt or covert aim of sex education is primarily restrictive or inhibitory, it is not likely to have much credibility with or effect on teenagers. Youngsters must be told the facts and given appropriate guidance. They must be helped to learn how to make sexual decisions, and to be mindful of the consequences. Their autonomy must be respected, but they must be taught to take responsibility for their actions.

Parents, teachers, and representatives of society have the right and the obligation to express their own sexual values, provided they have thought them through. It is indeed the duty of adults to set limits and to help teenagers learn to say no (68). But if teenagers are going to say no to some choices, they must also be told in what cases they can say yes. This is a matter not of making concessions but of providing youngsters with reasonable choices.

The family and the school both have a crucial role to play in the sexual education of adolescents. But there are limitations on what each of them can do. Perhaps the most effective avenues for sex education are through the mass media, especially television. Much criticism has been leveled at the portrayal of sexuality on television. These criticisms are well taken, but what is called for are programs that do a better job of conveying healthier, more realistic, and more informative messages. It took the threat of AIDS to get condoms mentioned on television; the same impetus can be used to produce more significant educational developments.

Public Policy

There is at present precious little in the way of public policy regarding adolescent sexuality. Young people are potentially at risk with regard to AIDS because of their patterns of sexual activity and erratic use of effective precautionary measures. Should there be a general outbreak of AIDS among the nation's youth, we may see policies generated in a hurry to deal with it. Meanwhile, and regardless of the threat of AIDS, responsible policy-making bodies and professionals must be ready to confront the realities of adolescent sexuality for today's youth in today's world.

The field of sexuality has made impressive strides over the past several decades, but it remains peripheral to the academic and research mainstream. That needs to change. Sex is too important to be left to sexologists; it should be part of everyone's business, especially when it concerns youth.

Groups that have tackled more specific issues such as teenage pregnancy have come up with detailed guidelines for research, policies, and programs. The set of recommendations by the Panel on Adolescent Pregnancy and Childbearing is a good example, and one that is highly pertinent to our concerns here (59). They call for the reduction of unintended pregnancies, especially among school-age teenagers, through contraceptive use; the enhancement of life options and more specific approaches for delaying the initiation of sexual activity; and the prevention of the high-risk consequences of sex. We need similar efforts by experts of comparable stature to set a national agenda to deal with the normative developmental aspects of adolescent sexual behavior and its ramifications.

This is the conventional approach. There is much to say for it. But we may also need to consider a whole new perspective on adolescent sexuality, a radical rethinking of our conceptual models and sexual values. We must recognize changing realities as sex becomes increasingly decoupled from reproduction, as gender roles become restructured, and as other forces of social change transform sexual relationships. Most of all, we need to recognize the importance of sexuality for the health and happiness of today's youth—for their own sake and for the sake of generations to come.

14

SELF AND IDENTITY DEVELOPMENT

Susan Harter

Suppose that we asked a typical 15-year-old to describe herself as a person, to present a verbal portrait of the self. What features would she emphasize, and how would such a description provide us with insights into the adolescent's self-concept? What follows is such a portrayal of the self, culled from self-descriptions representing the most salient themes that emerge.

What am I like as a person? Complicated! I'm sensitive, friendly, outgoing, popular, and tolerant, though I can also be shy, self-conscious, and even obnoxious. Obnoxious! I'd *like* to be friendly and tolerant all of the time. That's the kind of person I *want* to be, and I'm disappointed when I'm not. I'm responsible, even studious every now and then, but on the other hand I'm a goof-off too, because if you're too studious, you won't be popular. I don't usually do that well at school. I'm a pretty cheerful person, especially with my friends, where I can even get rowdy. At home I'm more likely to be anxious around my parents. They expect me to get all A's. It's not fair! I worry about how I probably *should* get better grades. But I'd be mortified in the eyes of my friends. So I'm usually pretty stressed-out at home, or sarcastic, since my parents are always on my case. But I really don't understand how I can switch so fast. I mean, how can I be cheerful one minute, anxious the next, and then be sarcastic? Which one is the *real* me? Sometimes I feel phony, especially around boys. Say I think some guy might be interested in asking me out. I try to act different, like Madonna. I'll be flirtatious and fun-loving. And then everybody, I mean *everybody* else is looking at me like they think I'm totally weird! Then I get self-conscious and embarrassed and become radically introverted, and I don't know who I really am! Am I just trying to impress them or what? But I don't really care what they think anyway. I don't *want* to care, that is. I just want to know what my close friends think. I can be my true self with my close friends. I can't be my real self with my parents. They don't understand me. What do *they* know about what it's like to be a teenager? They treat me like I'm still a kid. At least at school people treat you more like you're an adult. That gets confusing, though. I mean, which am I, a kid or an adult? It's scary, too, because I don't have any idea what I want to be when I grow up. I mean, I have lots of *ideas*. My friend Sheryl and I talk about whether we'll be stewardesses, or teachers, or nurses, veterinarians, maybe mothers, or actresses. I know I *don't* want to be a waitress or a secretary. But how do you decide all of this? I really don't know. I mean, I think about it a lot, but I can't resolve it. There are days when I wish I could just become immune to myself!

This personal narrative exemplifies numerous prototypic features of self-description during middle adolescence, features that are unique to this fascinating transitional period of development. We witness an introspective self-portrait that is couched in the language of traits of the self—obnoxious, tolerant, introverted, popular, cheerful, depressed—many of which appear to be contradictory. We glean that the display of different selves in different social contexts is cause for concern, as the adolescent struggles to reconcile these different selves as well as determine which is the "real me." Experimenting with one's persona, and determining whether this brings affirmation or denigration from others, is typically an emotional experience for the adolescent preoccupied with the challenge of self-definition. Such self-reflection is not restricted to the present but extends to one's future self, what one would like to become.

These processes do not occur, however, within an introspective vacuum. The self is a social construction. For example, the peer group looms large as a source of values, directives, feedback, and social comparison. Parental expectations, evaluations, and exhortations also play a major role and may well conflict with the values of the peer culture. "In Search of Self," therefore, defines a major drama that unfolds on center stage during adolescence, with a complicated cast of characters who do not always speak with a single voice.

In this chapter I shall first examine those factors that produce these typical features of the adolescent self-concept. Adolescence represents a fascinating transitional period, marked by the emergence of newfound cognitive capacities and changing societal expectations that, in consort, profoundly shape and alter the very nature of the self-concept. Teenagers who successfully navigate the journey of self-development should acquire a clear and consolidated sense of true self that is realistic and internalized, one that will lay the basis for further identity development. Failure to chart these waters successfully may result in a number of potential psychological risks, among them a distorted or unrealistic self-concept, failure to integrate the self across multiple roles, conflict over seeming contradictions within the self, maladaptive or distressing displays of false selves, and definitions of the self that rely primarily on the standards and desires of others. Any one of these may preclude the development of an integrated, internalized sense of self that will foster the search for a meaningful future identity.

I shall then delve into the issue of self-evaluation, focusing on adolescent self-esteem. Why do some youths hold the self in high regard, whereas others have very poor self-esteem? What causes these differences, and on what basis are specific as well as general evaluations of the self formed? Are such attitudes relatively stable, or are they susceptible to change?

Moreover, what impact, if any, does high or low self-esteem have on adolescents' emotional reactions and behavior? What function does self-esteem serve in the lives of teenagers? The literature reveals that positive self-esteem serves as a buffer against stress and is typically associated with a wide range of productive coping strategies (138). In addition, it is clearly linked to enhanced motivation and positive emotional states. In contrast, individuals with low self-esteem are more at risk for emotional and behavioral disorders such as anxiety, depression, and lack of motivation or energy. Behavioral manifestations can frequently be seen in suicidal tendencies, delinquency and conduct problems, and eating disorders. In this chapter we shall consider two specific processes and related behavioral outcomes that have mental-health implications: processes of turning against the self, which lead to depression and suicidal behavior, and processes in which the self turns against others or society, resulting in conduct problems and delinquency.

Finally we shall turn to self-definition within the context of identity formation. That is, not only must adolescents come to define, integrate, and evaluate specific self-attributes, but they must also consider the more general roles they will adopt within the larger society, including occupational, religious, and political identities. We shall explore the processes that conspire to provoke identity crises and their resolution in forming a new identity, as well as examine the competing psychological context—namely, the need to preserve a sense of the continuity of the self over time. Throughout the chapter attention will be directed to the role of both gender and ethnicity as they influence self and identity development.

The Nature of the Adolescent Self-Concept

Considerable evidence reveals that there is a developmental shift from relatively concrete descriptions of one's social and behavioral exterior in childhood to more abstract self-portraits that describe one's psychological interior in adolescence (30, 32, 59, 132, 134). As the narrative that began this chapter revealed, self-descriptions typically include a variety of personal and interpersonal traits: friendly, obnoxious, tolerant, popular, self-conscious, rowdy, responsible. In addition, teenagers will usually describe emotions, wishes, motives, attitudes, and beliefs, as in the introductive narrative where the adolescent described herself as embarrassed, depressed, cheerful, a goof-off, studious, and included ideas about how she wanted to be and did not want to be. Thus the self-reflective gaze is turned inward toward those private attributes of the self that are largely invisible—inner thoughts and feelings, some of which are real, others of which are hypothetical. Many of the attributes that emerge in later adolescence involve beliefs and moral standards that gradually become integrated into a personal philosophy with implications for one's identity development (31).

Self-descriptions often represent *abstractions* about the self—higher-order generalizations made possible by the cognitive advances that emerge during the period Piaget labeled *formal operational thought* (124, 125). That is, the adolescent can now integrate concrete descriptions of the self (for instance, good listener, able to see another's point of view) into a higher-order generalization about the self such as "tolerant," although the individual is unlikely to appreciate fully the building blocks of these abstractions. To consider oneself "sensitive," one must potentially combine such attributes as being understanding, friendly, and caring. The judgment that one is "moral" requires a complex integration of one's behaviors in relation to one's own or society's values. Such abstract generalizations about the self are typically unobservable and often hypothetical; that is, they require more inferences about one's latent characteristics than do the concrete self-descriptions of children.

Interestingly, this newfound ability to describe the self more abstractly is a double-edged sword. Although abstractions are developmentally advanced cognitive structures, they are removed from concrete, observable behaviors and are therefore more susceptible to distortion. The adoles-

356 · *Susan Harter*

cent's self-concept therefore becomes more difficult to verify, and often less realistic. Here we encounter an interesting developmental paradox: namely that advances to new cognitive levels may bring about certain *liabilities*. Thus, adolescents are at particular risk for developing inaccurate self-concepts, which in turn may lead to a variety of maladaptive behaviors. For example, overestimations of one's ability may lead on the one hand to the zealous choice of challenges that are doomed to failure or, on the other hand, to the avoidance of challenge in order to protect a fragile and unrealistic sense of competence. Those who *devalue* their abilities are also prone to avoid challenges, and to develop emotional reactions, such as anxiety or depression, that may further interfere with their functioning (62).

What factors may mitigate against an adolescent's developing such an unrealistic self-concept, given the potential liabilities ushered in by abstract thinking? As our prototypical narrative reveals, comparison with others, the reliance on normative standards, and sensitivity to others' opinions are powerful socializers in the process of forming a self-concept (137). The self is a social construction; that is, the self-concept represents, in large part, the incorporation of the attitudes that significant others hold about the self (62). Parents, classmates, and close friends, in particular, represent the primary source of such feedback. These reflected self-appraisals come to define what Cooley labeled the "looking-glass self" (26). Mead also described how one incorporates opinions in the form of a "generalized other," pooling these attitudes, as it were, in constructing the self (109). Thus, to the extent that the adolescent is attuned to the opinions of significant others, such feedback may offset introspective tendencies toward distortion. But to the extent that the opinions of others are distorted or perhaps in conflict with one another, thus making it difficult to construct a *generalized* other, the adolescent may well have difficulty in establishing a relatively realistic self-portrait.

Damon and Hart's analysis provides an interesting developmental perspective on these processes (31). They note that in childhood and early adolescence, self-judgments depend heavily on social comparison, normative standards, social similarities, and behaviors that enhance interpersonal interactions and social appeal. There is an expected normative shift, however, in late adolescence, toward self-attributes defined in terms of personal beliefs and internalized standards. Their analysis implies that individuals who do not move into this stage but instead continue to rely primarily on social standards and comparisons may well be at risk because they have not developed the internalized, relatively stable sense of self that will form the basis for subsequent identity development.

Differentiation of the Self into Multiple Domains

In addition to developmental changes in the nature of self-attributes, the self also undergoes differentiation, a process that characterizes most developmental systems (59, 95, 112, 113, 139, 134, 158). The categories of self-description proliferate with development as more trait labels and abstractions become available. The need for an increasing number of domains of self-description and evaluation has been documented by those espousing a multidimensional approach (62, 104, 114). For example, Harter's self-perception profile for adolescents identifies eight specific domains discriminable through factor-analytic procedures: scholastic competence, job competence, athletic competence, physical appearance, social acceptance, close friendship, romantic appeal, and conduct (60). In contrast, Harter's instruments for children require fewer domains.

Further support for the increasing differentiation of the self-concept in adolescence is evident from findings revealing that self-descriptions vary across different social roles or contexts, for example, self with father, mother, close friend, romantic relationship, and peers, as well as self in the role of student, on the job, and as athlete (46, 52, 57, 61, 147). Socialization pressures require teenagers to develop different selves in different roles. As the narrative beginning the chapter revealed, the self with parents may be depressed, sarcastic, and responsible; the self with friends may be sensitive, cheerful, and rowdy; while with someone in whom one is romantically interested the self may be fun-loving and flirtatious, as well as embarrassed and self-conscious. Although the differentiation of the self represents a developmental advance, a related developmental task remains: to integrate these multiple self-concepts into a unified, consistent theory of self. The period of adolescence poses special challenges in this regard.

Integrating Multiple Self-Concepts into a Unified Self-Theory

A major theme in the literature on the adult self is the need to integrate one's multiple attributes into a theory of self or personality that is coherent and unified (5, 6, 16, 39, 77, 83, 91, 105, 128). Epstein has cogently argued that the self-theory, like any formal scientific theory, must meet certain criteria, one of which is *internal consistency* (39). That is, one's self-theory will be threatened by evidence that is inconsistent with the portrait one has constructed of the self or by postulates within the theory that appear to be contradictory.

Given the creation of multiple self-concepts during adolescence, the task of integrating these diverse self-perceptions becomes particularly problematic. For at the same time the adolescent is faced with socialization pressures toward differentiating the self into multiple roles, cognitive advances with the emergence of formal operations press for *integration* and the formation of an internally consistent, coherent theory of the self. Yet these budding formal operational skills also represent a liability. The teenager appears first to develop the conceptual tools to *detect* inconsistencies in the self across roles, and only later develops the cognitive capacity to *integrate* these apparent contradictions. The sample narrative illustrates the first dilemma in that this girl, in middle adolescence, does not understand how she can be cheerful yet also depressed and sarcastic, wondering "which is the real me."

Developmental studies document that during middle adolescence (ages 14 to 15), individuals not only detect inconsistencies across their various role-related selves (with parents, friends, romantic partners), but are also extremely troubled and conflicted over these contradictions, much more so than are the youngest (ages 11 to 12) or oldest (ages 17 to 18) groups (31, 61, 111).

Typical comments from young adolescents, unconcerned about potential contradiction, include: "Well, you are nice to your friends and then mean to people who don't treat you nicely; there's no problem." "I guess I just think about one thing about myself at a time and don't think about the other until the next day." When asked why opposing attributes did not bother her, one 13-year-old exclaimed: "That's a stupid question; I don't fight with myself!" (61, p. 45).

Among middle adolescents, however, the comments tell quite a different story: "I really think I am a happy person and I want to be that way with everyone, but I get depressed with my family and it really bugs me because that's not what I want to be like," remarked one 14-year-old. In describing a conflict within her romantic relationships, a 15-year-old exclaimed: "I hate the fact that I get so nervous! I wish I wasn't so inhibited. The real me is talkative; I just want to be natural, but I can't" (61, p. 45).

Older adolescents, no longer experiencing conflict, gave the following kinds of explanations: "Sometimes it's fun to be rowdy but at other times you just want to be in a quiet mood; you really need to do both with really good friends." "You can be shy on a date, and then outgoing with friends because you are just different with different people; you can't always be the same person and probably shouldn't be." "Sometimes I'm really happy and sometimes I get depressed, I'm just a moody person" (61, p. 45).

Why should the detection of and distress over inconsistencies within one's self-theory peak in middle adolescence? Fischer's cognitive-developmental theory provides a partial answer (44). Fischer distinguishes several levels within formal operational thought. At the first level of "single abstractions" young adolescents can *construct* abstractions about the self (for example, tolerant, obnoxious, empathic, sarcastic, outgoing, self-conscious, cheerful, depressed). But they cannot yet cognitively *compare* these abstractions to one another. As a result, young adolescents tend not to detect or be concerned over self-attributes that are potential opposites.

The cognitive skills necessary to compare such abstractions ("abstract mappings" in Fischer's terms) do not emerge until middle adolescence. With the advent of the ability to relate attributes to one another, the individual can now evaluate the postulates of his or her self-theory and determine whether they are internally consistent. As a result, opposing self-attributes (such as tolerant versus obnoxious, cheerful versus depressed) become salient and very troublesome.

Conflict should diminish, according to Fischer's theory, in later adolescence with the emergence of "abstract systems." This new cognitive level brings with it the ability to integrate single abstractions into compatible higher-order abstractions about the self. Thus, cheerful and depressive attributes can be combined into the higher-order abstraction of "moody." The older adolescent can also resolve contradictory attributes across roles by asserting that he or she is flexible or adaptive, thereby subsuming apparent inconsistencies under generalized abstractions about the self. Thus, more advanced cognitive skills allow the older adolescent to coordinate and interpret diverse self-attributes.

Another strategy for reducing the potential conflict between opposing self-attributes is to adopt a philosophical stance toward the desirability or normality of behaving differently in different roles (65). For example, older adolescents assert that "it wouldn't be normal to act the same way with everyone; you act one way with your friends and a different way with your parents, that's the way it should be"; or "It's good to be able to be different with different people in your life, you'd be pretty strange and also pretty boring if you weren't" (65, p. 23). In adopting such a stance, older adolescents appear to shift to the model espoused for adults (47, 154), namely that consistency *within* a role may be desirable, but not necessarily consistency *across* roles. In fact, Vallacher argues that the construction of different selves represents *differentiation* rather than inconsistency per se (154).

Young people face potential risks as they move through these developmental stages of differentiating and then integrating multiple self-concepts. Failure to integrate these self-concepts may result in a self that is pathologically fragmented. Another possibility is that the conflict caused by one's awareness of multiple self-concepts may not abate, leading to the continuation of distress, which may be maladaptive. Interestingly, conflict over opposing attributes associated with different roles tends to diminish in later adolescence for boys but not for girls (65). For the latter, typically concerned with creating harmony across multiple relationships in different roles, opposing attributes within the self may become particularly salient as well as problematic. Boys, however, seem to move more facilely among their multiple selves in different roles, for it has been demonstrated that their roles are viewed as more independent of one another; therefore they have less need to regard their relationships, and thus themselves, as harmoniously integrated (48).

Constructing Actual and Ideal Selves

We have seen how the creation of role-related multiple selves poses challenges to the development of a unified, coherent self. Another such challenge comes with the adolescent's emerging ability to construct ideal or imagined selves in addition to actual ones. With the advent of formal operations comes the capacity to think about the *hypothetical,* a penchant that is often directed toward the self. Thus, adolescent self-descriptions include references to future selves (139), including both positive and negative images of what one might become (102), as our initial narrative revealed. Most studies have examined positive ideals or aspirations as well as the lack of consistency between ideal and real selves.

While the ability to construct such a discrepancy represents a cognitive advance (49), the magnitude of the inconsistency between one's actual and ideal selves has also been considered an index of maladjustment (129). It has further been suggested that different types of discrepancies will produce different forms of distress (75). Thus, a lack of consistency between one's actual self and the self that one would *like* to be produces dejection-related emotions such as disappointment, dissatisfaction, depression (from our narrative: "I'd *like* to be friendly and tolerant all of the time. That's the kind of person I *want* to be, and I'm disappointed when I'm not"). In contrast, the discrepancy between one's real self and the self that one feels one *ought* to be produces agitation-related emotions such as fear, a sense of threat, restlessness ("I worry about how I probably *should* get better grades").

Research findings reveal that during middle adolescence the difference between one's ideal and one's actual self is larger than in early or late adolescence (149). Although much of the literature suggests that such a discrepancy is debilitating, Markus and Nurius have introduced the concept of "possible selves," suggesting a *motivational* function (102). That is, possible selves represent both the hoped-for as well as the dreaded self and function as incentives clarifying which selves are to be approached and which avoided. From this perspective it is most desirable for the teenager to achieve a balance between positive, expected selves and negative, feared selves so that attributes of positive selves (for example, landing a well-paying job, being loved by one's family, being recognized and admired) can give direction toward desired future states, whereas attributes of negative possible selves (unemployed, lonely, socially ignored) can clarify what is to be avoided.

Possible selves need to relate not only to distant future goals but also to desired or feared self-attributes in the present. In fact, adolescents commonly act out these possible selves, donning the characteristics of desired, and at times undesired, alternative selves (41, 134). Such role experimentation may usher in another potential source of tension among multiple selves in the form of concern and confusion over one's true and false selves, which are often seen as divided. Our narrative self-description exemplifies such conflicts.

Research by Harter and Lee reveals that adolescents clearly distinguish between their true and false selves (67). They are most likely to display false-self behavior in romantic or dating situations and with classmates, and least likely to display it with close friends, while the level with parents falls in between. The motivations for engaging in false-self behavior are varied. There are four primary reasons: to impress others; to try out new behaviors or roles; because others force one to; and because others do not understand or like one's true self. In certain cases teenagers report disliking their false-self behavior, whereas in other cases they find it acceptable.

Little is known, however, about the extent to which false selves may be normatively adaptive forms of experimentation or protection as opposed to maladaptive, "driven" manifestations that are perceived as phony, empty facades. Within the clinical literature "false-self" phenomena stem from disruptions in the normal processes of identifying with parental values, which lead to a sense of alienation from the real or validated core self (14, 159). These pathological avenues to a sense of false self need to be distinguished from the stage-appropriate behavior of adolescents who are experimenting with different persona in the search for their true self. Despite limited normative evidence we can nevertheless appreciate how the need to cope with true versus false selves, as well as actual versus ideal and present versus future selves, constitutes a formidable task. These challenges contribute heavily to the adolescent's preoccupation with understanding the self.

Preoccupation with the Self

The period of adolescence brings about a dramatic shift toward introspection (41, 42, 45, 132). The unreflective self-acceptance of childhood vanishes, and "what were formerly unquestioned self-truths now become problematic self-hypotheses and the search for the truth about the self is on" (132, p. 255).

In describing the tortuous self-consciousness of this period, Erikson observed that teenagers, in their quest for a coherent self, are often morbidly preoccupied with what they appear to be in the eyes of others and with how to connect their earlier cultivated roles and skills with the ideal prototypes of the day (41, 42). More recent theorizing on this self-reflection portrays *early* adolescence as a period in which there is an awkward concern over convincing the self *that* I am (18, 19, 34, 89, 141). The individual is particularly preoccupied with the existence and function of the *mental* self, including both conscious and unconscious processes. During *later* adolescence there is a shift to the issue of *what* or *who* I am (20) as one seeks to establish self-boundaries and more clearly sort out the multiple "Me's" that provide a very crowded self-landscape.

The advent of formal operational thought (see Chapter 3 in this volume) is considered by most to be a prerequisite for adolescent self-reflection. The very ability to think about one's thinking, to reflect on internal events, does not become fully developed until this period. Selman suggests that the acquisition of perspective taking is also essential since one must first be aware that others are observing and evaluating the self (141). By adopting the perspective of the observing other, the individual is able to observe, reflect on, and evaluate the self.

With the advent of any new cognitive capacities comes difficulty in controlling and applying them effectively. Such a liability can be seen in the application of perspective-taking and self-reflective judgment skills. For example, the teenager has difficulty differentiating his or her own mental preoccupations from what others are thinking about him or her, leading to a form of egocentrism known as the "imaginary audience" (34). Adolescents falsely assume that others are as preoccupied with their behavior and appearance as they are themselves. In our illustrative narrative the speaker feels that "everybody, I mean *everybody* else is looking at me like they think I am totally weird!"

Interestingly, the inability to control and effectively apply new cognitive structures can result not only in a lack of differentiation between the self and others, as in the imaginary audience, but also in excessive or unrealistic differentiation. The latter penchant can be seen in another form of egocentrism that Elkind has identified as the "personal fable" (34). In recreating one's life story the adolescent asserts that his or her thoughts and feelings are uniquely experienced. No one else can possibly understand or experience the ecstasy of his or her rapture, the intensity of his or her despair. Parents are particularly likely to be singled out in this regard. As our adolescent narrator exclaims: "My parents . . . don't understand me. What do *they* know about what it's like to be a teenager?"

The imaginary audience and the personal fable can also be interpreted within a more psychodynamic framework (15, 89). Tremendous conflict is produced by the need to relinquish the omnipotent, internalized parent, whose love must be replaced by narcissistic visions of the self (81). From this perspective the imaginary audience performs a restorative function, contributing to these visions of the self. While the youth wishes to remain connected to the parent, there is also the push to separate, to differentiate, and to establish clear, if not rigid, self-boundaries. The construction of a personal fable, in which one's own experiences are so different as to be unique, represents an understandably extreme interpretation that serves to force the necessary boundaries between self and others. Josselson has identified yet another function of adolescent self-preoccupation, which is to provide an arena wherein one can discover which aspects of the self are malleable (82). We turn to this issue next.

Fluctuations in the Self

Given the adolescent's active struggle with multiple role-related selves, including discrepancies between actual and ideal selves as well as tension between true and false ones, it is not surprising that the adolescent self fluctuates over time and situation. In our illustrative narrative the adolescent is perplexed by these vacillations: "I really don't understand how I can switch so fast. I mean, how can I be cheerful one minute, anxious the next, and then be sarcastic?" The distress that fluctuations in self-attributes cause during middle adolescence was previously described from a cognitive-developmental perspective (61). Movement to any new stage typically results in difficulties in controlling newly acquired cognitive structures, which are often manifested in all-or-none thinking. Thus the adolescent may experience one attribute in a given situation, the opposite attribute in a different situation, and be unable to cognitively coordinate these disparate self-perceptions.

Rosenberg, in his metaphoric reference to the "barometric self-concept" of the adolescent, focuses on how socialization factors influence the volatility of the self during this period (134). The adolescent is tremendously concerned with the impression that he or she is making on others, given the dependence on what others think of the self. But he or she also has difficulty in divining others' impressions, and this leads to ambiguity over what the self is really like. Moreover, volatility of the self-concept is also fostered by the fact that different people in different roles or contexts have different impressions of the self. This complexity creates contradictory feedback, which results in uncertainty about the self. In addition, the attempt at role experimentation leads one to adopt tentatively, and as readily abandon, a variety of roles. Our prototypic teenager, for example, poignantly describes her attempts to adopt the persona of Madonna. To the extent that one observes oneself enacting these varying and often contradictory roles, one comes to experience the self as highly mutable.

Finally, the ambiguous status of adolescence within American society contributes to the confusion (9, 132). Since there are no clear age markers that signal when this period begins or ends, one may be treated like a child by some, like an adult by others, and of uncertain status by still other people with whom one interacts. In our prototypic self-description the narrator expresses her confusion over how she is treated like a "kid" by her parents but more like an adult at school. Given such fluctuations, in the face of adolescents' dependence on the opinions of others, their own appraisals of the self will undoubtedly vary.

In this section I have dealt primarily with short-term fluctuations in adolescent self-descriptions, indicating how factors conspire to produce a sense of self-as-chameleon across different social roles. Next I will examine the more self-evaluative judgments that teenagers make about their specific attributes and how these affect levels of overall self-esteem.

Adolescent Self-Esteem

Suppose that we now ask the same adolescent who provided the earlier narrative describing the self to *evaluate* that same self, to indicate what *causes* her to like and to dislike herself as a person. The typical dimensions along which adolescents evaluate the self are captured in the narrative account that follows.

> How much do I *like* the kind of person I am? Well, I like some things about me, but I don't like others. I'm glad that I'm popular since it's really important to me to have friends. But in school I don't do as well as the really smart kids. That's OK, because if you're too smart you'll lose your friends. So being smart is just not that important. Except to my parents. I feel like I'm letting

them down when I don't do as well as they want. But what's really important to me is how I look. If I like the way I look, then I really like the kind of person I am. Don't get me wrong. I mean, I don't exactly look like Madonna even though I try to act like her. But compared to the other girls in my school, I'm sort of good-looking. There's another thing about how much I like the kind of person I am. It matters what other people think, especially the other kids at school. It matters whether they like you. I care about what my parents think about me too. I've also changed. It started when I went to junior high school. I got really depressed. I thought it was going to be so great, like I'd feel so grown-up, and then I saw all of these new, older kids who really had it together and I didn't. So I felt terrible. There was this one day when I hated the way I looked, and I didn't get invited to this really important party, and then I got an awful report card, so for a couple of days I thought it would be best to just end it all. I mean, why bother getting up the next morning? What's the point? Who cares? I was letting my parents down, I wasn't good-looking anymore, and I wasn't that popular after all, and things were never going to get better. I talked to Sheryl, my best friend, and that helped some, but what does she really know? I mean, she's my best friend, so of course she likes me! I mean, her opinion doesn't really count. It's what all the other kids think and want that counts. It was a lot easier for my brother. He got involved in this gang and just decided that what they thought was what was really important, and he stopped caring about the kids in school, or my parents, or even society. That's what he did, and he likes himself fine. But I really don't, not right now.

Factors Influencing Global Self-Esteem

Despite hundreds of studies on adolescent self-esteem (117, 161), this body of research has not, until recently, led to a comprehensive or cohesive picture (117, 160). Ambiguous definitions of the construct, inadequate measuring instruments, and lack of theory have plagued self-esteem research. There is now a growing consensus (58, 62, 132, 134) that self-esteem is poorly captured by measures that combine evaluations across diverse domains—such as scholastic competence, social acceptance, behavioral conduct, and appearance—into a single summary score (as in the Coopersmith Self-Esteem Inventory; see 28). Such a procedure masks important evaluative distinctions that adolescents are capable of making, rendering a total score ambiguous at best, and meaningless at worst. A more fruitful approach is to tap discrete domains of the self-concept separately, since adolescents typically have different self-concepts in each of these areas. In addition, they possess a concept of global self-esteem (that is, how much they like, accept, or respect the self as a person) that can be tapped independently by its own set of questionnaire items (58, 62, 103, 104, 132).

The field has also shifted its emphasis from the mere demonstration of the *correlates* of self-esteem to a more thoughtful consideration of its *determinants*. Two theoretically based programs of research, one by Harter (62, 63, 64) and one by Rosenberg (132, 134), employing assessment procedures that meet many of the objections raised earlier, address the question of what causes some adolescents to like themselves as persons while others do not. Each draws on the theoretical legacies of William James (79) and Charles Horton Cooley (26).

For James, individuals possess a general sense of self-esteem as well as more discrete self-judgments about their competencies within specific domains. One's overall sense of esteem is based upon how adequately one performs in domains where one considers success to be important. High self-esteem would result, he reasoned, if one performed adequately in those domains deemed important. Low self-esteem would ensue if one felt inadequate in those same domains. Success in areas judged unimportant by the individual would have little impact on self-esteem. As our prototypical teenager notes, popularity and appearance are far more important to how much she likes herself as a person than scholastic competence.

In contrast, Cooley, as well as Mead, postulated that the self was a *social construction* involving the incorporation of the attitudes of significant others. Thus, the individual imitates the attitudes that others hold toward him or her; these reflected appraisals then define what Cooley metaphorically described as the "looking-glass-self." Or, as our prototypical narrator says: "It matters what other people think, especially the other kids at school. It matters whether *they* like you."

There is increasing evidence that both theoretical formulations are relevant to an understanding of the determinants of adolescent self-esteem. Harter's and Rosenberg's work reveals that self-esteem is directly influenced by how adequate adolescents feel in those domains where success is considered important. Those with high self-esteem feel very adequate in such domains, whereas those who feel inadequate experience low self-esteem. Thus the *discrepancy* between one's expectations or ideal self, as was described earlier, and the perception of one's actual adequacy have a major effect on self-esteem (75, 132, 143, 152).

There is also increasing evidence in support of Cooley's looking-glass model of self-esteem. Both Harter and Rosenberg have demonstrated that adolescents' perceptions of the attitudes of significant others are highly related to global self-esteem (62, 63, 132). Thus, the teenager who feels that he or she is receiving support and positive regard from significant others such as parents and peers will express positive regard for the self in the form of high self-esteem. Conversely, lack of perceived support and regard from significant others will take its toll in the form of low self-esteem (107).

Domains of Competence Contributing to Self-Esteem

Of the particular domains that contribute most to global self-esteem—how much one likes oneself as a person overall—there is considerable consensus that physical appearance heads the list (1, 66, 92, 93, 143, 146). As our prototypical adolescent reports: "What's really important to me is how I look. If I like the way I look, then I really like the kind of person I am." Among teenagers, physical appearance consistently correlates most highly with global self-esteem (66). Peer social acceptance is the second most significant domain. Less influential are scholastic competence, athletic competence, and conduct. Interestingly, the relationship between perceived appearance and self-esteem is not confined to adolescence but is extremely robust across the life span. These findings are consistent with research documenting the importance that our society attaches to physical appearance from infancy through adulthood (35, 69, 88, 94).

There is increasing evidence that during adolescence looks are more critical for girls than boys. Girls consider physical attractiveness to be more important than do boys, yet girls are also more dissatisfied with their appearance than are boys (143). As a result, according to the Jamesian discrepancy model, their self-esteem suffers. In fact, girls have lower self-esteem than boys, feel less attractive, and experience greater discrepancy between their perceived physical attractiveness and the importance that they attach to appearance (162). Other findings document the negative attitudes that adolescent girls hold toward their physical appearance (80, 117). Thus there is a constellation of related perceptions among girls, including a less favorable body image, greater self-consciousness, feelings of unattractiveness, and more negative attitudes toward their own gender, which, in consort with the value placed on appearance, take their toll on the self-esteem of adolescent females. Furthermore, teenage girls report more physical changes as a result of puberty, and have more difficulty adjusting to these changes, a fact that contributes to the greater self-concept disturbance or volatility noted among girls than among boys (143).

Given that the opinion of significant others also has a major impact on self-esteem, one can ask *which* significant others have the most influence. Our prototypical adolescent notes that the opinions of other kids at school are especially important, although parents' perceptions also matter. There appears to be a developmental shift in the amount of influence parents have on self-esteem; for children, perceived parental attitudes toward the self are of almost exclusive significance for self-esteem, while during adolescence, classmate support becomes more predictive (66, 132). By the college years, peers (in campus organizations) far outstrip parents in their impact on self-esteem (66).

Interestingly, classmates have considerably more influence on self-esteem than do close friends (66). Acknowledgment from peers in the public domain seems more critical than the personal regard of close friends, because close friends, by definition, provide support, and their positive feedback may not be perceived as necessarily self-enhancing. As our narrator puts it: "She's my best friend, so of course she likes me! I mean, her opinion doesn't really count. It's what all the other kids think and want that counts." Thus, it would appear that the adolescent must turn to somewhat more objective sources of support—to the social mirror, as it were—in order to validate the self.

Self-Esteem among Ethnic Minorities

The literature on the self-esteem of ethnic minorities deals primarily with African-Americans, although even within this group there has been until relatively recently a confusing mix of theoretical expectations and seemingly contradictory findings. Many of the conclusions about African-American children's self-concept were based on the doll preference studies by Clark and Clark (24). It was assumed that their preference for white dolls revealed negative self-attitudes, including low self-esteem and self-hatred. Such an interpretation was consistent with those formulations emphasizing the internalization of the attitudes of others toward the self (26, 109) as well as with social comparison theory (43). Given that African-Americans were held in low regard by white society as a whole and compared unfavorably to whites with regard to educational achievement, occupational status, and economic variables such as income, it was expected that African-Americans would manifest low self-esteem.

More recent findings, however, reveal a different picture, in that African-Americans, and African-American adolescents in particular, do not report low levels of global self-esteem (29, 51, 135, 148, 150, 160). Several thoughtful analyses have illuminated the reasons for this apparent contradiction (29, 133, 150). Earlier studies did not distinguish between *reference-group orientation* and *personal identity* (29). Reference-group orientation involves racial attitudes, group identity, racial preference, or racial image for the group, while personal identity involves the individual's self-esteem, self-confidence, perceived competence, and personality. It has been argued that the early doll preference studies tapped children's sense of racial or reference-group orientation and therefore spoke to the issue of African-American identity but not to the individual's sense of personal identity. Failure to make this distinction led to the erroneous conclusion that African-Americans *personally* suffered from low self-esteem and self-hatred. More recent studies find that positive self-esteem can exist in the face of potentially negative racial attitudes held by society.

The process underlying self-esteem formation among African-American adolescents appears to be no different from that of white adolescents (135, 150). Given the notion that one incorporates the attitudes of significant others toward the self, the context for self-esteem development in African-Americans involves the African-American family and community. Thus, African-American children internalize the opinions of parents and siblings, as well as African-American friends and teachers, who serve as their primary social reference group. Interestingly, the relationship between the attitudes of significant others toward the self and self-esteem has been found to be somewhat stronger among African-Americans than among white adolescents (135). It has been suggested that not only is the African-American community a source of positive self-concept in African-American children, but also that under certain conditions the African-American family can filter out destructive racist messages from the white community, supplanting such messages with more positive feedback that will enhance self-esteem (8).

James's formulation can also help to explain the comparable self-esteem of African-Americans (56). To the extent that African-American values differ from those of whites, different domains will be judged important. For example, there is a stronger connection between school grades and self-esteem among whites than among African-Americans, which suggests that the two racial groups may well base their self-esteem on different attributes (38). If we assume that people value those things they do well and try to do well at those things they value, we see that African-American adolescents come to value those nonschool areas in which they feel they excel and over which they have control, and devalue their negative academic experiences (56). Similarly, it has been suggested that African-American boys, in particular, maintain a positive self-image not so much by rejecting conventional values and institutions as by substituting compensatory values in areas where they can perform competently (78). For example, athletic prowess, musical talent, acting ability, sexuality, and certain antisocial behaviors may become more highly valued than academic performance.

Several studies suggest that when African-American students attend racially integrated schools, they may have more difficulty defending their own value system, which in turn leads to lowered self-esteem. These studies find that African-American students in segregated or racially isolated minority schools have higher self-concepts than African-Americans in desegregated schools (126, 127, 135). There are also regional differences: African-American students in racially segregated schools in the South have higher self-esteem than those in the North (127). These findings have been interpreted as suggesting that in segregated settings more cultural and psychological cohesion is provided by community and family, as well as by the shared values of school administrators and parents (25, 127).

Moreover, the racially integrated environment appears to foster social comparisons that are detrimental to the African-American students' self-image. Students who are in the majority by virtue of race, socioeconomic status, religion, and family structure (that is, two-parent versus single-parent homes) often cause those in the minority to feel pressured, out of place, or inferior, and these negative judgments can take their toll on self-esteem (131, 135). Such effects can also be cumulative. For example, it was found that African-American students from one-parent families who attended predominantly African-American schools had much higher self-esteem than their counterparts attending integrated schools with a large proportion of white students predominantly from two-parent families. These differences were not nearly as great, however, for African-American students from two-parent families in the two school settings (144).

Context, therefore, can provide for differences in social support, in the values, and in the network of social comparison, which can in turn affect self-esteem. Unfortunately, however, little research has been conducted on contextual factors among other ethnic groups. One cannot merely extrapolate from the findings with African-Americans. Moreover, research with African-Americans has been limited in that it does not take factors such as social class or economic stratification into account. Thus, a far more differentiated approach to ethnicity is needed—one that recognizes the potentially diverse pathways to self-esteem.

Changes in Self-Esteem during Adolescence

Carefully conducted longitudinal studies reveal gradual and systematic improvements in self-esteem over grades seven through twelve (36, 108, 118, 134, 146). Several interpretations of the overall gains have been suggested (97). Increasing realism about the ideal self may, in keeping with the Jamesian analysis, reduce the discrepancy between the ideal and actual self-image. Gains in personal autonomy and freedom of choice over the adolescent years may also play a role. Again, a Jamesian analysis is appropriate in that the individual has more opportunity to select performance domains in which he or she is competent. Such freedom may also provide the older adolescent with more opportunity to select those support groups that will provide the positive regard necessary to promote or enhance self-esteem, according to the looking-glass-self formulation. Increased role-taking ability may also lead teenagers to behave in more socially acceptable ways that enhance the evaluation of the self by others.

The picture of change in early adolescence is less sanguine, however. The findings suggest that self-esteem begins to decline at age 11 and reaches its low point between the ages of 12 and 13 (134). As our prototypical adolescent recounts, she changed ("I felt terrible") when she went to junior high school. The extent of change depends in large part on shifts in the school environment, as well as on pubertal change (143). Children making the shift to junior high in the seventh grade show greater losses of self-esteem than those who make the school transition later, after eighth grade. Moreover, students making the earlier change, particularly girls, do not recover these losses in self-esteem during the high school years. A developmental-readiness hypothesis has been proposed to explain this pattern, suggesting that children can be thrust into an environment before they are psychologically equipped to deal with the social and academic demands of the new school structure (143). The low self-esteem of our prototypical adolescent girl is the sort that can result from both social and academic failures experienced on entering junior high school, effects from which the narrator appears not to have recovered.

The timing of puberty can also have an effect (17, 143). Early-maturing girls appear to fare the worst in general. They are the most dissatisfied with their body image, particularly their weight and figure, and this has a major effect on feelings of self-esteem. Earlier-maturing girls tend to be somewhat heavier than later maturers and thus do not fit the cultural stereotype of female attractiveness (121). Furthermore, according to the developmental-readiness hypothesis, early-maturing girls are not yet emotionally prepared to deal with the social expectations that surround dating and the greater independence that early maturity often demands. The effects of pubertal level and timing of school transitions can be cumulative (143). Detrimental effects on self-esteem can result if changes occurs at too early an age, if one is off-time in terms of normal pubertal development (significantly earlier or later to mature than others), if a school transition places one in the lowest ranks of a new environment, and if the change is marked by sharp discontinuity.

A more theoretically driven approach has characterized Harter's (62) longitudinal efforts to determine whether changes in self-esteem are systematically related to changes in competence in domains judged important (a notion derived from Jamesian theory), as well as to changes in social support, as predicted by the looking-glass theory of Cooley. The findings revealed that for students making the transition from sixth grade (elementary school) to seventh grade (junior high school), changes in self-esteem were directly predicted both by corresponding self-reported changes in competence in domains deemed important and changes in social support. Thus, students whose self-esteem *increased* across this transition displayed greater competence in domains of importance and reported greater social support in the new school environment. Students whose self-esteem *decreased* displayed a decline in competence for valued domains and reported less social support after the transition. Students showing no changes in self-esteem reported minimal changes in both competence and social support.

These findings suggest that new school environments provide new social-comparison groups that may provoke a reevaluation of one's competence as well as of the importance of success in various domains. Also, alterations in the social network will in turn lead to new opportunities and/or challenges for obtaining social support. Each of these factors can have a dramatic effect on an individual's self-esteem. Such an approach also points to strategies for maintaining or enhancing self-esteem. These include valuing areas of competence and discounting areas of incompetence (62, 63), selecting social-comparison groups that are more similar to the self (151, 152), and choosing supportive peers who can provide affirmation that can be internalized as positive self-regard.

How the Self-Concept Influences Negative Behavior

In addition to examining the developmental, environmental, and related psychological factors that affect self-concept formation, one must ask whether the self-concept, so formed, performs a *functional* role in affecting the adolescent's behavior. It is commonly assumed that a positive sense of self is central to promoting and maintaining psychological health and successful adaptation (13, 39, 116). Less attention, however, has been directed at the role of the self in producing more negative outcomes. We shall next examine how low self-esteem, imbalances within the self-system, and/or immature levels of self-understanding during adolescence negatively influence two behavioral outcomes that have mental health implications: *depressive and suicidal* behavior, in which the individual turns against the self, and *delinquent* behavior, in which the individual turns against others or society.

Depressive and suicidal behavior. A growing body of literature reveals that low self-esteem and negative self-attributions are correlates of depression (10, 62, 66, 134, 140), and that low self-esteem in conjunction with depression and hopelessness appear to be precursors of suicidal behavior (22, 66, 68, 85, 86, 122). Much of this literature has reconstructed these relationships through a "psychological autopsy" of suicide victims, or has focused primarily on clinical populations.

One recent effort by Harter and Marold has looked more directly at a theory-based model of risk factors that affect self-esteem, depression, and thoughts of suicide among normative samples of adolescents (68). Several of the factors predictive of high self-esteem have already been identified (competence in domains deemed important, positive regard from others). Not only is competence in domains of importance to the self critical, but so is competence in domains of importance to parents. In addition to the impact of parental support, peer support is also crucial. Furthermore, not only is the *level* of support important, but so is the extent to which support is *contingent* on either meeting high parental expectations or conforming to peer demands. Each of these factors can lead to a specific feeling of hopelessness, according to the Harter and Merold model. These in turn determine an adolescent's level of depression on a composite defined by low self-esteem, feelings of depression, and general hopelessness about the future. Adolescents who rank high on this composite are likely to be engaged in suicidal ideation. Our prototypical narrative reveals a number of these features.

The findings supporting this model suggest a cameo portrait of the suicidal adolescent: he or she is not performing well in areas that are important to the self as well as to parents and is letting parents down in the face of support that is conditional on meeting their high expectations. Peer support also appears to be conditional. Feelings of hopelessness about ever being able to turn any of these circumstances around leads to low self-esteem, feelings of depression, and a sense of hopelessness about the future, culminating in thoughts of suicide as the only way out. While there are undoubtedly other paths to suicidal thinking and behavior in adolescents (122), this particular profile is instructive since it points to the crucial functional role played by self-esteem in mediating depressive and suicidal reactions among many teenagers who are distressed about their personal attributes and the availability of social support.

Delinquent behavior. While it is assumed that low self-esteem is associated with negative outcomes, the pattern among delinquents is not that straightforward. There is no direct relationship between self-esteem and adolescent delinquent behavior, for delinquents do not invariably report low self-esteem. In fact, many seem to have a relatively high level of self-esteem. Thus, hypotheses positing a more direct relationship need revision (21). One such hypothesis, based on the theory of reflected appraisals attributed earlier to Cooley and Mead, asserts that the deviant individual, who violates the basic values of society, should come to internalize negative attitudes toward the self, a process leading to low self-esteem (130). In other words, delinquency causes low self-esteem.

An alternative hypothesis reverses the directionality of effects, suggesting that low self-esteem causes delinquent behavior (84). In other words, failure to meet the standards of the dominant membership group leads to negative self-attitudes, which in turn impel the individual to seek out teenage groups in which prevalent standards are ignored and delinquent behaviors are admired. Presumably the motivational force is to elevate or restore one's level of esteem within the delinquent peer group that serves as a model and that grants its approval to antisocial actions (130).

Evidence seems to support the second rather than the first hypothesis. Research employing causal modeling techniques with longitudinal data suggests that among males entering high school with low self-esteem, the effects of delinquent behavior tend to be self-enhancing. Boys who suffered from the largest reduction in self-esteem when they entered high school seemed to be able to restore their self-esteem by engaging in delinquent behavior. As adolescents move through high school, however, these effects weaken, and other factors such as success, toughness, and sexual precocity come to play an increasingly important role in determining male self-esteem (21).

In another vein, the work of Markus on the functional role of "possible selves" (described earlier) has recently been applied to delinquent behavior among adolescents (102, 120). Markus' findings support the contention that there is no direct, linear relationship between self-esteem and delinquency. In selecting four groups of adolescents representing a continuum from public school youths who have never engaged in delinquent acts to teenagers confined for repeated severe offenses, the two extreme groups reported the highest levels of self-esteem, whereas the two groups in the middle range reported only moderate levels.

Markus suggests that her construct of possible selves may bear a more direct and meaningful relationship to delinquent behavior than does self-esteem. Specifically, the *balance* between positive and negative selves should be associated with the least delinquency. A positive image toward which one aspires (for example, professional achievement) coupled with a negative image of what one should avoid (lack of respect in the community) should represent the most adaptive combination. Delinquent behavior is more likely to result in the absence of such a balance. If one's negative possible self is not checked or countered by a positive possible self, one may be more likely to engage in antisocial behaviors consistent with one's negative self. In addition, if lack of balance is the result of an unrealistic, dangerous, or inappropriate positive self that is not held in check by feared negative possible selves, a variety of deviant behaviors may be fostered. Imbalance between possible selves predicts self-reported delinquent acts such as vandalism and assault, as well as less violent crimes (102).

Finally, Damon and Hart's developmental model of self-understanding also generates predictions about delinquent behavior (30). They suggest that the developmental level of self-understanding may be a better predictor of delinquency than self-esteem. Interview data revealed that conduct-disordered adolescents were more likely to describe future and ideal selves that involved low levels of self-understanding than were nondelinquent adolescents (110). That is, the delinquents were more likely to give *concrete* and *social-comparative* descriptions of their behavior (levels 1 and 2 in the Damon and Hart model) than references to *interpersonal* goals such as obtaining the approval of others and integrating oneself into the network of family and community (level 3). Because delinquents appear to be less connected to conventional social contexts, they experience fewer inhibitions about engaging in acts that inevitably result in social estrangement. The consequences of the social and legal difficulties the delinquent then faces, including social rejection, may make it stressful to shift to a higher level calling for concern with acceptance by others. Rather, the result may be the solidification of a level-2 understanding of the self (31). This approach, therefore, provides another perspective on how the self, specifically the level of self-understanding, may affect delinquent behavior.

Identity Formation

As the introductory self-description of our prototypical teenager reveals, the adolescent must not only define the self in terms of specific attributes but must also consider the more general roles that he or she will adopt within the larger society upon becoming an adult. Our teenager agonizes over various occupational choices with little sense of just how to make such decisions. Thus at this stage of life the creation of one's self-portrait is shifted to a larger canvas, where broad brush strokes are used to define occupational and gender identities as well as the religious and political identities that one will assume. The opposition among attributes within the self are recast as potentially conflicting identities, just as the need to experiment with different personas and to create an integrated theory of self shifts to the level of broader societal roles.

For Erikson the challenge of both creating and consolidating these identities was captured in the adolescent crisis of identity versus identity diffusion (40, 42). To experiment with different roles and identities, Erikson observed, the adolescent needs a *psychological moratorium,* a period of time without excessive responsibilities or obligations to restrict the pursuit of self-discovery.

The process of identity formation also involves the selective repudiation of possible roles or selves (81). One must not only make a commitment to certain choices but also give up others. William James articulated this very point in lamenting that the many roles to which he aspired (athlete, bon vivant, lady-killer, philosopher, philanthropist, statesman, warrior, African explorer, tone poet, and saint!) could not possibly coexist in the same person. As he knowingly concluded, in anticipating one of the struggles in the adolescent's search for identity: "So the seeker of his truest, strongest, deepest self must review the list carefully, and pick out the one on which to stake his salvation" (79, p. 174).

A major task in this process involves the challenge of preserving one's sense of *personal continuity* over time, of establishing a sense of sameness of oneself, despite the necessary changes that one must undergo in terms of redefining the self. James emphasized the importance of perceiving that the self of the past, the self of the present, and the potential self are all continuous. For Erikson this concern becomes paramount in adolescence, since the continuity of the self is naturally threatened by marked physical changes, cognitive advances, and shifting societal expectations. Erikson captures this concern in quoting a slogan he once observed: "I ain't what I ought to be, I ain't what I'm going to be, but I ain't what I was!" (41, p. 19).

Theorists of adolescent identity consistently emphasize the need to *integrate* the various identities that one selects into a coherent theory of self, a theme that was introduced earlier in the treatment of multiple selves. The task of identity formation is much broader, however, requiring the consolidation of societal roles, not merely self-attributes. This task must take place within the larger context of society. There must be a sense of *mutuality* between the individual's conception of the self and those that significant others hold about him or her; and the commitment to occupational, sexual, religious, and political identities must guarantee one's productive integration into society (41, 42).

Another facet of identity formation involves the need for distinctiveness and uniqueness, a theme that was introduced in an earlier section on preoccupation with the self. There is an obvious tension between this goal and the need to construct an identity that will receive the support of significant others as well as society. While earlier developmental tasks involve identification with parents, identity formation requires an individuation process in which one differentiates the self from parents, yet without becoming totally disconnected (13, 53, 54, 72, 81). The immersion in peer identifications and conformity to stereotypes during this period is considered by these theorists to be a manifestation of the need for alternatives in the face of pressure to abandon parental identifications.

From a broad cultural perspective one can appreciate why these several tasks of identity formation may appear to be rather formidable for the modern teenager. In their historical analysis of adolescence Baumeister and Tice observe that at the end of the nineteenth century there was a shift in the locus and burden of self-definition (9). Prior to this transition one's adult identity was primarily determined by family, community, and shared cultural values. More recently young people have been forced to fashion their occupational and personal identities out of a myriad of options. Liberal educational policies that provide a wide spectrum of choices, and Western society's loss of ideological consensus regarding fundamental religious, moral, and political truths, have conspired to produce the need for a protracted adolescent moratorium.

Most theorists agree on the arenas that are the major focus of identity formation. These include selecting and preparing for a future career, re-evaluating religious and moral beliefs, working out a political ideology, and adopting a set of social roles, including a social sex role and anticipation of marriage and parenthood (156). With regard to the crisis involved in making these decisions, Erikson anticipated that within each of these domains the adolescent should first experience identity *diffusion,* followed by experimentation during a *moratorium* period, culminating in identity *formation* involving choice, commitment, and consolidation.

The bulk of empirical work examining this formulation has been stimulated by Marcia's research on *identity statuses* (98, 99, 100, 101). Marcia sought to capture both the process involved in identity formation as well as individual differences in coping with identity issues. His four statuses are defined in terms of two dimensions: crisis (or exploration) and commitment. *Identity achievement,* the ideal form of identity resolution, applies to the individual who, after a period of crisis and exploration, emerges with relatively firm identity commitments. This represents the ideal form of identity resolution. The *moratorium* status is defined as an active period of crisis during which one seeks among alternatives in an attempt to arrive at a choice. As a normative process of experimentation during middle adolescence it is considered adaptive, as in the case of our prototypical teenager. But it is maladaptive if it represents an end point in lieu of a more stable sense of identity achievement.

Those in the *foreclosure* status have adopted the identities prescribed by parents or other authority figures with a keen sense of commitment, without ever exploring options or experiencing an identity crisis. While foreclosure represents commitment, and in that sense gives firm direction to the individual's pursuits, nevertheless it is considered somewhat maladaptive if it involves a premature constriction that precludes other possible choices. The status of *identity diffusion* refers to individuals who have little sense of commitment and are not actively seeking to make decisions. This status is developmentally appropriate at the beginning of adolescence; but if it represents the outcome of one's identity struggles in later adolescence, it constitutes lack of resolution and is considered to be maladaptive.

Initially Marcia intended these categories to represent a typology of individual differences (98); investigators have more recently emphasized, however, that shifts in these statuses represent normative developmental change (72, 99, 106, 156). Waterman and his colleagues have conducted the most extensive research in this area and have also aggregated the findings from numerous studies in order to provide a general picture of identity development. Across five developmental periods, from the years preceding high school through the college upperclass years, there is a relatively orderly increase in the percentage of those attaining the status of identity achievement, and an anticipated decrease in the percentage of those in the identity-diffusion stage, particularly in terms of vocational choice. For religious beliefs and political ideology, fewer have reached identity achievement in college, and a substantial number of students occupy the foreclosure as well as the diffusion status (156). Thus, it would appear that the timing of identity processes may differ depending on the particular arena, and that during the college years many students are still wrestling with ideological commitments.

Although there is some evidence of normative movement through these statuses, the cross-sectional findings mask alternative trajectories manifested by individuals or subgroups, since they do not follow the same individuals over time. Waterman has suggested a model that captures shifts in identity status, identifying various possible patterns that may characterize identity formation (155). For example, individuals in the moratorium stage may revert to diffusion, and those who have presumably reached identity achievement may question their decisions and revert to either moratorium or diffusion. There is some evidence on these and other pathways, although more longitudinal data following the potential changes in the same individuals over the course of development are needed to provide strong support for these hypotheses.

In keeping with earlier themes highlighting the need to integrate multiple roles as well as maintain continuity of the self over time, Hauser's approach to these identity statuses is illuminating in its emphasis on processes that involve the *structural integration* of self-images as well as their *continuity* over time (71, 72, 74). Those adolescents who forge a path of progressive identity *formation* are increasingly able to integrate their various self-images as well as to view the self as continuous over time. In contrast, those experiencing identity *diffusion* display declines in these processes. Identity *foreclosure* is often seen in stable self-images over time that do not become integrated. Those experiencing psychological *moratorium* often manifest fluctuations in their self-images rather than integration or continuity over time.

Hauser has also related these identity statuses directly to a model of ego development based on Loevinger's stages, which define a progression of increasingly mature levels of functioning (96). Not surprisingly, Hauser finds that the greatest number of individuals at *low* levels of ego development are within the identity diffusion status, whereas identity achievement is associated with higher stages of ego development (2, 71, 72).

Identity Formation in Males versus Females

In Erikson's classic treatment of identity formation, the division of labor between the sexes was underscored in that males' aspirations were typically directed toward career and ideological commitments, whereas females' aspirations centered around marriage and child rearing (42). Earlier studies found some support for Erikson's claims, since vocational concerns seemed to play a greater role in identity formation for males (11), whereas identity formation was more closely related to affiliation in women (32). A review of this literature suggests that, historically, identity formation in males has reflected the cultural expectations of autonomy and differentiation from others, whereas female identity has reflected the cultural expectation of connectedness and the establishment of intimate relationships (7, 12, 48, 77, 82).

It has also been suggested that the order of the stages postulated by Erikson is different for males and females. Some have argued that for males identity formation precedes the stage of intimacy, whereas for females issues involving intimacy are dealt with prior to those involved in identity (32). These suggestions are, on the surface, consistent with analyses showing how the socialization of females involves concern for relationships and emotional bonds, whereas males are encouraged to forge a path of independence, autonomy, and individual achievement (48, 136). There are challenges to the notion that the ordering of these stages is different for women and men, however. In order truly to establish intimacy, in the context of a meaningful reciprocal relationship, it can be argued that *both* sexes must have a clear sense of identity, although its content may well be different.

Other findings have suggested that the actual experience of the identity crisis is different for women and men. For example, in some studies self-esteem appears to be highest among women in the foreclosure status, which may best fit cultural expectations, and lowest among women in the identity-achievement status, perhaps because they become alienated from potential sources of support (101, 153). For men, however, adjustment and self-esteem seem to be highest in the identity-achievement status, compared to foreclosure and the less stable statuses (7).

Of particular interest is whether these gender differences will persist in the face of the sociological changes urged by the women's movement. Foreclosure may no longer be associated with optimal levels of self-esteem in women. Findings have revealed that for both males and females an androgynous orientation (high levels of both masculine and feminine traits) was more conducive to identity achievement and high self-esteem, whereas an undifferentiated sex-role orientation (low on both kinds of traits) was associated with identity diffusion and low self-esteem (119). A similar study found that females high in masculine traits reported higher self-esteem than females low in these qualities (23).

Other findings also indicate that the percentage of men and women in the various identity statuses differs depending on the particular domain. Males and females do not differ in distribution of identity statuses in the domains of vocational choice, religious beliefs, political ideology, and gender identity (155, 156). But women are *more* likely than men to be in the identity-achievement and moratorium statuses and less likely to be foreclosed or diffuse, in the domains of family priorities (7) and sexuality (157).

The most recent literature implies that the task of identity exploration and commitment may be more complex for females than males, to the extent that women may attempt to establish identities in a greater number of domains. The options for women may well have become more numerous and therefore potentially more confusing and conflicting (99). For those who aspire to a career the challenge is to integrate their work and family roles, whereas for most men career development still appears to be the primary issue (7, 55).

Ethnic Differences in Identity Formation

By far the most extensive treatment of this issue has been presented by Hauser and Kasendorf, whose findings indicate that African-American adolescents are more likely to occupy the identity-foreclosure status than are whites (73). Their interpretation focuses on both sociocultural and psychological influences. From historical and sociocultural perspectives, African-American youths have faced real restrictions limiting their occupational choices (70). For adolescents from the lower socioeconomic classes, pressing economic needs preclude an extensive moratorium during which to explore potential careers (55). Another environmental constraint that Hauser and Kasendorf have identified is the lack of African-American heroes to admire and emulate. African-American youth are far more likely than whites to be confronted with culturally devalued stereotypes. Hauser and Kasendorf also interpret the prevalence of identity foreclosure among African-Americans in terms of Erikson's developmental model. They suggest that the prior stage on which identity must be built—industry versus inferiority—is more typically resolved in the direction of inferiority for African-Americans rather than the work identification that characterizes a sense of industry.

Hauser and Kasendorf urge that we adopt a "functional/adaptational" model rather than a "deficit/pathological" model. They view identity foreclosure among African-Americans as a functional adaptation to a set of conditions that limit their opportunities. From this perspective cultural changes that improve the social, economic, and political climate for African-Americans should in turn have implications for alternative identity statuses that African-Americans can realistically achieve.

Influence of Parenting Styles and Family Interactions

Adolescents clearly differ in how they experience and cope with identity issues, and evidence links these individual differences to parenting styles and patterns of family interaction. One strategy has been to examine identity status in relation to typologies of parenting that distinguish between *democratic, autocratic,* and *permissive* child-rearing styles (33). Across several studies a certain pattern of findings has emerged (3, 12, 32, 37, 99, 155).

Democratic parents, who encourage teenagers to participate in the decision-making process and consider alternatives, are most likely to foster progress toward identity *achievement. Autocratic* parents, who regulate their children's behavior without allowing them to express their opinions, promote identity *foreclosure* rather than movement through moratorium to identity achievement. *Permissive* parents, who provide little guidance in the consideration of alternatives, allowing their children freedom to make all of their own decisions, tend to produce adolescents who remain mired in identity *diffusion.*

Other approaches have focused on the psychological *processes* involved in identity formation, relating them to attachment-theory constructs that involve separation and individuation (99). According to attachment theory, secure attachment allows one to explore, as well as to develop a separate sense of self (4, 97). Thus, this style is the most likely to provoke individuation and identity achievement. Identity diffusion is most likely to be observed in individuals who feel alienated from their parents. Marcia observes that an anxious, ambivalent attachment is likely to be mirrored by the tenacious hold that adolescents in identity foreclosure maintain on their conditionally loving parents (100).

A compelling research program has been conducted by Cooper and Grotevant in their efforts to unravel the specific interactive processes within the family and the relationship of these processes to identity outcomes (27, 54, 55). The strength of their approach is an emphasis on both *individuality* and *connectedness,* which they observed in the context of actual family interactions. Their framework emphasizes the fact that while one task of the adolescent is to individuate from the parents, he or she must also remain psychologically connected to the family in the process (76). Grotevant and Cooper assessed two dimensions of individuality: *self-assertion,* or the ability to have and communicate a point of view, and *separateness,* or the use of communication patterns that express how one is different from others. They also assessed two dimensions of connectedness: *permeability,* or openness to the views of others, and *mutuality,* or sensitivity to the views and needs of others.

After interviewing family members, they analyzed references to the exploration and active consideration of alternative possibilities, and to commitment, or the certainty of one's decisions. In general, the findings indicate that identity formation is facilitated by individuated family relationships characterized by both separateness, which gives the adolescent permission to develop his or her point of view, and connectedness, which provides a secure base from which to explore options outside the family.

An emphasis on the processes that underlie individuation and identity formation can also be seen in the efforts of Hauser and his colleagues (71, 72, 74) as well as of Sigel (142). Hauser's group, in studies of parent-child interaction, distinguishes between behaviors that are *constraining* (judging, distracting, devaluing) and those that are *enabling* (explaining, accepting, providing empathy). Their findings indicate that adolescent ego development is facilitated by enabling behaviors and hindered by constraint.

Sigel's efforts have been directed toward determining the conditions that allow the child to distance himself or herself cognitively from the parent, a process that involves the internalization of one's experience in order to function more independently (142). Such a process underlies individuation and identity formation. Sigel has demonstrated that parents who ask questions and also *sanction* questions from their children, as opposed to merely answering questions, promote the most adaptive distancing. Thus, one can see convergence across these research programs leading to the conclusion that interactive styles that give the adolescent permission to question, to be different, within a context of support and mutuality will foster the healthiest patterns of identity formation.

Policy Implications and Future Directions

Our exploration of the self began with those normative developmental processes responsible for changes in self-understanding provoked by both cognitive-developmental advances and the reactions of others who define the social milieu of the adolescent. These factors combine to cause the typical teenager to become preoccupied with the "search for self." Defining who one is in relation to multiple others, determining what one will become, and discovering which of one's many selves is the "true self" are the normative developmental tasks of this period. The search is often punctuated by conflict, contradiction, and confusion as the adolescent tries to create a consistent, unified self-portrait that possesses some continuity over time. While the ability to create hypothetical selves represents a major advance, in that the individual becomes able to imagine future options and directions of personal growth, it also constitutes a double-edged sword, since it threatens the coherence and continuity of the self at any given time. The myth that developmental advances during adolescence necessarily produce happy outcomes in the short run must be challenged (40).

Yet we need to foster development along this path. Failure to do so may result in a youth whose development is arrested. Those remaining at earlier levels of development may well stay rooted in self-definitions that rely primarily on the standards and desires of others rather than the development of their own standards (31). Several possible outcomes may ensue, including premature foreclosure of identity choices or an uncritical obedience to the behavioral norms of others that may put one at risk for a variety of pathological conditions. For example, both delinquency and certain eating disorders may result from developmentally immature forms of self-definition (31). Also, in certain individuals definitions of the self that rely largely on the dictates of others may lead to considerable distress over the fact that one is not responding to the call of one's true self.

How can we best foster adolescents' explorations of true selves, possible selves, and ideal selves within a framework based in reality? How can we promote personal standards that are internalized rather than imposed? How can we encourage values that are selected rather than conferred? Recent findings indicate that such development is most likely to be promoted by adults who model, as well as encourage, the communication of a personal point of view that may be different from others' while simultaneously retaining an openness to the views of others. Such displays are not likely to occur naturally among adolescents, given their penchant for black-and-white thinking. Self versus parent, child versus adult, individual versus institution—these are the distinctions that commonly define adolescent thought. Thus, it may be necessary to create milieus, be they informal opportunities for interaction or more formal programs, that foster the simultaneous coordination of *assertion* as well as *perspective-taking* skills. While programs designed to enhance awareness of the self and others have been developed, those that involve active role taking and modeling of the coordination of such seemingly contradictory skills by adults as well as other teenagers would appear to hold the most promise.

Programs designed to promote the *active* and *realistic* exploration of broad identity goals, such as educational and occupational choices, should also be encouraged. These may take the form of on-the-job experience, as in the Boston Compact Youth Incentive Program, which gives students access to high-paying summer jobs if they maintain a record of good school attendance and performance. Another model is the program instituted by Lang and Rivera, which not only provides monetary support but does so within the context of strengthening the links between high school activities and the world of work, providing for the exploration of alternatives (87). This program places emphasis on adolescents' choice of areas in which they are both interested and competent, allowing them to select educational opportunities that further their development in these domains. These suggestions are consistent with the model of self-esteem that I have discussed. The highest levels of self-esteem are found in individuals who are performing competently in domains that are important to the self. Thus, programs designed to aid individual adolescents to identify as well as to value areas of competence will be the most likely to foster self-esteem.

From a societal perspective, these goals will require respect for the wide range of domains in which success may be achieved, and an appreciation of diversity. At the same time, there is a need to recognize the fact that "dare to be different" is hardly the call of the adolescent. Emulation of others, particularly cultural heroes of the day, is by far the normative pattern. Yet we can capitalize on the penchant for emulation by providing a broad, diverse array of role models with whom it is acceptable to identify.

Within this spirit, schools have been urged to recognize the positive benefits of activities outside the realm of academic performance (21). Since educational failure in high school is very damaging to self-esteem, there is a need to reduce the competitive pressure on teenagers to achieve school-defined goals at all costs and to recognize other forms of worth (50). For minority youth especially it has been noted that if schoolwork is perceived to be incongruent with a student's cultural commitments, self-esteem may suffer (115).

This issue is obviously controversial, since many minority spokespersons would argue that education is the primary means for achieving opportunity and equality. The inspiration of the Hispanic high school teacher Jaime Escalante (documented in the movie *Stand and Deliver*) and the African-American high school principal Joe Clark (depicted in the movie *Lean on Me*) is a testimonial to this point of view. According to a study on ethnic identity in African-American and white youth, education and self-confidence are seen by many contemporary African-American students as a way of acquiring opportunities and overcoming prejudice (123). As one African-American eighth-grader commented: "If you get good grades, you can do whatever you want" (p. 271). It would appear, therefore, that attitudes and policies that encourage the exploration of talents in fields such as athletics, musical and artistic endeavors, and interpersonal skills that may lead to human services involvement, in the context of reasonable educational expectations and goals, represent the best approach. The insistence that high school and college athletes maintain a respectable grade average, for example, is a policy within this spirit, as is the requirement that students maintain a good record of attendance and performance at school in order to participate in jobs programs.

386 · Susan Harter

The need to encourage greater appreciation of diversity in order to maintain and enhance self-esteem is also evident within the domain of physical appearance. The findings indicate a dramatic effect of self-evaluations of appearance on self-esteem, particularly for adolescent females. As a society we need to alter the perception that narrowly defined cultural stereotypes of attractiveness are the measure of a woman's (or man's) worth, and permit a range of appearances, as well as other qualities and competencies, to form the basis for self-esteem. The "black is beautiful" theme is but one example of how prejudicial attitudes, be they within or across ethnic groups, can be altered.

The research also indicates that social support in the form of approval and confirmation from others exerts a powerful influence on self-esteem. Yet for many youths suffering from dysfunctional families or conditions of abuse and neglect such support is unavailable. In certain cases alternative sources of support can be substituted, either informally, through the encouragement of a teacher, coach, or similar significant adult, or more formally, through programs such as Big Brothers and Big Sisters. While it is clear that peer approval becomes increasingly important during the adolescent years, the findings debunk the myth that parental and adult support diminish greatly in their contribution to teenagers' self-esteem. Efforts to ensure both peer and adult support, therefore, will maximize the internalization of positive self-attitudes.

The identification of the *sources* of self-esteem, namely competence in domains important to the self, as well as social support, is critical in its implications for intervention. The findings suggest that in order to maintain or promote positive self-esteem, one needs to touch these sources directly. The self-esteem–enhancement programs of the 1960s, in which self-esteem itself was the target, and children and adolescents were encouraged to believe that they were worthwhile, were simply not effective. Rather, we need to intervene at the level of the *causes* of self-esteem if we are to have a major impact on changing these attitudes.

The findings on adolescents' transitions to new educational environments provides another approach to change, focusing on context effects and their impact on self-esteem. Recognizing the difficulty that many young adolescents have in making the transition from elementary school to junior high school, Simmons and Blyth suggest that an earlier transition to middle schools, particularly ones that are smaller in size than typical junior high schools, may offset the debilitating effects on self-esteem (143). Underlying these suggestions is the assumption that earlier transition of this type will result in a more gradual change, with fewer cumulative effects at any one time, an assumption that requires additional research.

School effects obtained with minority youth also point to social policy implications. While the myth that African-Americans in general necessarily suffer from low self-esteem now receives little support, findings indicate that racially integrated schools typically produce deficits in self-esteem for African-Americans. Comer and Hill argue that school integration alone was not sufficient (25). Rather, school integration will be successful only to the extent that there is an accompanying national policy of political and economic integration, as well as a pattern of housing desegregation. Powell's analysis further suggests that one needs to consider the congruence between the educational goals and strategies of parents and school administrators, since dissonance invariably leads to a pattern of disillusionment, alienation, and low self-esteem among African-American students (127).

Alienation from society, in terms of lack of economic and political clout, represents another cause of disillusionment, not only for African-Americans but also for women. African-Americans have been relegated to the lowest rungs of the socioeconomic ladder, a status that constricts their choices of potential identities, as is evidenced by the fact that the greatest number of African-Americans occupy the identity status of foreclosure. Until recently, cultural expectations and stereotypes have constrained women's identity choices as well, confining them primarily to the roles of wife and mother, or to relatively low-paying positions of providing services for others. That there has been some positive change, promoted by feminist consciousness-raising efforts, is evidenced by the fact that the foreclosure status is no longer the most prevalent nor the preferred status for women. Nonetheless, continued social change, in the form of an expanded array of opportunities and appropriate role models, is essential if more women and minorities are to forge paths of identity that will enhance both the individual and society. Not only will these groups be positively affected, but it is to be hoped that such change will raise the collective consciousness, and therefore the self-esteem, of society as a whole.

15

STRESS, COPING, AND ADAPTATION

Stuart T. Hauser and Mary Kay Bowlds

During adolescence a multifaceted developmental transition is set in motion: biological, psychological, and social forces intersect as the individual advances from childhood toward adulthood. This transition is rarely smooth or straightforward; adolescence is perplexing and disquieting for many young people as well as for the adults around them, such as parents and teachers. Yet the numerous changes experienced by the teenager do not lead to unique or more pervasive psychopathology than is found at other phases of the life cycle (106, 109, 114), an observation that serves as the point of departure for this chapter. We consider four interrelated questions: How do adolescents cope with the special, and by no means minimal, demands that arise during this phase of development? How do individual differences in developmental paths and personality shape this behavior? How does the family influence and respond to coping? How can we understand adolescents who are unable to surmount the challenges posed during these years, as well as those who are highly effective in dealing with the changes?

Coping with and within Adolescence

Despite current interest in questions involving coping, the specific meaning of this concept remains elusive (25, 113). Problems associated with the study of this issue are pervasive; they range from a lack of consensus about basic definitions to inconsistent criteria for evaluating coping. Among the numerous definitions, one of the clearest is offered by Lazarus and Folkman: "Coping is a process of managing demands (external or internal) that are appraised as taxing or exceeding the resources of a person" (85, p. 610). This conceptualization is noteworthy in several respects. First, no distinction is made between coping and defensive processes. Second, coping is seen as a *process* or a set of responses rather than as an enduring trait or style of the individual. Finally, this definition emphasizes *management* of stress rather than mastery. There are many sources of stress in a young person's life that must be adapted to and lived with, such as the divorce of one's parents or a chronic illness; these cannot be "solved" or completely overcome.

The process-oriented view recognizes that coping involves both stability and change. From this vantage point several individual distinctions come to mind when we consider a teenager's repertoire of coping skills: the resources to which he or she has access, the strategies he or she uses most often, the aspects of particular situations, and the time frame (23). For example, the death of a parent leads to bereavement, a complex set of processes that can last several years. Over time, as development continues and resources change, there may be significant shifts in the ways an individual copes with such a severe personal loss. Coping processes, then, refer to how an individual responds to *specific situations*.[1]

Coping processes may be characterized as stable or fluid. Yet consistency is ultimately in the eyes of the beholder. "Stability is probably more evident in the ways people would like to respond than in the way they do respond to any given situation" (95, p. 96). Interestingly, adolescents have been seen to show moderate levels of consistency in coping strategies over a nine-month interval (28). It may be (perhaps counter to our intuitions) that in particular ways young people are more consistent than adults, an observation that certainly warrants further investigation.

A widely used classification of coping processes distinguishes between problem-solving and emotion-regulating coping strategies (23, 25, 85). Problem-solving strategies, such as reframing, address environmental or internal difficulties that pose a threat. In contrast, emotion-regulating strategies are directed toward distress that comes about as a result of the threat. The latter strategies (such as denial and distraction) are sometimes seen as less effective forms of coping, since they treat the symptom rather than the cause of a problem. Yet in certain circumstances such strategies can lead to positive adaptive outcomes (for example, denial of a chronic

---

1. Connections between coping processes (which emphasize situational demands) and aspects of adolescent personality and development more explicitly linked with coping styles (which are consistent across diverse situations) are not obvious. Concerted theoretical and linked empirical investigations are needed to elucidate the significant relations among these aspects of individual functioning. Rather than being theoretically incompatible, it is more likely that these differing frameworks (developmental, personality, coping process) are responsive to different features of the complex phenomena involved in the transient and long-term adaptation of adolescents to stressful circumstances.

illness), contributing to emotional equilibrium (23). A teenager from our study of development and coping (58), recalling how he handled missing his family, illustrates two coping strategies—distracting and reframing—and the probable influence of parents as sources of coping strategies:

> *Interviewer:* When you were feeling homesick, was there any way that you tried to handle it or to make it change in some way?
>
> *Adolescent:* Well, I had this really strange thing. I have this infatuation with sky and clouds and rainbows, and when I draw, I love to draw things like that. So I would just kind of look at the sky and think, well, that might have been over my house a day ago. Maybe that worked. My father says that works for him. When he was in the army he did that, so it really is weird.
>
> *Interviewer:* What way did that work? What did that do for you?
>
> *Adolescent:* After looking at the sky, I would kind of start to smile and think of my family and start to laugh or something. I don't know, it really works.

As in this excerpt, both problem-solving and emotion-regulating strategies are used in nearly all stressful situations. The use of a specific strategy and its success are strongly influenced by the circumstances. Reframing strategies are often most effective in situations over which the adolescent has some degree of control (25). For example, school-related stressors are generally dealt with by problem-solving coping, whereas health stressors are associated with emotion-regulating methods. While the distinctions between these types of coping are apparent conceptually, we do not understand their ties to adolescent development and experience well enough to integrate the coping-processes perspective with analyses of the vicissitudes of adolescent development and adaptation.

How does one determine if the ways a teenager copes are adaptive? Coping processes cannot simply be labeled inherently "good" or "bad"; the specific context must be considered. A strategy that is effective for one problem or person may not work at all for another. The effectiveness of a given response may also vary over time; a coping strategy that is at first beneficial may become maladaptive if used continuously.

In order to identify *successful* adolescent adaptation, we need criteria for evaluating coping efforts. One approach is to focus on behavioral competence as a significant dimension of adaptation (7, 44, 113). *Competence* is used in reference to manifest behaviors such as school performance or peer relationships. School records, teacher reports, and peer ratings are utilized to make such assessments.

Another significant question about teenage coping concerns *differences* among adolescents. How do different paths of adolescent development influence coping patterns and adaptive outcomes? Before dealing more extensively with this intertwining of individual differences, coping, and varied adaptive outcomes, we turn to the broader question of how adolescent development gives rise to new and continuing issues that must—in some way—be dealt with by the growing teenager.

Stress and Change

Adolescence can be disturbing for both the youth and his or her family, as new dialogues, tensions, and dilemmas surface, sometimes unexpectedly. Established familial patterns may give way under the influence of cognitive, biological, and social changes. Cognitive transformations are salient; many adolescents engage readily in abstract thought and delight in new logical analyses, opening the way to intricate reflections and questions regarding family relationships and traditions. Biological changes are often associated with body and self-image conflicts (12, 16, 107), leading to new or intensified demands for parental assistance. In addition, parents experience their own complex pleasures, misgivings, and conflicts over their teenager's new intellectual prowess and adultlike body (70, 71, 123). Finally, adolescent confusion over new social opportunities and competing or inconsistent sexual norms and behaviors is frequently expressed in struggles over family rules and limits.

We know that adolescents vary dramatically in how they cope with these powerful changes. The psychiatric literature abounds with examples of difficult passages from child to adult status (12). But there is evidence of diversity in the normal range as well. For many years researchers have drawn our attention to the striking variations in development during the teenage years. They describe a rich landscape, defined by major differences in impulse control, autonomy, and relationships with family and peers (9, 12, 98).

Adolescence as Turmoil

An early, and now controversial, understanding of adolescent development depicted youth as a time when individuals experience profound inner turmoil and outward conflict—a time of "storm and stress" ("To be normal during the adolescent period is by itself abnormal," 42, p. 275). This view, still held by some clinical and lay observers, focuses on the often intense emotional upheavals experienced by adolescents. Many of the behaviors interpreted as signs of serious mental illness in adults or children are, in this vision, seen as normal for teenagers (109). They are expected to be extremely moody—depressed one day, elated the next. Highly charged conflict with family, friends, and authorities is commonplace. Shaping this perspective are major contributions of clinical theorists, from the early writing of G. Stanley Hall (54) to the more recent work of Peter Blos (12, 13) and Erik Erikson (34, 35). Basing their conclusions largely on their experience with patients, these observers depicted adolescence as a time of intermittent psychological crises, as young people struggle to deal with the psychological and societal tasks of this phase of life: namely, reducing psychological dependence on family of origin, separating from this family, and developing new intimate relationships with peers.

Several insights have been gained from the storm-and-stress perspective. First, it has called attention to the cumulative physical, social, and psychological changes experienced by adolescents and to their attempts to manage and master the many simultaneous demands. Second, there has been a burgeoning of empirical research based on nonclinical populations (see, for example, 32, 99, 105). The findings of these studies emphasize diversity, thus challenging the view that adolescence is *necessarily* a time of emotional upheaval and unpredictable behavior (1, 33, 37, 98, 99, 109, 114).

These new research programs take up the question of whether the majority of teenagers experience serious psychological turmoil. Although there is agreement that adolescence is a time of many changes, only about 10% to 20% of adolescents evince severe emotional disturbance—approximately the same percentage as in the adult population (100, 105). There is a growing consensus that, for most, the teenage years are not ordinarily a time of *severe* psychological turmoil (109).

Normative Stresses

Significant environmental and biological changes occur at the start of adolescence. If the young teenager entering middle school or junior high must simultaneously deal with other serious demands, this school transition may be especially burdensome (107, 120; and see also Chapter 8 in this volume). Potentially exacerbating the stresses associated with the new school environment are the biological changes of puberty, involving dramatic endocrine shifts and physical changes (see Chapter 2). Concerns about body size and shape and sexual appetites and fears can be exacerbated by the demands of the new environment, with its unfamiliar teachers and system, as well as peer pressures. In addition, the timing of puberty brings still other difficulties; being out of step with peers by being either precocious or delayed in physical development can be a source of significant disturbance (17, 107).

Beginning in the early adolescent years, and especially prominent by middle adolescence, is the mounting pressure to conform. This does not necessarily mean that parents lose their influence. More accurately, friends gain significantly more importance during this period (3, 107; and see Chapter 11). Accompanying these more pervasive peer influences are heightened temptations to experiment in risky areas, such as with drugs, alcohol, sex, and reckless driving. Many powerful stresses of middle adolescence are associated with peer relationships, as the teenager becomes increasingly involved in dating and in new negotiations with parents about curfews, cars, and freedom. For the first time many individuals develop intimate heterosexual and same-sex relationships (see Chapter 13). Dating expectations can be distressing, leading to fears of rejection, performance anxiety, and self-consciousness over sexuality and lack of experience (86, 91, 107).

As adolescents grow to adult size, their new physical stature can alter their relationship with parents. Especially if the teenager is the firstborn, parents may be painfully reminded of their own advancing age and mortality (86, 107). Moreover, it becomes increasingly clear as adolescence unfolds that parents and children will soon separate, a moment that can be dreaded or eagerly anticipated. Sexual overtones in the parent-child relationship may also be problematic. Whether parents are frightened and become physically more distant, or whether they express these feelings in more muted ways, many teenagers become anxious and rebellious, as they are unprepared to deal with these charged conflicts with mothers and fathers. The ability of the parents themselves to change and remain flexible is a key to determining the outcome of this phase of development.

Various other changes appear during middle adolescence: moodiness, self-absorption, self-aggrandizement, and daydreaming. Along with a generally heightened sense of awareness of talents and interests, a search for new meanings may also commence.

Nonnormative Stresses

In addition to these pervasive and often deep changes, there are also nonnormative stressors, or "risk factors," which increase the likelihood of maladaptive outcomes.[2] Familial stresses have been studied extensively. If

2. Although the nonnormative stresses discussed here are limited to those of a familial nature, there are also individual nonnormative stressors, such as a handicap or chronic illness. The unique problems and special coping strategies used by handicapped adolescents are described by Graham (50). Hauser and colleagues (62, 63) are engaged in longitudinal studies of the adaptation of chronically ill (diabetic) adolescents.

the family situation is unstable, or if there is severe marital discord, the adolescent is considered at risk for difficulties (112, 129). Extreme cases of marital disharmony result in divorce—a growing phenomenon in contemporary American society.[3] The burgeoning research addressing the effects of divorce on children (68, 69, 127, 128) points to how developmental and situational factors influence adolescents' adjustment to parental separation.

Teenagers exhibit marked individual differences in their reactions to their parents' divorce and remarriage (68). In general, early and middle adolescents express resistance to remarriage, while younger children tend to be less affected by marital disruptions and reorganizations. Perhaps because young children have fewer conscious memories of their parents' conflict and their own emotional distress, they may experience fewer disruptive long-term consequences. Most young children adapt reasonably well to marital transitions, provided no further stressors are encountered. Adolescents who have vivid recollections of familial tensions, however, experience more divorce-related difficulties, including depression, impulsive aggressive and sexual behaviors, academic distress, and problems with peer and dating relationships (69). One coping strategy especially prominent in older adolescents (found in approximately one-third of those studied) is disengagement from the family following a divorce and remarriage (68).

Divorce and life in a single-parent family appears to be less detrimental to girls than to boys, who have higher rates of behavior disorders and difficulties in interpersonal relationships both at home and at school. The sons of divorced parents are also more likely to be aggressive than boys from intact families up to three years after the divorce. Although the problems that girls experience in social and emotional functioning generally subside within two years, underlying tensions often reemerge in adolescence, manifesting themselves in precocious sexual behavior and difficulties with dating relationships. Some studies suggest that while it is harder for boys to adapt to divorce, girls have more severe problems coping with a parent's remarriage (69).

An adolescent's coping skills may be influenced by, and may influence, his or her adjustment to divorce (78). In a study of primarily white adolescents 14 to 17 years of age, subjects were asked to write about a stressful experience and describe the coping strategies they had used. Adolescents from di-

3. Although the impact of divorce on adolescents is covered in Chapter 6 in this volume, the discussion here highlights the interplay of risk factors and coping that is specific to divorce.

vorced families reported feeling less in control of stressful situations, used a greater proportion of "less mature, maladaptive coping strategies" (hostile reactions, escape-avoidance, confrontive coping, self-blame, distancing), and appeared to be more vulnerable to stress than those from intact families (78, p. 144). They also reported more stress associated with relationships. The teenagers from divorced families may have used less active, more emotion-regulating strategies because they had less control over situations affecting them (78).

Divorce does not invariably have negative effects. The majority of adolescents from divorced families adapt well, and children function better in a stable single-parent family or stepfamily than in an intact family fraught with constant conflict (68, 69, 89). High levels of continuous conflict, regardless of marital status, have an adverse effect on the social adjustment of children and teenagers (39). But if parents refrain from expressing their anger in front of their children and successfully negotiate their differences, the children are much more likely to adapt constructively to divorce (69).

The adjustment of an adolescent to parental divorce and remarriage is enhanced when he or she maintains positive relationships with both parents. Adaptation to these changes is also influenced by the quality of the new family situation, the effectiveness of available support systems, specific individual characteristics such as intelligence and temperament, and existing friendships (involving at least one close friend) (68).

A second familial risk factor is parental psychiatric disorder. Past research has focused overwhelmingly on maternal, as opposed to paternal, psychosis (112, 129). One study comparing the children of psychotic mothers to those of normal controls found that the most competent children of psychotic mothers were far more "competent, colorful, creative, and talented" than those from the control group (80). The strongest predictor of which children became "super-competent" was whether or not they had a warm, supportive relationship with their mother. These highly competent children also more frequently reported having an intense supportive relationship with an unrelated adult, had more intimate relationships with peers, showed better mental health, and had more interesting hobbies and vocations than did those from the control group. Although children of schizophrenic mothers fared better in general than those of depressed mothers, the key differentiating aspect was not the clinical diagnosis but the mother's current level of functioning (80).

Many other family risk factors have been identified: loss of or separation from either parent or other significant figures; a record of child abuse, or of being placed in the care of local authorities; a paternal record of criminality; perinatal stress and complications or chronic illness; and low level of parental education (112, 129). In his studies on the Isle of Wight and in inner London boroughs, Rutter found that the risk for maladaptive outcomes increased exponentially as the number of stressors the youth was exposed to expanded. There was a multiplicative effect: "It appeared that even with chronic family stresses the children were not particularly at psychiatric risk so long as it was really a single stress on its own. On the other hand, when any two of the stresses occurred together, the risk went up no less than fourfold . . . In other words, the stresses *potentiated* each other so that the combination of chronic stresses provided very much more than a summation of the effects of the separate stresses considered singly" (112, pp. 52–53).

Besides these specific normative and nonnormative stressors, there are other familial and social burdens that can intensify or bring new demands upon adolescents. The broader social context within which the family is embedded—minority group membership, social-class status—generates complex challenges and strains on the family system. These strains are transmitted to the developing adolescent, as Diane Slaughter's *Black Children and Poverty: A Developmental Perspective* illustrates (121). Family financial troubles stemming from unemployment or sustained poverty may be experienced as uncontrollable and pervasive disturbances by the teenager. In addition, disruption of the neighborhood or a move to a new neighborhood can lead to perturbation for the family and the adolescent. While these contextual stresses can arise from many sources, minority group membership is especially noteworthy. Consider the chain of disturbances that can be unleashed and sustained as the effects of institutional and individual racial prejudice lead to unemployment, discrimination and failure at school, subsequent school and family moves, and mounting, pervasive demoralization of the family and the teenager.

Observers from many quarters, then, concur in recognizing that adolescence is a time for striking growth and change on an array of physical and psychological fronts, and a time of obvious vulnerability, linked with individual change as well as special social conditions. An impressive collection of demands, conflicts, and opportunities are associated with the normative and nonnormative stresses occurring within this period.[4] How do adolescents cope with these dilemmas and conflicts? And why do most remain so resilient in the face of all the potential strain and adversity?

4. While it is meaningful to identify and track the possible impacts of developmental and contextual stressors on adolescent coping and functioning, the causal connections are by no means simple ones. Findings by Cohen and colleagues (22) call attention to the fact that aspects of adolescent functioning (depression, anxiety, low self-esteem) can lead to, rather than result from, transient and ongoing stressful situations (for example, school difficulties or substance abuse).

Influences on Coping

Several factors influence both how an adolescent copes and the consequences of his or her efforts. Development—psychological (level of ego development) as well as physical (pubertal maturity)—is related to adaptive functioning and emotional well-being (16, 96). Timing can be especially critical in determining how stressful the event is perceived to be (that is, "on-time" versus precocious or delayed pubertal changes; 107, 113). The sociocultural meaning attributed to being on time with regard to aspects of pubertal development can have a significant impact on adolescents' self-image (18, 82). Cross-cultural studies of pubertal change show that the timing of maturational events may vary not only by individuals but by country. For example, age of menarche can differ widely both within a society and between societies. In addition, there is now evidence that hormonal changes accompanying puberty may themselves influence emotions and behaviors in early and middle adolescence (97, 125).

Cognitive development and temperament can also affect coping efforts and their outcomes. As an adolescent's reasoning becomes progressively more complex, he or she can view dilemmas from multiple perspectives, thus increasing the potential repertoire of coping strategies, specifically those involving appraisal of events, anticipation, and cognitive problem solving.[5] Temperament influences the possible range of coping strategies restricting or increasing envisioned options for dealing with difficulties. It also has an impact on which events are recognized by an individual as stressful. The degree to which temperament directly influences the strategies employed by adolescents in a stressful encounter remains uncertain (25).

Age is another factor that underlies differences in outcomes. Older teenagers generally have a broader range of coping strategies, especially problem-solving ones, and the coping mechanisms they choose are more similar to those of adults than children. A recent study found that emotion-focused coping increased from the sixth to the eighth grade, while the use of problem-focused coping remained essentially the same. In addition, girls employed more emotion-focused strategies than boys in dealing with academic stress (28). A study of college-age men who were subsequently observed during middle age found that defenses and types of coping strategies changed during the adult years as new biological and social stresses were encountered (126).

Are there specific coping styles and processes uniquely or primarily

---

5. The interested reader can find more extended discussion of adolescent cognitive development in Chapter 3 of this volume.

associated with the adolescent era, and with differences *among* adolescents? This question has been dealt with most fully by clinical observers and theorists, beginning with Anna Freud (41) and continuing in the work of Blos (13). Their observations have emphasized the importance of such coping (or, in their terms, "defense") strategies as intellectualization, asceticism, and acting out. But it has been immensely difficult to advance from these rich clinical formulations, based on intensive study of small and special (psychiatrically disturbed) groups, to systematic studies of adolescents (57). Some early attempts were made to translate the clinically generated constructs into empirical definitions (7, 79, 104, 126). The next stage of work, to assess directly age-specific coping profiles and their variations within adolescence, will require representative cross-sectional samples of children and young adults as well as teenagers.

The interesting question of how gender may influence adolescent coping and adaptation is still unanswered. Recent speculations suggest that important aspects of relationship development may differ between male and female adolescents (cf. 46). It is reasonable to suspect that these differences may also be linked with variations in coping. With the number of coping investigations in adolescence increasing, we should begin to find consistent gender-linked patterns, such as a possibly greater impact of social-support disruptions on the adaptation of teenage boys. In several studies of younger children boys have been found to be more vulnerable than girls with respect to stress caused by hospital admission, birth of a sibling, parental discord or divorce, and day care (113).

In any account of differences in coping strategies several unique characteristics of the individual teenager must also be recognized. Developmental history, past experiences with stressors, the particular coping strategies used, and the relative degree of success achieved will all influence how a given adolescent approaches and resolves significant difficulties. Aspects of cognitive and social development that can be relevant include self-perceptions, self-efficacy beliefs, self-control, self-esteem, intelligence, problem-solving and interpersonal skills, temperament, and locus of control (25). Problem-solving and interpersonal skills are especially significant, since they provide a broad repertoire of coping strategies that can be used in particular situations.

In terms of environment, there is evidence, largely resulting from studies of adults, of a positive connection between social support and health or buffering effects on stress (24, 77). With the exception of Cauce's work describing influences of social networks on social competence among minority groups and high-risk youth (20, 21), there are few empirical studies of the effects of social support on the coping and adaptation of teenagers

(15). Theoretically and intuitively we would expect interactive social supports to be a key determinant of health and well-being during adolescence as well, since social support provides emotional sustenance, informational guidance, and tangible assistance (74, 77, 107). Potential sources of social support for youth are numerous: parents, siblings, adults outside the home, and peers. In adolescence the picture may be especially complex, given the intensified significance of peer relationships. As supports are lost or broken, or a friend within one's support network becomes disabled, there may be increased stress on the individual and consequent shifts or increases in coping efforts.

Developmental Paths and Adolescent Coping

Intertwined with these individual and environmental factors is the issue of socioemotional development. Our own work has focused on the varying paths or profiles of ego development during the high school years (58, 65, 66). By ego development we mean qualitatively differing psychosocial stages through which an adolescent progresses (87). General trends incorporated within these stages include internalization of the rules of social intercourse, increasing cognitive complexity and tolerance of ambiguity, and growing objectivity. In addition, impulse control becomes guided by self-chosen long-term intentions, and there is an increased respect for individual autonomy together with an interest in genuine mutuality.

In samples of patients and nonpatients we have distinguished a variety of developmental paths, which we term ego development trajectories (65). Each trajectory type identifies the base level of ego development for subjects in early adolescence and characterizes their form of progression, or stability, in development throughout high school. These trajectories represent the configuration of development or the profile of stages that the adolescent shows over a period of several years. Some boys and girls begin their teenage years in the earliest stages of ego development; they continue to be highly dependent on their parents and almost unaware of differences between themselves and others, and they relate to peers and adults through largely exploitative styles of behavior. In addition, these young people use relatively simple cognitive constructions, responding to situations and questions with few options (either-or, black-and-white thinking). If they remain at these stages for two years or more, they are said to be following the *severely arrested* path of ego development.

A second group of adolescents are intensely concerned with acceptance by friends and compliance with prevailing social rules. Their awareness of individual differences and complex views is, at best, limited, and they live by socially prized categories and slogans, which they rarely question. In terms of ego development, these students are at the conformist stages, frequently found during the adolescent years. If they do not advance to higher stages, they are referred to as following the *steady conformist* path.

A third trajectory includes adolescents who express higher, postconformist ego stages. They show adherence to norms based on inner standards, increased distance or autonomy from parental views, an abiding interest in mutuality with others, and a strong interest in complexity of experience and in paradox or contradiction. These high-level behaviors are typical of *accelerated* ego development, and contrast most strikingly with those of adolescents who are severely arrested in their development.

Finally, a fourth trajectory is *progressive* ego development, in which the individual switches from functioning at the earliest preconformist stages to the conformist stages, or from conformist to postconformist stages, or—most dramatically—from the earliest to the most advanced stages.

These developmental paths are associated with various coping styles. Our first observations in this area are based on ego-development trajectories and clinical research interviews. Using Q-sort ratings of coping and defense repertoires (52), made by raters who were unaware of adolescents' ego-development paths, we found the strongest differences between accelerated and arrested individuals. The accelerated adolescents expressed the highest levels of empathy, objectivity, and intellectuality, while the arrested teenagers exhibited low levels of these qualities. Youths arrested in their ego development (58) utilized primarily those defenses (detachment, rationalization, displacement) believed to be associated with problematic adaptation.

The continuing longitudinal studies of the Blocks' research team (9, 10, 102) provide yet another way of understanding and measuring differences among adolescents. Although they employed a different theoretical perspective, there are important parallels between this work and research on paths of ego development. In the Blocks' perspective the two organizing constructs are *ego control* and *ego resiliency*. Ego control refers to characteristic styles of controlling or modulating impulses, feelings, and desires (60); ego resiliency focuses on the adolescent's elasticity, or the ability to adapt flexibly to changing circumstances and to modify ego control. These basic personality characteristics strongly influence responses to inner motivations and external forces. From long-term longitudinal observations Block identified several adolescent personality types that incorporate combinations of these basic dimensions, ranging from marked undercontrol to overcontrol (9). Among these are *ego resilients, belated adjusters, anomic extroverts,* and *vulnerable undercontrollers.* Ongoing research is in the early phases of clarifying connections between these subgroups and certain coping processes. A number of predictive studies have suggested that variations in the basic underlying dimensions of ego control and resiliency forecast such phenomena as drug abuse (11) and depression (48). More generally, a growing number of contributions are also delineating how adolescent personality and developmental paths may underlie coping styles and adaptation during the teenage years. More detailed consideration of this issue can be found in the reports of several groups working in this area (9, 10, 11, 58, 99, 106).

Familial Influences

Studies of family dynamics focus attention on several questions relevant to adaptation: How does daily family experience, and the overall fabric of family relationships, contribute to adolescent development and adaptation? What family strengths enhance a teenager's autonomy and connectedness with others? In what ways do families, whether intentionally or inadvertently, obstruct individual development and the evolution of family ties compatible with the demands and opportunities of late adolescence?

Two aspects of psychosocial development, autonomy and intimacy, are especially germane to the topics of coping and adaptation in adolescence. Earlier theoretical formulations equated autonomy with detachment from parents, more specifically with *freedom from* parental attachments and influence (72, 124). There is now strong theoretical and empirical support for an alternative view, one that does not assume that major psychological or behavioral disruption in family relations underlies or reflects adolescent autonomy. These studies address the interplay between transformations in autonomy and transformations in family relationships.

Baumrind's studies of parental authority suggest potential connections between parental style and adolescent autonomy (2, 4). She found that *traditional* parents "value a sense of continuity and order more than innovation and risk-taking. They accept the pattern of understanding and value judgements that have been worked out over time by previous generations" (4, p. 111). Adolescents from such families have been described as generally more attached to their parents, more conforming, more achievement oriented; they may also bypass major conflicts in their teenage years (4).

Authoritarian-restrictive parents shape, control, and evaluate their adolescent in line with fairly inflexible standards derived from religious or higher secular authorities. Obedience is a virtue. Authoritarian parents "do not willingly share power and responsibility evenly with their adolescents, and in this sense violate the implicit contract in which parental authority is exercised to benefit primarily the child rather than the parent" (4, p. 111). Related to the authoritarian orientation is the more *punitive* parenting style, in which harsh discipline is favored to curb willfulness (autonomy strivings). This last pattern is associated with major deflections in autonomous development and problematic adolescent behaviors (4).

In contrast, *authoritative* parents do not regard their standards or themselves as divinely inspired or infallible. They are supportive and committed and show differentiated responsiveness. Context and individual differences guide their support for autonomous expression and emphasis on "disciplined conformity" (5). They are affectively responsive (loving, supportive, committed) and cognitively responsive (in providing a stimulating and challenging environment) (4). In short, "the authoritative parent combines limit-setting with negotiation, thus encouraging the child's contribution to the discipline process" (51, p. 84). While Baumrind's published findings to date involve familial antecedents of competent functioning in early and middle childhood, results from other studies support the conclusion that authoritative parenting also predicts greater autonomy in adolescents (70, 71). Despite this clear association between a particular kind of parenting and adolescent development, a vital qualification must be kept in mind. In the absence of longitudinal studies on parenting in the preadolescent years, we cannot know whether these connections represent parental contributions to autonomy or parents' *responses* to their more autonomous teenagers. When we have access to data from Baumrind's observations, we will be in a better position to understand the extent to which these parenting practices function as antecedents of autonomous development.

Other pertinent findings about parental contributions describe the role of parents' ego development (62, 63, 64). Parents at higher levels of ego development (with greater awareness of self and increasing appreciation of individual differences among people) exhibit more explaining, curiosity, and problem solving in family discussions with their teenage children and spouses. This observation is of interest for at least two reasons. First, it suggests that authoritative parents may be functioning at relatively high levels of ego development. In addition, we begin to perceive mechanisms through which the specific behaviors shown by these parents in ongoing family interactions may influence adolescent coping.

The newest studies tracing the development of autonomy are also based on observed family interactions. Results from Grotevant and Cooper (30, 51) underscore how individuality and connectedness in family relationships are linked with adolescent identity exploration and perspective taking. Young people expressing high levels of identity exploration were found to have fathers who were sensitive to the views and needs of others and who were accepting of different viewpoints. In addition, the mothers of these teenagers were aware of clear boundaries between them and their children. These adolescents tended to be members of families that flourished by examining their differences, but within the context of connectedness. In contrast, youths with minimal levels of identity formation and perspective taking were found in families that blurred the boundaries between members and avoided disagreements.

In our research program we also find strong ties between ego development and responsiveness toward parents, along the lines of cognitive (focusing, problem-solving) and affective (accepting, empathy) interactions (64, 108). Similarly, parents' affective responsiveness was associated with adolescent ego development. The meaning of these cross-sectional findings is illuminated by longitudinal analyses pointing to significant links between adolescents accustomed to these family interactions at age 14 and subsequent ego-development trajectories. For instance, teenagers showing arrested ego development were less responsive in family discussions than any of the other adolescents. Thus, initial family discussions indicated which young people were likely to show arrested or unstable development in subsequent years. There were also signs that parental behaviors may contribute to subsequent adaptation. Both mothers and fathers are least responsive toward those adolescents who later display arrested ego development, while parents express more explanation, acceptance, and empathy toward adolescents who go on to show trajectories of progressive development.

These observations highlight the significance of specific kinds of family relationships in the unfolding of adolescent development paths—paths that are associated with varied coping and adaptive outcomes. We cannot yet draw complete pictures of families associated with different trajectories of development, for each of the family dyads (mother-child, father-child, and father-mother) contributes in different ways to the development of adolescent autonomy. This caveat is not meant to rule out the eventual possibility of identifying which family environments may be most effective in promoting particular paths of autonomy development. For the present, though, more is to be gained from understanding the fine texture of family relations than from smoothing out this texture to create a readily comprehensible account of the role of this complex social system in shaping certain paths.

Family life also influences teenagers' abilities to form and maintain intimate or close relationships. Distinctive adolescent dilemmas arise from attempts to maintain meaningful family and peer attachments in the midst of rapid pubertal, cognitive, and environmental (for example, school) change. Gilligan notes the "problems of disconnection in adolescence: As the balance of power between child and parent shifts with the child's coming of age, so too the experience and meaning of connection change. What constitutes attachment in early childhood does not constitute attachment in adolescence, given the sexual changes of puberty and the growth of subjective and reflexive thought" (46, p. 80). Two penetrating questions are posed: "What are the analogues in adolescence to the responsive engagement psychologists find so striking in infancy and early childhood? What constitutes genuine connection in the adolescent years?" (46, p. 80).

Once we focus on significant adolescent attachments, we can see several possible links to family influences. First, there is the issue of *transformations* in family relationships. Investigators of pubertal change have examined this topic, pointing out how family relationships alter with the onset of puberty, and how these relationships may themselves contribute to pubertal change (123). But there is a further question, taken up by Smetana: How do parent-child relations change in light of the often rapid advances in the adolescent's self-reflective capacities (122)? More specifically, what family features facilitate growth, promoting greater differentiation while not jeopardizing, or rupturing, enduring family ties? Preliminary responses to this fundamental question take note of the importance of interactions that permit conflict between members in a context of support (4, 108), acceptance and active understanding from parents (62, 63, 64), and parental expressions of individuality and connectedness (51). These are qualities of family life that provide maximum responsiveness during a challenging and potentially troublesome time in the life of the adolescent child. Authoritative parenting styles may be exquisitely well matched for coping with such challenges, while others, such as authoritarian and punitive styles, may fail dismally. What we do not yet know is whether and how these parenting styles evolve during adolescence, and whether unique parenting forms emerge in the teenage years.

In addition to parent-adolescent bonds, developments in peer relationships bring with them new stresses and emerging opportunities. Children and teenagers differ in their skills at negotiating social relationships, in initiating, diversifying, sustaining, and deepening such ties. In two pioneering papers Cooper and her colleagues mapped links between family and peer relationships (29, 31). One relevant finding was that adolescents who experience individuated relationships within their families are more likely than others to engage in perspective taking, a valuable competence in actual social relationships. Longitudinal observations, together with more intensive observations of friendships in field settings (such as Gottman's study of children; 49) are likely to provide us with a fuller understanding of how family relations shape and are shaped by adolescent peer relationships.

Outcomes of Adolescent Coping

Most teenagers are able to handle the varied stresses and challenges of this phase of life without unusual duress. Yet some are unable to cope effectively. The unfavorable outcomes can appear in numerous guises, ranging from behavioral (delinquency, truancy) and emotional problems (eating disorders, depression), to academic distress or physical complications (67). It is beyond the scope of this chapter—and volume—to discuss this array of pathology. Instead, we single out one particularly dramatic and disturbing event in adolescence for more detailed consideration.

Severe Dysfunction: Suicide

The most disastrous response to stress is suicide.[6] We shall consider suicide from the perspective of stress and coping, and conceptualize it as a failure of coping. Suicide is the second leading cause of death in young people aged 15 to 24 (14). It may actually rank even higher, since these deaths are vastly underreported owing to continuing social taboos. The overall rate tripled between 1970 and 1990, and even more so for white males, whose death rate by suicide is two to three times greater than that for females (47). Several studies found that over 50% of adolescents who attempted or committed suicide had previously either attempted or threatened to kill themselves (47, 117, 118). Shaffer, for instance, reports that eight out of thirty teenagers had threatened suicide within twenty-four hours of their death. In a sample composed mainly of white boys, nearly all had previously expressed suicidal ideation (117). Other important correlates include emotional problems, experience of suicidal behavior, parental absence, and history of parental abusiveness (118). In one study of school and family concomitants, nearly half of the adolescents who attempted suicide were either truant or not attending school at all; half were at least one grade behind agemates; and only 20% currently lived with both natural parents (47).

6. Different aspects of suicide are covered in other chapters within this volume, specifically in Chapters 14 and 17.

There is a paucity of systematic psychosocial research dealing with child and adolescent suicide, in part because reports have concentrated on official statistics such as methods and the sex and age of the individual rather than on motivations. While researchers have used data drawn from coroners', educational, medical, social service, and psychiatric records, they rarely interview immediate family members (117). Nonetheless, drawing on past studies and his own observations, Shaffer concludes that "what finally determines a child's death by suicide is a degree of conceptual maturity; disturbed family background; depressed mental state; a precipitating incident, often of a humiliating kind; access to the means of suicide and opportunity to use these in isolation; and in addition close experience of suicidal behaviour either through its occurrence in his own family, within his peer group or at a fantasy level" (117, p. 289).

More recently, sensitive researchers aware of the relevance of family data are gathering interview material from willing family members and friends. Combining this information with the results of earlier studies, investigators are attempting to formulate a "psychological autopsy" of suicide (118). From the standpoint of this orientation, findings from earlier studies are being challenged. For instance, a study based on adolescents who committed suicide and a group of matched-pair control subjects found that there were no significant differences with respect to such variables as having demanding parents, coming from a broken home, living in an over-crowded household, having parents who abuse drugs or alcohol, performing poorly in school, not being in the age-appropriate grade, or being a school dropout (118). In their review of teenage suicide Blumenthal and Kupfer summarize five major risk factors: psychiatric diagnosis, personality, psychosocial forces, genetic and family dimensions, and biological variables (14). As the number of risk factors increases, the suicide risk also rises.

An extremely large percentage of adolescents who commit suicide have suffered a psychiatric illness, including major affective disorders, conduct disorders, and substance abuse. Antisocial behavior together with depression is an especially lethal combination. In one study, 95% of the adolescents who attempted suicide had a diagnosed psychiatric disorder: 76% had an affective disorder, 70% had a drug or alcohol problem, and 70% had a history of antisocial behavior, while 65% demonstrated an "inhibited" personality (118).

Adolescent personality traits predictive of suicide are similar to those that predict suicide in adulthood. Those who attempt suicide tend to be withdrawn, either aloof or aggressive, impulsive, perfectionistic, and rigid. A study of depressed hospitalized patients revealed that hopelessness was the emotion most strongly correlated with long-term suicide risk, and those who eventually committed suicide were described as having been more isolated, more disturbed, and less visible than the previous attempters (103).

A variety of psychosocial factors are predictive of adolescent suicide. Changes within the nuclear family, death of a parent, discord, divorce or separation, or a generally troubled relationship with parents is frequently present. There may be a history of losses, especially early ones, and recent humiliating experiences, usually involving parents or peers. One study of adolescents who attempted suicide found that the majority had experienced an unusual number of major stresses, including several in the previous year and many in the previous month. Of these attempts 40% appeared to follow an immediate precipitating event, and 78% were actually made in the presence of others, or in close proximity (47). Other factors such as decreased social support or personal resources and physical illness are also associated with increased risk (14). An exposure to suicide through family, friends, or the mass media is also considered a risk factor, because of the belief that suicide may be "contagious." The adolescent in these circumstances identifies with and imitates the person who has committed suicide.[7]

While it is important to be aware of risk factors generally associated with adolescent suicide, it is crucial to be alert for warning signs signaling that a particular teenager may be contemplating it. Such warning signs include alterations in appetite or sleep patterns, sudden changes in behavior, impulsivity, decreased concentration, social withdrawal, and a loss of interest in usual activities (14). Similarly, persistent feelings of guilt, self-reproach, or hopelessness, a recent humiliating experience, making a will or giving away prized possessions, or talking about suicide must be taken seriously as warnings.

Intervention programs should be organized within the educational system to develop the coping skills and increase the self-esteem of both children and adolescents. A critical first step is to conduct rigorous research on intervention techniques. As Blumenthal and Kupfer state: "There is no dearth of literature on intervention techniques for youth

---

7. Although the topic is beyond the scope of this chapter, genetic factors related to suicide ought to be considered. Through families, genetic factors for psychiatric illness, and possibly for suicide itself, are transmitted. Research is exploring whether or not there is a genetic link for a vulnerability to suicide (14). An extremely high rate has been found for suicide in identical but not fraternal twins. Is there a biological abnormality that creates a propensity toward suicide? Preliminary research has shown an alteration in one brain neurotransmitter, serotonin: attempters have decreased levels (14).

suicidal behavior, [but] the results of studies to date are compromised by poor methodology, lack of control groups, lack of evaluation and follow-up, and by the fact that many of these interventions are not based on a theoretical model of detection and intervention" (14, p. 13). Additional evaluations of existing intervention programs, as well as research that recognizes individual differences and specifies factors that make certain adolescents vulnerable to suicide, are needed if we are to develop improved interventions. By more precisely determining what may either lead to or increase the chance of adolescent suicide or interfere with suicide attempts, we put ourselves in a better position to help those who are at risk.

Resilient Adolescents

Why are some adolescents highly effective in dealing with stressors while others cannot surmount the challenges posed during their teenage years? Our knowledge of stress resistance in adolescence is in its earliest stages. In recent years there has been a surge of interest in the contributions of individual and contextual forces to resilient outcomes.

> The exploration of protective factors in children's responses to stress and disadvantage has only just begun. We are nowhere near the stage when any kind of overall conclusions can be drawn . . . the explanation will probably include the patterning of stresses, individual differences caused by both constitutional and experiential factors, compensating experiences outside the home, the development of self-esteem, the scope and range of available opportunities and appropriate degree of environmental structure and control, the availability of personal bonds and intimate relationships, and the acquisition of coping skills. (112, p. 70)

Invulnerable or resilient children are those who, "despite exposure to significant risk factors, show few or no signs of developmental impairment" (67). Several prominent theorists have focused on different aspects of resilience and have proposed varying approaches to how it should be assessed. For some, resilience involves social, school, and cognitive competence (44). For others it is the "capacity to cope effectively with the internal stress of [their] vulnerabilities and external stresses" such as illness, major losses, and dissolution of the family (129, p. 4). In general, children who were exposed to multiple risk factors at an early age but subsequently had no severe psychological, learning, or behavioral disturbances are labeled stress resistant. These are "individuals who overcome adversity, who survive stress, and who rise above disadvantage" (112, p. 3). Variables that differentiate children who develop behavioral and psychological difficulties from those who remain free of any disturbances are called protective factors. In slightly different terms, "ego-resiliency" is contrasted with "ego-brittleness" in the work of Block and Block (10).

Resiliency research inquires into the factors that support stress resistance. Investigators seek to answer questions such as: Who remains invulnerable in the face of stress (minor or extreme) and why? How can groups at-risk be identified? What interventions can be designed to protect them? We must keep in mind that only a small percentage of all the children exposed to risk will develop serious problems. Stress resistance rather than maladjustment appears to be the norm, as Bleuler argues: "It must be emphasized, that only a minority of the children . . . are in any way abnormal or socially incompetent . . . One is even left with the impression that pain and suffering has a steeling—a hardening—effect on the personalities of some children, making them capable of mastering their lives with all its obstacles, in defiance of all their disadvantages" (8, p. 400).

Protective factors are forces that significantly buffer the effects of stress—"those attributes of persons, environments, situations, and events that appear to temper predictions of psychopathology based upon an individual's at-risk status" (43, p. 73). Yet little of the literature on stress resistance has examined *how* resilient youth cope. Instead, researchers have attempted to identify overall characteristics that differentiate the resilient from those who are not able to respond as adaptively to stress (25). The few studies that have been done on coping processes have highlighted three kinds of protective factors: family environments, support networks, and personality characteristics.

Supportive family environments characterized by parental warmth, cohesiveness, and closeness can serve a protective function for at-risk adolescents (25, 67). Parents who help their children develop social and cognitive skills and general competence, while themselves remaining flexible, encourage traits such as self-confidence and self-control, which are associated with resilient behavior (115). Parents who express concern about their children's education and give them room for self-direction and autonomy without being severely critical, possessive, or anxious can help them become stress resistant (67).

Familial interactions are also crucial: "clearly focused, flexible, well-structured and task-appropriate communications" foster competent school and social performance (67, p. 88). Even in a turbulent home the presence of one parent who has an affectionate, warm, supportive, and noncritical relationship with the child is conducive to stress resistance (44). Resilient adolescents have better relationships with parents and receive more parental support. The parents are less often absent from the home; and the children are raised in an environment where there is respect for individuality and family closeness as well as rule setting, discipline, and defined roles within the family (129). Consistently enforced rules, good supervision, and well-balanced discipline combined with a supportive, understanding relationship are key determinants of resilient behavior (67).

The community can provide support for the adolescent as well. The quality of the school and the extent to which the teachers and guidance counselors are involved with the students can be extremely influential. An external support system encourages and reinforces a teenager's coping efforts while demonstrating positive values (112). Resilient adolescents often have extensive contacts outside the immediate family with concerned and caring ministers, teachers, and older friends, as well as peers (67, 129).

Many personality or dispositional characteristics can temper the impacts of stress; these include social skills, coping styles, temperament, self-esteem, locus of control, autonomy, self-efficacy, and self-confidence. The research on personality characteristics indicates that being sensitive, cooperative, socially responsible, and emotionally stable and participating in activities are positively related to resiliency (67).

Various patterns of coping contribute to resilient outcomes. Delaying gratification, regulating impulse drives, being oriented to the future, and depending on personal resources are examples of such coping styles. Curiosity, adaptability, and malleability are also relevant characteristics (67). In addition, behavioral efforts to deal with the challenge and cognitive attempts to manage one's appraisal of a threat are effective (74, p. 740). Finally, information seeking, problem-solving actions, self-reliance, and controlled reflectiveness are associated with resilience.

An easygoing disposition buffers the effects of stress. Similarly an internal locus of control and high scholastic performance (which has been associated with high self-esteem) are protective factors that can counterbalance stress (25, 74). Self-efficacy has predicted coping, achievement strivings, and lack of resignation in the face of failure, while high self-confidence and self-esteem are related positively to resilient behavior (74). Resilient adolescents also display good communication and cognitive skills: they appear to have a sense of control over the environment and some feeling of personal power as opposed to powerlessness (44, 67, 94, 113, 129).

Studies of black children from inner-city ghettos have distinguished key differences between resilient and nonresilient children. The former were active, sensitive, socially responsive, intelligent, and cooperative. In addition, they had high levels of self-esteem and positive self-images and were not sullen or restless. The family environments of resilient adolescents were neat and not cluttered; books were available; and family relationships were described as warm and cohesive. If the mother headed a single-parent home, she was actively concerned about her child's competency; she helped with homework; and she recognized and reinforced the child's goals, interests, and striving toward self-direction (44). While at least one significant positive role model was present in the lives of all of these resilient youth, the number of additional caretakers or social supports was particularly influential in single-parent households.

Public Policy and Future Research

Historically children have not been a high priority for the government. A 1977 Carnegie Council report on children concluded: "Today . . . virtually the last question we ask of any public policy is how it will affect children. It should be the first question" (115, p. 325). Funding for research has not been forthcoming, although there is a significant need to support and develop research programs at several levels. First, the basic questions about environmental factors and individual development that we have touched on in this chapter must be addressed. We do not know which environmental units affect adolescent development the most, how environmental experience connects with adolescent development, or how individual differences interact with environmental experience. These questions have clear connections to broad and urgent societal concerns:

> Our society is experiencing increasing stress . . . The problems of crime and violence and social disarray defy easy solution . . . In the face of the frustration and fear that stalk many communities, there is a danger that facile explanations of genetic factors will substitute for the more complex understandings needed to solve the problems . . . It is therefore urgent that we keep before us the perspective that behavioral development is the result of a complex interplay of genetic, biological, and environmental factors. That urgency must be translated into a research agenda that includes a commitment to understand how best to characterize the environment as it functions in the complex relationships of organism to environment. (76, p. 443)

At a more specific level, we have emphasized the need to study various contexts and to target adolescents other than college-bound whites from suburban middle-class families. Numerous questions demand further attention. For example, what interlocking social and psychological stressors do these groups of teenagers encounter? And what community, family, and individual characteristics contribute to successful coping, to developmental paths undisrupted by severe psychopathology (suicide, substance abuse) or social dysfunction (dropping out of school, criminal careers)?

Finally, there is much to be learned about *interventions* for at-risk adolescents and their families. The most effective interventions will likely be derived from more precise understandings of environment-development relations. Once these interventions, or "treatments," are in place, a new knowledge of environmental impacts surfaces, as well as important evaluative questions. We must refine our ideas about *when* to intervene. As we become more sophisticated about causes of unfavorable outcomes, the best ages (whether preadolescence or early childhood) and contexts (school or family) for interventions should become more apparent. Identifying the interventions, however, will require well-designed evaluative programs. We will need prospective longitudinal designs that incorporate rigorous sampling (control groups, comparison groups), consistent observational procedures, and appropriate timing of observations (baseline, during the intervention, and at near and distant points following interventions).

Yet the best-designed research, both basic and evaluative, will be of little practical social value if the results are not disseminated properly. "Mental health research is not an end in itself. It acquires value only when its findings are used, whether the users are scientists, science administrators, practitioners, social agency managers, or the general public" (115, p. 303). Findings must be transmitted to legislators, social-service agencies, and legal practitioners. The factors that enhance or obstruct communication between researchers and these other groups are of obvious significance but beyond the scope of this chapter. The interested reader can find extended discussion of these issues in G. Melton's book *Reforming the Law: Impacts of Child Development Research* (90), and in the essay "Children as Futures" by F. D. Horowitz and M. O'Brien (76).

Within the adult literature efforts have been under way to integrate conceptualizations and measurements of stress and coping. Yet such work is only in its beginnings in studies of adolescents (25). Researchers must arrive at agreed-upon constructs, distinctions among theoretical perspectives, and linked empirical definitions so that more intensive studies of diverse samples can be designed and implemented by means of the multisite collaborative model well known in medical and psychiatric research.

If such basic issues can in fact be successfully resolved, the field can advance to investigate more specific questions. We need further research to delineate specific adolescent coping strategies: Which strategies are most effective for which stressors, and at what particular stages of dealing with the stressor? Coping measures should be developed that will allow comparisons of individual differences among adolescents as they respond to acute and persistent difficulties. So too, we need to know how an individual's coping shifts—or remains constant—as he or she continues to deal with different versions of the same stressor. Similarly, we must detail more fully the relations between patterns of coping and the varied paths of adolescent development (cf. 58).

There are unresolved questions of developmental specificity, such as how to determine the predominant coping styles and processes used by adolescents and the functions these various strategies serve. In resiliency research, general characteristics that differentiate those who cope effectively under stress from those who become impaired or are overwhelmed are distinguished. We must also determine what strategies stress-resistant youth utilize.

The extensive, multilayered connections between the family and adolescent coping and adaptation must be more precisely conceptualized and studied. Throughout this chapter we have emphasized the complex ways in which the teenager and the family reciprocally influence one another. At each juncture—coping strategies, varying outcomes, risk factors, protective factors, development of autonomy and intimacy—we have explored implications with respect to the family system and individual parents. Closely related to the topic of family influence are the larger questions of key environmental units. One significant aspect of the environment is social support, a domain repeatedly linked with health and well-being in adults (77). A future task is to determine its significance in adolescence, to discover how family members and peers are intermeshed with social support and new kinds of close relationships through transformations in autonomy and intimacy.

These policy and research topics point to an admittedly grand agenda, one that demands a lessening of conceptual rivalries leading to artificial polarities, such as psychodynamic versus transactional views of coping. The phenomena of stress, adaptation, and growth during adolescence are too complex, and the need to understand successful outcomes under adverse conditions too urgent, to permit the inevitable waste of effort caused by parochial theoretical controversies. The domain of stress, adaptation, and development calls for the very best in collaborative efforts in order to strengthen relevant theory and build ambitious, inclusive empirical research.

16

PROBLEM BEHAVIORS

Joan McCord*

Common opinion holds that breaking adult rules is a normal occurrence during adolescence. Yet common opinion also views such behavior as a sign of maladjustment. This paradox serves as a backdrop to the fact that adolescence has been found to be the period of greatest risk for initiation of drug use, for arrests (both in terms of the numbers of adolescents arrested and in terms of the frequency of being arrested), for committing serious street crimes, and for developing serious drinking problems. Adolescence is also the period during which sexuality is most likely to create problems, when people are most likely to begin smoking, and when youngsters may decide to terminate their education prematurely. Although many theories purport to explain why so many teenagers run into trouble, no one theory has gained overwhelming acceptance by those familiar with the evidence. Nor is there broad agreement about interpreting the interrelationship among various forms of problem behaviors.

Drinking, smoking, drug use, delinquency, and sexual activity have been considered elements of a deviant adolescent life-style. Partly for this reason, some researchers (Jessor and Jessor, Kaplan, Robins) believe that various manifestations of deviance should be considered in terms of a single underlying tendency (90, 101, 102, 159–164). Others (Bachman, Cohen and Brook, Elliott, Kandel, McCord) believe that different sets of deviant behaviors represent diverse underlying difficulties (6, 7, 45, 55–58, 93–100, 123–128).

In part the difference is one of emphasis. Those who consider drug use, delinquency, and other forms of deviance facets of a single "problem behaviors syndrome" may leave out of their account the conditions under

*The author wishes to thank Denise Kandel, David Farrington, and two anonymous reviewers for their cogent criticisms of an earlier draft.

which particular forms of deviance appear. The selection of type may, of course, be largely opportunistic. Those who emphasize the common elements believe that reducing problem behaviors depends on the amelioration or prevention of a common underlying trait.

In showing the rise and fall of initiation into drug use as related to tours of duty in Vietnam, Robins (159) demonstrated interacting effects between predisposing factors and environmental conditions that promoted the use of drugs. Changes in the availability of drugs also appear to account for shifts in the prevalence of drug use within a single neighborhood (30). Similar issues of availability in terms of targets or accomplices seem to account for some neighborhood differences in crime rates (44, 156, 183). These results are consonant with the theory that a single underlying trait motivates problem behaviors.

Yet if different types of problem behaviors represent diverse underlying difficulties, a single strategy might fail to ameliorate the problems of most individuals. Several longitudinal data sets have been used to try to identify the determinants of different forms of deviance. In one project children first studied between the ages of 5 and 10 were restudied eight years later (45). Measures of substance use, externalization (including aggressiveness), and internalization (including depression) were correlated. Risk factors measured prospectively nonetheless indicated different sources for the three types of problem behaviors. A combination of maternal inattention and neighborhood crime predicted substance abuse; neighborhood crime, residential instability, parental sociopathy or mental illness, parental remarriage, and power-assertive discipline predicted externalization of problems; social isolation, parent's mental illness, parental remarriage, and lax or inconsistent rules predicted internalization of problems. In another study youths aged 11 to 17 in 1976 were restudied periodically through 1983 (57). In this sample teenagers who used drugs typically also committed minor delinquencies, but there was little overlap between drug use and serious criminal activity. Although the paths crossed in various ways, different trajectories seemed to account for serious crime, substance abuse, and mental health problems. Probably the most direct attack on the question of specificity comes from a study tracing high school seniors to ages 21 or 22 (142). The study attempted to explain criminal behavior, heavy drinking, marijuana use, use of other illicit drugs, and dangerous driving. A general tendency toward deviance, becoming less significant over time, accounted for more of the variance in criminal behavior than in the other forms of problem behaviors. The common factor accounted for most of the covariation among behaviors, although the data showed strong stability for specific types of problems.

Prevalence of Problem Behaviors

Collecting accurate information about the ecology of problem behaviors is particularly difficult because both official data and self-reports are suspect. Official statistics give information only after a crime has been reported or detected. Figures therefore reflect public attitudes as well as practices of enforcement agencies. Some evidence suggests that bias enters at these levels. For example, comparison of rape victims' reports with official reports shows that black offenders are considerably more likely to be reported to police than are white offenders (81).

New laws, politics, and social conditions have marked effects on crime statistics (46). So, too, do policies regarding the treatment of confessions and other police practices (65). Opportunities for bias in the criminal justice system occur at such points as deciding whether to report an offense, whether to arrest, whether to bring an accused offender to court, whether to detain an accused person prior to trial, whether to adjudicate the accused as culpable and, if so, for what charge, and what disposition will be imposed. Evidence of racial and sex biases have been detected in some, but not in all, jurisdictions. Bias has been found to be more prevalent at the early stages of the criminal justice process (49, 81, 201), although evidence of racial bias has been identified at each of the choice points. The authors of one study comparing youths sent to correctional institutions with those sent to mental hospitals in the same jurisdiction summarized the results succinctly: "Violent, disturbed adolescent blacks were incarcerated; violent, disturbed whites were hospitalized" (111, p. 306).

To overcome some of the problems involved in using official records, researchers have turned to reports by those whose behavior is being studied. Such self-reports of problem behaviors can offer information about undetected activities, but they are subject to both underreporting and overreporting. Relation to expected covariates has been used to validate self-report scales, but these tests may reflect consistent differences in the willingness to report, along with differences in actual behavior. Self-reports must also rely on voluntary cooperation, and those people most heavily involved in delinquency and drug use are least likely to participate in the studies (36, 84, 92, 94, 98).

In addition to the problem of winning cooperation from possibly reluctant adolescents, self-report studies also face problems of memory and honesty. Underreporting of delinquent behavior and drug use is related to ethnicity (82, 87, 134, 193), with blacks reporting less of their officially recorded deviant behavior than whites. It remains unclear, however,

whether the error should be attributed to the official or to the self-reported information (57). Slight changes in wording or format influence
responses (21), especially for frequency of offending (63). Some reporting
errors seem to be due to the respondent's desire to appear respectable (77,
134). A first arrest increases a delinquent's veracity about his crimes (61);
one explanation is that prior to arrest, a delinquent tries to maintain the
appearance of respectability.

Absent hidden observers to record what really happens, accurate figures
regarding crime, drug use, underage drinking, and other problem behaviors remain elusive. Probably some combination of methods yields more
accurate information than does any single method used alone. By pooling
data from a variety of sources, we begin to gain a picture of the prevalence
of various types of problems among teenagers.

The National Youth Survey gathered information on families, behavior,
and attitudes from a probability sample of boys and girls between the ages
of 11 and 17 in 1976 (57). Because conventional people are more likely to
consent to being studied, the fact that more than a quarter of the selected
sample refused to participate almost surely resulted in underestimates of
problem behaviors. The degree to which reported delinquent activities
represent behavior serious enough to result in arrest had the activities
been known by the police remains a question.

The National Youth Survey figures resulted in classification of about
30% of the males and 10% of the females as serious violent offenders
because they reported at least three violent offenses within a year before
reaching age 18. As active delinquents, the boys averaged around nine and
the girls around five violent offenses per year. Girls committed fewer
crimes than boys and participated most actively in violent crimes at an
earlier age.

Various estimates of arrests for serious (index) crimes compiled by the
National Academy of Sciences Panel on Research on Criminal Careers
indicate that between 12% and 18% of males had been arrested prior to age
18 (21). The annual rate for male juvenile offenders was estimated as 1.84
nontraffic offenses, including 1.32 violent offenses. Male-to-female ratios
for index-offense arrests are approximately 5 to 1 (21, p. 40). Male-to-female
ratios of drug use, like those for delinquency, are higher for more serious
forms of deviance (94).

The rate of index arrests of juveniles increased markedly from the
mid-1960s to a peak in 1974, when they began an irregular decline. Since
the early 1970s estimates based on a national sample of high school seniors
reporting on their own behavior showed increases in the use of marijuana
and other illicit drugs. Between 1983 and 1988, however, these surveys

showed slight declines in drug use. Data from the class of 1988 indicated that 21.4% had used only marijuana and 32.5% had used other illicit drugs at some period in their lives (91). Because many teenagers who use drugs drop out of high school (92, 133, 159, 161, 200), however, figures based on high school students understate the proportion of adolescents who have used marijuana or other drugs.

According to the reports of high school seniors, almost 5% of the class of 1987 used alcohol daily, and 37.5% had taken at least five drinks in succession at some time within the two weeks prior to the survey (91). Almost 20% smoked tobacco daily, and over 11% smoked at least half a pack per day. These figures indicate no decline in tobacco use for several years. Again, based as they are on high school students, the data may well underestimate the prevalence of both drinking and smoking among adolescents.

Since 1972 the National Institute on Drug Abuse has surveyed house-holds in the forty-eight contiguous states, sampling by age categories. In 1985 about 31% of males and 28% of females aged 12 to 17 reported having used illicit drugs. For both sexes the proportions were higher for non-Hispanic whites than for either blacks or Hispanics. Other studies have shown that West Indian blacks are less likely to use drugs than are American blacks, and that American blacks are less likely to use illicit drugs than are American whites (57, 94, 96, 107, 200).

Among ethnic minorities, American Indians have historically been prone to drug use (94). Asian teenagers, until recently, appeared to be relatively immune to drugs and crime. The revised laws of 1965 that expanded the immigration of Asians, causing partial integration of ethnic communities and changing their demographic characteristics, seem to have resulted in an increase in antisocial activities among Filipinos, Koreans, Chinese, Asian Indians, and Vietnamese (38, 112).

Although blacks are overrepresented in official crime rates, the figures may misrepresent racial differences. Data from the National Youth Survey suggest that when black and white youths commit similar crimes, the black youths are considerably more likely to be charged with a serious offense (88). Even official records indicate, however, that blacks are no more likely than whites to be rearrested for serious crimes (23).

Estimates of the age at which adolescents initiate sexual intercourse have been based on a national sample of men and women interviewed retrospectively in 1984, when they were 26 years of age. Half the men in the sample reported that they had experienced coitus by age 16.9, as had half the women by age 18.3. A sample from New York State, interviewed retrospectively when they were about a year younger than those in the national sample, provided similar information. Half the men in the sample reported that they had had intercourse by age 17.2, as had half the women by age 18.3. In both samples black males reported initiating coitus at earlier ages than did Hispanics or other whites (95). Among a sample of adolescent students in Baltimore, 12% of the white males and 50% of the black males reported having been sexually active prior to age 13. In addition, 1% of the white women and 10% of the black women reported being sexually active at age 12 or under. As students in grades seven through twelve, 15% of the black women and 9% of the white women reported that they had been pregnant, and 16% of the black males plus 10% of the white males reported having fathered a child (200).

The National Youth Survey indicated that youths engaged in violent crimes were also likely to be involved in felony thefts (48%), drug sales (22%), and drug use (20%). Many of those classified as serious nonviolent offenders (youths who reported at least three felonies but not three violent offenses in a year) also participated in drug sales (25%) and used illicit drugs (21%). These proportions can be compared with data from nonoffenders (youths who reported fewer than three delinquencies of any kind and no serious street crimes) showing 0.3% involved in drug sales and 1.8% using illicit drugs. In one study over 80% of the incarcerated delinquents reported having used marijuana and almost half had used other illicit drugs (80). Compared with same-age peers, sexually active young teenagers are more likely to smoke tobacco (200), use illicit drugs (52, 200), and commit crimes (197).

According to reports of high school seniors, those living in the West and Northeast are more likely to use illicit drugs than those living in north central or southern regions (91). Alcohol was the drug of choice in each of the four regions, followed in prevalence by tobacco and then marijuana. Whether preference or availability or some combination of the two creates the difference is unknown, but PCP, cocaine, and opiates are more commonly used in the West than elsewhere in the country, while marijuana, LSD, and other hallucinogens are more prevalent in the Northeast.

Sources other than self-reports and official records exist for some types of problem behaviors. For example, clinic registries and urinalyses yield alternative estimates of drug use. Clinic samples, of course, omit people not seeking treatment; in addition, rates of remission for clinic samples are lower than in the general population (94, 159). Urinalysis was used by Robins to study Vietnam veterans (159), and it also has been used with groups such as athletes and arrestees, populations among which drug abuse is probably more common than in the general population. Victim reports, third-person accounts, and observational records have also provided data for studies of problem behaviors.

One of the difficulties with discussions about the prevalence of adolescent problem behavior is that there is no consensus regarding what should count as a problem. For some purposes, committing any action proscribed by law constitutes delinquency. Most teenagers have played truant, trespassed, or committed traffic offenses at one time or another. Only a minority, however, have committed serious crimes. Most adolescents have tasted alcohol, and a majority appear to be regular drinkers, but only a minority have become problem drinkers or incipient alcoholics. A majority of adolescents have experimented with marijuana, though only a minority have tried other illicit drugs. In the remainder of this chapter the discussion will focus on the minority behaviors that clearly constitute problems.

Explanations for Deviance

Explanations of adolescent deviance lend themselves to organization by focus: on social and community factors that influence opportunities, biogenetic susceptibilities, personality and character traits, parental inadequacies, and vulnerability to peer influences.

Social and Community Factors

A number of classic theories about deviance emphasize the lack of legitimate opportunities for success available to those who manifest problem behaviors (40, 42, 135). This lack of socially acceptable opportunities, it has been suggested, leads to frustration and sometimes a search for alternative means to success. Evidence available through official records of the criminal justice system shows an inverse relationship between social class and crime rates. Self-report studies of behavior serious enough to result in arrest, and studies of multiple offenders, also generally show an inverse relation between social class and crime rates (25, 55, 193).

Frustration may explain why delinquents and drug users typically have poor school records (10, 56, 84, 161). Some poor students may be frustrated by requirements they cannot meet, and others may be frustrated because success in school seems pointless. The latter may explain why early promise of academic success among black males was found to predict drug use a decade later (103). Reports that delinquent activities decrease after adolescents drop out of school can be interpreted as evidence that frustrating school experiences promote deviant behavior (7, 29, 58). Studies that fail to find criminality decreasing once individuals leave school raise the possibility, however, that the relationship may be a function of age (186) or of the availability of alternative opportunities (151).

Despite a link between school failure and problem behaviors, theories suggesting that crime is primarily a response to the frustrated desire for success run into difficulties in the face of two types of evidence: first, improved opportunities for legitimate success do not consistently reduce delinquency (see, for example, 72, 76, 136, 155, 165), and second, rates of serious crime and drug use have been found to be consistently low for one group whose opportunities for legitimate success have traditionally been circumscribed: women (41, 89, 94, 178, 192).

Success in school may not matter to those who later use drugs, become delinquents, or have early sexual experiences; for them, then, school failure may not be experienced as frustrating. Evidence that teenagers who are about to try marijuana devalue academic achievement (90), that it is misbehavior rather than poor academic performance in primary school that predicts serious adolescent delinquency (177), and that students who drop out of school have generally been truants since the primary grades (164) lends credibility to this interpretation.

Opportunities influence behavior in ways other than as pathways to success. Neighborhood standards convey what forms of behavior are accepted; for example, they seem to account for high rates of teenage pregnancy in some communities (4) and for a high incidence of gang activity in others (48, 85). Television and movies also provide means by which the adolescent's repertoire of behavior can be shaped (60, 143). Although there is some evidence that the effects of television viewing are related to prior aggressiveness, it has been reported that "high exposure to television violence increases the degree to which boys engage in serious violence" (13, p. 15).

Employment environments may also affect opportunities. Some evidence suggests that holding a part-time job increases the likelihood of smoking tobacco and marijuana and may encourage some types of delinquency (74). By contrast, the availability of employment opportunities for adolescents appears to reduce the amount of serious crime among disadvantaged males (2, 151). The former effect may be due to absence of supervision, alienation, anticipatory role adaptation, or to newly perceived opportunities to commit crimes. Experimental evidence suggests that the latter effect may be related more directly to the problems of poverty and the perceived need for goods (16) or the possibility for achieving desired goals (109). Research suggests that the effects of community quality vary in relation to individual characteristics (73). Crowding, incivility, and the general pace of life affect opportunities in a variety of ways (198). These conditions probably influence problem behaviors as well. More research is necessary before we can understand their impact.

Biogenetic Susceptibilities

Evidence of family resemblance regarding problem behaviors may be explained by sociological and psychological theories. In order to place this evidence in a biogenetic context, some researchers have studied twins and adoptees. In twin studies, genetic contributions to behavior are estimated from comparisons between pairs of twins who have identical genes and those who share only the number expected for siblings, estimated at 50%. The former are monozygotic and the latter are dizygotic pairs. If environmental similarities are assumed to be irrelevant, differences between the similarities in monozygotic and dizygotic pairs yield a basis for estimating genetic contribution. In adoption studies, genetic contributions to behavior are estimated from comparisons between the resemblance of offspring to their biological and to their adoptive families.

Although at least one study found delinquent activities no more closely linked in monozygotic twins than in dizygotic twins (166), overall, monozygotic twins seem to be more similar than dizygotic twins and biological families more similar than adoptive families in terms of propensity toward alcoholism and criminal behavior (32, 131). Critics note, however, that samples have been small and may not be representative of the general population (174, 187).

The mechanism by which genetic transfer occurs has been elusive (11). The strongest evidence favoring a biogenetic theory about problem behaviors has been adduced in studies of alcoholism, where research has indicated that adolescent sons of alcoholics differ from sons of nonalcoholics in the speed with which they metabolize alcohol and in how they experience its effects (172, 173). Some evidence suggests that addiction to drugs may also be affected by differential biological responses to controlled substances (132).

The persistence of sex differences in crime rates has led to a search for sex-linked causes of delinquency. Males seem to be more aggressive across many cultures and types of situations (115), and aggressiveness appears to be transmitted through family lines (86). Furthermore, studies in several cultures have shown that, along with social and psychological factors, heightened levels of aggression presage delinquency and drug use (see, for example, 103, 118, 126, 152, 195, 197). Data from recent studies show, however, that aggressiveness alone (that is, in the absence of additional problems) may not be predictive of deviant behavior (117, 141).

Sex-linked hormones have been suggested as a basis for biogenetic differences in behavior. Studies of teenage sexuality indicate that testosterone levels influence sexual ideation and sexual activity in males, though not in females (189, 190). Testosterone levels do not seem to be related to criminal behavior (140, 171).

Early sexual maturation among females may lead to their selection of older friends and to increases in family conflict (117, 180), either of which can produce troublesome behavior. Only among girls with older friends was there greater use of illegal drugs, drunkenness, and delinquency in relation to early menarche (117).

Adrenaline secretion, which is related to arousal, may be rewarding for those who typically have low levels of cortical arousal (140, 169). If so, then differences in the adrenal medullary system could account for why some people are attracted to activities that increase arousal. The evidence is mixed. A variety of studies have found that criminals have low autonomic arousal (78, 113), although other studies have failed to confirm this finding (83, 120). A difficult problem for theoretical development regarding the relationship between adrenal cortical arousal and behavior involves sorting through cause and effect. Environmental factors influence cortical secretions (8, 191). Exposure to violence can desensitize (39, 185), and criminals are typically reared by punitive parents (9, 62, 126).

Other possible biogenetic sources of problem behaviors include neurological abnormalities. Evidence regarding the biological basis for attention deficit disorder—a syndrome sometimes considered minimum brain damage, sometimes hyperactivity—continues to be debated (5, 129). Some neurological abnormalities can impede learning or affect the integration of experiences, and a combination of neurological difficulties and parental abuse or rejection appears to promote serious criminal behavior (110, 137).

Personality and Character Traits

Evidence suggests that individuals follow alternate paths to problem behaviors. Sensation seeking and impulsivity seem to characterize one such path. A desire to be accepted, perhaps coupled with poor social skills, depression, and low self-esteem, appears to typify another.

Impulsivity and sensation-seeking or risk-taking behavior are characteristic of persistent delinquents (15, 20, 153, 202). Furthermore, when these attributes have been measured prior to adolescence, they have been found to be predictive of adolescent delinquency (66, 169, 170). Both patterns have been observed among adults who use hallucinogens (104), and the pattern of sensation seeking is related to drug use among adolescent girls as well as boys (26, 27, 184). Evidence from emergency rooms suggests, however, that males are more likely to use drugs for their psychoactive effects, but females are more likely to be suicidally motivated (138).

While the first path represents an active seeking of experience—a proactive path—the second path might be viewed as passive or reactive. Along the latter path deviant behavior can be seen as an attempt to cope with experiences. Young children who get into trouble because of their behavior typically lack the social skills prevalent among their classmates (51, 144). Such children are also likely to have been exposed to rejecting, punitive parents (150). Depression as well as low self-esteem may be a consequence of the heavy dose of negative feedback they seem to receive. Drug use appears to be a means for coping with depression (145, 179) and situational stress (37, 108, 139, 184).

Some researchers argue that problem behaviors increase self-esteem (14, 71, 101, 102). Yet the claim remains controversial (122, 194). Perhaps the clearest attack on the question of how delinquency and self-esteem are related came from analysis of data collected in the Youth in Transition project (31). The project began with boys in tenth grade in public high schools. Analyses were based on responses from those who participated in 1966, 1968, and 1969. Among those with low self-esteem in tenth grade, some support was found for Kaplan's theory that delinquency increases self-esteem (101, 102). Overall, however, the analyses showed that "self-esteem appears to play hardly any part in mediating the effects of behavior from one time to the next" (31, p. 428).

Some of the controversy may be due to the impact of cultural differences either on the effects of drugs or on expectations for behavior when a person is depressed. Among high school students in New York, for example, girls were more likely to use drugs if they were depressed, while black and Puerto Rican boys were more likely to use drugs if they were not depressed (145). The authors noted: "In no group, however, do psychological factors seem to be a strong determinant of adolescent drug use" (p. 197).

Parental Inadequacies

Psychodynamic and learning theories converge on parental inadequacies as explanations for crime and drug abuse. Crime, drug use, adolescent pregnancy, and single-parent family structure are prevalent in high-density, poor urban areas. This coincidence has helped to fuel the belief that children reared without a standard nuclear family will have difficulties as they reach adolescence. The relative frequency with which paternal absence, maternal rejection, and inadequate or punitive discipline have been found in delinquent or drug-using populations has contributed to the identification of these variables as causes of problem behaviors (see, for example, 28, 94, 114).

Relationships between family and biogenetic factors and among family variables are not well understood. A few studies have focused on the effects children have on parents. The results suggest that troubled children have previously been troublesome, and that even their nondeviant behavior may have elicited negative responses from their parents (12, 34, 116, 146, 154, 188).

The effect of parental inadequacies on adolescent deviance has been evident through longitudinal studies. Variables typically considered in these studies include rejection, conflict, deviance, and inadequate discipline. The evidence seems clearest in showing that conflict between parents and inadequate discipline increase the probability of delinquency, early sexual activity, and drug use. Prior conflict and absence of supervision seem at least partly responsible for the problems of children reared by single parents (3, 54, 59, 125, 167). Broken homes are associated with paternal crime and alcoholism as well as with conflict and lack of supervision (125). Paternal alcoholism and drug use are also associated with various poor child-rearing practices (50, 128). Both paternal deviance and the associated child-rearing practices may contribute to the problem behaviors found among teenagers from disturbed homes (62, 75, 94, 131, 147, 162).

Despite the wealth of evidence, difficulties ensue from using these studies for identifying specific causal links. These arise from the fact that prior conditions, which may be biological, can influence observed relations, and that families having problems along one dimension typically have problems along many. Statistical solutions for collinearity can be invoked, but these cannot overcome problems of measurement.

Retrospective studies, some of which have failed to show a relationship between parental inadequacies and adolescent deviance, may encourage biases toward presenting a socially acceptable picture of one's family. Even a longitudinal approach, of course, cannot protect against the misidentification of relevant variables. To date, longitudinal studies have been carried out in societies that share a Judeo-Christian orientation, that value individual achievement, and that deify the nuclear family. The degree to which these factors (or related ones) interact with differences in child rearing remains to be examined.

Vulnerability to Peer Influence

The theory of differential association (182) suggests that people acquire their behavioral orientations by learning to define experiences through the eyes of their associates. This theory and the related social learning theory

(1, 9, 130) place a premium on the idea that peer groups shape the behavior of adolescents (see also Chapter 7 in this volume).

Similarities among peer associates have been demonstrated in studies of delinquency (56, 149), drinking (52, 97), and drug use (90, 94, 158). These similarities have sometimes been used to support the peer-influence theories that predict such similarities. More direct evidence of influence comes from longitudinal studies. In one, among adolescents who had not been arrested, having delinquent friends predicted a first arrest within the following three years (176). In two others, among adolescents who had not smoked marijuana, those whose friends had done so were found likely to begin within the next six months (99) or the following year (90).

Descriptions of peer relations of youths suggest that friendships among delinquents involve closer ties as well as greater mutual influence than do friendships among nondelinquents (24, 70). Although aggressive youngsters may be unpopular with their more conventionally behaved classmates, they do seem to acquire friends who share their aggressive attitudes or deviant behaviors (33, 119).

Co-offending, or committing a crime with others, is a common phenomenon among adolescents (42, 157, 168). Much of it occurs in relatively unstable pairings or small groups (105, 157). The fact that teengers commit most of their crimes in pairs or groups does not, of course, prove that peers influence delinquency. Such an influence may be deduced, however, from the increase in crime that followed successful organization of gangs in Los Angeles (105).

Studies of gang participants suggest that, as compared with offenders who are not gang members, gang offenders tend to be younger when they begin their criminal careers, are more likely to be violent in public places, and are more likely to use guns (121). A relatively new phenomenon in urban areas is the emergence of Asian gangs. Developed originally for self-protection, these gangs now participate in robbery, drug traffic, gambling, and extortion (38).

The degree to which peers affect adolescent deviance seems to depend on other conditions. Susceptibility to peer influence is inversely related to interaction with parents (94, 97, 181). Furthermore, evidence from several studies indicates that a sizable proportion of agreement among friends results from adolescents' tendency to choose friends who are similar to themselves (43, 93). As compared with peers, parents seem to have more influence on the use of drugs among the working class than among the middle class, and among blacks more than whites (19). Parents also appear to be more influential for the initial decision whether to use any drugs than for ongoing decisions about how and when to use them (97; see also Chapter 11 in this volume).

Precursors and Progressions

Problem behaviors during adolescence typically receive attention in proportion to the apparent seriousness of the concurrent problems they create. Unfortunately, by the time some problems become serious, it is too late to effect a cure, and others that appear to be minor may signal grave difficulties in later years.

Childhood aggression and misbehavior operate as relatively efficient predictors of problems in adolescence. Yet many children outgrow their difficulties (64, 103, 126, 144, 163). Furthermore, some teenagers with severe problems seem to have been normal children. More research should be directed toward identifying childhood symptoms that signal enduring problems and recognizing the more subtle cues that might presage adolescent difficulties.

Arrests, truancy, drinking alcohol, fighting, promiscuity, dropping out of school, associating with bad friends, and taking drugs predict poor adult outcomes, including early parenthood, alcoholism, crime, drug abuse, violence, poor health, and unemployment (63, 100, 123, 160). Overall, studies show that the more serious the juvenile record, the more likely the individual is to continue having difficulties as an adult. Much more needs to be learned, however, about rehabilitating conditions.

Adult difficulties may be consequences of adolescent deviance, of social responses to adolescent deviance, or of factors such as insecurity or impulsiveness that are related to problems in both adolescence and adulthood. More research should be directed toward identifying the conditions under which adolescent problems are most likely to be overcome.

Some studies indicate that marriage to a nondeviant spouse tends to reduce deviance (6, 196). What little evidence is available suggests that selection factors account for this effect: by the time a person is ready to take on the responsibilities of marriage, deviance is already abating. If this view is correct, a key to learning about protective factors may be found by focusing on the selection of mates.

Research is also needed for understanding the dynamics of different forms of deviant behavior. Work on criminal recidivism can be a useful prototype. Criminologists have specified models to identify subgroups that have different probabilities of offending at different rates (22). A similar approach may be fruitful for understanding patterns of deviant behavior across the domains of drug use, alcoholism, and delinquency.

Intervention and Prevention

Studies consistently indicate that incarceration fails to deter crime (47, 127, 199). Yet diversion programs, which were developed in the hope of reducing crime by avoiding labeling a youth as delinquent, have been a disappointment. Not only have diversion programs failed to reduce recidivism, but they have also brought within the jurisdiction of the courts youngsters who might otherwise have been corrected by less formal sanctions (69, 106, 175).

Job programs and counseling, used as preventive techniques, have also failed to live up to their promise (76, 165). One of the better-known programs, the Cambridge-Somerville Youth Study, attempted to prevent delinquency by providing counseling and a variety of assistance over an extended period of time. Evaluation of the program, which included a matched control group and random selection for treatment, uncovered discouraging results. The treatment actually appears to have been harmful, in that those in the treatment group were more likely to become recidivist criminals, mentally ill, or alcoholics (124). Evaluations of other counseling programs have also indicated that treated cases often fare worse than untreated ones (35, 68, 195).

Some evidence suggests that success in school reduces the likelihood of drug use (29) as well as delinquency (64, 167). Yet several attempts to intervene with educational and social skills programs have been unsuccessful in terms of lessening adolescent deviance (72).

Short-term benefits from projects aimed at decreasing criminal recidivism have been obtained from several approaches. These include parent training, teacher instruction, and the use of peer groups whose behavior is conventional. One parent-training approach had brought down the rate of unacceptable behaviors in the home by the time treatment was concluded, but follow-up checks indicated that treated boys were no less likely to be arrested than were those from the control group (148). One school intervention program trained some teachers to use proactive classroom-management techniques. Students in classes where teachers actually used the techniques seemed to respond by increasing on-task behaviors. Nevertheless, the authors concluded: "Virtually no relationships were found between the use of the teaching practices . . . and student self-reports of truancy, theft from desks or lockers, or the frequency of getting in trouble at school for drugs or alcohol" (79, p. 265). The peer project involved mixing inner-city delinquents with middle-class youths. At termination of the program there was more conforming behavior among the referred boys, and the referring agencies for the inner-city boys reported improvements, but the planned follow-up a year later produced little useful data (67). One reasonable strategy would aim at developing techniques to maintain what have been short-term gains.

Working with younger children may prove more promising. A preliminary study found positive results from interventions with mothers of premature infants. These women were taught how to be responsive to their babies. Compared with randomly assigned control parents, they were more self-confident and satisfied with their parental roles and with their infants. In addition, their children showed improved cognitive development at age 4 (154). If parental affection or cognitive factors influence adolescent behavior problems, this program may have intervened successfully.

Probably the most promising plan for preventing later problems has been the Perry Preschool Program (17). This program used preschool as a time to promote self-reliance and to help educate mothers in child rearing. An evaluation carried out once the children had reached 19 to 24 years of age showed that the program had not only improved school performance but had also reduced rates of delinquency and premarital pregnancy (18). Replication of the intervention, together with assessments that include random assignments, should be a top priority, for without such replication we will not be able to identify which features of the program were relevant to its effectiveness.

Challenges for the Future

We have looked at evidence about the distribution of adolescent deviance. Enough has been learned about the problems of bias, underreporting, and voluntary participation to permit rough comparisons among groups for which descriptive parameters are known. Enough is probably known too about the questionable bases for pursuing accurate figures across different domains of participants. Other problems deserve more attention. The real challenge for the future lies in understanding adolescent behavior well enough to be able to offer effective help to those who choose to seek it.

None of the traditional theories adduced in explanation for adolescent deviance can be considered totally satisfactory. We need to learn more about the conditions under which adolescent deviance develops and wanes. Cross-cultural comparisons can be helpful in this endeavor. The influx into the United States of families from Asia, for example, could be used to test hypotheses about parental warmth and supervision. Some of these immigrants make up cohesive families in which the father and mother live apart for years. Sometimes a father or mother has come to the United States in anticipation of being followed after some considerable time by the other. These two-household families can provide information about how socially acceptable parental absence differs from the traditional forms of single-parent families. Another variant is the family in which both parents work long hours and cannot supervise their children but have high expectations for them. The variety among Asian immigrants raises a possibility for testing what we think we learn by replicating studies in different Asian cultures.

A reasonable strategy for discovering how to improve the lives of adolescents would involve using longitudinal studies of individuals in family and school settings. Such a study should include intervention projects introduced at different ages. These interventions would be designed to test theories about the development of problem behavior. They would also be pilot programs for testing techniques to aid adolescents in need of assistance. The longitudinal projects should be complimented by studies investigating the effects of cultural and community differences. Apart from information regarding the distribution of problem behaviors, little is known about how communities affect their teenagers.

The next wave of research should be not only interesting but also fruitful in helping adolescents through their difficult years.

17

ADOLESCENT HEALTH

Susan G. Millstein and Iris F. Litt

Before embarking on a discussion of adolescent health and the factors that influence it, it is useful to consider the concept of health and issues relevant to the health of adolescents or any other population. Definitions of health and the boundaries of the concept have shifted over time. The Chinese and the Greeks, for example, viewed health as a state of dynamic balance between interrelated biological, psychosocial, and environmental components. As late as the mid-nineteenth century this sociomedical paradigm was the model for medical thinking (114).

In the latter part of the century a major shift in medical models directed attention away from this broad conceptualization toward a focus on the human organism and its physical parts. The emphasis on germ theory shaped the methods and technology of modern medical science. Over time, however, the limitations of germ theory have been revealed. Realizing that germs are often a necessary but not a sufficient condition for disease, medical scientists have once again adopted a broader perspective (114).

For most lay people, including adolescents, social and behavioral factors are included in the definition of health (14). Typically, adolescents view health as being more than simply the absence of illness; being healthy includes living up to one's potential; being able to function physically, mentally, and socially; and experiencing positive emotional states (14, 31, 107, 126). In fact, "not being sick" reflects less than 30% of the content of their concepts of health (101). The health concerns of young people also reflect a wide range of nontraditional health problems, involving, for example, concerns related to social interaction and emotional needs (119, 139).

In conceptualizing health and defining its elements and boundaries, a systems perspective is useful. Within this perspective living systems of all types form a hierarchy of interdependent units. Individuals operate as parts of multiple social units such as families, communities, cultural groups, economic classes, and so on. Similarly, individuals themselves comprise a variety of systems, among them biological, cognitive, and behavioral. Health, then, can be examined from the standpoint either of one given system or of the interaction between multiple systems.

Some of the broader systems that have particular relevance to health include the biological system, the cognitive system, the behavioral system, social systems, and environmental systems. The biological system plays a prominent role in current thinking about health, and for many years was the sole element of the concept. Although it is not discussed in detail in this chapter, the biological system plays a crucial role both by itself and in concert with other living systems. The cognitive system is critical in determining how individuals attend to certain information, interpret it, and use it to make decisions about future action. The behavioral system is especially important in regard to adolescent health: mortality and morbidity during adolescence is largely behaviorally based, and many of the behavioral practices adopted in adolescence are linked to disease later in life. Social systems affect health by establishing a social climate that favors the expression of specific behaviors. Social networks may also play a role by modifying the effects of stressful events. As for the environment, two particularly salient health-related issues emerge: the effect of poverty on health and the availability and accessibility of health services for youth.

Using the systems perspective and the models that have been used with them, we now turn toward an examination of adolescent health.

Adolescent Health Status

Mortality and morbidity data[1] offer rough estimates of health in the adolescent population, although such indicators probably significantly overestimate the health of the adolescent population. Measures such as utilization of physicians' services, hospital discharge rates, and conditions cited in visits to office-based physicians emphasize short-term physical outcomes. Sources of morbidity associated with behavioral factors or with longer-term outcomes such as heart disease are often unmeasured, and thus unrecognized (57). Furthermore, these data essentially restrict us to estimating the prevalence of treated conditions; problems that go untreated may not be measured or included. In populations with high levels of unmet needs, these indicators will give an unduly optimistic picture of health status.

Despite these limitations, mortality and morbidity data highlight areas

1. Mortality data reflect causes of death. Morbidity data reflect health problems.

of adolescent health that merit concern. In contrast to mortality among children and adults, adolescent mortality primarily arises not from disease but from preventable social, environmental, and behavioral factors. Behavioral factors also rank high among causes of morbidity in adolescents.

Causes of Mortality

The mortality rate for adolescents in 1984 was 31 per 100,000 population between ages 12 and 14, 66 per 100,000 between ages 15 and 17, and 102 per 100,000 for youths aged 18 and 19 (77). Mortality rates in males are nearly twice that for females (57). A significant difference in the life expectancy of black and white adolescents exists, with black males showing the lowest life expectancy (150). Seventy-five percent of adolescent deaths can be accounted for by three causes of mortality: accidents, suicide, and homicide (110, 131, 132).

Accidents. More than half of all deaths among young people aged 10 to 19 are due to accidents, and most of these involve motor vehicles (53). This is especially true among older adolescents (77), who account for a greater proportion of motor vehicle fatalities than would be expected from their representation in the population (91). Risky driving habits such as speeding, tailgating, and driving under the influence of alcohol or other drugs may be a more significant cause of these accidents than is lack of driving experience (63). In about half of the motor vehicle fatalities involving an adolescent driver, the driver has a blood alcohol level above 0.100% (15, 16, 17, 18, 53, 105), twice the level considered "under the influence" in some states. Studies have also shown high rates of intoxication among samples of adolescents who die as pedestrians or while using recreational vehicles (38, 122).

Suicide. Suicide accounts for 6% of deaths in the 10-to-14 age group, a rate of 1.3 per 100,000 population. At ages 15 to 19 suicide accounts for 12% of deaths, or 9 per 100,000 population. Among white youth a dramatic increase in suicide occurs during later adolescence, making it the second leading cause of death. This is especially true for white males, whose rate of suicide is 14 per 100,000. In contrast, suicide ranks as the fifth leading cause of death among black adolescents between 15 and 19 years of age (21).

Adolescents who commit suicide have usually made previous attempts. Also common are histories of substance use, aggressive outbursts alternating with depression, and learning disorders. Among vulnerable youth, common stressors such as school programs or arguments with parents may be sufficient to trigger suicidal behavior (134; see also Chapter 15 in this volume).

Homicide. Homicide is the leading cause of death among black males aged 15 to 19, accounting for 33% of deaths in this group (21). In contrast, homicide among older white males accounts for less than 7% of deaths (19). Youth who live in impoverished, high-density metropolitan areas are especially likely to be victims. Homicides generally occur during arguments and in other noncriminal circumstances, and usually involve firearms. Because fighting and arguments between young males are common (140), a key factor affecting homicide is whether lethal weapons are present during altercations. National samples indicate that weapons are often at hand. Among males aged 13 to 16, 23% reported having taken a knife to school at least once during the previous year (108).

Other sources of mortality. The most frequent nontraumatic causes of mortality during adolescence are malignant neoplasms (3.5 deaths per 100,000 population) and cardiovascular disease (1.4 deaths per 100,000) (77).

Causes of Morbidity

The incidence of acute conditions among adolescents is higher than in any other age group except younger children (22). Illness and injury account for an average of nine days of restricted activity per year, five days of school absence, and four days in bed. Hospital discharges in 1984 were 64 per 1,000 (ages 12 to 17), with an average length of stay of five days (77).

Accidents. Nonfatal injuries resulting from accidents account for the largest number of hospital days among adolescents ages 12 to 17 (77, 109). Motor vehicle and recreational vehicle accidents are most frequently cited, and again usually involve the use of alcohol. Fully one-third of eighth-grade students and 44% of tenth-graders reported having ridden in a car during the previous month with a driver who was under the influence of alcohol or other drugs (108). Among young people aged 11 to 18, 7% reported having operated a car while under the influence, and twice that number reported having used bicycles or skateboards while under the influence of alcohol or other drugs (102).

Substance use. Although estimates of the prevalence of use of some substances are decreasing, rates still remain high. A 1988 study found that 92% of high school seniors had used alcohol, 47% had used marijuana, and 12% had used cocaine at least once (61). Daily cigarette smoking was reported by 18% of the sample. Usage rates for different substances vary by age and gender, with higher rates in older adolescents and, for most substances, among males (62). Research on substance use in different racial and ethnic groups has generally yielded negative or inconclusive findings (46).

Sexual activity. More than 77% of males and 62% of females have had sexual intercourse by age 19 (49). The primary health problems associated with sexual behavior in the adolescent population are sexually transmitted diseases (STD) and the social and economic consequences of pregnancy. STD rates are higher among sexually active adolescents than in any other age group; one-fourth of all sexually active adolescents are infected with an STD before graduating from high school (4, 111). Risk factors for STDs include early age of onset of sexual activity, multiple sexual partners, and failure to use barrier methods such as condoms (141). Sexually active black adolescents have significantly higher STD rates than do white adolescents, for reasons that are unknown (133, 141).

Approximately 1 million teenagers become pregnant and 480,000 give birth each year (47). Many premarital pregnancies occur within six months of the initiation of sexual intercourse. Most adolescents do not use contraception at first intercourse (153). In fact, only 29% of sexually active teenagers aged 15 to 19 use contraception consistently (152). Factors influencing nonuse include underestimates of their own fertility, negative attitudes toward contraception, and the often unplanned nature of their sexual activity (104).

Chronic illness. Two million adolescents (6%) between the ages of 10 and 18 suffer from chronic conditions that limit their ability to perform their usual activities (113). The most common causes of chronic illness are mental disorders (32%), diseases of the respiratory system, such as asthma (21%), and diseases of the musculoskeletal system (15%). Disability rates are highest among younger adolescents (10 to 14), males, and those living in poverty. Although chronic illness can interfere with physical, emotional, and social development, for many young people it does not have a negative impact on psychosocial adjustment (70).

Sexual abuse. Sexual abuse of adolescents has been recognized as a national problem. Although data on the prevalence of sexual abuse is limited and the event is probably underreported, it is estimated that 18% to 30% of the female population experience sexual abuse before the age of 18. Initial effects include negative affective responses (fear, anxiety, depression), poor social functioning (difficulties at school, running away from home), and inappropriate sexual behavior. Long-term effects include a variety of psychiatric symptoms (for example, depression and anxiety), self-destructive behaviors, substance abuse, poor self-esteem, and sexual dysfunction (11). Negative physical and psychological outcomes associated with sexual abuse vary depending on the nature of the abuse. Sexual abuse that occurs over a long period of time, involves the use of force, or is perpetrated by a trusted individual yields the most negative outcomes (11, 89).

Other sources of morbidity. Common health problems that occur more frequently among adolescents than among other age groups include acne, painful menstrual periods (dysmenorrhea), Epstein-Barr virus infection (infectious mononucleosis), and disorders of the skeletal system such as Osgood-Schlatter disease, slipped capital femoral epiphysis, and idiopathic scoliosis. Less common disorders that appear among adolescents include malignant tumors of the vagina, testicles, thyroid, and bone (84).

Mental Health

There appears to be a peak in the incidence of mental disorders during the adolescent years. Overall rates of mental disorders are the same for males and females, but frequencies within diagnostic categories do differ by gender. Most notably, females are more often diagnosed with major depressive disorders than are males. This contrasts with the situation in childhood, when males have much higher rates of many mental disorders and equal rates of depression (52).

Depression. Mood fluctuations and transient depressive feelings are common during adolescence. A national survey reported mild depressive symptoms in 34% of the females and 15% of the males studied (108). For some young people, however, depressive symptoms are part of a more serious disturbance and constitute clinical depression. The incidence of depressive disorders among adolescents remains unclear, but it appears to exceed 5% of the population and may be increasing (125). In one study 20% of the sample had experienced three or more depressive symptoms within a one-year period (140); 6% of the sample were considered to have significant depressive symptoms, 24% reported suicidal thoughts, and 4% had made actual suicide attempts. The risk of suicide among depressed adolescents is significantly increased in those who exhibit antisocial behavior, other mental disorders, or signs of substance abuse (134; see also Chapter 15 in this volume).

The hormonal and other neuroendocrine changes of puberty, along with major changes in the social environment, are thought to contribute to the increased incidence of depression during the adolescent years. For females, the timing of menarche, which often coincides with transition to middle school, may constitute an additional source of stress. The hypothesis that the endocrine changes of puberty may be associated with alterations in neuropeptide and neurotransmitter production is based largely on data from subhuman primates and has not yet been documented in humans (142). Alternative hypotheses emphasize changes in role expectations, self-image, and social systems.

Eating disorders. Approximately 0.5% of females aged 12 to 18 develop anorexia nervosa, and at least 5% to 18% are afflicted with bulimia (48). Most patients with eating disorders are female, although bulimia is distributed somewhat more equally between males and females, while anorexia is uncommon in boys. Eating disorders may be precipitated by feelings about body changes that occur during adolescence, but the general increase in these disorders over the past few decades may be related to the growing societal emphasis on thinness as the ideal body image. Both anorexia and bulimia can cause serious medical complications (117); anorexia alone is associated with a mortality rate of 10% to 15%. Obesity, which occurs in approximately 15% of adolescents, may be caused by excess number or size of fat cells (123). The most common form of adolescent obesity may result from chronic overeating in depressed, passive individuals with low self-esteem, particularly when they are under stress (95). With the exception of morbid obesity, there are no known adverse medical consequences of obesity during adolescence. The likelihood of its continuation into adulthood, however, makes it a hazard to future health. Research on psychosocial symptoms and consequences is inconclusive (69, 129). Successful strategies designed to lower body weight have combined behavioral modification with exercise and diet prescriptions (120).

Adolescents' Perceptions of Their Health Needs

Although most young people consider themselves fairly healthy, they identify a variety of health concerns reflecting both common medical problems and psychosocial issues. Although these issues differ with age, gender, race, ethnicity, and socioeconomic factors, the similarities are more striking than the differences.

Common concerns among a socioeconomically mixed sample of 1,400 adolescents included acne, obesity, menstruation, headaches, sexuality, sexually transmitted disease, substance use, "nervousness," dental problems, school problems, and family issues (139). Similar results have been reported for suburban middle-class youth (88) and for samples of white, black, and Hispanic youth (119). It is of interest, and perhaps reassuring, to note that the health issues most frequently identified by professionals are also recognized by adolescents, including drug use, sex, birth control, sexually transmitted disease, pregnancy, and menstruation. But also of interest are the diversity and range of other pressing concerns across many systems.

Mental health consistently ranks high among adolescents' health concerns (5, 88, 119, 139). In a sample of white, Hispanic, and black youths of varying socioeconomic backgrounds, 20% reported being concerned about depression, sadness, or nervousness (119). Females were twice as likely to report mental health concerns as were males, and white adolescents reported mental health issues more often (27%) than did Hispanic (22%) or black adolescents (20%). Whether these racial and ethnic differences generalize to other samples is unknown.

More generally, young people seem to have health concerns in four broad categories (146): school and career; health, appearance, and substance use; private self; and social self. Among older adolescents, issues of schooling and future career are perceived as most worrisome, while younger adolescents are most concerned about smoking and drug abuse. Females report more concerns about appearance than do males.

Adolescents' views about health and health problems do not always correspond with those of adults (79). A prime example involves differences in perceptions of dental health. Across studies, young people consistently rank dental concerns as being of great importance (119, 139), yet this topic rarely receives attention in discussions of adolescent health.

Developmental and Sociodemographic Variations

As is evident from these data on the health status of adolescents, there is considerable variation among different ages, races, ethnicities, and genders. Reporting data for adolescents as a group—a common practice—obscures significant dissimilarities in health status within the age group. Marked racial and ethnic differences emerge across a variety of health status measures, including life expectancy, morbidity rates, and functional disability. In general, these measures point to poorer health among black and Hispanic adolescents than among whites.

Age variations exist in both the rates and the causes of mortality during adolescence. Between early (ages 10 to 14) and late (ages 15–19) adolescence, mortality rates more than triple as causes of mortality change, with a shift toward more violent causes of death. Among whites a dramatic increase in suicide occurs; for older black adolescents homicide becomes the most likely cause of death.

Male adolescents die at a rate more than twice that of their female peers (57), primarily as a result of their involvement in motor vehicle accidents. Females show higher rates of morbidity on indicators such as utilization of physicians' services and hospitalization, primarily as a function of reproductive health care needs.

The Cognitive System and Adolescent Health

Many of the threats to adolescent health are the direct or indirect result of volitional behaviors. Such behaviors often are viewed within the framework of cognitive decision-making theories. Cognitive aspects of adolescent health also are salient because of changes in cognitive capacities that emerge during adolescence (see Chapter 3 in this volume). Decision making becomes increasingly important as the social environment grants the adolescent expanding autonomy over many domains, including health. In concert with emotional states, cognitive processes allow the individual to filter available health information and interpret this information through existing conceptual schemes, such as common-sense models of health and illness (78, 82).

Health and Illness Concepts

Concepts of health and illness seem to develop according to a fairly predictable course that is consistent with Piaget's theory of cognitive development (7, 13, 30). Young children view health and illness in relatively simplistic terms, describing vague feelings and relying on the judgment of others to determine when they are ill. They cannot distinguish the symptoms of illness from its causes, and they may not be able to define the concept of health except vis à vis illness. As children get older, they can conceive of multiple causes of illness, although they may still demonstrate reliance on external validation. Their attributions of causal factors usually focus on contagion from single causes.

By early adolescence young people still may not recognize the possibility of multiple and coexisting causes of illness. Relatively concrete thinking about illness predominates, usually in relation to specific diseases and disorders (14, 98). Concepts of health show a similar lack of abstraction. By late adolescence some youths exhibit formal operational thinking. They can conceptualize both health and illness in hypothetical and abstract terms. They are now more likely to describe illness and health in terms of psychological, affective, and social components, and to consider personal behavior as salient to health (31, 101, 107, 126).

Processing of Health Information

Cognitive processes also influence health-related outcomes as they affect the interpretation and processing of health-related information. Research has identified cognitive biases that affect the interpretation of information (67, 144, 148), but few studies have focused on the adolescent population or on other factors such as cultural context that may influence interpretation. Since providing information constitutes a large part of health education practices, the lack of research on the topic is unfortunate.

Age variations in concepts of health and illness suggest that young adolescents and older teenagers may interpret the same health information quite differently. Individuals may also process information differently as a function of its source. Although young people report receiving health information from various sources such as the mass media, friends, family, schools, and health care providers (104), they report relying most on parents and physicians (80). Cultural factors are also likely sources of influence, and the variations may be more extensive than those caused simply by language differences (116). It is important to discover how the meaning of a recommendation such as "know your partner" differs as a function of the cultural group to which it is addressed. Similarly, a recommendation to "seek professional help" may suggest a variety of health and allied professionals, depending on the cultural context in which it is delivered.

Interpreting Symptoms

Studies of symptom reporting have shown that most people experience symptoms fairly often but seek care for only a fraction of them. Two processes that are significant in determining whether an individual will seek medical attention in the presence of symptomatology are the recognition of altered bodily states and the interpretation of those states.

Attentional processes. Medical professionals have viewed the ability of adolescents to recognize alterations in bodily states in somewhat paradoxical ways. On the one hand, young people are thought to minimize deviations from what is normal through the process of denial. Clinical observations have suggested that denial may be most likely to accompany emotionally charged symptoms such as those relating to sexual activity or drug use. Still, no data supports the contention that adolescents are any different from adults in this regard. On the other hand, youth also have been viewed as exaggerating and dwelling on symptoms. Adolescence is characterized by increasing self-consciousness and heightened self-awareness, which may extend to bodily symptomatology. Young people who score relatively high on measures of introspection have been found to report more symptoms and higher levels of use of the health care system (93, 94). Again, however, this phenomenon may also exist among adults (42).

Appraisal process. After an event is recognized as being unusual, individuals must appraise its significance. Those that occur frequently or are familiar are often judged harmless and may not be labeled as symptoms. The appraisal process may thus change as a function of differences in the perceived frequency of specific symptoms in certain populations (75, 155). Although adolescents report a relatively high frequency of symptomatology, as many as one-third report that they never visit a doctor because they are never sick (139).

Cultural differences in the appraisal of bodily states have been well described (155). A series of studies has shown marked differences in the perception and tolerance of pain and responses to medication among adults of different ethnic backgrounds (75, 94, 151, 155). Similar studies have not been conducted on adolescents.

Both adolescents and adults appear to be susceptible to bias in interpreting the cause of symptoms (90). In a study of young people with chest pain, a majority of the sample thought they were experiencing a heart attack or heart disease despite never having known someone their age who had had such an illness (118). This finding may reflect the tendency to overestimate the prevalence of illnesses that occur frequently in the general population.

The study of attributional biases has been carried out almost exclusively among adults. Thus it is not clear whether these biases have a developmental component.

Beliefs about Health

Beliefs about vulnerability. A widely held conception about young people is that they perceive themselves as invulnerable to harm, and that this is a direct result of their level of cognitive development. Despite frequent references to this "adolescent" invulnerability and its developmental basis in both professional and popular literature, no empirical work supports the assumption (96). Adolescents, like adults, evidence significant optimistic bias when asked to estimate their personal vulnerability to harm (68). Informal comparisons of the degree of optimistic bias in studies of adolescents and adults suggest that differences between these groups are not large. Furthermore, perceived vulnerability seems to be a relatively stable personality trait (41). Clinical observations of youth that imply differences in the awareness of susceptibility have not been followed by careful examination of the observed differences and their source. This remains a critical gap in research on adolescent development, because expectations of perceived invulnerability not only influence the development of intervention models but also have significant implications for informed consent definitions in this population.

Although some research shows no differences in perceived vulnerability as a function of race and ethnicity (41), other studies do report cultural variations. Black youth may perceive themselves to be less susceptible to cancer (124) but more susceptible to pregnancy than do whites (29).

Results are equivocal on how perceptions of vulnerability affect behavior. Although some research shows feelings of vulnerability to be associated with increased health-protective behavior (29, 58), exactly the opposite results have also been reported (149).

Beliefs about behavior. Adolescents generally recognize as potential health hazards behaviors such as substance abuse and sexual activity, as well as more general threats such as air pollution and nuclear war (12, 99). They also identify health threats in areas that fall outside constrictive definitions of health, including family and peer relations and school problems (88, 119, 139). Differences emerge when they are asked about general threats to youth as opposed to personal behaviors that place them at risk. Like adults, adolescents probably underestimate the potentially negative consequences of their behavior. Adolescents also anticipate, sometimes incorrectly, that the risks associated with certain behaviors will diminish with increased age (99).

Behaviors that young people identify as protective of health include exercise, adequate sleep, cleanliness, tooth brushing, proper nutrition, and keeping emergency numbers by the telephone (100).

Health knowledge. The best evidence available suggests that knowledge is a necessary but insufficient condition for influencing health-related behaviors. Thus, the provision of information about health is an important element of health education, but it cannot be considered sufficient by itself. Adolescents who correctly identify condoms as a means of protection against sexually transmitted disease, for example, do not necessarily understand why this is the case, or how the condom must be used. Health education must teach young people the skills they need to translate their decisions into behavior, and provide opportunities to practice those behaviors.

The young are generally poorly informed about health issues and demonstrate significant misperceptions (20, 104). Knowledge levels vary as a function of age and race; younger adolescents possess less factual knowledge about a variety of health topics than older ones (104). Examination of racial and ethnic differences has been infrequent but does suggest that blacks are less knowledgeable than their white peers in relation to knowledge about AIDS, contraception, and cancer (26, 104, 124). These studies have not, however, disentangled the effects of race from those of social class.

Adolescent Health Behaviors

A wide range of behaviors is included under the rubric of health behavior. In the absence of specific illness, certain behaviors may be undertaken to maintain health, avoid disease, or increase one's sense of well-being. These behaviors may be motivated by an interest in preventing illness (dressing properly for the weather, undergoing screening examinations) or in enhancing health (improving functional status through exercise). In the presence of symptomatology or illness, adolescents may engage in behaviors directed toward the restoration of health. These include adopting the sick role (staying home from school), seeking professional or nonprofessional help or advice, following medical recommendations, or undertaking other behaviors that are perceived as health restoring.

Other kinds of behaviors usually included in discussions of adolescent health are those such as substance use and behavior leading to accidents, which account for most of the morbidity and mortality. These behaviors should perhaps be described as health related because engaging in them can adversely affect health but need not do so immediately. An important conceptual distinction separates the avoidance of behaviors that may be deleterious to health and the adoption of behaviors that may enhance it. Factors that predict preventive behaviors differ from those that predict sick-role behaviors (58). Similarly, models that predict one type of behavior may not be appropriate for predicting other types. Although there is reason to speculate that individuals who engage in health-promoting behaviors are less likely to engage in others that are health damaging (27), the evidence to date shows conflicting results (73).

Models of Health Behavior

Just as a range of behaviors fits under the umbrella of health actions, so too has a range of theoretical models been invoked to describe these behaviors. But few models of health behavior have been tested in adolescent populations or have addressed the potential for developmental variation in their applicability. Even fewer have been applied across different racial and ethnic groups.

One widely tested formal model of health behavior that has been used on adolescent populations is the health belief model (3). The model posits that people will be motivated to undertake action to avoid disease when they believe that, first, they are personally susceptible to the disease; second, the disease would have a negative impact on their life; third, specific preventive measures exist that could reduce susceptibility; and fourth, the benefits of taking preventive action outweigh potential costs. The model has been used to explore adolescent compliance, cigarette smoking, and sexual behavior, with mixed results.

A number of more general social and behavioral models have also been applied to explore health actions. The theory of reasoned action is a cognitively based model similar to the health belief model, but it emphasizes the role of social norms in decision making (34). It also differs from the health belief model in its focus on behavioral intention, rather than behavior, as the dependent variable of interest, since the individual's intentions are viewed as the best predictor of actual behavior.

The application of developmental theory to models of health behavior has emerged mainly in attempts to understand health beliefs and health-compromising behaviors. Piaget's theory of cognitive development has been used to explain the development of adolescents' concepts of health and illness (7, 121). Similarly, health-compromising behaviors during adolescence have been considered developmentally based, emerging as a result of young people's normal developmental needs for autonomy, experimentation, and limit testing (2, 136). A different application of developmental considerations can be seen in stress-reactance models, which posit that adolescents, who are subject to rapid development and change, experience increased stress and engage in risky behaviors as a means of coping with stressors in their lives (43). Variations of this model focus on the specific stress of pubertal change: these include models that argue for direct effects of puberty on behavior (71, 72) or for biological effects mediated by cognitive or sociocultural factors (56, 64, 65, 106).

Other models posit that, regardless of the source of stress, the emergence of health-compromising behavior as a coping mechanism is a reflection of inadequate coping. They consider the emergence of risky behavior a result of maladaptive forms of coping that have their origins in early childhood (128) and that are reflected in such individual characteristics as degree of self-esteem, need for social approval, locus of control, and level of anxiety.

Finally, models that point to the importance of the social environment have also been applied to understanding adolescent health behaviors. These include models that focus on the role of social systems in maintaining and enhancing health, on the role of social norms and expectations, and on social learning theories of behavior (1, 31).

Preventive Health Behavior

Preventive behaviors refer to behaviors undertaken in the absence of illness in order to enhance or maintain wellness. It is the perception that is critical, and not whether the behavior is demonstrably effective at promoting health. Models that attempt to explain preventive health behavior in terms of individuals' belief systems should similarly emphasize the importance of perception and beliefs, whether or not a rational basis for the belief exists. Only then are health behavior models likely to be generalizable to a range of social and cultural settings.

Little research has specifically examined preventive health behaviors among adolescents. One study that examined the use of tampons in relation to information about toxic shock syndrome found that adolescents and adults exhibited similar preventive actions: both showed an identical 21% decrease in tampon use following media coverage of the disease (55). Although young women differed in their initial rates of tampon use as a function of race and ethnicity, behavior change, reflected by decreases in tampon use, was uniform across racial and ethnic groups.

Empirical evidence supporting the health benefits of specific behaviors is not always available. A case in point is exercise as a health-promoting behavior. The health benefits of regular physical activity have been demonstrated primarily for adults. Yet many people firmly believe that regular exercise during adolescence establishes a pattern that lasts into adulthood, promotes generalizable health-protective behaviors, inhibits health-compromising behaviors, and leads to improved health status. Available data are still inconclusive on these points (10). Mechanic's longitudinal study reported no relationship between levels of exercise during childhood and levels in early adulthood (94). Adolescents who engage in sports as a form of exercise are less likely on the whole to smoke cigarettes but may be more likely to use smokeless tobacco (66). For some female athletes, involvement in strenuous physical activity may be detrimental to health, as is evidenced by sports amenorrhea and nutritional deficiencies (83, 127).

Utilization of Health Services

Although adolescents experience a greater number of acute conditions than do adults (22), their utilization of private physician services is lower than for any other age group (25). Given their level of need, adolescents also underutilize other health care systems (97). Differences in utilization patterns as a function of sociodemographic factors point to pockets of underserved adolescents, with more unmet needs among younger adolescents, minority group members, and those living in poverty (131, 132). Research on this aspect of health care systems has not been extensive but has called attention to a number of barriers that are believed to affect the use adolescents make of health care. Among the chief barriers are cost, poor organization and availability of health services,[2] and problems concerning confidentiality of care. Utilization rates may also reflect the nature of the care adolescents receive. Few providers get specialized training in serving this age group. Many health-care providers report feeling unprepared to provide services such as contraceptive counseling, evaluation of psychopathology, general counseling, and treatment of dysmenorrhea (23, 54). Providers may convey to adolescent patients their discomfort in discussing topics such as sexuality, which may result in adolescents' unwillingness to raise sensitive issues that concern them. Because young people are frequently considered difficult to work with, practitioners may not want to devote the time needed to establish good rapport with them. These factors are important, because the interpersonal relationship between patient and provider is a major influence on patients' satisfaction and compliance with health care recommendations (51).

Adherence to Recommendations

The widely held notion that adolescents are less compliant with recommended therapy than are patients of other ages had not been supported by available data (85). As with adults, approximately half of all adolescent patients fail to follow medical advice. The factors associated with noncompliance may differ, however, from those affecting adults, because of the unique psychosocial characteristics of this developmental period (39).

Compared to adults, adolescents may have more difficulty accepting treatments that have adverse effects on physical appearance. Studies of young people with cancer and those who have undergone transplants have documented nonadherence to steroid medication, even among those well informed about their illness and the consequences of failing to adhere to the treatment (76, 138). The effects of steroids, including weight gain and distorted features, overrode the risk of any hypothetical outcome, including death. Adolescents who are insecure in their self-image may have the greatest difficulty adhering to regimens that highlight differences between them and their peers (86, 87, 112).

---

2. A more complete discussion of financial barriers to health care and the organization of health services can be found later in this chapter in the section on the organization of health services for adolescents.

The cognitive development of younger adolescents may influence their ability to conceptualize theoretical consequences of their behavior and hence to follow instructions. Coping strategies for dealing with stress often include denial and intellectualization, both of which have been shown to be associated with nonadherence to diabetes treatment (154).

Adherence is enhanced in the presence of good provider-patient interactions (51). The adolescent's perception that the provider cares appears to be a particularly powerful predictor of satisfaction (137). Peers can also be influential in promoting adherence, as is evidenced by the positive effects of peer counseling on compliance with the use of contraceptives (59).

Health and the Social System

Social relationships influence health through their role in setting cultural norms about health, by providing emotional support, and by encouraging healthy or unhealthy behaviors. The expanding radius of social relationships during adolescence suggests the possibility of a wide range of socially mediated health effects. Teenagers themselves recognize the importance of these issues in relation to health, and they rank family and peer relationships high on their list of health concerns (88, 119, 139).

Cultural and Ethnic Variations

A critical aspect of the social environment that has received little attention in the literature on adolescent health and development is that of race and ethnicity. Racial and ethnic variations emerge across a variety of health and health-related indicators such as physical health status, responses to illness, health cognitions, and health behaviors. These studies, however, are few in number and suggest no overall pattern. The differences that have been identified probably are mediated by the cultural and environmental settings in which they emerge, although little research has examined such issues directly. Specific elements of the environment that are correlated, including race, ethnicity, and economic status, are rarely disentangled.

Social Support Networks

Social supports have long been viewed as playing an important role in health. Research has consistently indicated that people with fewer social ties than the average have higher age-adjusted death rates as well as higher rates of mental and physical illness (50). Social supports also enhance recovery from illness, reduce surgical complications, and promote adherence to therapeutic regimens (44, 147). Although the specific mechanisms that link social relationships to health are not well understood, social support is thought to exert positive effects by facilitating healthy behaviors and/or effective coping mechanisms.

The relationship between social supports and health status in adolescents has been less extensively studied, but there is little reason to believe it is any less instrumental (45). During adolescence major reconfigurations of familial and extrafamilial relationships take place, which may argue for the importance of social supports during this potentially stressful period.

Research is also needed on the avenues of social support available to adolescents. Little information exists as to whom the young view as supportive or what constitutes effective support for adolescents in general. It seems likely that there are cultural differences in the meaning of support, but this question needs study.

Role of the Family and Peers

The erosion of family support networks for many young people has focused attention on the role of the family in adolescent development. Families are crucial to the provision of support. Although growth during adolescence requires that youths reformulate their family relationships, these reformulations do not lessen the need for parental support. Healthy development requires that the individual develop a sense of autonomy, which is best accomplished within a supportive family context (see Chapter 6 in this volume).

In addition to providing social support, parents and siblings are key models for children. The strongest research data for the role of parental modeling in adolescent health behaviors emerge in the relationship between parental smoking and adolescent smoking. Parental and other familial influences are strongest during the early years of childhood, weakening as children broaden their social circle and are exposed to more general social attitudes and messages (135).

Peers represent an important source of positive support but may function as negative influences if they promote unhealthy behaviors. Numerous studies have documented an association between unhealthy behaviors in adolescents and their friends, although the association may not be causal. It is possible, for example, that youths specifically choose peers who support behaviors in which they have already decided to engage.

Although peers may not be the primary source of motivation for engaging in or abstaining from specific behaviors, they do function as an influence. Adolescents who have a limited capacity to refuse dares, for example, may be more likely than others to engage in risk-taking behavior (6). Studies have also highlighted the functions that substance use serves, such as in initiating and maintaining peer relationships and activities (24, 60).

Intervening in Adolescent Health Behaviors

The range of models used to explain adolescents' health-related behaviors are associated with a similarly wide array of intervention approaches. A perspective on the evolution of prevention models emerges from consideration of those used to prevent cigarette smoking and to encourage contraceptive use.

Prevention of Cigarette Smoking

Early attempts to intervene in this area focused on presenting information about the dangers of cigarette smoking. That is, adolescents were viewed as uninformed, requiring only the facts in order to make healthy decisions. Informational and fear-based approaches continue to play a role in contemporary health education, despite evidence of their limitations. Although carefully presented informational interventions can be effective in changing adolescents' knowledge and attitudes, they fail to influence changes beyond the cognitive level to actual behavior (143). Interventions that have been shown to be successful in affecting adolescent smoking recognize that multiple factors influence the choice whether or not to smoke. These interventions typically are comprehensive in nature, incorporating elements that reflect a wide range of theoretical perspectives. Interventions using a social-influence model deem both the attitudes and behavior of family members and peers and the general social norms portrayed through the mass media to be key influences on adolescents' behavior. Recognizing the role of social factors in the initiation of smoking led to interventions that focused on increasing adolescents' awareness of these social influences and teaching them specific skills for resisting the messages (33, 92). As these models have evolved, they have become more comprehensive, including elements of behavioral learning techniques (role playing, practice, and reinforcement) and the use of peer educators to further utilize the social-influences paradigm (35). In contrast, the "Just Say No" campaign popular during the 1980s, although sensitive to the effects of social influences on substance use, has failed to include other critical components such as specific practice in refusal skills. Providing the concrete skills for countering peer pressure requires systematic instruction and role playing over a period of time.

Another comprehensive approach that has enjoyed considerable success in preventing adolescent smoking is based on the premise that problem behaviors are related to a set of similar causal factors that mainly reflect a lack of competence in personal and social functioning (8). The covariation among health-compromising behaviors during adolescence is viewed as evidence of a common causal factor (27) and an argument for interventions that target these postulated underlying determinants (see Chapter 16 in this volume).[3] These "life skills" and "social skills" interventions are intended to improve adolescents' decision-making skills, social skills, and coping skills. Central elements of these programs include training in problem solving, self-control, stress reduction, self-esteem enhancement, and general interpersonal skills.

Although preventing the individual from initiating smoking almost certainly is the optimal way to deter the practice, efforts to intervene with adolescents who already have experimented with smoking also are important. Leventhal and Cleary posit that becoming a smoker is a long and complex process and therefore requires different forms of intervention at different stages and for different types of smokers (81). Using a cognitive-developmental framework, they describe four stages of smoking behavior: preparation, initiation, becoming a smoker, and maintenance. These stages interact with three types of motivational "sets" for engaging in smoking: social compliance, which is perhaps closest to the social-influences model; regulation of emotions or mood; and self-definition (40). Initial results of interventions based on the model have been promising.

Prevention of Adolescent Pregnancy

Efforts to decrease the rate of adolescent pregnancy have included both primary prevention (delaying the onset of sexual activity) and secondary prevention (increasing effective contraceptive use). Delaying the onset of sexual activity not only decreases the absolute number of adolescents who engage in sexual activity but also indirectly affects pregnancy rates, because those who delay the onset of sexual activity usually become more effective users of contraceptives.

Prevention of adolescent pregnancy typically lags behind techniques and strategies developed for substance use, with the exception of the skills-based approach of Schinke (130). Although most schools provide some form of sex education, few interventions have incorporated psychological principles in their development (37). Most programs have focused

---

3. The presence of covariation across a range of health-damaging behaviors may or may not reflect a set of underlying causal factors. Furthermore, it is not clear whether targeting these underlying factors rather than specific behaviors is a more effective approach for altering behavior.

on increasing access to contraception and on providing knowledge about sexuality and contraception, at least partly in response to evidence of widespread misinformation among adolescents in relation to contraceptive use (104). Unfortunately there is little reason to believe that correcting this misinformation will by itself affect behaviors.

In part, this lag in prevention practice related to contraception has been due to a lack of knowledge about adolescents' sexual practices, basic motivational issues related to sexuality, and the meaning of sexuality during adolescence (9). Research has been hampered by societal ambivalence about sexuality in general and adolescent sexuality in particular. Although concern about AIDS has led to some loosening of restrictions on informational content, little progress has been made in bringing skills-based approaches to sexuality interventions (115).

The Future of Intervention

Research on preventive interventions during adolescence has highlighted a number of issues for further consideration. There is a need for theory-based interventions, especially in the areas of sexual behavior (36). Specifically, interventions that integrate theories of development, social influences, and behavior change are most likely to influence subsequent behavior.

Interventions must be developed and evaluated for their effectiveness in different groups of adolescents, including low-income minority youth. This is especially important when the probability of negative outcomes is distributed differentially across groups. The probability of contracting AIDS, for example, is far greater for economically disadvantaged youth living in inner cities than it is for middle-class suburban youth. Interventions tailored for these vulnerable populations that can change behavior are desperately needed.

Finally, evaluation of interventions must move beyond mere examination of knowledge and attitudinal change to incorporate assessment of actual behavioral outcomes over time (115). A substantial body of research has demonstrated repeatedly the limitations of examining these variables alone, and there is little justification for continuing to fund studies that do not include analysis of behavioral outcomes. Exceptions would be reasonable in cases where knowledge and attitudes are good predictors of behavior.

Environmental Contributions to Adolescent Health

The environment has long been recognized as a significant influence on health status. Early sanitation drives highlighted the role of the environment in causing disease, and environmental issues continue to be in the forefront, as is evidenced by public interest in toxic environmental effects. Environmental issues of particular salience to adolescent health include the availability and accessibility of health services for youth and the effects of poverty on health.

Organization of Health Services

The current health care system, like many social service systems, is primarily categorical in nature: health services are fragmented into many different specialties and subspecialties. Determining the proper point of entry into the health care system for adolescents poses particular difficulties, because their problems may not be reflected in the presenting complaint, and multiple problems often exist simultaneously. Even when a proper point of entry is clear, young people left to negotiate the health system on their own often fail to do so.

The cost of health services constitutes a major barrier for many adolescents. Among young people aged 10 to 18, 14% have no health insurance, with cost being the major reason for lack of coverage (113). Among ethnic minorities and youth living in poverty the situation is far worse. Even low-cost clinics are beyond the means of many.

Insurance coverage itself does not guarantee access; adolescents who are covered by family health insurance may be reluctant to use it if they are concerned about their parents' learning of their health care visit (88). Adolescents are not always aware that, depending on law and local practices, they can receive confidential care from health providers. Even where the law allows adolescents to consent to their own care and guarantees confidentiality, however, access is dependent on a source of payment (32). Furthermore, many services are offered at times when adolescents are in school and thus require a note from parents explaining their absence.

Legal consent issues may affect accessibility as well. Many states will allow adolescents to consent to treatment in cases of emergency or "sensitive" services in cases such as pregnancy, sexually transmitted disease, and substance use (32). But not all adolescent health needs fall into these categories. Furthermore, some of these services, because of their sensitive nature, may be perceived as inaccessible by virtue of the stigma attached to them (96).

Alternate Models of Health Care Delivery

A consideration of the complex nature of adolescent health problems and the barriers adolescents face in obtaining health care has led to the development of a number of alternative models of health care delivery for youth. These include models of comprehensive health care based in communities or in schools.

Early models of comprehensive community-based adolescent health care such as the Haight-Ashbury Free Clinic were developed to offer free, one-stop confidential health services for the many homeless and alienated young people of the 1960s (28, 74). Subsequent developments included the addition of adolescent health services to existing community-based clinics and the consolidation of services for high-risk youth within communities.

Recent years have also witnessed a revival of a historic trend in child health services, that of school-based health care. Whereas early models focused mainly on providing limited services through school nurses, current school-based clinics offer far more comprehensive care. More than 125 school-based adolescent health clinics have been established in the United States, primarily in poor communities with high levels of unmet health needs. The services range from traditional health care to ancillary services such as vocational counseling, employment training, parenting education, and school dropout prevention. Although some evaluations report promising results, data remain limited. The strongest results show high levels of utilization and a relatively low cost for school-based health services (97); the paucity of rigorous evaluation studies, however, constitutes a significant barrier to the funding and expansion of these programs.

Models of comprehensive care, wherever they are based, share an emphasis on providing services to adolescents that cover the range of health problems they experience. They also aim to satisfy other criteria that are considered important in the provision of adolescent health care, for example, accessibility, assurance of confidentiality, and reduction of costs. Although these attributes apply to community-based and school-based comprehensive health programs, they may also characterize other health care delivery systems, such as hospital-based adolescent clinics or health maintenance organizations. No comparative studies have been conducted under different conditions and for different subsets of the adolescent population, so the question cannot yet be answered as to which approaches provide the most effective provision of health care to young people.

Poverty and Health

A major environmental factor that will affect the health of adolescents during the current decade and beyond is poverty. The sociodemographic composition of this group is undergoing dramatic change. The future adolescent population will include increasing numbers of poorly educated, non–English-speaking youths living in impoverished metropolitan areas.

A higher proportion will belong to racial and ethnic minorities, and many will have been raised in poverty by a single parent. By the year 2000 an estimated 20 million children will be living in poverty—an increase of about 37% since 1985. Of these children one-third will be adolescents, with the highest rates among blacks and subgroups of Hispanics. Fewer than 10% of all adolescents will have been raised in the kind of household that was once considered the norm, with a working father, a housewife mother, and two or more school-age children (103).

The well-documented association between poverty and health status suggests that these youths are likely to have high rates of unmet medical needs, poorer health in general, and more chronic limitations on levels of activity. Services available to serve adolescents may be cut back even further if the absolute size of the adolescent population declines as expected.

Changes in the causes of morbidity and mortality may also occur. The concentration of adolescents in large metropolitan areas is likely to result in increasing rates of violence against and among youth. Suicide rates, which are associated with poverty, may also increase. The greater incidence of poverty may also generate higher rates of alcoholism, other forms of substance use, premature sexuality, sexually transmitted disease, and unplanned pregnancy.

Future Directions

An overarching need exists to improve the adequacy of national statistics on the health status of youth. Data relevant to the health care needs of young people often are not collected on adolescents less than 15 years of age. When such data are collected, surveys are inconsistent in terms of how adolescence is defined; younger adolescents often are combined with children and older adolescents with young adults. A national monitoring system on the health behaviors of youth, including controversial behaviors such as sexual practices, is needed if we are to evaluate the effects of health policies.

Research Needs

Despite the frequency among youth of behaviors that can have immediate and lifelong adverse consequences, relatively little work has been done to improve our understanding of the natural history of such behaviors and their meaning to the adolescent or to delineate the specific needs fulfilled by different types of behaviors, as well as alternative means of meeting those needs. To better understand the meaning of risk from the adolescent's perspective, we need studies that use qualitative approaches. It will also be necessary to identify factors affecting adolescents' perceptions of their vulnerability to harm. Research on covariation among high-risk behaviors should move beyond exploring simple relationships and examine trends within population subgroups.

The types of protective environments that foster optimal psychosocial development should be studied, with attention to successful adaptation and coping with adversity. A better understanding of adolescents who are able to overcome difficult life circumstances could have important implications for intervention, especially given the expected increases in the number of young people who will be raised in poverty.

In terms of health and illness, few investigators have examined adolescents' beliefs about health-promoting behaviors, conceptual schemata used in interpreting body sensation and symptomatology, decision-making in relation to health, or beliefs about the health care system. Behavioral research on the health practices of youth, their treatment-seeking behavior, and their sick-role behavior is also warranted. In addition, little is known about the development of health behaviors or about how individual, family, and cultural norms and beliefs influence these behaviors. Studies on the effect of social policies on health-related beliefs and behavior would also be illuminating. Research is also needed to delineate the effects of chronic and acute illness on family functioning and specific family members. Too little is known about the secondary effects of chronic illness on cognitive function, school performance, and social interaction.

Research on health care delivery systems that focuses on the adolescent age group is almost nonexistent. There is an urgent need for comparative studies of different methods of organizing, financing, and delivering health care services for adolescents, and on the effects of different approaches on utilization and health status.

The role of the family is another important research topic, particularly in view of the changing nature of the American family. Areas of special relevance for adolescent health include family violence and neglect, family mediators of health behavior and outcomes, and the impact on health of changes in family structure.

Design, Implementation, and Evaluation of Interventions

Given the health problems of adolescents, intervention needs emerge most clearly in the areas of mental health, adoption of high-risk behaviors, health service utilization, and adherence to medical recommendations. There is a clear need for the continuing development of theory-based interventions that incorporate principles of learning, behavior, and development, and evaluations of the impact of these interventions on health status.

A number of promising behavioral intervention models have been developed to reduce the rate of behaviors such as smoking in adolescents. Such models require further implementation and testing across a variety of problem areas and within different population subgroups. Bringing these interventions to some groups such as the disenfranchised, or developing them for problems such as mental health, will require outreach efforts, including the development of methods to identify at-risk adolescents without stigmatization. A critical examination of current health education in the schools and other youth settings would also be useful for identifying gaps between what is known about effective health-promotion strategies and what is actually taking place in schools and communities.

Behavioral scientists with an understanding of how systems operate can play a leading role in facilitating the transition of programs from conception to organizational settings. This calls for individuals who understand the culture of the environment in which they hope to implement programs. Case studies of projects that have overcome obstacles and been successfully implemented would be useful. The need for careful evaluation of programs cannot be overstated. Problems at both a practical and a methodological level that are typically uncovered in evaluation will require creative solutions.

18

YOUTH IN RELATION TO
SOCIAL INSTITUTIONS

Judith Torney-Purta

Social issues and political institutions are not high on the interest agenda of adolescents. The current research agenda of social scientists in the United States also gives low priority to young people's beliefs about what they can expect from society or the contributions they might make to the polity or the community. In the 1960s and early 1970s a large volume of research on adolescent political socialization was published, stimulated partly by a wish to understand the sources of student political activism. Relatively little research has appeared since. Some believe this is because there has been no attention-getting political crisis involving the student generation. Others have been disappointed that earlier research failed to show continuity between adolescent and adult political beliefs. Still others note that questions about political and social issues are considered too controversial by school administrators, whose cooperation is required for most studies.

Whatever the reason, the collection of empirical data about adolescents' political attitudes has declined and been replaced by debates about the way schools can shape students' values. Concern with these values has emerged recently in response to the low rate of voting by young people aged 18 to 20 (2) and to uneasiness about self-centered values among the current generation (8).

Two types of research on adolescent sociopolitical development will be reviewed in this chapter. *Political socialization* research has focused on the way young people develop a regard for their national government, its leaders, and the rule of law. It also investigates how they learn about political and economic institutions, and about their own roles as citizens in exercising critical judgment about leaders and policies. Much of this research, organized around "agents of socialization," has been preoccupied with such questions as whether families or schools are more influential. Political socialization research has been conducted primarily by political scientists, sociologists, and social studies educators, who rely on surveys of knowledge and attitudes.

Moral development research has focused on young people's ability to recognize and reason about moral dilemmas and to make choices based on moral principles and reasoning. This research has been conducted primarily by psychologists using interviews about moral dilemmas, with a large proportion of research in the United States based on Kohlberg's stage theory of moral reasoning.

The two areas are seldom considered together, in part because of the different disciplinary orientations. Furthermore, political socialization research has focused on attitudes related to national institutions and on actions such as voting and writing letters to officials, which are at least one step removed from face-to-face interaction. In contrast, moral development research has taken a more individualistic approach, focusing on direct interaction with peers and on local institutions such as the school.

Recently this contrast has become less pronounced. Some political socialization research has demonstrated the importance of local issues to adolescents (73); differences have been noted between the political attitudes and actions of individuals growing up in different kinds of communities (45, 47); and the importance of face-to-face negotiation of political roles in schools has increasingly been recognized (59). At the same time, moral development research has moved beyond a focus on age and cognitive stage to acknowledge the importance of collective norms in schools (69). The mature individual, both politically and morally, is being viewed as someone able to balance self-interest with support for institutions such as the school, the local community, and the national government. Research on political socialization considered together with research on moral development as it relates to institutions reflects a growing trend.[1]

The review of political socialization and moral development research presented in this chapter focuses primarily on the ways adolescents think about these issues and not on their attitudes. Some researchers, noting a declining interest in research on political socialization, have commented that future research should attend to political cognitions, since "individuals must know what something is before they can say how they feel about it" (26, p. 1081).

Two terms borrowed from cognitive psychology that will be used exten-

---

1. Handbooks on adolescence frequently include either a chapter on moral development (67) or separate chapters on political socialization (34) and on values (31).

sively throughout the chapter need to be defined at the outset. *Domain-specific* research is that which studies the knowledge and kind of thinking individuals engage in when considering a specific area such as society or politics. When more general cognitive abilities developed in logical or scientific thinking are used to explain one's understanding of society and politics, this is *domain-general* research.

A logical way to introduce a cognitive approach to political socialization and moral development is to discuss the role of discrete elements of knowledge as the building blocks of political and societal awareness. The first section of the chapter will therefore address the question: What is the research evidence concerning elements of knowledge about social and political institutions? The second section will deal with research that considers the influence of general cognitive abilities or stages on political awareness. This section, on domain-general research, will address the question: What evidence is there that general stages of cognitive development can be applied to understanding adolescents' political and social knowledge and behavior? The third section will deal with research on thinking specific to the domain of political or social institutions. It will answer the question: Do teenagers develop ways of thinking specific to understanding social, political, or moral behavior? A fourth section will link knowledge and experience to political attitudes and will answer the question: What do we know about adolescents' political attachments or alienation and their political participation or behavior?

The contexts and influences represented by family, school, mass media, and peers (often called the agents of socialization) will be considered in each section.

Discrete Cognitive Elements

The most basic way of viewing the outcomes of political socialization is as discrete elements of knowledge about politics and society. This section will attempt to discover what "facts" adolescents know about social and political institutions. This research has generally focused on bits of information assessed by multiple-choice tests.

Research on Knowledge Elements

In 1971 a cross-national study of knowledge elements, the IEA Civic Education Survey, was conducted by an international consortium of educational research institutes. Multiple-choice tests of factual knowledge about political institutions were administered to stratified national samples in Western European countries and the United States. The 14-year-old students in the United States answered 24.7 out of 47 items correctly, ranking fourth out of eight industrialized countries (79).

Studies in the United States have had similar results. In a 1987 multiple-choice test weighted with twentieth-century history, a national sample of 17-year-olds attained an average score of 54.6%, with African-American and Hispanic students scoring lower than white students (70). Similarly, in a 1974 study of one thousand Pennsylvania high school seniors the average score was about 50% on a fifteen-item current events test. It was found, however, that 100% of the students could mention a current political issue, the most common being Watergate, inflation, and the energy crisis (73).

In summary, adolescents lack many of those elements of knowledge that educators consider important. The mean scores of 40% to 60% may be a somewhat low estimate of existing knowledge, however, since many items are included in these tests because they are "good discriminators" (that is, they are selected for the test because about half the students on which the tests were developed could answer them correctly).

Influences on Knowledge Elements

There is substantial agreement concerning the factors that influence the acquisition of these discrete bits of information. Students from classrooms where teachers encourage discussion of controversial issues and promote students' expression of their own opinions, even if the students disagree with the view of the teacher, perform at a higher level on these tests of discrete knowledge (79, 84). High-scoring students come from more highly educated families, an influence probably mediated through the availability of reading material in the home and through family discussions. The absence of such discussions of American politics in Mexican-American homes may contribute to these students' lower political awareness (52). Males score higher than females (80, 81, 84).

Reading the newspaper and watching television news are also significant predictors of the amount of political information adolescents possess, as judged by multiple-choice tests (22, 35, 81). How well teenagers think they understand television news has been a significant predictor of knowledge and is a factor deserving further research (9, 10).

Domain-General Cognitive Abilities

In this section I shall address the question: What evidence is there that the general stages of cognitive development apply to adolescents' concepts and behaviors relating to political and social institutions? Three theories have been used by researchers to study this issue: Piaget's theory delineating stages in logical and mathematical thinking, Kohlberg's theory of stages for judging hypothetical moral dilemmas, and Selman's theory of interpersonal negotiations.

Research Relating to Piaget's Theory

A number of studies have attempted to find stages in political thinking that parallel the stages described by Piaget in logical and mathematical thought. Evidence that the concrete and formal operational stages in thinking also operate in the specific domain of politics usually consists of surface similarities between responses to political issues and responses to Piagetian logical or mathematical tasks (60). For example, a modest relationship has been found between political or socioeconomic awareness and performance on tests of Piagetian formal operational reasoning (46, 58).

In general, studies have failed to present convincing evidence of strong connections between reasoning about scientific phenomena and reasoning about political issues. Indeed, psychologists currently question whether there are general stages of inferential abilities that characterize reasoning across different subjects because people seem to use different kinds of reasoning for different kinds of tasks (36).

Research Relating to Kohlberg's Theory

Kohlberg's theory of moral development, which was built on the moral development theory of Piaget, describes six stages in the development of moral judgment. These stages are used in ways that imply that the individual who responds to a moral issue at a given level should also respond to other social or political issues at the same level (71). It is primarily a domain-general theory.

Here we focus on how Kohlberg's theory deals with the relationship of the adolescent to society. For example, in stage 3 adolescents reason about moral decisions in terms of conformity to society's conventions. In contrast, at stage 4 moral choice involves considering the impact of personal action on the social system. The limitation of this theory for understanding political and societal thinking is that most research has used hypothetical moral dilemmas framed at the personal level. Some research, however, has inquired into images of rules, laws, and legal institutions (77).

Among the issues raised by psychologists such as Gilligan are whether Kohlberg's theory applies to males but not females (38), and whether moral dilemmas with a real-life basis are judged differently from hypothetical dilemmas. One study on those issues investigated triads of parents and their children in grades one to ten, using both hypothetical and real-life dilemmas (87). Impersonal conflicts, involving institutions or persons they did not know well, were mentioned by slightly more than a third of the respondents when they were asked to recall "a recent situation of moral conflict where you had to make a decision about what was right." The moral judgments given in response to real-life dilemmas were less advanced than responses to hypothetical dilemmas. These researchers failed to confirm Gilligan's prediction that women would give responses based on a caring conception of morality while men would use a "rights" orientation based on a justice conception of morality. Rather, they found that individuals of both sexes tended to solve impersonal dilemmas using a rights orientation and personal dilemmas using a caring orientation.

Kohlberg's theory does not give clear guidance to policy or practice because of the breadth of the domains that it attempts to cover. Turiel is somewhat more specific because he distinguishes the moral domain from the social-conventional domain. Moral transgressions are those acts that would be wrong even if there were no law against them, such as threats of physical or psychological harm (86). Social-conventional transgressions are those that depend on social organizations or institutions for their definition, such as calling adults by their first name or leaving one's assigned seat in school. Different aspects of the individual's social experience contribute to the construction of ideas about these two domains. Turiel suggests that early adolescents negate conventions by seeing them as arbitrary and "nothing but" someone's expectation, while older teenagers see conventions as useful for the orderly and smooth functioning of society. Although this theory grew out of Kohlberg's domain-general stage theory, it moves closer to a domain-specific approach for understanding adolescents' social concepts and behavior.

Research Relating to Selman's Theory

Although there has been extensive research on how young people react in face-to-face encounters, there have been few attempts to apply ideas about interpersonal interactions gained from this research to understanding political interactions. Selman's work suggests that there are four stages of skills in interpersonal negotiation, ranging from dealing with an incident impulsively (for example, fighting), to a one-way negotiation (giving in), to a reciprocal negotiation (asking for reasons from the person with whom one disagrees), to mutual or collaborative negotiations (working out the problem in terms of mutual needs) (17, 72).

In responding to hypothetical situations of interpersonal conflict, youths aged 14 to 16 were much more likely to use reciprocal strategies than were younger adolescents aged 11 to 13. There has been some success in teaching teenagers more advanced negotiation strategies by asking them to consider the societal perspective (30). Observations of social and political organization conducted in high schools by educational anthropologists often highlight negotiation strategies (27, 59). Selman's theory of the development of interpersonal negotiation deserves further attention in understanding how young people relate to rules and to political situations in which negotiation occurs in real-life settings.

Influences on Domain-General Thinking

Those who have conducted domain-general research have not devoted much attention to the influences of families or schools. Some have speculated that not until adolescents reach Piaget's formal operational level will they benefit from discussions of politics in the classroom. In practical terms, if one waited until the majority of class members were at the formal operational level, no citizenship education would take place in some schools. Furthermore, not only are young adolescents interested in discussions of politics, but such discussions may actually stimulate both general cognitive development and political thinking (75). Finally, students operating at concrete cognitive levels can still incorporate information from observational learning, direct teaching, and discussion (15).

The most substantial attempts to understand the influence of stages of moral development on political reasoning have come through research on moral education. Programs based on Kohlberg's theory are organized as follows: their major goal is to encourage higher levels of principled moral reasoning; their method is the stimulation of cognitive conflict through discussion of hypothetical moral dilemmas; the educator or teacher is a Socratic facilitator who asks questions and challenges statements rather than presenting answers (55). The most frequently used technique is the "plus-one" discussion, in which arguments one stage above the individual's current level of functioning are presented in peer-led or teacher-led groups. When used with junior high or high school students over periods of several weeks, the "plus-one" treatment results in advances in moral reasoning. Some psychologists argue, however, that these represent changes in students' ability to express a reasonable answer rather than development in underlying moral competence (29). Discussion of moral dilemmas is sometimes difficult to integrate into social studies classes because schools specify that certain historical or geographical content be covered (43). And school administrators often express concern that these discussions about morality do not promote specific values or behavior. Some moral education programs in Britain and Canada have adopted a more directive focus, specifying value content while still using discussions in which perspectives conflict (76, 80).

Kohlberg's group has helped a number of schools to restructure themselves as "just-community schools," in which the appeal of the collective is balanced with the rights of individual students and the promotion of their moral growth (69). These micropolitical environments involve high levels of student responsibility for setting and accepting rules in areas such as drug use and respect for property. They also provide firsthand experience with alternative perspectives and with conflict between the individual's desires, the group's wishes, and the power structure of the outside world. Teachers serve as group leaders, encouraging students to see others' perspectives and raising issues of fairness and morality in school meetings. A study of three of these alternative high schools with ethnographic as well as structured methods found that moral maturity appeared to be stimulated in the just-community school. The increases, however, were about the same as those produced by moral discussions in the classroom and were not as substantial as expected, given that the whole school environment had been restructured. Strong collective norms were the most powerful aspect of the school's moral culture.

Others have studied adolescents' experiences in activities that have been promoted as building moral character, such as work and team sports. In fact it has been found that substantial proportions of teenage employees give away goods or services (usually to their friends) or take things from the workplace. High levels of materialistic values and cynicism about commitment to employment are associated with these behaviors (40). Furthermore, adolescents who participated in team sports were compared in terms of their moral judgments to others who were not team members. Given a hypothetical sports dilemma, such as whether to accept a coach's suggestion to injure an opposing player, athletes were more likely to use lower-level reasoning here than for solving other dilemmas (16). By contrast, there was no difference in responses to the sports and nonsports dilemmas by nonathletes.

In summary, research on Piaget's general cognitive stages has been of limited assistance in understanding adolescents' relations to society and polity. Research on Kohlberg's theory of moral development and on Sel-

man's theory has explored interesting avenues but is still somewhat difficult to apply.

Thinking Specific to the Political Domain

Although few researchers have explicitly investigated the nature of adolescents' thinking in the domain of politics, such an approach helps to clarify
the process by which individuals relate to the polity, the society, and the
community.

Research Relating to Domain-Specific Thinking

According to Connell, thinking about the physical world through direct
contact with objects is different from thinking about the specific domain
of politics, with which the young person has only indirect contact (24).
He found that young Australian children have idiosyncratic and partial
images of the political world, and that they "twist, chop, and fricassee
political material with a sublime disregard for . . . political fact" (p. 233).
At about the age of 10 most of those he interviewed were beginning to
notice political alternatives, although at first relatively isolated from one
another; they also realized that opposing policy positions exist. Some
adolescents possessed a schema of the political order in which multiple
relationships among political actors were possible. For a small group of
older students there was also an ideological stage involving abstract
thought about political arguments (24). Connell's work illustrates domain-specific political thinking.

Clear examples of the domain-specific nature of preadolescents' thinking are also found in a study of young people's understanding of economic
concepts (14). Italian children and youth did not demonstrate a generalized level of reasoning about economics. Young children could give an
organized account of the distribution of goods in shops, but only preadolescents could do the same for the production process in a factory. The
concept of work and production, which includes bosses and workers, was
not connected to the concept of buying and selling, which includes consumers and shopkeepers, until at least age 11. For preadolescents, concepts
such as government and state were "assimilated to a very general idea of
someone who commands or provides for other people" (p. 184). Adolescents understood these as public institutions related to collective services.
The young person's ability to distinguish actors in the economic system
(owner from boss, seller from producer) as well as the ability to see

connections between different aspects of economic and political activity showed the development of more complex thinking in this domain.

Political and economic thinking has been studied by asking individuals to think aloud while solving a hypothetical problem. A graphic model representing an individual's underlying image of the political system is then constructed from these responses. For example, gifted students aged 13 to 17 were asked to imagine that they were the finance minister of a developing country unable to pay interest on its debt (83). A graphic model of concepts represented by their responses included three types of elements: *actors* in the political or economic system (such as banks holding the loans), *actions* in which these actors could engage (for example, rescheduling the loan), and *constraints* on these actions (such as the bank's unwillingness to lose profits). In addition to conveying individual differences in the complexity of economic and political concepts, these interviews and associated graphic models showed how students restructure their concepts of the political and economic system as a result of their participation in an educational program, in this case an international simulation (82).

The work of Adelson and his colleagues can also be interpreted as domain-specific political cognition (3, 4). Students were presented with hypothetical problems confronting a group marooned on a Pacific island. There were substantial contrasts between the responses of young people aged 11 to 13 and those of 15-year-olds. The older respondents spoke from a coherent view of the political order and referred to a sense of community and the social contract (3, 33). In other words, the older students possessed a more complex understanding of the political system, one that involved seeing the points of view of others as both individuals and community members. They could envision an expanded network of potential social actors, including institutions as well as persons. Older students were also able to trace the long-range consequences of actions, seeing future as well as present constraints.

Weinreich-Haste presented two contrasting models (88, 89). In her domain-general model, logical operations (such as those described by Piaget) would lead to social perspective taking (as described by Selman), which would lead to moral reasoning (as described by Kohlberg), which would in turn lead to political reasoning. Research on the contrasting domain-specific model showed that British adolescents were able to apply logical reasoning abilities and social perspective-taking abilities in the social domain, the moral domain, or the political domain. In responding to Adelson's Pacific island dilemma and one of Kohlberg's moral dilemmas, the younger adolescents saw individuals as both sources of and solutions for problems. At higher levels of social-political reasoning, interpersonal issues involving the community as a collective entity were discussed. Older teenagers also recognized ways in which the social order might produce, rather than merely solve, economic and political inequality.

Weinreich-Haste, and to some extent those who do research on Kohlberg's theory, are moving away from viewing moral reasoning as prior to social or political reasoning, and toward seeing two domains that are distinct but related. This trend, together with the opportunity to interpret research using graphic concept maps, is promising for understanding adolescents' relationship to institutions.

Influences on Domain-Specific Thinking

There are only scattered findings on the influence of contexts and socialization agents on domain-specific cognitions. For example, whereas African-American and white students in the United States differ minimally in levels of conceptualization of the political system (34), youth in England, West Germany, and the United States differ more substantially, perhaps because of different schooling experiences (33). Families in which the young person is encouraged to talk about moral and political issues and consider alternative positions also influence the political thinking of youth (24, 89).

Experiences in the classroom, especially those in which conflicting perspectives are discussed, also influence economic and political reasoning. Some beliefs appear resistant to instruction, however. For example, a study of Italian youth found that one barrier to understanding banks' profits was the persistent norm for reciprocity between individuals, which made it seem unfair for a bank to charge for loans (14).

In summary, the most comprehensive research on political thinking has either been conducted outside the United States or is more than twenty years old. Although many of the difficulties British, Italian, and Australian young people demonstrated in forming complex and connected concepts of politics and economics would probably apply to American youth today, comparable research on political thinking is needed across a wide range of adolescents in the United States.

Political Thinking, Attitudes, and Participation

This chapter has been organized around modes of thinking in political socialization in order to redress the balance of previous reviews of political socialization that have focused on broadly defined attitudes. This section will answer the question: What are the findings of research that links political concepts to political attitudes and participation?

There is considerable evidence from both ethnographic accounts and surveys that many American young people are politically alienated, in the sense that politics is of little salience to them and that, at least since Watergate, they express relatively low levels of trust in the political system (11, 12, 53, 63, 74). Political scientists who study both conventional types of political participation (voting, writing letters to elected officials) and more unconventional participation (taking part in boycotts, demonstrations, or violent political activity) have documented relatively low levels of involvement among adolescents and young adults. This section will review some of the research that connects these attitudes and behaviors with reasoning.

Research Linking Political Concepts to Attitudes

Some studies of socialization have considered cognition, attitudes, and participation. High school seniors interviewed in 1974 felt "proud of America most of the time but ashamed sometimes" (73, p. 75). Their understanding of democracy was assessed by asking them how they would explain the American government to someone from a country without a democratic system. Most students repeated slogans regarding individuals' freedom to do as they pleased without government interference, or rule by the people rather than by an authoritarian leader. It appeared that some teenagers' conceptions of democracy were projections of their own desire to do as they wished without interference from authority. The rare student could name two features of democracy and relate them to each other. Students who had a more sophisticated image of democracy were also found more likely to apply democratic principles to everyday problems.

In addition, adolescents were presented with three hypothetical situations dealing with a local factory polluting the air, a state official revoking drivers' licenses for those under 21, and a proposed national policy drastically restricting citizens' freedom to be critical of the government (73). Most made suggestions for appropriate political action. Demonstrations and other unconventional political activities had a prominent place in the repertoire of political actions in the late 1970s, in contrast to responses of adolescents collected in the 1950s. It was the unusual respondent, however, who actually reported engaging on a regular basis in participation that required much effort. Only about a third of these adolescents were at all active in politics; the remainder ranged from being apathetic (about 30%) to attending to politics and participating only if an issue was of direct personal concern. Working-class youth were especially likely to be passive.

American adolescents share many ideas about political influence with their peers in other industrialized countries. A cross-national survey of perceived power structures conducted in 1971 found that 14-year-olds in eight countries believed union leaders and rich people to be almost as influential as elected officials (79). Newspaper editors and radio or television commentators were rated ninth or tenth out of ten institutional leaders in their influence on laws and policy. Variation between nations was greatest in the rating given the "average person," who was seen as moderately influential in the United States but lacking in influence in West Germany. Most 14-year-olds had a clear image of only one or two institutions (for example, the police).

Adolescents aged 17 to 19 in the cross-national study were more likely than those in other age ranges to recognize differences of opinion among groups in society, to participate in political discussion, to realize the power of the mass media, and to acknowledge that institutions sometimes oppress individuals. Boys were more aware of political conflict than girls, and were also more likely to participate in political discussions. Students in the United States reported relatively frequent participation in political discussion in school; but they tended not to initiate such conversations outside the classroom with peers or parents, an activity much more commonly reported in West Germany and Finland. On a general measure of feelings of trust in the national government, students in the United States (as well as those in Israel) scored very high, in contrast to more negative attitudes among students from West Germany and Finland.

Attitudes among Minority Youth

Research on minority youth presents an opportunity to examine the effects of perceptions of the opportunity to hold economic or political power, sometimes called the *opportunity structure*. In a study assessing political knowledge and attitudes, one thousand Chicano adolescents from three cities were asked what they knew about specific political ideologies—capitalism or liberal democracy, Chicano nationalism (separatism), communism, and socialism—and whether they felt positively or negatively toward each one (47).

Substantial differences among cities were noted, in contrast to earlier findings of similar patterns in eight U.S. cities (42). In San Antonio students were best able to describe capitalism or liberal democracy, apparently because of a required course in the public schools on the free-enterprise system, but they had little knowledge of Chicano nationalism (47). In contrast, in Los Angeles and Albuquerque many were most familiar with Chicano nationalism, usually as a result of contacts with speakers or literature outside the school or from discussions with parents, and many students were positive toward this ideology. In these two cities capitalism or liberal democracy tended to be associated with Anglos. Those from the middle socioeconomic class and longtime residents from the lower socioeconomic class tended to be negative about liberal democratic and capitalistic idealogy (see also 5). Only two groups in Los Angeles viewed capitalism or liberal democracy positively—those of high socioeconomic status (SES) and those of low SES who were recent immigrants and still saw economic and political opportunities for themselves.

Many minority youth viewed conventional political activity as ineffective. In San Antonio, a city with a relatively conservative political atmosphere, voting was seen by middle-class Hispanic students as the major way to influence policy. By contrast, middle-class students in Los Angeles and Albuquerque considered protests against poor schools, economic boycotts, and even riots to be effective approaches, although these upwardly mobile young people were not themselves likely to participate in the more violent or illegal activities. Lower-class students in all three cities not only supported unconventional political participation in principle but also engaged in both legal and illegal activity as a way to communicate the urgent need for change to those in power. The youths who were most positive about Chicano nationalism tended to be most supportive of all forms of political protest, even extending, in a few cases, to violence.

There are many similarities between Hispanic and African-American students in their views of government and associated institutions. For example, African-American adolescents in St. Louis perceived pervasive racial discrimination and showed substantially higher levels of political distrust than white adolescents (57; see also 18 and 56). African-American youth, especially those of low SES and those doing poorly in school, were willing to support confrontational tactics to bring about political change.

Jennings and Niemi examined changes in attitudes of African-American adolescents as they became young adults (49). In 1965, at the beginning of a longitudinal study, nonwhite high school students expressed little pride in the civil rights record of the United States. On other items, however, their pride in the government equaled that of their white peers. At a later point in the longitudinal study, in 1973, a much more cynical attitude characterized African-American young adults, who were then far more willing than whites to support changes in the American form of government to solve the country's problems (50).

By 1973 about 14% of the whites and 30% of the nonwhites had participated in some sort of political demonstration. Responses in the 1965 interviews on items such as perception of the good citizen as active or trust in the government did not differentiate between those who would later be protestors or nonprotestors, although there were differences between racial groups on these questions in 1973 (50). The young protestors' view of the government had become associated with cynicism, while their view of the citizen had become associated with political activity—both unconventional activities such as demonstrations and conventional ones such as writing letters to the editor.

What accounts for these racial differences in feelings of political efficacy (perceived responsiveness of the government to citizens) and political trust? In a review of thirty-eight studies of African-Americans, Abramson found little support for the view that teachers or school curricula fail to stress political participation for African-Americans (1). Similarly, there was only moderate evidence that poor economic circumstances and the resulting social deprivation contributed to low self-confidence, and blaming of political authorities, since racial differences in political efficacy and trust tended to persist even when socioeconomic status was controlled.

Abramson concluded that there was good empirical support for the view that racial differences in political socialization resulted from the realities of the political environment and the structure of political opportunity with which African-Americans live. African-Americans citizens actually had less power than whites to influence national political leaders, and political leaders behaved in untrustworthy ways with respect to their interests. African-American adolescents either learned this from their own experience or were told it by adults. The support for this explanation included data showing that feelings of political effectiveness and trust were lower among African-Americans who understood political realities as measured by knowledge tests (2). Furthermore, the information learned in high school civics courses, as well as participation in political discussions, tended to make minority students cynical.

This interpretation, related to the actual opportunities that African-Americans have to influence politics, fits with Ogbu's general explanation of how members of "castelike groups," such as African-Americans and some Hispanics in the United States, become aware of ceilings placed on their occupational, political, and educational achievement and respond with peer-group-enforced cultural identities that devalue or oppose achievement (66). Just as attempts to achieve in school may be defined as "trying to act white," conventional political behavior may also be defined as inappropriate. Rather than developing an "oppositional identity," immigrant minority groups, such as Sikhs in California, have been found to develop a collective social identity that accepts the need for obtaining school credentials; they do not perceive ceilings on occupational achievement or political power (37). The studies reviewed in this section corroborate Ianni's conclusion from a study of ten American communities that lack of access to opportunity was an important factor leading to pessimistic future orientations among urban minority youth (45). Coles arrived at similar conclusions as a result of interviews with minority youth (23).

Influences on Political Thinking, Attitudes, and Participation

Research on how the family shapes adolescents' views has not provided clear-cut answers. Parents and their teenage children usually have similar party affiliations and attitudes toward partisan political issues (13, 49), a similarity that appears to be greater in white than in African-American families (21, 50). The recognition that individuals shape their own political concepts and attitudes based on their experiences has led researchers away from looking for direct transmission between parents and children. Furthermore, much of the research has had methodological shortcomings, in that it relies on young people's reports of parents' attitudes and fails to consider issues such as differing family power relationships experienced by adolescents of different ages.

The movement of young people since the 1970s toward more self-centered values is partially attributed to family influence. Alwin studied family values over a fifty-year period in a midwestern community. In the 1970s parents wanted their children to be autonomous and independent, whereas in the 1920s parents had stressed obedience to adult and institutional authority (loyalty to the church and patriotism) (6). Jennings, interpreting data collected from individuals in 1965, 1973, and 1982, pointed to effects of the particular historical period in which individuals came of age politically (48).

The mass media also influence political knowledge and participation. Although most adolescents are not regular readers of newspapers or regular watchers of news or public affairs television, those with this type of media exposure generally have a more complex view of the world. Connell noted, however, that television transmits more detailed information about national events than about local events, in which the adolescent might become more directly involved (24). A study of the influence of entertainment television found that frequent viewing of crime shows by young people in grades six through twelve led to an image of a mean world in which people cannot be trusted (20). Such an image of social reality was associated with opposition to civil liberties for accused persons.

The impact of social studies courses on adolescents' political and social understanding has also been investigated (7). Students who had the most complex images of democracy (73) or the most complete international knowledge (81) were found to have taken more social studies courses than other students. Other research has been concerned with identifying which aspects of social studies classes are most effective. In light of current beliefs that students actively construct meaning, attention has focused on the role of classroom discussion.

Two studies conducted in the social psychology laboratory and the classroom illustrate the complexity of classroom discussion. The nature of exchanges depends in part on the gender of the participants. For example, in discussions of nuclear disarmament, partners in female pairs supported and extended each other's comments, while male pairs critiqued or challenged each other's ideas. Male-female pairs combined these two types of interchanges (54).

Classroom lessons in which higher-order thinking skills were observed in students (thoughtful classes) have been contrasted with lessons in which such skills were rare (64). Thoughtful classes were dominated by the use of Socratic questioning coupled with the careful consideration of reasons and explanations for events on the part of teachers. A number of studies, which have used surveys, interviews, simulated peer discussions, and educational programs, confirm the value of discussion and dialogue (14, 28, 32, 79, 82).

With respect to political participation, the formal curriculum concentrates on conventional modes (voting, letter writing), although since the middle 1970s students have begun to consider a wider range of political activities. Some studies show that female adolescents tend to be less positive toward unconventional and conflict-related types of political participation than males (73, 79).

Other aspects of school may also be instrumental in the development of political knowledge and attitudes. Consider, for example, the high school rule structure. On the basis of a longitudinal study, schools with an implicit or expectation-oriented social contract were distinguished from those with an explicit or rule-oriented social contract. The schools with an implicit social contract were more successful in getting students to become committed to socially integrative roles (44). Furthermore, it has been proposed that smaller high schools foster a greater sense of community and may thus promote greater integration of students into responsible roles (63).

The peer group can be of special significance as an influence on political participation. For example, among African-Americans in Chicago in the 1960s there was strong peer group influence on participation in race-conscious activities in both school and neighborhood (68). A researcher who returned in 1979 to a high school in Pennsylvania that had been studied in 1970 found that the salience of political topics in peer group and classroom discussion as well as participation in unconventional political activity had declined (85). This decline was attributed to the end of the Vietnam War and the emergence of a more politically conservative climate. In fact, recent research shows that political issues other than marijuana laws and racial attitudes are seldom discussed in informal peer get-togethers (19, 78).

The local community is increasingly recognized as a context for young people's learning about politics and society. Community service by youth, either required for high school graduation or designated as the major avenue to college financial support, has been proposed by national political leaders as well as by social scientists and educators. Youth programs, whose major purpose is providing jobs or job training to unemployed youth, appear to have less long-term value than programs that emphasize civic content and enhance social bonding to the community and its institutions (61). One study of CETA volunteers has demonstrated the unexpected positive influence of this job training program on political attitudes and participation (62).

Ianni proposes that each community devise a youth charter to make explicit the expectations and commitments of both adults and young people to mutual well-being (45). He recommends expanding mentor relationships in the form of networks in which adults and youth work together on real community problems rather than in authority-based relationships. This is of special importance in urban minority communities, where powerlessness and lack of opportunity dampen youth investment in society. The Grant Foundation's proposals for expanded youth service opportunities are similar (39).

Although these initiatives are promising, there is little research to document either young people's motivation to participate in them or the ways in which the programs may be organized for the most effective impact on adolescents' civic values. An effective community service program can have four types of impact: on personal psychological development, by providing a transition from dependence to independence; on intellectual development, by enhancing one's ability to use information in everyday problem solving; on social development, by increasing the sense of empathy and bonding to social institutions; and on social obligation, by increasing the individual's willingness to contribute to, and not merely take from, society (65). Only a few studies assess these diverse effects (25, 41).

Future Directions

This chapter has conceptualized political socialization as a process by which young people acquire knowledge concerning social and political institutions and develop an increasingly complex understanding of these institutions. It is clear, however, that many adolescents approach young adulthood with only rudimentary knowledge and with concepts that are relatively poorly developed. They do not make connections, for example, between the actions of government and those of citizens or between different parts of the political and economic systems. Furthermore, many adolescents habitually reason about everyday moral issues at relatively low levels and find it difficult to see connections between ethical principles and their own lives or political issues involving the common good. In addition, many cannot focus easily on concepts outside their personal experience or perceive reciprocity and mutual interest. When faced with a crisis or an issue that threatens their own well-being, some will respond with political activity. But a generalized sense of alienation often accompanied by cynicism exists in substantial proportions of adolescents, especially among African-American and Hispanic youth. A small proportion believe that only confrontation can serve to awaken public officials to serious problems. Reviews of research suggest that in some cases these adolescents are responding to political reality and a limited opportunity structure.

This is not a new situation, but it is one that should be of concern to policy makers. Yet there has been a decade-long gap in political socialization research. Although educators are currently showing renewed interest in civic and values education, coordinated research describing adolescents in the United States today is lacking. Because of the considerable importance of the political context (who the president is, the major issues on the public agenda), research more than fifteen years old should probably be replicated before being used as the basis of policy. And generalizing from research conducted in other political or economic systems to the United States ignores the influence of the sociohistorical context. Although the proportion of adolescents who are African-American and Hispanic is increasing, minority youth have not been extensively studied. Also, in spite of the influx of immigrant youth, there is almost no published work on the political knowledge, attitudes, or participation of these groups.

The movement toward more concern for political reasoning and for collective norms in studies of moral development and moral education is promising. But there are a number of problems to be solved before that research can advance our understanding of adolescents' relations to social and political institutions.

Many existing studies fail to bridge the wide gap between elementary or middle school students and secondary school youth. Samples frequently include students in fourth to eighth grades, or tenth to twelfth grades, without attending to the transitions between early and late adolescence.

More longitudinal studies, even if short term, would help clarify developmental, educational, and social influences as well as the role of the political and socioeconomic context. Although gender differences in knowledge about and interest in politics have been reported, we have little understanding of these differences—why they are so persistent or what impact they have on the lives of young people once they become adults. It is possible that the same perceptions of a limited opportunity structure that dampen minority-group political activity also have a negative influence on the participation of females.

Our current understanding of the influence of various agents of socialization is little advanced from that of a decade ago. The mass media are influential, but little is known about how young people relate what they see, hear, or read to their existing knowledge. What motivates some to listen to the news and to discuss it with their friends and families while others are not interested? Intriguing hypotheses exist as to how family context and values influence the child to feel an obligation to participate in society in a socially responsible fashion. It has been suggested that family discussion of politics fosters knowledge of political institutions and political action, although relevant studies have not been conducted with sophisticated methodologies. A similar statement could be made about studies of peer group influence. Although social policy in the United States cannot directly shape either the mass media or the actions of parents and peers, enlightened policy can have an impact on community organizations, especially those that are involved in coordinating programs for youth serving as volunteers.

Research that can be related to educational policy, by contrast, can have a relatively direct effect. There is considerable evidence that current classroom experience, especially in grades six to twelve, neither advances adolescents' social and political knowledge nor raises the students' interest in national politics or community participation. Much of the knowledge is taught and tested as unrelated pieces of information, and not surprisingly it is remembered relatively poorly and in a disconnected fashion.

One finding of political socialization research has been consistently replicated despite varying methodologies. Students' active involvement in grappling with controversial issues or dilemmas in which they must construct and defend their own positions while remaining aware of the views of others has a positive effect on political awareness and moral development.

The implications of the research reviewed here are not limited to formal schooling. Those responsible for policy making in social service agencies or youth organizations are often in a better position than educators to deal with problems of political and moral alienation in adolescents, to provide opportunities to discuss social and political problems, and to develop closer ties between school and community institutions. Youth service to the community appears to be an idea whose time has come, and it should be coordinated with a solid program of research.

Research within the domain-specific cognitive framework described in this chapter has a great potential for enhancing our understanding of the links between political socialization and moral development. Further attempts should be made to connect cognition to attitudes or behavior, linking knowledge and understanding to participation in the polity and the community.

Qualitative and ethnographic research has been helpful in identifying the underlying values or "hidden curriculum" in formal and informal educational settings. Among the best existing research on adolescents' relations to political and social institutions is that which has combined written questionnaires with interviews. The expanded use of observational methods in political socialization would be an important next step. Furthermore, some of the promising methods developed to study cognition, family processes, and peer relations could be grafted onto research on young people's relations to, and understanding of, social and political institutions.

The burst of interest in research on moral development in the early 1960s was stimulated in part by concern over atrocities committed in the Second World War and the enthusiasm with which many German and Japanese young people supported the war. The burst of interest in research on political socialization in the early 1970s was stimulated in part by a desire to understand the roots of student protest. One can only hope that researchers will be able to anticipate rather than react to the next crisis of politics and morality among adolescents.

19

PROGRESS AND PROMISE OF RESEARCH ON ADOLESCENCE

S. Shirley Feldman and Glen R. Elliott

Society has many reasons to treasure adolescents as a national resource, not the least of which is their inherent promise as the next generation of adults. The preceding chapters document both the intricacies of normal adolescent development and the advances being made in understanding those complexities. The current explosion of interest in the topic among researchers promises to provide the much-needed scientific underpinnings for those who wish to optimize the adolescent experience.

In this chapter we undertake the rather formidable task of pulling together the significant themes and broader issues that emerged from this project. Of necessity we focus here on broad topics of general concern; reviews of other issues relevant to adolescent development are provided in earlier chapters. We first emphasize some of the new and important findings that have arisen out of recent research. Next we consider three key areas that cut across the entire spectrum of adolescent research for which greater attention seems especially urgent and promising. Finally we draw attention to several other strategies and notable topics that merit further study.

New Insights

The contributors to this volume have emphasized research that helps to clarify the adolescent experience in the United States today. The picture that emerges from such a summary suggests a need to reassess popular conceptions. Teenagers today confront demands and expectations, as well as risks and temptations, that seem more numerous and more complex than any facing youth only a generation ago. Yet, despite marked changes in personal and societal conditions, the majority of children still seem to traverse successfully through adolescence into adulthood. Moreover, both the most significant sources of risk and the resources available to the average adolescent are becoming more apparent.

Substantive causes for concern are easily identified. Influences that offer stability in the lives of the young appear to be evaporating. High rates of divorce, increased numbers of unwed mothers, and continuing geographic mobility have diminished the number of adolescents who grow up in a fixed nuclear and extended family. Other societal changes also are disconcerting. As a result of increased social acceptance and widespread media coverage, young people face a bewildering array of life-style options. Many must deal with the temptations and pressures of such weighty matters as drug, alcohol, and tobacco use or sexual activity at a distressingly early age. A number of them choose behaviors that create risks for their immediate and long-term welfare. Even the physical environments of school and community are demonstrably less safe than they once were. Such alarming trends have helped stimulate the current encouraging interest in adolescence.

Against the manifest reasons for concern, there is reassuring evidence that many adolescents continue to fare well. Most become adults who function competently within our society. In fact, by some measures the majority of teenagers are better off now than they were only ten or twenty years ago. For example, adolescents today are much less likely to die of infectious illnesses. After climbing for several years, accident and homicide rates now have decreased somewhat, as have rates of drug use, juvenile delinquency, and teenage pregnancy among black females. Also, more adolescents finish high school than ever before, especially minority youth. Furthermore, young people have far more expendable income. For many who deal regularly with adolescents, however, such encouraging statistics provide added urgency to concerns about teenagers who are in or headed for trouble.

These observations underscore an important reality: adolescents are not a single, homogeneous entity. Rather, regional, ethnic, cultural, gender, socioeconomic, age, and life-style differences profoundly influence the actual life trajectory of each individual. Quite different pictures can emerge depending on which adolescents are considered. A challenge for researchers, then, is to determine which characteristics are most salient for particular developmental processes.

Social Attitudes

Public attitudes about adolescence arise from a blend of personal experience and media portrayals; neither source offers the objectivity needed to understand how normal development is evolving in this country. Many individuals measure the behaviors of today's teenagers against the often distorted memories of their own youth. Depending on the selectiveness of those memories, adolescents today may seem more rebellious, less respectful, and more prone to getting into trouble; or they may seem more assertive and adventurous, headed for a bright future. The mass media often focus on the sensational, so young people who are in trouble or who oppose social conventions are much more likely to be considered newsworthy than are those who function well within the mainstream. Recurrent exposure to such coverage may create the impression that substantial majorities of youth are engaged in deviant behaviors. Actually, a relatively small number account for much of the total incidence of socially unacceptable behavior.

Researchers have made gratifying strides toward clarifying what adolescence is. At another level, however, that work has underscored the widely different views of various elements of society about what this stage of life should and should not be. Some cherish and promote the perceived freedom of the young to be daring and innovative; others look to adolescents to fulfill their own unmet goals. At times, expectations about the young are based on adult idealizations that may be unrealistic, at least as reflected in typical adult behaviors. A few examples may help to illustrate how such a mixture of expectations can serve to complicate efforts to understand the adolescent process:

• The degree of legal autonomy that adolescents have varies not only by age and task but sometimes by geographic location. In most states teenagers cannot drive until age 16, vote until age 18, or drink until age 21; yet in some states 14-year-olds can choose the parent with whom they will live after a divorce and can override parental wishes about medical matters such as abortion or psychiatric care. Rationales for these specific age limits are seldom well articulated or compelling.

• Societal attitudes about adolescent sexuality are especially powerful and conflicted. Children are expected to be sexually naive, while adults are supposed to become sexually active in a caring interpersonal context. Adolescents must somehow traverse this chasm, remaining innocent while becoming knowledgeable. Some members of society exalt youth as a time of experimentation, others as a time for inculcating high standards of maturity and personal safety. Heated debates continue about how much and what kind of explicit sex education adolescents should receive and about the suitability and potential consequences of graphic depictions of sexuality in the mass media.

• Parents and social institutions urge adolescents to look toward the ideal of entering a monogamous marriage and having children—in that order. Yet teenagers confront the reality that nearly half of all marriages end in divorce, that nonmarital liaisons are increasingly common, and that a growing number of individuals in this society neither embody nor embrace that ideal, including those who choose not to marry, those who marry but elect to remain childless, and homosexuals.

• Society proscribes the use of alcohol, tobacco, or other recreational drugs for youth; yet many adults not only accept such activities as normal but passively or actively support often extravagant alcohol and drug use, especially among older adolescents. Teenagers must sift through competing messages that they should seek out such substances as essential elements of the good life, that they should "just say no," or that they should try to establish patterns of moderate use of socially approved drugs.

• Parents and schools promote formal education as essential and general erudition as valuable for success in adulthood. But adolescents note the rewards that those with exceptional athletic prowess or business acumen can garner. Many conclude that *having* a diploma is somehow more important than the process of *earning* it, especially when they interact with adults who place little value on learning.

Dedramatization of the Adolescent Experience

For most of the twentieth century the United States and other Western cultures have treated adolescence as an inherently problematic and largely unpredictable stage of life to be endured—preferably with patience and humor—by youth, their families, and society. Today many parents, educators, researchers, public officials, and community leaders share a perception that adolescents are at risk, individually and as a group. Yet it seems reasonable to conclude from the material presented in this volume that most American youths and their families find this stage to be neither as arduous nor as perilous as was once thought. Instead, for the majority it is a time of marked physical, psychological, and social growth that provides tremendous challenge as well as much excitement.

A key research finding is that teenagers and their parents have far less stormy relationships than was once believed (see Chapter 10 in this volume). Investigators have found that adolescence need not—and typically does not—mark the onset of open or covert conflict as youth seek to establish a sense of autonomy. Rather, parents remain an important influence throughout these critical years, helping adolescents mold their sense of self and shape future life choices. Although they have to adapt to changes that accompany adolescence, successful parents remain actively involved with their children. Moreover, most young people still feel close to their parents, despite widespread increases in minor disagreements between the two generations. What does change is how interactions are structured to acknowledge and accommodate growing autonomy.

In parallel fashion, researchers now better appreciate the ways in which adolescents interact with their peers (see Chapters 7, 11). The so-called youth culture is not nearly as monolithic and countercultural as was once thought, nor is it uniformly hedonistic and self-centered. In fact, peer groups often support traditional parental attitudes and beliefs and frequently work in concert with, rather than in automatic opposition to, adult goals. Peer influences may be critically important, especially for youths whose access to parental influences is impaired.

As researchers have reexamined the adolescent process, the degree to which youth reflect societal values and behaviors has become more fully apparent. For example, both adolescent drug and alcohol use and sexual activity and contraceptive use seem to be interconnected with shifts in attitudes among adults. Yet issues of timing and modes of transmission for such attitudinal shifts remain poorly understood. Studies are needed not only of how current behavior among teenagers predicts their future but also of how it reflects our society's past and present. Of particular interest may be the degree to which broad changes occur in adolescent development as a direct result of modifications of general social agendas and of attitudes toward youth. At the same time, shifting ideologies and concerns of its young people can affect a society itself, as was forcefully demonstrated during the political agitation that characterized much of the 1960s (see Chapter 18).

The Biological and Psychosocial Interface

Until quite recently, biological studies of adolescence have been limited by the unavailability of safe, meaningful measures of relevant biological states. Progress in many areas has begun to make such inquiries more feasible and potentially informative (see Chapter 2). New techniques are available for assessing stages of maturation, assaying hormones, monitoring brain electrical and metabolic activity, and even obtaining images of brain structures in living human beings. Many of these methodologies pose minimal risk for the subject, thus enabling researchers to use them as part of studies of normal development in children and adolescents.

Recent findings suggest that no one-to-one mapping exists between biology and behavior. Although adolescence is a time of extraordinary physical and endocrinological change, even the behavioral manifestations of the "raging hormones" characteristic of this life stage are influenced by past and present effects of socialization. For example, repeated studies of the association between hormones such as testosterone and behaviors such as aggressiveness or sexual arousal have failed to show strong and uniform associations. The observed effects of changing hormones on such behaviors, when detectible, have been small and typically seem to be affected by psychological and social factors (see Chapter 2).

Researchers are beginning to explore how factors such as personal perceptions and expectations, previous socialization patterns, specific personality traits, and the reactions of peers and adults alter the transition through puberty. For example, negative experiences of menarche are more common for girls who are unprepared for it or who have received prior information that it will be unpleasant (see Chapter 2). Links also have been made between the cultural emphasis on slimness and teenagers' preoccupation with dieting, as well as with the growing problems of eating disorders such as anorexia nervosa and bulimia (see Chapter 17). These and other findings suggest that positive interventions to smooth the transition into at least some aspects of early adolescence may be imminently feasible and highly desirable.

Research on adolescent health has benefited especially from a more integrated appreciation of both biological and psychosocial influences. Increasingly the health concerns and problems of this age group are the consequence of choices that adolescents make and behaviors they adopt (see Chapter 17). The most pressing health concerns are now accidents, homicides, depression and suicide, alcohol and drug abuse, sexual abuse, and eating disorders. Even the relatively new infectious disorders in this age group, including sexually transmitted diseases and acquired immune deficiency syndrome (AIDS), evoke significant behavioral issues. Furthermore, during adolescence many individuals establish patterns of eating, alcohol use, smoking, exercise, and other preventive practices that may influence their health for the rest of their lives. As a result, researchers are increasingly attentive to such issues as decision making, impulse control, autonomy and affiliation, and perceptions about treatment.

Adolescent sex differences have long provided rich materials for those interested in the interface between biology and environment. Adolescent boys differ from adolescent girls along numerous dimensions. For instance, on average, girls are shorter and lighter than boys, enter puberty earlier, and are less interested in science, mathematics, and computers. Still, some previously well-established sex differences are diminishing or even reversing; thus, girls now have an increased likelihood of graduating from school, working part-time, engaging in autonomy-seeking behavior, and having strained relations with parents, with rates quite similar to those for boys. Other differences—for example, initiation of smoking and alcohol use—are of particular concern both because of their potential consequences and because more young women seem to be engaging in such behaviors even as fewer young men are doing so.

The shifting patterns of sex differences serve to emphasize that simplistic explanations that evoke either strictly biological or sociological causes must be eschewed. Possible effects of such key social changes as more employment among adult females, wider professional opportunities for women, and changed ideologies engendered by the women's movement simply have yet to be examined. Empirical investigation of why some sex differences are vanishing while others remain would be of great value. Also needed is a better understanding of how changes in concepts about sex roles for men and women alter the perceived life options and goals of adolescents.

The Complexity of Adolescent Development

As researchers delve more deeply into the adolescent process, efforts to invoke a single developmental model meet with limited success. The most general model of development, going back over forty years, posits that young people explore alternatives and experiment with choices as they forge an identity. Although such a paradigm may account for numerous observed behaviors among white, middle-class youth, it works much less well for the poor, the school dropout, the unemployed, and the homeless. For these youths development often seems to be most influenced by happenstance or by social and racial barriers, by discrimination and prejudice (see Chapters 4, 5).

More generally, adolescents face changes in essentially all aspects of their lives; their ability to cope with those changes depends not only on intrinsic strengths and external supports but also on the timing of the stresses. If disruptions are too numerous or require too much change in too little time, they may be hazardous (see Chapter 15). Concurrent major changes—for instance, going through puberty while entering a new school and losing an established circle of peer relationships—may be more than many adolescents can handle (see Chapter 8). Some of the problems associated with poverty may arise from the degree to which it promulgates changes over which neither adolescents nor their families can exert control.

Detailed scrutiny is demonstrating that even seemingly straightforward aspects of development are complicated. Whether a given outcome is good or bad may depend on such factors as context, age, ethnicity, and gender. For instance, helping adolescents gain a sense of autonomy typically promotes responsibility in youth, but autonomy granted too early seems to promote deviance. Similarly, in the United States high self-esteem is a trait that is usually associated with positive outcomes; yet delinquents nearly always have high levels of self-esteem. Good school performance has major benefits in both the short and long term for most youths; still, for some it may entail high personal and social costs. For example, poor African-Americans or Hispanics who perform well in school may face social ostracism (see Chapter 5), as may some young women who excel in math or science (see Chapter 8). More attention is being given to identifying such interactive effects and considering their role in adolescent development.

Of particular importance is the increasing recognition that socio-economic status and ethnicity may play major roles in helping to shape the adolescent psychological and social experience. In the United States two distinct groups of youth have emerged, one markedly more advantaged than the other. Since the early 1970s the gap between these two groups has grown. This division is linked to a worrisome degree to ethnicity and minority status (see Chapters 1, 5). This division is linked to a worrisome degree to ethnicity and minority status (see Chapters 1, 5). Even apart from poverty, minority status affects adolescents and their environments in multiple ways. For example, compared with their European-American counterparts, Asian-American youth, especially first-generation and second-generation immigrants, spend longer hours studying and strikingly less time with peers, begin dating at a much later age, have less autonomy, and are more influenced by and obedient to their parents. Such structural and behavioral differences can alter the nature of the adolescent experience and enhance or detract from the ability of a given teenager to get through this period successfully. More precise information about the nature and impact of such differences could advance the ability of investigators to understand key components of development and to identify points at which the individual may be especially sensitive to disruption from various sources.

One consequence of the heightened awareness among investigators of the diversity of adolescent experiences has been a general move away from the search for unified developmental processes, with greater attention to processes that may be specific to a given situation. Examples of such research abound in this volume. For instance, earlier investigators believed that teenagers developed characteristic modes of thinking and moral reasoning in a predictable, linear fashion (see Chapter 3). They further believed that, as those modes of reasoning developed, adolescents could use them across a full range of situations and problems. Instead, adolescents reason at more advanced levels with familiar than with unfamiliar material and they do not reason about abstract moral dilemmas in the same way that they view familiar interpersonal situations (see Chapters 3, 18). Similarly, decision-making skills once were thought to reflect general strategies gained with age and experience that were readily generalizable; on closer examination, such skills were found to transfer only modestly from one circumstance to others that are not closely linked to it, and adolescents are apt to revert to less mature strategies when under stress (see Chapter 3). Researchers have gained additional information about self-esteem by looking at key components of self-concept such as the physical, interpersonal, and academic (see Chapter 14). In yet another domain, investigators initially had hoped that changes in amounts of such hormones as testosterone, estrogen, and growth hormone would provide fixed, valid indicators of key pubertal processes; now it is clear that hormonal influences, though real and pervasive, account for only a small part of the multiple changes that characterize adolescence (see Chapter 2). Although it is perhaps less gratifying than the search for "universal" phenomena, the elaboration of such multiple processes raises the possibility of identifying rules for understanding exactly how youth are influenced by specific situations and settings and, in turn, influence them.

Cross-Cutting Issues for Future Research

Three topics—minority populations, contexts, and the developmental perspective—have emerged as important directions for future research into essentially all aspects of normal adolescent development. Each promises to make our understanding of the adolescent experience both richer and more complex. Each demands that investigators push beyond the simplifying assumptions that have typified research, even in recent years. Although presented separately, these issues complement one another in that each inevitably is influenced by the other two.

Learning More about Nonwhite Youth

As Chapter 1 noted, minority populations are expanding rapidly, to the point that minority youth have already become the majority in their age range in some states. The picture of minority adolescents that emerges from this volume is sobering, especially in light of the reasonably positive situation for most adolescents. Even though scant information exists in many areas, enough is available to indicate that many minority teenagers are not faring well in America. It also is clear that little is known about minority youth raised in more advantaged settings.

Overshadowing whatever benefits or disadvantages may accrue to them as a result of their ethnic heritage is the reality that minority youth are overrepresented among a number of groups known not to be doing well. Too many are poor and are reared in single-parent families (but see Chapter 16; see also Chapter 6). In addition, they are overrepresented among school dropouts and among adolescents manifesting problem behaviors such as delinquency and teenage pregnancy. The strong associations between minority status and other profound influences on development greatly confound efforts to understand potentially unique contributions to the adolescent experience of being part of an ethnic minority. Overcoming the resulting complications for researchers will be arduous but worthwhile.

Studying normal development in minority adolescents. Perhaps the most striking observation across all the chapters in this volume is the degree to which research on normal development has been restricted to middle-class whites. Far too little information is available about African-Americans and Hispanics, and even less is known about other minority groups. Only the chapter on problem behaviors (Chapter 16) covers a body of literature that focuses largely on minority youth. This anomaly reflects the reality that most existing research on minority youth is based on a deviance or deficit perspective: these groups typically are studied when the topic of interest is a problem behavior rather than an aspect of normal development (see Chapter 5).

The lack of good information about the development of minority adolescents is highly disadvantageous. Many of the basic psychological and social changes that occur during the teenage years may be especially prone to the influences of ethnicity and minority status. For instance, the search for identity demands some efforts to recognize and accommodate to one's origins, ethnicity, and place in society. Also, the advent of dating brings new, emotionally laden overtones to social relations. One common result is increased de facto racial segregation even in ostensibly integrated settings. In theory, entry into larger, more heterogeneous middle schools and high schools should expand opportunities for ethnically diverse contacts, in comparison with those available in smaller neighborhood elementary schools. The more common outcome, however, is that peer groups increasingly become defined by ethnicity (see Chapter 7). Furthermore, at least for ethnic groups such as Hispanics, African-Americans, and American Indians, teenagers become more sensitive to inconsistencies between society's implied promises of future opportunities and the limited range of adult roles actually available (see Chapter 5).

There are many reasons to study minority youth, not the least of which is their importance in this society. Models of adolescence based on white, middle-class youth are too limiting. Inclusion of ethnic populations in research diversifies the contexts in which investigators can explore how developmental processes emerge and resolve themselves. Although many of these processes probably are unchanged across different settings, this hypothesis remains largely untested. Some may prove to be quite domain specific, and ethnic variability is likely to offer a rich natural resource for gathering empirical data about different modes by which a process such as decision making or moral judgment may evolve.

Overcoming obstacles to studying minority youth. Simply noting the paucity of high-quality research on minority youth is insufficient, as would be a call for more and better studies. The lack of such work is not merely an oversight but rather a result of problems ranging from the absence of an overarching theory about the effects of minority status on development, through the scarcity of investigators engaged in pursuing these important questions, to the complexities of actually carrying out the needed studies. Most problems noted here are not unique to research on minority adolescents; yet throughout the field the shortage of information typically is most marked for minorities.

Few studies of minorities define ethnic groups precisely. Minority youth usually are classified in broad categories such as Hispanic, African-American, or Asian-American. Yet it helps little to refer to "Asians" when Japanese, Chinese, Korean, Vietnamese, and many other clearly distinct cultures exist within this ethnic classification. As is true also for the American Indians and Hispanics, broad ethnic categories encompass large differences in language, immigration history, and cultural values that may overwhelm more superficial similarities. For example, Cuban adolescents have a higher rate of school completion than do Puerto Ricans (see Chapter 5). Although both are classified as Hispanic, averaging across these two groups would distort any results of studies of minority status and school performance.

Designing and conducting the kinds of studies of minority adolescents that are needed will not be easy. Many confounding variables have yet to be disentangled from minority status per se. The most obvious of these is socioeconomic status, especially poverty. Thus, researchers have reported that African-Americans are more likely than European-Americans to engage in authoritarian and punitive parenting styles; but closer scrutiny has shown that this style of parenting is characteristic of families in poverty, while middle-class African-American parents use styles like those of middle-class European-Americans (see Chapter 5). Similar points can be made for other factors that are closely linked to ethnicity, including the effects of migration and the cascade of changes that occur across generations; the influence of language and the trade-offs to ethnic groups of maintaining their native tongue, rapidly adopting English, or encouraging bilingualism; and the importance of readily identifiable external markers such as skin color or facial features in fostering and maintaining social biases.

Some questions can be addressed most directly by studying minority youth who have grown up in socioeconomically advantaged settings, so that a number of the complicating issues can be bypassed. But investigators still face many practical obstacles in the study of minority youth. Members of an ethnic population may see little reason to trust outsiders and have much to fear from them. Efforts of researchers to probe into their lives may be met with distrust and provoke either outright refusals to participate in studies or covert resistance. Language barriers can be daunting, requiring close collaboration with sophisticated translators to ensure that little is lost during the interpretive process. To the extent that studies extend to poor or truant youth, among other groups, innovative methods may be needed even to identify subjects and persuade them to participate. For instance, one investigator paid local youth to recruit school dropouts for the study. Each such novel approach unfortunately imposes additional demands on researchers to maintain high standards in their research methodology, so that both the applicability and limitations of any findings are clear.

Explanations for why researchers do or do not study ethnic minority youth are many and varied. Possible barriers for researchers who do not have a minority background include a perception that work on other aspects of adolescence is more readily rewarded and less politically sensitive. Those researchers who do focus on minority adolescents often are associated with institutions that lack extensive resources to support research, and many of them carry large teaching and administrative loads. A more detailed assessment of real and imagined obstacles to attracting researchers in the field might well be informative. Whatever they may be, however, continued efforts are needed to enlarge the pool of scientists who are willing to tackle pressing questions about minority adolescents in the United States.

At present much of the research on minority youth is conducted by academicians who are studying adolescents with the same ethnic background as their own. Often such individuals bring invaluable perspectives gained from personal experience, and the shared heritage sometimes facilitates making connections with potential research subjects. Even so, efforts are needed to promote minority research that crosses ethnic lines. Such work is vital to attempts to identify patterns of specificity and generality within the effects of minority status on adolescent development. Conferences and other forums are needed to aid researchers from different minority groups in integrating isolated and disconnected bodies of research on specific ethnic groups.

Examining Contexts

This volume devotes an entire section to the role of the contexts of normal adolescent development. Researchers have begun to clarify key aspects of specific settings and circumstances relevant to adolescence, and their results emphasize the striking degree to which development is embedded in individual and social contexts. Many aspects of context remain virtually unstudied, however, and investigators continue to face the challenge of exploring how contexts and developmental processes intertwine.

As children enter adolescence, they increasingly interact autonomously with their environment. They spend ever-greater amounts of time with people outside the family and steadily gain control over where, how, and with whom they spend their time. Many social forces favor these changes. For example, adolescents move from relatively small, local grade schools to larger, typically more diverse middle or junior high schools. They also have available a variety of outside activities, organized or spontaneous, in which they can participate with varying degrees of adult supervision. Adolescence seems to be a time for group activities, whether in school-sponsored sports or clubs, social organizations such as scouting or church groups, or merely informal get-togethers in teenage "hangouts" such as video arcades and malls. As their mobility increases with the use of public transportation or the availability of cars and friends who can drive, adolescents further augment their options for exposing themselves to the wider world.

Because of the key role of contexts, researchers must familiarize themselves both with the specifics of past and current environmental circumstances and with the ways in which those circumstances alter and are altered by adolescent development. The study of history has important contributions to make in distinguishing transitory from more enduring features of adolescence across time and circumstance. In some instances changes are more a matter of form than of substance—for example, the particular mode of dress or style of music that adolescents use to underscore their distinctiveness from adults (see Chapter 9). Other modifications seem more substantive, as is the case with the role of work. In the past, young people worked because they were an integral part of the family and their labor was necessary to its well-being; now, most teenagers who work do so to earn discretionary income (see Chapters 4, 9).

The changing circumstances of Today's Youth. Even the briefest contemplation of the social settings in which adolescent development occurs today underscores the enormous changes that have taken place since the 1960s (see Chapter 1). Nearly half of all youth have experienced a divorce in the immediate family and will spend at least a portion of their lives in a single-parent household, in shared custody, or in one or more reconstituted families (see Chapter 6). Moreover, steadily higher proportions of mothers are employed, a trend that alters the structure of household activities and the availability of adult support and supervision for the adolescent even in intact families.

Similarly, continuing immigration and the relatively high birth rates of low-income families highlight the critical need to understand how adolescence unfolds among the entire range of youth. Issues raised by ethnic diversity have already been discussed. The poor youth of this nation receive little explicit attention in this volume, but they pose pressing issues for the nation. Detailed study of the specific mechanisms by which poverty alters the contexts and experience of adolescence will broaden our understanding of the nature of this stage of life and may offer new insights into ways of easing some of the adverse effects of poverty.

The exposure of adolescents to disparate social models has also grown over the years. Surprisingly little attention has been given even to documenting how adolescents spend their time; less has been learned about where they acquire their beliefs about acceptable and unacceptable social behaviors (see Chapter 9). Such innovations as cable television and videocassette recorders have transformed the ease with which young people gain access to materials that parents might previously have proscribed. Analogously, changing social mores about drug, alcohol, and tobacco use inevitably affect both the degree to which adolescents feel free to experiment with mind-altering substances and the specific drugs they use.

The ability to separate sex from procreation also has resulted in pervasive shifts in social attitudes that inevitably have affected the adolescent experience in many ways (see Chapters 13, 17). At least in part, the availability of protected sex helped fuel a deregulation of sexual activity among adults, with increasingly explicit consideration of sex in the mass media. Through the media, adolescents receive early and repeated messages about the allure of sexual activity, almost always divorced from any realistic consideration of its possible costs (see Chapter 9). In fact, the conflicting attitudes of various segments of society about teenage sexuality has resulted in many adolescents being saturated in its mystique while remaining ignorant about its practical aspects. Increasing numbers are experiencing sexual intercourse at an early age (see Chapter 13) but without protection against pregnancy or sexually transmitted diseases (see Chapter 17).

Changes in society undoubtedly will continue to alter the setting in which teenagers are developing. Pivotal changes often are not readily identifiable in advance, nor are their effects. Therefore, it will be important for researchers to monitor actual conditions regularly to ensure early detection of major shifts in conditions. In this regard, the historical perspective may be invaluable in identifying both recurrent patterns and unique constellations of circumstances. For example, have there been times in the past when adolescents faced comparable concerns that their training is poorly matched to probable adult roles? If so, what light do earlier crises shed on current concerns?

Studying the contexts. Until relatively recently investigators studying normal adolescent development have treated the context in which this development occurs largely as a nuisance variable. With the recognition that some key processes may be domain specific, however, context itself is becoming of interest (but see Chapter 18). Even so, relatively few investigators have begun to study the adolescent context and the ways in which it affects normal development.

One useful if overly simple approach to contexts subdivides them into proximal and distal influences. The former include the family, peers, schools, and other social organizations with which an individual has direct contact. Distal contexts are imposed as a result of the specific time and circumstance into which the individual is born; they reflect era, culture, and ethnicity, as well as socioeconomic status and choice of community. Although the effects of distal contexts are quite real, their impact on the individual is presumably filtered through proximal contexts by mechanisms that are themselves worthwhile subjects for research.

Some proximal contexts have received considerable study, as we have seen in the chapters on parents, peers, and schools. Yet even on those topics much remains to be done. Notably absent in the existing literature is any systematic assessment of organized youth activities, including sports groups such as Little League and soccer, music groups, formal youth clubs such as boy Scouts and Girl Scouts or 4-H, and church groups. For many teenagers such organizations are major sources of structured leisure-time activities and of friends and role models. Also, little information is available about the nature and meaning of friendships between members of the opposite sex, either within or outside the dating relationship.

Physical aspects of proximal contexts have been largely neglected. Few investigators have considered even the question of how to describe and specify key features of the environment. Researchers must develop ways of studying the effects on the adolescent experience of factors such as the availability of hangouts (parks or malls), relative ease of transportation, density of living, or physical safety of the neighborhood. Even more, a conceptual framework is needed that will enable investigators to identify commonalities across settings, so that changes in specific circumstances do not create overwhelming complexity in the study of contexts.

Interpersonal proximal contexts have received more study, especially those involving interactions between adolescents and parents (see Chapter 10). Even so, the equally abundant interactions between teenagers and their siblings and the less frequent but sometimes pivotal interactions with extended-family members such as grandparents have received scant attention. Of great interest is the possibility of learning how different interpersonal proximal contexts complement or interfere with one another. Studies of peer influences, for example, suggest that peers are much more supportive of parental goals than was once believed (see Chapter 7). A better understanding of how family and school influences interact might also do much to inform the ongoing debate about appropriate non-academic functions for schools in fostering development.

Few studies are available on distal contexts of adolescence (but see Chapter 18). Oddly, the role of distal contexts seems simultaneously to be taken for granted and dismissed. Few would deny the impact on all society of such events as the depression, the world wars, or the social upheaval of the 1960s. Yet there is a widespread assumption that research done on adolescents during those earlier eras applies equally well within the contexts and circumstances of today.

Even casual reflection suggests that the results of some previous research must be applied with caution, if at all, to today's youth. For example, studies of minorities that were conducted in the United States before the mid-1960s may not be relevant to youth born after the civil rights movement and the Black Power movement (see Chapter 5). Similarly, conclusions drawn from research on the politically active youth of the 1960s may not apply to the more quiescent youth of subsequent decades (see Chapter 18). Likewise, old correlational data linking premarital sexual intercourse with problem outcomes may have little relevance for an era in which the majority have had sexual intercourse by age 16 (see Chapter 16). These and many other examples emphasize that old findings need continuing reassessment and revalidation when they may be affected by changes in larger social contexts. Also, systematic evaluation is needed of the potential impact on adolescent development of such changes as the declining position of the United States in the world and the perceived risk of nuclear war.

As a way of simplifying their research, investigators regularly have dealt with such contexts as the family, school, or peer group as if their effects on individuals were essentially uniform. (Results of this type are summarized in earlier chapters.) And yet, within any of these settings individuals may have vastly different personal experiences. Even the most prestigious upper-middle-class schools with high academic expectations contain peer groups that value drugs, deviance, and defiance. Conversely, even schools in poor rural areas where most students devalue intellectual accomplishment have subgroups that esteem academic achievement and are involved in student government and similar activities. Efforts are needed to develop more accurate methods of identifying the specific contexts for discrete individuals.

Researchers also must consider the contexts themselves in greater detail than has been customary. For example, parents are not a monolithic entity. They, too, are subject to developmental pressures that may alter their interactions with their adolescent children in significant ways. Some researchers have suggested that certain interactive patterns between teenagers and their parents arise from their being at developmental stages that mirror each other: young people are exploring what they can do with their lives even as parents are reviewing what they have done with their own; the former may be trying to cope with rapidly rising sexual awareness and drives as the latter face declines (see Chapter 6). Much more detailed assessments are needed if we are to consider how contexts are connected with outcomes. For example, do parents who are significantly older or younger than average interact with their adolescents in ways that are consonant with the parents' own developmental issues? Do adults who experience turbulent midlife appraisals also have turbulent interactions with their teenage children?

Future research will need to examine in detail the role of the individual in shaping particular contexts. Lack of homogeneity within contexts gives individuals considerable latitude in shaping their own situations, at least within certain constraints. Too often adolescents are portrayed as passive recipients of circumstances and resources that others make available to them. In reality they play an active role in choosing and shaping the contexts in which they operate—their friends, their activities, and their life-styles. The desires of parents and society to provide environments that promote healthy development might be simplified if researchers could gain a clearer understanding of why and how teenagers either resist or cooperate with such efforts. Of particular relevance in this regard may be studies of those youth who seem either especially resilient or vulnerable. Why do some adolescents function successfully as adults despite having grown up in poverty or in a broken home, contexts that are known to be associated with generally negative outcomes? Conversely, why do others fail despite coming from settings that seem to offer every advantage? Some work has already begun to ask these questions (see Chapters 15, 16).

A further complication of studying contexts is their fluidity. Contexts change, sometimes rapidly, sometimes slowly. Even the family is not an immutable entity. During the second decade of life many adolescents experience a diversity of family structures. Size, stability, and specific components of this key structure are subject to the vagaries of family conflict, separation, divorce, cohabitation, remarriage, and reconstitution. Other major contexts may be even more prone to recurrent modification. Given the geographic mobility common in the United States, many adolescents must cope with one or more major disruptions in schools, peer groups, and neighborhoods. Some changes in contexts are more gradual or predictable, for example, the organization and structure of formal schooling or the departure and intermittent return of older siblings. To study any of these issues, investigators must develop ways of surveying changes over time.

Researchers cannot address many of the questions identified here with conventional methods that examine a group of subjects once, or even twice. To the extent that specific contexts change over time, it may be necessary to track populations of youth repeatedly over fairly prolonged intervals in order to assess both the nature of the changes and their short-term and long-term effects. For instance, a study in California tracked custody arrangements over three years for divorced families with young children and adolescents. The proportion of families with shared legal custody was high and remained relatively stable over the course of the study; the families with true shared custody, however, were not nearly as stable, and relatively few children and adolescents experienced that arrangement throughout the entire study. This type of longitudinal research is complex and expensive, and it requires a support structure that can ensure stability of the project over a number of years. Few academic institutions or funding agencies have been prepared to back such efforts. Nonetheless, longitudinal studies have great potential for enabling the field to advance our knowledge of adolescent development.

The developmental perspective. In considering how contexts shape and are shaped by the adolescent experience, researchers are just beginning to deal with the ways in which the adolescent's developmental phase modifies the impact of any given context. Most studies have examined how a context such as parental divorce, low socioeconomic status, or exposure to violence in the mass media influences adolescents as a whole. But just as the biological changes of puberty have proven to have only modest explanatory power in and of themselves, so too are contextual factors—no matter how well specified—unlikely to have broad effects common across all youth. Even the well-documented adversities of poverty fail to produce uniformly bad outcomes for all adolescents.

For many contextual influences the most that scientists are apt to accomplish is documenting a range of probable outcomes for known circumstances at particular stages of development. For example, a large proportion of adolescents experiment with drugs in their mid-teens; but the likelihood that a given individual will do so is influenced not only by age but also by the attitudes and practices of his or her closest friends (see Chapters 11, 16). For many events such as the loss of a parent through death or divorce, the immediate and long-term impact will depend to some degree on the age of the adolescent. Family dissolution produces quite different patterns of disruption and almost certainly results in different perceptions and reactions for an older adolescent who already has left home, a younger teenager who still is dependent on the family, and a preschooler. Similarly, experimentation with recreational drugs will not have the same meaning for and impact on a 12-year-old as for a 19-year-old.

Identifying mechanisms by which contexts produce their effects. A major challenge for those studying adolescent development is to elucidate pathways or mechanisms by which contexts exert their effects. It no longer is adequate simply to document that certain contexts are associated with particular outcomes. For example, why is poverty associated with so many ill effects on youth? Is a lack of socially desirable role models a key factor? Do interactions with peers contribute to the problems of poor adolescents or provide some level of protection for them (see Chapters 11, 16)? Work in several disparate areas shows the feasibility of asking such questions. For example, investigators have begun to explore processes that may help to account for the poor educational attainment of African-American and Hispanic adolescents; parenting styles that are more properly linked to economic disadvantage than to ethnicity appear to play a role, as may systematic differences in the response of peers to an adolescent's investment in educational pursuits (see Chapter 5). A second example can be found in efforts to explore the potential mismatches between specific features of middle schools and high schools and ongoing developmental needs of the students enrolled in them (see Chapter 8). At times the most important factor in determining how well an adolescent is doing may simply be the sheer number and magnitude of changes with which he or she must cope (see Chapter 15). Considerably more analysis at this level is needed across the entire spectrum of adolescent research.

Deliberate interventions offer investigators a powerful strategy in the search for specific mechanisms. Associations between processes and out-comes—even quite strong ones—are not enough to establish a causal relationship between the two. At a minimum, researchers will need to demonstrate that altering the process affects the outcome in predictable ways. For example, if conflicts between parents and their teenage children are thought to arise from young people's need for autonomy, then it should be possible to show that helping adolescents achieve a sense of autonomy in other ways decreases the frequency of conflicts (see Chapter 10). Similarly, if teenagers are thought to have trouble making friends because they lack adequate social skills, then it should be possible to provide training in these skills that would improve their peer relationships (see Chapters 11, 16). Naturally, such research is of interest because of the insights it may offer into basic processes; in addition, it may suggest ways of enhancing the adolescent experience, especially in areas that can be especially problematic for some youth.

Considering Adolescence as Part of the Life Course

As investigators delimit pivotal aspects of normal adolescent develop-ment, it will become increasingly urgent to consider how those processes are affected by the experiences of childhood. A recent resurgence of such work is encouraging, but more is needed. Often, questions have been framed as though puberty and other important aspects of adolescent development might be expected to overwhelm all previous influences. For instance, investigators have asked, "What is the effect of puberty on self-image or depression or family relations?" "What is the effect of age on decision-making abilities or strategies?" This research approach unques-tionably should continue. Some fields have advanced sufficiently, however, to enable investigators to explore within the context of adolescence the degree to which specific developmental outcomes are predictable from conditions and behaviors existing earlier in life.

With an increasing acceptance of a life-course perspective, investigators are directing attention once again to links between childhood and adoles-cence (see Chapters 15, 16). Similar results have been found in England, the United States, and the Scandinavian countries, offering exciting and provocative data that suggest that problem behaviors in adolescence and even in adulthood often are foreshadowed by adjustment difficulties in childhood and by problematic parent-child relations (Chapter 16). Asso-ciations between behavioral problems may be much stronger and longer lasting than are the continuities of normal development. Yet discon-tinuities, with difficult children doing well as adults or vice versa, also present compelling research questions (Chapter 16).

Of equal interest is the connection between adolescence and adulthood. Again, available studies consider continuities of problem behaviors. Several suggest that problems in youth portend difficulties during adulthood. For instance, one study successfully predicted which youth would engage in criminal activities of various types as adults on the basis of how aggressive they were as teenagers and how their families responded to them (see Chapter 16). Such findings raise questions about the conventional wisdom which dismisses some forms of antisocial behavior as being a normal part of adolescence. Still, observed associations are not strong, and they equally suggest that many youth with early problems are able to change in ways that make the adult outcomes better than anticipated. Studying why those children did well might help to suggest useful intervention strategies.

Oddly, a central question that remains unanswered concerns the extent to which adolescents remain malleable. An extreme view would posit that good or bad outcomes in adolescence result from earlier childhood experiences and that efforts to intervene during the teenage years will have imperceptible effects on adult outcomes. Perhaps, it could be argued, the early foundations created by biology and environmental influences simply manifest themselves in new, noteworthy ways as the child enters adolescence. Such a hypothesis seems as unlikely as the equally extreme view that nothing in an adolescent's past matters. Once again, placing the research squarely within a developmental framework will enable researchers to assess the unique contribution of the adolescent experience to the developmental process.

Key Opportunities for Facilitating Research on Normal Adolescence

Various needs and promising research directions emerged repeatedly during the preparation of this volume. The ones described here serve to suggest the wide range of levels at which progress seems to be within reach. Even these few examples illustrate the stimulating opportunities that exist within the field for productive work, as do the many promising lines of research detailed in earlier chapters in the volume that relate more directly to specific areas.

Monitoring the Adolescent Experience

For a variety of fiscal and policy reasons, this nation has markedly fewer mechanisms in place now for monitoring demographic trends than it did until the late 1970s. The continued rapid changes in adolescent contexts and behaviors argues strongly for reconsideration of such policies. Repeatedly contributors to this volume have noted significant aspects of the adolescent experience about which information is either unavailable or outdated. Data about how and how often teenagers use various types of electronic media are a case in point (Chapter 9), as is information about political awareness and involvement (Chapter 18).

Recurrent assessments of a number of physical, psychological, and social factors for a representative national sample would be an invaluable, ongoing resource for many researchers. Some regional samples do exist, as does a national sample for high school and beyond. What is needed is a national survey that extends down into early adolescence and is explicitly designed to ensure appropriate coverage of diverse ethnic and cultural groups. Attention also could be given to ensuring that data are reported in ways that are most useful to researchers. For example, many older surveys consolidate their results by reporting on two groups: children and adolescents up to about age 15, and older adolescents plus youth in their early twenties (see Chapter 17). These clusters do not correspond well with more typical age groupings, such as early, middle, and late adolescence; moreover, they frustrate the efforts of investigators looking for systematic trends in contexts or behaviors as a function of age.

Developing and Applying Innovative Research Methodologies

Early research on adolescent development relied heavily on interviews, questionnaires, and rating scales, as researchers accumulated data of questionable relevance, reliability, or even validity. Often studies have relied on only a single informant—usually the adolescent—without benefit of confirming evidence from other sources. Gradually such approaches are yielding to more sophisticated methodologies that hold the promise of offering far more useful and informative results. New measures of physical parameters of development that now are available were mentioned earlier. Especially exciting techniques from the psychological and social sciences include direct observation of behaviors in natural and laboratory settings, assessment of individuals using random sampling of behavior over the course of days or weeks, and discourse analyses. Also effective has been the use of spatial representational models to help adolescents and their families reliably describe such complex issues as family connectedness. Although available methods are helpful, more innovations are needed to enhance the ability of investigators to observe and record the adolescent condition. Borrowing from anthropology, a few researchers are using participant observers who live with or spend extensive blocks of time with adolescents, thereby becoming a part of their routine and an eyewitness to the natural process.

As investigators expand the complexity of their questions about adolescent development, so too must their methods become increasingly complex. Key components of such studies will include the use of multiple informants and the assessment of significant phenomena by several independent methods. Projects also may need to recruit participants across multiple sites in order to ensure adequate representation of various subgroups. Although this volume focuses on youth in the United States, multinational collaborations can further enrich some aspects of the research, for example, by disclosing aspects of the adolescent experience that may be peculiar to this nation. Done properly, such approaches can improve the reliability and generalizability of the research findings; any differences that emerge from the use of different informants or subjects from different regions or nationalities can themselves provide valuable insights into the effects of contexts on developmental processes.

Developing Conceptual Frameworks

Many earlier hypotheses that seemed to describe universal processes in adolescent development have not been as robust as they were once believed to be. The resulting move toward empiricism has had beneficial effects, but it also has had its costs. The field now is handicapped by a lack of theories to guide its questions. Some theories usefully can be imported from related areas of study, and efforts to foster such cross-fertilization would be worthwhile. But continued support of innovative attempts to identify and elaborate upon key underlying processes also is needed, and few mechanisms exist to encourage such efforts.

Work by Dweck on motivation and achievement offers a timely example of how process-oriented research can lead from observation to hypothesis to hypothesis testing (see Chapter 12). She has explored the interplay between individual self-perception and actual performance in various settings. Although it is clearly only one of several possible explanations, her hypothesis has helped to stimulate research in several directions. Other important areas summarized in this volume, including sexuality, schools, political development, and ethnicity, continue to be swamped with empirical data in the absence of an organizing framework.

Links across Developmental Processes and Contexts

This volume is subdivided much as research on adolescence is organized— that is, topically. Thus, chapters address issues such as motivation, sexuality, problem behaviors, peers, and so on. This structure, like the research it reviews, slights the associative links that exist across topics. Still, some investigators are trying to identify and characterize such links. Recent work has explored how family variables affect functioning in other domains including peer relations and school performance (see Chapters 8, 11), as well as the role cognitive changes may have in affecting the interactions of adolescents with their families (see Chapter 10). Also important are the possible age-dependent effects of school organization as a disruptive influence on the development and maintenance of stable peer relationships (see Chapter 11). Similar potential links need to be considered with regard to the effect of family relations on friendship and dating patterns, or the impact of pervasive media messages about sex and normal interactions between the sexes in terms of dating expectations and conduct, or the influence of hormonal changes on school motivation or interest in dating. Often these types of studies have the salutary effect of encouraging collaborations among researchers who typically work in different areas and with sometimes complementary approaches.

Investigators are beginning to delineate more precisely how adolescents learn about and incorporate social expectations about acceptable and deviant behaviors (see Chapters 3, 16). Social maturation does not proceed as directly or as smoothly as was once thought. Rather, adolescents engage in a series of experimentations as circumstances permit, advancing in some contexts while temporarily retreating in others. Even so, it seems possible to identify patterns of behavior acquisition in at least some instances. Studies of socially deviant or risky behaviors in adolescence offer a powerful example of such interconnections. Both deviant behaviors and the individuals engaging in them form distinctive groupings. Hence, an adolescent who begins smoking cigarettes at an early age has a greatly increased likelihood of engaging in early use of alcohol, drug experimentation, and precocious sex. The identification of early signal events and behavioral patterns that cluster together may suggest directions for future research on useful intervention strategies. Clarification of exactly how teenagers incorporate what they see and hear in the mass media into their daily life also would be of value (see Chapter 16).

Learning about Adolescence from the Adolescent's Perspective

Although researchers are rapidly acquiring much useful information about the tasks and manifestations of adolescence, they have been less successful at capturing its essence, as experienced by adolescents themselves. The distinction is at times crucial. For instance, risk-taking behavior has long been of interest in research because many young people adopt or at least experiment with a variety of behaviors such as smoking, drug use, unprotected sex, or high-speed driving that pose a risk to their immediate or future well-being. Their responses to direct questions suggest that adolescents do not appear to engage in such behaviors because they are unduly attracted to danger (see Chapter 17). Not unlike adults, teenagers typically adopt a behavior because they believe it helps them achieve some desired end such as peer acceptance; in doing so they are likely to ignore or discount evidence that the behavior poses any real threat to them. For example, the willingness to start smoking or to have unprotected sex is markedly affected by beliefs adolescents hold about peer expectations and practices (see Chapter 17). In these instances and many others, a single behavior such as smoking may serve a wide range of purposes ranging from projecting a desired image to emulating or defying an important adult figure. Conversely, seemingly dissimilar behaviors may serve a single purpose; for example, in the desire to acquire a stable peer group one adolescent may become active in school government or church groups and another may drop out of school to join a street gang. In fact, little is known, still, about what impels teenagers to join peer groups and what they value and dislike about such associations (see Chapters 11, 16). By simply accepting observed behaviors as indicators of underlying motivation, investigators sometimes find themselves being led far afield.

Learning how to elicit information on what adolescents think and feel about themselves, about events in their lives, and about their understanding of what they are doing would be an enormous benefit to research. Apart from the subject of depression (see Chapters 14, 15), little information is available about emotional development during adolescence. How do young people learn to recognize, categorize, and calibrate such diverse affective states as elation, despair, disgust, anticipation, love? When and in what ways do they compare and contrast their own feelings with those of peers or adults? How does their experience of adolescence—good and bad—color their understanding of such emotional states? Are their emotions continuous or discontinuous with childhood emotions?

Equally interesting and also poorly understood are the processes by which teenagers acquire their individual social expectations and values. On what examples do they draw in adopting their own code of ethics, including elements such as honor and integrity? Can adolescents learn to articulate such processes as they occur both in face-to-face interactions and in relation to more distant societal institutions? If so, investigators could augment existing work on moral stages, which focuses more on cognitive underpinnings of such ethics (see Chapter 18). Such information has great practical significance because it may suggest ways for adults to facilitate transmission of shared social values to the next generation.

The type of research recommended here is difficult. At the very least, adolescents, like adults, often are reluctant or even unable to talk about their thoughts and feelings. Still, the potential insights that would come out of such studies justify considerable effort. Initially, investigators may have to use diverse research approaches, including working with a few subjects quite extensively for a long time. As suggestive patterns emerge, it should be possible to construct additional studies that begin the search for commonalities across adolescents of different ages and for contextual variations that influence them.

Promoting Carefully Planned Longitudinal Studies

Longitudinal studies inevitably must be a significant component of any thoughtful research agenda on normal adolescent development. They are central to any effort to clarify how one aspect of development connects with another, or how a present intervention may change future events. Specific needs for longitudinal studies vary widely. Some can be completed in only a few years; others may need to last a lifetime. Some may appropriately be done with intensive study of a small, homogeneous group of subjects; others may require large numbers of subjects who must be recruited from several distinct geographic locations so that questions about links between key contexts and processes can be answered definitively. Some will entail only naturalistic observations of subjects; others may involve careful study of specific interventions. All will provide settings in which researchers truly can focus on adolescence as a developmental process.

The extant long-term longitudinal studies of children have been extremely influential in the field, but new ones are required. As we noted earlier, social and historical change demands a continuing assessment of adolescent development. Also, the availability of new research techniques creates new possibilities about the sorts of information that can reasonably be gathered. Such studies may be supplemented usefully with shorter-term longitudinal projects, especially ones that follow multiple groups over several years. Such a design can help disentangle specific developmental changes from externally induced changes that arise, for example, from shifts in social attitudes or practices.

Given the expense of such studies and the large demand for them, mechanisms are needed to provide sustained support for the projects while also encouraging multidisciplinary and cross-institutional collaborations that will ensure maximum feasible utilization of these valuable resources. Carefully done, such arrangements can also help minimize the chronic problems that plague these kinds of studies, including sampling bias and socioeconomic, ethnic, and regional influences.

As if reflecting the subject of its own inquiry, research on normal development stands at an interesting juncture. Sufficient progress has been made in enough areas to convey a clear sense of the promise of the inquiries; yet so much remains to be done that thoughtful guidance seems both feasible and appropriate. The chapters in this volume portray the vigorous growth in many directions, as well as the awkwardness and immaturity that often go with such rapid expansion. Like adolescents themselves, the field is doing quite well in many respects, but it needs a nurturing environment that will continue to foster development.

Much of the work done to date can be characterized as being either descriptive or correlative. Both are essential elements for progress, with the former providing a solid base of knowledge about the contexts and processes of adolescence and the latter identifying interconnections among them. Although many interesting issues remain to be delineated, recent progress is heartening. Building on that expanding body of information, investigators now have the opportunity and challenge of characterizing the sources of those interconnections and studying them within the dynamic context of development. Although such work is formidable, the successes cited in this volume demonstrate its feasibility.

To realize its full potential, research on adolescence must continue to attract and incorporate contributions from a large number of specialties— psychology, sociology, anthropology, pediatrics, child psychiatry, history, epidemiology, education, and more. In part this volume is intended to provide a meeting ground on which researchers from such fields can pause to consider how they might usefully contribute to an understanding of the adolescent experience. To the extent that it captures the importance of this stage of life both for individuals and for society and conveys a sense of the momentum that has been building so powerfully in recent years, it will have succeeded.

REFERENCES

CONTRIBUTORS

INDEX

REFERENCES

2. The Role of Pubertal Processes

1. Abel, T., & Joffe, N. F. (1950). Cultural background of female puberty. *American Journal of Psychotherapy, 4,* 90–113.
2. *Accent on you,* Lake Success, N.Y.: Tampax, Inc.
3. Adams, L. A.; Vician, L.; Clifton, D. K.; & Steiner, R. A. (1987). Gonadotropin-releasing hormone (GnRH) mRNA content in GnRH neurons is similar in the brains of juvenile and adult male monkeys. In *Macaca fasciculares.* Proceedings of the 69th Annual Meeting of the Endocrine Society, 1987.
4. Alther, L. (1976). *Kinflicks.* New York: Knopf.
5. Attie, I., & Brooks-Gunn, J. (1987). Weight-related concerns in women: A response to or a cause of stress? In R. C. Barnett, L. Biener, & G. K. Baruch, eds., *Gender and stress.* New York: Free Press, pp. 218–254.
6. Attie, I., & Brooks-Gunn, J. (1989). The development of eating problems in adolescent girls: A longitudinal study. *Developmental Psychology, 25*(1), 70–79.
7. Baydar, N.; Brooks-Gunn, J.; & Warren, M. P. (in press). Determinants of depressive symptoms in adolescent girls: A four-year longitudinal study. *Developmental Psychology.*
8. Beach, F. A. (1975). Behavioral endocrinology: An emerging discipline. *American Scientist, 63,* 178–187.
9. Blyth, D.; Simmons, R.; & Zakin, D. (1985). Satisfaction with body image for early adolescent females: The impact of pubertal timing within different school environments. *Journal of Youth and Adolescence, 14*(3), 207–225.
10. Brackbill, Y., & Nevill, D. (1981). Parental expectations of achievement as affected by children's height. *Merrill-Palmer Quarterly, 27,* 429–441.
11. Brooks-Gunn, J. (1984). The psychological significance of different pubertal events to young girls. *Journal of Early Adolescence, 4*(4), 315–327.
12. Brooks-Gunn, J. (1987). Pubertal processes and girls' psychological adaptation. In R. Lerner & T. T. Foch, eds., *Biological-psychosocial interactions in early adolescence: A life-span perspective.* Hillsdale, N.J.: Erlbaum, pp. 123–153.
13. Brooks-Gunn, J. (1988a). Transition to early adolescence. In M. Gunnar &

W. A. Collins, eds., *Development during transition to adolescence: Minnesota symposia on child psychology.* Vol. 21. Hillsdale, N.J.: Erlbaum, pp. 189–208.

14. Brooks-Gunn, J. (1988b). Antecedents and consequences of variations in girls' maturational timing. *Journal of Adolescent Health Care, 9*(5), 1–9.

15. Brooks-Gunn, J. (1989a). Pubertal processes and the early adolescent transition. In W. Damon, ed., *Child development today and tomorrow.* San Francisco: Jossey-Bass, pp. 155–176.

16. Brooks-Gunn, J. (1989b). Adolescents as children and as parents: A developmental perspective. In I. E. Sigel & G. H. Brody, eds., *Family Research.* Vol. 1. Hillsdale, N.J.: Erlbaum, pp. 213–248.

17. Brooks-Gunn, J. (1990). Barriers and impediments to conducting research with young adolescents. *Journal of Youth and Adolescence, 19*(5).

18. Brooks-Gunn, J.; Boyer, C. B.; & Hein, K. (1988). Preventing HIV infection and AIDS in children and adolescents: Behavioral research and intervention strategies. *American Psychologist, 43*(11), 958–964.

19. Brooks-Gunn, J., & Furstenberg, F. F., Jr. (1989). Adolescent sexual behavior. *American Psychologist, 44*(2), 249–257.

20. Brooks-Gunn, J., & Matthews, W. (1979). *He and she: How children develop their sex-role identity.* Englewood Cliffs, N.J.: Prentice-Hall.

21. Brooks-Gunn, J.; Newman, D.; & Warren, M. P. (1989). Significance of breast growth. Unpublished manuscript.

22. Brooks-Gunn, J., & Paikoff, R. L. (in press). Taking no chances: Teenage pregnancy prevention programs. *American Psychologist.*

23. Brooks-Gunn, J., & Petersen, A. C., eds. (1983). *Girls at puberty: Biological and psychosocial perspectives.* New York: Plenum Press.

24. Brooks-Gunn, J.; Petersen, A. C.; & Eichorn, D. (1985). The study of maturational timing effects in adolescence. Special issue. *Journal of Youth and Adolescence, 14*(3, 4).

25. Brooks-Gunn, J., & Petersen, A. C. (1991, in press). The emergence of depression in adolescence. Special issue. *Journal of Youth and Adolescence.*

26. Brooks-Gunn, J., & Ruble, D. N. (1980). Menarche: The interaction of physiology, cultural, and social factors. In A. J. Dan, E. A. Graham, & C. P. Beecher, eds., *The menstrual cycle: A synthesis of interdisciplinary research.* New York: Springer, pp. 141–159.

27. Brooks-Gunn, J., & Ruble, D. N. (1982). The development of menstrual-related beliefs and behaviors during early adolescence. *Child Development, 53,* 1567–77.

28. Brooks-Gunn, J.; Samelson, M.; Warren, M. P.; & Fox, R. (1986). Physical similarity of and disclosure of menarcheal status to friends: Effects of age and pubertal status. *Journal of Early Adolescence, 6*(1), 3–14.

29. Brooks-Gunn, J., & Warren, M. P. (1985a). Measuring physical status and timing in early adolescence: A developmental perspective. *Journal of Youth and Adolescence, 14*(3), 163–189.

30. Brooks-Gunn, J., & Warren, M. P. (1985b). Effects of delayed menarche in different contexts: Dance and nondance students. *Journal of Youth and Adolescence, 14*(4), 285–300.

31. Brooks-Gunn, J., & Warren, M. P. (1988). The psychological significance of secondary sexual characteristics in 9- to 11-year-old girls. *Child Development, 59,* 161–169.
32. Brooks-Gunn, J., & Warren, M. P. (1989). Biological contributions to affective expression in young adolescent girls. *Child Development, 60,* 372–385.
33. Brooks-Gunn, J.; Warren, M. P.; & Rosso, J. T. (1991, in press). The impact of pubertal and social events upon girls' problem behavior. *Journal of Youth and Adolescence.*
34. Brooks-Gunn, J., & Zahaykevich, M. (1989). Parent-child relationships in early adolescence: A developmental perspective. In K. Kreppner & R. M. Lerner, eds., *Family systems and life-span development.* Hillsdale, N.J.: Erlbaum, pp. 223–246.
35. Brown, J. K. (1963). A cross-cultural study of female initiation rites. *American Anthropologist, 65,* 837–853.
36. Bruch, H. (1978). *The golden cage.* Cambridge, Mass.: Harvard University Press.
37. Cameron, J. L.; Koerker, D. J.; & Steiner, R. A. (1985). Metabolic changes during maturation of male monkeys: Possible signals for onset of puberty. *American Journal of Physiology, 249,* 385–391.
38. Cantwell, D. P., & Baker, L. (1991, in press). Manifestations of depressive affect in adolescence. *Journal of Youth and Adolescence.*
39. Carey, S.; Diamond, R.; & Woods, B. (1980). Development of face recognition—a maturational component? *Developmental Psychology, 16,* 257–269.
40. Chodorow, N. (1978). *The reproduction of mothering: Psychoanalysis and sociology of gender.* Berkeley: University of California Press.
41. Clausen, J. A. (1975). The social meaning of differential physical and sexual maturation. In S. E. Dragastin & G. H. Elder, Jr., eds., *Adolescence in the life cycle: Psychological change and the social context.* New York: Halstead.
42. Conel, J. L. (1939–1967). *The postnatal development of the human cerebral cortex.* Vols. 1–87. Cambridge, Mass.: Harvard University Press.
43. Crawford, J. D., & Osler, D. C. (1975). Body composition at menarche: The Frisch-Revelle hypothesis revisited. *Pediatrics, 56*(3), 449–458.
44. de Beauvoir, S. (1968). *The second sex.* New York: Knopf.
45. Deutsch, H. (1944). *The psychology of women.* Vol. 1. New York: Grune & Stratton.
46. Dobbing, J., & Sands, J. (1973). Quantitative growth and development of the human brain. *Archives of Diseases in Childhood, 48,* 757–767.
47. Dornbusch, S. M.; Carlsmith, J. M.; Gross, R. T.; Martin, J. A.; Jennings, D.; Rosenberg, A.; & Duke, P. (1981). Sexual development, age, and dating: A comparison of biological and social influences upon one set of behaviors. *Child Development, 52,* 179–185.
48. Dornbusch, S. M.; Carlsmith, J. M.; Duncan, P. D.; Gross, R. T.; Martin, J. A.; Ritter, P. L.; Siegel-Gorelick, B. (1984). Sexual maturation, social class, and the desire to be thin among adolescent females. *Developmental and Behavioral Pediatrics, 5*(6), 308–314.
49. Dubas, J. S.; Crockett, L. J.; & Petersen, A. C. (1990). Longitudinal investi-

gation of sex and individual differences in cognitive abilities during early adolescence: The role of personality and the timing of puberty. Manuscript submitted for publication.

50. Duke, P. M.; Jennings, D. J.; Dornbusch, S. M.; & Siegel-Gorelick, B. (1982). Educational correlates of early and late sexual maturation in adolescence. *Journal of Pediatrics, 100*(4), 633–637.

51. Duncan, P. D.; Ritter, P. L.; Dornbusch, S. M.; Gross, R. T.; & Carlsmith, J. (1985). The effects of pubertal timing on body image, school behavior, and deviance. *Journal of Youth and Adolescence, 14,* 227–235.

52. Eichorn, D. H., & Bayley, N. (1962). Growth in head circumference from birth through young adulthood. *Child Development, 33,* 257–271.

53. Elliot, D. S., & Voss, H. L. (1974). *Delinquency and dropout.* Lexington, Mass.: D. C. Heath.

54. Epstein, H. T. (1974). Phrenoblysis: Special brain and mind growth periods. Pt. 2. Human mental development. *Developmental Psychobiology, 7,* 217–224.

55. Epstein, H. T. (1986). Stages in human brain development. *Developments in Brain Research, 30,* 114–119.

56. Epstein, H. T. & Toepfer, C. F. (1978). A neuroscience basis for reorganizing middle grades education. *Educational Leadership, 35,* 656–660.

57. Eveleth, P. B., & Tanner, J. M. (1976). *Worldwide variation in human growth.* London: Cambridge University Press.

58. Faust, M. S. (1983). Alternative constructions of adolescent growth. In J. Brooks-Gunn & A. C. Petersen, eds., *Girls at puberty: Biological and psychosocial perspectives.* New York: Plenum, pp. 105–125.

59. Frank, A. (1972). *The diary of a young girl.* New York: Pocket Books.

60. Frisch, R. E. (1984). Body fat, puberty, and fertility. *Biology Review, 59*(2), 161–188.

61. Frisch, R. E.; Wyshak, G.; & Vincent, L. (1980). Delayed menarche and amenorrhea in ballet dancers. *New England Journal of Medicine, 303*(1), 17–19.

62. Gaddis, A., & Brooks-Gunn, J. (1985). The male experience of pubertal change. *Journal of Youth and Adolescence, 14*(1), 61–69.

63. Gargiulo, J.; Attie, I.; Brooks-Gunn, J.; & Warren, M. P. (1987). Dating middle-school girls: Effects of social context, maturation, and grade. *Developmental Psychology, 23*(5), 730–737.

64. Garn, S. M. (1980). Continuities and change in maturational timing. In O. Brim & J. Kagan, eds., *Constancy and change in human development.* Cambridge, Mass.: Harvard University Press, pp. 113–162.

65. Garwood, S. G., & Allen, L. (1979). Self-concept and identified problem differences between pre- and post-menarcheal adolescents. *Journal of Clinical Psychology, 35,* 527–528.

66. Gay, V. L., & Plant, T. M. (1987). N-methyl-D,L aspartate elicits hypothalamic gonadotropin-releasing hormone release in prepubertal male rhesus monkeys (*Macaca mulatta*). *Endocrinology, 120,* 2289–96.

67. Gilligan, C. (1982). *In a different voice.* Cambridge, Mass.: Harvard University Press.

68. Gjerde, P. F., & Block, J. (1991, in press). The early personality context of

adolescent dysthymia: A prospective study of gender differences. *Journal of Youth and Adolescence.*

69. Graber, J. A., & Petersen, A. C. (1991, in press). Cognitive changes at adolescence: Biological perspectives. In K. Gibson & A. C. Petersen, eds., *Brain maturation and behavior development: Biosocial dimensions.* New York: Aldine.

70. Greenough, W. T.; Black, J. E.; & Wallace, C. S. (1987). Experience and brain development. *Child Development, 58,* 539–559.

71. Grief, E. B., & Ulman, K. J. (1982). The psychological impact of menarche on early adolescent females: A review of the literature. *Child Development, 53,* 1413–30.

72. Grotevant, H. D., & Cooper, C. R. (1986). Individuation in family relationships. *Human Development, 29,* 82–100.

73. *Growing up and liking it.* (1976). Milltown, N.J.: Personal Products.

74. Grumbach, M. M. (1985). True or central precocious puberty. In D. T. Krieger & C. W. Barden, eds., *Current therapy in endocrinology and metabolism.* Philadelphia: B. C. Decker, pp. 4–8.

75. Grumbach, M. M., & Sizonenko, P. C., eds. (1986). *Control of the onset of puberty.* Vol. 2. New York: Academic Press.

76. Gunnar, M. A., & Collins, W. A. (1988). *Development during the transitions in adolescence: Minnesota symposia on child psychology.* Vol. 21. Hillsdale, N.J.: Erlbaum.

77. Hall, G. S. (1904). *Adolescence: Its psychology and its relation to psychology, anthropology, sociology, sex, crime, religion, and education.* Englewood Cliffs, N.J.: Prentice-Hall.

78. Halmi, K. A. (1980). Eating disorders. In H. I. Kaplan, A. M. Freedman, & B. J. Sadock, eds., *Comprehensive textbook of psychiatry.* Vol. 3. Baltimore: Williams and Wilkins.

79. Hamburg, B. A. (1974). Coping in early adolescence. In S. Arieti, ed., *American handbook of psychiatry.* 2nd ed. New York: Basic Books, pp. 212–236.

80. Hamburg, B. A. (1980). Early adolescence as a life stress. In S. Levine and H. Ursin, eds., *Coping and health.* New York: Plenum Press, pp. 121–143.

81. Hamilton, L. H.; Brooks-Gunn, J.; Warren, M. P.; & Hamilton, W. G. (1988). The role of selectivity in the pathogenesis of eating disorders. *Medicine and Science in Sports and Exercise, 20*(6), 560–565.

82. Harris Poll. (1988). Report card for parents: When AIDs comes to school. *Children's Magazine,* pp. 1–8.

83. Harley, G. W. (1941). Notes on the Poro in Liberia. In B. B. Sommer, ed., *Puberty and adolescence.* New York: Oxford University Press, p. 24.

84. Hayes, C. D., ed. (1987). *Risking the future: Adolescent sexuality, pregnancy, and childbearing.* Vol. 1. Washington, D.C.: National Academy of Sciences Press.

85. Hill, J. P. (1982). Early adolescence. Special issue. *Child Development, 53*(6).

86. Hill, J. P. (1988). Adapting to menarche: Familial control and conflict. In M. R. Gunnar & W. A. Collins, eds., *Development during the transition to adolescence.* Vol. 21. Hillsdale, N.J.: Erlbaum, pp. 43–77.

87. Hill, J. P., & Lynch, M. E. (1983). The intensification of gender-related role

expectations during early adolescence. In J. Brooks-Gunn & A. C. Petersen, eds., *Girls at puberty: Biological and psychosocial perspectives*. New York: Plenum, pp. 201–228.

88. Hofferth, S. L., & Hayes, C. D., eds., (1987). *Risking the future: Adolescent sexuality, pregnancy, and childbearing*. Vol. 2. Washington, D.C.: National Academy of Sciences Press.

89. Holland, B. A.; Haas, D. K.; Norman, D.; Brant-Zawadzki, M.; & Newton, T. H. (1986). MRI of normal brain maturation. *American Journal of Neuroradiology, 7,* 201–208.

90. Irwin, C., ed. (1987). *New directions for child development*. San Francisco: Jossey-Bass.

91. Jessor, S. L., & Jessor, R. (1975). Transition from virginity to nonvirginity among youth: A social-psychological study over time. *Developmental Psychology, 11*(4), 473–484.

92. Jones, E.; Forrest, J. D.; Henshaw, S. K.; Silverman, J.; & Torres, A. (1988). Unintended pregnancy, contraceptive practice, and family planning services in developed countries. *Family Planning Perspectives, 20*(2), 53–67.

93. Josselson, R. L. (1980). Psychodynamic aspects of identity formation in college women. *Journal of Youth and Adolescence, 2,* 3–52.

94. Kaplan, S. L.; Grumbach, M. M.; & Aubert, M. L. (1976). The ontogenesis of pituitary hormones and hypothalamic factors in the human fetus: Maturation of the central nervous system regulation of anterior pituitary function. *Recent Progress in Hormone Research, 32,* 161–243.

95. Kirby, D. (1984). *Sexuality education: An evaluation of programs and their effects*. Santa Cruz: Network Publications.

96. Koff, E.; Rierdan, J.; & Silverstone, E. (1978). Changes in representation of body image as a function of menarcheal status. *Developmental Psychology, 14,* 635–642.

97. Kretschmann, H. J.; Kammradt, G.; Krauthausen, I.; Sauer, B.; & Wingert, F. (1986). Brain growth in man. *Bibliotheca Anatomica, 28,* 1–26.

98. Kulin, H. E.; Buibo, N.; Mutie, D.; & Sorter, S. (1982). The effect of chronic childhood malnutrition on pubertal growth and development. *American Journal of Clinical Nutrition, 36,* 527–536.

99. Laron, Z.; Arad, J.; Gurewitz, R.; Grunebaum, M.; & Dickerman, Z. (1980). Age at first conscious ejaculation: A milestone in male puberty. *Helvetica Paediatrica Acta, 5,* 13–20.

100. Larsen, V. L. (1961). Sources of menstrual information: A comparison of age groups. *Family Life Coordinator, 10,* 41–43.

101. Lerner, R. M., & Foch, T. T., eds. (1987). *Biological-psychosocial interactions in early adolescence: A life-span perspective*. Hillsdale, N.J.: Erlbaum Associates.

102. Liestol, K. (1982). Social conditions and menarcheal age: The importance of the early years of life. *Annals of Human Biology, 9,* 521–536.

103. Linn, M. C., & Petersen, A. C. (1985). Emergence and characterization of sex differences in spatial ability: A meta-analysis. *Child Development, 56,* 1479–98.

104. Lipsitz, J. (1977). *Growing up forgotten: A review of research and programs concerning young adolescents*. Lexington, Mass.: D. C. Heath.

105. Magnusson, D.; Strattin, H.; & Allen, V. L. (1985). Biological maturation and

social development: A longitudinal study of some adjustment processes from midadolescence to adulthood. *Journal of Youth and Adolescence, 14*(4), 267–283.

106. Magnusson, D., et al. (1988). *Individual development from an interactional perspective: A longitudinal study.* Hillsdale, N.J.: Erlbaum.

107. Malina, R. M. (1983). Menarche in athletes: A synthesis and hypothesis. *Annals of Human Biology, 10*(1), 1–24.

108. Marsh, R. W. (1985). Phrenoblysis: Real or chimera? *Child Development, 56,* 1059–61.

109. Marshall, W. A., & Tanner, J. M. (1969). Variations in pattern of pubertal changes in girls. *Archives of Diseases in Childhood, 44,* 291–303.

110. Marshall, W. A., & Tanner, J. M. (1970). Variations in the pattern of pubertal changes in girls. *Archives of Diseases in Childhood, 45,* 13–23.

111. McArnery, E. R., & Levine, M., eds. (1987). *Early adolescent transitions.* New York: Heath Publications.

112. McCall, R. B.; Meyers, E. C., Jr.; Hartman, J.; & Roche, A. F. (1983). Developmental changes in head-circumference and mental-performance growth rates: A test of Epstein's hypothesis. *Developmental Psychobiology, 16,* 457–468.

113. Mead, M. (1935). *Sex and temperament.* New York: William Morrow and Co.

114. Money, J., & Ehrhardt, A. A. (1972). *Man and woman, boy and girl.* Baltimore: Johns Hopkins University Press.

115. Morris, N. M., & Udry, J. R. (1980). Validation of a self-administered instrument to assess stage of adolescent development. *Journal of Youth and Adolescence, 9,* 275–276.

116. Mussen, P. H., & Jones, M. C. (1957). Self-conceptions, motivations, and interpersonal attitudes of late- and early-maturing boys. *Child Development, 28,* 243–256.

117. Nesselroade, J. R., & Baltes, P. B. (1974). Adolescent personality development and historical change: 1970–1972. *Monographs of the Society for Research in Child Development, 39*(1), ser. no. 154.

118. Newcombe, N., & Dubas, J. S. (1987). Individual differences in cognitive ability: Are they related to timing of puberty? In R. M. Lerner & T. T. Foch, eds., *Biological-psychosocial interactions in early adolescence.* Hillsdale, N.J.: Erlbaum.

119. Nolen-Hoeksema, S.; Girgus, J. S.; & Seligman, M. E. P. (1991, in press). Sex differences in depression and explanatory style in children. *Journal of Youth and Adolescence.*

120. Offer, D. (1987). In defense of adolescents. *Journal of the American Medical Association, 257*(24), 3407–8.

121. Olweus, D. (1984). Stability in aggressive and withdrawal inhibited behavior patterns. In R. Kaplan, V. Konecni, & R. Novaco, eds., *Aggression in children and youth.* Boston: Martinus Nijhoff Publishers, pp. 162–174.

122. Paige, K. E. (1983). A bargaining theory of menarcheal responses in preindustrial cultures. In J. Brooks-Gunn & A. C. Petersen, eds., *Girls at puberty: Biological and psychosocial perspectives.* New York: Plenum Press, pp. 301–322.

123. Paikoff, R. L., & Brooks-Gunn, J. (1989). Physiological processes: What role do they play during the transition to adolescence? In R. Montemayor, G. Adams, & T. Gullotta, eds., *Advances in adolescent development.* Vol. 2. *The*

transition from childhood to adolescence. Beverly Hills: Sage Publications, pp. 63–81.

124. Parlee, M. B. (1973). The premenstrual syndrome. *Psychological Bulletin, 80*(6), 454–465.
125. Peskin, H. (1967). Pubertal onset and ego functioning. *Journal of Abnormal Psychology, 72,* 1–15.
126. Petersen, A. C. (1983). Pubertal change and cognition. In J. Brooks-Gunn & A. C. Petersen, eds., *Girls at puberty: Biological and psychosocial perspectives.* New York: Plenum, pp. 179–198.
127. Petersen, A. C. (1987). The nature of biological-psychosocial interactions: The sample case of early adolescence. In R. M. Lerner & T. T. Foch, eds., *Biological-psychosocial interactions in early adolescence: A life-span perspective.* Hillsdale, N.J.: Erlbaum, pp. 35–61.
128. Petersen, A. C. (1988). Adolescent development. In M. R. Rosenzweig, ed., *Annual review of psychology.* Palo Alto: Annual Reviews, pp. 583–607.
129. Petersen, A. C., & Crockett, L. (1985). Pubertal timing and grade effects on adjustment. *Journal of Youth and Adolescence, 14*(3), 191–206.
130. Plant, T. M. (1986). Gonadal regulation of hypothalamic-gonadotropin releasing hormone release in primates. *Endocrine Review, 7,* 75–88.
131. Plant, T. M. (1988). Puberty in primates. In E. Knobil and J. Neill, eds., *The Physiology of Reproduction.* Vol. 2. New York: Raven Press, pp. 1763–88.
132. Pratt, D. I.; Finkelstein, J. S.; O'Dey, St. L.; Badger, T. M.; Rau, P. N.; Campbell, J. D.; & Crowley, W. F. (1986). Long-term administration of gonadotropin-releasing hormones in men with idiopathic hypogonadotropic hypogonadism. *Annals of Internal Medicine, 105,* 848–855.
133. Puig-Antich, J. (1987). Affective disorders in children and adolescents: Diagnosis validity and psychobiology. In H. Meltzer, ed., *Psychopharmacology: The third generation of progress.* New York: Raven Press.
134. Rabinowicz, T. (1986). The differentiated maturation of the cerebral cortex. In F. Falkner & J. M. Tanner, eds., *Human growth: A comprehensive treatise.* Vol. 2. New York: Plenum, pp. 385–410.
135. Reiter, E. O. (1987). Neuroendocrine control process: Pubertal onset and progression. *Journal of Adolescent Health Care, 8,* 479–491.
136. Reiter, E. O., & Grumbach, M. M. (1982). Neuroendocrine control mechanisms and the onset of puberty. *Annual Review of Physiology, 44,* 595–613.
137. Robins, L. N. (1966). *Deviant children grown up: A sociological and psychiatric study of sociopathic personality.* Baltimore: Williams and Wilkins.
138. Ruble, D. N., & Brooks-Gunn, J. (1979). Menstrual symptoms: A social cognitive analysis. *Journal of Behavioral Medicine, 2,* 171–194.
139. Ruble, D. N., & Brooks-Gunn, J. (1982). The experience of menarche. *Child Development, 53,* 1557–66.
140. Rutter, M.; Graham, P.; Chadwick, O. F.; & Yule, W. (1976). Adolescent turmoil: Fact or fiction. *Journal of Child Psychology and Psychiatry, 17,* 35–56.
141. Shipman, G. (1971). The psychodynamics of sex education. In R. E. Muuss, ed., *Adolescent behavior and society: A book of readings.* New York: Random House, pp. 326–336.

142. Shulman, A. K. (1976). *Memoirs of an ex-prom queen*. New York: Bantam Books.

143. Simmons, R. G., & Blyth, D. A. (1987). *Moving into adolescence: The impact of pubertal change and school context*. New York: Aldine-De Gruyter.

144. Simmons, R. G.; Blyth, D. A.; & McKinney, K. L. (1983). The social and psychological effects of puberty on white females. In J. Brooks-Gunn & A. C. Petersen, eds., *Girls at puberty: Biological and psychosocial perspectives*. New York: Plenum, pp. 229–272.

145. Simmons, R. G.; Burgeson, R.; & Reef, M. J. (1988). Cumulative change at entry to adolescence. In M. A. Gunnar & W. A. Collins, eds., *Development during transition to adolescence: Minnesota symposia on child psychology*. Vol. 21. Hillsdale, N.J.: Erlbaum, pp. 123–47.

146. Sisk, C. L., & Bronson, F. H. (1986). Effects of food restriction and restoration on gonadotropin and growth hormone secretion in immature female rats. *Biological Reproduction, 35,* 554–561.

147. Smetana, J. G. (1988). Concepts of self and social convention: Adolescents' and parents' reasoning about hypothetical and actual family conflicts. In M. A. Gunnar & W. A. Collins, eds., *Development during transition to adolescence: Minnesota symposia on child psychology*. Vol. 21. Hillsdale, N.J.: Erlbaum, pp. 79–119.

148. Steinberg, L. (1988). Reciprocal relation between parent-child distance and pubertal maturation. *Developmental Psychology, 24*(1), 122–128.

149. Steinberg, L. D., & Hill, J. P. (1978). Patterns of family interaction as a function of age, the onset of puberty, and formal thinking. *Developmental Psychology, 14,* 683–684.

150. Steiner, R. A.; Cameron, J. L.; McNeill, T. H.; et al. (1983). Metabolic signals for the onset of puberty. In R. L. Norman, ed., *Neuroendocrine aspects of reproduction*. New York: Academic Press, pp. 183–227.

151. Stunkard, A. J.; Sorensen, T. I. A.; Hanis, D.; Teasdale, T. W.; Chakraborty, R.; Schull, W. J.; & Schulsinger, F. (1986). An adoption study of obesity. *New England Journal of Medicine, 314,* 193–198.

152. Susman, E. J.; Inoff-Germain, G.; Nottelmann, E. D.; Loriaux, D. L.; Cutler, G. B.; & Chrousos, G. P. (1987). Hormones, emotional dispositions, and aggressive attributes in young adolescents. *Child Development, 58,* 1114–34.

153. Tanner, J. M. (1962). *Growth at adolescence*. New York: Lippincott.

154. Tanner, J. M. (1981). *A history of the study of human growth*. Cambridge: Cambridge University Press.

155. Tanner, J. M., & Davies, P. S. W. (1985). Clinical longitudinal standards for height and height velocity for North American children. *Journal of Pediatrics, 107,* 317–329.

156. Tanner, J. M.; Whitehouse, R. H.; & Takaishi, M. (1966). Standards from birth to maturity for height, weight, height velocity, and weight velocity: British children, 1965. *Archives of Disease in Childhood, 41,* 454–471, 613–635.

157. Thatcher, R. W.; Walker, R. A.; & Giudice, S. (1987). Human cerebral hemispheres develop at different rates and ages. *Science, 236,* 1110–13.

158. Thornberry, O. T.; Wilson, R. W.; & Golden, P. (1986). Health promotion and

disease prevention provisional data from the National Health Interview Survey: United States, January–June 1985. *Vital and Health Statistics of the National Center for Health Statistics, 119*, 1–16.

159. Udry, J. R.; Richard, L. T.; & Morris, N. M. (1986). Biosocial foundations for adolescent female sexuality. *Demography, 23*(2) 217–230.

160. Udry, J. R.; Billy, J. O.; Morris, N. M.; Groff, T. R.; & Raj, M. H. (1985). Serum androgenic hormones motivate sexual behavior in adolescent boys. *Fertility and Sterility, 43*(1), 90–94.

161. Waber, D. P. (1976). Sex differences in cognition: A function of maturation rate? *Science, 192*, 572–574.

162. Waber, D. P. (1977). Sex differences in mental abilities, hemisphere lateralization, and rate of physical growth at adolescence. *Developmental Psychology, 13*, 29–38.

163. Warren, M. (1980). The effects of exercise on pubertal progression and reproductive function in girls. *Journal of Clinical Endocrinology and Metabolism, 51*, 1150–57.

164. Warren, M. P. (1985). When weight loss accompanies amenorrhea. *Contemporary Obstetrics and Gynecology, 28*(3), 588–597.

165. Warren, M. P.; Brooks-Gunn, J.; Hamilton, L. H.; Hamilton, W. G.; & Warren, L. F. (1986). Scoliosis and fractures in young ballet dancers: Relation to delayed menarche and secondary amenorrhea. *New England Journal of Medicine, 314*, 1348–53.

166. Weideger, P. (1975). *Menstruation and menopause*. New York: Knopf.

167. Wooley, S. C., & Wooley, O. W. (1985). Intensive outpatient and residential treatment for bulimia. In D. M. Garner & P. E. Garfinkel, eds., *Handbook of psychotherapy for anorexia nervosa and bulimia*. New York: Guilford Press, pp. 391–430.

168. Zindel, P. (1971). *My darling, my hamburger*. New York: Bantam.

3. Adolescent Thinking

1. Alexander, K. L., & Entwisle, D. R. (1989). Achievement in the first two years of school: Patterns and processes. *Monographs of the Society for Research in Child Development, 53*(2), ser. no. 218.

2. Anderson, D. (1984). In F. Morrison, C. Lord, & D. Keating, eds., *Applied developmental psychology*. Vol. 1. New York: Academic Press, pp. 116–163.

3. Baker, D. P., & Entwisle, D. R. (1987). The influence of mothers on the academic expectations of young children: A longitudinal study of how gender differences arise. *Social Forces, 65*, 670–695.

4. Baltes, P. B. (1987). Theoretical propositions of life-span developmental psychology: On the dynamics between growth and decline. *Developmental Psychology, 23*, 611–626.

5. Barenboim, C. (1981). The development of person perception in childhood and adolescence: From behavioral comparisons to psychological constructs to psychological constructions. *Child Development, 52*, 129–144.

6. Benbow, C. P., & Stanley, J. C. (1980). Sex differences in mathematical ability: Fact or artifact? *Science, 210,* 1262.
7. Bennett, S. (1987). *New dimensions in research on class size and academic achievement.* Madison, Wis.: National Center on Effective Secondary Schools.
8. Bloom, B., ed. (1985). *Developing talent in young people.* New York: Ballantine Books.
9. Bowles, S., & Gintis, H. (1976). *Schooling in capitalist America.* New York: Basic Books.
10. Braine, M. D. S., & Rumain, B. (1983). Logical reasoning. In J. H. Flavell & E. M. Markman, eds., *Handbook of child psychology.* Vol. 3. New York: Wiley, pp. 263–340.
11. Bransford, J. D.; Arbitman-Smith, R.; Stein, B. S.; & Vye, N. J. (1985). Improving thinking and learning skills: An analysis of three approaches. In J. W. Segal, S. F. Chipman, & R. Glaser, eds., *Thinking and learning skills.* Vol. 1. Hillsdale, N.J.: Erlbaum, pp. 133–206.
12. Bronfenbrenner, U., & Crouter, A. (1983). The evolution of environmental models in developmental research. In P. Mussen, ed., *Handbook of child psychology.* Vol. 1. New York: Wiley.
13. Brown, A. L.; Bransford, J. D.; Ferrara, R. A.; & Campione, J. C. (1983). Learning, remembering, and understanding. In J. H. Flavell & E. M. Markman, eds., *Handbook of child psychology.* Vol. 3. New York: Wiley, pp. 77–166.
14. Byrnes, J. P. (1988). Formal operations: A systematic reformulation. *Developmental Review, 8,* 1–22.
15. Byrnes, J. P., & Overton, W. F. (1986). Reasoning about certainty and uncertainty in concrete, causal, and propositional contexts. *Developmental Psychology, 22,* 793–799.
16. Campione, J. C., & Armbruster, B. B. (1985). Acquiring information from texts: An analysis of four approaches. In J. W. Segal, S. F. Chipman, & R. Glaser, eds., *Thinking and learning skills.* Vol. 1. Hillsdale, N.J.: Erlbaum, pp. 317–359.
17. Carey, S. (1986). Cognitive science and science education. *American Psychologist, 41,* 1123–30.
18. Case, R. (1978). Intellectual development from birth to adulthood: A neo-Piagetian interpretation. In R. S. Siegler, ed., *Children's thinking: What develops?* Hillsdale, N.J.: Erlbaum.
19. Case, R. (1985). *Intellectual development: Birth to adulthood.* New York: Academic Press.
20. Case, R., & Sowder, J. T. (in press). The development of computational estimation: A neo-Piagetian analysis. *Cognition and Instruction.*
21. Cavanaugh, J. C., & Perlmutter, M. (1982). Metamemory: A critical reexamination. *Child Development, 53,* 11–28.
22. Chance, P. (1986). *Thinking in the classroom: A survey of programs.* New York: Teachers College Press.
23. Chandler, M. (1987). The Othello effect: Essay on the emergence and eclipse of skeptical doubt. *Human Development, 30,* 137–159.

24. Cheng, P. W.; Holyoak, K. J.; Nisbett, R. E.; & Oliver, L. M. (1986). Pragmatic versus syntactic approaches to training deductive reasoning. *Cognitive Psychology, 18,* 293–328.

25. Chi, M. T. H. (1978). Knowledge structures and memory development. In R. S. Siegler, ed., *Children's thinking: What develops?* Hillsdale, N.J.: Erlbaum.

26. Chi, M. T. H.; Glaser, R.; & Rees, E. (1982). Expertise in problem solving. In R. J. Sternberg, ed., *Advances in the psychology of human intelligence.* Vol. 1. Hillsdale, N.J.: Erlbaum, pp. 7–75.

27. Colby, A.; Kohlberg, L.; Gibbs, J.; & Lieberman, M. A. (1983). A longitudinal study of moral judgment. *Monographs of the Society for Research in Child Development,* ser. no. 200.

28. Cole, M., & Means, B. (1981). *Comparative studies of how people think.* Cambridge, Mass.: Harvard University Press.

29. Compas, B. E. (1987). Coping with stress during childhood and adolescence. *Psychological Bulletin, 101,* 393–403.

30. diSessa, A. A. (1988). Knowledge in pieces. In G. Forman & P. Pufall, eds., *Constructivism in the computer age.* Hillsdale, N.J.: Erlbaum.

31. Elkind, D. (1967). Egocentrism in adolescence. *Child Development, 38,* 1025–34.

32. Epstein, H. T. (1974). Phrenoblysis: Special brain and mind growth periods. *Developmental Psychobiology, 7,* 207–216.

33. Epstein, H. T., & Toepfer, C. F., Jr. (1978). A neuroscience basis for reorganizing middle grades education. *Educational Leadership, 35,* 656–660.

34. Eylon, B., & Linn, M. (forthcoming). Learning and instruction: An examination of four research perspectives in science education. *Review of Educational Research.*

35. Feldman, D. (1986). *Nature's gambit.* New York: Basic Books.

36. Fischer, K. W., & Pipp, S. L. (1984). Processes of cognitive development: Optimal level and skill acquisition. In R. J. Sternberg, ed., *Mechanisms of cognitive development.* New York: Freeman & Co., pp. 45–80.

37. Ford, M. E. (1982). Social cognition and social competence in adolescence. *Developmental Psychology, 18,* 323–340.

38. Frederiksen, N. (1984). The real test bias: Influences of testing on teaching and learning. *American Psychologist, 39,* 193–202.

39. Gardner, H. (1983). *Frames of mind.* New York: Basic Books.

40. Gelman, R., & Baillargeon, R. (1983). A review of some Piagetian concepts. In J. H. Flavell & E. M. Markman, eds., *Handbook of child psychology.* Vol. 3. New York: Wiley, pp. 167–230.

41. Gilligan, C. (1982). *In a different voice.* Cambridge, Mass.: Harvard University Press.

42. Glaser, R. (1984). Education and thinking: The role of knowledge. *American Psychologist, 39,* 93–104.

43. Goodlad, J. (1984). *A place called school.* New York: McGraw-Hill.

44. Gouze, K. R.; Strauss, D.; & Keating, D. P. (1986). Adolescents' conceptions of stress and coping. Paper presented at the Biennial Meeting of the Society for Research in Adolescence, Madison, Wis.

45. Greenough, W. T.; Black, J. E.; & Wallace, C. S. (1987). Experience and brain development. *Child Development, 58,* 539–559.

46. Grotevant, H. D., & Cooper, C. R. (1988). The role of family experience in career exploration: A life-span perspective. In P. B. Baltes, D. L. Featherman, & R. M. Lerner, eds., *Life-span development and behavior.* Vol. 8. Hillsdale, N.J.: Erlbaum, pp. 231–258.
47. Hahn, W. K. (1987). Cerebral lateralization of function: From infancy through childhood. *Psychological Bulletin, 101,* 376–392.
48. Hakuta, K. (1987). Degree of bilingualism and cognitive ability in mainland Puerto Rican children. *Child Development, 58,* 1372–88.
49. Herrnstein, R.; Nickerson, R.; de Sanchez, M.; & Swets, J. (1986). Teaching thinking skills. *American Psychologist, 41,* 1279–89.
50. Hyde, J. S., & Linn, M. C. (1988). Gender differences in verbal ability: A meta-analysis. *Psychological Bulletin, 104,* 53–69.
51. Inhelder, B., & Piaget, J. (1958). *The growth of logical thinking from childhood to adolescence.* New York: Basic Books.
52. Jensen, A. R. (1980). *Bias in mental testing.* New York: Free Press.
53. Keating, D. P. (1974). The study of mathematically precocious youth. In J. C. Stanley, D. P. Keating, & L. H. Fox, eds., *Mathematical talent: Discovery, description, and development.* Baltimore, Md.: Johns Hopkins University Press.
54. Keating, D. P. (1975). Precocious cognitive development at the level of formal operations. *Child Development, 46,* 476–480.
55. Keating, D. P. (1980a). Four faces of creativity: The continuing plight of the intellectually underserved. *Gifted Child Quarterly, 24,* 56–61.
56. Keating, D. P. (1980b). Thinking processes in adolescence. In J. Adelson, ed., *Handbook of adolescent psychology.* New York: Wiley, pp. 211–246.
57. Keating, D. P. (1988a). *Adolescents' ability to engage in critical thinking.* Madison, Wis.: National Center for Effective Secondary Education.
58. Keating, D. P. (1988b). Byrnes' reformulation of Piaget's formal operations: Is what's left what's right? *Developmental Review, 8,* 376–384.
59. Keating, D. P. (forthcoming). Structuralism, deconstruction, reconstruction: The limits of reasoning. In W. F. Overton, ed., *Reasoning, necessity, and logic: Developmental perspectives.* Hillsdale, N.J.: Erlbaum.
60. Keating, D. P., & Bobbitt, B. L. (1978). Individual and developmental differences in cognitive-processing components of mental ability. *Child Development, 49,* 155–167.
61. Keating, D. P., & Clark, L. V. (1980). Development of physical and social reasoning in adolescence. *Developmental Psychology, 16,* 23–30.
62. Keating, D. P., & MacLean, D. J. (1987). Cognitive ability, cognitive processing, and development: A reconsideration. In P. A. Vernon, ed., *Speed of information-processing and intelligence.* Norwood, N.J.: Ablex.
63. Keating, D. P., & MacLean, D. J. (1988). Reconstruction in cognitive development: A post-structuralist agenda. In P. B. Baltes, D. L. Featherman, and R. M. Lerner, eds., *Life span development and behavior.* Vol. 8. Hillsdale, N.J.: Erlbaum.
64. Kegan, R. (1982). *The evolving self.* Cambridge, Mass.: Harvard University Press.
65. Kegan, R. (1983). A neo-Piagetian approach to object relations. In B. Lee &

G. Noam, eds., *Developmental approaches to the self.* New York: Plenum, pp. 267–307.

66. Kitchener, K. S., & King, P. M. (1981). Reflective judgment: Concepts of justification and their relation to age and education. *Journal of Applied Developmental Psychology, 2,* 89–116.

67. Klayman, J. (1985). Children's decision strategies and their adaptation to task characteristics. *Organizational Behavior and Human Decision Process, 35,* 179–201.

68. Kline, M. (1984). *Mathematics: The loss of certainty.* New York: Oxford University Press.

69. Kohlberg, L. (1958). The development of modes of moral thinking and choice in the years 10 to 16. Ph.D. dissertation, University of Chicago.

70. Kohn, M. L., & Schooler, C. (1985). *Work and personality.* Norwood, N.J.: Ablex.

71. Koslowski, B., & Okagaki, L. (1986). Non-Humean indices of causation in problem-solving situations: Causal mechanism, analogous effects, and the status of alternative rival accounts. *Child Development, 57,* 1100–8.

72. Koslowski, B.; Okagaki, L.; Lorenz, C.; & Umbach, D. (in press). When covariation isn't enough: The role of causal mechanism, sampling method, and sample size in causal reasoning. *Child Development.*

73. Kuhn, D.; Amsel, E.; & O'Loughlin, M. (1988). *The development of scientific thinking skills.* San Diego: Academic Press.

74. Kuhn, D.; Ho, V.; & Adams, C. (1979). Formal reasoning among pre- and late adolescents. *Child Development, 50,* 1128–35.

75. Lapsley, D. K.; Milstead, M.; Quintana, S. M.; Flannery, D.; & Buss, R. R. (1986). Adolescent egocentrism and formal operations: Tests of a theoretical assumption. *Developmental Psychology, 22,* 800–807.

76. Lewis, C. C. (1981). How adolescents approach decisions: Changes over grades seven to twelve and policy implications. *Child Development, 52,* 538–554.

77. Linn, M. C. (1983). Content, context, and process in reasoning during adolescence: Selecting a model. *Journal of Early Adolescence, 3,* 63–82.

78. Linn, M. C.; Delucchi, K. L.; & deBenedictis, T. (1984). Adolescent reasoning about advertisements: Relevance of product claims. *Journal of Early Adolescence, 4,* 371–385.

79. Linn, M. C., & Petersen, A. C. (1985). Emergence and characterization of sex differences in spatial ability. *Child Development, 56,* 1479–98.

80. Manis, F. R.; Keating, D. P.; & Morrison, F. J. (1980). Developmental differences in the allocation of processing capacity. *Journal of Experimental Child Psychology, 29,* 156–169.

81. Mann, L.; Harmoni, R.; & Power, C. N. (in press). Adolescent decision making: The development of competence. *Journal of Adolescence.*

82. Mann, L.; Harmoni, R. V.; Power, C. N.; Beswick, G.; & Ormond, C. (1988). Effectiveness of the GOFER course in decision making for high school students. *Journal of Behavioral Decision Making, 1,* 159–168.

83. Marsh, R. W. (1985). Phrenoblysis: Real or chimera? *Child Development, 56,* 1059–61.

84. Morrison, F. J.; Lord, C. A.; & Keating, D. P. (1984). Applied developmental

psychology. In F. Morrison, C. Lord, & D. Keating, eds., *Applied Developmental Psychology*. Vol. 1. New York: Academic Press, pp. 1–20.

85. Moshman, D., & Franks, B. A. (1986). Development of the concept of inferential validity. *Child Development*, 57, 153–165.

86. Neville, R. C. (1981). *Reconstruction of thinking*. Albany: SUNY Press.

87. Newmann, F. M. (forthcoming). Higher order thinking in the teaching of social studies: Connections between theory and practice. In D. Perkins, J. Segal, & J. Voss, eds., *Informal reasoning and education*. Hillsdale, N.J.: Erlbaum.

88. Nickerson, R. S. (in press). On improving thinking through instruction. *Review of Research in Education*.

89. Nickerson, R. S.; Perkins, D. N.; & Smith, E. E. (1985). *The teaching of thinking*. Hillsdale, N.J.: Erlbaum.

90. Nisbett, R. E.; Fong, G. T.; Lehman, D. R.; & Cheng, P. W. (1987). Teaching reasoning. *Science*, 237, 625–631.

91. Olson, D. (1986). Intelligence and literacy. In R. Sternberg & R. Wagner, eds. *Practical intelligence*. New York: Cambridge University Press.

92. Overton, W. F.; Ward, S. L.; Noveck, I. A.; Black, J.; & O'Brien, D. P. (1987). Form and content in the development of deductive reasoning. *Developmental Psychology*, 23, 22–30.

93. Palincsar, A. S., & Brown, A. L. (1984). Reciprocal teaching of comprehension-fostering and monitoring activities. *Cognition and Instruction*, 1, 117–175.

94. Parsons, J. E.; Adler, T. F.; & Kaczala, C. M. (1982). Socialization of achievement attitudes and beliefs: Parental influences. *Child Development*, 53, 310–321.

95. Parsons, J. E.; Kaczala, C. M.; & Meece, J. L. (1982). Socialization of achievement attitudes and beliefs: Classroom influences. *Child Development*, 53, 322–339.

96. Petersen, A. C. (1988). Adolescent development. *Annual Review of Psychology*, 39, 583–607.

97. Piaget, J. (1972). Intellectual evolution from adolescence to adulthood. *Human Development*, 15, 1–12.

98. Plomin, R., & Thompson, L. (1988). Life-span developmental behavioral genetics. In P. B. Baltes, D. L. Featherman, & R. M. Lerner, eds., *Life-span development and behavior*. Vol. 8. Hillsdale, N.J.: Erlbaum, pp. 1–31.

99. Potvin, L.; Champagne, F.; & Laberge-Nadeau, C. (1988). Mandatory driver training and road safety: The Quebec experience. *American Journal of Public Health*, 78, 1206–12.

100. *Profile of American youth* (1982). Washington, D.C.: U.S. Government. Department of Defense.

101. Resnick, L. B. (1986). *Education and learning to think*. Washington, D.C.: National Research Council.

102. Rest, J. R. (1983). Morality. In J. H. Flavell & E. M. Markman, eds., *Handbook of child psychology*. Vol. 3. New York: Wiley, pp. 556–629.

103. Robertson, L. S. (1984). Federal funds and state motor vehicle deaths. *Journal of Public Health Policy*, 5, 376–386.

104. Rossiter, J. R. (1980). Source effects and self-concept appeals in children's television advertising. In R. P. Adler et al., eds., *The effects of television*. Lexington, Mass.: Lexington Books.

105. Scardamalia, M.; Bereiter, C.; McLean, R. S.; Swallow, J.; & Woodruff, E. (1989). Computer supported intentional learning environments. *Journal of Educational Computing Research, 5,* 51–68.
106. Schrag, F. (1987). Thoughtfulness: Is high school the place for thinking? *National Center on Effective Secondary Schools Newsletter, 2,* 2–4.
107. Selman, R. L. (1980). *The growth of interpersonal understanding.* New York: Academic Press.
108. Selman, R. L.; Beardslee, W.; Schultz, L. H.; Krupa, M.; & Podorefsky, D. (1986). Assessing adolescent interpersonal negotiation strategies: Toward the integration of structural and functional models. *Developmental Psychology, 22,* 450–459.
109. Shantz, C. U. (1983). Social cognition. In J. H. Flavell & E. M. Markman, eds., *Handbook of child psychology.* Vol. 3. New York: Wiley, pp. 495–555.
110. Shimp, T. A. (1979). Social psychological (mis)representations in television advertising. *Journal of Consumer Affairs, 13,* 28–40.
111. Shor, I. (1987). *Critical teaching and everyday life.* Chicago: University of Chicago Press.
112. Spivack, G., & Shure, M. B. (1982). The cognition of social adjustment: Interpersonal cognitive problem-solving thinking. In B. B. Lahey & A. E. Kazdin, eds., *Advances in clinical child psychology.* Vol. 5. New York: Plenum, pp. 323–372.
113. Sternberg, R. J. (1988). *The triarchic mind.* New York: Viking.
114. Sternberg, R. J., & Powell, J. S. (1983). The development of intelligence. In J. H. Flavell & E. M. Markman, eds., *Handbook of child psychology.* Vol. 3. New York: Wiley, pp. 341–419.
115. Thatcher, R. W.; Walker, R. A.; & Giudice, S. (1987). Human cerebral hemispheres develop at different rates and ages. *Science, 236,* 1110–13.
116. Turiel, E. (1989). Domain-specific social judgments and domain ambiguities. *Merrill-Palmer Quarterly, 35,* 89–114.
117. Vygotsky, L. S. (1978). *Mind in society.* Cambridge, Mass.: Harvard University Press.
118. Waber, D. P. (1976). Sex differences in cognition: A function of maturation rate? *Science, 192,* 572–574.
119. Waber, D. P. (1977). Sex differences in mental abilities, hemispheric lateralization, and rate of physical growth at adolescence. *Developmental Psychology, 13,* 29–38.
120. Weithorn, L. A., & Campbell, S. B. (1982). The competency of children to make informed treatment decisions. *Child Development, 53,* 1589–98.
121. White, V. Y. (in press). ThinkerTools: Causal models, conceptual change, and science education. *Cognition and Instruction.*

4. Historical Perspectives

1. Addams, J. (1909). *The spirit of youth and the city streets.* New York: Macmillan.
2. Addams, J. (1910). *Twenty years at Hull-House.* New York: Macmillan.
3. Allmendinger, D. F., Jr. (1975). *Paupers and scholars: The transformation of student life in nineteenth-century New England.* New York: St. Martin's.

4. Atkinson, P., et al. (1982). Social and life skills: The latest case of compensatory education. In T. L. Rees and P. Atkinson, eds., *Youth unemployment and state intervention*. London: Routledge & Kegan Paul.

5. Bailey, B. L. (1988). *From front porch to back seat: Courtship in twentieth-century America*. Baltimore: Johns Hopkins University Press.

6. Barker-Benfield, G. J. (1976). *The horrors of the half-known life: Male attitudes toward women and sexuality in nineteenth-century America*. New York: Harper and Row.

7. Berkner, L. K. (1972). The stem family and the developmental cycle of the peasant household: An 18th-century Austrian example. *American Historical Review, 77,* 398–418.

8. Blumenthal, A. (1932). *Small town stuff*. Chicago: University of Chicago Press.

9. Brumberg, J. J. (1988). *Fasting girls: The emergence of anorexia nervosa as a modern disease*. Cambridge, Mass.: Harvard University Press.

10. Buchmann, M. (1989). *The script of life in modern society*. Chicago: University of Chicago Press.

11. Carter, M. P. (1962). *Home, school, and work*. New York: Macmillan.

12. Coffield, F. (1987). From the celebration to the marginalization of youth. In G. Cohen, ed., *Social change and the life course*. London: Tavistock.

13. Coffield, F.; Borrill, C.; & Marshall, S. (1986). *Growing up at the margins*. Milton Keynes, England: Open University Press.

14. Coleman, J. S. (1961). *The adolescent society*. New York: Free Press of Glencoe.

15. Coleman, J. S.; Campbell, E. Q.; Hobson, C. J.; McPartland, J.; Mood, A. M.; Weinfeld, F. D.; & York, R. L. (1966). *Equality of educational opportunity*. Report no. OE-38001. U.S. Department of Health, Education, and Welfare, Office of Education. Washington, D.C.

16. Coleman, J. S.; Hoffer, T.; & Kilgore, S. (1982). *High school achievement: Public, Catholic, and private schools compared*. New York: Basic Books.

17. Cott, N. F. (1985). Women in the second great awakening. In Harvey Graff, ed., *Growing up in America*. Detroit: Wayne State University Press.

18. Davies, B. (1986). *Threatening youth: Toward a national youth policy*. Milton Keynes, England: Open University Press.

19. Davis, N. Z. (1975). *Society and culture in early modern France*. Stanford: Stanford University Press.

20. Demos, J. (1986). *Past, present, and personal*. New York: Oxford University Press.

21. Demos, J., & Demos, V. (1969). Adolescence in historical perspective. *Journal of Marriage and the Family, 31,* 632–638.

22. Dornbusch, S. M.; Carlsmith, J. M.; Gross, R. T.; Martin, J. A.; Jennings, D.; Rosenberg, A.; & Duke, P. (1981). Sexual development, age, and dating: A comparison of biological and social influences upon one set of behaviors. *Child Development, 52,* 179–185.

23. Dyhouse, C. (1981). *Girls growing up in late Victorian and Edwardian England*. London: Routledge & Kegan Paul.

24. Eckert, R. E., & Marshall, T. O. (1938). *When youth leave school*. New York: McGraw-Hill.

25. Elder, G. H., Jr. (1980). Adolescence in historical perspective. In Joseph Adelson, ed., *Handbook of adolescent psychology*. New York: Wiley and Sons.
26. Fass, P. (1977). *The damned and the beautiful*. New York: Oxford University Press.
27. Featherman, D. L., & Hauser, R. M. (1978). *Opportunity and chance*. New York: Academic Press.
28. Floud, J. (1954). The educational experience of the adult population of England and Wales as of July 1949. In D. V. Glass, ed., *Social mobility in Britain*. London: Routledge & Kegan Paul.
29. Floud, J. E.; Halsey, A. H.; & Martin, F. M. (1976). *Social class and educational opportunity*. Westport, Conn.: Greenwood Press. Originally published 1957.
30. Fogelman, K., ed. (1983). *Growing up in Great Britain: Papers from the national child development study*. London: Macmillan, for the National Children's Bureau.
31. Freeman, A. (1980). *Boy life and labour: The manufacture of inefficiency*. New York: Garland Publishing. Originally published 1914.
32. Frith, S. (1981). *Sound effects: Youth, leisure, and the politics of rock 'n' roll*. New York: Pantheon.
33. Gilbert, J. (1986). *A cycle of outrage: America's reaction to the juvenile delinquent in the 1950s*. New York: Oxford University Press.
34. Gillis, J. (1974). *Youth and history: Tradition and change in European age relations, 1770-present*. New York: Academic Press.
35. Gillis, J. (1975). The evolution of juvenile delinquency in England, 1890–1914. *Past and Present, 67,* 96–126.
36. Graebner, W. (1987). Outlawing teenage populism: The campaign against secret societies in the American high school, 1900–1960. *Journal of American History, 4,* 411–437.
37. Greenberger, E., & Steinberg, L. (1986). *When teenagers work*. New York: Basic Books.
38. Greven, P. J. (1970). *Four generations: Population, land, and family in colonial Andover, Massachusetts*. Ithaca: Cornell University Press.
39. Greven, P. J. (1977). *The Protestant temperament*. New York: New American Library.
40. Hall, G. S. (1904). *Adolescence: Its psychology and its relations to anthropology, sex, crime, religion, and education*. New York: Appleton.
41. Halsey, A. H.; Heath, A. F.; & Ridge, J. M. (1980). *Origins and destinations: Family, class, and education in modern Britain*. Oxford: Clarendon Press.
42. Himmelweit, H. T.; Halsey, H. A.; & Oppenheim, A. N. (1952). The view of adolescents on some aspects of social class structure. *British Journal of Sociology, 3,* 148–172.
43. Hiner, R. N. (1975). Adolescence in eighteenth-century America. *History of Childhood Quarterly, 3,* 253–280.
44. Hogan, D. (1981). *Transitions and social change*. New York: Academic Press.
45. Hollingshead, A. B. (1949). *Elmtown's youth: The impact of social classes on adolescents*. New York: Wiley.
46. Humphries, S. (1981). *Hooligans or rebels? An oral history of working-class childhood and youth, 1889–1939*. Oxford: Basil Blackwell.

47. Jordan, W. D. (1976). Searching for adulthood in America. *Daedalus, 105,* 1–11.
48. Katz, M. B. (1975). *The people of Hamilton, Canada West: Family and class in a mid-nineteenth-century city.* Cambridge, Mass.: Harvard University Press.
49. Katz, M.; Doucet, M. J.; & Stern, M. J. (1982). *The social organization of early industrial capitalism.* Cambridge, Mass.: Harvard University Press.
50. Kett, J. (1977). *Rites of passage: Adolescence in America, 1790 to the present.* New York: Basic Books.
51. Kett, J. (1978). Curing the disease of precocity. In J. Demos & S. S. Boocock, eds., *Turning points: Historical and sociological essays on the family.* Chicago: University of Chicago Press.
52. Lacey, C. (1970). *Hightown Grammar: The school as a social system.* Manchester, England: Manchester University Press.
53. Lawson, J., & Silver, H. (1973). *A social history of education in England.* London: Methuen.
54. Lazerson, M. (1971). *Origins of the urban school.* Cambridge, Mass.: Harvard University Press.
55. Leonard, D. (1980). *Sex and generation: A study of courtship and weddings.* London: Tavistock.
56. Lowe, D. M. (1982). *A history of bourgeois perception.* Chicago: University of Chicago Press.
57. Macleod, D. (1983). *Building character in the American boy: The Boy Scouts and their forerunners, 1870–1920.* Madison: University of Wisconsin Press.
58. Maclure, S. (1979). *Education and youth employment in Great Britain.* Berkeley: Carnegie Council on Policy Studies in Higher Education.
59. Maizels, J. (1970). *Adolescent needs and the transition from school to work.* London: Athlone Press.
60. Mays, J. B. (1964). *Growing up in the city.* New York: Wiley. Originally published 1954.
61. Meacham, S. (1977). *A life apart: The English working class, 1890–1914.* Cambridge, Mass.: Harvard University Press.
62. Modell, J. (1989). *Into one's own: From youth to adulthood in the United States, 1920–1975.* Berkeley: University of California Press.
63. Modell, J.; Furstenberg, F. F., Jr.; & Hershberg, T. (1976). Transitions to adulthood in historical perspective. *Journal of Family History, 1,* 7–32.
64. Nasaw, D. (1985). *Children of the city.* New York: Oxford University Press.
65. O'Donnell, J. M. (1985). *The origins of behaviorism: American psychology, 1870–1920.* New York: New York University Press.
66. Platt, A. M. (1977). *The child savers: The invention of delinquency.* 2nd ed. Chicago: University of Chicago Press.
67. Pollock, L. (1981). *Forgotten children: Parent-child relations from 1500–1900.* New York: Cambridge University Press.
68. Reubens, B. G.; Harrisson, J. A. C.; & Rupp, K. (1981). *The youth labor force, 1945–1955: A cross-national analysis.* Totowa, N.J.: Allanheld, Osmun.
69. Ross, D. (1972). *G. Stanley Hall: The psychologist as prophet.* Chicago: University of Chicago Press.
70. Rubinstein, D., & Simon, B. (1973). *The evolution of the comprehensive school, 1926–1972.* London: Routledge & Kegan Paul.

71. Ryan, M. P. (1981). *Cradle of the middle class: The family in Oneida County, New York, 1790–1865.* New York: Cambridge University Press.
72. Scanlon, J. (1975). Self-reported health behavior and attitudes of youths 12–17 Years. In *Vital and health statistics.* Ser. 11, no. 147. Washington, D.C.: National Center for Health Statistics.
73. Schlossman, S. L. (1977). *Love and the American delinquent: The theory and practice of "progressive" juvenile justice, 1825–1920.* Chicago: University of Chicago Press.
74. Schofield, M. (1965). *The sexual behavior of young people.* Boston: Little, Brown.
75. Sennett, R. (1970). *The fall of public man: On the social psychology of capitalism.* New York: Vintage.
76. Sewell, W. H., & Hauser, R. M. (1975). *Education, occupation, and earnings.* New York: Academic Press.
77. Smith, D. S. (1973). Parental power and marriage patterns: An analysis of historical trends in Hingham, Massachusetts. *Journal of Marriage and the Family, 35,* 419–428.
78. Smith-Rosenberg, C. (1978). Sex as a symbol in Victorian purity: An ethnohistorical analysis of Jacksonian America. In J. Demos and S. S. Boocock, eds., *Turning points: Historical and sociological essays on the family.* Chicago: University of Chicago Press.
79. Springhall, J. (1986). *Coming of age: Adolescence in Britain, 1860–1960.* Dublin: Gill & Macmillan.
80. Stansell, C. (1986). *City of women.* Urbana: University of Illinois Press.
81. Stearns, C. Z., & Stearns, P. N. (1986). *Anger: The struggle for emotional control in America's history.* Chicago: University of Chicago Press.
82. Stinchcombe, A. L. (1964). *Rebellion in a high school.* Chicago: Quadrangle Press.
83. Stone, L. (1977). *The family, sex, and marriage in England, 1500–1800.* New York: Harper and Row.
84. Sugarman, B. (1967). Involvement in youth culture, academic achievement, and conformity in school. *British Journal of Sociology, 18,* 151–164.
85. Trexler, R. C. (1974). Adolescence and salvation in the Renaissance. In H. A. Oberman, ed., *The pursuit of holiness in late medieval and Renaissance religion.* Leiden: E. J. Brill.
86. Troen, S. K. (1987). The discovery of the adolescent by American educational reformers, 1900–1920: An economic perspective. In H. J. Graff, ed., *Growing up in America.* Detroit: Wayne State University Press. Originally published 1976.
87. Trow, M. (1960). The second transformation of American secondary education. In R. Bendix and S. M. Lipset, eds., *Class, status, and power.* 2nd ed. Glencoe, Ill.: Free Press.
88. Trumbach, R. (1978). *The rise of the egalitarian family.* New York: Academic Press.
89. Turner, R. H. (1960). Sponsored and contest mobility and the school system. *American Sociological Review, 25,* 121–139.

90. Tyack, D. (1974). *The one best system: A history of American urban education.* Cambridge, Mass.: Harvard University Press.
91. Ueda, R. (1987). *Avenues to adulthood: The origins of the high school and social mobility in an American suburb.* New York: Cambridge University Press.
92. White House Conference on Child Health and Protection (1934). *The adolescent in the family: A study of personality development in the home environment.* New York: Appleton-Century Company.
93. Whyte, W. F. (1943). *Street corner society: The social structure of an Italian slum.* Chicago: University of Chicago Press.
94. Willmott, P. (1969). *Adolescent boys of East London.* Baltimore: Penguin. Originally published 1966.
95. Wohl, R. R. (1969). The "country boy" myth and its place in American urban culture: The nineteenth-century contribution. *Perspectives in American History, 3,* 77–158.
96. Zelizer, V. (1985). *Pricing the priceless child: The changing social value of children.* New York: Basic Books.

5. Challenges in Studying Minority Youth

1. Ames, R. A. (1950). Protest and irony in Negro folksong. *Science and Society, 14,* 193–213.
2. Aponte, R.; Neckerman, K.; & Wilson, W. (1985). *Race, family structure, and social policy: Race and policy.* Working Paper 7, National Conference on Social Welfare. Washington, D.C.: Project on the Federal Role.
3. Arce, C. H. (1981). A reconsideration of Chicano culture and identity. *Daedalus, 110*(2), 177–192.
4. Baltes, P. B. (1973). On life-span development research paradigms: Retrospects and prospects. In P. B. Baltes & K. W. Schaie, eds., *Life-span developmental psychology: Personality and socialization.* New York: Academic Press, pp. 366–396.
5. Baltes, P. B., & Schaie, K. W., eds. (1973). *Life-span developmental psychology: Personality and socialization.* New York: Academic Press.
6. Banks, J. A. (1984). Black youths in predominantly white suburbs: An exploratory study of their attitudes and self-concepts. *Journal of Negro Education, 53* (1), 3–17.
7. Barnes, E. J. (1980). The black community as the source of positive self-concept for black children: A theoretical perspective. In R. Jones, eds., *Black psychology.* New York: Harper and Row, pp. 106–130.
8. Baron, R.; Tom, D.; & Cooper, H. (1985). Social class, race, and teacher expectations. In J. Dusek & G. Joseph, eds., *Teacher expectancies.* Hillsdale, N.J.: Erlbaum, pp. 251–269.
9. Bartz, K. W., & Levine, E. S. (1978). Childrearing by black parents: A description and comparison to Anglo and Chicano parents. *Journal of Marriage and the Family, 40,* 709–719.
10. Bell-Scott, P., & Taylor, R. L. (1989). Introduction: The multiple ecologies of black development. In P. Bell-Scott & R. L. Taylor, eds., *Journal of Adolescent*

Research: Special Edition on Black Adolescents (April), 119–124. Newbury Park, Calif.: Sage Publications.

11. Billingsley, A. (1968). Black families in white America. Englewood Cliffs, N.J.: Prentice-Hall.

12. Blau, Z. S. (1981). Black children/white children: Competence, socialization, and social structure. New York: Free Press.

13. Bowman, P. J., & Howard, C. (1985). Race-related socialization, motivation, and academic achievement: A study of black youths in three-generation families. Journal of the American Academy of Child Psychiatry, 24(2), 134–141.

14. Boykin, A. W. (1986). The triple quandary and the schooling of Afro-American children. In U. Neisser, ed., The school achievement of minority children: New perspectives. Hillsdale, N.J.: Erlbaum, pp. 57–92.

15. Bronfenbrenner, U. (1979). The ecology of human development: Experiments by nature and design. Cambridge, Mass.: Harvard University Press.

16. Bronfenbrenner, U. (1985). Summary. In M. B. Spencer, G. K. Brooks, & W. R. Allen, eds., Beginnings: The social and affective development of black children. Hillsdale, N.J.: Erlbaum, pp. 67–78.

17. Caplan, N.; Whitmore, J. K.; & Choy, M. H. (1989). The boat people and achievement in America. Ann Arbor: University of Michigan Press.

18. Chestang, L. W. (1972). Character development in a hostile environment. Occasional Paper no. 3. Chicago: University of Chicago Press, pp. 1–12.

19. Clark, R. (1983). Family life and school achievement: Why poor black children succeed or fail. Chicago: University of Chicago Press.

20. Coles, R. (1964). Children of crisis. Boston: Little, Brown.

21. Colletta, N. D., & Lee, D. (1983). The impact of support for black adolescent mothers. Journal of Family Issues, 4, 127–143.

22. Comer, J. P. (1972). Beyond black and white. New York: Quadrangle Books.

23. Comer, J. P. (1988). Educating poor minority children. Scientific American, 259 (5), 42–48.

24. Committee for Economic Development (1987). Children in need: Investment strategies for the educationally disadvantaged. Washington, D.C.: Committee for Economic Development.

25. Cooley, C. H. (1902). Human nature and the social order. In C. H. Cooley, ed., Two major works: Social organization and human nature and the social order. Glencoe, Ill.: Free Press.

26. Cross, W. E., Jr. (1985). Black identity: Rediscovering the distinction between personal identity and reference group orientation. In M. B. Spencer, G. K. Brookins, & W. R. Allen, eds., Beginnings: The social and affective development of black children. Hillsdale, N.J.: Erlbaum, pp. 155–171.

27. Cross, W. E., Jr. (1987). A two-factor theory of black identity: Implications for the study of identity development in minority children. In J. S. Phinney & M. J. Rotheram, eds., Ethnic socialization: Pluralism and development. Newbury Park, Calif.: Sage Publications, pp. 117–133.

28. DeVos, G. A. (1980). Ethnic adaptations and minority status. Journal of Cross-Cultural Psychology, 11(1), 101–124.

29. DeVos, G. A., & Romanucci-Ross, L., eds. (1982). Ethnic identity: Cultural continuity and change. Chicago: University of Chicago Press.

30. Deyhle, D. (1986). Break dancing and breaking out: Anglos, Utes, and Navajos in a border reservation high school. *Anthropology and Education Quarterly, 17,* 111–127.
31. Dornbusch, S. M.; Carlsmith, J. M.; Bushwall, S. J.; Ritter, P. L.; Leiderman, P. H.; Hastorf, A. H.; & Gross, R. T. (1985). Single parents, extended households, and the control of adolescents. *Child Development, 56,* 326–341.
32. Dornbusch, S. M.; Ritter, P. L.; Leiderman, P. H.; Roberts, D. F.; & Fraleigh, M. J. (1987). The relation of parenting style to adolescent school performance. *Child Development, 58,* 1244–57.
33. Dressler, W. (1985). Extended family relationships, social support, and mental health in a southern black community. *Journal of Health and Social Behavior, 26,* 39–48.
34. Du Bois, W. E. B. (1961). *The souls of black folk.* Greenwich, Conn.: Fawcett Publications. Originally published 1903.
35. Entwisle, D. R. (1990). Schools and adolescence. In S. S. Feldman & G. R. Elliott, eds., *At the threshold: The developing adolescent.* Cambridge, Mass.: Harvard University Press.
36. Erickson, E. H. (1968). *Identity: Youth and crisis.* New York: W. W. Norton.
37. Farley, R., & Allan, W. (1987). *The color line and quality of life in America.* New York: Russell Sage Foundation.
38. Fillmore, L. W., & Britsch, S. (1988). Early education for children from linguistic and cultural minority families. Paper presented for the Early Education Task Force of the National Association of State Boards of Education, Alexandria, Va.
39. Ford Foundation (1984). *Ford Foundation Letter, 15*(5).
40. Fordham, S., & Ogbu, J. U. (1986). Black students' school success: Coping with the "burden of 'acting white.'" *Urban Review, 18*(3), 176–206.
41. Frazier, E. F. (1962). *Black bourgeoisie: The rise of a new middle class in the United States.* New York: Collier Books.
42. Furstenberg, F. F., & Crawford, A. G. (1978). Family support: Helping teenage mothers to cope. *Family Planning Perspectives, 10*(6), 322–333.
43. Gallimore, R.; Boggs, J. W.; & Jordan, C. (1974). *Culture, behavior, and education: A study of Hawaiian-Americans.* Beverly Hills: Sage Publications.
44. Garbarino, J. (1982). *Children and families in the social environment.* New York: Aldine.
45. Gibbs, J. T. (1988). *Young, black, and male in America: An endangered species.* Dover, Mass.: Auburn House.
46. Gibbs, J. T., & Huang, L. N., eds. (1989). *Children of color: Psychological interventions with minority youth.* San Francisco: Jossey-Bass.
47. Gibson, M. A. (1987). The school performance of immigrant minorities: A comparative view. *Anthropology & Education Quarterly, 18*(4), 262–275.
48. Hakuta, K. (1986). *Mirror of language.* New York: Basic Books.
49. Hale-Benson, J. E. (1980). The socialization of black children. *Dimensions, 9,* 43–48.
50. Hale-Benson, J. E. (1982). *Black children: Their roots, culture, and learning styles.* Baltimore: Johns Hopkins University Press.

51. Hare, B. R., & Castenell, L. A., Jr. (1985). No place to run, no place to hide: Comparative status and future prospects of black boys. In M. B. Spencer, G. K. Brookins, & W. R. Allen, eds., *Beginnings: The social and affective development of black children.* Hillsdale, N.J.: Erlbaum, pp. 201–214.

52. Harter, S. (1990). Adolescent self and identity development. In S. S. Feldman & G. R. Elliott, eds., *At the threshold: The developing adolescent.* Cambridge, Mass.: Harvard University Press.

53. Henderson, V. L., & Dweck, C. S. (1990). Motivation and achievement in adolescence: Toward a model of motivational processes. In S. S. Feldman & G. R. Elliott, eds., *At the threshold: The developing adolescent.* Cambridge, Mass.: Harvard University Press.

54. Hernandez, J. (1980). Social science and the Puerto Rican community. In E. Rodriguez, V. S. Korrol, & J. O. Alers, eds., *The Puerto Rican struggle: Essays on survival in the U.S.* New York: Puerto Rican Migration Research Consortium, pp. 11–19.

55. Hill, R. (1972). *The strengths of black families.* New York: Emerson-Hall.

56. Hofferth, S. L. (1984). Kin network, race, and family structure. *Journal of Marriage and the Family, 46,* 791–806.

57. Huang, L. N. (1989). Southeast Asian refugee children and adolescents. In J. T. Gibbs & L. N. Huang, eds., *Children of color: Psychological interventions with minority youth.* San Francisco: Jossey-Bass, pp. 278–321.

58. Johnson, D. J. (1988). Racial socialization strategies of parents in three black private schools. In D. T. Slaughter & D. J. Johnson, eds., *Visible now: Blacks in private schools.* New York: Greenwood Press, pp. 251–276.

59. Jordan, C. (1984). Cultural compatibility and the education of ethnic minority children. *Educational Research Quarterly, 8*(4), 59–71.

60. Jordan, C., & Tharp, R. G. (1979). Culture and education. In A. J. Marsella, R. G. Tharp, & T. J. Ciborowski, eds., *Perspectives on cross-cultural psychology.* New York: Academic Press, pp. 265–285.

61. Kasarda, J. (1983). Caught in the web of change. *Society, 21,* 4–7.

62. Keating, D. P. (1990). Adolescent thinking. In S. S. Feldman & G. R. Elliott, eds., *At the threshold: The developing adolescent.* Cambridge, Mass.: Harvard University Press.

63. Keefe, S. E., & Padilla, A. M. (1987). *Chicano ethnicity.* Albuquerque: University of New Mexico Press.

64. Kellam, S.; Ensminger, M. E.; & Turner, R. (1977). Family structure and the mental health of children. *Archives of General Psychiatry, 34,* 1012–22.

65. LaFromboise, T. D. (1988). American Indian mental health policy. *American Psychologist,* 388–397.

66. Landry, B. (1987). *The new black middle class.* Berkeley: University of California Press.

67. Lee, C. C. (1985). Successful rural black adolescents: A psychological profile. *Adolescence, 20*(77), 129–142.

68. Lee, E. (1988). Cultural factors in working with Southeast Asian refugee adolescents. *Journal of Adolescence, 11,* 167–179.

69. Lewis, J. M., & Looney, J. G., eds. (1983). *The long struggle: Well-functioning working-class black families.* New York: Brunner/Mazel.

70. Lightfoot, S. L. (1978). *Worlds apart: Relationships between families and schools.* New York: Basic Books.
71. Looney, J. G., & Lewis, J. M. (1983). Competent adolescents from different socioeconomic and ethnic contexts. *Adolescent Psychiatry, 11,* 64–74.
72. MacLeod, J. (1987). *Ain't no makin' it.* Boulder: Westview Press.
73. Madsen, M. (1964). The alcoholic agringado. *American Anthropologist, 66,* 355–361.
74. Martin, E. P., & Martin, J. M. (1978). *The black extended family.* Chicago: University of Chicago Press.
75. Massey, G. C; Scott, M. V.; Dornbusch, S. M. (1975). Racism without racists: Institutional racism in urban schools. *The Black Scholar, 7*(3), 10–19.
76. Matute-Bianchi, M. E. (1986). Ethnic identity and patterns of school success and failures among Mexican-descendant and Japanese-American students in a California high school: An ethnographic analysis. *American Journal of Education, 95,* 233–255.
77. McDermott, R. P. (1987a). The explanation of minority school failure, again. *Anthropology & Education Quarterly, 18,* 361–364.
78. McDermott, R. P. (1987b). Achieving school failure: An anthropological approach to illiteracy and social stratification. In G. D. Spindler, ed., *Education and cultural process.* Prospect Heights, Ill.: Waveland Press, pp. 173–209.
79. McFee, M. (1968). The 150% man, a product of Blackfeet acculturation. *American Anthropologist, 70,* 1096–1103.
80. McGoldrick, M. (1982). Normal families: An ethnic perspective. In F. Walsh, ed., *Normal family processes.* New York: Guilford Press, pp. 399–424.
81. McKenry, P. C.; Everett, J. E.; Ramseur, H. P.; & Carter, C. J. (1989). Research on black adolescents. In P. Bell-Scott & R. L. Taylor, eds., *Journal of Adolescent Research: Special Edition on Black Adolescents.* Newbury Park, Calif.: Sage Publications, pp. 254–258.
82. McLanahan, S. (1983). Family structure and stress: A longitudinal comparison of two-parent and female-headed families. *Journal of Marriage and the Family, 45,* 347–357.
83. McLoyd, V. (forthcoming). The declining fortunes of black children: Psychological distress, parenting, and socioemotional development in the context of economic hardship. *Child Development.*
84. Means, R. (1980). Fighting words on the future of the earth. *Mother Jones, 5* (10), 12–38.
85. Messer, M. M., & Rasmussen, N. H. (1986). Southeast Asian children in America: The impact of change. *Pediatrics, 78,* 323–329.
86. Mindel, C. H. (1980). Extended familism among urban Mexican-American Anglos and blacks. *Hispanic Journal of Behavior Science, 2,* 21–34.
87. Monroe, S.; Goldman, P.; & Smith, V. E. (1988). *Brothers: Black and poor—a true story of courage and survival.* New York: Morrow.
88. Mont-Reynaud, R. (1989). Personal communication.
89. Moore, J. W. (1981). Minorities in the American class system. *Daedalus, 110,* 275–298.
90. Moore, J., & Pachon, H. (1985). *Hispanics in the United States.* Englewood Cliffs, N.J.: Prentice-Hall.

91. Muga, D. (1984). Academic subcultural theory and the problematic of ethnicity: A tentative critique. *Journal of Ethnic Studies, 12,* 1–51.
92. Nagata, D. K. (1989). Japanese-American children and adolescents. In J. T. Gibbs & L. N. Huang, eds., *Children of color: Psychological interventions with minority youth.* San Francisco: Jossey-Bass, pp. 67–113.
93. Natriello, G., & Dornbusch, S. M. (1984). *Teacher evaluative standards and student effort.* New York: Longmans.
94. Nidorf, J. F. (1985). Mental health and refugee youths: A model for diagnostic training. In T. C. Owen, ed., *Southeast Asian mental health: Treatment, prevention, services, training, and research.* Washington, D.C.: National Institute of Mental Health, pp. 391–427.
95. Ogbu, J. U. (1974). *The next generation: An ethnography of education in an urban neighborhood.* New York: Academic Press.
96. Ogbu, J. U. (1978). *Minority education and caste.* New York: Academic Press.
97. Ogbu, J. U. (1981). Origins of human competence: A cultural-ecological perspective. *Child Development, 52,* 413–429.
98. Ogbu, J. U. (1983). Minority status and schooling in plural societies. *Comparative Education Review, 27*(2), 168–190.
99. Ogbu, J. U. (1986). The consequences of the American caste system. In U. Neisser, ed., *The school achievement of minority children: New perspectives.* Hillsdale, N.J.: Erlbaum, pp. 19–56.
100. Ogbu, J. U. (1987a). Variability in minority school performance: A problem in search of an explanation. *Anthropology & Education Quarterly, 18,* 312–334.
101. Ogbu, J. U. (1987b). Social stratification in the United States. In P. Hockings, ed., *Dimensions of social life: Essays in honor of David G. Mandelbaum.* New York: Mouton de Gruyter, pp. 585–597.
102. Padilla, A. M. (1980). The role of cultural awareness and ethnic loyalty in acculturation. In A. M. Padilla, ed., *Acculturation.* Boulder: Westview Press, pp. 47–84.
103. Phinney, J. S. (1989). Stages of ethnic identity development in minority-group adolescents. *Journal of Early Adolescence, 9,* 34–49.
104. Phinney, J. S.; Lochner, B. T.; & Murphy, R. (forthcoming). Ethnic identity development and psychological adjustment in adolescence. In A. Stiffman & L. Davis, eds., *Advances in adolescent mental health.* Vol. 5. *Ethnic issues.* Greenwich, Conn.: JAI Press.
105. Portes, P.; Dunham, R.; & Williams, S. (1986). Assessing child-rearing style in ecological settings: Its relation to culture, social class, early-age intervention, and scholastic achievement. *Adolescence, 21,* 723–735.
106. Pugh, R. W. (1972). *Psychology and the black experience.* Monterey, Calif.: Brooks/Cole.
107. Ramirez, M. (1984). Assessing and understanding biculturalism-multiculturalism in Mexican-American adults. In J. L. Mendoza & R. H. Mendoza, eds., *Chicano psychology.* New York: Academic Press, pp. 77–94.
108. Ramirez, M., & Castaneda, A. (1974). *Cultural democracy, bicognitive development, and education.* Orlando, Fla.: Academic Press.

109. Reed, R. (1988). Education and achievement of young black males. In J. T. Gibbs, ed., *Young, black, and male in America: An endangered species*. Dover, Mass.: Auburn House.
110. Rist, R. C. (1970). Student social class and teacher expectations: The self-fulfilling prophecy in ghetto education. *Harvard Education Review, 40* (August), 411–451.
111. Ritter, P. L.; Mont-Reynaud, R.; & Dornbusch, S. M. (forthcoming). In N. F. Chavkin, ed., *Minority parents and the schools*. New York: Teachers College Press.
112. Rosenthal, D. (1987). Ethnic identity development in adolescents. In J. S. Phinney & M. J. Rotheram, eds., *Children's ethnic socialization: Pluralism and development*. Newbury Park, Calif.: Sage Publications, pp. 156–179.
113. Rotheram, M. J., & Phinney, J. S. (1987). Introduction: Definitions and perspectives in the study of children's ethnic socialization. In J. S. Phinney & M. J. Rotheram, eds., *Children's ethnic socialization: Pluralism and development*. Newbury Park, Calif.: Sage Publications, pp. 10–28.
114. Samuda, R. (1975). *Psychological testing of American minorities: Issues and consequences*. New York: Dodd, Mead.
115. Scanzoni, J. H. (1971). *The black family in modern society*. Boston: Allyn & Bacon.
116. Select Committee on Children, Youth, and Families, House of Representatives, 100th Congress (1987). *Race relations and adolescence: Coping with new realities*. Report no. 73-234. Hearing held in Washington, D.C., March 27. Washington, D.C.: U.S. Government Printing Office.
117. Semaj, L. T. (1985). Afrikanity, cognition, and extended self-identity. In M. B. Spencer, G. K. Brookins, & W. R. Allen, eds., *Beginnings: The social and affective development of black children*. Hillsdale, N.J.: Erlbaum, pp. 173–183.
118. Slaughter, D. T., & Johnson, D. J. (1988). *Visible now: Blacks in private schools*. Westport, Conn.: Greenwood Press.
119. Spencer, M. B. (1983). Children's cultural values and parental child-rearing strategies. *Developmental Review, 3*, 351–370.
120. Spencer, M. B. (1987). Black children's ethnic identity formation: Risk and resilience of castelike minorities. In J. S. Phinney & M. J. Rotheram, eds., *Children's ethnic socialization: Pluralism and development*. Newbury Park, Calif.: Sage Publications, pp. 103–116.
121. Spencer, M. B. (1990). Parental values transmission: Implications for black child development. In J. B. Stewart & H. Cheatham, eds., *Interdisciplinary perspectives on black families*. Atlanta: Transaction, pp. 111–131.
122. Spencer, M. B.; Brookins, G. K.; & Allen, W. R., eds. (1985). *Beginnings: The social and affective development of black children*. Hillsdale, N.J.: Erlbaum.
123. Stack, C. B. (1974). *All our kin*. New York: Harper & Row.
124. Stonequist, E. V. (1964). The marginal man: A study in personality and culture conflict. In E. Burgess & D. J. Bogue, eds., *Contributions to urban sociology*. Chicago: University of Chicago Press, pp. 327–345.
125. Suarez-Orozco, M. M. (1987). Towards a psychosocial understanding of Hispanic adaptation to American schooling. In H. T. Trueba, ed., *Success or*

failure: Linguistic minority children at home and in school. New York: Harper & Row, pp. 156–168.

126. Sung, B. L. (1985). Bicultural conflicts in Chinese immigrant children. *Journal of Comparative Family Studies, 16*(2), 255–270.

127. Szapocnik, J., & Kurstnes, W. (1980). Acculturation, biculturalism, and adjustment among Cuban-Americans. In A. M. Padilla, ed., *Acculturation*. Boulder: Westview Press.

128. Tan, A. (1989). *The Joy Luck Club.* New York: G. P. Putnam's Sons.

129. Thomas, P. (1967). *Down these mean streets.* New York: Alfred A. Knopf.

130. Tienda, M., & Angel, R. (1982). Headship and household composition among blacks, Hispanics, and other whites, *Social Forces, 61,* 508–531.

131. Trueba, H. T. (1988). Culturally based explanations of minority students' academic achievement. *Anthropology & Education Quarterly, 19*(3), 270–287.

132. U.S. Bureau of the Census (1985). *Marital status and living arrangements.* Current Population Reports, ser. P-20, March. Washington, D.C.: U.S. Government Printing Office.

133. U.S. Commission on Civil Rights (1982). *Disadvantaged women and their children.* Washington, D.C.: U.S. Government Printing Office.

134. U.S. Commission on Civil Rights (1983). *A growing crisis: Disadvantaged women and their children.* Washington, D.C.: U.S. Government Printing Office.

135. Vaughan, G. M. (1987). A social-psychological model of ethnic identity development. In J. S. Phinney & M. J. Rotheram, eds., *Children's ethnic socialization: Pluralism and development.* Newbury Park, Calif.: Sage Publications, pp. 73–91.

136. Walker, H. A. (1988). Black-white differences in marriage and family patterns. In S. M. Dornbusch & M. H. Strober, eds., *Feminism, children, and the new families.* New York: Guilford Press, pp. 87–112.

137. Wilson, J. W. (1987). *The truly disadvantaged: The inner city, the underclass, and public policy.* Chicago: University of Chicago Press.

138. Wilson, M. N. (1986). The black extended family: An analytical consideration. *Developmental Psychology, 22*(2), 246–258.

139. Wilson, M. N. (1989). Child development in the context of the black extended family. *American Psychologist, 44*(2), 380–383.

140. Wilson, W. J., & Neckerman, K. (1986). Poverty and family structure: The widening gap between evidence and public policy issues. In S. Danziger & D. Weinberg, eds., *Fighting poverty: What works and what doesn't.* Cambridge, Mass.: Harvard University Press, pp. 232–259.

6. Coming of Age in a Changing Family System

1. Arendell, T. (1986). *Mothers and divorce: Legal, economic, and social dilemmas.* Berkeley: University of California Press.

2. Baldwin, W. H., & Cain, V. S. (1980). The children of teenage parents. *Family Planning Perspectives, 12*(2), 3–41.

3. Baldwin, W. H., & Nord, C. W. (1984). Delayed childbearing in the U.S.: Facts and fiction. *Population Bulletin, 39*(4), 3–41.

4. Bianchi, S., & Spain, D. (1986). *American women in transition*. New York: Russell Sage Foundation.
5. Blake, J. (1981). Family size and the quality of children. *Demography, 18,* 421–422.
6. Block, J.; Block, J. H.; & Gjerde, P. F. (1988). *Parental functioning and the home environment in families of divorce: Perspective and concurrent analysis*. Study supported by the National Institute of Mental Health, Grant #MH16080.
7. Bumpass, L. (1984). Some characteristics of children's second families. *American Journal of Sociology, 90,* 608–623.
8. Bumpass, L. (1984). Children and marital dissolution. *Demography, 21,* 71–82.
9. Carter, H., & Glick, P. C. (1976). *Marriage and divorce: A social and economic study*. Cambridge, Mass.: Harvard University Press.
10. Castro, T., & Bumpass, L. (1989). Recent trends in marital disruption. *Demography, 26*(1), 37–51.
11. Chase-Lansdale, P. L., & Hetherington, E. M. (in press). The impact of divorce on life-span development: Short- and long-term effects. *Life-Span Behavior and Development*.
12. Cherlin, A. J. (1981). *Marriage, divorce, remarriage*. Cambridge, Mass.: Harvard University Press.
13. Cherlin, A. J. (1988). The weakening link between marriage and the care of children. *Family Planning perspectives, 20*(6), 302–306.
14. Cherlin, A. J., & Furstenberg, F. F., Jr. (1986). *The new American grandparent: A place in the family, a life apart*. New York: Basic Books.
15. Cherlin, A. J., & Furstenberg, F. F., Jr. (1988). The changing European family: Lessons for the American reader. *Journal of Family Issues, 9*(3), 291–297.
16. Coleman, J. S. (1974). *Youth: Transition to adulthood*. Chicago: University of Chicago Press.
17. Daniels, P., & Weingarten, K. (1982). *Sooner or later: The timing of parenthood in adult lives*. New York: Norton.
18. Davis, K., ed. (1985). *Contemporary marriage*. New York: Russell Sage Foundation.
19. Deglar, C. N. (1980). *At odds: Women and the family in America from the Revolution to the present*. New York: Oxford University Press.
20. Demos, J. (1986). *Past, present, and personal: The family and the life course in American history*. New York: Oxford University Press.
21. Ellwood, D. (1988). *Poor support: Poverty in the American family*. New York: Basic Books.
22. Emery, R. E. (1988). *Marriage, divorce, and children's adjustment*. Beverly Hills: Sage Publications.
23. Espanshade, T. J. (1985). The recent decline of American marriage: Blacks and whites in comparative perspective. In K. Davis, ed., *Contemporary Marriage*. New York: Russell Sage Foundation, pp. 53–90.
24. Farley, R., & Allen, W. (1987). *The color line and the quality of life in America*. New York: Russell Sage Foundation.
25. Flacks, R. (1971). *Youth and social change*. Chicago: Markham Publishing.
26. Fox, G. L. (1982). *The childbearing decision: Fertility attitudes and behavior*. Beverly Hills: Sage Publications.

27. Furstenberg, F. F., Jr. (1987). The new extended family: Experiences in step-families. In K. Pasley & M. Ininger-Tallman, eds., *Remarriage and stepparenting: Current research and theory*. New York: Guilford Press, pp. 42–61.
28. Furstenberg, F. F., Jr. (1988). Good dads–bad dads: The two faces of fatherhood. In A. J. Cherlin, ed., *The changing American family and public policy*. Washington, D.C.: Urban Institute Press, pp. 193–218.
29. Furstenberg, F. F., Jr. (1989). The emergence of conjugal succession. In H. Bershady, ed., *Social class and democratic leadership*. Philadelphia: University of Pennsylvania Press.
30. Furstenberg, F. F., Jr., & Brooks-Gunn, J. (1986). Children of adolescent mothers: Physical, academic, and psychological outcomes. *Developmental Review, 6,* 224–251.
31. Furstenberg, F. F., Jr.; Brooks-Gunn, J.; & Morgan, S. P. (1987). *Adolescent mothers in later life*. New York: Cambridge University Press.
32. Furstenberg, F. F., Jr., & Condran, G. A. (1988). Family change and adolescent well-being. A reexamination of U.S. trends. In A. Cherlin, ed., *The changing American family and public policy*. Washington, D.C.: Urban Institute Press, pp. 117–155.
33. Furstenberg, F. F., Jr.; Lincoln, R.; & Menken, J., eds. (1981). *Teenage sexuality, pregnancy, and childbearing*. Philadelphia: University of Pennsylvania Press.
34. Furstenberg, F. F., Jr.; Morgan, S. P.; Allison, P. A. (1987). Paternal participation and children's well-being after marital dissolution. *American Sociological Review, 52,* 695–701.
35. Furstenberg, F. F., Jr.; Nord, C. W.; Peterson, J. L.; & Zill, N. (1983). The life course of children and divorce: Marital disruption and parental conflict. *American Sociological Review, 48*(5), 656–668.
36. Furstenberg, F. F., Jr., & Spanier, G. B. (1984). *Recycling the family: Remarriage after divorce*. Beverly Hills: Sage Publications.
37. Garfinkel, I., & McLanahan, S. (1986). *Single mothers and their children*. Washington, D.C.: Urban Institute Press.
38. Glenn, N. D., & Kramer, K. B. (1985). Psychological well-being of adult children of divorce. *Journal of Marriage and the Family, 47*(4), 905–912.
39. Glenn, N. D., & Kramer, K. B. (1987). The marriages and divorces of the children of divorce. *Journal of Marriage and the Family, 49,* 811–825.
40. Goode, W. J. (1982). Why men resist. In A. S. Skolnick, & J. H. Skolnick, eds., *Family in transition*. Boston: Little, Brown, pp. 201–218.
41. Gordon, M., ed. (1983). *The American family in social-historical perspective*. New York: St. Martin's.
42. Hareven, T., ed. (1978). *Transitions: The family and the life course in historical perspective*. New York: Academic Press.
43. Hayes, C. D., ed. (1987). *Risking the future*. Vol. 1. Washington, D.C.: National Academy Press.
44. Hayes, C. D., & Kamerman, S. B., eds. (1983). *Children of working parents: Experiences and outcomes*. Washington, D. C.: National Academy Press.
45. Hernandez, D. J. (1986). Childhood in sociodemographic perspective. *Annual Review of Sociology, 12,* 159–180.
46. Hetherington, E. M.; Camara, K. A.; & Featherman, D. L. (1982). Achieve-

ment and intellectual functioning of children in one-parent households. In J. Spence, ed., *Assessing achievement*. San Francisco: W. H. Freeman & Co.

47. Hetherington, E. M.; Lerner, R. M.; & Perlmutter, M. (1988). *Child development in life-span perspective*. Hillsdale, N.J.: Erlbaum.

48. Hofferth, S. L. (1985). Updating children's life course. *Journal of Marriage and the Family, 47*(1), 93–115.

49. Hofferth, S. L. (1987). The effects of programs and policies on adolescent pregnancy and childbearing. In S. L. Hofferth & C. D. Hayes, eds., *Risking the future: Adolescent sexuality, pregnancy, and childbearing*. Vol. 2. Washington, D.C.: National Academy Press, pp. 207–263.

50. Hofferth, S. L., & Hayes, C. D., eds. (1987). *Risking the future: Adolescent sexuality, pregnancy, and childbearing*. Vol. 2. Washington, D.C.: National Academy Press.

51. Huber, J., & Spitze, G. (1988). Trends in family sociology. In N. J. Smelser, ed., *Handbook of Sociology*. Beverly Hills: Sage Publications, pp. 425–448.

52. Johnson, C. (1988). *Ex familia: Grandparents, parents, and children adjust to divorce*. New Brunswick, N.J.: Rutgers University Press.

53. Jones, E. F.; Forrest, J. D.; Henshaw, S. K.; Silverman, J.; & Torres, A. (1988). Unintended pregnancy, contraceptive practice, and family planning services in developed countries. *Family Planning Perspectives, 20*(2), 53–67.

54. Kahn, A. J., & Kamerman, S. B. (1988). *Child support: From debt collection to social policy*. Beverly Hills: Sage Publications.

55. Keniston, K. (1968). *Young radicals: Notes on committed youth*. New York: Harcourt, Brace and World.

56. Lamb, M., ed. (1982). *Nontraditional families: Parenting and child development*. Hillsdale, N.J.: Erlbaum.

57. Lamb, M.; Pleck, J. H.; & Levine, J. A. (1987). Effects of increased paternal involvement on fathers and mothers. In C. Lewis and M. O'Brien, eds., *Reassuring fatherhood*. Beverly Hills: Sage Publications, pp. 109–125.

58. Lamb, M., & Sagi, A., eds. (1983). *Fatherhood and family policy*. Hillsdale, N.J.: Erlbaum.

59. Lesthaeghe, R. (1983). A century of demographic and cultural change in Western Europe. *Population and Development Review, 9*, 411–435.

60. McLanahan, S. (1985). Family structure and the reproduction of poverty. *American Journal of Sociology, 90*, 873–901.

61. Miller, B.; McCoy, J. K.; Olson, T. D.; & Wallace, C. M. (1986). Parental discipline and control attempts in relation to adolescent sexual attitudes and behavior. *Journal of Marriage and the Family, 48*, 503–512.

62. Modell, J. (1980). Normative aspects of American marriage timing since World War II. *Journal of Family History, 5*, 210–234.

63. National Center for Health Statistics (1987). Advance report of final natality statistics, 1985. *Monthly Vital Statistics Report, 36*(4) July 17. DHHS Publication no. PHS 87-1120, Washington, D.C.

64. National Center for Health Statistics (1988). Advance report of final natality statistics, 1986. *Monthly Vital Statistics Report, 37*(3) Suppl. July 12. DHHS Publication no. 88-1120, Washington, D.C.

65. Nord, C. W. (1988). Delayed childbearing in the United States: An exploration

for women's and children's lives. Ph.D. dissertation, University of Pennsylvania.

66. Norton, A., & Moorman, J. E. (1987). Current trends in marriage and divorce among American women. *Journal of Marriage and the Family, 49,* 3–14.

67. O'Connell, M., & Rogers, C. C. (1984). Out-of-wedlock births, premarital pregnancies, and their effect on family formation and dissolution. *Family Planning Perspectives, 16*(4), 157–162.

68. Parke, R. (1988). In search of fathers: A narrative of an empirical journey. In I. E. Siegel & G. H. Brody, eds., *Family research.* Vol. 1. *Research on marriage and the family.* Hillsdale, N.J.: Erlbaum.

69. Pasley, K., & Ininger-Tallman, M. Eds., (1987). *Marriage and step-parenting: Current research and theory.* New York: Guilford Press.

70. Peterson, J. L., & Zill, N. (1986). Marital disruption, parent-child relationship, and behavior problems in children. *Journal of Marriage and the Family, 48,* 295–307.

71. Preston, S. (1984). Children and the elderly: Divergent paths for America's dependents. *Demography, 21*(4), 435–457.

72. Rossi, A. S. (1985). *Gender and the life course.* New York: Aldine Publishing.

73. Shorter, E. (1975). *The making of the modern family.* New York: Basic Books.

74. Skolnick, A. S. (1983). *The intimate environment: Exploring marriage and the family.* Boston: Little, Brown.

75. Smith, H. L. (1988). Relationship of sibling size of birth cohorts to the fertility of corresponding maternal generations. Paper presented at the 1988 annual meeting of the Population Association of America, New Orleans.

76. Stack, C. B. (1974). *All our kin.* New York: Harper & Row.

77. Stone, L. (1977). *The family, sex, and marriage in England, 1500–1800.* New York: Harper & Row.

78. Sweet, J. A., & Bumpass, L. L. (1987). *American families and households.* New York: Russell Sage Foundation.

79. Thornton, A. (1989). Changing attitudes towards family issues in the United States. *Journal of Marriage and the Family, 51,* 873–893.

80. Tufte, V., & Myerhoff, B. (1979). *Changing images of the family.* New Haven: Yale University Press.

81. Uhlenberg, P. (1983). Death and the family. In M. Gordon, ed., *The American family in social-historical perspective.* New York: St. Martin's, pp. 169–178.

82. Uhlenberg, P., & Eggebeen, D. (1986). The declining well-being of American adolescents. *Public Interest, 82,* 25–38.

83. U.S. Bureau of the Census (1988). Marital status and living arrangements: March 1987. *Current Population Reports,* ser. P-20, no. 423. Washington, D.C.: U.S. Government Printing Office.

84. U.S. Bureau of the Census (1989). Marital status and living arrangements: March 1988. *Current Population Reports,* ser. P-20, no. 433. Washington, D.C.: U.S. Government Printing Office.

85. Wallerstein, J. S., & Blakeslee, S. (1989). *Second chances: Men, women, and children a decade after divorce.* New York: Ticknor & Fields.

86. Wallerstein, J. S., & Kelly, J. B. (1980). *Surviving the breakup; How children and parents cope with divorce.* New York: Basic Books.

87. Weitzman, L. J. (1985). *The divorce revolution: The unexpected social and economic consequences for women and children in America.* New York: Free Press.
88. Zaslow, M. J. (1987). Sex differences in children's response to parental divorce. Paper presented at the Symposium on Sex Differences in Children's Responses to Psychosocial Stress, Woods Hole, Mass., September.
89. Zelizer, V. A. (1985). *Pricing the priceless child.* New York: Basic Books.
90. Zelnik, M.; Kantner, J. F.; & Ford, K. (1981). *Sex and pregnancy in adolescence.* Beverly Hills: Sage Publications.
91. Zill, N., & Rogers, C. C. (1988). Recent trends in the well-being of children in the United States and their implications for public policy. In A. Cherlin, ed., *The changing American family and public policy.* Washington, D.C.: Urban Institute Press, pp. 31–115.

7. Peer Groups and Peer Cultures

1. Asher, S. R., & Gottman, J. M., eds. (1981). *The development of children's friendships.* Cambridge: Cambridge University Press.
2. Ball, S. J. (1981). *Beachside comprehensive.* Cambridge: Cambridge University Press.
3. Bandura, A. (1964). The stormy decade: Fact or fiction? *Psychology in the Schools, 1,* 224–231.
4. Barenboim, C. (1981). Development of person perception in childhood and adolescence: From behavioral comparisons to psychological constructs to psychological comparisons. *Child Development, 52,* 129–141.
5. Bauman, K. E., & Fisher, L. A. (1986). On the measurement of friend behavior in research on friend influence and selection: Findings from longitudinal studies of adolescent smoking and drinking. *Journal of Youth and Adolescence, 15,* 345–353.
6. Bealer, R. C.; Willits, F. K.; & Maida, P. R. (1971). The rebelliousness of youth culture—a myth. In R. E. Muus, ed., *Adolescent behavior and society: A book of readings.* New York: Random House, pp. 454–463.
7. Berndt, T. (1979). Developmental changes in conformity to peers and parents. *Developmental Psychology, 15,* 606–616.
8. Berndt, T. (1989). Effects of friendship on achievement motivation and classroom behavior. Paper presented at the annual meeting of the American Educational Research Association, San Francisco, March.
9. Berndt, T. J., & Hawkins, J. A. (1987). The contributions of supportive friendships to adjustment after the transition to junior high school. Unpublished manuscript, Department of Psychological Sciences, Purdue University.
10. Bixenstine, V. E.; DeCorte, M. S.; & Bixenstine, B. A. (1976). Conformity to peer-sponsored misconduct at four grade levels. *Developmental Psychology, 12,* 226–236.
11. Blyth, D. A.; Hill, J. P.; & Thiel, K. S. (1982). Early adolescents' significant others: Grade and gender differences in perceived relationships with familial and nonfamilial adults and young people. *Journal of Youth and Adolescence, 11,* 425–450.

12. Bratton, R. D. (1977). Participation in school and community sports by adolescents from a Calgary junior high school. *CAPHER Journal, 44,* 6–14.
13. Brittain, C. V. (1963). Adolescent choices and parent-peer cross-pressures. *American Sociological Review, 28,* 385–391.
14. Brown, B. B. (1982). The extent and effects of peer pressure among high school students: A retrospective analysis. *Journal of Youth and Adolescence, 11,* 121–133.
15. Brown, B. B. (1989a). Can nerds and druggies be friends? Mapping "social distance" between adolescent peer groups. Paper presented at the annual meeting of the American Educational Research Association, San Francisco, March.
16. Brown, B. B. (1989b). Skirting the "brain-nerd" connection": How high achievers save face among peers. Paper presented at the annual meetings of the American Educational Research Association, San Francisco, March.
17. Brown, B. B. (1989c). The role of peer groups in adolescents' adjustment to secondary school. In T. J. Berndt & G. W. Ladd, eds., *Peer relationships in child development.* New York: Wiley, pp. 188–215.
18. Brown, B. B., & Clasen, D. R. (1986). Develomental changes in adolescents' conceptions of peer groups. Paper presented at the biennial meetings of the Society for Research in Adolescence, Madison, Wisconsin, March.
19. Brown, B. B.; Clasen, D. R.; & Eicher, S. A. (1986). Perceptions of peer pressure, peer conformity dispositions, and self-reported behavior among adolescents. *Developmental Psychology, 22,* 521–530.
20. Brown, B. B.; Clasen, D. R.; & Niess, J. (1987). Smoke in the looking glass: Adolescents' perceptions of their peer group status. Paper presented at the biennial meetings of the Society for Research in Child Development, Baltimore, April.
21. Brown, B. B.; Eicher, S. A.; & Petrie, S. (1986). The importance of peer group ("crowd") affiliation in adolescence. *Journal of Adolescence, 9,* 73–96.
22. Brown, B. B., & Lohr, M. J. (1987). Peer group affiliation and adolescent self-esteem: An integration of ego-identity and symbolic interaction theories. *Journal of Personality and Social Psychology, 52,* 47–55.
23. Brown, B. B.; Lohr, M. J.; & McClenahan, E. L. (1986). Early adolescents' perceptions of peer pressure. *Journal of Early Adolescence, 6,* 139–154.
24. Brown, B. B.; Lohr, M. J.; & Trujillo, C. M. (1990). Multiple crowds and multiple lifestyles: Adolescents' perceptions of peer group characteristics. In R. E. Muuss, ed., *Adolescent behavior and society: A book of readings.* New York: Random House, pp. 30–36.
25. Brown, B. B., & Mounts, N. (1989). Peer group structures in single versus multi-ethnic high schools. Paper presented at the biennial meetings of the Society for Research in Child Development, Kansas City, April.
26. Buff, S. A. (1970). Greasers, dupers, and hippies: Three responses to the adult world. In L. Howe, ed., *The white majority.* New York: Random House, pp. 60–77.
27. Burlingame, W. V. (1970). The youth culture. In E. D. Evans, ed., *Adolescents: Readings in behavior and development.* Hinsdale, Ill.: Dryden Press, pp. 131–149.

28. Butcher, J. (1986). Longitudinal analysis of adolescent girls' aspirations at school and perceptions of popularity. *Adolescence, 21,* 133–143.
29. Cairns, R. B., & Cairns, B. D. (forthcoming). Social cognition and social networks: A developmental perspective. In D. Peplar & K. H. Rubin, eds., *Aggression in childhood.*
30. Cairns, R. B.; Cairns, B. D.; Neckerman, H. J.; Gest, S. D.; & Gariepy, J. L. (1988). Social networks and aggressive behavior: Peer support or peer rejection? *Developmental Psychology, 24,* 815–823.
31. Cairns, R. B.; Neckerman, H. J.; & Cairns, B. D. (1989). Social networks and the shadows of synchrony. In G. R. Adams, R. Montemayor, & T. P. Gullotta, eds., *Biology of adolescent behavior and development.* Newbury Park, Calif.: Sage Publications, pp. 275–305.
32. Cairns, R. B.; Perrin, J. E.; & Cairns, B. D. (1985). Social structure and social cognition in early adolescence: Affiliative patterns. *Journal of Early Adolescence, 5,* 339–355.
33. Clarke, J.; Hall, S.; Jefferson, T.; & Roberts, B. (1976). Subcultures, cultures, and class. In S. Hall & T. Jefferson, eds., *Resistance through ritual.* London: Hutchinson, pp. 9–74.
34. Clasen, D. R., & Brown, B. B. (1985). The multidimensionality of peer pressure in adolescence. *Journal of Youth and Adolescence, 14,* 451–468.
35. Clasen, D. R., & Brown, B. B. (1987). Understanding peer pressure in middle school. In D. B. Strahn, ed., *Middle school research: Selected studies, 1987.* Columbus: National Middle School Association, pp. 65–75.
36. Cohen, A. K. (1955). *Delinquent boys: The culture of the gang.* New York: Free Press.
37. Cohen, J. (1977). Sources of peer group homogeneity. *Sociology of Education, 50,* 227–241.
38. Cohen, J. (1979). High school subcultures and the adult world. *Adolescence, 14,* 491–502.
39. Coleman, J. C. (1974). *Relationships in adolescence.* Boston: Routledge & Kegan Paul.
40. Coleman, J. S. (1961). *The adolescent society.* New York: Free Press.
41. Collins, J. K., & Thomas, N. T. (1972). Age and susceptibility to same-sex peer pressure. *British Journal of Educational Psychology, 42,* 83–85.
42. Cooper, C. R.; Grotevant, H. D.; & Ayers-Lopez, S. (1988). Links between patterns of negotiation in adolescents' family and peer interaction. Unpublished manuscript, University of California, Santa Cruz.
43. Costanzo, P. R. (1970). Conformity development as a function of self-blame. *Journal of Personality and Social Psychology, 14,* 366–374.
44. Costanzo, P. R., & Shaw, M. E. (1966). Conformity as a function of age level. *Child Development, 37,* 967–975.
45. Crocket, L.; Losoff, M.; & Petersen, A. C. (1984). Perceptions of the peer group and friendship in early adolescence. *Journal of Early Adolescence, 4,* 155–181.
46. Csikszentmihalyi, M., & Larson, R. (1974). *Being adolescent.* New York: Basic Books.

47. Cusick, P. A. (1973). *Inside high school.* New York: Holt, Rinehart, and Winston.

48. Delgado-Gaitan, C. (1986). Adolescent peer influences and differential school performance. *Journal of Adolescent Research, 1,* 449–462.

49. Deutsch, M., & Gerard, H. B. (1955). A study of normative and informational social influences upon social judgment. *Journal of Abnormal and Social Psychology, 51,* 629–636.

50. Devereaux, E. C. (1970). The role of peer group experience in moral development. In J. P. Hill, ed., *Minnesota symposia on child development.* Vol. 4. Minneapolis: University of Minnesota Press, pp. 94–140.

51. Dishion, T. J.; Patterson, G. R.; & Skinner, M. L. (1989). Parent monitoring and peer relations in the drift to deviant peers: From middle childhood to early adolescence. Paper presented at the biennial meetings of the Society for Research in Child Development, Kansas City, April.

52. Dornbusch, S. M. (1987). Individual moral choices and social evaluations: A research odyssey. In E. J. Lawler & B. Markovski, eds., *Advances in group processes: Theory and research.* Vol. 4. Greenwich, Conn.: JAI Press, pp. 271–307.

53. Douvan, E., & Adelson, J. (1966). *The adolescent experience.* New York: Wiley.

54. Downs. W. R. (1985). Using panel data to examine sex differences in causal relationships among adolescent alcohol use, norms, and peer alcohol use. *Journal of Youth and Adolescence, 14,* 469–486.

55. Dunphy, D. (1963). The social structure of urban adolescent peer groups. *Sociometry, 26,* 230–246.

56. Eder, D. (1985). The cycle of popularity: Interpersonal relations among female adolescents. *Sociology of Education, 58,* 154–165.

57. Eicher, S. A. (1988). The influence of perceived family cohesion and adaptability on adolescents' peer investment. M.S. thesis, Department of Educational Psychology, University of Wisconsin-Madison.

58. Eichhorn, D. H. (1980). The school. In M. Johnson, ed., *Toward adolescence; The middle school years.* Chicago: National Society for the Study of Education (University of Chicago Press), pp. 56–73.

59. Eisenstadt, S. N. (1956). *From generation to generation: Age groups and social structure.* London: Collier-Macmillan.

60. Eitzen, D. S. (1975). Athletics in the status system of male adolescents: A replication of Coleman's *The adolescent society. Adolescence, 10,* 267–276.

61. Elkin, F., & Westley, W. A. (1955). The myth of the adolescent culture. *American Sociological Review, 20,* 680–684.

62. Erikson, E. H. (1968). *Identity, youth, and crisis.* New York: Norton.

63. Feltz, D. L. (1978). Athletics in the status system of female adolescents. *Review of Sport and Leisure, 4,* 110–118.

64. Foot, H. C.; Chapman, A. J.; & Smith, J. R., eds. (1980). *Friendship and social relations in children.* New York: Wiley.

65. Fordham, S., & Oghu, J. U. (1986). Black students' school success: Coping with the burden of "acting white." *Urban Review, 18,* 176–206.

66. French, D. C. (1988). Heterogeneity of peer-rejected boys: Aggressive and non-aggressive subtypes. *Child Development, 59,* 976–985.

67. Friedenberg, E. Z. (1959). *The vanishing adolescent*. Boston: Beacon Press.
68. Friesen, D. (1968). Academic-athletic-popularity syndrome in the Canadian high school society. *Adolescence, 3,* 39–52.
69. Fuller, M. (1984). Black girls in a London comprehensive school. In M. Hammersley & P. Woods, eds., *Life in school: The sociology of pupil culture*. New York: Open University Press, pp. 77–88.
70. Garbarino, J.; Burston, N.; Raber, S.; Russel, R.; & Crouter, A. (1978). The social maps of children approaching adolescence: Studying the ecology of youth development. *Journal of Youth and Adolescence, 7,* 417–428.
71. Goodman, P. (1966). A social critic on "moral youth in an immoral society." In *The young Americans*. New York: *Time* Books, pp. 18–19.
72. Hall, S., & Jefferson, T., eds. (1976). *Resistance through ritual*. London: Hutchinson.
73. Hallinan, M. T. (1980). Patterns of cliquing among youth. In H. C. Foote, A. J. Chapman, & J. R. Smith, eds., *Friendship and social relations in children*. New York: Wiley, pp. 321–342.
74. Hansell, S. (1981). Ego development and peer friendship networks. *Sociology of Education, 54,* 51–63.
75. Hansell, S. (1985). Adolescent friendship networks and distress in school. *Social Forces, 63,* 698–715.
76. Hargreaves, D. (1967). *Social relations in a secondary school*. London: Routledge & Kegan Paul.
77. Hartup, W. W. (1983). Peer relations. In P. H. Mussen, ed., *Handbook of child psychology*. Vol. 4. *Socialization*. New York: Wiley, pp. 103–196.
78. Hill, J. P., & Holmbeck, G. N. (1985). Familial adaptation to pubertal change. Paper presented at the biennial meeting of the Society for Research in Child Development, Toronto, April.
79. Hill, J. P., & Palmquist, W. J. (1978). Social cognition and social relationships in early adolescence. *International Journal of Behavioral Development, 1,* 1–36.
80. Hollingshead, A. B. (1949). *Elmtown's youth*. New York: Wiley.
81. Ianni, F. A. J. (1983). *Home, school, and community in adolescent education*. New York: Clearinghouse on Urban Education.
82. Johnson, J. A. (1987). Influence of adolescent social crowds on the development of vocational identity. *Journal of Vocational Behavior, 31,* 182–199.
83. Johnston, L. D.; Bachman, J. G.; & O'Malley, P. M. (1982). *Monitoring the future: Questionnaire responses from the nation's high school seniors, 1981*. Ann Arbor: Institute for Social Research, University of Michigan.
84. Kandel, D. B. (1978). Homophily, selection, and socialization in adolescent friendships. *American Journal of Sociology, 84,* 427–436.
85. Kandel, D. B. (1986). Processes of peer influence in adolescence. In R. K. Silbereisen et al., eds., *Development as action in context*. Berlin: Springer-Verlag, pp. 203–277.
86. Kandel, D., & Lesser, G. S. (1972). *Youth in two worlds*. San Francisco: Jossey-Bass.
87. Keniston, K. (1965). *The uncommitted*. New York: Harcourt, Brace, and World.
88. Keniston, K. (1968). *Young radicals*. New York: Harcourt, Brace, and World.

89. Krosnick, J. A., & Judd, C. M. (1982). Transitions in social influence at adolescence: Who induces cigarette smoking. *Developmental Psychology, 18,* 359–368.

90. Lacey, C. (1970). *Hightown Grammar.* Manchester, England: Manchester University Press.

91. Landsbaum, J., & Willis, R. (1971). Conformity in early and late adolescence. *Developmental Psychology, 4,* 334–337.

92. Larkin, R. W. (1979). *Suburban youth in cultural crisis.* New York: Oxford University Press.

93. Larson, L. E. (1972). The influence of parents and peers during adolescence: The situation hypothesis revisited. *Journal of Marriage and the Family, 36,* 123–138.

94. Loeb, R. (1973). Adolescent groups. *Sociology and Social Research, 58,* 13–22.

95. Magnusson, D. (1988). *Individual development from an interactional perspective.* Hillsdale, N.J.: Erlbaum.

96. Marsland, D., & Perry, M. (1973). Variations in 'adolescent societies': Exploratory analyses of the orientations of young people. *Youth and Society, 5,* 61–83.

97. Montemayor, R. (1982). The relationship between parent-adolescent conflict and the amount of time adolescents spend alone and with parents and peers. *Child Development, 53,* 1512–19.

98. Moreland, R. L., & Levine, J. M. (1982). Socialization in small groups: Temporal changes in individual-group relations. In L. Berkowitz, ed., *Advances in experimental social psychology.* Vol. 15. New York: Academic Press, pp. 137–192.

99. Mosbach, P., & Leventhal, H. (1988). Peer group identification and smoking: Implications for intervention. *Journal of Abnormal Psychology, 97,* 238–245.

100. Newman, P. R., & Newman, B. M. (1976). Early adolescence and its conflict: Group identity versus alienation. *Adolescence, 11,* 261–274.

101. O'Brien, S. F., & Bierman, K. L. (1988). Conceptions and perceived influence of peer groups: Interviews with preadolescents and adolescents. *Child Development, 59,* 1360–65.

102. Oetting, E. R., & Beauvais, F. (1986). Peer cluster theory: Drugs and the adolescent. *Journal of Counseling and Development, 65,* 17–22.

103. Offer, D. (1969). *The psychological world of the teenager.* New York: Basic Books. Books.

104. O'Mahoney, J. F. (1986). Development of person description over adolescence. *Journal of Youth and Adolescence, 15,* 389–413.

105. Opie, I. A., & Opie, P. (1959). *The lore and language of school children.* Oxford: Oxford University Press.

106. Parsons, T. (1942). Age and sex in the social structure of the United States. *American Sociological Review, 7,* 604–616.

107. Patterson, G. R., & Dishion, T. J. (1985). Contributions of families and peers to delinquency. *Criminology, 23,* 63–79.

108. Polk, K. (1975). A reassessment of middle-class delinquency. In H. D. Thornburg, ed., *Contemporary adolescence: Readings.* 2nd ed. Monterey, Calif.: Brooks/Cole, pp. 420–433.

109. Riester, A. E., & Zucker, R. A. (1968). Adolescent social structure and drinking behavior. *Personnel and Guidance Journal, 47,* 304–312.

110. Rigsby, L. C., & McDill, E. L. (1975). Value orientations of high school students. In H. R. Stub, ed., *The sociology of education: A sourcebook*. Homewood, Ill.: Dorsey Press, pp. 53–75.

111. Rubin, K. H., & Ross, H. S., eds. (1982). *Peer relations and social skills in childhood*. New York: Springer-Verlag.

112. Rutter, M. (1983). School effects on pupil progress: Research findings and policy implications. *Child Development, 54*, 1–29.

113. Savin-Williams, R. C. (1980). Social interactions of adolescent females in natural groups. In H. C. Foot, A. J. Chapman, & J. R. Smith, eds., *Friendship and social relations in children*. New York: Wiley, pp. 343–364.

114. Savin-Williams, R. C. (1987). *Adolescence: An ethological perspective*. New York: Springer-Verlag.

115. Schwartz, F. (1981). Supporting or subverting learning? Peer group patterns in four tracked high schools. *Anthropology and Education Quarterly, 12*, 99–121.

116. Sebald, H., & White, B. (1980). Teenagers' divided reference groups: Uneven alignment with parents and peers. *Adolescence, 15*, 979–984.

117. Selman, R. L. (1980). *The growth of interpersonal understanding: Developmental and clinical analyses*. New York: Academic Press.

118. Serafica, F. C., & Blyth, D. A. (1985). Continuities and changes in the study of friendship and peer groups during early adolescence. *Journal of Early Adolescence, 5*, 267–283.

119. Sherif, M., & Sherif, C. W. (1964). *Reference groups*. Chicago: Regnery.

120. Sherif, M.; White, B. J.; & Harvey, O. J. (1955). Status in experimentally produced groups. *American Journal of Sociology, 60*, 370–390.

121. Shrum, W., & Cheek, N. H. (1987). Social structure during the school years: Onset of the degrouping process. *American Sociological Review, 52*, 218–223.

122. Smith, D. M. (1987). Peers, subcultures, and schools. In D. Marsland, ed., *Education and Youth*. London: Falmer Press, pp. 41–64.

123. Snyder, E. E. (1972). High school student perceptions of prestige criteria. *Adolescence, 6*, 129–136.

124. Steinberg, L. (1981). Transformations in family relations at puberty. *Developmental Psychology, 17*, 833–840.

125. Steinberg, L. (1987). Single parents, stepparents, and the susceptibility of adolescents to antisocial peer pressure. *Child Development, 58*, 269–275.

126. Sussman, S.; Dent, C. W.; Raynor, A.; Stacy, A.; Charlin, V.; Craig, S.; Hansen, W. B.; Burton, D.; & Flay, B. R. (1988). The relevance of peer group association to adolescent tobacco use. Paper presented at the Third Behaviour Therapy World Conference, August, Edinburgh.

127. Thurnher, M.; Spence, D.; & Fiske, M. (1974). Value confluence and behavioral conflict in intergenerational relations. *Journal of Marriage and the Family, 36*, 308–319.

128. Varenne, H. (1982). Jocks and freaks: The symbolic structure of the expression of social interaction among American senior high school students. In G. Spindler, ed., *Doing the ethnography of schooling*. New York: Holt, Rinehart, and Winston, pp. 213–235.

129. Westley, W. A., & Elkin, F. (1956). The protective environment and adolescent socialization. *Social Forces, 35*, 243–249.

130. Williams, J. M., & White, K. A. (1983). Adolescent status system for males and females at three age levels. *Adolescence, 18,* 381–390.
131. Willis, P. (1977). *Learning to labor.* London: Columbia University Press.
132. Yankelovich, D., & Clark, R. (1974). College and noncollege youth values. *Change, 6*(7), 45–46.
133. Youniss, J. (1980). *Parents and peers in social development.* Chicago: University of Chicago Press.
134. Youniss, J., & Smollar, J. (1985). *Adolescents' relations with mothers, fathers, and friends.* Chicago: University of Chicago Press.

8. Schools and the Adolescent

1. Alexander, K. L. (1988). In defense of ivory-towerism: Confessions of an unreconstructed basic researcher. Paper presented at the New York Education Policy Seminar, New York, November.
2. Alexander, K. L., & Eckland, B. (1975). School experience and status attainment. In S. E. Dragastin & G. H. Elder, Jr., eds., *Adolescence in the life cycle.* Washington, D.C.: Hemisphere Publishing Corporation, pp. 171–210.
3. Alwin, D. F., & Otto, L. B. (1977). High school context effects on aspiration. *Sociology of Education, 50,* 259–273.
4. Barker, R. G., & Gump, P. V. (1964). *Big school, small school: High school size and student behavior.* Stanford: Stanford University Press.
5. Barr, K., & Dreeben, R. (1983). *How schools work.* Chicago: University of Chicago Press.
6. Becker, H. (1987). *Addressing the needs of different groups of early adolescents: Effects of varying school and classroom organizational practices on students from different social backgrounds and abilities.* Report no. 16. Baltimore: Johns Hopkins University, Center for Research on Elementary and Middle Schools.
7. Bishop, J. L. (1989). Why the apathy in American high schools? *Educational Researcher, 18,* 6–10, 42.
8. Bowman, P. J., & Howard, C. (1985). Race-related socialization, motivation, and academic achievement: A study of black youths in three-generation families. *Journal of the American Academy of Child Psychiatry, 24,* 134–141.
9. Boyer, E. L. (1983). *High school.* New York: Harper and Row.
10. Braddock, J. H.; McPartland, J. M.; & Wu, S. (1988). *School organization in the middle grades: National variations and effects.* Report no. 24. Baltimore: Johns Hopkins University, Center for Research on Elementary and Middle Schools.
11. Brophy, J. (1979). Teacher behavior and its effects. *Journal of Educational Psychology, 71,* 733–750.
12. Brophy, J. (1985). Interactions of male and female students with male and female teachers. In L. C. Wilkinson & C. B. Marrett, eds., *Gender influences in classroom interaction.* New York: Academic Press, pp. 115–142.
13. Coleman, J. S. (1961). *The adolescent society.* New York: Free Press.
14. Coleman, J. S.; Campbell, E. Q.; Hobson, C. J.; McPartland, J.; Mood, A.; Weinfeld, F. D.; & York, R. L. (1966). *Equality of educational opportunity.* Washington, D.C.: U.S. Government Printing Office.

15. Coleman, J. S., & Hoffer, T. (1987). *Public and private high schools*. New York: Basic Books.
16. Coleman, J. S.; Hoffer, T.; & Kilgore, S. (1982). *High school achievement: Public, Catholic, and private schools compared*. New York: Basic Books.
17. Conant, J. B. (1959). *The American high school today*. New York: McGraw-Hill.
18. Crain, R. L., & Mehard, R. E. (1981). Minority achievement: Policy implications of research. In W. D. Hawley, ed., *Effective school desegregation*. Beverly Hills: Sage Publications, pp. 55–84.
19. DeBord, L. W.; Griffin, L.; & Clark, M. (1977). Race and sex influences in the schooling processes of rural and small town youth. *Sociology of Education, 50,* 85–102.
20. Duncan, G. J. (1984). *Years of poverty, years of plenty*. Ann Arbor: University of Michigan, Institute for Social Research.
21. Eccles (Parsons), J. (1984). Sex differences in mathematics participation. In M. W. Steinkamp & M. L. Maehr, eds., *Advances in motivation and achievement*. Vol. 2. *Women in science*. Greenwich, Conn.: JAI Press, pp. 93–138.
22. Eccles (Parsons), J.; Adler, T.; & Meece, J. L. (1984). Sex differences in achievement: A test of alternate theories. *Journal of Personality and Social Psychology, 46,* 26–43.
23. Eccles, J. S., & Midgley, C. (1989). Stage/environment fit: Developmentally appropriate classrooms for early adolescents. In R. E. Ames & C. Ames, eds., *Research on motivation in education*. Vol. 3. *Goals and cognition*. New York: Academic Press.
24. Eccles, J.; Midgley, C.; & Adler, T. (1984). Grade-related changes in the school environment: Effects on achievement motivation. In J. J. Nicholls, ed., *Advances in motivation and achievement*. Vol. 3. Greenwich, Conn.: JAI Press, pp. 283–331.
25. Eccles, J. S.; Midgley, C.; Feldlaufer, H.; Reuman, D.; Wigfield, A.; & MacIver, D. (1988). Developmental mismatch and the junior high school transition. Paper presented at the Biannual Meeting of the Society for Research on Adolescence. Alexandria, Va., March.
26. Elder, G. H. (1965). Family structure and educational attainment: A cross-national analysis. *American Sociological Review, 30,* 81–96.
27. Entwisle, D. R., & Alexander, K. L. (1989). Early schooling as a "critical period" phenomenon. In K. Namboodiri and R. G. Corwin, eds., *Sociology of education and socialization*. Vol. 8. *Selected methodological issues*. Greenwich, Conn.: JAI Press, pp. 27–55.
28. Entwisle, D. R., and Baker, D. P. (1983). Gender and young children's expectations for performance in arithmetic. *Developmental Psychology, 19,* 200–209.
29. Entwisle, D. R., & Hayduk, L. A. (1988). Lasting effects of elementary school. *Sociology of Education, 61,* 147–159.
30. Epps, E. (1981). Minority children: Desegregation, self-evaluation, and achievement orientation. In W. D. Hawley, ed., *Effective school desegregation: Equity, quality, and feasibility*. Beverly Hills: Sage Publications, pp. 85–106.
31. Epstein, J. H. (1984). A longitudinal study of school and family effects on

student development. In S. A. Mednick, H. Harway, & K. M. Finello, eds., *Longitudinal research in the U.S.* New York: Praeger, pp. 381–397.

32. Epstein, J. (1987). Parent involvement: What research says to administrators. *Education and Urban Society, 19,* 119–136.

33. Feingold, A. (1988). Cognitive gender differences are disappearing. *American Psychologist, 43,* 95–103.

34. Felner, R. D., & Adan, A. M. (forthcoming). The school transitional environment project: An ecological intervention and evaluation. In R. H. Price, E. L. Cowen, R. P. Lorion, I. Serrano-Garcia, & B. Hitchens, eds., *A casebook of exemplary prevention, promotion, and intervention alternatives.* Washington, D.C.: American Psychological Association.

35. Felner, R. D.; Ginter, M.; & Primavera, J. (1982). Primary prevention during school transitions: Social support and environmental structure. *American Journal of Community Psychology, 10,* 277–290.

36. Furstenberg, F. (1987). The new extended family: The experience of parents and children after remarriage. In K. Pasley & M. Ininger-Tallman, eds., *Remarriage and stepparenting: Current research and theory.* New York: Guilford, pp. 42–61.

37. Furstenberg, F. F.; Brooks-Gunn, J.; & Morgan, S. P. (1987). *Adolescent mothers in later life.* New York: Cambridge University Press.

38. Gamoran, A., & Berends, M. (1987). The effects of stratification in secondary schools: Synthesis of survey and ethnographic research. *Review of Educational Research, 57,* 415–435.

39. Gamoran, A., & Mare, R. D. (1989). Secondary school tracking and educational inequality: Compensation, reinforcement, or neutrality? *American Journal of Sociology, 94,* 1146–83.

40. Gottfredson, D. L. (1981). Black-white differences in the educational attainment process: What have we learned? *American Sociological Review, 46,* 542–557.

41. Gottfredson, D. L. (1982). Personality and persistence in education: A longitudinal study. *Journal of Personality and Social Psychology, 43,* 532–545.

42. Granovetter, M. (1986). The micro-structure of school desegregation. In J. Prager, D. Longshore, & M. Seeman, eds., *School desegregation research.* New York: Plenum, pp. 81–110.

43. Hallinan, M. T., & Sorenson, A. B. (1987). Ability grouping and sex differences in mathematics achievement. *Sociology of Education, 60,* 63–72.

44. Hanks, M. P., & Eckland, B. K. (1976). Athletics and social participation in the educational attainment process. *Sociology of Education, 49,* 271–294.

45. Harter, S. (forthcoming). Causes, correlates and the functional role of global self-worth: A life-span perspective. In R. Sternberg & J. Kolligan, eds., *Perceptions of competence and incompetence across the life span.* New Haven: Yale University Press.

46. Hawley, W. D., ed. (1981). *Effective school desegregation.* Beverly Hills: Sage Publications.

47. Hess, R. D.; Holloway, S. D.; Dickson, W. P.; & Price, G. G. (1984). Maternal variables as predictors of children's school readiness and later achievement in vocabulary and mathematics in sixth grade. *Child Development, 55,* 1902–12.

48. Hetherington, E. M.; Camara, K. A.; & Featherman, D. L. (1983). Achievement and intellectual functioning of children in one-parent households. In J. Spence, ed., *Achievement and achievement motives.* San Francisco: W. H. Freeman, pp. 205–284.

49. Heyns, B. (1982). The influence of parents' work on children's school achievement. In S. B. Kamerman & C. D. Hayes, eds., *Families that work: Children in a changing world.* Washington, D.C.: National Academy Press, pp. 229–267.

50. Hoelter, J. W. (1982). Segregation and rationality in black status aspiration processes. *Sociology of Education, 55,* 31–39.

51. Hout, M., & Morgan, W. R. (1975). Race and sex variations in the causes of expected attainments of high school seniors. *American Journal of Sociology, 81,* 364–394.

52. Jencks, C. (1972). *Inequality: A reassessment of the effects of family and schooling in America.* New York: Basic Books.

53. Jencks, C. (1985). How much do high school students learn? *Sociology of Education, 58,* 128–135.

54. Jencks, C., & Mayer, S. (1988). *The social consequences of growing up in a poor neighborhood: A review.* Evanston, Ill.: Northwestern University, Center for Urban Affairs and Policy Research.

55. Jones, L. V.; Burton, N. W.; & Davenport, E. C., Jr. (1982). *Mathematics achievement levels of black and white youth.* Report no. 165. Chapel Hill: L. L. Thurstone Psychometric Laboratory, University of North Carolina.

56. Keith, T. A., & Page, E. B. (1985). Do Catholic high schools improve minority student achievement? *American Educational Research Journal, 22,* 337–349.

57. Keith, V. M., & Finlay, B. (1988). The impact of parental divorce on children's educational attainment, marital timing, and likelihood of divorce. *Journal of Marriage and the Family, 50,* 797–809.

58. Kellam, S. G.; Ensminger, M. E.; & Turner, J. (1977). Family structures and the mental health of children. *Archives of General Psychiatry, 34,* 1012–22.

59. Kerckhoff, A. C., & Campbell, R. T. (1977). Black-white differences in the educational attainment process. *Sociology of Education, 50,* 15–27.

60. Kimmel, D. C., & Weiner, I. B. (1985). *Adolescence: A developmental transition.* Hillsdale, N.J.: Erlbaum.

61. Lazar, I., & Darlington, R. (1982). Lasting effects of early education: A report from the Consortium for Longitudinal Studies. *Monographs of the Society for Research in Child Development, 47*(2–3), serial no. 195.

62. Lee, V., & Bryk, A. (1986). Effects of single-sex secondary schools on student achievement and attitudes. *Psychological Bulletin, 78,* 381–395.

63. Leinhardt, G.; Seewald, A. M.; & Engel, M. (1979). Learning what's taught: Sex differences in instruction. *Journal of Educational Psychology, 71,* 432–439.

64. Levin, H. M. (1980). Educational production theory and teacher inputs. In C. E. Bidwill & D. M. Windham, eds., *The analysis of educational productivity.* Vol. 2. *Issues in macroanalysis.* Cambridge, Mass.: Ballinger, pp. 203–231.

65. Lichter, D. T. (1988). Racial differences in underemployment in American cities. *American Journal of Sociology, 93,* 771–792.

66. Lightfoot, S. L. (1983). *The good high school.* New York: Basic Books.

67. Lindsay, P. (1984). High school size, participation in activities, and young adult social participation: Some enduring effects of schooling. *Educational Evaluation and Policy Analysis, 6,* 73–83.

68. Lipsitz, J. (1984). *Successful schools for young adolescents.* New Brunswick, N.J.: Transaction.

69. Lloyd, D. N. (1978). Prediction of school failure from third-grade data. *Educational and Psychological Measurement, 38,* 1193–1200.

70. Longshore, D., & Prager, J. (1985). The impact of school desegregation: A situational analysis. *Annual Review of Sociology, 11,* 75–91.

71. Mare, R. D. (1980). Social background and school continuation decisions. *Journal of the American Statistical Association, 75,* 295–305.

72. Mare, R. D., & Winship, C. (1988). Ethnic and racial patterns of educational attainment and school enrollment. In G. D. Sandefur & M. Tienda, eds., *Divided opportunities.* New York: Plenum, pp. 173–195.

73. McCarthy, E. D. (1979). Family structure: Its relation to social class and child behavior. In R. G. Simmons, ed., *Research in community and mental health.* Vol. 1. Greenwich, Conn.: JAI Press, pp. 138–146.

74. McClelland, K. A. (1982). Adolescent subculture in the schools. In T. M. Field, A. Huston, H. C. Quay, L. Troll, & G. E. Finley, eds., *Review of human development.* New York: Wiley, pp. 395–417.

75. McLanahan S. S. (1983). Family structure and stress: A longitudinal comparison of two-parent and female-headed families. *Journal of Marriage and the Family, 45,* 347–357.

76. McLanahan, S. S. (1985). Family structure and the reproduction of poverty. *American Journal of Sociology, 90,* 873–901.

77. McLanahan, S. S., & Bumpass, L. (1988). Comment: A note on the effect of family structure on school enrollment. In G. D. Sandefur & M. Tienda, eds., *Divided opportunities.* New York: Plenum, pp. 195–201.

78. McPartland, J. M., & Braddock, J. H. (1981). Going to college and getting a good job: The impact of desegregation. In W. D. Hawley, ed., *Effective school desegregation.* Beverly Hills: Sage Publications, pp. 141–154.

79. McPartland, J. M.; Coldiron, J. R.; & Braddock, J. H. (1987). *School structures and classroom practices in elementary, middle, and secondary schools.* Report no. 14. Baltimore: Center for Research on Elementary and Middle Schools, Johns Hopkins University.

80. McPartland, J. M., & McDill, E. L. (1976). *The unique role of schools in the causes of youthful crime.* Baltimore: Johns Hopkins University Press.

81. McPartland, J. M., & McDill, E. L. (1977). Research on crime in schools. In J. M. McPartland & E. L. McDill, eds., *Violence in schools.* Lexington, Mass.: Lexington Books, pp. 3–33.

82. Meyer, R. J., & Haggerty, R. J. (1962). Streptococcal infections in families: Factors altering individual susceptibility. *Pediatrics, 29,* 539–549.

83. Midgley, C.; Feldlaufer, H.; & Eccles, J. S. (1988). Change in teacher efficacy and student self- and task-related beliefs in mathematics during the transition to junior high school. Unpublished paper, Institute for Social Research, Ann Arbor.

84. Mueser, P. (1979). The effects of non-cognitive traits. In C. Jencks, H. Smith, H. Acland, M. J. Bane, D. Cohen, H. Gintis, B. Heyns, & Y. S. Michelson, eds., *Who gets ahead? The determinants of economic success in America.* New York: Basic Books, pp. 122–158.

85. Natriello, G., & Dornbusch, G. M. (1984). *Teacher evaluative standards and student effort.* New York: Longman.

86. Nottelmann, E. D. (1987). Competence and self-esteem during transition from childhood to adolescence. *Developmental Psychology, 23,* 441–450.

87. Pallas, A. M. (1984). The determinants of high school dropout. Ph.D. dissertation, Johns Hopkins University.

88. Parker, J. G., & Asher, S. R. (1987). Peer relations and later personal adjustment: Are low-accepted children at risk? *Psychological Bulletin, 102,* 357–389.

89. Parsons, J. E. (1983). Attributional processes as mediators of sex differences in achievement. *Journal of Educational Equity and Leadership, 3,* 19–27.

90. Portes, A., & Wilson, K. L. (1976). Black-white differences in educational attainment. *American Sociological Review, 41,* 414–431.

91. Prager, J.; Longshore, D.; & Seeman, M. (1986). *School desegregation research: New approaches to situational analyses.* New York: Plenum.

92. Purkey, S. C., & Smith, M. S. (1983). Effective schools: A review. *Elementary School Journal, 83,* 427–452.

93. Riordan, C. (forthcoming). *Boys and girls in school: Together or separate.* New York: Teachers College Press.

94. Rosenberg, M., & Simmons, R. G. (1972). *Black and white self-esteem: The urban school child.* Arnold M. and Caroline Rose Monograph Series. Washington, D.C.: American Sociological Association.

95. Rowan, B.; Bossert, S. T.; & Dwyer, D. C. (1983). Research on effective schools: A cautionary note. *Educational Researcher, 12,* 24–31.

96. Rutter, M. (1983). School effects on pupil progress: Research findings and policy implications. *Child Development, 54,* 1–29.

97. Rutter, M.; Maughan, B.; Mortimore, P.; Ouston, J.; & Smith, A. (1979). *Fifteen thousand hours: Secondary schools and their effects on children.* Cambridge, Mass.: Harvard University Press.

98. St. John, N. (1975). *School desegregation: Outcomes for children.* New York: Wiley.

99. Scheinfeld, D. R. (1983). Family relationships and school achievement among boys of lower-income urban black families. *American Journal of Orthopsychiatry, 53,* 127–143.

100. Schwartz, F. (1981). Supporting or subverting learning: Peer-group patterns in four tracked schools. *Anthropology & Education Quarterly, 12,* 99–120.

101. Seltzer, J. A. (1981). *Familial sources of children's psychological well-being.* Ph.D. dissertation, University of Michigan.

102. Sewell, W. H.; Haller, A. O.; & Ohlendorf, G. W. (1970). The educational and early occupational attainment process: Replication and revision. *American Sociological Review, 35,* 1014–27.

103. Sewell, W. H.; Haller, A. O.; & Portes, A. (1969). The educational and early occupational attainment process. *American Sociological Review, 34,* 82–91.

104. Sewell, W. H., & Hauser, R. M. (1972). Causes and consequences of higher education: Models of the status attainment process. *American Journal of Agricultural Economics, 54,* 851–861.
105. Simmons, R. G., & Blyth, G. A. (1987). *Moving into adolescence: The impact of pubertal change and school context.* New York: Aldine de Gruyter.
106. Simmons, R.; Blyth, D.; Van Cleaves, E.; & Bush, R. (1979). Entry into early adolescence: The impact of school structure, puberty, and early dating. *American Sociological Review, 44,* 948–967.
107. Simmons, R.; Brown, L.; Bush, D.; & Blyth, D. (1978). Self-esteem and achievement of black and white adolescents. *Social Problems, 26,* 86–96.
108. Simmons, R. G.; Burgeson, R.; Carlton-Ford, S.; & Blyth, D. A. (1987). The impact of cumulative change in adolescence. *Child Development, 58,* 1220–34.
109. Slavin, R. E. (1983). *Cooperative learning.* New York: Longman.
110. Steinberg, L.; Blinde, P. L.; & Chan, K. S. (1984). Dropping out among language minority youth. *Review of Educational Research, 54,* 113–132.
111. Stephan, W. G. (1978). School desegregation: An analysis of predictions made in *Brown vs. Board of Education. Psychological Bulletin, 85,* 217–238.
112. Stevenson, D. L., & Baker, D. P. (1987). The family-school relation and the child's school performance. *Child Development, 58,* 1348–57.
113. Stevenson, H. W., & Newman, R. S. (1986). Long-term prediction of achievement and attitudes in mathematics and reading. *Child Development, 57,* 646–659.
114. Stinchcombe, A. L. (1964). *Rebellion in a high school.* Chicago: Quadrangle.
115. Stroup, A. L., & Robins, L. B. (1972). Elementary school predictors of high school dropout among black males. *Sociology of Education, 45,* 212–222.
116. Travers, K. J., ed. (1985). *U.S. summary report: Second international mathematics study.* Champaign, Ill.: Stipes.
117. Travers, K. J. (1988). Opportunity to learn mathematics in eighth-grade classrooms in the United States. In R. R. Cocking and J. P. Mestre, eds., *Linguistic and cultural influences on learning mathematics.* Hillsdale, N.J.: Erlbaum, pp. 187–200.
118. U.S. Dept. of Commerce, Bureau of the Census (1987). *Statistical Abstract of the U.S.* Washington, D.C.: U.S. Government Printing Office.
119. Weitzman, M.; Alpert, J. J.; Klerman, L. V.; Kayne, H.; Lamb, G. A.; Geromini, K. R.; Kane, K. T.; & Rose, L. (1986). High-risk youth and health: The case of excessive school absence. *Pediatrics, 78,* 313–322.
120. William T. Grant Foundation Commission on Work, Family, and Citizenship (1988). *The forgotten half: Non-college youth in America.* Washington, D.C.
121. Willms, J. D. (1987). Patterns of academic achievement in public and private schools: Implications for public policy and future research. In E. H. Haertel, T. James, & H. M. Levin, eds., *Comparing public and private schools.* Vol. 2. *School achievement.* New York: Falmer, pp. 113–134.
122. Yinger, J. M. (1986). The research agenda: New directions for desegregation studies. In J. Prager, D. Longshore, & M. Seeman, eds., *School desegregation research.* New York: Plenum, pp. 229–254.
123. Zaslow, M., & Hayes, C. D. (1986). Sex differences in children's response to

psychosocial stress: Toward a cross-context analysis. In M. E. Lamb, N. L. Brown, & B. Rogoff, eds., *Advances in development*. Hillsdale, N.J.: Erlbaum, pp. 285–337.

9. Leisure, Work, and the Mass Media

1. Adams, G. R., & Gullotta, T. (1983). *Adolescent life experiences*. Monterey, Calif.: Brooks/Cole.
2. Alexander, A. (1985). Adolescents' soap opera viewing and relational perceptions. *Journal of Broadcasting and Electronic Media, 29,* 295–308.
3. Amuchie, F. A. (1982). Age and sex differences among adolescent participants in recreational activities. *International Review of Sport Sociology, 17,* 79–84.
4. Anderson, E. (1978). *A place on the corner*. Chicago: University of Chicago Press.
5. Anson, R. (1977). Recreational deviance: Some mainline hypotheses. *Journal of Leisure Research, 8,* 177–180.
6. Anthony, K. (1985). The shopping mall: A teenage hangout. *Adolescence, 20,* 307–312.
7. Bachman, J. G. (1987). Adolescence: An eye on the future. *Psychology Today, 21,* 6–8.
8. Bachman, J. G.; Johnston, L. D.; & O'Malley, P. M. (1987). *Monitoring the future: Questionnaire responses from the nation's high school seniors, 1986*. Ann Arbor: Survey Research Center, Institute for Social Research.
9. Ball-Rokeach, S. (1976). A dependency model of mass media effects. *Communication Research, 3,* 3–21.
10. Bandura, A. (1986). *Social foundations of thought and action: A social cognitive theory*. Englewood Cliffs, N.J.: Prentice-Hall.
11. Bandura, A. (in press). Social cognitive theory of mass communication. In J. Groebel & P. Winterhoff, eds., *Empirische medienpsychologie*. Munich: Psychologie Verlags Union.
12. Bar-Haim, G. (1987). The meaning of Western commercial artifacts for Eastern European youth. *Journal of Contemporary Ethnography, 16,* 205–226.
13. Bennett, H. S. (1980). *On becoming a rock musician*. Amherst, Mass.: University of Massachusetts Press.
14. Bogart, L. (1978). *Children, mothers, and newspapers*. New York: Newspaper Advertising Bureau.
15. Brake, M. (1985). *Comparative youth culture*. London: Routledge & Kegan Paul.
16. Bronfenbrenner, U. (1979). *The ecology of human development*. Cambridge, Mass.: Harvard University Press.
17. Brown, B. B. (1990). Peer groups and peer cultures. In S. Shirley Feldman & Glen R. Elliott, eds., *At the threshold: The developing adolescent*. Cambridge, Mass.: Harvard University Press.
18. Brown, J. D.; Childers, K. W.; Bauman, K.; & Koch, G. (1990). The influence of new media and family structure on young adolescents' TV and radio use. *Communication Research, 17,* 65–82.

19. Brown, J. D.; Bauman, K.; Lentz, G. M.; & Koch, G. (1987). Young adolescents' use of radio and television in the 1980s. Paper presented at the Annual Convention of International Communication Association, Montreal, May.

20. Brown, J. D.; Campbell, K.; & Fischer, L. (1986). American adolescents and music videos: Why do they watch? *Gazette, 37*(1/2), 19–32.

21. Bryson, L. (1987). Sport and the maintenance of masculine hegemony. *Women's Studies International Forum, 10,* 349–360.

22. Carlson, J. M. (1983). Crime show viewing by preadults: The impact on attitudes toward civil liberties. *Communication Research, 10,* 529–552.

23. Carnegie Council on Policy Studies in Higher Education (1980). *Giving youth a better chance.* San Francisco: Jossey-Bass.

24. Carrington, B.; Chivers, T.; & Williams, T. (1987). Gender, leisure, sport: A case-study of young people of South Asian descent. *Leisure Studies, 6,* 265–279.

25. Chaffee, S. H., & McLeod, J. (1972). Adolescent television use in the family context. In G. A. Comstock & E. A. Rubinstein, eds., *Television and social behavior.* Vol. 3. *Television and adolescent aggressiveness.* Washington, D.C.: U.S. Government Printing Office, pp. 149–172.

26. Chaffee, S. H., & Yang, S. M. (1990). Communication and political socialization, In O. Ichilov, ed., *Political socialization, citizen education, and democracy.* New York: Columbia University Teachers College Press, pp. 137–157.

27. Charner, I. D., & Fraser, B. S. (1988). *Youth and work: What we know; What we don't know; What we need to know.* Washington, D.C.: National Institute for Work and Learning.

28. Christenson, P. G., & Lindlof, T. R. (1985). Children's use of audio media. *Communication Research, 12,* 327–343.

29. Christenson, P. G., & Roberts, D. F. (1983). The role of television in the formation of children's social attitudes. In M. J. A. Howe, ed., *Learning from television: Psychological and educational research.* London: Academic Press, pp. 79–99.

30. Clark, R. M. (1974). The dance party as a socialization mechanism for black urban preadolescents and adolescents. *Sociology and Social Research, 58,* 145–154.

31. Clarke, J.; Hall, S.; Jefferson, T.; & Roberts, B. (1976). Subcultures, cultures, and class: A theoretical overview. In S. Hall & T. Jefferson, eds., *Resistance through rituals.* London: Hutchinson, pp. 9–74.

32. Cobb, C. (1986). Patterns of newspaper readership among teenagers. *Communication Research, 13,* 299–326.

33. Coffield, F., & Borrill, C. (1983). Entree and exit. *Sociological Review, 31,* 520–545.

34. Coleman, J. S. (1961). *The adolescent society.* New York: Free Press.

35. Colley, A. (1984). Sex roles and explanations of leisure behavior. *Leisure Studies, 3,* 335–341.

36. Comstock, G.; Chaffee, S.; Katzman, N.; McCombs, M.; & Roberts, D. F. (1978). *Television and human behavior.* New York: Columbia University Press.

37. Conger, J. J., & Petersen, A. C. (1984). *Adolescence and youth: Psychological development in a changing world.* 3rd ed. New York: Harper & Row.

38. Cottle, T. S. (1972). The connections of adolescence. In J. Kagan & R. Coles, eds., *12 to 16: Early adolescence*. New York: W. W. Norton, pp. 294–336.
39. Crites, J. O. (1965). Measurement of vocational maturity in adolescence: I. Attitude test of the vocational development inventory. *Psychological Monographs, 79*(2), 1–36.
40. Csikszentmihalyi, M., & Larson, R. (1984). *Being adolescent*. New York: Basic Books.
41. D'Amico, R. (1984). Does employment during high school impair academic progress? *Sociology of Education, 57*, 152–164.
42. Denisoff, R. S. (1986). *Tarnished gold*. New Brunswick, N.J.: Transaction.
43. Dominick, J. (1974). Children's viewing of crime shows and attitudes on law enforcement. *Journalism Quarterly, 51*, 5–12.
44. Downes, D. M. (1966). *The delinquent solution*. London: Routledge & Kegan Paul.
45. Dreeben, R. (1968). *On what is learned in school*. Reading, Mass.: Addison-Wesley.
46. Eder, D. (1985). The cycle of popularity: Interpersonal relations among female adolescents. *Sociology of Education, 58*, 154–165.
47. Eitzen, D. S. (1976). Sport and social status in American public secondary education. *Review of Sport and Leisure, 1*, 139–155.
48. Elder, G. H., Jr. (1974). *Children of the Great Depression*. Chicago: University of Chicago Press.
49. Elder, G. H., Jr., & Rockwell, R. C. (1979). Economic depression and postwar opportunity in men's lives: A study of life patterns and health. In R. G. Simmons, ed., *Research in community and mental health*. Vol. 1. Greenwich, Conn.: JAI Press, pp. 249–303.
50. Ellis, G. D., & Rademacher, C. (1987). Development of a typology of common adolescent free time activities. *Journal of Leisure Research, 19*, 284–292.
51. Engstrom, L. M. (1974). Physical activities during leisure. *International Review of Sport Sociology, 9*, 83–102.
52. Erikson, E. H. (1963). *Childhood and society*. 2nd ed. New York: W. W. Norton.
53. Everhart, R. B. (1983). *Reading, writing, and resistance*. Boston: Routledge & Kegan Paul.
54. Faber, R. J.; Brown, J. D.; & McLeod, J. M. (1979). Coming of age in the global village: Television and adolescence. In E. Wartella, ed., *Children communicating: Media and development of thought, speech, understanding*. Beverly Hills: Sage Publications, pp. 215–249.
55. Featherman, D. L. (1980). Schooling and occupational careers: Constancy and change in worldly success. In O. G. Brim, Jr., & J. Kagan, eds., *Constancy and change in human development*. Cambridge, Mass.: Harvard University Press.
56. Finch, M. D., & Mortimer, J. T. (1985). Adolescent work hours and the process of achievement. In A. C. Kerckhoff, ed., *Research in sociology of education and socialization*. Vol. 5. Greenwich, Conn.: JAI Press, pp. 171–196.
57. Finch, M. D., & Mortimer, J. T. (1989). Interrelationships of autonomy, overload, and stress among working men and women. Paper presented at the Midwest Sociological Society Meeting, St. Louis.

58. Fine, G. A. (1981). Friends, impression management, and preadolescent behavior. In S. R. Asher & J. M. Gottman, eds., *The development of children's friendships*. New York: Cambridge University Press, pp. 29–52.
59. Fine, G. A. (1983). *Shared fantasy*. Chicago: University of Chicago Press.
60. Fine, G. A. (1989). Mobilizing fun: Provisioning resources in leisure worlds. *Sport Sociology Journal, 6*, 319–334.
61. Fine, G. A., & Kleinman, S. (1979). Rethinking subculture. *American Journal of Sociology, 85*, 1–20.
62. Flegle, M. J. M. (1972). The use of leisure time by high school students in the suburbs of Detroit, Michigan. Ph.D. dissertation, University of Michigan.
63. Florian, V., & Har-Even D. (1984). Cultural patterns in the choice of leisure time activity frameworks. *Journal of Leisure Research, 16*, 330–337.
64. Fox, J. F. (1934). Leisure-time social backgrounds in a suburban community. *Journal of Educational Sociology, 7*, 493–503.
65. Freeman, R. B., & Wise, D. A. (1979). *Youth unemployment*. Cambridge, Mass.: National Bureau of Economic Research.
66. Frye, B. V. (1981). Leisure attitudes among middle school and high school students. Ph.D. dissertation, University of North Carolina at Greensboro.
67. Gans, H. (1962). *Urban villagers*. New York: Free Press.
68. Garton, A. F., & Pratt, C. (1987). Participation and interest in leisure activities by adolescent school children. *Journal of Adolescence, 10*, 341–351.
69. Gillis, J. R. (1974). *Youth and history*. New York: Academic Press.
70. Glancy, M.; Willits, F.; & Farrell, P. (1986). Adolescent activities and adult success and happiness: Twenty-four years later. *Sociology and Social Research, 70*, 242–247.
71. Goldstein, E. (1979). An exploration of the relationships between the leisure attitudes and leisure activities of an adolescent group. Ph.D. dissertation, Columbia University Teachers College.
72. Gore, T. (1987). *Raising PG kids in an X-rated society*. Nashville: Abingdon Press.
73. Gottfredson, L. S. (1981). Circumscription and compromise: A developmental theory of occupational aspirations. *Journal of Counselling Psychology Monograph, 28*, 545–579.
74. Gras, F. (1976). Problems of the social structure of children and young people participating in youth spartakiads. *International Review of Sport Sociology, 11*, 47–52.
75. Greenberg, B. S. (1982). Television and role socialization: An overview. In D. Pearl, L. Bouthilet, & J. Lazar, eds., *Television and behavior: Ten years of scientific progress and implications for the eighties*. Vol. 2. *Technical reviews*. Rockville, Md.: U.S. Department of Health and Human Services, pp. 179–190.
76. Greenberg, B. S. (1988). Mass media and adolescents: A review of research reported from 1980–1987. Manuscript prepared for Carnegie Council on Adolescent Development. Department of Communication, Michigan State University.
77. Greenberger, E. (1984). Children, families, and work. In N. D. Reppucci, L. A. Weithorn, E. P. Mulvey, & J. Monahan, eds., *Children, mental health, and the law*. Beverly Hills: Sage Publications, pp. 103–122.

78. Greenberger, E. (1988). Working in teenage America. In J. T. Mortimer & K. M. Borman, eds., *Work experience and psychological development through the life span.* Boulder: Westview Press, pp. 21–50.

79. Greenberger, E., & Steinberg, L. D. (1981). The workplace as a context for the socialization of youth. *Journal of Youth and Adolescence, 10,* 185–210.

80. Greenberger, E., & Steinberg, L. D. (1983). Sex differences in early labor force experience: Harbinger of things to come. *Social Forces, 62,* 467–486.

81. Greenberger, E., & Steinberg, L. D. (1986). *When teenagers work: The psychological and social costs of adolescent employment.* New York: Basic Books.

82. Greenberger, E.; Steinberg, L. D.; & Ruggiero, M. (1982). A job is a job is a job . . . or is it? *Work and Occupations, 9,* 79–96.

83. Greenberger, E.; Steinberg, L. D.; & Vaux, A. (1981). Adolescents who work: Health and behavioral consequences of job stress. *Developmental Psychology, 17,* 691–703.

84. Greenberger E.; Steinberg, L. D.; Vaux, A.; & McAuliffe, S. (1980). Adolescents who work: Effects of part-time employment on family and peer relations. *Journal of Youth and Adolescence, 9,* 189–202.

85. Greendorfer, S., & Lewko, J. (1978). The role of family members in the sport socialization of children. *Research Quarterly, 46,* 146–152.

86. Grossberg, L. (1986). Is there rock after punk? *Critical Studies in Mass Communication, 4,* 37–50.

87. Hall, D. T. (1971). A theoretical model of career subidentity development in organizational settings. *Organizational Behavior and Human Performance, 6,* 50–76.

88. Hamilton, S. F., & Crouter, A. C. (1980). Work and growth: A review of research on the impact of work experience on adolescent development. *Journal of Youth and Adolescence, 9,* 323–338.

89. Hanks, M., & Eckland, B. K. (1978). Adult voluntary associations and adolescent socialization. *Sociological Quarterly, 19,* 481–490.

90. Hannerz, U. (1969). *Soulside.* New York: Columbia University Press.

91. Hebdige, D. (1979). *Subcultures: The meaning of style.* London: Methuen.

92. Hendry, L. B.; Raymond, M.; & Stewart, C. (1984). Unemployment, school, and leisure; An adolescent study. *Leisure Studies, 3,* 175–187.

93. Hinsching, J. (1981). Sport as a leisure pursuit of older school youth. *International Review of Sport Sociology, 16,* 97–103.

94. Hornik, R. C. (1981). Out-of-school television and schooling: Hypotheses and methods. *Review of Educational Research, 51,* 199–214.

95. Horowitz, R. (1983). *Honor and the American dream.* New Brunswick, N.J.: Rutgers University Press.

96. Hotchkiss, L. (1982). *Effects of work time on school activities and career expectations.* Columbus: National Center for Research in Vocational Education.

97. Irwin, J. (1977). *Scenes.* Beverly Hills: Sage Publications.

98. Iso-Ahola, S. (1975). Leisure patterns of American and Finnish youth. *International Review of Sport Sociology, 10,* 63–85.

99. Jacobs, J. (1984). *The mall: An attempted escape from everyday life.* Prospect Heights, Ill.: Waveland Press.

100. Kelly, J. R. (1982). *Leisure.* Englewood Cliffs, N.J.: Prentice-Hall.

101. Kestenbaum, G. I., & Wernstein, L. (1983). Personality, psychopathology, and developmental issues in male adolescent video game use. *Journal of the American Academy of Child Psychiatry, 24,* 329–337.
102. Kett, J. E. (1977). *Rites of passage: Adolescence in America, 1790 to the present.* New York: Basic Books.
103. Kleiber, D. A., & Hemmer, J. D. (1981). Sex differences in the relationship of locus of control and recreational sport participation. *Sex Roles, 7,* 801–810.
104. Kleiber, D. A.; Larson, R.; & Csikszentmihalyi, M. (1986). The experience of leisure in adolescence. *Journal of Leisure Research, 18,* 169–176.
105. Kleiber, D. A., & Rickards, W. H. (1985). Leisure and recreation in adolescence: Limitations and potential. In M. G. Wade, ed., *Constraints on leisure.* Springfield, Ill.: Charles C. Thomas, pp. 289–317.
106. Kohn, M. L., & Schooler, C. (1983). *Work and personality: An inquiry into the impact of social stratification.* Norwood, N.J.: Albex.
107. Kotarba, J. A., & Wells, L. (1987). Studies of adolescent participation in an all-ages rock 'n' roll nightclub. *Youth and Society, 18,* 398–417.
108. Larson, R., & Kubey, R. (1983). Television and music: Contrasting media in adolescent life. *Youth and Society, 15,* 13–31.
109. Larson, R.; Kubey, R.; & Colletti, J. (in press). Changing channels: Early adolescent media choices and shifting investments. *Journal of Youth and Adolescence.*
110. Lewin-Epstein, N. (1971). *Youth employment during high school.* Washington, D.C.: National Center for Educational Statistics.
111. Lorence, J., & Mortimer, J. T. (1985). Work involvement through the life course: A panel study of three age groups. *American Sociological Review, 50,* 618–638.
112. Lyle, J., & Hoffman, H. R. (1972). Children's use of television and other media. In E. A. Rubinstein, G. A. Comstock, & J. P. Murray, eds., *Television and social behavior: Reports and papers.* Vol. 4. *Television in day-to-day life: Patterns of use.* Washington, D.C.: U.S. Government Printing Office, pp. 129–256.
113. Manning, P. K., & Campbell, B. (1973). Pinball as game, fad, synedoche. *Youth and Society, 4,* 333–358.
114. Marsh, H. W. (1988). Employment during high school: Character building or a subversion of academic goals. Unpublished manuscript.
115. Marsh, P.; Rosser, E.; & Harre, R. (1978). *The rules of disorder.* London: Routledge & Kegan Paul.
116. Marsland, D. (1982). It's my life: Young people and leisure. *Leisure Studies, 1,* 305–322.
117. Martinson, F. M. (1981). Preadolescent sexuality: Latent or manifest. In L. Constantine & F. Martinson, eds., *Children and sex.* Boston: Little, Brown, pp. 83–93.
118. McGuire, W. J. (1986). The myth of massive media impact: Savagings and salvagings. In G. A. Comstock, ed., *Public Communication and behavior.* Vol. 1. Orlando, Fla.: Academic Press, pp. 173–257.
119. McRobbie, A., & Garber, J. (1976). Girls and subculture: An exploration. In

S. Hall & T. Jefferson, eds., *Resistance through ritual*. London: Hutchinson, pp. 209–222.

120. Medrich, E. A. (1979). Constant television: A background to daily life. *Journal of Communication, 29,* 171–176.

121. Meyer, R. M., & Wise, D. A. (1982). High school preparation and early labor force experience. In R. B. Freeman & D. A. Wise, eds., *The youth labor market problem: Its nature, causes, and consequences.* Chicago: University of Chicago Press, pp. 277–347.

122. Mortimer, J. T.; Dunnigan, T.; Owens, T.; & Martin, D. (1989). Report of a longitudinal study of the vocational acculturation of Hmong adolescents: Preliminary first-wave findings. Paper presented at the American Sociological Association Meeting, San Francisco, August.

123. Mortimer, J. T., & Finch, M. D. (1983). Autonomy as a source of self-esteem in adolescence. Paper presented at the American Sociological Association Meeting, August, Detroit.

124. Mortimer, J. T., & Finch, M. D. (1986). The effects of part-time work on self-concept and achievement. In K. M. Borman & J. Reisman, eds., *Becoming a worker.* Norwood, N.J.: Ablex, pp. 66–89.

125. Mortimer, J. T., & Finch, M. D. (1988). Youth development study: Wave I survey. Unpublished data, University of Minnesota.

126. Mortimer, J. T.; Finch, M. D.; & Maruyama, G. (1988). Work experience and job satisfaction: Variation by age and gender. In J. T. Mortimer & K. M. Borman, eds., *Work experience and psychological development through the life span: American Association of Advancement of Science Selected Symposium 107.* Boulder: Westview Press, pp. 109–155.

127. Mortimer, J. T.; Finch, M. D.; Owens, T.; Shanahan, M.; & Kemper, M. (1989). The nature and correlates of early adolescent work experience. Paper presented at the American Sociological Association Meeting, San Francisco, August.

128. Mortimer, J. T.; Lorence, J.; & Kumka, D. (1986). *Work, family, and personality: Transition to adulthood.* Norwood, N.J.: Ablex.

129. Mortimer, J. T., & Yamoor, C. (1987). Interrelations and parallels of school and work as sources of psychological development. *Research in the Sociology of Education and Socialization, 7,* 221–246. Greenwich, Conn.: JAI Press.

130. Mungham, G., & Pearson, G. (1976). Troubled youth, troubled world. In G. Mungham & G. Pearson, eds., *Working class youth culture.* London: Routledge & Kegan Paul, pp. 1–9.

131. Musgrove, F. (1969). The problem of youth and the structure of society in England. *Youth and Society, 1,* 38–58.

132. Mutz, D.; Roberts, D. F.; & Van Vuuren, D. P. (1988). Reconsidering the displacement hypothesis: The South African case. Paper presented at the annual convention of the International Communication Association, New Orleans, May.

133. National Commission on Youth (1980). *The transition to adulthood: A bridge too long.* Boulder: Westview Press.

134. Nava. M. (1984). Youth service provision, social order, and the question of

girls. In A. M. Robbie & M. Nava, eds., *Gender and generation*. Houndsmills, England: Macmillan, pp. 1–30.

135. Neulinger, J. (1974). *The psychology of leisure*. Springfield, Ill.: Charles C. Thomas.

136. Ng, D., & June, L. (1985). Electronic leisure and youth: Kitchener arcade video game players. *Society and Leisure, 8,* 537–548.

137. Nicholson, N. (1984). A theory of work role transitions. *Administrative Science Quarterly, 29,* 172–191.

138. Noe, F. (1969). An instrumental conception of leisure for the adolescent. *Adolescence, 4,* 385–400.

139. Noe, F., & Elifson, K. (1976). The pleasures of youth: Parent and peer compliance toward discretionary time. *Journal of Youth and Adolescence, 5,* 37–58.

140. Olmsted, A. D. (1988). Morally controversial leisure: The social world of gun collectors. *Symbolic Interaction, 11,* 277–287.

141. Osterman, P. (1980). *Getting started: The youth labor market*. Cambridge, Mass.: Massachusetts Institute of Technology Press.

142. Otto, L. B. (1975). Extracurricular activities in the educational attainment process. *Rural Sociology, 40,* 162–176.

143. Otto, L. B., & Alwin, D. F. (1977). Athletics, aspirations, and attainment. *Sociology of Education, 50,* 102–113.

144. Panel on Youth of the President's Science Advisory Committee (1974). *Youth: Transition to adulthood*. Chicago: University of Chicago Press.

145. Panelas, T. (1983). Adolescents and video games: Consumption of leisure and the social construction of the peer group. *Youth and Society, 15,* 51–65.

146. Parsons, T. (1942). Age and sex in the social structure of the United States. *American Sociological Review, 7,* 604–616.

147. Pearl, D.; Bouthilet, L.; & Lazar, J. (1982). *Television and behavior*. Vol. 2. *Ten years of scientific progress and implications for the eighties*. Technical Reviews. Rockville, Md.: U.S. Department of Health and Human Services.

148. Peterson, E. (1987). Media consumption and girls who want to have fun. *Critical Studies in Mass Communication, 4,* 37–50.

149. Poole, M. E. (1983). *Youth: Expectations and transitions*. Melbourne: Routledge & Kegan Paul.

150. Porter, R. T. (1967). Sports and adolescence. In G. Slovenko & J. Knight, eds., *Motivation in play, games, and sport*. Springfield, Ill.: Charles C. Thomas, pp. 73–90.

151. Postman, N. (1985). *Amusing ourselves to death: Public discourse in the age of show business*. New York: Viking.

152. Ralbovsky, M. (1973). *Destiny's darlings*. New York: Hawthorne Books.

153. Ritchie, D.; Price, V.; & Roberts, D. F. (1987). Television, reading and reading achievement: A reappraisal. *Communication Research, 14,* 292–315.

154. Roberts, D. F. (1982). Children and commercials: Issues, evidence, interventions. *Prevention in Human Services, 2,* 19–35.

155. Roberts, D. F., & Maccoby, N. (1984). Effects of mass communication. In G. Lindzey & E. Aronson, eds., *Handbook of social psychology*. Vol. 2 3rd ed. *Special fields and applications*. Reading, Mass.: Addison-Wesley, pp. 539–598.

156. Roberts, J., & Sutton-Smith, B. (1962). Child training and game involvement. *Ethnology, 1,* 166–185.
157. Roberts, K. (1983). *Youth and leisure.* London: George Allen and Unwin.
158. Roberts, K.; Noble, M.; & Duggan, J. (1982). Youth unemployment: An old problem or a new life-style. *Leisure Studies, 1,* 171–182.
159. Roe, K. (1987). The school and music in adolescent socialization. In J. Lull, ed., *Popular music and communication.* Beverly Hills: Sage Publications, pp. 212–230.
160. Rosenmayr, L. (1967). Sport as leisure activity of young people. *International Review of Sport Sociology, 1,* 19–32.
161. Ruggiero, M. (1984). Work as an impetus to delinquency: An examination of theoretical and empirical connections. Ph.D. dissertation, University of California, Irvine.
162. Ruggiero, M.; Greenberger, E.; & Steinberg, L. D. (1982). Occupational deviance among first-time workers. *Youth and Society, 13,* 423–448.
163. Sanders, C. R. (1974). Psyching out the crowd: Folk performers and their audiences. *Urban Life and Culture, 3,* 264–282.
164. Sato, I. (1988). Play theory of delinquency: Toward a general theory of action. *Symbolic Interaction, 11,* 191–212.
165. Schill, W. J.; McCartin, R.; & Meyer, K. (1985). Youth employment: Its relationship to academic and family variables. *Journal of Vocational Behavior, 26,* 155–163.
166. Schramm, W.; Lyle, J.; & Parker, E. B. (1961). *Television in the lives of our children.* Stanford: Stanford University Press.
167. Schwartz, P., & Lever, J. (1976). Fear and loathing at a college mixer. *Urban Life, 4,* 413–431.
168. Sherif, M., & Sherif, C. (1964). *Reference groups.* New York: Harper & Row.
169. Simons, E. R. (1980). The slumber party as folk ritual: An analysis of the informal sex education of pre-adolescents. Master's thesis, University of California, Berkeley.
170. Siskind, J. B. (1983). Leisure and vocational interests of secondary school students. Ph.D. dissertation, University of Florida.
171. Smith, C. S. (1973). Adolescence. In M. A. Smith, S. Parker, & C. S. Smith, eds., *Leisure and society in Britain.* London: Allen Lane, pp. 148–158.
172. Smith, D. M. (1987). Some patterns of reported leisure behavior of young people. *Youth and Society, 18,* 255–281.
173. Snedeker, B. (1982). *Hard knocks: Preparing youth for work.* Baltimore: Johns Hopkins University Press.
174. Spady, W. G. (1970). Lament for the letterman: Effects of peer status and extracurricular activities on goals and achievement. *American Journal of Sociology, 75,* 680–702.
175. Steinberg, L. D.; Greenberger, E.; Garduque, L.; & McAuliffe, S. (1982). High school students in the labor force: Some costs and benefits to schooling and learning. *Education Evaluation and Policy Analysis, 4,* 363–372.
176. Steinberg, L. D.; Greenberger, E.; Garduque, L.; Ruggiero, M.; & Vaux, A. (1982). Effects of working on adolescent development. *Developmental Psychology, 18,* 385–395.

177. Stoll, C. S., & Inbar, M. (1970). Games and socialization: An exploratory study of race differences. *Sociological Quarterly, 11,* 374–381.

178. Sun, S. W., & Lull, J. (1986). The adolescent audience for music videos and why they watch. *Journal of Communication, 36,* 115–125.

179. Sutton-Smith, B. (1959). The kissing games of adolescence in Ohio. *Midwest Folklore, 9,* 189–211.

180. Tanner, J. (1978). New directions for subcultural theory. *Youth and Society, 9,* 343–372.

181. Taylor, L. (1971). *Deviance and society.* London: Joseph.

182. Thrasher, F. (1927). *The gang.* Chicago: University of Chicago Press.

183. U.S. Department of Labor (1985). *Handbook of Labor Statistics, Bureau of Labor Statistics Bulletin 2217.* Washington, D.C.: U.S. Government Printing Office.

184. U.S. Department of Labor (1987). *Employment and Earnings.* Vol. 34, no. 10. Washington, D.C.: U.S. Government Printing Office.

185. Van Maanen, J., & Schein, E. (1979). Toward a theory of organizational socialization. *Research in Organizational Behavior, 1,* 209–264.

186. Varpalotai, A. (1987). The hidden curriculum in leisure: An analysis of a girls' sport subculture. *Women's Studies International Forum, 10,* 411–422.

187. Vaz, E. (1982). *The professionalization of young hockey players.* Lincoln: University of Nebraska Press.

188. Wartella, E.; Heintz, K.; Aidman, A.; & Mazzarella, S. (1990). Television and beyond: Children's video media in one community. *Communication research, 17,* 45–64.

189. Watson, G. G., & Collis, R. (1982). Adolescent values in sport: A case of conflicting interests. *International Review of Sport Sociology, 17,* 73–90.

190. White, E. (1982). *A boy's own story.* New York: Dutton.

191. Williams, T., & Kornblum, W. (1985). *Growing up poor.* Lexington, Mass.: Lexington Books.

192. Willis, P. (1981). *Learning to labor.* New York: Columbia University Press.

193. Winn, M. (1977). *The plug-in drug.* New York: Viking.

194. Wirtz, W. (1975). *The boundless resource: A prospectus for an education/work policy.* Washington, D.C.: New Republic Book Company.

195. Wulff, H. (1988). *Twenty girls: Growing up, ethnicity, and excitement in a South London microculture.* Stockholm: Stockholm Studies in Social Anthropology.

196. Yamoor, C., & Mortimer, J. T. (1989). An investigation of age and gender differences in the effects of employment on adolescent achievement and well-being. Paper presented at the Midwest Sociological Society Annual Meeting, St. Louis.

197. Young, A. M. (1979). The difference a year makes in the nation's youth work force. *Monthly Labor Review, 102,* 34–38.

198. Young, R. A. (1983). Career development of adolescents: An ecological perspective. *Journal of Youth and Adolescence, 12,* 401–417.

10. Autonomy, Conflict, and Harmony in the Family Relationship

1. Adelson, J., & Doehrman, M. (1980). The psychodynamic approach to adolescence. In J. Adelson, ed., *Handbook of adolescent psychology.* New York: Wiley, pp. 99–116.

2. Atkinson, B., & Bell, N. (1986). Attachment and autonomy in adolescence. Paper presented at the biennial meetings of the Society for Research on Adolescence, March, Madison, Wis.

3. Ballenski, C., & Cook, A. (1982). Mothers' perceptions of their competence in managing selected parenting tasks. *Family Relations, 31,* 489–494.

4. Barnes, G. (1984). Adolescent alcohol abuse and other problem behaviors: Their relationship and common parental influences. *Journal of Youth and Adolescence, 13,* 329–348.

5. Baumrind, D. (1967). Child care practices anteceding three patterns of preschool behavior. *Genetic Psychology Monographs, 75,* 43–88.

6. Bell-Scott, P. (1987). Family-adolescent relationships. In *Black adolescence: Topical summaries and annotated bibliographies of research.* Storrs, Conn.: Consortium for Research on Black Adolescence, University of Connecticut.

7. Blos, P. (1979). *The adolescent passage.* New York: International Universities Press.

8. Bowlby, J. (1981). *Attachment and loss.* Vol. 3. *Loss, sadness, and depression.* New York: Basic Books.

9. Bronfenbrenner, U. (1986). Ecology of the family as a context for human development: Research perspectives. *Developmental Psychology, 22,* 723–742.

10. Buchanan, C.; Eccles, J.; Flanagan, C.; Midgley, C.; Feldlaufer, H.; & Goldsmith, R. (1988). Parents' and teachers' beliefs about adolescents: Effects of sex and experience. Manuscript under review. Stanford University Center for the Study of Families, Children, and Youth.

11. Collins, W. A. (1988). Research on the transition to adolescence. Continuity in the study of developmental processes. In M. Gunnar, ed., *21st Minnesota symposium on child psychology.* Hillsdale, N.J.: Erlbaum, pp. 1–15.

12. Collins, W. A. (1989). Parent-child relationships in the transition to adolescence: Continuity and change in interaction, affect, and cognition. In R. Montemayor, G. Adams, & T. Gullotta, eds., *Advances in adolescent development.* Vol. 2. *The transition from childhood to adolescence.* Beverly Hills: Sage Publications.

13. Conger, J. (1981). Freedom and commitment: Families, youth, and social change. *American Psychologist, 36,* 1475–84.

14. Cooper, C. (1988). Commentary: The role of conflict in adolescent-parent relationships. In M. Gunnar, ed., *21st Minnesota symposium on child psychology.* Hillsdale, N.J.: Erlbaum, pp. 181–187.

15. Cooper, C.; Grotevant, H.; & Condon, S. (1983). Individuality and connectedness in the family as a context for adolescent identity formation and role taking-skill. In H. Grotevant & C. Cooper, eds., *Adolescent development in the family.* San Francisco: Jossey-Bass, pp. 43–60.

16. Dornbusch, S.; Carlsmith, J.; Bushwall, S.; Ritter, P.; Leiderman, P.; Hastorf, A.; & Gross, R. (1985). Single parents, extended households, and the control of adolescents. *Child Development, 56,* 326–341.

17. Dornbusch, S.; Ritter, P.; Liederman, P.; Roberts, D.; & Fraleigh, M. (1987). The relation of parenting style to adolescent school performance. *Child Development, 58,* 1244–57.

18. Douvan, E., & Adelson, J. (1966). *The adolescent experience.* New York: Wiley.

19. Enright, R.; Levy, V.; Harris, D.; & Lapsley, D. (1987). Do economic conditions influence how theorists view adolescents? *Journal of Youth and Adolescence, 16,* 541–560.
20. Feldman, S., & Gehring, T. (1988). Changing perceptions of family cohesion and power across adolescence. *Child Development, 59,* 1034–45.
21. Feldman, S., & Quatman, T. (in press). Factors influencing age expectations for adolescent autonomy: A study of early adolescents and parents. *Journal of Early Adolescence.*
22. Feldman, S.; Rubenstein, J.; & Rubin, C. (in press). Depressive affect and restraint in early adolescents: Relationships with family structure, family process, and friendship support. *Journal of Early Adolescence.*
23. Freud, A. (1958). Adolescence. *Psychoanalytic Study of the Child, 13,* 255–278.
24. Garbarino, J.; Sebes, J.; & Schellenbach, C. (1984). Families at risk for destructive parent-child relations in adolescence. *Child Development, 55,* 174–183.
25. Gjerde, P. (1986). The interpersonal structure of family interaction settings: Parent-adolescent relations in dyads and triads. *Developmental Psychology, 22,* 297–304.
26. Greenberg, M.; Siegel, J.; & Leitch, C. (1983). The nature and importance of attachment relationships to parents and peers during adolescence. *Journal of Youth and Adolescence, 12,* 373–386.
27. Grotevant, H., & Cooper, C. (1986). Individuation in family relationships: A perspective on individual differences in the development of identity and role-taking skill in adolescence. *Human Development, 29,* 82–100.
28. Harter, S. (1983). Developmental perspectives on the self-system. In E. M. Hetherington, ed., *Handbook of child psychology.* Vol. 4. *Socialization, personality, and social development.* New York: Wiley, pp. 275–385.
29. Hauser, S.; Book, B.; Houlihan, J.; Powers, S.; Weiss-Perry, B.; Follansbee, D.; Jacobson, A.; & Noam, G. (1987). Sex differences within the family: Studies of adolescent- and parent-family interactions. *Journal of Youth and Adolescence, 16,* 199–220.
30. Hauser, S.; Powers, S.; Noam, G.; Jacobson, A.; Weiss, B.; & Follansbee, D. (1984). Familial contexts of adolescent ego development. *Child Development, 55,* 195–213.
31. Hetherington, E. M., & Camara, K. (1984). Families in transition: The processes of dissolution and reconstitution. In R. Parke, ed., *Review of child development research.* Vol. 7. Chicago: University of Chicago Press, pp. 398–437.
32. Hill, J. P. (1980). The family. In M. Johnson, ed., *Toward adolescence: The middle school years.* Seventy-ninth yearbook of the National Society for the Study of Education. Chicago: University of Chicago Press, pp. 32–55.
33. Hill, J. (1988). Adapting to menarche: Familial control and conflict. In M. Gunnar, ed., *21st Minnesota symposium on child psychology.* Hillsdale, N.J.: Erlbaum, pp. 43–77.
34. Hill, J., & Holmbeck, G. (1986). Attachment and autonomy during adolescence. In G. Whitehurst, ed., *Annals of child development.* Greenwich, Conn.: JAI Press.

35. Hoffman, L. W., & Manis, J. D. (1978). Influences of children on marital and parental satisfactions and dissatisfactions. In R. M. Lerner & G. B. Spanier, eds., *Child influences on marital and family interaction: A life-span perspective.* New York: Academic Press, pp. 165–213.

36. Holmbeck, G., & Hill, J. (1988). The role of familial conflict in adaptation to menarche: Sequential analysis of family interaction. Unpublished manuscript, Department of Psychology, Temple University.

37. Jessor, R., & Jessor, S. (1977). *Problem behavior and psychosocial development: A longitudinal study of youth.* New York: Academic Press.

38. Josselson, R. (1980). Ego development in adolescence. In J. Adelson, ed., *Handbook of adolescent psychology.* New York: Wiley, pp. 188–210.

39. Kaplan, L. (1984). *Adolescence: The farewell to childhood.* New York: Simon and Schuster.

40. Kandel, D., & Lesser, G. (1972). *Youth in two worlds.* San Francisco: Jossey-Bass.

41. Kobak, R., & Sceery, A. (1988). Attachment in late adolescence: Working models, affect regulation, and representations of self and others. *Child Development, 59,* 135–146.

42. Loeber, R., & Stouthamer-Loeber, M. (1986). Family factors as correlates and predictors of juvenile conduct problems and delinquency. In M. Tonry & N. Morris, eds., *Crime and justice.* Vol. 7. Chicago: University of Chicago Press, pp. 29–149.

43. Maccoby, E., & Martin, J. (1983). Socialization in the context of the family: Parent-child interaction. In E. M. Hetherington, ed., *Handbook of child psychology.* Vol. 4. *Socialization, personality, and social development.* New York: Wiley, pp. 1–101.

44. Minuchin, S. (1974). *Families and family therapy.* Cambridge, Mass.: Harvard University Press.

45. Montemayor, R. (1983). Parents and adolescents in conflict: All families some of the time and some families most of the time. *Journal of Early Adolescence, 3,* 83–103.

46. Montemayor, R. (1985). Some thoughts about conflict and power in the parent-adolescent relationship. Paper presented at the Third Biennial Conference on Adolescent Research, March, Tucson.

47. Montemayor, R. (1986). Family variation in parent-adolescent storm and stress. *Journal of Adolescent Research, 1,* 15–31.

48. Montemayor, R., & Hanson, E. (1985). A naturalistic view of conflict between adolescents and their parents and siblings. *Journal of Early Adolescence, 5,* 23–30.

49. Offer, D. (1969). *The psychological world of the teenager.* New York: Basic Books.

50. Offer, D.; Ostrov, E.; & Howard, K. (1981). *The adolescent: A psychological self-portrait.* New York: Basic Books.

51. Papini, D., & Sebby, R. (1987). Adolescent pubertal status and affective family relationships: A multivariate assessment. *Journal of Youth and Adolescence, 16,* 1–15.

52. Patterson, G. (1986). Performance models for antisocial boys. *American Psychologist, 41,* 432–444.
53. President's Science Advisory Committee (1973). *Youth: Transition to adulthood.* Chicago: University of Chicago Press.
54. Rutter, M.; Graham, P.; Chadwick, F.; & Yule, W. (1976). Adolescent turmoil: Fact or fiction? *Journal of Child Psychology and Psychiatry, 17,* 35–56.
55. Ryan, R., & Lynch, J. (1989). Emotional autonomy versus detachment: Revisiting the vicissitudes of adolescence and young adulthood. *Child Development, 60,* 340–356.
56. Santrock, J.; Warshak, R.; Lindbergh, C.; Meadows, L. (1982). Children's and parents' observed social behavior in stepfather families. *Child Development, 53,* 472–480.
57. Silverberg, S., & Steinberg, L. (1987). Adolescent autonomy, parent-adolescent conflict, and parental well-being. *Journal of Youth and Adolescence, 16,* 293–312.
58. Silverberg, S., & Steinberg, L. (in press). Psychological well-being of parents at midlife: The impact of early adolescent children. *Developmental Psychology.*
59. Small, S.; Eastman, G.; & Cornelius, S. (1988). Adolescent autonomy and parental stress. *Journal of Youth and Adolescence, 17,* 377–392.
60. Smetana, J. (1988). Concepts of self and social convention: Adolescents' and parents' reasoning about hypothetical and actual family conflicts. In M. Gunnar, ed., *21st Minnesota symposium on child psychology.* Hillsdale, N.J.: Erlbaum, pp. 79–122.
61. Smollar, J., & Youniss, J. (1985). Transformation in adolescents' perception of parents. Paper presented at the biennial meetings of the Society for Research in Child Development, April, Toronto.
62. Steinberg, L. (1987). The impact of puberty on family relations: Effects of pubertal status and pubertal timing. *Developmental Psychology, 23,* 451–460.
63. Steinberg, L. (1988). Reciprocal relation between parent-child distance and pubertal maturation. *Developmental Psychology, 24,* 122–128.
64. Steinberg, L. (1989). Pubertal maturation and parent-adolescent distance: An evolutionary perspective. In G. Adams, R. Montemayor, & T. Gullotta, eds., *Advances in adolescent development.* Vol. 1. Beverly Hills: Sage Publications.
65. Steinberg, L., & Silverberg, S. (1986). The vicissitudes of autonomy in early adolescence. *Child Development, 57,* 841–851.
66. Steinberg, L., & Silverberg, S. (1987). Influences on marital satisfaction during the middle stages of the family life cycle. *Journal of Marriage and the Family, 49,* 751–760.
67. Susman, E.; Inhoff-Germain, G.; Nottelmann, E.; Loriaux, D.; Cutler, G., Jr.; & Chrousos, G. (1987). Hormones, emotional dispositions, and aggressive attributes in young adolescents. *Child Development, 58,* 1114–34.
68. Veroff, J., & Feld, S. (1970). *Marriage and work in America.* New York: Van Nostrand Reinhold.
69. Wetzel, J. (1987). *American youth: A statistical snapshot.* Washington, D.C.: William T. Grant Foundation Commission on Work, Family, and Citizenship.
70. White, K.; Speisman, J.; Costos, D.; & Smith, A. (1987). Relationship matu-

rity: A conceptual and empirical approach. In J. Meacham, ed., *Contributions to human development*. Vol. 18. New York: Karger, pp. 81–101.
71. Youniss, J. (1988). *Mutuality in parent-adolescent relationships*. Washington, D.C.: William T. Grant Foundation Commission on Work, Family, and Citizenship.
72. Youniss, J., & Smollar, J. (1985). *Adolescent relations with mothers, fathers, and friends*. Chicago: University of Chicago Press.

11. Friendship and Peer Relations

1. Ball, S. J. (1981). *Beachside comprehensive*. Cambridge: Cambridge University Press.
2. Bell, A. P.; Weinberg, M. S.; & Hammersmith, S. K. (1981). *Sexual preference: Its development in men and women*. Bloomington: Indiana University Press.
3. Berndt, T. J. (1981). Effects of friendship on prosocial intentions and behavior. *Child Development, 52*, 636–643.
4. Berndt, T. J. (1982). The features and effects of friendships in early adolescence. *Child Development, 53*, 1447–60.
5. Berndt, T. J. (1986). Sharing between friends: Contexts and consequences. In E. C. Mueller & C. R. Cooper, eds., *Process and outcome in peer relationships*. New York: Academic Press, pp. 105–127.
6. Berndt, T. J. (1988). The nature and significance of children's friendships. In R. Vasta, ed., *Annals of child development*. Vol. 5. Greenwich, Conn.: JAI Press, pp. 155–186.
7. Berndt, T. J. (forthcoming). Obtaining support from friends in childhood and adolescence. In D. Belle, eds., *The social support needs of school-aged children*. New York: Wiley.
8. Berndt, T. J., & Hawkins, J. A. (1987). The contribution of supportive friendships to adjustment after the transition to junior high school. Unpublished manuscript, Purdue University.
9. Berndt, T. J.; Hawkins, J. A.; & Hoyle, S. G. (1986). Changes in friendship during a school year: Effects on children's and adolescents' impressions of friendship and sharing with friends. *Child Development, 57*, 1284–97.
10. Berndt, T. J., & Hoyle, S. G. (1985). Stability and change in childhood and adolescent friendships. *Developmental Psychology, 21*, 1007–15.
11. Berndt, T. J.; McCartney, K.; Caparulo, B. K.; & Moore, A. M. (1983–84). The effects of group discussions on children's moral decisions. *Social Cognition, 2*, 343–360.
12. Berzon, B., & Leighton, R., eds. (1979). *Positively gay*. Millbrae, Calif.: Celestial Arts.
13. Bierman, K. L. (1986). The relationship between social aggression and peer rejection in middle childhood. In R. Prinz, ed., *Advances in behavioral assessment of children and families*. Vol. 2. Greenwich, Conn.: JAI Press, pp. 151–178.
14. Bierman, K. L., & Furman, W. F. (1984). The effects of social skills training and peer involvement on the social adjustment of preadolescents. *Child Development, 55*, 151–162.

15. Bierman, K. L., & McCauley, E. (1987). Children's descriptions of their peer interactions: Useful information for clinical child assessment. *Journal of Clinical Child Psychology, 16,* 9–18.
16. Bierman, K. L.; Miller, C. M.; & Stabb, S. (1987) Improving the social behavior and peer acceptance of rejected boys: Effects of social skill training with instructions and prohibitions. *Journal of Consulting and Clinical Psychology, 55,* 194–200.
17. Bigelow, B. J., & LaGaipa, J. J. (1980). The development of friendship values and choice. In H. C. Foot; A. J. Chapman; & J. R. Smith, eds., *Friendship and social relations in children.* New York: Wiley, pp. 15–44.
18. Billy, J. O. G.; Rodgers, J. L.; & Udry, J. R. (1984). Adolescent sexual behavior and friendship choice. *Social Forces, 62,* 653–678.
19. Bronfenbrenner, U., & Crouter, A. C. (1983). The evolution of environmental models in developmental research. In P. H. Mussen, eds., *Handbook of child psychology.* Vol. 1. *History, theory, and methods,* ed. W. Kessen. New York: Wiley, pp. 357–414.
20. Brown, B. B.; Clasen, D. R.; & Eicher, S. A. (1986). Perceptions of peer pressure, peer conformity dispositions, and self-reported behavior among adolescents. *Developmental Psychology, 22,* 521–530.
21. Buhrmester, D., & Furman, W. (1986). The changing functions of children's friendships: A neo-Sullivanian perspective. In V. Derlega & B. Winstead, eds., *Friendships and social interaction.* New York: Springer, pp. 41–62.
22. Buhrmester, D., & Furman, W. (1987). The development of companionship and intimacy. *Child Development, 50,* 1101–15.
23. Bukowski, W. M., & Hoza, B. (1989). Popularity and friendship: Issues in theory, measurement, and outcome. In T. J. Berndt & G. W. Ladd, eds., *Peer relationships in child development.* New York: John Wiley & Sons, pp. 15–45.
24. Bukowski, W. M., & Newcomb, A. F. (1984). Stability and determinants of sociometric status and friendship choice: A longitudinal perspective. *Developmental Psychology, 20,* 941–952.
25. Bukowski, W. M.; Newcomb, A. F.; & Hoza, B. (1987). Friendship conceptions among early adolescents: A longitudinal study of stability and change. *Journal of Early Adolescence, 7,* 143–152.
26. Cairns, R. B.; Cairns, B. D.; Neckerman, H. J.; Gest, S. D.; & Gariepy, J. L. (1988). Social networks and aggressive behavior: Peer support or peer rejection? *Developmental Psychology, 24,* 815–823.
27. Cauce, A. M. (1986). Social networks and social competence: Exploring the effects of early adolescent friendships. *American Journal of Community Psychology, 14,* 607–628.
28. Cauce, A. M. (1987). Social and peer competence in early adolescence: A test of domain-specific self-perceived competence, *Developmental Psychology, 23,* 287–291.
29. Cauce, A. M.; Felner, R. D.; & Primavera, J. (1982). Social support in high-risk adolescents: Structural components and adaptive impact. *American Journal of Community Psychology, 10,* 417–428.
30. Chassin, L.; Presson, C. C.; Montello, D.; Sherman, S. J.; & McGrew, J.

(1986). Changes in peer and parent influence during adolescence: Longitudinal versus cross-sectional perspectives on smoking initiation. *Developmental Psychology, 22,* 327–334.

31. Clark, M. L. & Ayers, M. (1988). The role of reciprocity and proximity in junior high school friendships. *Journal of Youth and Adolescence, 17,* 403–411.

32. Coates, D. L. (1985). Relationships between self-concept measures and social network characteristics for black adolescents. *Journal of Early Adolescence, 5,* 319–338.

33. Coates, D. L. (1987). Gender differences in the structure and support characteristics of black adolescents' social networks. *Sex Roles, 17,* 667–687.

34. Cohen, J. (1977). Sources of peer homogeneity. *Sociology of Education, 50,* 227–241.

35. Cohen, J. (1983). Commentary: The relationship between friendship selection and peer influence. In J. Epstein & N. Karweit, eds., *Friends in school: Patterns of selection and influence in secondary schools.* New York: Academic Press, pp. 163–174.

36. Cohen, S., & Wills, T. A. (1985). Stress, social support, and the buffering hypothesis. *Psychological Bulletin, 98,* 310–357.

37. Cole, J. D., & Dodge, K. A. (1983). Continuities and changes in children's social status: A five-year longitudinal study. *Merrill Palmer Quarterly, 29,* 261–282.

38. Coleman, J. S. (1961). *The adolescent society.* New York: Free Press.

39. Condry, J., & Siman, M. L. (1974). Characteristics of peer- and adult-oriented children. *Journal of Marriage and the Family, 36,* 543–554.

40. Csikszentmihalyi, M., & Larson, R. (1984). *Being adolescent.* New York: Basic Books.

41. Davies, B. (1982). *Life in the classroom and playground.* London: Routledge & Kegan Paul.

42. Douvan, E., & Adelson, J. (1966). *The adolescent experience.* New York: Wiley.

43. Dunn, S. E.; Putallaz, M.; Sheppard, B. H.; & Lindstrom, R. (1987). Social support and adjustment in gifted adolescents. *Journal of Educational Psychology, 79,* 467–473.

44. Dunphy, D. C. (1963). The social structure of urban adolescent peer groups. *Sociometry, 26,* 230–246.

45. East, P. L.; Hess, L. E.; & Lerner, R. M. (1987). Peer social support and adjustment of early adolescent peer groups. *Journal of Early Adolescence, 7,* 153–163.

46. Eder, D. (1985). The cycle of popularity: Interpersonal relations among female adolescents. *Sociology of Education, 58,* 154–165.

47. Eder, D. (1986). Serious and playful disputes: Variation in conflict talk among female adolescents. In A. D. Grimshaw, ed., *Conflict talk; Sociolinguistic investigations of arguments in conversations.* Cambridge: Cambridge University Press.

48. Eder, D. (1987). The role of teasing in adolescent peer group culture. Paper presented at the Conference on Ethnographic Approaches to Children's Worlds and Peer Cultures, Trondheim, Norway.

49. Eder, D., & Hallinan, M. T. (1978). Sex differences in children's friendships. *American Sociological Review, 43,* 237–250.

50. Eder, D., & Sanford, S. (1986). The development and maintenance of interactional norms among early adolescents. In P. Adler, ed., *Sociological studies of child development.* Vol. 1. Greenwich, Conn.: JAI Press, pp. 283–300.

51. Epstein, J. L. (1983a). The influence of friends on achievement and affective outcomes. In J. L. Epstein & N. L. Karweit, eds., *Friends in school.* New York: Academic Press, pp. 177–200.

52. Epstein, J. L. (1983b). Examining theories of adolescent friendship. In J. L. Epstein & N. L. Karweit, eds. *Friends in school.* New York: Academic Press, pp. 39–61.

53. Epstein, J. L. (1983c). Selection of friends in differently organized schools and classrooms. In J. L. Epstein & N. L. Karweit, eds., *Friends in school.* New York: Academic Press, pp. 73–92.

54. Epstein, J. L. (1983d). School environment and student friendships: Issues, implications, and interventions. In J. L. Epstein & N. L. Karweit, eds., *Friends in school.* New York: Academic Press, pp. 235–253.

55. Epstein, J. L. (1986). Friendship selection: Developmental and environmental influences. In R. C. Mueller & C. R. Cooper, eds., *Process and outcome in peer relationships.* New York: Academic Press, pp. 129–160.

56. Epstein, J. L. (1989). The selection of friends: Changes across the grades and in different school environments. In T. J. Berndt & G. W. Ladd, eds., *Peer relationships in child development.* New York: Wiley, pp. 158–187.

57. Feltham, R. F; Doyle, A. B.; Schwartzman, A. E.; Serbin, L. A.; & Ledingham, J. E. (1985). Friendship in normal and socially deviant children. *Journal of Early Adolescence, 5,* 371–382.

58. Fine, G. A. (1980). The natural history of preadolescent male friendship groups. In H. C. Foot, A. J. Chapman, & J. R. Smith, eds., *Friendship and social relations in children.* New York: Wiley, pp. 293–320.

59. French, J. R. P., & Raven, B. (1959). The bases of social power. In D. C. Cartwright, ed., *Studies in social power.* Ann Arbor: University of Michigan Press, pp. 150–167.

60. Fuligni, A. J., & Savin-Williams, R. C. (1989). An exploratory study of adolescent peer teasing and ridicule. Paper presented at the Fifth Biennial Conference on Adolescent Research, Tucson.

61. Furman, W., & Buhrmester, D. (1985). Children's perceptions of the personal relationships in their social networks. *Developmental Psychology, 21,* 1016–24.

62. Glynn, T. J. (1981). From family to peer: A review of transitions of influence among drug-using youth. *Journal of Youth and Adolescence, 10,* 363–383.

63. Gold, M., & Yanof, D. S. (1985). Mothers, daughters, and girlfriends. *Journal of Personality and Social Psychology, 49,* 654–659.

64. Goodwin, M. H. (1980). He-said-she-said: Formal cultural procedures for the construction of a gossip dispute activity. *American Ethnologist, 7,* 674–695.

65. Hallinan, M. T. (1978–79). The process of friendship formation. *Social Networks, 1,* 193–210.

66. Hansell, S. (1982). The adolescent friendship network as a source of stress and

support in school. Paper presented at the National Conference on Social Stress, University of New Hampshire.

67. Hartup, W. W. (1978). Children and their friends. In H. McGurk, ed., *Issues in childhood social development.* London: Methuen.

68. Hartup, W. W. (1983). Peer relations. In E. M. Hetherington, ed., *Handbook of child psychology.* Vol. 4. New York: Wiley, pp. 103–196.

69. Hirsch, B. J., & Reischl, T. M. (1985). Social networks and developmental psychopathology: A comparison of adolescent children of a depressed, arthritic, or normal parent. *Journal of Abnormal Psychology, 94,* 272–281.

70. Hirsch, B. J., & Renders, R. J. (1986). The challenge of adolescent friendships: A study of Lisa and her friends. In S. E. Hobfoll, ed., *Stress, social support, and women.* Washington, D.C.: Hemisphere, pp. 17–27.

71. Kandel, D. B. (1973). Adolescent marijuana use: Roles of parents and peers, *Science, 181,* 1067–70.

72. Kandel, D. B. (1978). Homophily, selection, and socialization in adolescent friendships. *American Journal of Sociology, 84,* 427–436.

73. Kandel, D. B. (1978). Similarity in real-life adolescent friendship pairs. *Journal of Personality and Social Psychology, 36,* 306–312.

74. Kandel, D., & Lesser, G. S. (1972). *Youth in two worlds.* San Francisco: Jossey-Bass.

75. Karweit, N. (1983). Extracurricular activities and friendship selection. In J. L. Epstein & N. Karweit, eds., *Friends in school; Patterns of selection and influence in secondary schools.* New York: Academic Press, pp. 131–139.

76. Kessler, R. C.; Price, R. H.; & Wortman, C. B. (1985). Social factors in psychopathology: Stress, social support, and coping processes. *Annual Review of Psychology, 36,* 531–572.

77. Maccoby, E. E. (1988). Gender as a social category. *Developmental Psychology, 24,* 755–765.

78. Magnusson, D. (1988). *Individual development from an interactional perspective: A longitudinal study.* Hillsdale, N.J.: Erlbaum.

79. Mannarino, A. P. (1980). The development of children's friendships. In H. C. Foot, A. J. Chapman, & J. K. Smith, eds., *Friendship and social relations in children.* New York: Wiley, pp. 45–64.

80. McGuire, K. D., & Weisz, J. R. (1982). Social cognition and behavior correlates of preadolescent chumships. *Child Development, 53,* 1478–84.

81. Mechanic, D. (1983). Adolescent health and illness behavior: Review of the literature and a new hypothesis for the study of stress. *Journal of Human Stress, 9,* 4–13.

82. Miller, K. E., & Berndt, T. J. (1987). Adolescent friendship and school orientation. Paper presented at the Society for Research in Child Development, Baltimore.

83. Oden, S., & Asher, S. R. (1977). Coaching children in social skills for friendship making. *Child Development, 48,* 495–506.

84. Offer, D., & Offer, J. B. (1975). *From teenage to young manhood: A psychological study.* New York: Basic Books.

85. Olweus, D. (1984). Aggressors and their victims: Bullying at school. In N.

Frude & Gault, eds., *Disruptive behaviour in schools*. London: John Wiley & Sons, pp. 57–76.

86. Olweus, D. (1987). Bully/victim problems among school children in Scandinavia. In J. P. Myklebust & R. Ommundsen, eds., *Psykologprofesjonen mot ar 2000*. Oslo: Universitetsforlaget, pp. 345–413.

87. Paikoff, R. L. (1987). Causal and consequential thinking about adolescent pregnancy: Developmental and individual factors. Ph.D. dissertation, University of Minnesota.

88. Parker, J. G., & Asher, S. R. (1987). Peer relations and later personal adjustment: Are low-accepted children "at risk?" *Psychological Bulletin, 102,* 357–389.

89. Pearlin, L. E. (1985). Social structure and processes of social support. In S. Cohen & S. L. Syme, eds., *Social support and health*. New York: Academic Press, pp. 43–60.

90. Perry, D. G.; Kusel, S. J.; & Perry, L. C. (1988). Victims of peer aggression. *Developmental Psychology, 24,* 807–814.

91. Perry, T. B. (1987). The relation of adolescents' self-perceptions to their social relationships. Ph.D. dissertation, University of Oklahoma.

92. Reisman, J. M. (1985). Friendship and its implications for mental health or social competence. *Journal of Early Adolescence, 5,* 383–391.

93. Reisman, J. M., & Shorr, S. I. (1978). Friendship claims and expectations among children and adults. *Child Development, 49,* 913–916.

94. Rivenbark, W. H. (1971). Self-disclosure among adolescents. *Psychological Reports, 28,* 35–42.

95. Rubin, Z. (1980). *Children's friendships*. Cambridge, Mass.: Harvard University Press.

96. Rubin, Z., & Sloman, J. (1984). How parents influence their children's friendships. In M. Lewis & L. Rosenblum, eds., *Beyond the dyad*. New York: Plenum.

97. Savin-Williams, R. C. (1987). *Adolescence: An ethological perspective*. New York: Springer-Verlag.

98. Savin-Williams, R. C. (1990). *Gay and lesbian youths: Expressions of identity*. Washington, D.C.: Hemisphere.

99. Scarr, S., & McCartney, K. (1983). How people make their own environments: A theory of genotype environment effects. *Child Development, 54,* 424–435.

100. Schofield, J. W. (1981). Complementary and conflicting identities: Images and interactions in an interracial school. In S. R. Asher & J. M. Gottman, eds., *The development of children's friendships*. Cambridge: Cambridge University Press, pp. 53–90.

101. Schofield, J. W. (1982). *Black and white in school: Trust, tension, or tolerance?* New York: Praeger.

102. Sebald, H. (1986). Adolescents' shifting orientation toward parents and peers: A curvilinear trend over recent decades. *Journal of Marriage and the Family, 48,* 5–13.

103. Selman, R. L. (1976). Social-cognitive understanding: A guide to educational and clinical practice. In T. Lickona, ed., *Moral development and behavior*. New York: Holt, Rinehart & Winston.

104. Selman, R. L. (1980). *The growth of interpersonal understanding*. New York: Academic Press.

105. Selman, R. L. (1981). The child as a friendship philosopher: A case study in the growth of interpersonal understanding. In S. R. Asher & J. M. Gottman, eds., *The development of children's friendships*. Cambridge: Cambridge University Press, pp. 242–272.

106. Sharabany, R. (1974). Intimate friendship among kibbutz and city children and its measurement. *Dissertation Abstracts International, 35,* 1028B–1029B. University Microfilms no. 74-17, 682.

107. Sharabany, R. (1984). The development of capacity for altruism as a function of object relations development and vicissitudes. In E. Staub, D. Bar-Tal, J. Karilowski, & J. Reykowski, eds., *Development and maintenance of prosocial behavior*. New York: Plenum Press.

108. Sharabany, R.; Gershoni, R.; & Hofman, J. E. (1981). Girlfriend, boyfriend: Age and sex differences in intimate friendships. *Developmental Psychology, 17,* 800–808.

109. Shaver, P.; Furman, W.; & Buhrmester, D. (1985). Transition to college: Network changes, social skills, and loneliness. In S. Duck & D. Perlman, eds., *Understanding personal relationships: An interdisciplinary approach*. London: Sage, pp. 193–219.

110. Sherif, M., & Sherif, C. (1964). *Reference groups: Exploration into conformity and deviance of adolescents*. New York: Harper & Row.

111. Simmons, R. G., & Blyth, D. A. (1987). *Moving into adolescence: The impact of pubertal change and social context*. Hawthorne, N.Y.: Aldine de Gruyter.

112. Skipper, J. K., & Nass, G. (1966). Dating behavior: A framework for analysis and an illustration. *Journal of Marriage and the Family, 28,* 412–420.

113. Sternberg, R. J., & Grajek, S. (1984). The nature of love. *Journal of Personality and Social Psychology, 47,* 312–329.

114. Sullivan, H. S. (1953). *The interpersonal theory of psychiatry*. New York: Norton.

115. Tesser, A. (1984). Self-evaluation maintenance processes: Implications for relationships and for development. In J. C. Masters & K. Yarkin-Levin, eds., *Boundary areas in social and developmental psychology*. New York: Academic Press, pp. 271–299.

116. Tesser, A.; Campbell, J.; & Smith, M. (1984). Friendship choice and performance: Self-esteem maintenance in children. *Journal of Personality and Social Psychology, 46,* 561–574.

117. Thoits, P. A. (1985). Social support and psychological well-being: Theoretical possibilities. In I. G. Sarason & B. R. Sarason, eds., *Social support: Theory, research, and applications*. Dordrecht: Martinus Nijhoff, pp. 51–72.

118. Tietjen, A. M. (1982). The social networks of preadolescent children in Sweden. *International Journal of Behavioral Development, 5,* 111–130.

119. Whiting, B. (1986). The effect of experience on peer relationships. In E. Mueller & C. Cooper, eds., *Process and outcome in peer relationships*. New York: Academic Press, pp. 77–99.

120. Youniss, J. (1980). *Parents and peers in social development*. Chicago: University of Chicago Press.

121. Youniss, J., & Smollar, J. (1985). *Adolescent relations with mothers, fathers, and friends*. Chicago: University of Chicago Press.

12. Motivation and Achievement

1. Ames, C. (1984). Achievement attributions and self-instruction under competitive and individualistic goal structures. *Journal of Educational Psychology*, 76, 478–487.
2. Ames, C.; Ames, R.; & Felker, D. W. (1977). Effects of competitive reward structure and valence of outcome on children's achievement attributions. *Journal of Educational Psychology*, 69, 1–8.
3. Ames, C. & Ames, R., eds. (1985). *Research on motivation in education*. Vol. 2. *The classroom milieu*. Orlando, Fla.: Academic Press.
4. Ames, C., & Ames, R., eds. (1989). *Research on motivation in education*. Vol. 3. *Goals and cognitions*. San Diego: Academic Press.
5. Ames, C., & Archer, J. (1988). Achievement goals in the classrooms: Students' learning strategies and motivation processes. *Journal of Educational Psychology*, 80, 260–267.
6. Ames, R., & Ames, C., eds. (1984). *Research on motivation in education*. Vol. 1. *Student motivation*. San Diego: Academic Press.
7. Andrews, G. R., & Debus, R. L. (1978). Persistence and the causal attribution of failure: Modifying cognitive attributions. *Journal of Educational Psychology*, 71, 85–93.
8. Astin, H. (1974). Sex differences in scientific and mathematical precocity. In J. C. Stanley, D. P. Keating, & L. H. Fox, eds., *Mathematical talent: Discovery, description, and development*. Baltimore: John Hopkins University Press.
9. Atkinson, J. W. (1964). *An introduction to motivation*. Princeton: Van Nostrand.
10. Bandura, M., & Dweck, C. S. (1985). The relationship of conceptions of intelligence and achievement goals to achievement-related cognition, affect, and behavior. Unpublished manuscript.
11. Bowman, P. J., & Howard, C. (1985). Race-related socialization, motivation, and academic achievement: A study of black youths in three-generation families. *Journal of the American Academy of Child Psychiatry*, 24, 134–141.
12. Byrn, B. M., & Shavelson, R. J. (1986). On the structure of adolescent self-concept. *Journal of Educational Psychology*, 78, 473–481.
13. Castinell, L. A. (1983). Achievement motivation: An investigation of adolescents' achievement patterns. *American Educational Research Journal*, 20, 503–510.
14. Chapin, M., & Dyck, D. (1976). Persistence in children's reading behavior as a function of N length and attribution retraining. *Journal of Abnormal Psychology*, 35, 511–515.
15. Chung, Y., & Hwang, K. (1981). Attribution of performance and characteristics of learning helplessness in junior high school students. *Acta Psychologica Taiwanica*, 23, 155–164.
16. Curtis, W. M. J. (1978). The black adolescent's self-concept and academic performance. *Western Journal of Black Studies*, 2, 125–131.

17. Deci, E. L., & Ryan, R. M. (1985). *Intrinsic motivation and self-determination in human behavior.* New York: Plenum.

18. Diener, C. I., & Dweck, C. S. (1978). An analysis of learned helplessness: Continuous changes in performance, strategy, and achievement cognitions following failure. *Journal of Personality and Social Psychology, 36,* 451–462.

19. Diener, C. I., & Dweck, C. S. (1980). An analysis of learned helplessness: II. The processing of success. *Journal of Personality and Social Psychology, 39,* 940–952.

20. Donlon, T.; Ekstrom, R.; & Lockheed, M. (1976). Comparing the sexes on achievement items of varying content. Paper presented at the meeting of the American Psychological Association, September, Washington, D.C.

21. Duda, J. L. (1985). Goals and achievement orientations of Anglo and Mexican-American adolescents in sport and the classroom. *International Journal of Intercultural Relations, 9,* 131–150.

22. Dweck, C. S. (1975). The role of expectations and attributions in the alleviation of learned helplessness. *Journal of Personality and Social Psychology, 31,* 674–685.

23. Dweck, C. S., & Bempechat, J. (1983). Children's theories of intelligence. In S. Paris, G. Olson, & H. Stevenson, eds., *Learning and motivation in the classroom.* Hillsdale, N.J.: Erlbaum, pp. 239–256.

24. Dweck, C. S.; Davidson, W.; Nelson, S.; & Enna, B. (1978). Sex differences in learned helplessness: II: The contingencies of evaluative feedback in the classroom, and III: An experimental analysis. *Developmental Psychology, 14,* 268–276.

25. Dweck, C. S., & Elliott, E. S. (1983). Achievement motivation. In P. Mussen, gen. ed., and E. M. Hetherington, vol. ed., *Handbook of Child Psychology.* Vol. 4. New York: Wiley, pp. 643–691.

26. Dweck, C. S., & Leggett, E. L. (1988). A social-cognitive approach to motivation and personality. *Psychological Review, 95,* 256–272.

27. Dweck, C. S., & Reppucci, N. D. (1973). Learned helplessness and reinforcement responsibility in children. *Journal of Personality and Social Psychology, 25,* 109–116.

28. Eccles (Parsons), J. (1983). Expectancies, values, and academic behaviors. In J. T. Spence, ed., *Achievement and achievement motives.* San Francisco: Witt, Freeman, and Co.

29. Ekstrom, R.; Donlon, T.; & Lockheed, M. (1976). The effect of sex-biased performance. Paper presented at the meeting of American Educational Research Association, April, San Francisco.

30. Elliott, E. S., & Dweck, C. S. (1988). Goals: An approach to motivation and achievement. *Journal of Personality and Social Psychology, 54,* 5–12.

31. Fennema, E., & Sherman, J. (1977). Sex-related differences in mathematics achievement, spatial visualization, and affective factors. *American Educational Research Journal, 14,* 51–71.

32. Ford, M. E., & Thompson, R. A. (1985). Perceptions of personal agency and infant attachment: Toward a life-span perspective on competence development. *International Journal of Behavior Development, 8,* 377–406.

33. Fordham, S. (1982). Cultural inversion and black children's school perfor-

mance. Paper presented at the annual meeting of the American Anthropological Association, December, Washington, D.C.

34. Gill, D. L.; Gross, J. B.; & Huddleston, S. (1983). Participation motivation in youth sports. *International Journal of Sport Psychology, 14,* 1–14.

35. Goetz, T. E., & Dweck, C. S. (1980). Learned helplessness in social situations. *Journal of Personality and Social Psychology, 39,* 249–255.

36. Gottfried, A. E. (1985). Academic intrinsic motivation in elementary and junior high school students. *Journal of Educational Psychology, 77,* 631–645.

37. Greene, I. C. (1985). Relationships among learning and attribution theory motivation variables. *American Educational Research Journal, 23,* 65–78.

38. Haertel, G. D.; Walberg, H. J.; Junker, L.; & Pascarella, E. J. (1981). Early adolescent sex differences in science learning: Evidence from the National Assessment of Educational Progress. *American Educational Research Journal, 18,* 329–341.

39. Hagen, U., with H. Frankel (1973). *Respect for acting.* New York: Macmillan.

40. Hall, V. C.; Merkel, S.; Howe, A.; & Lederman, N. (1986). Behavior, motivation, and achievement in desegregated junior high school science classes. *Journal of Educational Psychology, 78,* 108–115.

41. Hamilton, M. A. (1985). Performance levels in science and other subjects for Jamaican adolescents attending single-sex and coeducational high schools. *Science Education, 69,* 535–547.

42. Handley, H. M., & Morse, L. W. (1984). Two-year study relating adolescents' self-concepts and gender role perceptions to achievement and attitudes toward science. *Journal of Research in Science Teaching, 21,* 599–607.

43. Harackiewicz, J. M.; Sansone, C.; & Manderlink, G. (1985). Competence, achievement orientation, and intrinsic motivation: A process analysis. *Journal of Personality and Social Psychology, 48,* 493–508.

44. Haynes, N. M.; Comer, J. P.; & Hamilton-Lee, M. (1988). Gender and achievement status differences on learning factors among black high school students. *Journal of Educational Research, 81,* 233–237.

45. Heckhausen, H.; Schmalt, H.; & Schneider, K. (1985). *Achievement motivation in perspective,* trans. M. Woodruff & R. Wicklund. Orlando, Fla.: Academic Press.

46. Henderson, V. L.; Cain, K. M.; & Dweck, C. S. (1987). Theories of intelligence and their dimensions. Unpublished raw data.

47. Henderson, V. L., & Dweck, C. S. (1989). Predicting individual differences in school anxiety in early adolescence. Paper presented at the biennial meeting of the Society for Research in Child Development, April, Kansas City.

48. Hess, R. D.; Azuma, K. K.; Dickson, W. P.; Nagano, S.; Holloway, S.; Miyake, K.; Price, G.; Hatano, G.; & McDevitt, T. (1986). Family influences on school readiness and achievement in Japan and the United States: An overview of a longitudinal study. In H. Stevenson, H. Azuma, & K. Hakuta, eds., *Child development and education in Japan.* New York: W. H. Freeman.

49. Hilton, T., & Berglund, G. (1974). Sex differences in mathematics achievement: A longitudinal study. *Journal of Educational Research, 67,* 231–237.

50. Holloway, S. D. (1988). Concepts of ability and effort in Japan and the United States. *Review of Educational Research, 58,* 327–345.
51. Ichikawa, S. (1986). American perceptions of Japanese education. In W. K. Cummings, E. R. Beauchamp, S. Ichikawa, V. N. Kobayashi, and M. Ushiago, eds., *Educational policies in crisis: Japanese and American perspectives.* New York: Praeger.
52. Ishiyama, F. I., & Chabassol, D. J. (1985). Adolescents' fear of social consequences of academic success as a function of age and sex. *Journal of Youth and Adolescence, 14,* 37–46.
53. Jencks, C., & Mayer, S. (1988). The social consequences of growing up in a poor neighborhood: A review. Manuscript in preparation.
54. Jones, J. C.; Dennis, C. C.; & Shallcrass, J. (1971). Effects of coeducation on adolescent values. Paper presented at the Annual Meeting of the American Educational Research Association.
55. Jordan, T. J. (1981). Self-concepts, motivation, and academic achievement of black adolescents. *Journal of Educational Psychology, 74,* 509–517.
56. Lee, C. C. (1984). An investigation of psychosocial variables related to academic success for rural black adolescents. *Journal of Negro Education, 53,* 424–434.
57. Lee, C. C. (1985). Successful rural black adolescents: A psychosocial profile. *Adolescence, 20,* 129–142.
58. Lee, V. E., & Bryk, A. A. (1986). Effects of single-sex secondary schools on student achievement and attitudes. *Journal of Educational Psychology, 78,* 381–395.
59. Lefcourt, H. M. (1982). *Locus of control: Current trends in theory and research.* 2nd ed. Hillsdale, N.J.: Erlbaum.
60. Leggett, E. L. (1985). Children's entity and incremental theories of intelligence: Relationship to achievement behavior. Paper presented at the annual meeting of the Eastern Psychological Association, March, Boston.
61. Leggett, E. L., & Dweck, C. S. (1986). Goals and inference rules: Sources of causal judgment. Unpublished manuscript.
62. Licht, B. G., & Dweck, C. S. (1983). Sex differences in achievement orientations: Consequences for academic choices and attainments. In M. Marland, ed., *Sex differentation and schooling.* London: Heinemann.
63. Licht, B. G., & Dweck, C. S. (1984). Determinants of academic achievement: The interaction of children's achievement orientations with skill area. *Developmental Psychology, 20,* 628–636.
64. Licht, B. G., & Shapiro, S. H. (1982). Sex differences in attributions among high achievers. Paper presented at the meeting of the American Psychological Association, August, Washington, D.C.
65. Lloyd, J., & Barenblatt, L. (1984). Intrinsic intellectuality: Its relations to social class, intelligence, and achievement. *Journal of Personality and Social Psychology, 46,* 646–654.
66. Loomis, C. C.; Hines, F. A.; Erdley, C. A.; & Cain, K. M. (1989). The effects of goals on children's social behavior. Paper presented at the biennial meeting of the Society for Research in Child Development, April, Kansas City.

67. Maccoby, E. E., & Jacklin, C. N. (1974). *The psychology of sex differences.* Stanford: Stanford University Press.
68. Maehr, M. L. (1974). Culture and achievement motivation. *American Psychologist, 29,* 887–896.
69. Marsh, H. W. (1984). Relations among dimensions of self-attribution, dimensions of self-concept, and academic achievements. *Journal of Educational Psychology, 76,* 3–32.
70. Marsh, H. W. (1986). Self-serving effect (bias?) in academic attributions: Its relation to academic achievement and self-concept. *Journal of Educational Psychology, 78,* 190–200.
71. Marsh, H. W. (1989). Effects of attending single-sex and coeducational high schools on achievement, attitudes, behaviors, and sex differences. *Journal of Educational Psychology, 81,* 70–85.
72. Mboya, M. M. (1986). Black adolescents: A descriptive study of the self-concepts and academic achievement. *Adolescence, 21,* 689–696.
73. McClelland, D. C.; Atkinson, J. W.; Clark, R. A.; & Lowell, E. L. (1953; reprinted 1976). *The achievement motive.* New York: Appleton-Century-Crofts.
74. Metcalfe, R. J., & Dobson, C. B. (1983). Factorial structure and dispositional correlates of "locus of control" in children. *Research in Education, 30,* 53–63.
75. Nicholls, J. G. (1984). Achievement motivation: Conceptions of ability, subjective experience, task choice, and performance. *Psychological Review, 91,* 328–346.
76. Olshefsky, L. M.; Erdley, C. A.; & Dweck, C. S. (1987). Self-conceptions and goals in social situations. Unpublished manuscript.
77. Petersen, A. C. (1986). Early adolescence: A critical development transition? Paper presented at the annual meeting of the American Education Research Association, April, San Francisco.
78. Prawat, R. S.; Grissom, S.; & Parish, T. S. (1979). Affective development in children, grades 3 through 12. *Journal of Genetic Psychology, 135,* 37–49.
79. Prawat, R. S.; Jones, H.; & Hampton, J. (1979). Longitudinal study of attitude development in pre-, early, and later adolescent samples. *Journal of Educational Psychology, 71,* 363–369.
80. Ramirez, M., III, & Castaneda, A. (1974). *Cultural democracy, bicognitive development, and education.* New York: Academic Press.
81. Rotella, R. J. (1980). Psychological processes for achieving and coping with stress in sports. Paper presented at the Preconvention Symposium of the National Association for Sport and Physical Education Sport Psychology, April.
82. Rothbaum, F.; Weisz, J. R.; & Snyder, S. S. (1982). Changing the world and changing the self: A two-process model of perceived control. *Journal of Personality and Social Psychology, 42,* 5–37.
83. Schunk, D. H. (1982). Effects of effort attributional feedback on children's perceived self-efficacy and achievement. *Journal of Educational Psychology, 74,* 548–566.
84. Schunk, D. H., & Gunn, T. P. (1985). Modeled importance of task strategies

and achievement beliefs: Effect on self-efficacy and skill development. *Journal of Early Adolescence, 5,* 247–258.

85. Sewell, T. E.; Farley, F. H.; Manni, J. L.; & Hunt, P. (1982). Motivation, social reinforcement, and intelligence as predictors of academic achievement in black adolescents. *Adolescence, 17,* 647–656.

86. Shaw, R. A. (1983). Academic achievement and self-concept of academic ability: A four-year longitudinal study. Paper presented at the annual convention of the American Psychological Association, August, Anaheim.

87. Smith, S. N. (1979). Recent cross-ethnic research on the adolescent. *Journal of Negro Education, 48,* 306–323.

88. Song, I. S., & Hattie, J. (1984). Home environment, self-concept, and academic achievement: A causal modeling approach. *Journal of Educational Psychology, 76,* 1269–81.

89. Spears, W. D., & Deese, M. E. (1973). Self-concept as a cause. *Educational Theory, 23,* 144–152.

90. Stanislavski, C. (1948). *An actor prepares,* trans. E. R. Hapgood. New York: Theatre Arts Books, Robert M. MacGregor.

91. Steinkamp, M. W., & Maehr, M. L. (1984). Gender differences in motivational orientations toward achievement in school science: A quantitative synthesis. *American Educational Research Journal, 21,* 39–59.

92. Stenner, A. J., & Katzenmeyer, W. G. (1976). Self-concept, ability, and achievement in a sample of sixth-grade students. *Journal of Educational Research, 69,* 270–273.

93. Stevenson, H. W.; Lee, S.; & Stigler, J. W. (1986). Mathematics achievement of Chinese, Japanese, and American children. *Science, 231,* 693–699.

94. Stevenson, H.; Stigler, J. W.; Lee, S.; Kitamura, S.; Kimura, S.; & Kato, T. (1986). Achievement in mathematics. In H. Stevenson, H. Azuma, and K. Hakuta, eds., *Child development and education in Japan.* New York: W. H. Freeman.

95. Stipek, D. J., & Hoffman, J. M. (1980). Children's achievement-related expectancies as a function of academic performance histories and sex. *Journal of Educational Psychology, 72,* 861–865.

96. Stipek, D. J., & Weisz, J. R. (1981). Perceived personal control and achievement. *Review of Educational Research, 51,* 101–137.

97. Stoddard, E. R. (1973). *Mexican-Americans.* New York: Random House.

98. Tsukada, M. (1986). A factual overview of Japanese and American education. In W. K. Cummings, E. R. Beauchamp, S. Ichikawa, V. N. Kobayashi, & M. Ushiogi, eds., *Educational policies in crisis: Japanese and American perspectives.* New York: Praeger.

99. U.S. Department of Education (1987). *Japanese education today.* DOE Publication no. OR 87-500. Washington, D.C.: U.S. Government Printing Office.

100. Watkins, D., & Astilla, E. (1986). Causal dominance among self-concept, locus of causality, and academic achievement. *Journal of Psychology, 120,* 627–633.

101. Weiner, B., ed. (1974). *Achievement motivation and attribution theory.* Morristown, N.J.: General Learning Press.

102. White, M. I., & LeVine, R. A. (1986). What is an *ii ko* (good child)? In H. Stevenson, H. Azuma, & K. Hakuta, eds., *Child development and education in Japan*. New York: W. H. Freeman.

103. Whitehead, J. (1984). Motives for higher education: A study of intrinsic and extrinsic motivation in relation to academic attainment. *Cambridge Journal of Education, 14,* 26–34.

104. Wolf, F. M., & Savickas, M. L. (1985). Time perspective and causal attributions for achievement. *Journal of Educational Psychology, 77,* 471–480.

13. Sexuality

1. Abrahamse, A. F.; Morrison, P. A.; & Waite, L. J. (1985). How family characteristics deter early unwed parenthood. Paper presented at the annual meeting of the Population Association of America, Boston.

2. Attorney General's Commission on Pornography (1987). *Final Report.* Washington, D.C.: U.S. Government Printing Office.

3. Bancroft, J. (1989). *Human sexuality and its problems.* 2nd ed. Edinburgh: Churchill-Livingstone.

4. Bauman, K., & Udry, J. R. (1981). Subjective expected utility and adolescent sexual behavior. *Adolescence, 14,* 527–538.

5. Bell, A. P.; Weinberg, M. S.; & Hammersmith, S. K. (1981). *Sexual preference: Its development in men and women.* Bloomington: Indiana University Press.

6. Billy, J. O.; Rodgers, J. L.; & Udry, J. R. (1984). Adolescent sexual behavior and friendship choice. *Social Forces, 62,* 653–678.

7. Billy, J. O., & Udry, J. R. (1983). The effects of age and pubertal development on adolescent sexual behavior. Unpublished manuscript. Cited in *National Research Council* (1987).

8. Billy, J. O., & Udry, J. R. (1985). Patterns of adolescent friendship and effects on sexual behavior. *Social Psychological Quarterly, 48,* 27–41.

9. Brooks-Gunn, J.; Boyer, C. B.; & Hein, K. (1988). Preventing HIV infection and AIDS in children and adolescents: Behavioral research and intervention strategies. *American Psychologist, 43*(11).

10. Brooks-Gunn, J., & Furstenberg, F. F., Jr. (1988). Adolescent sexual behavior. *American Psychologist, 4*(22).

11. Chilman, C. (1980). Toward a reconceptualization of adolescent sexuality. In C. Chilman, ed., *Adolescent pregnancy and childbearing: Findings from research.* Washington, D.C.: U.S. Department of Health and Human Services.

12. Chilman, C. (1983). *Adolescent sexuality in a changing American society: Social and psychological perspectives for the human services professions.* 2nd ed. New York: Wiley.

13. Coles, R., & Stokes, G. (1985). *Sex and the American teenager.* New York: Harper & Row.

14. Conn, J., & Kanner, L. (1940). Spontaneous erections in childhood. *Journal of Pediatrics, 16,* 237–240.

15. Cvetkovich, G., & Grote, B. (1980). Psychological development and the social program of teenage illegitimacy. In C. Chilman, ed., *Adolescent pregnancy and*

childbearing: Findings from research. Washington, D.C.: U.S. Department of Health and Human Services.

16. Dement, W. C. (1965). An essay on dreams. In F. Barron, ed., *New directions in psychology*. Vol. 2. New York: Holt, Rinehart, and Winston.

17. Devaney, B. L., & Hubley, K. S. (1981). *The determinants of adolescent pregnancy and childbearing*. Final report to the National Institute of Child Health and Human Development. Washington, D.C.: Mathematica Policy Research.

18. Diepold, J., Jr., & Young, R. D. (1979). Empirical studies of adolescent sexual behavior: A critical review. *Adolescence, 14*, 45–64.

19. Donnerstein, E.; Linz, D.; & Penrod, S. (1987). *The question of pornography*. New York: Free Press.

20. Dornbusch, S. M.; Carlsmith, J. M.; Gross, R. T.; Martin, J. A.; Jennings, D.; Rosenberg, A.; & Duke, P. (1981). Sexual development, age, and dating: A comparison of biological and social influences upon one set of behaviors. *Child Development, 52*, 179–185.

21. Elder, G. H. (1980). Adolescence in historical perspective. In J. Adelson, ed., *Handbook of adolescent psychology*. New York: Wiley.

22. Fisher, C.; Cohen, H. D.; Schiavi, R. C.; Davis, D.; Ferman, B.; Ward, K.; Edwards, A.; & Cunningham, J. (1983). Patterns of female sexual arousal during sleep and waking: Vaginal thermo-conductance studies. *Archives of Sexual Behavior, 12*(2).

23. Ford, C. S., & Beach, F. A. (1951). *Patterns of sexual behavior*. New York: Harper & Row.

24. Furstenberg, F. F., Jr., & Brooks-Gunn, J. (1985). Adolescent fertility: Causes, consequences, and remedies. In L. Aiken & D. Mechanic, eds., *Applications of social science to clinical medicine and health policy*. New Brunswick, N.J.: Rutgers University Press.

25. Furstenberg, F. F., Jr.; Brooks-Gunn, J.; & Chase-Lansdale, L. (1988). Adolescent fertility and public policy. *American Psychologist 43*(8).

26. Furstenberg, F. F., Jr.; Moore, K. A.; & Peterson, J. L. (1986). Sex education and sexual experience among adolescents. *American Journal of Public Health, 75*, 1221–22.

27. Gagnon, J., & Simon, W. (1973). *Sexual conduct*. Chicago: Aldine.

28. Gallup, G. (1978). *Epidemic of teenage pregnancies: Growing number of Americans favor discussion of sex in classrooms*. News release. Princeton, N.J.: Gallup Poll.

29. Garguilo, J.; Attie, I.; Brooks-Gunn, J.; & Warren, M. P. (1987). Dating in middle school girls: Effects of social context, maturation, and grade. *Developmental Psychology, 23*(5), 730–737.

30. Giovacchini, P. L. (1986). Promiscuity in adolescents and young adults. *Medical Aspects of Human Sexuality, 20*(5), 24–31.

31. Goldman, R. J., & Goldman, J. D. G. (1982). How children perceive the origin of babies and the roles of mothers and fathers in procreation: A cross-national study. *Child Development, 53*, 491–504.

32. Gregersen, E. (1983). *Sexual practices*. New York: Watts.

33. Haas, A. (1979). *Teenage sexuality*. New York: Macmillan.

34. Hofferth, S. L. (1987a). Initiation of sexual intercourse. In *National Research Council*. Washington, D.C.: National Academy Press.
35. Hofferth, S. L., ed. (1987b). *Risking the future: Adolescent sexuality, pregnancy, and childbearing.* Vol. 2. Washington, D.C.: National Academy Press.
36. Hogan, D. P., & Kitagawa, E. M. (1983). Family factors in the fertility of black adolescents. Paper presented at the annual meeting of the Population Association of America. Cited in *National Research Council* (1987).
37. Inazu, J. K., & Fox, G. L. (1980). Maternal influence on the sexual behavior of teenage daughters. *Journal of Family Issues, 1,* 81–102.
38. Jessor, R.; Costa, F.; Jessor, L.; & Donovan, J. E. (1983). The time of first intercourse: A prospective study. *Journal of Personality and Social Psychology, 44,* 608–626.
39. Jessor, R., & Jessor, S. L. (1977). *Problem behavior and psychosocial development.* New York: Academic Press.
40. Jessor, S. L., & Jessor, R. (1975). Transition from virginity to nonvirginity among youth: A social-psychological study over time. *Developmental Psychology, 11,* 473–484.
41. Kahn, J.; Smith, K.; & Roberts, E. (1984). *Familial communication and adolescent sexual behavior: Final report to the Office of Adolescent Pregnancy Programs.* Cambridge, Mass.: American Institutes for Research.
42. Kantner, J. F., & Zelnik, M. (1972). Sexual experience of young unmarried women in the United States. *Family Planning Perspectives, 4,* 9–18.
43. Katchadourian, H. (1989). *Fundamentals of human sexuality.* 5th ed. New York: Holt, Rinehart, and Winston.
44. Katchadourian, H., & Martin, J., eds. (1979). *Human sexuality: A comparative and developmental perspective.* Berkeley: University of California Press.
45. Kelley, K., ed. (1987). *Females, males, and sexuality.* Albany: State University of New York.
46. Kenney, A. M., & Orr, M. T. (1984). Sex education: An overview of current programs, policies, and research. *Phi Delta Kappa* (March), 491–497.
47. Kinsey, A. C.; Pomeroy, W. B.; & Martin, C. E. (1948). *Sexual behavior in the human male.* Philadelphia: Saunders.
48. Kinsey, A. C.; Pomeroy, W. B.; Martin, C. E.; & Gebhard, P. H. (1953). *Sexual behavior in the human female.* Philadelphia: Saunders.
49. Kirby, D. (1984). *Sexuality education: An evaluation of programs and their effects.* Santa Cruz, Calif.: Network Publications.
50. Lancaster, J. B., & Hamburg, B. A. (1986). *School-age pregnancy and parenthood.* Hawthorne, N.Y.: Aldine.
51. Langfeldt, T. (1981). Sexual development in children. In M. Cook & K. Howells, eds., *Adult sexual interest in children.* London: Academic Press.
52. McAnarney, E. R. (1983). *Premature adolescent pregnancy and parenthood.* New York: Grune and Stratton.
53. Melton, G. B., & Pliner, A. J. (1986). Adolescent abortion: A psychological analysis. In G. B. Melton, ed., *Adolescent abortion: Psychological and legal issues.* Lincoln: University of Nebraska Press.

54. Miller, P. Y., & Simon, W. (1974). Adolescent sexual behavior: Context and change. *Social Problems, 22,* 58–76.
55. Miller, P., & Simon, W. (1980). Adolescent sexual development. In J. Adelson, ed., *The handbook of adolescent psychology.* New York: Wiley.
56. Money, J., & Erhardt, A. A. (1972). *Man and woman, boy and girl.* Baltimore: Johns Hopkins University Press.
57. Moore, K. A.; Simms, M. C.; & Betsey, C. L. (1986). *Choice and circumstances: Racial differences in adolescent sexuality and fertility.* New Brunswick, N.J.: Transition Books.
58. Mot F. L. (1983). Early fertility behavior among American youth: Evidence from the 1982 national longitudinal surveys of labor force behavior of youth. Paper presented at the annual meeting of the American Public Health Association.
59. National Research Council (1987a). *Risking the future: Adolescent sexuality, pregnancy, and childbearing.* Washington, D.C.: National Academy Press.
60. National Research Council (1987b). *Risking the future: Adolescent sexuality, pregnancy, and childbearing: Working papers.* Washington, D.C.: National Academy Press.
61. NBC News (1982). Poll Results, no. 74, February 5.
62. Newcomb, M. D.; Huba, G. J.; & Bentler, P. M. (1986). Determinants of sexual and dating behaviors among adolescents. *Journal of Personality and Social Psychology, 50,* 428–438.
63. Newcomer, S. F., & Udry, J. R. (1983). Adolescent sexual behavior and popularity. *Adolescence, 18,* 515–522.
64. Newcomer, S. F., & Udry, J. R. (1985). Oral sex in an adolescent population. *Archives of Sexual Behavior, 14,* 41–56.
65. Norman, J., and Harris, M. (1981). *The private life of the American teenager.* New York: Rawson Wade.
66. Ooms, T., ed. (1981). *Teenage pregnancy in a family context: Implications for policy.* Philadelphia: Temple University Press.
67. Orr, M. (1982). Sex education and contraceptive education in U.S. public high schools. *Family Planning Perspectives, 14,* 304–313.
68. Peterson, L. (1988). The issue and controversy surrounding adolescent sexuality and abstinence. *SIECUS Report, 17*(1), 1–8.
69. Reinisch, J. R.; Rosenblum, L. A.; & Sanders, S. A. (1987). *Masculinity and femininity.* New York: Oxford University Press.
70. Remafedi, G. (1987). Adolescent sexuality: Psychosocial and medical implications. *Pediatrics, 79*(3), 326–330.
71. Roberts, E. J. (1980). *Childhood sexual learning: The unwritten curriculum.* Cambridge, Mass.: Ballinger.
72. Roberts, E. J.; Kline, D.; & Gagnon, J. (1978). *Family life and sexual learning,* Vol. 10. Cambridge, Mass.: Population Education.
73. Rosenfeld, A.; Wenegrat, A.; Haavic, D.; & Wenegrat, B. (1982). Parents' fears of their children's developing sexuality. *Medical Aspects of Human Sexuality, 16* (10).

74. Simon, W., & Gagnon, J. H. (1986). Sexual scripts: Permanence and change. *Archives of Sexual Behavior, 15*(2), 97–120.
75. Smith, E. A.; Udry, J. R.; & Morris, N. M. (1985). Pubertal development and friends: A biosocial explanation of adolescent sexual behavior. *Journal of Health and Social Behavior, 26,* 183–192.
76. Sonnenstein, F., & Pittman, K. (1982). Sex education in public schools: A look at the big U.S. cities. Paper presented to the annual meeting of the National Council on Family Relations, Washington, D.C.
77. Sorensen, R. C. (1973). *Adolescent sexuality in contemporary America.* New York: World.
78. St. John, C., & Grasmick, H. G. (1982). Racial differences in the fertility process: An elaboration of the minority group status hypothesis. Unpublished manuscript. Cited in *National Research Council* (1987a).
79. Thorne, B., & Luria, Z. (1986). Sexuality and gender in children's daily worlds. *Social Problems, 33,* 166–190.
80. Udry, J. R. (1979). Age at menarche, at first intercourse, and at first pregnancy. *Journal of Biological Science 11,* 411–433.
81. Udry, J. R.; Billy, J. O.; Morris, N. M.; Groff, T. R.; & Raj, M. S. (1985). Serum androgenic hormones motivate sexual behavior in adolescent boys. *Fertility and Sterility, 43,* 90–94.
82. Udry, J. R.; Talbert, L.; & Morris, N. M. (1986). Biosocial foundations of adolescent female sexuality. Paper presented at the annual meeting of the American Sociological Association, Washington, D.C.
83. Westney, O. E.; Jenkins, R. R.; & Benjamin, C. (1983). Sociosexual development of preadolescents. In J. Brooks-Gunn & J. Peterson, eds., *Girls at puberty.* New York: Plenum, pp. 273–300.
84. Zelnik, M. (1983). Sexual activity among adolescents: Perspective of a decade. In E. R. McAnarney, ed., *Premature adolescent pregnancy and parenthood.* New York: Grune & Stratton.
85. Zelnik, M., & Kantner, J. F. (1977). Sexual and contraceptive experience of young unmarried women in the United States, 1976 and 1971. *Family Planning Perspectives, 9,* 55–71.
86. Zelnik, M., & Kantner, J. F. (1980). Sexual activity, contraceptive use, and pregnancy among metropolitan-area teenagers. 1971–1979. *Family Planning Perspectives, 12*(5), 230–231, 233–237.
87. Zelnik, M.; Kantner, J.; & Ford, K. (1981). *Sex and pregnancy in adolescence.* Beverly Hills: Sage Publications.
88. Zelnik, M., and Kim, Y. J. (1982). Sex education and its association with teenage sexual activity, pregnancy, and contraceptive use. *Family Planning Perspectives 14,* 117–126.

14. Self and Identity Development

1. Adams, G. (1977). Physical attractiveness research. *Human Development, 20,* 217–239.

2. Adams, G. R., & Shea, J. A. (1979). The relationship between identity status, locus of control, and age development. *Journal of Youth and Adolescence, 8,* 81–89.

3. Adams, R. R., & Jones, R. M. (1983). Female adolescents' identity development: Age comparisons and perceived child-rearing experience. *Developmental Psychology, 1,* 249–256.

4. Ainsworth, M. D. S; Blehar, M.; Waters, E.; & Wall, E. (1978). *Patterns of attachment.* Hillsdale, N.J.: Erlbaum.

5. Allport, G. W. (1955). *Becoming: Basic considerations for a psychology of personality.* New Haven: Yale University Press.

6. Allport, G. W. (1961). *Pattern and growth in personality.* New York: Holt, Rinehart & Winston.

7. Archer, S. L. (1985). Identity and the choice of social roles. In A. S. Waterman, ed., *Identity in adolescence: Processes and contents.* San Francisco: Jossey-Bass, pp. 79–100.

8. Barnes, E. J. (1980). The black community as the source of positive self-concept for black children: A theoretical perspective. In R. Jones, ed., *Black psychology.* New York: Harper & Row, pp. 106–130.

9. Baumeister, R., & Tice, D. (1986). How adolescence became the struggle for self: A historical transformation of psychological development. In J. Suls & A. Greenwald, eds., *Psychological perspectives on the self.* Vol. 3. Hillsdale, N.J.: Erlbaum, pp. 183–201.

10. Beck, A. (1967). *Depression: Causes and treatment.* Philadelphia: University of Pennsylvania Press.

11. Bell, A. P. (1969). Role modeling of fathers in adolescence and adulthood. *Journal of Counseling Psychology, 16,* 30–35.

12. Bernard, H. S. (1981). Identity formation during late adolescence: A review of some empirical findings, *Adolescence, 16,* 349–358.

13. Blasi, A. (1988). Identity and the development of self. In D. K. Lapsley & F. C. Power, eds., *Self, ego, and identity: Integrative approaches.* New York: Springer Verlag, pp. 226–242.

14. Bleiberg, E. (1984). Narcissistic disorders in children. *Bulletin of the Menninger Clinic, 48,* 501–517.

15. Blos, P. (1962). *On adolescence.* New York: Free Press.

16. Brim, O. G. (1976). Life span development of the theory of oneself: Implications for child development. In H. W. Reese, ed., *Advances in child development and behavior.* Vol. 2. New York: Academic Press, pp. 241–251.

17. Brooks-Gunn, J., & Peterson, A. (1983). *Girls at puberty: Biological and psychological perspectives.* New York: Plenum.

18. Broughton, J. (1977). Beyond formal operations: Theoretical thought in adolescence. *Teachers College Record, 79,* 87–96.

19. Broughton, J. (1978). The development of the concepts of self, mind, reality, and knowledge. In W. Damon, ed., *Social Cognition.* San Francisco: Jossey-Bass, pp. 75–100.

20. Broughton, J. (1981). The divided self in adolescence. *Human Development, 24,* 13–32.

21. Bynner, J. M.; O'Malley, P. M.; & Bachman, J. C. (1981). Self-esteem and delinquency revisited. *Journal of Youth and Adolescence, 10,* 407–441.
22. Cantor, P. (producer and director) (1987). *Young people in crisis: How you can help.* Film. National Committee on Youth Suicide Prevention and American Association of Suicidology, in consultation with Harvard Medical School, Dept. of Psychiatry, Cambridge City Hospital, Cambridge, Mass.
23. Cate, R., & Sugawara, A. I. (1986). Sex-role orientation and dimensions of self-esteem among middle adolescents. *Sex Roles, 15,* 145–158.
24. Clark, K. B., & Clark, M. K. (1947). Racial identification and preference in Negro children. In G. S. Swanson, T. M. Newcomb, & E. L. Harley, eds., *Readings in social psychology.* Rev. ed. New York: Holt, pp. 551–560.
25. Comer, J. P., & Hill, H. (1985). Social policy and the mental health of black children. *Journal of the American Academy of Child Psychiatry, 24*(2), 175–181.
26. Cooley, C. H. (1902). *Human nature and the social order.* New York: Charles Scribner & Sons.
27. Cooper, C. R.; Grotevant, H. D.; & Condon, S. M. (1983). Individuality and connectedness both foster adolescent identity formation and role taking skills. In H. D. Grotevant & C. R. Cooper, eds., *Adolescent development in the family: New directions for child development.* San Francisco: Jossey-Bass, pp. 43–59.
28. Coopersmith, S. (1967). *The antecedents of self-esteem.* San Francisco: W. H. Freeman.
29. Cross, W. E. (1985). Black identity: Rediscovering the distinction between personal identity and reference group orientation. In M. B. Spencer, G. K. Brookins, & W. R. Allen, eds., *Beginnings: The social and affective development of black children.* Hillsdale, N.J.: Erlbaum, pp. 155–171.
30. Damon, W., & Hart, D. (1982). The development of self-understanding from infancy through adolescence. *Child Development, 53,* 841–864.
31. Damon, W., & Hart, D. (1988). *Self-understanding in childhood and adolescence.* New York: Cambridge University Press.
32. Douvan, E., & Adelson, J. (1966). *The adolescence experience.* New York: Wiley.
33. Elder, G. H. (1962). Sociocultural variations in the child-rearing relationship. *Sociometry, 25,* 241–262.
34. Elkind, D. (1967). Egocentrism in adolescence. *Child Development, 38,* 1025–34.
35. Elkind, D. (1984). Growing up faster. *Psychology Today, 12,* 38–45.
36. Engel, M. (1959). The stability of the self-concept in adolescence. *Journal of Abnormal and Social Psychology, 58,* 211–217.
37. Enright, R. D.; Lapsley, D. K.; Dricas, A. S.; & Fehr, L. A. (1980). Parental influence on the development of adolescent autonomy and identity. *Journal of Youth and Adolescence 9,* 529–546.
38. Epps, E. (1975). Impact of school desegregation on aspirations, self-concept, and other aspects of personality. *Law and Contemporary Problems, 50,* 300–313.
39. Epstein, S. (1973). The self-concept revisited, or a theory of a theory. *American Psychologist, 28,* 405–416.
40. Erikson, E. H. (1950). *Childhood and Society.* New York: Norton.

41. Erikson, E. (1959). Identity and the life cycle. *Psychological Issues, 1,* 18–164.
42. Erikson, E. (1968). *Identity, youth, and crisis.* New York: Norton.
43. Festinger, L. A. (1954). A theory of social comparison processes. *Human Relations, 7,* 117–140.
44. Fischer, K. W. (1980). A theory of cognitive development: The control and construction of hierarchies of skills. *Psychological Review, 87,* 477–531.
45. Freud, A. (1965). *Normality and pathology in childhood.* New York: International Universities Press.
46. Gecas, V. (1972). Parental behavior and contextual variations in adolescent self-esteem. *Sociometry, 35,* 332–345.
47. Gergen, K. J. (1968). Personal consistency and the presentation of self. In C. Gordon & J. Gergen, eds., *The self in social interaction.* New York: Wiley, pp. 299–308.
48. Gilligan, C. (1982). *In a different voice.* Cambridge, Mass.: Harvard University Press.
49. Glick, M., & Zigler, E. (1985). Self-image: A cognitive-developmental approach. In R. L. Leahy, ed., *The development of self.* New York: Academic Press, pp. 1–53.
50. Gold, M. (1978). Self-esteem and delinquent behavior: A theory of alternative schools. *Crime and Delinquency Literature* (July), 290–308.
51. Gordon, V. V. (1978). *The self-concept of black Americans.* Washington, D.C.: American Sociological Association.
52. Griffin, N.; Chassin, L.; & Young, R. D. (1981). Measurement of global self-concept versus multiple role-specific self-concepts in adolescents. *Adolescence, 16,* 49–56.
53. Grotevant, H. D., & Cooper, C. R. (1983). *Adolescent development in the family.* New Directions for Child Development. San Francisco: Jossey-Bass.
54. Grotevant, H. D., & Cooper, C. R. (1985). Patterns of interaction in family relationships and the development of identity exploration in adolescence. *Child Development, 56,* 415–428.
55. Grotevant, H. D., & Cooper, C. R. (1986). Individuation in family relationships. *Human Development, 29,* 83–100.
56. Hare, B. R., & Castenell, L. A., Jr. (1985). No place to run, no place to hide: Comparative status and future prospects of black boys. In M. B. Spender, G. K. Brookins, & W. R. Allen, eds., *Beginnings: The social and affective development of black children.* Hillsdale, N.J.: Erlbaum, pp. 201–214.
57. Hart, D. (1988). The adolescent self-concept in social context. In D. K. Lapsley & F. C. Power, eds., *Self, ego, and identity.* New York: Springer Verlag, pp. 71–90.
58. Harter, S. (1982). The perceived competence scale for children. *Child Development, 53,* 87–97.
59. Harter, S. (1983). Developmental perspectives on the self-system. In E. M. Hetherington, ed., *Handbook of child psychology.* Vol. 4. *Socialization, personality, and social development.* New York: Wiley.
60. Harter, S. (1985). The self-perception profile for adolescents. Unpublished manuscript, University of Denver.

61. Harter, S. (1986a). Cognitive-developmental processes in the integration of concepts about emotion and the self. *Social Cognition, 4,* 119–151.
62. Harter, S. (1986b). Processes underlying the construction, maintenance, and enhancement of the self-concept in children. In J. Suls & A. Greenwald, eds., *Psychological perspectives on the self.* Vol. 3. Hillsdale, N.J.: Erlbaum, pp. 137–181.
63. Harter, S. (1987). The determinants and mediational role of global self-worth in children. In N. Eisenberg, ed., *Contemporary Issues in Developmental Psychology.* New York: Wiley, pp. 219–242.
64. Harter, S. (1988a). The construction and conservation of the self: James and Cooley revisited. In D. K. Lapsley & F. C. Power, eds., *Self, ego, and identity: Integrative approaches.* New York: Springer-Verlag, pp. 43–70.
65. Harter, S. (1988b). Developmental and dynamic changes in the nature of the self-concept: Implications for child psychotherapy. In S. Shirk, ed., *Cognitive development and child psychotherapy.* New York: Plenum, pp. 119–160.
66. Harter, S. (1989). Causes, correlates, and the functional role of global self-worth: A life-span perspective. In J. Kolligian & R. Sternberg, eds., *Perceptions of competence and incompetence across the life-span.* New Haven: Yale University Press.
67. Harter, S., & Lee, L. (1989). Manifestations of true and false selves in early adolescence. Presentation, Society for Research in Child Development, Kansas City.
68. Harter, S., & Marold, D. (1989). A model of risk factors in adolescent suicide. Presentation, Society for Research in Child Development, Kansas City.
69. Hatfield, E., & Sprechner, S. (1986). *Mirror, mirror: The importance of looks in everyday life.* Albany: State University of New York Press.
70. Hauser, S. T. (1971). *Black and white identity formation.* New York: Wiley.
71. Hauser, S. T. (1976). Self-image complexity and identity formation in adolescence longitudinal studies. *Journal of Youth and Adolescence, 5,* 161–177.
72. Hauser, S. T., & Follansbee, D. J. (1984). Developing identity: Ego growth and change during adolescence. In H. E. Fitzgerald, B. M. Laster, & M. W. Yogman, eds., *Theory and research in behavioral pediatrics.* Vol. 2. New York: Plenum, pp. 207–268.
73. Hauser, S. T., & Kasendorf, E. (1983). *Black and white identity formation.* Malabar, Fla.: Robert E. Krieger.
74. Hauser, S. T.; Powers, S. I.; Noam, G. G.; Jacobson, A. M.; Weisse, B.; & Follansbee, D. J. (1984). Familial contexts of adolescent ego development. *Child Development, 55,* 195–213.
75. Higgins, E. T. (1987). Self-discrepancy: A theory relating self and affect. *Psychological Review, 94,* 319–340.
76. Hill, J. P., & Holmbeck, G. N. (1986). Attachment and autonomy during adolescence. In G. J. Whitehurst, ed., *Annals of Child Development.* Vol. 3. Greenwich, Conn.: JAI Press, pp. 145–189.
77. Horney, K. (1950). *Neurosis and human growth.* New York: Norton.
78. Hunt, J. M., & Hunt, L. (1977). Racial inequality and self-image: Identity maintenance as identity diffusion. *Sociology and Social Research, 61,* 539–559.
79. James, W. (1982). *Psychology: The briefer course.* New York: Holt, Rinehart, & Winston.

80. Jersild, A. T.; Brook, J. S.; & Brook, D. W. (1978). *The psychology of adolescence.* 3rd ed. New York: Macmillan.

81. Josselson, R. (1980). Ego development in adolescence. In J. Adelson, ed., *Handbook of adolescent psychology.* New York: Wiley, pp. 188–210.

82. Josselson, R.; Greenberger, E., & McConochie, D. (1977). Phenomenological aspects of psychosocial maturity in adolescents. Pt. 2: Girls. *Journal of Youth and Adolescence, 6,* 145–167.

83. Jung, C. G. (1928). *Two essays on analytical psychology.* New York: Dodd, Mead.

84. Kaplan, H. B. (1975). *Self-attitudes and deviant behavior.* Pacific Palisades, Calif.: Goodyear.

85. Kaplan, H. B., & Pokorny, A. D. (1976). Self-attitudes and suicidal behavior. *Suicide and Life-Threatening Behavior, 6,* 23–35.

86. Kazdin, A. E.; French, N. H.; Unis, A. S.; Esveldt-Dawson, K.; & Sherrich, R. B. (1983). Hopelessness, depression, and suicidal intent among psychiatrically disturbed in-patient children. *Journal of Consulting and Clinical Psychology, 51,* 504–510.

87. Lang, E., & Rivera, J. (1987). In Harlem: Millionaire's promise still inspires. *New York Times,* June 20, 53.

88. Langlois, J. H. (1981). Beauty and the beast: The role of physical attractiveness in the development of peer relations and social behavior. In S. S. Brehn, S. M. Kassin, & F. X. Gibbons, eds., *Developmental social psychology: Theory and research.* New York: Oxford University Press.

89. Lapsley, D. K., & Rice, K. (1988). The "new look" at the imaginary audience and personal fable: Toward a general model of adolescent ego development. In D. K. Lapsley & F. C. Power, Eds., *Self, ego, and identity: Integrative approaches.* New York: Springer Verlag, pp. 109–129.

90. Leahy, R. L. (1985). The costs of development: Clinical implications. In R. L. Leahy, ed., *The development of the self.* New York: Academic Press.

91. Lecky, P. (1945). *Self-consistency: A theory of personality.* New York: Island Press.

92. Lerner, R. M., & Brackney, B. E. (1978). The importance of inner and outer body parts attitudes in the self-concept of late adolescents. *Sex Roles, 4,* 225–237.

93. Lerner, R. M.; Orlos, J. B.; & Knapp, J. (1976). Physical attractiveness, physical effectiveness, and self-concept of late adolescents. *Adolescence, 11,* 313–326.

94. Lewis, M., & Brooks-Gunn, J. (1979). *Social cognition and the acquisition of self.* New York: Plenum.

95. Livesley, W. J., & Bromley, D. B. (1973). *Person perception in childhood and adolescence.* London: Wiley.

96. Loevinger, J. (1979). *Scientific ways in the study of ego development.* Worcester, Mass.: Clark University Press.

97. Mahler, M. S.; Pine, F.; & Berman, A. (1975). *The psychological birth of the human infant.* New York: Basic Books.

98. Marcia, J. E. (1966). Development and validation of ego-identity status. *Journal of Personality and Social Psychology, 3,* 551–558.

99. Marcia, J. E. (1980). Identity in adolescence. In J. Adelson, ed., *Handbook of adolescent psychology.* New York: Wiley, pp. 159–177.

100. Marcia, J. E. (1988). Common processes underlying ego identity, cog-

nitive/normal development, and individuation. In D. K. Lapsley & F. C. Power, eds., *Self, ego, and identity.* New York: Springer Verlag, pp. 211–225.

101. Marcia, J. E., & Friedman, M. L. (1970). Ego identity status in college women. *Journal of Personality, 38,* 249–263.

102. Markus, H., & Nurius, P. (1986). Possible selves. *American Psychologist, 41,* 954–969.

103. Marsh, H. W. (1986). Global self-esteem: Its relation to specific facets of self-concept and their importance. *Journal of Personality and Social Psychology, 51,* 1224–36.

104. Marsh, H. W., & O'Neill, R. (1984). Self-description questionnaire III (SDQ III): The construct validity of multidimensional self-concept ratings by late adolescents. *Journal of Educational Measurement, 21,* 153–174.

105. Maslow, A. H. (1961). Peak-experience as acute identity-experiences. *American Journal of Psychoanalysis, 21,* 254–260.

106. Mattleson, D. R. (1977). Exploration and commitment: Sex differences and methodological problems in the use of identity status categories. *Journal of Youth and Adolescence, 6,* 353–374.

107. May, R. (1967). *Psychology and the human dilemma.* Princeton: Van Nostrand.

108. McCarthy, J., & Hoge, D. (1982). Analysis of age effects in longitudinal studies of adolescent self-esteem. *Developmental Psychology, 18,* 372–379.

109. Mead, G. H. (1934). *Mind, self, and society.* Chicago: University of Chicago Press.

110. Meicher, B. (1986). Moral reasoning, self-identity, and moral action: A study of conduct disorder in adolescence. Ph.D. dissertation, University of Pittsburgh.

111. Monsour, A. (1985). The structure and dynamics of the adolescent self-concept. Ph.D. dissertation, University of Denver.

112. Montemayor, R., & Eisen, M. (1977). The development of self-conceptions from childhood to adolescence. *Developmental Psychology, 13,* 314–319.

113. Mullener, N., & Laird, J. D. (1971). Some developmental changes in the organization of self-evaluations. *Developmental Psychology, 5,* 233–236.

114. Neemann, J., & Harter, S. (1986). The self-perception profile for college students. Unpublished manuscript, University of Denver.

115. Newman, F. M. (1981). Reducing student alienation in high schools: Implications of theory. *Harvard Educational Review, 51,* 546–564.

116. Noam, G. G.; Kohlberg, L.; & Snarey, J. (1983). *Steps toward a model of the self.* In B. Lee & G. G. Noam, eds., *Developmental approaches to the self.* New York: Plenum, pp. 59–142.

117. Offer, D.; & Ostrov, E.; & Howard, K. (1981). *The adolescent: A psychological self-portrait.* New York: Basic Books.

118. O'Malley, P., & Bachman, J. (1983). Self-esteem: Change and stability between ages 13 and 23. *Developmental Psychology, 19,* 257–268.

119. Orlofsky, J. L. (1977). Sex-role orientation, identity formation, and self-esteem in college men and women. *Sex Roles, 3,* 561–575.

120. Oyserman, D., & Markus, H. (1987). Possible selves, motivation, and delinquency. Unpublished manuscript, University of Michigan.

121. Peterson, A. C., & Taylor, B. (1980). Puberty: Biological change and psychological adaption. In J. Adelson, ed., *Handbook of adolescent psychology*. New York: Wiley, pp. 117–158.

122. Pfeffer, C. (1986). *The suicidal child*. New York: Guilford Press.

123. Phinney, J. S., & Tarver, S. (1988). Ethnic identity search and commitment in black and white eighth-graders. *Journal of Adolescence, 8,* 265–277.

124. Piaget, J. (1960). *The psychology of intelligence*. Paterson, N.J.: Littlefield, Adams.

125. Piaget, J. (1963). *The origins of intelligence in children*. New York: Norton.

126. Powell, G. J. (1983). *Black Monday's children: The psychological effects of school desegregation on southern schoolchildren*. New York: Appleton-Century-Croft.

127. Powell, G. J. (1985). Self-concepts among Afro-American students in racially isolated minority schools: Some regional differences. *Journal of the American Academy of Child Psychiatry, 24,* 142–149.

128. Rogers, C. R. (1950). The significance of the self-regarding attitudes and perceptions. M. L. Reymart, ed., *Feelings and emotions: The Mooseheart symposium*. New York: McGraw-Hill, pp. 78–99.

129. Rogers, C., & Dymond, R. (1954). *Psychotherapy and personality change*. Chicago: University of Chicago Press.

130. Rosenberg, F. R., & Rosenberg, M. (1978). Self-esteem and delinquency. *Journal of Youth and Adolescence, 7,* 279–291.

131. Rosenberg, M. (1975). The dissonant context and the adolescent self-concept. In S. Dragastin & G. Elder, Jr., eds., *Adolescence in the life cycle*. Washington, D.C.: Hemisphere, pp. 76–102.

132. Rosenberg, M. (1979). *Conceiving the self*. New York: Basic Books.

133. Rosenberg, M. (1985). Summary on identity. In M. B. Spencer, G. K. Brookings, and W. R. Allen, eds., *Beginnings: The social and affective development of black children*. Hillsdale, N.J.: Erlbaum, pp. 231–234.

134. Rosenberg, M. (1986). Self-concept from middle childhood through adolescence. In J. Suls & A. G. Greenwald, eds., *Psychological perspective on the self*. Hillsdale, N.J.: Erlbaum, pp. 182–205.

135. Rosenberg, M., & Simmons, R. G. (1972). *Black and white self-esteem: The urban schoolchild*. Arnold and Caroline Rose Monograph Series. Washington, D.C.: American Sociological Association.

136. Rubin, L. B. (1985). *Just friends*. New York: Harper & Row.

137. Ruble, D. (1983). The development of social comparison processes and their role in achievement-related self-socialization. In T. Higgins, D. Ruble, & W. Hartup, eds., *Social cognitive development: A social-cultural perspective*. New York: Cambridge University Press.

138. Rutter, M. (1987). Psychosocial resilience and protective mechanisms. *American Journal of Orthopsychiatry, 57,* 47–61.

139. Secord, P., & Peevers, B. (1974). The development of person concepts. In T. Mischel, ed., *Understanding other persons*. Oxford: Blackwell, pp. 117–142.

140. Seligman, M. E. P. (1976). *Helplessness: On depression, development, and death*. San Francisco: Freeman.

141. Selman, R. (1980). *The growth of interpersonal understanding*. New York: Academic Press.
142. Sigel, I. E. (1984). Reflections on action theory and distancing theory. *Human Development, 27,* 188–193.
143. Simmons, R. G., & Blyth, D. A. (1987). *Moving into adolescence: The impact of pubertal change and school context*. New York: Aldine de Gruyter.
144. Simmons, R.; Brown, L.; Bush, D.; & Blyth, D. (1979). Self-esteem and achievement of black and white adolescents. *Social Problems, 25,* 86–96.
145. Simmons, R. G.; Rosenberg, F.; & Rosenberg, M. (1973). Disturbance in the self-image at adolescence. *American Sociological Review, 38,* 553–568.
146. Simmons, R. G., & Rosenberg, F. (1975). Sex, sex-roles, and self-image. *Journal of Youth and Adolescence, 4*(3), 229–258.
147. Smollar, J., & Youniss, J. (1985). Adolescent self-concept development. In R. L. Leahy, ed., *The development of self*. New York: Academic Press.
148. Spencer, M. B. (1985). Cultural cognition and social cognition as identity correlates of black children's personal-social development. In M. B. Spencer, G. K. Brookins, and W. R. Allen, eds., *Beginnings: The social and affective development of black children*. Hillsdale, N.J.: Erlbaum, pp. 215–230.
149. Strachen, A., & Jones, D. (1982). Changes in identification during adolescence: A personal construct theory approach. *Journal of Personality Assessment, 46,* 139–148.
150. Taylor, R. L. (1976). Psychosocial development among black children and youth: A reexamination. *American Journal of Orthopsychiatry, 46*(1), 4–19.
151. Tesser, A., & Campbell, J. (1980). Self-definition: The impact of the relative performance and similarity of others. *Social Psychology Quarterly. 43,* 341–347.
152. Tesser, A., & Campbell, J. (1983). Self-definition and self-evaluation maintenance. In J. Suls & A. G. Greenwald, eds., *Psychological perspectives on the self.* Vol. 2. Hillsdale, N.J.: Erlbaum, pp. 1–30.
153. Toder, N. L., & Marcia, J. E. (1973). Ego identity status and response to conformity pressure in college women. *Journal of Personality and Social Psychology, 26,* 287–294.
154. Vallacher, R. R. (1980). An introduction to self-theory. In D. M. Wegner & R. R. Vallacher, eds., *The self in social psychology*. New York: Oxford University Press, pp. 3–30.
155. Waterman, A. S. (1982). Identity development from adolescence to adulthood: An extension of theory and review of research. *Developmental Psychology, 18,* 341–358.
156. Waterman, A. S. (1985). Identity in the context of adolescent psychology. In A. S. Waterman, ed., *Identity in adolescence: Processes and contents*. San Francisco: Jossey-Bass, pp. 5–24.
157. Waterman, C. K., & Nevid, J. (1977). Sex differences in the resolution of the identity crisis. *Journal of Youth and Adolescence, 6,* 337–342.
158. Werner, H. (1957). The concept of development from a comparative and organismic view. In D. B. Harris, ed., *The concept of development*. Minneapolis: University of Minnesota Press, pp. 125–148.
159. Winnicott, D. (1965). *The maturational processes and the facilitating environment*. New York: International Universities Press.

160. Wylie, R. (1974). *The self-concept.* Rev. ed. Vol. 1. *A review of methodological considerations and measuring instruments.* Lincoln: University of Nebraska Press.

161. Wylie, R. (1979). *The self-concept.* Vol. 2. *Theory and research on selected topics.* Lincoln: University of Nebraska Press.

162. Zumpf, C., & Harter, S. (1989). Mirror, mirror, on the wall: The relationship between appearance and self-worth in adolescent males and females. Presentation, Society for Research in Child Development, Kansas City.

15. Stress, Coping, and Adaptation

1. Bandura, A. (1964). The stormy decade: Fact or fiction? *Psychology in the Schools, 1,* 224–231.

2. Baumrind, D. (1968). Authoritarian vs. authoritative control. *Adolescence, 3,* 255–272.

3. Baumrind, D. (1985). Familial antecedents of adolescent drug use: A developmental perspective. In C. L. Jones & R. J. Battjes, eds., *Etiology of adolescent drug abuse: Implications for prevention.* NIDA Research Monograph no. 56. Rockville, Md.: National Institute on Drug Abuse.

4. Baumrind, D. (1987). A developmental perspective on adolescent risk taking in contemporary America. In C. E. Irwin, Jr., ed., *Adolescent social behavior and health.* New Directions for Child Development no. 37. San Francisco: Jossey-Bass, pp. 93–125.

5. Baumrind, D. (1989). Rearing competent children. In W. Damon, ed., *Child development today and tomorrow.* New Directions for Child Development. San Francisco: Jossey-Bass.

6. Beardslee, W. R., & Podorefsky, D. (1988). Resilient adolescents whose parents have serious affective and other psychiatric disorders: Importance of self-understanding and relationships. *American Journal of Psychiatry, 145,* 63–69.

7. Beardslee, W. R.; Jacobson, A. M.; Hauser, S. T.; Noam, G. V.; & Powers, S. (1985). An approach to evaluating adolescent adaptive processes: Scale development and reliability. *Journal of the American Academy of Child Psychiatry, 24,* 637–642.

8. Bleuler, M. (1978). *The schizophrenic disorders: Long-term patient and family studies.* New Haven: Yale University Press.

9. Block, J. (1971). *Lives through time.* Berkeley: Bancroft Books.

10. Block, J. H., & Block, J. (1980). The role of ego-control and ego-resiliency in the organization of behavior. In W. A. Collins, ed., *Development of cognition, affect, and social relations. Minnesota symposia on child psychology.* Vol. 13. Hillsdale, N.J.: Erlbaum, pp. 39–101.

11. Block, J.; Block, J. H.; & Keyes, S. (1988). Longitudinally foretelling drug usage in adolescence: Early childhood and environmental precursors. *Child Development, 59,* 339–355.

12. Blos, P. (1962). *On adolescence: A psychoanalytic interpretation.* New York: Free Press.

13. Blos, P. (1984). *Adolescent passages.* New York: Free Press.

14. Blumenthal, S. J., & Kupfer, D. J. (1988). Overview of early detection and

treatment strategies for suicidal behavior in young people. *Journal of Youth and Adolescence, 17,* 1–23.

15. Boyce, W. T. (1985). Social support, family, and children. In S. Cohen & S. L. Syme, eds., *Social support and health.* New York: Academic Press.
16. Brooks-Gunn, J., & Petersen, A. C., eds. (1983). *Girls at puberty: Biological and psychological perspectives.* New York: Plenum.
17. Brooks-Gunn, J.; Petersen, A. C.; & Eichorn, D., eds. (1985). Time of maturation and psychosocial functioning in adolescence. Special issue. *Journal of Youth and Adolescence, 14,* 149–264.
18. Brooks-Gunn, J., & Ruble, D. N. (1983). The experience of menarche from a developmental perspective. In J. Brooks-Gunn & A. C. Petersen, eds., *Girls at puberty: Biological and psychosocial perspectives.* New York: Plenum, pp. 155–178.
19. Browning, D. L. (1987). Ego development, authoritarianism, and social status: An investigation of the incremental validity of Loevinger's Sentence Completion Test (short form). *Journal of Personality and Social Psychology, 53,* 113–118.
20. Cauce, A. M. (1986). Social networks and social competence: Exploring the effects of early adolescent friendships. *American Journal of Community Psychology, 14,* 607–628.
21. Cauce, A. M. (1987). School and peer competence in early adolescence: A test of domain-specific self-perceived competence. *Developmental Psychology, 23,* 287–291.
22. Cohen, L. H.; Burt, C. E.; & Bjorck, J. P. (1987). Life stress and adjustment: Effects of life events experienced by young adolescents and their parents. *Developmental Psychology, 23,* 583–592.
23. Cohen, F., & Lazarus, R. S. (1983). Coping and adaptation in health and illness. In D. Mechanic, ed., *Handbook of health, health care, and the health professions.* New York: Free Press, pp. 608–635.
24. Cohen, S., & Syme, S. L., eds. (1985). *Social support and health.* New York: Academic Press.
25. Compas, B. E. (1987a). Coping with stress during childhood and adolescence. *Psychological Bulletin, 101,* 393–403.
26. Compas, B. E. (1987b). Stress and life events during childhood and adolescence. *Clinical Psychology Review, 7,* 275–302.
27. Compas, B. E.; Davis, G. E.; Forsythe, C. J.; & Wagner, B. M. (1987). Assessment of major and daily stressful life events during adolescence: The Adolescent Perceived Events Scale. *Journal of Consulting and Clinical Psychology, 55,* 534–541.
28. Compas, B. E.; Malcarne, V. L.; & Fondacaro, K. M. (1988). Coping with stressful events in older children and young adolescents. *Journal of Consulting and Clinical Psychology, 56,* 405–411.
29. Cooper, C. R., & Ayers-Lopez, S. (1985). Family and peer systems in early adolescence: New models of the role of relationships in development. *Journal of Early Adolescence, 5,* 9–21.
30. Cooper, C.; Grotevant, H. D.; & Condon, S. M. (1983). Individuality and connectedness in the family as a context for adolescent identity and role-taking skills. In H. D. Grotevant & C. R. Cooper, eds., *Adolescent development*

in the family. New Directions for Child Development. San Francisco: Jossey-Bass.

31. Cooper, C. R., & Grotevant, H. D. (1987). Gender issues at the interface of family experience and adolescents' friendship and dating identity. *Journal of Youth and Adolescence, 16,* 247–264.

32. Csikszentmihaly, M., & Larson, R. (1984). *Being adolescent.* New York: Basic Books.

33. Douvan, E., & Adelson, J. (1966). *The adolescent experience.* New York: Wiley.

34. Erikson, E. H. (1959). Identity and the life cycle. *Psychological Issues, 1,* 1–171.

35. Erikson, E. H. (1968). *Identity, youth, and crisis.* New York: W. W. Norton.

36. Farber, S. S.; Felner, R. D.; & Primavera, J. (1985). Parental separation/divorce and adolescents: An examination of factors mediating adaptation. *American Journal of Community Psychology, 13,* 171–185.

37. Flaste, R. (1988). The myth about teen-agers. *New York Times Magazine: Good Health Supplement* (October 8), 19, 76, 80, 85.

38. Folkman, S.; Lazarus, R. S.; Dunkel-Schetter, C.; DeLongis, A.; & Gruen, R. J. (1986). Dynamics of a stressful encounter: Cognitive appraisal, coping, and encounter outcomes. *Journal of Personality and Social Psychology, 50,* 992–1003.

39. Forehand, R.; McCombs, A.; Long, N.; Brody, G.; & Fauber, R. (1988). Early adolescent adjustment to recent parental divorce: The role of interparental conflict and adolescent sex as mediating variables. *Journal of Consulting and Clinical Psychology, 56,* 624–627.

40. Frank, S., & Quinlan, D. (1976). Ego development and female delinquency: A cognitive-developmental approach. *Journal of Abnormal Psychology, 85,* 505–510.

41. Freud, A. (1936). *The ego and the mechanisms of defense.* New York: International Universities Press.

42. Freud, A. (1958). Adolescence. In *Psychoanalytic Study of the Child.* Vol. 13. New York: International Universities Press, pp. 255–278.

43. Garmezy, N. (1983). Stressors of childhood. In N. Garmezy & M. Rutter, eds., *Stress, coping, and development in children.* New York: Wiley Interscience, pp. 43–84.

44. Garmezy, N. (1984). Stress-resistant children: The search for protective factors. In J. E. Stevenson, ed., *Recent research in developmental psychopathology. Journal of Child Psychology and Psychiatry* Book Supplement, no. 4. Oxford: Pergamon Press, pp. 213–233.

45. Garmezy, N. (1987). Stress, competence, and development: Continuities in the study of schizophrenic adults, children vulnerable to psychopathology, and the search for stress-resistant children. *American Journal of Orthopsychiatry, 57,* 159–174.

46. Gilligan, C. (1987). Adolescent development reconsidered. In C. E. Irwin, ed., *Adolescent social behavior and health.* New Directions for Child Development, no. 37. San Francisco: Jossey-Bass, pp. 63–92.

47. Gispert, M.; Wheeler, K.; Marsh, L.; & Davis, M. S. (1985). Suicidal adolescents: Factors in evaluation. *Adolescence, 20,* 753–762.

48. Gjerde, P.; Block, J.; & Block, J. H. (in press). Depressive symptoms and

personality during late adolescence: Gender differences in the externalization-internalization of symptom expression. *Journal of Abnormal Psychology*.

49. Gottman, J. M. (1983). How children become friends. *Monographs of the Society for Research in Child Development, 48*(3), ser. no. 201.

50. Graham, P. (1985). Handling stress in the handicapped adolescent. *Developmental Medicine and Child Neurology, 27,* 389–391.

51. Grotevant, H. D., & Cooper, C. R. (1986). Individuation in family relationships. *Human Development, 29,* 82–100.

52. Haan, N. (1977). *Coping and defending: Processes of self-environment organization.* New York: Academic.

53. Haan, N.; Aerts, E.; & Cooper, B. A. B. (1985). *On moral grounds: The search for practical morality.* New York: New York University Press.

54. Hall, G. S. (1904). *Adolescence.* New York: Appleton and Company.

55. Hartmann, H. (1939). *Ego psychology and the problem of adaptation.* New York: International Universities Press.

56. Hauser, S. T. (1976). Loevinger's model and measure of ego development: A critical review. *Psychological Bulletin, 83,* 928–955.

57. Hauser, S. T. (1986). Conceptual and empirical dilemmas in the assessment of defenses. In G. E. Vaillant, ed., *Empirical studies of ego mechanisms of defense.* Washington, D.C.: American Psychiatric Press, pp. 89–99.

58. Hauser, S. T.; Borman, E.; Bowlds, M. K.; Powers, S.; Jacobson, A.; Noam, G.; & Knoebber, K. (forthcoming). Understanding coping within adolescence: Stages and paths of development. In A. L. Greene, E. M. Cummings, & K. Karraker, eds., *Life-span developmental psychology: Perspectives on stress and coping.* Hillsdale, N.J.: Erlbaum.

59. Hauser, S. T., & Daffner, K. R. (1980). Ego functions and development: Empirical research and clinical relevance. *McLean Hospital Journal, 5,* 87–109.

60. Hauser, S. T., & Follansbee, D. (1984). Developing identity: Ego growth and change during adolescence. In H. Fitzgerald, B. Lester, & M. Yogman, eds., *Theory and research in behavioral pediatrics.* New York: Plenum.

61. Hauser, S. T., & Greene, W. (forthcoming). Passages from late adolescence to early adulthood. In G. Pollock and S. Greenspan, eds., *The course of life.* New York: International University Press.

62. Hauser, S. T.; Houlihan, J.; Powers, S. I.; Jacobson, A. M.; Noam, G.; Weiss-Perry, B.; & Follansbee, D. (1987). Interaction sequences in families of psychiatrically hospitalized and nonpatient adolescents. *Psychiatry, 50,* 308–319.

63. Hauser, S. T.; Houlihan, J.; Powers, S. I.; Jacobson, A. M.; Noam, G. G.; Weiss-Perry, B.; Follansbee, D.; & Book, B. K. (in press). Adolescent ego development within the family: Family styles and family sequences. *International Journal of Behavioral Development.*

64. Hauser, S. T.; Powers, S.; Noam, G.; Jacobson, A.; Weiss, B.; & Follansbee, D. (1984). Familial contexts of adolescent ego development. *Child Development, 55,* 195–213.

65. Hauser, S. T.; Powers, S. I.; Noam, G.; & Bowlds, M. K. (1987). Family interiors of adolescent ego-development trajectories. *Family Perspective, 21,* 263–282.

66. Hauser, S. T.; with Powers, S., & Noam, G. (forthcoming). *Separating and connecting: Paths of teenage development in families.* New York: Free Press.
67. Hauser, S. T.; Vieyra, M. A. B.; Jacobson, A. M.; & Wertlieb, D. (1985). Vulnerability and resilience in adolescence: Views from the family. *Journal of Early Adolescence, 5,* 81–100.
68. Hetherington, E. M. (1989). Coping with family transitions: Winners, losers, and survivors. *Child Development, 60,* 1–14.
69. Hetherington, E. M.; Stanley-Hagan, M.; & Anderson, E. R. (1989). Marital transitions: A child's perspective. *American Psychologist, 44,* 303–312.
70. Hill, J. P. (1980). The family. In M. Johnson, ed., *Toward adolescence: The middle school years. Seventy-Ninth Yearbook of the National Society for the Study of Education.* Chicago: University of Chicago Press.
71. Hill, J. P. (1987). Research on adolescents and their families: Past and prospect. In C. E. Irwin, ed., *Adolescent social behavior and health.* New Directions for Child Development no. 37. San Francisco: Jossey-Bass.
72. Hill, J. P., & Holmbeck, G. N. (1986). Attachment and autonomy during adolescence. In G. W. Whitehurst, ed., *Annals of Child Development.* Vol. 3. Greenwich, Conn.: JAI Press.
73. Hirsch, B. J. (1985). Adolescent coping and support across multiple social environments. *American Journal of Community Psychology, 13,* 381–392.
74. Holahan, C. J., & Moos, R. H. (1985). Life stress and health: Personality, coping, and family support in stress resistance. *Journal of Personality and Social Psychology, 49,* 739–747.
75. Holahan, C. J., & Moos, R. H. (1987). Risk, resistance, and psychological distress: A longitudinal analysis with adults and children. *Journal of Abnormal Psychology, 96,* 3–13.
76. Horowitz, F. D., & O'Brien, M. (1989). Children as futures: In the interest of the nation: A reflective essay on the state of our knowledge and the challenges before us. *American Psychologist, 44,* 441–445.
77. House, J. S.; Landis, K. R.; & Umberson, D. (1988). Social relationships and health. *Science, 241,* 540–545.
78. Irion, J. C.; Coon, R. C.; & Blanchard-Fields, F. (1988). The influence of divorce on coping in adolescence. *Journal of Youth and Adolescence, 17,* 135–145.
79. Jacobson, A. M.; Beardslee, W.; Hauser, S. T.; Noam, G. G.; & Powers, S. I. (1986). An approach to evaluating adolescent ego-defense mechanisms using clinical interviews. In G. E. Vaillant, ed., *Empirical studies of ego mechanisms of defense.* Washington, D.C.: American Psychiatric Press, pp. 47–59.
80. Kauffman, C.; Grunebaum, H.; Cohler, B.; & Gamer, E. (1979). Superkids: Competent children of psychotic mothers. *American Journal of Psychiatry, 136,* 1398–1402.
81. Kessler, R. C.; Price, R. H.; & Wortman, C. B. (1985). Social factors in psychopathology: Stress, social support, and coping processes. *Annual Review of Psychology, 36,* 531–572.
82. Klein, J. R., & Litt, I. (1983). Menarche and dysmenorrhea. In J. Brooks-Gunn & A. C. Petersen, eds., *Girls at puberty: Biological and psychosocial perspectives.* New York: Plenum, pp. 73–88.

83. Kobasa, S. C. (1982). Commitment and coping in stress resistance among lawyers. *Journal of Personality and Social Psychology, 42,* 707–717.

84. Labouvie-Vief, G.; Hakim-Larson, J.; & Hobart, C. J. (1987). Age, ego level, and the life-span development of coping and defense processes. *Psychology and Aging, 2,* 286–293.

85. Lazarus, R. S., & Folkman, S., eds. (1984). *Stress, appraisal, and coping.* New York: Springer.

86. Levi, L. D.; Stierlin, H.; & Savard, R. J. (1972). Fathers and sons: The interlocking crises of integrity and identity. *Psychiatry, 35,* 48–56.

87. Loevinger, J. (1976). *Ego development: Conceptions and theories.* San Francisco: Jossey-Bass.

88. Loevinger, J. (1979). Construct validity of the sentence-completion test of ego development. *Applied Psychological Measurement, 3,* 281–311.

89. Long, N.; Forehand, R.; Fauber, R.; & Brody, G. H. (1987). Self-perceived and independently observed competence of young adolescents as a function of parental marital conflict and recent divorce. *Journal of Abnormal Child Psychology, 15,* 15–27.

90. Melton, G. (1987). *Reforming the law: Impacts of child development research.* New York: Guilford.

91. Mishne, J. M. (1986). *Clinical work with adolescents.* New York: Free Press.

92. Moriarty, A. E., & Toussieng, P. W. (1976). *Adolescent coping.* New York: Grune & Stratton.

93. Murphy, L. B. (1974). Coping, vulnerability, and resilience in childhood. In G. V. Coelho, D. A. Hamburg, & J. E. Adams, eds., *Coping and adaptation.* New York: Basic Books, pp. 69–100.

94. Murphy, L. B., & Moriarty, A. E. (1976). *Vulnerability, coping, and growth: From infancy to adolescence.* New Haven: Yale University Press.

95. Newman, B. M.; Newman, P. R.; & Stewart, L. W. (1980). Crisis and coping. In *Personality development through the life span.* Monterey, Calif.: Brooks/Cole, pp. 80–97.

96. Noam, G., Hauser, S. T.; Santostefano, S.; Garrison, W.; Jacobson, A.; Powers, S.; & Mead, M. (1984). Ego development and psychopathology: A study of hospitalized adolescents. *Child Development, 55,* 184–194.

97. Nottelman, E.; Susman, E.; Inoff-Germain, G.; Cutler, G.; Loriaux, D.; & Chrousos, G. (1987). Developmental processes in early adolescence: Relationships between adolescent adjustment problems and chronological age, pubertal stage, and puberty-related serum hormone levels. *Journal of Pediatrics, 110,* 473–480.

98. Offer, D. (1969). *The psychological world of the teenager: A study of normal adolescent boys.* New York: Basic Books.

99. Offer, D., & Offer, J. (1975). *From teenage to young manhood: A study of normal adolescent boys.* New York: Basic Books.

100. Offer, D.; Ostrov, E.; & Howard, I. (1981). *The adolescent: A psychological self-portrait.* New York: Basic Books.

101. Offer, D., & Sabshin, M. (1984). *Normality and the life cycle.* New York: Basic Books.

102. Ozer, D., & Gjerde, P. (in press). Patterns of personality consistency and change from childhood through adolescence. *Journal of Personality*.

103. Patsiokas, A. T.; Clum, G. A.; & Luscomb, R. L. (1979). Cognitive characteristics of suicide attempters. *Journal of Consulting and Clinical Psychology*, *47*, 478–484.

104. Perry, J. C., & Cooper, S. H. (1986). What do cross-sectional measures of defense mechanisms predict? In G. E. Vaillant, ed., *Empirical studies of ego mechanisms of defense*. Washington, D.C.: American Psychiatric Press, pp. 31–46.

105. Petersen, A. C. (1987). Adolescent development. *Annual Review of Psychology*, *39*, 583–607.

106. Petersen, A. C., & Hamburg, B. A. (1986). Adolescence: A developmental approach to problems and psychopathology. *Behavior Therapy*, *17*, 480–499.

107. Petersen, A. C., & Spiga, R. (1982). Adolescence and stress. In L. Goldberger & S. Breznitz, eds., *Handbook of stress: Theoretical and clinical aspects*. New York: Free Press, pp. 515–528.

108. Powers, S. I.; Hauser, S. T.; Schwartz J.; Noam, G. G.; & Jacobson, A. (1983). Adolescent ego development and family interaction: A structural-developmental perspective. In H. D. Grotevant & C. R. Cooper, eds., *Adolescent development in the family*. New Directions for Child Development, no. 22. San Francisco: Jossey-Bass.

109. Powers, S. I.; Hauser, S. T.; & Kilner, L. A. (1989). Adolescent mental health. *American Psychologist*, *44*, 200–208.

110. Proulx, J., & Koulack, D. (1987). The effect of parental divorce on parent-adolescent separation. *Journal of Youth and Adolescence*, *16*, 473–480.

111. Rosznafsky, J. (1981). The relationship of level of ego development to Q-sort personality ratings. *Journal of Personality and Social Psychology*, *41*, 99–120.

112. Rutter, M. (1979). Protective factors in children's responses to stress and disadvantage. In M. W. Kent & J. E. Rolf, eds., *Primary prevention of psychopathology*. Vol. 3. *Social competence in children*. Hanover, N.H.: University Press of New England, pp. 49–74.

113. Rutter, M. (1983). Stress, coping, and development: Some issues and some questions. In N. Garmezy & M. Rutter, eds., *Stress, coping, and development in children*. New York: McGraw-Hill, pp. 1–41.

114. Rutter, M.; Graham, P.; Chadwick, O. F. D.; & Yule, W. (1976). Adolescent turmoil: Fact or fiction? *Journal of Child Psychology and Psychiatry*, *17*, 35–56.

115. Segal, J. (1983). Utilization of stress and coping research: Issues of public education and public policy. In N. Garmezy & M. Rutter, eds., *Stress, coping, and development in children*. New York: McGraw-Hill, pp. 303–334.

116. Selye, H. (1976). *The stress of life*. New York: McGraw-Hill. Originally published 1956.

117. Shaffer, D. (1974). Suicide in childhood and early adolescence. *Journal of Child Psychology and Psychiatry*, *15*, 275–291.

118. Shafii, M., Carrigan, S.; Whittinghill, J. R.; & Derrick, A. (1985). Psychological autopsy of completed suicide in children and adolescents. *American Journal of Psychiatry*, *142*, 1061–64.

119. Shneidman, E. (1985). *Definition of suicide.* New York: Wiley.
120. Simmons, R. G.; Burgeson, R.; Carlton-Ford, S.; & Blyth, D. A. (1987). The impact of cumulative change in early adolescence. *Child Development, 58,* 1220–34.
121. Slaughter, D. T., ed. (1988). *Black children and poverty: A developmental perspective.* San Francisco: Jossey-Bass.
122. Smetana, J. G. (1988). Adolescents' and parents' conceptions of parental authority. *Child Development, 59,* 321–335.
123. Steinberg, L. (1988). Reciprocal relations between parent-child distance and pubertal maturation. *Developmental Psychology, 24,* 122–128.
124. Steinberg, L., & Silverberg, S. (1986). The vicissitudes of autonomy in adolescence. *Child Development, 57,* 841–851.
125. Susman, E.; Inoff-Germain, G.; Nottelman, E.; Loriaux, D.; Cutler, G.; & Chrousos, G. (1987). Hormones, emotional dispositions, and aggressive attributes in young adolescents. *Child Development, 58,* 1114–34.
126. Vaillant, G. E. (1977). *Adaptation to life.* Boston: Little, Brown.
127. Wallerstein, J. S., & Blakeslee, S. (1989). *Second chances.* New York: Ticknor & Fields.
128. Wallerstein, J. S., & Kelly, J. B. (1980). *Surviving the breakup: How children and parents cope with divorce.* New York: Basic Books.
129. Werner, E. E., & Smith, R. S. (1982). *Vulnerable but invincible: A study of resilient children.* New York: McGraw-Hill.

16. Problem Behaviors

1. Akers, R. L. (1973). *Deviant behavior: A social learning approach.* Belmont, Calif.: Wadsworth.
2. Allan, E. A., & Steffensmeier, D. J. (1989). Youth, underemployment, and property crime: Differential effects of job availability and job quality on juvenile and young adult arrest rates. *American Sociological Review, 54,* 107–123.
3. Amato, P. R. (1987). Family process in one-parent, stepparent, and intact families: The child's point of view. *Journal of Marriage and the Family, 49,* 327–337.
4. Anderson, E. (1989). Sex codes and family life among poor inner-city youths. *Annals of the American Academy of Political and Social Science, 501,* 59–78.
5. August, G. J., & Stewart, M. A. (1982). Is there a syndrome of pure hyperactivity? *British Journal of Psychiatry, 140,* 305–311.
6. Bachman, J. G. (1987). Changes in deviant behavior during late adolescence and early adulthood. Paper presented at the ninth biennial meetings of the International Society for the Study of Behavioral Development, July, Tokyo.
7. Bachman, J. G.; Green, S.; & Wirtanen, I. (1971). *Youth in transition.* Vol. 3. *Dropping out: Problem or symptom?* Ann Arbor: Institute for Social Research.
8. Bandura, A.; Taylor, C. B.; Williams, S. L.; Mefford, I. N.; & Barchas, J. D. (1985). Catecholamine secretion as a function of perceived coping self-efficacy. *Journal of Consulting and Clinical Psychology, 53,* 406–414.
9. Bandura, A., & Walters, R. H. (1959). *Adolescent aggression.* New York: Ronald.

10. Barnes, G. M., & Welte, J. W. (1986). Patterns and predictors of alcohol use among 7th–12th grade students in New York State. *Journal of Studies on Alcohol, 47,* 53–62.
11. Bell, B.; Mednick, S. A.; Gottesman, I. I.; & Sergeant, J. (1977). Electrodermal parameters in male twins. In S. A. Mednick & K. O. Christiansen, eds., *Biosocial bases of criminal behavior.* New York: Gardner Press, pp. 217–225.
12. Bell, R. Q. (1986). Age-specific manifestations in changing psychosocial risk. In D. C. Farvan & J. D. McKinney, eds., *Risk in intellectual and psychosocial development.* Orlando, Fla.: Academic Press, pp. 169–185.
13. Belson, W. A. (1978). *Television violence and the adolescent boy.* Westwood, England: Saxon House.
14. Bentler, P. M. (1987). Drug use and personality in adolescence and young adulthood: Structural models with nonnormal variables. *Child Development, 58,* 65–79.
15. Berg, N. L. (1974). Self-concept of neurotic and sociopathic criminal offenders. *Psychological Reports, 34,* 622.
16. Berk, R. A.; Lenihan, K. J.; & Rossi, P. H. (1980). Crime and poverty: Some experimental evidence from ex-offenders. *American Sociological Review, 45,* 766–786.
17. Berrueta-Clement, J. R.; Schweinhart, L. J.; Barnett, W. S.; Epstein, A. S.; & Weikart, D. P. (1984). *Changed lives: The effects of the Perry Preschool Program on youths through age 19.* Ypsilanti, Mich.: High Scope Press.
18. Berrueta-Clement, J. R.; Schweinhart, L. J.; Barnett, W. S.; & Weikart, D. P. (1987). The effects of early educational intervention on crime and delinquency in adolescence and early adulthood. In J. D. Burchard & S. N. Burchard, eds., *Prevention of Delinquent Behavior.* Newbury Park, Calif.: Sage Publications, pp. 220–240.
19. Biddle, B. J.; Bank, B. J.; & Marlin, M. J. (1980). Social determinants of adolescent drinking. *Journal of Studies on Alcohol, 41,* 215–240.
20. Blackburn, R. (1978). Psychopathy, arousal, and the need for stimulation. In R. D. Hare & D. Schalling, eds., *Psychopathic behavior.* Chichester: Wiley, pp. 157–164.
21. Blumstein, A.; Cohen, J.; Roth, J. A.; & Visher, C. A. (1986). *Criminal careers and career criminals.* Vol. 1. Washington, D.C.: National Academy Press.
22. Blumstein, A.; Farrington, D. P.; & Moitra, S. (1985). Delinquency careers: Innocents, desisters, and persisters. In M. Tonry & N. Morris, eds., *Crime and Justice.* Vol. 6. Chicago: University of Chicago Press, pp. 187–219.
23. Blumstein, A., & Graddy, E. (1981–82). Prevalence and recidivism in index arrests: A feedback model. *Law and Society Review, 16,* 265–290.
24. Bowker, L. H., & Klein, M. W. (1983). The etiology of female juvenile delinquency and gang membership. *Adolescence, 18,* 739–751.
25. Braithwaite, J. (1981). The myth of social class and criminality reconsidered. *American Sociological Review, 46,* 36–57.
26. Brook, J. S.; Whiteman, M.; & Gordon, A. S.; & Brook, D. W. (1984a). Identification with paternal attributes and its relationship to the son's personality and drug use. *Developmental Psychology, 20,* 1111–19.
27. Brook, J. S.; Whiteman, M.; Gordon, A. S.; & Brook, D. W. (1984b). Paternal

determinants of female adolescent's marijuana use. *Developmental Psychology, 20,* 1032–43.

28. Brook, J. S.; Whiteman, M.; & Gordon, A. S. (1985). Father absence, perceived family characteristics, and stage of drug use in adolescence. *British Journal of Developmental Psychology, 2,* 87–94.

29. Brook, J. S.; Whiteman, M.; Gordon, A. S.; & Cohen, P. (1986). Dynamics of childhood and adolescent personality traits and adolescent drug use. *Developmental Psychology, 22,* 403–414.

30. Brunswick, A. F.; Merzel, C. R.; & Messeri, P. A. (1985). Drug use initiation among urban black youth: A seven-year follow-up of developmental and secular influences. *Youth & Society, 17,* 189–216.

31. Bynner, J. M.; O'Malley, P.; & Bachman, J. G. (1981). Self-esteem and delinquency revisited. *Journal of Youth and Adolescence, 10,* 407–441.

32. Cadoret, R.; Troughton, E.; & O'Gorman, T. W. (1987). Genetic and environmental factors in alcohol abuse and antisocial personality. *Journal of Studies on Alcohol, 48,* 1–8.

33. Cairns, R. B.; Cairns, B. D.; Neckerman, H. J.; Gest, S. D.; & Gariépy, J. (1988). Social networks and aggressive behavior: Peer support or peer rejection? *Developmental Psychology, 24,* 815–823.

34. Cantor, N. L., & Gelfand, D. M. (1977). Effects of responsiveness and sex of children on adults' behavior. *Child Development, 48,* 232–238.

35. Cass, L. K., & Thomas, C. B. (1979). *Childhood pathology and later adjustment.* New York: Wiley.

36. Cernkovich, S. A.; Giordano, P. C.; & Pugh, M. D. (1985). Chronic offenders: The missing cases in self-report delinquency research. *Journal of Criminal Law and Criminology, 76,* 705–732.

37. Chassin, L.; Mann, L. M.; & Sher, K. J. (1988). Self-awareness theory, family history of alcoholism, and adolescent alcohol involvement. *Journal of Abnormal Psychology, 97,* 206–217.

38. Chin, K. (1988). Chinese gangs in New York City, 1965–1988. Paper presented at Social and Psychological Factors in Juvenile Delinquency: An International Conference between Republic of China and United States of America, August, Taipei.

39. Cline, V. B.; Croft, R. G.; & Courrier, S. (1973). Desensitization of children to television violence. *Journal of Personality and Social Psychology, 27,* 360–365.

40. Cloward, R. A., & Ohlin, L. E. (1960). *Delinquency and opportunity.* New York: Free Press.

41. Cockburn, J. J., & Maclay, I. (1965). Sex differentials in juvenile delinquency. *British Journal of Criminology, 5* (July), 289–308.

42. Cohen, A. K. (1955). *Delinquent boys.* Glencoe: Free Press.

43. Cohen, J. M. (1977). Sources of peer group homogeneity. *Sociology of Education, 50,* 227–241.

44. Cohen, L. E., & Felson, M. (1979). Social change and crime rate trends: A routine activity approach. *American Sociological Review, 44,* 588–608.

45. Cohen, P., Brook, J. E.; Cohen, J.; Velez, C. N.; & Garcia, M. (1990). Common and uncommon pathways to adolescent psychopathology and

problem behavior. In L. Robins & M. Rutter, eds. *Straight and devious pathways from childhood to adulthood.* Cambridge: Cambridge University Press.

46. Cook, P. J. (1980). Research in criminal deterence: Laying the groundwork for the second decade. In N. Morris & M. Tonry, eds., *Crime and justice*. Vol. 2. Chicago: University of Chicago Press, pp. 211–268.

47. Crowther, C. (1969). Crimes, penalties, and legislatures. *Annals of the American Academy of Political and Social Science, 381,* 147–158.

48. Curry, G. D., & Spergel, I. A. (1988). Gang homicide, delinquency, and community. *Criminology, 26,* 381–405.

49. Dannefer, D., & Schutt, R. K. (1982). Race and juvenile justice processing in court and police agencies. *American Journal of Sociology, 87,* 1113–31.

50. Dembo, R.; Grandon, G.; LaVoie, L.; Schmeidler, J.; & Burgos, W. (1986). Parents and drugs revisited: Some further evidence in support of social learning theory. *Criminology, 24,* 85–104.

51. Dodge, K. A. (1983). Behavioral antecedents of peer social status. *Child Development, 54,* 1386–99.

52. Donovan, J. E.; Jessor, R.; & Jessor, L. (1983). Problem drinking in adolescence and young adulthood. *Journal of Studies on Alcohol, 44,* 109–137.

53. Donovan, J. E.; Jessor, R. (1985). The structure of problem behavior in adolescence and young adulthood. *Journal of Consulting and Clinical Psychology, 53,* 890–904.

54. Dornbusch, S. M.; Carlsmith, J. M.; Bushwall, S. J.; Ritter, P. S.; Leiderman, H.; Hastorf, A. H.; & Gross, R. T. (1985). Single parents, extended households, and the control of adolescents. *Child Development, 56,* 326–341.

55. Elliott, D. S., & Ageton, S. S. (1980). Reconciling race and class differences in self-reported and official estimates of delinquency. *American Sociological Review, 45,* 95–110.

56. Elliott, D. S.; Huizinga, D.; & Ageton, S. S. (1985). *Explaining delinquency and drug use.* Beverly Hills: Sage Publications.

57. Elliott, D. S.; Huizinga, D.; & Menard, S. (1989). *Multiple-problem youth: Delinquency, substance use, and mental health problems.* New York: Springer Verlag.

58. Elliott, D. S., & Voss, H. L. (1974). *Delinquency and dropout* Lexington, Mass.: Heath.

59. Ensminger, M. E.; Kellam, S. G.; & Rubin, B. R. (1983). School and family origins of delinquency: Comparisons by sex. In K. T. Van Dusen & S. A. Mednick, eds., *Prospective studies of crime and delinquency.* Boston: Kluwer-Nijhoff, pp. 73–97.

60. Eron, L. D., & Huesmann, L. R. (1986). The role of television in the development of prosocial and antisocial behaviour. In D. Olweus, J. Block, & M. R. Yarrow, eds., *Development of antisocial and prosocial behavior.* New York: Academic Press, pp. 285–314.

61. Farrington, D. P. (1977). The effects of public labelling. *British Journal of Criminology, 17,* 112–125.

62. Farrington, D. P. (1978). The family backgrounds of aggressive youths. In L. A. Hersov & M. Berger, eds., *Aggression and antisocial behavior in childhood and adolescence.* Oxford: Pergamon, pp. 73–93.

63. Farrington, D. P. (1983). Offending from 10 to 25 years of age. In K. T. Van Dusen & S. A. Mednick, eds., *Prospective studies of crime and delinquency.* Boston: Kluwer-Nijhoff, pp. 73–97.
64. Farrington, D. P. (1986). Stepping stones to adult criminal careers. In D. Olweus, J. Block, & M. R. Yarrow, eds., *Development of antisocial and prosocial behavior.* New York: Academic Press, pp. 359–384.
65. Farrington, D. P., & Dowds, E. A. (1985). Disentangling criminal behaviour and police reaction. In D. P. Farrington & J. Gunn, eds., *Reaction to crime: The public, the police, courts, and prisons.* Chichester: Wiley, pp. 41–72.
66. Farrington, D. P., & Loeber, R. (1987). Long-term criminality of conduct disorder boys with or without impulsive-inattentive behavior. Paper presented at the Life History Research Society, October, St. Louis.
67. Feldman, R. A.; Caplinger, T. E.; & Wodarski, J. S. (1983). *The St. Louis conundrum.* Englewood Cliffs, N.J.: Prentice-Hall.
68. Gersten, J. C.; Langner, T. S.; & Simcha-Fagan, O. (1979). Developmental patterns of types of behavioral disturbance and secondary prevention. *International Journal of Mental Health, 7,* 132–149.
69. Gibbons, D. C., & Blake, G. F. (1976). Evaluating the impact of juvenile diversion programs. *Crime and Delinquency, 22,* 411–420.
70. Giordano, P. C.; Cernkovich, S. A.; & Pugh, M. D. (1986). Friendships and delinquency. *American Journal of Sociology, 91,* 1170–1202.
71. Gold, M., & Mann, D. (1972). Delinquency as defense. *American Journal of Orthopsychiatry, 42,* 463–479.
72. Gottfredson, G. D. (1987). Peer group interventions to reduce the risk of delinquent behavior: A selective review and a new evaluation. *Criminology, 25,* 671–714.
73. Gottfredson, S., & Taylor, R. B. (1986). Person-environment interactions in the prediction of recidivism. In R. Sampson & J. Byrne, eds., *The Social Ecology of Crime.* New York: Springer Verlag, pp. 133–155.
74. Greenberger, E., & Steinberg, L. (1986). *When teenagers work: The psychological and social costs of adolescent employment.* New York: Basic Books.
75. Guze, S. B.; Goodwin, D. W.; & Crane, J. B. (1970). A psychiatric study of the wives of convicted felons: An example of assortative mating. *American Journal of Psychiatry, 126,* 1773–76.
76. Hackler, J. C., & Hagan, J. L. (1975). Work and teaching machines as delinquency prevention tools: A four-year follow-up. *Social Service Review, 49,* 92–106.
77. Hardt, R. H., & Peterson-Hardt, S. (1977). On determining the quality of the delinquency self-report method. *Journal of Research in Crime and Delinquency, 14,* 247–261.
78. Hare, R. D. (1978). Electrodermal and cardiovascular correlates of psychopathy. In R. D. Hare & D. Schalling, eds., *Psychopathic behaviour.* Chichester: Wiley, pp. 107–143.
79. Hawkins, J. D., & Lam, T. (1987). Teacher practices, social development, and delinquency. In J. D. Burchard & S. N. Burchard, eds., *Prevention of delinquent behavior.* Newbury Park, Calif.: Sage Publications, pp. 241–274.
80. Hawkins, J. D.; Lishner, D. M.; Jenson, J. M.; & Catalano, R. F. (1987).

Delinquents and drugs: What the evidence suggests about prevention and treatment programming. In B. S. Brown & A. R. Mills, eds., *Youth at high risk for substance abuse*. Rockville, Md.: National Institute on Drug Abuse.
81. Hindelang, M. J. (1978). Race and involvement in common law personal crimes. *American Sociological Review, 43,* 93–109.
82. Hindelang, M. J.; Hirschi, T.; & Weis, J. G. (1981). *Measuring delinquency.* Beverly Hills: Sage Publications.
83. Hinton, J.; O'Neill, M.; Hamilton, S.; & Burke, M. (1980). Psychophysiological differentiation between psychopathic and schizophrenic abnormal offenders. *British Journal of Social and Clinical Psychology, 19,* 257–269.
84. Hirschi, T. (1969). *Causes of delinquency.* Berkeley: University of California Press.
85. Horowitz, R. (1987). Community tolerance of gang violence. *Social Problems, 34,* 437–450.
86. Huesmann, L. R.; Eron, L. D.; Lefkowitz, M. M.; & Walder, L. O. (1984). Stability of aggression over time and generations. *Developmental Psychology, 20,* 1120–34.
87. Huizinga, D., & Elliott, D. (1986). Reassessing the reliability and validity of self-report delinquency measures. *Journal of Quantitative Criminology, 2,* 293–327.
88. Huizinga, D., & Elliott, D. S. (1987). Juvenile offenders: Prevalence, offender incidence, and arrest rates by race. *Crime & Delinquency, 33,* 206–223.
89. Jensen, G. F., & Eve, R. (1976). Sex differences in delinquency. *Criminology, 13,* 427–448.
90. Jessor, R., & Jessor, S. (1978). Theory testing in longitudinal research on marijuana use. In D. B. Kandel, ed., *Longitudinal research on drug use.* New York: Wiley, pp. 41–71.
91. Johnston, L. D.; O'Malley, P. M.; & Bachman, J. G. (1988). *Illicit drug use, smoking, and drinking by America's high school students, college students, and young adults, 1975–1987.* Rockville, Md.: National Institute on Drug Abuse.
92. Josephson, E., & Rosen, M. A. (1978). Panel loss in a high school drug study. In D. B. Kandel, ed., *Longitudinal research on drug use.* New York: Wiley, pp. 115–133.
93. Kandel, D. B. (1978). Similarity in real-life adolescent friendship pairs, *Journal of Personality and Social Psychology, 36,* 306–312.
94. Kandel, D. B. (1980). Drug and drinking behavior among youth. *Annual Review of Sociology, 6,* 235–285.
95. Kandel, D. B. (1988). Age of onset into drugs and sexual behavior. Paper prepared for Onset Working Group Program on Human Development and Criminal Behavior, July, Montreal.
96. Kandel, D. B. (forthcoming). Cocaine use in a national sample of U.S. youth (NLSY): Epidemiology, predictors, and ethnic patterns. In *The epidemiology of cocaine use and abuse.* NIDA Research Monograph. Rockville, Md.: National Institute on Drug Abuse.
97. Kandel, D. B., & Andrews, K. (1987). Process of adolescent socialization by parents and peers. *International Journal of the Addictions, 22,* 319–342.
98. Kandel, D. B.; Davies, M.; Karus, D.; & Yamaguchi, K. (1986). The conse-

quences in young adulthood of adolescent drug involvement. *Archives of General Psychiatry*, *43*, 746–754.

99. Kandel, D. B.; Kessler, R. C.; & Margulies, R. Z. (1978). Antecedents of adolescent initiation into stages of drug use: A developmental analysis. In D. B. Kandel, ed., *Longitudinal research on drug use*. New York: Wiley, pp. 73–99.

100. Kandel, D. B., & Yamaguchi, K. (1987). Job mobility and drug use: An event history analysis. *American Journal of Sociology*, *92*, 836–878.

101. Kaplan, H. B. (1980). *Deviant behavior in defense of self*. New York: Academic Press.

102. Kaplan, H. B.; Johnson, R. J.; & Bailey, C. A. (1987). Deviant peers and deviant behavior: Further elaboration of a model. *Social Psychology Quarterly*, *50*, 277–284.

103. Kellam, S. G.; Simon, M. B.; & Ensminger, M. E. (1983). Antecedents in first grade of teenage substance use and psychological well-being: A ten-year community-wide prospective study. In D. F. Ricks and B. S. Dohrenwend, eds., *Origins of psychopathology*. Cambridge: Cambridge University Press, pp. 17–42.

104. Khavari, K. A.; Mabry, E.; & Humes, M. (1977). Personality correlates of hallucinogen use. *Journal of Abnormal Psychology*, *86*, 172–178.

105. Klein, M. W. (1971). *Street gangs and street workers*. Englewood Cliffs, N.J.: Prentice-Hall.

106. Klein, M. W. (1979). Deinstitutionalization and diversion of juvenile offenders: A litany of impediments. In N. Morris & M. Tonry, eds., *Crime and justice*. Vol. 1. Chicago: University of Chicago Press, pp. 145–201.

107. Kleinman, P. H., & Lukoff, I. F. (1978). Ethnic differences in factors related to drug use. *Journal of Health and Social Behavior*, *19*, 190–199.

108. Labouvie, E. W. (1986). Alcohol and marijuana use in relation to adolescent stress. *International Journal of the Addictions*, *21*, 333–345.

109. Lattimore, P.; Witte, A.; & Baker, J. (1989). An experimental assessment of an integrated vocational training program for youthful offenders. Working paper no. 2952, March. Cambridge, Mass.: National Bureau of Economic Research.

110. Lewis, D. O.; Pincus, J.; Lovely, R.; Spitzer, E.; & Moy, E. (1987). Biopsychosocial characteristics of matched samples of delinquents and nondelinquents. *Journal of the American Academy of Child and Adolescent Psychiatry*, *26*, 744–752.

111. Lewis, D. O., & Shanok, S. S. (1981). Racial factors influencing the diagnosis, disposition, and treatment of deviant adolescents. In D. O. Lewis, ed., *Vulnerabilities to delinquency*. New York: SP Medical and Scientific Books, pp. 295–311.

112. Liu, W. T. (1988). Asian-American teenagers: A research challenge. Paper presented at Social and Psychological Factors in Juvenile Delinquency: An International Conference between Republic of China and United States of America, August, Taipei.

113. Loeb, J., & Mednick, S. A. (1977). A prospective study of predictors of criminality: 3: Electrodermal response patterns. In S. A. Mednick & K. O. Chris-

tiansen, eds., *Biosocial bases of criminal behavior.* New York: Gardner, pp. 245–254.

114. Loeber, R., & Stouthamer-Loeber, M. (1986). Family factors as correlates and predictors of juvenile conduct problems and delinquency. In N. Morris & M. Tonry, eds., *Crime and justice.* Vol. 7. Chicago: University of Chicago Press, pp. 29–149.

115. Maccoby, E. E., & Jacklin, C. N. (1974). *The psychology of sex differences.* Stanford: Stanford University Press.

116. Maccoby, E. E., & Jacklin, C. N. (1982). The "person" characteristics of children and the family as environment. Paper presented at the Conference on Interaction of Person and Environment, June, Stockholm.

117. Magnusson, D. (1988). *Individual development from an interactional perspective.* Hillsdale, N.J.: Erlbaum.

118. Magnusson, D.; Stattin, J.; & Duner, A. (1983). Aggression and criminality in longitudinal perspective. In K. T. Van Dusen & S. A. Mednick, eds., *Prospective studies of crime and delinquency.* Boston: Kluwer-Nijhoff, pp. 277–301.

119. Magnusson, D.; Stattin, J.; & Allen, V. L. (1985). Biological maturation and social development: A longitudinal study of some adjustment processes from midadolescence to adulthood. *Journal of Youth and Adolescence, 14,* 267–283.

120. Mawson, A. R., & Mawson, C. D. (1977). Psychopathy and arousal: A new interpretation of the psychophysiological literature. *Biological Psychiatry, 12,* 49–74.

121. Maxson, C. L.; Gordon, M. A.; & Klein, M. W. (1985). Differences between gang and nongang homicides. *Criminology, 23,* 209–222.

122. McCarthy, J. D., & Hoge, D. R. (1984). The dynamics of self-esteem and delinquency. *American Journal of Sociology, 90,* 396–410.

123. McCord, J. (1979). Some child-rearing antecedents of criminal behavior in adult men. *Journal of Personality and Social Psychology, 37,* 1477–86.

124. McCord, J. (1981). Consideration of some effects of a counseling program. In S. E. Martin, L. B. Sechrest, & R. Redner, eds., *New directions in the rehabilitation of criminal offenders.* Washington, D.C.: National Academy of Sciences, pp. 394–405.

125. McCord, J. (1982). A longitudinal view of the relationship between paternal absence and crime. In J. Gunn & D. P. Farrington, eds., *Abnormal offenders, delinquency, and the criminal justice system.* Chichester: Wiley, pp. 113–128.

126. McCord, J. (1983). A longitudinal study of aggression and antisocial behavior. In K. T. Van Dusen & S. A. Mednick, eds., *Prospective studies of crime and delinquency.* Boston: Kluwer-Nijhoff, pp. 269–275.

127. McCord, J. (1985). Deterrence and the light touch of the law. In D. P. Farrington and J. Gunn, eds., *Reactions to crime: The public, the police, courts, and prisons.* London: Wiley, pp. 73–85.

128. McCord, J. (1988). Identifying developmental paradigms leading to alcoholism. *Journal of Studies on Alcohol, 49,* 357–362.

129. McGee, R., & Share, D. L. (1988). Attention deficit disorder-hyperactivity and academic failure: Which comes first and what should be treated? *Journal of the American Academy of Child and Adolescent Psychiatry, 27,* 318–325.

130. Mead, G. H. (1934). *Mind, self, and society from the standpoint of a social behaviorist.* Chicago: University of Chicago Press.
131. Mednick, S. A.; Gabrielli, W. F; & Hutchings, B. (1987). Genetic factors in the etiology of criminal behavior. In S. A. Mednick, T. E. Moffitt, & S. A. Stack, eds., *The causes of crime: New biological approaches.* Cambridge: Cambridge University Press, pp. 74–91.
132. Meller, W. H.; Rinehart, R.; Cadoret, R. J.; & Troughton, E. (1988). Specific familial transmission in substance abuse. *International Journal of the Addictions, 23,* 1029–39.
133. Mensch, B. S., & Kandel, D. B. (1988a). Dropping out of high school and drug involvement. *Sociology of Education, 61,* 95–113.
134. Mensch, B. S., & Kandel, D. B. (1988b). Underreporting of substance use in a national longitudinal youth cohort: Individual and interviewer effects. *Public Opinion Quarterly, 52,* 100–124.
135. Merton, R. K. (1938). Social structure and anomie. *American Sociological Review, 3,* 672–682.
136. Miller, W. B. (1962). The impact of a "total community" delinquency control project. *Social Problems, 10,* 168–191.
137. Moffitt, T. E., & Silva, P. A. (1988). Self-reported delinquency, neuropsychological deficit, and history of attention deficit disorder. *Journal of Abnormal Child Psychology, 16,* 553–569.
138. National Institute of Drug Abuse (1987). *National Survey on Drug Abuse: Population Estimates, 1985.* Rockville, Md.: National Institute on Drug Abuse.
139. Newcomb, M. D., & Bentler, P. M. (1989). Substance use and abuse among children and teenagers. *American Psychologist, 44,* 242–248.
140. Olweus, D. (1986). Aggression and hormones: Behavioral relationship with testosterone and adrenaline. In D. Olweus, J. Block, & M. R. Yarrow, eds., *Development of antisocial and prosocial behavior.* New York: Academic Press, pp. 51–72.
141. Olweus, D. (1988). Bully/victim problems among school children: Effects of an intervention program in Norway. Paper presented at the Earlscourt Symposium on Childhood Aggression, June, Toronto.
142. Osgood, D. W.; Johnston, L. D.; O'Malley, P. M.; & Backman, J. G. (1988). The generality of deviance in late adolescence and early adulthood. *American Sociological Review, 53,* 81–93.
143. Parke, R. D.; Berkowitz, L.; Leyens, J. P.; West, S. G.; & Sebastian, R. J. (1977). Some effects of violent and nonviolent movies on the behavior of juvenile delinquents. In L. Berkowitz ed., *Advances in experimental social psychology.* Vol. 10. New York: Academic Press, pp. 135–172.
144. Parker, J. G., & Asher, S. R. (1987). Peer relations and later personal adjustment: Are low-accepted children at risk? *Psychological Bulletin, 102,* 357–389.
145. Paton, S., & Kandel, D. B. (1978). Psychological factors and adolescent illicit drug use: Ethnicity and sex differences. *Adolescence, 13,* 187–198.
146. Patterson, G. R. (1976). The aggressive child: Victim and architect of a coercive system. In E. J. Mash, L. A. Hamerlynck, & L. C. Handy, eds., *Behavior modification and families.* Vol. 1. *Theory and Research.* New York: Brunner/Mazel, pp. 267–316.

147. Patterson, G. R. (1985). Beyond technology: The next stage in developing an empirical base for parent training. In L. L'Abate, ed., *Handbook of family psychology and therapy.* Vol. 2. Homewood, Ill.: Dorsey Press, pp. 1344–79.
148. Patterson, G. R.; Chamberlain, P.; & Reid, J. B. (1982). A comparative evaluation of a parent-training program. *Behavior Therapy, 13,* 638–650.
149. Patterson, G. R., & Dishion, T. J. (1985). Contributions of families and peers to delinquency. *Criminology, 23,* 63–79.
150. Pettit, G. S.; Dodge, K. A.; & Brown, M. M. (1988). Early family experience, social problem solving patterns, and children's social competence. *Child Development, 59,* 107–120.
151. Phillips, L., & Votey, H. L., Jr. (1987). Rational choice models of crimes by youth. *Review of Black Political Economy, 16,* 129–185.
152. Pulkkinen, L. (1983). Search for alternatives to aggression in Finland. In A. P. Goldstein & M. H. Segall, eds., *Aggression in global perspective.* Elmsford, N.Y.: Pergamon Press, pp. 104–144.
153. Quay, H. C. (1965). Psychopathic personality as pathological stimulation seeking. *American Journal of Psychiatry, 122,* 180–183.
154. Rauh, V. A.; Achenbach, T. M.; Nurcombe, B.; Howell, C. T.; & Teti, D. M. (1988). Minimizing adverse effects of low birthweight: Four-year results of an early intervention program. *Child Development, 59,* 544–553.
155. Reckless, W. C., & Dinitz, S. (1972). *The prevention of juvenile delinquency: An experiment.* Columbus: Ohio State University Press.
156. Reiss, A. J., Jr. (1986). Why are communities important in understanding crime? In A. J. Reiss & M. Tonry, eds., *Communities and crime.* Vol. 8. Chicago: University of Chicago Press, pp. 1–33.
157. Reiss, A. J., Jr. (1988). Co-offending and criminal careers. In N. Morris & M. Tonry, eds., *Crime and Justice.* Vol. 7. Chicago: University of Chicago Press, pp. 117–170.
158. Ried, L. D.; Martinson, D. B.; & Weaver, L. C. (1987). Factors associated with the drug use of fifth through eighth grade students. *Journal of Drug Education, 17,* 149–162.
159. Robins, L. N. (1978a). The interaction of setting and predisposition in explaining novel behavior: Drug initiations before, in, and after Vietnam. In D. B. Kandel, ed., *Longitudinal research on drug use.* New York: Wiley, pp. 179–196.
160. Robins, L. N. (1978b). Sturdy childhood predictors of adult antisocial behavior: Replications from longitudinal studies. *Psychological Medicine, 8,* 611–622.
161. Robins, L. N.; Darvish, H. S.; & Murphy, G. E. (1970). The long-term outcome for adolescent drug users: A follow-up study of 76 users and 146 nonusers. In J. Zubin & A. M. Freedman, eds., *The psychopathology of adolescence.* New York: Grune & Stratton, pp. 159–178.
162. Robins, L. N., & Lewis, R. G. (1966). The role of the antisocial family in school completion and delinquency: A three-generational study. *Sociological Quarterly, 7,* 500–514.
163. Robins, L. N., & Ratcliff, K. S. (1979). Risk factors in the continuation of childhood antisocial behavior into adulthood. *International Journal of Mental Health, 7,* 96–116.
164. Robins, L. N., & Wish, E. (1977). Childhood deviance as a developmental

process: A study of 223 urban black men from birth to 18. *Social Forces, 56,* 448–473.

165. Rossi, P. H.; Berk, R. A.; & Lenihan, K. J. (1980). *Money, work, and crime.* New York: Academic Press.

166. Rowe, D. (1986). Sibling interaction and self-reported delinquent behavior: A study of 265 twin pairs. *Criminology, 23,* 223–240.

167. Rutter, M. (1978). Family, area, and school influences in the genesis of conduct disorders. In L. A. Hersov & M. Berger, eds., *Aggression and anti-social behaviour in childhood and adolescence.* Oxford: Pergamon Press, pp. 95–113.

168. Sarnecki, J. (1986). *Delinquent networks.* Stockholm: National Council for Crime Prevention.

169. Satterfield, J. H. (1987). Childhood diagnostic and neurophysiological predictors of teenage arrest rates: An eight-year prospective study. In S. A. Mednick, T. E. Moffitt, & S. A. Stack, eds., *The causes of crime: New biological approaches.* Cambridge: Cambridge University Press, pp. 146–167.

170. Schachar, R.; Rutter, M.; & Smith, A. (1981). The characteristics of situationally and pervasively hyperactive children: Implications for syndrome definition. *Child Psychology and Psychiatry, 22,* 375–392.

171. Schalling, D. (1987). Personality correlates of plasma testosterone levels in young delinquents: An example of person-situation interaction? In S. A. Mednick, T. E. Moffitt, & S. A. Stack, eds., *The causes of crime: New biological approaches.* Cambridge: Cambridge University Press, pp. 283–291.

172. Schuckit, M. A. (1984). Subjective responses to alcohol in sons of alcoholics and controls. *Archives of General Psychiatry, 41,* 879–884.

173. Schuckit, M. A., & Rayses, V. (1979). Ethanol ingestion: Differences in blood acetaldehyde concentrations in relatives of alcoholics and controls. *Science, 203,* 54–55.

174. Searles, J. S. (1988). The role of genetics in the pathogenesis of alcoholism. *Journal of Abnormal Psychology, 97,* 153–167.

175. Severy, L., & Whitaker, J. M. (1982). Juvenile diversion: An experimental analysis of effectiveness. *Evaluation Review, 6,* 753–774.

176. Snyder, J.; Dishion, T. J.; & Patterson, G. R. (1986). Determinants and consequences of associating with deviant peers during preadolescence and adolescence. *Journal of Early Adolescence, 6,* 29–43.

177. Spivack, G., & Cianci, N. (1987). High-risk early behavior pattern and later delinquency. In J. D. Burchard & S. N. Burchard, eds., *Prevention of delinquent behavior.* Newbury Park, Calif.: Sage Publications, pp. 44–74.

178. Steffensmeier, D. J., & Steffensmeier, R. H. (1980). Trends in female delinquency: An examination of arrest, juvenile court, self-report, and field data. *Criminology, 18,* 62–85.

179. Stein, J. A.; Newcomb, M. D.; & Bentler, P. M. (1987). An 8-year study of multiple influences on drug use and drug consequences. *Journal of Personality and Social Psychology, 53,* 1094–1105.

180. Steinberg, L. (1987a). Impact of puberty on family relations: Effects of pubertal status and pubertal timing. *Developmental Psychology, 23,* 451–460.

181. Steinberg, L. (1987b). Single parents, stepparents, and the susceptibility of adolescents to antisocial peer pressure. *Child Development, 58,* 269–275.

182. Sutherland, E. H., & Cressey, D. R. (1974). *Criminology*. 9th ed. Philadelphia: Lippincott.
183. Taylor, R. B., & Gottfredson, S. (1986). Environmental design, crime, and prevention: An examination of community dynamics. In A. J. Reiss & M. Tonry, eds., *Communities and crime*. Vol. 8. Chicago: University of Chicago Press, pp. 387–416.
184. Teichman, M.; Barnea, Z.; & Ravav, G. (1989). Personality and substance use among adolescents: A longitudinal study. *British Journal of Addiction, 84,* 181–190.
185. Thomas, M. H.; Horton, R. W.; Lippincott, E. C.; & Drabman, R. S. (1977). Desensitization to portrayals of real-life aggression as a function of exposure to television violence. *Journal of Personality and Social Psychology, 35,* 450–458.
186. Thornberry, T.; Moore, M.; & Christenson, R. L. (1985). The effect of dropping out of high school on subsequent criminal behavior. *Criminology, 23,* 13–18.
187. Trasler, G. (1987). Some cautions for the biological approach to crime causation. In S. A. Mednick, T. E. Moffitt, & S. A. Stack, eds., *The causes of crime: New biological approaches*. Cambridge: Cambridge University Press, pp. 7–24.
188. Tremblay, R. E.; Larivée, S.; & Grégoire, J. C. (1985). The association between early adolescent boys' cognitive development, father attitudes, and nonverbal behavior. *Journal of Early Adolescence, 5,* 45–58.
189. Udry, J. R. (1988). Biological predispositions and social control in adolescent sexual behavior. *American Sociological Review, 53,* 709–722.
190. Udry, J. R., & Billy, J. O. G. (1987). Initiation of coitus in early adolescence. *American Sociological Review, 52,* 841–855.
191. Wadsworth, M. E. J. (1976). Delinquency, pulse rates, and early emotional deprivation. *British Journal of Criminology, 16,* 245–256.
192. Warren, M. Q. (1981). Gender comparisons in crime and delinquency. In M. Q. Warren, ed., *Comparing female and male offenders*. Beverly Hills: Sage Publications, pp. 73–88.
193. Weis, J. G. (1986). Issues in the measurement of criminal careers. *Criminal careers and career criminals*. Vol. 2. Washington, D.C.: National Academy Press, pp. 1–51.
194. Wells, L. E., & Rankin, J. H. (1983). Self-concept as a mediating factor in delinquency. *Social Psychology Quarterly, 46,* 11–22.
195. Werner, E. E., & Smith, R. S. (1977). *Kauai's children come of age*. Honolulu: University Press of Hawaii.
196. West, D. J. (1982). *Delinquency: Its roots, careers, and prospects*. Cambridge, Mass.: Harvard University Press.
197. West, D. J., & Farrington, D. P. (1977). *The delinquent way of life*. London: Heinemann.
198. Wilson, J. Q., & Herrnstein, R. J. (1985). *Crime and human nature*. New York: Simon and Schuster.
199. Wolfgang, M. E.; Figlio, R. M.; & Sellin, T. (1972). *Delinquency in a birth cohort*. Chicago: University of Chicago Press.
200. Zabin, L. S.; Hardy, J. B.; Smith, E. A.; & Hirsch, M. B. (1986). Substance

use and its relation to sexual activity among inner-city adolescents. *Journal of Adolescent Health Care, 7,* 320–331.

201. Zatz, M. S. (1987). The changing forms of racial/ethnic biases in sentencing. *Journal of Research in Crime and Delinquency, 21,* 69–89.

202. Zuckerman, M. (1978). Sensation seeking and psychopathy. In R. D. Hare & D. Schalling, eds., *Psychopathic behaviour.* Chichester: Wiley, pp. 165–185.

17. Adolescent Health

1. Bandura, A. (1977). *Social learning theory.* Englewood Cliffs, N.J.: Prentice-Hall.

2. Baumrind, D. (1986). A developmental perspective on adolescent risk-taking in contemporary America. Paper presented at the National Invitational Conference, Health Futures of Adolescents, Society for Adolescent Medicine, Daytona Beach, Fla.

3. Becker, M. H., ed. (1974). The health belief model and personal health behavior. *Health Education Monograph, 2,* 324–508.

4. Bell, T. A., & Holmes, K. K. (1984). Age-specific risks of syphilis, gonorrhea, and hospitalized pelvic inflammatory disease in sexually experienced U.S. women. *Sexually Transmitted Diseases, 11,* 291–295.

5. Benedict, V.; Lundeen, K. W.; & Morr, B. D. (1981). Self-assessment by adolescents of their health status and perceived health needs. *Health Values: Achieving High-Level Wellness, 5*(6), 239–245.

6. Berndt, T. J. (1979). Developmental changes in conformity to peers and parents. *Developmental Psychology, 15,* 608–616.

7. Bibace, R., & Walsh, M. (1980). Development of childrens' concepts of illness. *Pediatrics, 66,* 912–917.

8. Botvin, G. J., & Tortu, S. (1988). Preventing adolescent substance abuse through life skills training. In R. H. Price, E. L. Cowen, R. P. Lorion, & J. Ramos-McKay, eds., *14 Ounces of prevention.* Washington, D.C.: American Psychological Association.

9. Brooks-Gunn, J., & Furstenberg, F. F., Jr. (1989). Adolescent sexual behavior. *American Psychologist, 44*(2), 249–257.

10. Brown, J. D., & Siegel, J. M. (1988). Exercise as a buffer of life stress: A prospective study of adolescent health. *Health Psychology, 7*(4), 341–353.

11. Browne, A., & Finkelhor, D. (1986). Initial and long-term effect: A review of the research. In D. Finkelhor, S. Anaj, L. Baron, et al., eds., *A source book on child sexual abuse.* Beverly Hills: Sage Publications.

12. Brunswick, A. F. (1969). Health needs of adolescence: How the adolescent sees them. *American Journal of Public Health, 59,* 1730–45.

13. Burbach, D. J., & Peterson, L. (1986). Children's concepts of physical illness: A review and critique of the cognitive-developmental literature. *Health Psychology, 5,* 307–325.

14. Campbell, J. D. (1975). Illness is a point of view: The development of children's concepts of illness. *Child Development, 46,* 92–100.

15. Centers for Disease Control (1982). Accidental injury in the United States. *Morbidity and Mortality Weekly Reports, 31,* 110–111.

16. Centers for Disease Control (1983a). Patterns of alcohol use among teenage drivers in fatal motor vehicle accidents: United States, 1977–1981. *Morbidity and Mortality Weekly Reports, 32,* 344–347.
17. Centers for Disease Control (1983b). Alcohol as a risk factor for injuries: United States. *Morbidity and Mortality Weekly Reports, 32,* 61–62.
18. Centers for Disease Control (1984). Temporal patterns of motor-vehicle related fatalities associated with young drinking drivers: United States, 1983. *Morbidity and Mortality Weekly Reports, 33,* 699–701.
19. Centers for Disease Control (1985). Homicide among young black males: United States, 1970–1982. *Morbidity and Mortality Weekly Reports, 34,* 629–633.
20. Centers for Disease Control (1988). HIV-related beliefs, knowledge, and behaviors among high school students. *Morbidity and Mortality Weekly Reports, 37,* 717–721.
21. *Chartbook on adolescent health* (forthcoming). Rockville, Md.: Public Health Service, Health Resources and Services Administration, Bureau of Health Care Delivery and Assistance, Division of Maternal and Child Health.
22. Children's Defense Fund (1986). *Building health programs for teenagers.* Washington, D.C.
23. Cohen, M. I. (1980). Importance, implementation, and impact of the adolescent medicine components of the Task Force on Pediatric Education. *Journal of Adolescent Health Care, 1,* 1–8.
24. Covington, M. V. (1981). Strategies for smoking prevention and resistance among young adolescents. *Journal of Early Adolescence, 1,* 349–356.
25. Cypress, B. K. (1984). *Health care of adolescents by office-based physicians: National Ambulatory Care Survey, 1980–81.* DHHS, advance data, NCHS Publication no. 99. Washington, D.C.: U.S. Government Printing Office, pp. 1–8.
26. DiClemente, R. J.; Boyer, C. B.; & Morales, E. S. (1988). Minorities and AIDS: Knowledge, attitudes, and misconceptions among black and Latino adolescents. *American Journal of Public Health, 78,* 55–57.
27. Donovan, J. E.; Jessor, R.; & Costa, F. M. (forthcoming). Adolescent health behavior and conventionality-unconventionality: An extension of problem behavior theory. *Health Psychology.*
28. Dryfoos, J. G., & Klerman, L. V. (in press). School-based clinics: Their role in helping students meet the 1990 objectives. *Health Education Quarterly.*
29. Eisen, M.; Zellman, G. L.; & McAlister, A. L. (1985). A health belief model approach to adolescents' fertility control: Some pilot program findings. *Health Education Quarterly, 12*(2), 185–210.
30. Eiser, C. (1985). *The psychology of childhood illness.* New York: Springer Verlag.
31. Eiser, C.; Patterson, D.; & Eiser, J. R. (1983). Children's knowledge of health and illness: Implications for health education. *Child Care, Health, and Development, 9,* 285–292.
32. English, A. (1988). Health care for children and adolescents. *Youth Law News, 9,* 16–22.
33. Evans, R. I. (1976). Smoking in children: Developing a social psychological strategy for deterrence. *Preventive Medicine, 5,* 122–127.
34. Fishbein, M., & Ajzen, I. (1975). *Beliefs, attitudes, intention, and behavior: An introduction to theory and research.* Reading, Mass.: Addison-Wesley.

35. Flay, B. R. (1985). Psychosocial approaches to smoking prevention: A review of findings. *Health Psychology, 4*(5), 449–488.
36. Flora, J. A., & Thoresen, C. E. (1988). Reducing the risk of AIDS in adolescents. *American Psychologist, 43*(11), 965–970.
37. Forrest, J. D., & Silverman, J. (1989). What public school teachers teach about preventing pregnancy, AIDS, and sexually transmitted diseases. *Family Planning Perspectives, 21*(2), 65–72.
38. Friedman, I. (1985). Alcohol and youthful unnatural deaths. *Pediatrics, 76*, 191–193.
39. Friedman, I. M., & Litt, I. F. (1987). Adolescents' compliance with therapeutic regimens: Psychological and social aspects and intervention. *Journal of Adolescent Health Care, 85*, 2–67.
40. Glynn, K.; Leventhal, H.; & Hirschman, R. (1985). A cognitive developmental approach to smoking prevention. In C. S. Bell & R. Battjes, eds., *Prevention research: Deterring drug abuse among children and adolescents.* Washington, D.C.: Division of Clinical Research, National Institute on Drug Abuse.
41. Gochman, D. S. (1985). Family determinants of children's concepts of health and illness. In D. C. Turk & R. D. Kerns, eds., *Health, illness, and families: A life-span perspective.* New York: John Wiley & Sons.
42. Greeley, J. R., & Mechanic, D. (1976). Social selection in seeking help for psychological problems. *Journal of Health and Social Behavior, 17*, 249–262.
43. Hamburg, B. A., & Hamburg, D. A. (1975). Stressful transitions of adolescence: Endocrine and psychosocial aspects. In L. Levi, ed., *Society, stress, and disease.* Vol. 2. *Childhood and adolescence.* London: Oxford University Press.
44. Hamburg, D. A.; Elliott, G. R.; & Parron, D. L. (1982). Changes in human societies, families, social supports, and health. In D. A. Hamburg, G. R. Elliott, & D. L. Parron, eds., *Health and behavior: Frontiers of research in the biobehavioral sciences.* Washington, D.C.: National Academy Press.
45. Hamburg, D. A.; Mortimer, A. M.; & Nightingale, E. O. (forthcoming). The role of social support and social networks in improving the health of adolescents. In W. Hendee, ed., *The health of adolescents.* Chicago: American Medical Association.
46. Hawkins, J. D.; Lishner, D. M.; & Catalano, R. F. (1985). Childhood predictors and the prevention of adolescent substance abuse. In C. L. Jones & R. J. Battjes, eds., *Etiology of drug abuse: Implications for prevention.* NIDA Research Monograph no. 56, DHHS Publication no. ADM 85-1335. Washington, D.C.: U.S. Government Printing Office.
47. Hayes, C. D., ed. (1987). *Risking the future: Adolescent sexuality, pregnancy, and childbearing.* Vol. 1. National Research Council. Washington, D.C.: National Academy Press.
48. Herzog, D. M., & Copeland, P. M. (1985). Eating disorders. *New England Journal of Medicine, 313*, 295.
49. Hofferth, S. L., & Hayes, C. D., eds. (1987). *Risking the future: Adolescent sexuality, pregnancy, and childbearing.* Vol. 2. National Research Council. Washington, D.C.: National Academy Press.

50. House, J. S.; Landis, K. R.; & Umberson, D. (1988). Social relationships and health. *Science, 241,* 540–545.
51. Hulka, B. S. (1979). Patient-clinician interactions and compliance. In R. B. Haynes, D. W. Taylor, & D. L. Sackett, eds., *Compliance in health care.* Baltimore: Johns Hopkins University Press.
52. Institute of Medicine, Division of Mental Health and Behavioral Medicine (1989). *Research on children and adolescents with mental, behavioral, and developmental disorders: Mobilizing a national initiative.* Washington, D.C.: National Academy Press.
53. Insurance Institute for Highway Safety (1984). *Status report, 19*(7), 1–11.
54. Irwin, C. E. (1986). Why adolescent medicine? *Journal of Adolescent Health Care, 7,* 2S–12S.
55. Irwin, C. E., & Millstein, S. G. (1982). Emerging patterns of tampon use in the adolescent female: The impact of toxic shock syndrome. *American Journal of Public Health, 72*(5), 464–467.
56. Irwin, C. E., & Millstein, S. G. (1987). Biopsychosocial correlates of risk-taking behaviors during adolescence. *Journal of Adolescent Health Care, 7,* 82S–93S.
57. Irwin, C. E., & Vaughan, E. (1987). Emerging national issues and trends in adolescent health. Paper presented at Region 9, Regional Institute, High Priority Issues in Maternal and Child Health.
58. Janz, N. K., & Becker, M. H. (1984). The health belief model: A decade later. *Health Education Quarterly, 11*(1), 1–47.
59. Jay, M. S.; DuRant, R. H.; Litt, I. F.; et al. (1984). Effect of peer counselors on adolescent compliance with use of oral contraceptives. *Pediatrics, 73,* 126–131.
60. Jessor, R. (1982). Critical issues in research on adolescent health promotion. In T. Coates, A. Petersen, & C. Perry, eds., *Promoting adolescent health: A dialogue on research and practice.* New York: Academic Press, pp. 447–465.
61. Johnston, L. D.; Bachman, J. G.; & O'Malley, P. M. (1988). *Drug use, drinking, and smoking: National survey results from high school, college, and young adult populations.* Press release. Washington, D.C.: National Institute on Drug Abuse.
62. Johnston, L. D.; O'Malley, P. M.; & Bachman, J. G. (1987). *National trends in drug use and related factors among American high school students and young adults.* Washington, D.C.: National Institute on Drug Abuse.
63. Jonah, B. (1985). Adolescent risk and risk-taking behavior among young drivers: Relevant research. In *Proceedings of a conference on adolescent risk-taking behaviors.* Vancouver, British Columbia: University of British Columbia, Department of Pediatrics, pp. 26–38.
64. Jones, M. C. (1965). Psychosocial correlates of somatic development. *Child Development, 36,* 899–911.
65. Jones, M. C., & Mussen, P. H. (1958). Self-conceptions, motivations, and interpersonal attitudes of early- and late-maturing girls. *Child Development, 29,* 491–501.

66. Jones, R. B., & Moberg, P. (1988). Correlates of smokeless tobacco use in a male adolescent population. *American Journal of Public Health, 78,* 61–63.

67. Kahneman, D., & Tversky, A. (1972). Subjective probability: A judgment of representativeness. *Cognitive Psychology, 3,* 430–454.

68. Kamler, J.; Irwin, C. E.; Stone, G. C.; & Millstein, S. G. (1987). Optimistic bias in adolescent hemophiliacs. Paper presented at the annual meeting of the Society for Pediatric Research, May, Anaheim.

69. Kaplan, K. M., & Wadden, T. A. (1986). Childhood obesity and self-esteem. *Journal of Pediatrics, 109,* 367–370.

70. Kellerman, J.; Zeltzer, L.; & Ellenberg, L. (1980). Psychologic effects of illness in adolescence. Pt. 2: Impact of illness in adolescents: Crucial issues and coping styles. *Journal of Pediatrics, 97,* 126–131.

71. Kestenberg, J. (1967a). Phases of adolescence with suggestions for a correlation of psychic and hormonal organization. Pt. 1: Antecedents of adolescent organizations in childhood. *Journal of the American Academy of Child Psychiatry, 6,* 426–463.

72. Kestenberg, J. (1967b). Phases of adolescence with suggestions for a correlation of psychic and hormonal organizations. Pt. 2: Prepuberty, diffusion, and reintegration. *Journal of the American Academy of Child Psychiatry, 6,* 426–463.

73. Kirscht, J. P. (1983). Preventive health behavior: A review of research and issues. *Health Psychology, 2*(3), 277–301.

74. Klerman, L. V., & Stack, M. R. (1986). Problems in the organization of health services for adolescents. Paper presented at the National Invitational Conference, Health Futures of Adolescents, Society for Adolescent Medicine, April, Daytona Beach, Fla.

75. Koos, E. L. (1954). *The health of Regionville, New York.* New York: Columbia University Press.

76. Korsch, B. M.; Fine, R. N.; & Negrete, V. F. (1978). Noncompliance in children with renal transplants. *Pediatrics, 61,* 872–876.

77. Kovar, M. G., & Dawson, D. (1988). In H. M. Wallace et al., eds., *Maternal and child health practices.* Oakland: Third Party Publishing Company.

78. Lau, R. R., & Hartman, K. A. (1983). Common sense representations of common illnesses. *Health Psychology, 2*(2), 167–185.

79. Levenson, P. M.; Morrow, J. R.; Gregory, E. K.; & Pfefferbaum, B. J. (1984). Attitudes toward health and illness: A comparison of adolescent, physician, teacher, and school nurse views. *Journal of Adolescent Health Care, 5,* 254–260.

80. Levenson, P. M.; Morrow, J. R.; & Morgan, W. C. (1986). Health information sources and preferences as perceived by adolescents, pediatricians, teachers, and school nurses. *Journal of Early Adolescence, 6*(2), 183–195.

81. Leventhal, H., & Cleary, P. D. (1980). The smoking problem: A review of the research and theory in behavioral risk modification. *Psychological Bulletin, 88* (2), 370–405.

82. Leventhal, H., & Nerenz, D. (1982). Representations on threat and the control of stress. In D. Meichenbaum & M. Jaremko, eds., *Stress prevention and management: A cognitive behavioral approach.* New York: Plenum.

83. Litt, I. F. (1986). Amenorrhea in the adolescent athlete. *Postgraduate Medicine, 80,* 245–253.

84. Litt, I. F. (1987). Special problems during adolescence. In R. Behrman & V. C. Vaughan III, eds., *Nelson textbook of pediatrics.* 13th ed. Philadelphia: W. B. Saunders.

85. Litt, I. F. (forthcoming). Compliance with pediatric medication regimens. In S. J. Yaffe, ed., *Pediatric pharmacology: Therapeutic principles in practice.* Rev. ed. Philadelphia: Grune and Stratton.

86. Litt, I. F.; Cuskey, W. R.; & Rosenberg, A. (1982). The role of self-esteem and autonomy in determining medication compliance among adolescents with juvenile rheumatoid arthritis. *Pediatrics, 69,* 15–17.

87. Litt, I. F., & Cuskey, W. R. (1984). Satisfaction with health care: A predictor of adolescents' appointment-keeping. *Journal of Adolescent Health Care, 5,* 196–200.

88. Marks, A.; Malizio, J.; Hoch, J.; Brody, R.; & Fisher, M. (1983). Assessment of health needs and willingness to utilize health care resources of adolescents in a suburban population. *Journal of Pediatrics, 102*(3), 456–460.

89. Massie, M. E., & Johnson, S. M. (1989). The importance of recognizing a history of sexual abuse in female adolescents. *Journal of adolescent health care, 10,* 184–191.

90. Matthews, K. A.; Siegel, J. M.; Kuller, L. H.; Thompson, M.; & Varat, M. (1983). Determinants of decisions to seek medical treatment by patients with acute myocardial infarction symptoms. *Journal of Personality and Social Psychology, 44*(6), 1144–56.

91. Mayhew, D., & Simpson, H. H. (1982). Age, alcohol, and fatal crash risk. Paper presented at the Nineteenth annual meeting of the Traffic Injury Research Foundation of Canada, Toronto.

92. McGuire, W. J. (1969). The nature of attitude and attitude change. In G. Lindzay & E. Aronson, eds., *Handbook of social psychology.* 2nd ed. Vol. 3. Reading, Mass.: Addison-Wesley.

93. Mechanic, D. (1980). The experience and reporting of common physical complaints. *Journal of Health and Social Behavior, 21,* 146–155.

94. Mechanic, D. (1983). Adolescent health and illness behavior: Review of the literature and a new hypothesis for the study of stress. *Journal of Human Stress, 9,* 4–13.

95. Mellin, L. (1983). *Shapedown.* Weight Management Programs for Adolescents. San Francisco: Balboa Publishing Company.

96. Melton, G. B. (1988). Adolescents and prevention of AIDS. *American Psychologist, 19*(3), 403–408.

97. Millstein, S. G. (1988). *The potential of school-linked centers to promote adolescent health and development.* Washington, D.C.: Carnegie Council on Adolescent Development.

98. Millstein, S. G.; Adler, N. E.; & Irwin, C. E. (1981). Conceptions of illness in young adolescents. *Pediatrics, 68,* 834–839.

99. Millstein, S. G., & Irwin, C. E. (1985). Adolescent assessment of behavioral risk: Sex differences and maturation effects. *Pediatric Research, 19,* 112A.

100. Millstein, S. G., & Irwin, C. E. (1986). Health-protective and health-risk behaviors in adolescents. Unpublished manuscript.

101. Millstein, S. G., & Irwin, C. E. (1987). Concepts of health and illness: Different constructs or variations on a theme? *Health Psychology, 6*(6), 515–524.

102. Millstein, S. G., & Irwin, C. E. (1988). Accident-related behaviors in adolescents: A biopsychosocial view. *Alcohol, Drugs, and Driving, 4*(1), 21–29.

103. Millstein, S. G; Irwin, C. E.; & Brindis, C. (forthcoming). Sociodemographic trends and projections in the adolescent population. In W. Hendee, ed., *The health of adolescents*. Chicago: American Medical Association.

104. Morrison, D. M. (1985). Adolescent contraceptive behavior: A review. *Psychological Bulletin, 98*(3), 538–568.

105. Moscowitz, H. (1985). Marijuana and driving. *Accident Analysis and Prevention, 17,* 323–345.

106. Mussen, P. H., & Jones, M. C. (1957). Self-conceptions, motivations, and interpersonal attitudes of early- and late-maturing boys. *Child Development, 28,* 243–256.

107. Natapoff, J. N. (1978). Children's views of health: A developmental study. *American Journal of Public Health, 68*(10), 995–1000.

108. National Adolescent Student Health Survey (1988). *National survey reveals teen behavior, knowledge, and attitudes on health, sex topics.* Press release. Reston, Va.

109. National Center for Health Statistics (1981). *Vital and health statistics: Current estimates.* From the National Health Interview Survey, DHHS Publication no. 82-1567. Hyattsville, Md.

110. National Center for Health Statistics (1984). *Health, United States.* DHHS Publication no. PHS 85-1232. Washington, D.C.: U.S. Government Printing Office.

111. National Institutes on Allergies and Infectious Disease Study Group (1980). *Sexually transmitted diseases: Summary and recommendations.* Bethesda, Md.: National Institutes of Health.

112. Neel, E. U.; Jay, M. S.; & Litt, I. F. (1985). The relationship of self-concept and autonomy to oral contraceptive compliance among adolescents. *Journal of Adolescent Health Care, 6,* 445–447.

113. Newacheck, P. W., & McManus, M. A. (in press). Health insurance status of adolescents in the United States. *Pediatrics.*

114. Noack, H. (1987). Concepts of health and health promotion. In T. Abelin, Z. J. Brzezinski, & V. D. L. Carstairs, eds., *Measurement in health promotion and protection.* European Series no. 22. Copenhagen: WHO Regional Office for Europe.

115. Office of Technology Assessment (1988). *How effective is AIDS education?* Staff Paper no. 3. Washington, D.C.: Health Program, Office of Technology Assessment, U.S. Congress.

116. Orlandi, M. A. (1986). Community-based substance abuse prevention: A multicultural perspective. *Journal of School Health, 56*(9), 394–401.

117. Palla, B., & Litt, I. F. (1988). Medical complications of eating disorders in adolescents. *Pediatrics, 81,* 613–623.

118. Pantell, R. H., & Goodman, B. W. (1983). Adolescent chest pain: A perspective study. *Pediatrics, 71,* 881–887.

119. Parcel, G. S.; Nader, P. R.; & Meyer, M. P. (1972). Adolescent health concerns, problems, and patterns of utilization in a triethnic urban population. *Pediatrics, 60,* 157–164.
120. Peck, E. B., & Ullrich, H. D. (1985). *Children and weight: A changing perspective.* Berkeley: Nutrition Communications Associated.
121. Perrin, E., & Gerrity, P. S. (1981). There's a demon in your belly: Children's understanding of illness. *pediatrics, 67,* 841–849.
122. Pipkin, N. L.; Walker, L. G.; & Thomsason, M. H. (1989). Alcohol and vehicular injuries in adolescents. *Journal of Adolescent Health Care, 10,* 119–121.
123. Poissonet, C. M.; La Valle, M.; & Burdi, A. R. (1988). Growth and development of adipose tissue. *Journal of Pediatrics, 113,* 1–9.
124. Price, J. H.; Desmond, S. M.; Wallace, M.; Smith, D.; & Stewart, P. M. (1988). *Journal of School Health, 58*(2), 66–70.
125. Puig-Antich, J., & Rabinovich, H. (1983). Major child and adolescent psychiatric disorders. In M. D. Levine, W. B. Cavey, A. C. Crocker, et al., eds., *Developmental-behavioral pediatrics.* Philadelphia: W. B. Saunders.
126. Radius, S. M.; Dillman, T. E.; Becker, M. H.; Rosenstock, I. M.; & Horvath, W. J. (1980). Adolescent perspectives on health and illness. *Adolescence, 15,* 375–384.
127. Rowland, T. W.; Black, S. A.; & Kelleher, J. K. (1987). Iron deficiency in adolescent endurance athletes. *Journal of Adolescent Health Care, 8,* 322–326.
128. Rutter, M. (forthcoming). Psychosocial resilience and protective mechanism. In J. Rolf, A. Masten, D. Cicchetti, K. Nuechterlein, & S. Weintraub, eds., *Risk and protective factors in the development of psychopathology.* New York: Cambridge University Press.
129. Sallade, J. (1973). A comparison of the psychological adjustment of obese vs. nonobese children. *Journal of Psychosomatic Research, 17,* 89–96.
130. Schinke, S. P. (1984). Preventing teenage pregnancy. In M. Hensen, R. M. Eisler, & P. M. Miller, eds., *Progress in behavior modification.* Vol. 16. New York: Academic Press.
131. Select Panel for the Promotion of Child Health (1981a). *Better health for children: A national strategy.* DHHS Publication no. 79-55071. Vol. 2. Washington, D.C.: U.S. Government Printing Office.
132. Select Panel for the Promotion of Child Health (1981b). *Better health for children: A national strategy.* DHHS Publication no. 79-55071. Vol. 3. Washington, D.C.: U.S. Government Printing Office.
133. Shafer, M. A.; Blain, B.; Beck, A.; Dole, P.; Irwin, C. E.; Sweet, R.; & Schachter, S. (1984). Chlamydia trachomatis: Important relationships to race, contraceptive use, lower genital tract infection, and Papanicolaou smears. *Journal of Pediatrics, 104,* 141–146.
134. Shaffer, D.; Philips, I.; Garland, A.; & Bacon, K. (1988). Prevention issues in youth suicide. Paper prepared for Project Prevention, American Academy of Child and Adolescent Psychiatry.
135. Shute, R.; Pierre, R.; & Lubell, E. (1981). Smoking awareness and practices of urban preschool and first-grade children. *Journal of School Health, 5,* 347–351.
136. Silbereisen, R. K., & Noack, P. (1988). On the constructive role of problem behavior in adolescence. In N. Bolger, A. Caspi, G. Downey, & M. Moore-

house, eds., *Person and context: Developmental processes*. Cambridge: Cambridge University Press.

137. Slinkard, L.; Shalwitz, J.; Adler, N. E.; & Irwin, C. E. (1982). *Physician attributes preferred by adolescents*. New York: Society for Adolescent Medicine.

138. Smith, S. D., et al. (1979). A reliable method for evaluating drug compliance in children with cancer. *Cancer, 43*, 169–173.

139. Sternlieb, J. J., & Munan, L. (1972). A survey of health problems, practices, and needs of youth. *Pediatrics, 49*(2), 177–186.

140. Stiffman, A. R.; Earls, F.; Robins, L. N.; & Jung, K. G. (1988). Problems and help seeking in high-risk adolescent patients of health clinics. *Journal of Adolescent Health Care, 9*, 305–309.

141. Strobino, D. M. (1987). Consequences of early sexual and fertility behavior. In National Research Council, *Risking the future: Adolescent sexuality, pregnancy, and childbearing*. Vol. 2. Washington, D.C.: National Academy Press.

142. Susman, E. J.; Nottelman, E. D.; & Dorn, L. D. (forthcoming). The physiology of stress and behavioral development. In D. S. Palerno, ed., *Coping with uncertainty: Biological, behavioral, and developmental perspectives*. Hillsdale, N.J.: Erlbaum.

143. Thompson, E. L. (1978). Smoking reduction programs, 1960–1976. *American Journal of Public Health, 68*, 250–255.

144. Tversky, A., & Kahneman, D. (1973). Availability: A heuristic for judging frequency and probability. *Cognitive Psychology, 5*, 207–232.

145. Tversky, A., & Kahneman, D. (1974). Judgment under uncertainty: Heuristics and biases. *Science, 185*, 1124–31.

146. Violato, C., & Holden, W. B. (1988). A confirmatory factor analysis of a four-factor model of adolescent concerns. *Journal of Youth and Adolescence, 17*(1), 101–113.

147. Wallston, B. S.; Alagna, S. W.; DeVellis, B. M.; & DeVellis, R. F. (1983). Social support and physical health. *Health Psychology, 2*(4), 367–391.

148. Weinstein, N. D. (1984). Why it won't happen to me: Perceptions of risk factors and susceptibility. *Health Psychology, 3*(5), 431–458.

149. Weisenberg, M.; Kegeles, S. S.; & Lund, A. K. (1980). Children's health beliefs and acceptance of a dental preventive activity. *Journal of Health and Social Behavior, 21* (March), 59–74.

150. Wetzel, J. (1987). *American youth: A statistical snapshot*. Washington, D.C.: William T. Grant Foundation Commission on Work, Family, and Citizenship.

151. Zborowski, M. (1952). Cultural components in response to pain. *Journal of Social Issues, 8*, 16–30.

152. Zelnick, M., & Kantner, J. F. (1977). Sexual and contraceptive experience of young unmarried women in the United States: 1976 and 1971. *Family Planning Perspectives, 9*, 55–71.

153. Zelnick, M., & Shah, F. K. (1983). First intercourse among young Americans. *Family Planning Perspectives, 15*, 64–72.

154. Zeltzer, L.; Ellenberger, L.; & Rigler, D. (1980). Psychological effects of illness in adolescents. Pt. 2: Illness in adolescents: Crucial issues and coping styles. *Journal of Pediatrics, 97*, 132–137.

155. Zola, I. K. (1966). Culture and symptoms: An analysis of patients' presenting complaints. *American Sociological Review, 31,* 615–630.

18. Youth in Relation to Social Institutions

1. Abramson, P. (1977). *The political socialization of black Americans.* New York: Free Press.
2. Abramson, P. (1983). *Political attitudes in America.* San Francisco: Freeman.
3. Adelson, J.; Green, B.; & O'Neil, R. (1969). Growth of the idea of law in adolescence. *Developmental Psychology, 1,* 327–332.
4. Adelson, J., & O'Neil, R. (1966). Growth of political ideas in adolescence: The sense of community. *Journal of Personality and Social Psychology, 4,* 295–306.
5. Alva, S. (1985). The political acculturation of Mexican-American adolescents. *Hispanic Journal of Behavioral Science, 7,* 345–364.
6. Alwin, D. (1988). From obedience to autonomy: Changes in traits desired in children, 1924–1978. *Public Opinion Quarterly, 52,* 33–52.
7. Armento, B. (1986). Research on teaching social studies. In M. Wittrock, ed., *Handbook of research on teaching.* New York: Macmillan, pp. 942–951.
8. Astin, A.; Green, K.; & Korn, W. (1987). *The American freshman: Twenty-year trends, 1966–1985.* Los Angeles: University of California, Graduate School of Education.
9. Atkin, C. K. (1981). Communication and political socialization. In D. Nimmo & K. Sanders, eds., *Handbook of political communication.* Beverly Hills: Sage Publications, pp. 299–328.
10. Atkin, C., & Garramone, G. (1984). The role of foreign news coverage in adolescent political socialization. *Communication, 10,* 43–61.
11. Bachman, J.; Johnston, L.; & O'Malley, P. (1980). *Monitoring the future: Questionnaire response from the nation's high school seniors, 1976.* Ann Arbor: Institute for Survey Research.
12. Bachman, J.; Johnston, L; & O'Malley, P. (1987). *Monitoring the future: Questionnaire response from the nation's high school seniors, 1986* Ann Arbor: Institute for Survey Research.
13. Benson, P.; Williams, D.; & Johnson, A. (1987). *The quicksilver years.* New York: Harper and Row.
14. Berti, A., & Bombi, A. (1988). *The child's construction of economics.* Cambridge: Cambridge University Press.
15. Blasi, A., & Hoeffel, E. (1974). Adolescence and formal operations. *Human Development, 17,* 344–363.
16. Bredemeier, B. J., & Shields, D. (1987). Game reasoning and interactional morality. *Journal of Genetic Psychology, 147,* 257–272.
17. Brian-Meisels, S., & Selman, R. (1984). Early adolescent development of new interpersonal strategies. *School Psychology Review, 13,* 278–291.
18. Button, C. (1974). Political education for minority groups. In R. Niemi, ed., *The politics of future citizens.* San Francisco: Jossey-Bass, pp. 167–198.
19. Campbell, B. (1980). A theoretical approach to peer influence in adolescent socialization. *American Journal of Political Science, 24,* 324–344.

20. Carlson, J. (1985). *Prime time law enforcement: Crime show viewing and attitudes toward the criminal justice system.* New York: Praeger.
21. Carlson, J., & Iovini, J. (1985). The transmission of racial attitudes from fathers to sons: A study of blacks and whites. *Adolescence, 77,* 233–237.
22. Chafee, S., & Yang, S. (1990). Communication and political socialization. In O. Ichilov, ed., *Political socialization, citizenship and democracy.* New York: Teachers College Press.
23. Coles, R. (1986). *The political life of children.* Boston: Houghton Mifflin.
24. Connell, R. (1971). *The child's construction of politics.* Carleton, Virginia: Melbourne University Press.
25. Conrad, D., & Hedin, D. (1982). *Experiential education evaluation project.* St. Paul: University of Minnesota Press.
26. Cook, T. E. (1985). The bear market in political socialization. *American Political Science Review, 79,* 1079–91.
27. Davies, L. (1984). *Pupil power: Deviance and gender in school.* London: Falmer Press.
28. Ehman, L. (1980). The American school in the political socialization process. *Review of Educational Research, 50,* 99–119.
29. Enright, R.; Lapsley, D.; & Levy, V. (1983). Moral education strategies. In M. Pressley & J. Levin, eds., *Cognitive strategy research.* New York: Springer Verlag.
30. Enright, R.; Olson, L.; Ganiere, D.; Lapsley, D. K.; & Buss, R. (1984). A clinical model for enhancing adolescent identity. *Journal of Adolescence, 7,* 119–130.
31. Feather, N. (1980). Values in adolescence. In J. Adelson, ed., *Handbook of adolescent psychology.* New York: Wiley, pp. 247–294.
32. Furth, H. (1980). *The world of grown-ups.* New York: Elsevier-North Holland.
33. Gallatin, J. (1976). The conceptualization of rights: Psychological development and cross-national perspectives. In R. Claude, ed., *Comparative human rights.* Baltimore: Johns Hopkins University Press, pp. 302–325.
34. Gallatin, J. (1980). Political thinking in adolescence. In J. Adelson, ed., *Handbook of adolescent psychology.* New York: Wiley, pp. 344–382.
35. Garramone, G., & Atkin, C. (1986). Mass communication and political socialization: Specifying the effects. *Public Opinion Quarterly, 50,* 76–86.
36. Gelman, R., & Baillargeon, R. (1983). A review of some Piagetian concepts. In J. Flavell & E. Markman, eds., *Handbook of child psychology.* Vol. 3. P. Mussen, general ed. New York: Wiley, pp. 167–230.
37. Gibson, M. (1988). *Accommodation without assimilation: Sikh immigrants in an American high school.* Ithaca: Cornell University Press.
38. Gilligan, C. (1982). *In a different voice.* Cambridge, Mass.: Harvard University Press.
39. Grant Foundation Commission (1988). *Pathways to success for America's youth and young families.* Washington, D.C.: W. T. Grant Foundation.
40. Greenberger, E., & Steinberg, L. (1986). *When teenagers work: The psychological and social costs of adolescent employment.* New York: Basic Books.
41. Hamilton, S. (1988). The impact of volunteer experience on adolescent social

development: Evidence of program effects. *Journal of Adolescent Research, 3,* 65–80.

42. Hess, R. D., & Torney, J. V. (1967). *The development of political attitudes in children.* Chicago: Aldine.
43. Higgins, A. (1980). Research and measurement issues in moral education interventions. In R. L. Mosher, ed., *Moral education: A first generation of research and development.* New York: Praeger.
44. Hilles, W. S., & Kahle, L. (1985). Social contract and social integration in adolescent development. *Journal of Personality and Social Psychology, 49,* 1114–21.
45. Ianni, F. (1989). *Search for structure: A report on American youth today.* New York: Macmillan.
46. Jahoda, G. (1984). Levels of social and logicomathematical thinking: Their nature and interrelations. In W. Doise & W. Palamonari, eds., *Social interaction in individual development.* New York: Cambridge University Press, pp. 173–187.
47. Jankowski, M. S. (1986). *City bound: Urban life and political attitudes among Chicano youth.* Albuquerque: University of New Mexico Press.
48. Jennings, M. K. (1987). Residues of the movement: The aging of the American protest generation. *American Political Science Review, 81,* 367–382.
49. Jennings, M. K., & Niemi, R. (1971). *The political character of adolescence.* Princeton: Princeton University Press.
50. Jennings, M. K., & Niemi, R. (1981). *Generations and politics.* Princeton: Princeton University Press.
51. Kohlberg, L. (1969). Stage and sequence: The cognitive-developmental approach to moral education. In D. Goslin, ed., *Handbook of socialization theory and research.* Chicago: Rand-McNally.
52. Lamare, J. (1974). Language environment and political socialization of Mexican-American children. In R. Niemi, ed., *The politics of future citizens.* San Francisco: Jossey-Bass, pp. 63–72.
53. Larkin, R. (1979). *Suburban youth in cultural crisis.* New York: Oxford University Press.
54. Leadbetter, B. (1989). Relational processes in adolescent and adult dialogues: Assessing the intersubjective context of conversation. *Human Development, 31,* 313–326.
55. Leming, J. (1985). Kohlbergian programmes in moral education: A practical review and an assessment. In S. Modgil & C. Modgil, eds., *Lawrence Kohlberg: Consensus and controversy.* Philadelphia: Falmer Press, pp. 245–262.
56. Liebschutz, S., & Niemi, R. (1974). Political attitudes among black children. In R. Niemi, eds., *The politics of future citizens.* San Francisco: Jossey-Bass, pp. 83–102.
57. Long, S. (1983). Psychopolitical orientations of white and black youth. *Journal of Black Studies, 13,* 439–457.
58. Lonsky, E. (1983). Logical concept prerequisites to political development in adolescents. *Psychological Reports, 53,* 947–954.
59. McNeil, L. (1986). *Contradictions of control.* New York: Routledge & Kegan Paul.

60. Moore, S.; Lare, J.; & Wagner, K. (1985). *The child's political world: A longitudinal perspective.* New York: Praeger.

61. Moskos, C. (1988). *A call to civic service: National service for country and community.* New York: Free Press.

62. Nedwek, B. (1987). Political socialization and policy evaluation: The case of youth employment and training programs. *Evaluation and Program Planning, 10,* 35–42.

63. Newmann, F. (1981). Reducing student alienation in high schools: Implications of theory. *Harvard Educational Review, 51,* 546–564.

64. Newmann, F. (1988). The curriculum of thoughtful classes. Paper presented at the American Educational Research Association, New Orleans.

65. Newmann, F., & Rutter, R. (1983). *The effects of high school community service programs on students' social development.* Madison: Wisconsin Center for Education Research.

66. Ogbu, J. (1987). Variability in responses to schooling: Nonimmigrants vs. immigrants. In G. Spindler & L. Spindler, eds., *Interpretive ethnography of education.* Hillsdale, N.J.: Erlbaum, pp. 225–280.

67. Perlmutter, R., & Shapiro, E. (1987). Morals and values in adolescence. In V. Van Hasselt & M. Heisen eds., *Handbook of adolescent psychology.* New York: Pergamon, pp. 184–204.

68. Pitts, J. (1975–76). Self-direction and the political socialization of black youth. *Social Science Quarterly, 56,* 93–104.

69. Power, F. C.; Higgins, A.; & Kohlberg, L. (1989). *Lawrence Kohlberg's approach to moral education.* New York: Columbia University Press.

70. Ravitch, D., & Finn, C. (1987). *What do our 17-year-olds know?* New York: Harper & Row.

71. Rest, J. (1983). Morality. In J. H. Flavell & E. Markman, eds., *Handbook of child psychology.* Vol. 3. New York: Wiley, pp. 556–629.

72. Selman, R. L.; Beardslee, W.; Schultz, L. H.; Krupa, M.; & Podorefsky, D. (1986). Assessing adolescent interpersonal negotiation strategies: Toward the integration of structural and functional models. *Developmental Psychology, 22,* 450–459.

73. Sigel, R., & Hoskin, M. (1981). *The political involvement of adolescents.* New Brunswick, N.J.: Rutgers University Press.

74. Steinitz, V., & Solomon, E. (1986). *Starting out: Class and community in the lives of working-class youth.* Philadelphia: Temple University Press.

75. Stevens, O. (1982). *Children talking politics.* Oxford: Martin Robertson.

76. Sullivan, E. (1985). Kohlberg's stage theory as a progressive educational form for value development. In S. Modgil & C. Modgil, eds., *Lawrence Kohlberg: Consensus and controversy.* Philadelphia: Falmer Press, pp. 233–244.

77. Tapp, J., & Kohlberg, L. (1977). Developing senses of law and legal justice. In J. Tapp & F. Levine, eds., *Law, justice, and the individual in society.* New York: Holt, pp. 89–105.

78. Tedin, K. (1980). Assessing peer and parent influence on adolescent political attitudes. *American Journal of Political Science, 24,* 136–54.

79. Torney, J.; Oppenheim, A. N.; & Farnen, R. F. (1975). *Civic education in ten countries: An empirical study*. New York: Wiley.
80. Torney-Purta, J. (1984). Political socialization and policy: The U.S. in a cross-national context. In H. Stevenson & A. Siegel, eds., *Child development research and social policy*. Vol. 1. Chicago: University of Chicago Press, pp. 471–525.
81. Torney-Purta, J. (1985). *Predictors of global awareness and global concern among secondary school students*. Columbus: Mershon Center, Ohio State University, ERIC 271364.
82. Torney-Purta, J. (1989). Political cognition and its restructuring in young people. *Human Development, 32*, 14–23.
83. Torney-Purta, J. (1990). From attitudes to schemata: Expanding the outcomes of political socialization research. In O. Ichilov, ed., *Political socialization, citizenship and democracy*. New York: Teachers College Press, pp. 98–115.
84. Torney-Purta, J., & Landsdale, D. (1986). Classroom climate and process in international studies: Data from the American Schools and the World Project. Paper presented at the American Educational Research Association, San Francisco.
85. Travers, E. (1982). Ideology and political participation among high school students: Changes from 1970 to 1979. *Youth and Society, 13*, 327–352.
86. Turiel, E. (1983). *The development of social knowledge*. Cambridge: Cambridge University Press.
87. Walker, L. J.; de Vries, B.; & Trevethan, S. D. (1987). Moral stages and moral orientations in real-life and hypothetical dilemmas. *Child Development, 58*, 842–858.
88. Weinreich-Haste, H. (1984). Political, moral, and social reasoning. In A. Regenbogen, ed., *Moral und Politik-Soziales Bewusstsein als lernprozess*. Cologne: Paul Rugenstein Verlag.
89. Weinreich-Haste, H. (1985). Kohlberg's contribution to political psychology: A positive view. In S. Modgil & C. Modgil, eds., *Lawrence Kohlberg: Consensus and controversy*. Philadelphia: Falmer Press, pp. 337–362.

CONTRIBUTORS

Thomas J. Berndt is Professor of Developmental Psychology, Department of Psychological Sciences, Purdue University.

Mary Kay Bowlds is Research Coordinator, Harvard Medical School.

Jeanne Brooks-Gunn is Senior Research Scientist, Educational Testing Service, Princeton, New Jersey.

B. Bradford Brown is Associate Professor of Human Development, Department of Educational Psychology, University of Wisconsin, Madison.

Sanford M. Dornbusch is Reed-Hodgson Professor of Human Biology, Professor of Sociology and Education, and Director of the Stanford Center for the Study of Families, Children and Youth, Stanford University.

Carol S. Dweck is Professor of Psychology, Department of Psychology, Columbia University.

Glen R. Elliott is Associate Professor and Director, Child and Adolescent Psychiatry, Department of Psychiatry, University of California, San Francisco.

Doris R. Entwisle is Professor of Sociology, Sociology Department, Johns Hopkins University.

S. Shirley Feldman is Professor of Human Biology, Senior Research Scientist in Child Psychiatry, and Deputy Director of the Stanford Center for the Study of Families, Children and Youth, Stanford University.

Gary Alan Fine is Professor of Sociology, Department of Sociology, University of Minnesota.

Frank F. Furstenberg is Professor of Sociology, Department of Sociology, University of Pennsylvania.

Madeline Goodman is a doctoral student in the Department of History, Carnegie-Mellon University.

Susan Harter is Professor of Psychology and Area Head, Department of Developmental Psychology, University of Denver.

Stuart T. Hauser is Associate Professor of Psychiatry, Harvard Medical School, and Director, Clinical Research Training Program, Massachusetts Mental Health Center.

Valanne L. Henderson is a doctoral student in the Department of Psychology, University of Illinois, Champaign.

Herant Katchadourian is Professor of Psychiatry and Behavioral Sciences, Human Biology, and Education, Program in Human Biology, Stanford University.

Daniel P. Keating is Professor of Special Education and Applied Cognitive Science, Department of Special Education, Ontario Institute for Studies in Education.

Iris F. Litt is Professor of Pediatrics and Director, Division of Adolescent Medicine, Department of Pediatrics, Children's Hospital at Stanford.

Joan McCord is Professor of Criminal Justice, Department of Criminal Justice, Temple University.

Susan G. Millstein is Associate Director, Carnegie Council on Adolescent Development, and Assistant Professor of Pediatrics, University of California, San Francisco.

John Modell is Professor of History, Department of History, Carnegie-Mellon University.

Jeylan T. Mortimer is Professor of Sociology and Director, Life Course Center, University of Minnesota.

Edward O. Reiter is Professor of Pediatrics and Chairman of the Department of Pediatrics, Baystate Medical Center, Tufts University.

Donald F. Roberts is Professor of Communication and Director, Institute for Communication Research, Stanford University.

Ritch C. Savin-Williams is Associate Professor of Human Development and Family Studies, Department of Human Development and Family Studies, Cornell University.

Margaret Beale Spencer is Associate Professor of Psychology, Division of Educational Studies, Emory University.

Laurence Steinberg is Professor of Child and Family Studies, Department of Psychology, Temple University.

Judith Torney-Purta is Professor of Human Development, Department of Human Development, University of Maryland.

Index

Ability grouping. *See* Tracking, academic
Absenteeism, school, 218, 219, 221
Academic ability. *See* Academic achievement; Intellectual ability
Academic achievement, 48, 52, 77, 80–81, 193, 222, 223–224, 308–329, 341, 410; among minorities, 80–81, 126, 139–143, 145, 193, 200–201, 212, 325–328, 486; and popularity, 172, 173, 193; friendships and, 193, 290–291, 297; factors in, 199–201, 308–309; and work, 226, 239, 240–241; and theories of intelligence, 313–317, 319, 323–325, 328; predicting, 317–319. *See also* Intellectual ability
Accidents, motor vehicle, 433, 438
Achievement, 309–328; in nonacademic areas, 320–323, 385. *See also* Academic achievement
Achievement behavior, 308, 311–313
Achievement motivation, 309–316; in nonacademic areas, 320–323; gender differences in, 323–325; and ethnicity, 325–328
Adults, 2, 19, 40, 179, 180, 195–196, 235, 281, 499; and teen sexuality, 348, 350. *See also* Parents; Teachers
Advertising, television, 55, 78
African-Americans, 7, 13, 29, 80, 117, 125–126, 127, 138, 157, 168, 299, 304; academic performance of, 126, 139–143, 145, 193, 290, 327, 385, 496; and religion, 129–130; and identity development, 132–133; fami-

ly influences, 135–136, 137, 262; parenting style, 136–138, 140, 489, 497; peer influences and, 139–140, 193; earning and employment rates of, 142; erosion of marriage among, 151, 154, 155; dropout rates of, 201–202; and sexual behavior, 332, 338–339; and self-esteem, 368–370, 387; and resiliency, 410–411; and problem behaviors, 416–417; political attitudes of, 470–471, 473–474. *See also* Minorities; Race
Age: and legal autonomy, 4–5, 481; and employment, 244; as factor in coping, 397. *See also* Early/Middle/Late adolescence
Age effects: and marital disruption, 162–163; in peer groups, 191
Age grading, 208–209, 215
Aggression, 44, 51, 193, 422
AIDS, 45, 51, 349–350, 451, 484
Alcohol use, 133, 190, 192, 230, 418, 419, 482; and car accidents, 433, 434
Alienation, 118, 173, 387, 468
Anorexia nervosa, 44, 50, 100, 437, 484
Anxiety, school, 319–320
Apprenticeships, 96, 100, 113, 238
Arapesh (New Guinea) pubertal rites, 35–36
Arrested development, 384, 399, 400, 403
Arts, and achievement motivation, 322
Asian-Americans, 134, 140, 326, 486
Asians, 7, 28–29, 128, 134, 236, 418, 426,